Human Motor Development

HUMAN MOTOR DEVELOPMENT
A Lifespan Approach
THIRD EDITION

V. Gregory Payne
San Jose State University

Larry D. Isaacs
Wright State University

Mayfield Publishing Company
Mountain View, California
London • Toronto

Library of Congress Cataloging-in-Publication Data
Payne, V. Gregory.
      Human motor development : a lifespan approach / V. Gregory Payne,
Larry D. Isaacs. — 3rd ed.
         p. cm.
      Includes bibliographical references and index.
      ISBN 1 -55934-379-6
      1. Motor ability in children. 2. Child development. 3. Human
mechanics. I. Isaacs, Larry D. (Larry David).
II. Title
RJ133.P39 1994
155.4'123—dc20

Manufactured in the United States of America

10 9 8 7 6 5 4 3 2 1

Mayfield Publishing Company
1280 Villa Street
Mountain View, California 94041

Sponsoring editor, Serina Beauparlant; production management, The Cowans; copyeditor, Jeanine Ardourel; text designer, Richard Kharibian; cover designer, Joan Greenfield; illustrators, John Foster, Tara Winkler; manufacturing manager, Aimee Rutter. The text was set in 10/12 New Caledonia by The Cowans and printed on 50# Finch Opaque by R. R. Donnelley & Sons.

To Luke, the best motor development professor ever, and our hopes for a bright future. ITAYATT

V.G.P

To my children, Brooke and Timothy.
No words could ever adequately express my love for each of you.

L.D.I.

ABOUT THE AUTHORS

V. Gregory Payne is beginning his twelfth year at San Jose Sate University where he is professor in the Department of Human Performance. He received his undergraduate degree from Western Illinois University, a master's degree from the University of Iowa, and a doctoral degree specializing in motor development from Indiana University. Dr. Payne is the 1994-95 president of the California Association for Health, Physical Education, Recreation, and Dance and is currently serving as the Past Chair of AAHPERD's Motor Development Academy. He is a special advisor to California's Governor's Council on Physical Fitness and Sports, has been a fellow in the Research Consortium of AAHPERD since 1983, and has served as co-chair of the Research Committee of the Council on Aging and Adult Development. He recently received the *Research Quarterly for Exercise and Sport* writing award for meta-analysis conducted on children's exercise. He resides in San Jose's Almaden Valley with his wife, Barb, and their 5-year-old son, Luke.

Larry D. Isaacs is professor in the Exercise Science Program, Department of Biology, College of Science and Mathematics at Wright State University. Since receiving his doctorate in 1979 from the University of Maryland, Dr. Isaacs has served as a reviewer for many scholarly journals. In addition, he has published numerous scholarly articles and has written six textbooks. Over the past 16 years, his writings have been recognized by many organizations including the American Alliance for Health, Physical Education, Recreation, and Dance where he has received the status of Research Fellow. In 1993 Dr. Isaacs received national certification (Health-Fitness Track) with the American College of Sports Medicine. Presently Dr. Isaacs' research is focusing on the physiological basis of muscular strength development in both prepubescent and elderly individuals. He currently lives in Dayton with his wife, Joy, and two children, Brooke and Timothy, 14 and 10 years old, respectively.

Contents

PART FIVE: **Assessing Motor Development and Implementing a Program**

Preface

As in the first two editions of *Human Motor Development: A Lifespan Approach,* this new edition covers well-established undergraduate motor development material. Our approach to this subject is unique in many ways.

SPECIAL FEATURES AND ORGANIZATION

Unlike traditional motor development texts that present development as a concept that ceases at adulthood, our book approaches motor development as a lifelong process. This approach recognizes the dramatic changes occurring within our population and the increasing popularity of movement programs outside the school setting.

Another feature of our book is the underlying philosophy that movement influences *and is influenced by* social, cognitive, and physical aspects of human development. That philosophy is apparent throughout the book, and separate chapters are allocated to each of these areas of human development.

Chapter 15, Youth Sports, and Chapter 18, Planning and Conducting Developmental Movement Programs, present information often omitted in traditional motor development texts. In addition, Chapter 18 provides information for those who are interested in setting up their own developmental movement program.

A number of features assist both the student and instructor. For example, each chapter concludes with a summary and a list of key terms, and complete references, by chapter, are provided at the end of the book. In addition, we have created a new Instructor's Manual. The Manual includes a sample syllabus, multiple choice and essay questions for each chapter (more than 500 test items total), suggested assignments for each chapter, expanded assignments (such as case studies and program critiques), and more than 70 transparency masters highlighting key information.

The organization of our book remains straightforward. Part One provides an overview of human development and includes chapters on the developmental aspects mentioned above. Part Two covers factors affecting development, including the effects of early stimulation and deprivation. Part Three, Physical Changes Across the Lifespan, and Part Four, Movement Across the Lifespan, present the book's core concepts. We conclude with Part Five, Assessing and Implementing a Program, an expanded, two-chapter part.

NEW FEATURES

All of the chapters have been updated and modified to reflect current research in motor development and to improve readability for students. The following are some major modifications you will find in the new third edition:

- Chapter 1, Introduction to Motor Development, has several new tables. We have also expanded the section on research designs and incorporated a new section on current trends in motor development that discusses the lifespan approach and dynamical systems perspective.

- Chapter 3, Social and Motor Development, has been supplemented with several new tables, figures, and photos, an expanded discussion of the concept of socialization and a new section on the exercise-aging cycle.

- Chapter 4, Perceptual-Motor Development, has much more information on the development of postural control and has been thoroughly updated.

- Chapter 5, Prenatal Developmental Concerns, has many new tables, including a comprehensive table indicating normal fetal development. New sections have been added on maternal diseases, HIV, cystic fibrosis, and diabetes mellitus. The sections on maternal nutrition and exercise during pregnancy have been expanded.

- Chapter 6, Effects of Early Stimulation and Deprivation, now includes a discussion of an important policy statement on infant exercise from the American Academy of Pediatrics, an expanded discussion of classic research conducted by Wayne Dennis, and even more examples of classic cases of extreme deprivation and its effects.

- Chapter 8, Physiological Changes: Health-Related Physical Fitness, now has many more tables as well as expanded information on developmental changes in heart rate. We have also included a section on the effects of exercise on prepubescents and have incorporated important position statements from prominent professional associations concerning children's weight training. Finally, new sections on the elderly and resistance training and gender- and health-related fitness have been included.

- Chapter 9, Movement and the Changing Senses, now provides information about several modalities other than just vision and includes major sections on such senses as proprioception and touch.

- Chapter 10, Infant Reflexes and Stereotypies, now has two new tables and a section discussing the difference between lifespan and infant reflexes.

- Chapter 11, Voluntary Movements of Infancy, has newly expanded sections on attainment of upright posture and early reaching and grasping behavior.

- Chapter 12, Fine Motor Development, includes a number of new photos as well as new sections on current interpretations of the development of prehension and some exciting research on early exploratory hand movements and the development of haptic perception.

- Chapter 13, Fundamental Locomotion Skills of Childhood, and Chapter 14, Fundamental Object Control Skills of Childhood, have been expanded and separated into two chapters for ease of reading. In addition to the many other fundamental locomotor skills included in the previous edition, Chapter 13 now includes developmental information on galloping, sliding, and skipping. Chapter 14 adds one-handed catching to the list of non-locomotor skills that were previously included. Finally, sections have been added concerning gender differences in overarm throwing and the effects of instruction on non-locomotor skills.

- Chapter 15, Youth Sports, now includes many new tables and updated data on children's participation in sports programs. New information is provided about why children participate, and the section on youth sports injuries has been updated and expanded.

- Chapter 16, Movement in Adulthood, now includes more information about adult postural control and a discussion of the classic work of Lehman and age-of-peak proficiency in various movement activities. More importantly, the work of Lehman has been updated to include the nearly fifty years of information since his work was completed. A section on physical activity trends through adulthood has also been incorporated.

- Chapter 18, Planning and Conducting Developmental Movement Programs, now includes sections on playground injuries with many new tables accompanying this information. A section has also been added to address the need for precaution in blood management.

ACKNOWLEDGMENTS

A special thanks to Mayfield Publishing for, again, guiding us through the publication process in a friendly and focused manner. We also appreciate their willingness, upon our request, to solicit many more reviews than usual. These reviews were particularly useful in our efforts to meet the needs of instructors and students of motor development. We're grateful for the constructive comments from all the reviewers: Beverly J. Allen, Alabama State University; Judy M. Bohren, University of Tampa; Allen Burton, University of Minnesota; Stephen E. Butterfield, University of Maine; Nancy L. Carleton, San Jose State University; Tami Benham Deal, University of Wyoming; John L. Haubenstricker, Michigan State University; Robert E. Kraft, University of Delaware; George Luedke, Southern Illinois University at Edwardsville; Louise S. McCormack, Plymouth State College; Sally McGrath, Shippensburg University; and Mary Painter, California State University at Northridge. One reviewer in particular surpassed all expectations. Dr. Allen Burton of the University of Minnesota provided us with supremely constructive comments with detailed rationale and references. Improvements in this edition are, in part, a function of Dr. Burton's critical insights into motor development.

We also acknowledge the work of Dr. Karyn Nelson of the University of Hawaii, who wrote large portions of our Instructor's Manual. Knowing Dr. Nelson's compassion as an instructor and her interest and expertise in motor development and written-test construction, we were always confident that our Instructor's Manual would be the quality we sought. Dr. Nelson produced a wide variety of carefully constructed test questions with many clever and creative assignments. All of our students will prosper from her work. Thanks, Karyn!

Lastly, we would again like to thank Dr. John Haubenstricker, Dr. Vern Seefeldt, and colleagues at Michigan State University for providing us with the research data and supporting studies pertaining to the "total body approach" for describing developmental sequences (presented in Chapters 13, 14, and 17). Although we had used these sequences in previous editions, we now include even more of the findings from the work conducted at Michigan State University. We would also like to again acknowledge that the film tracings that accompany much of this work were done by Dr. Joy Kiger, a former doctoral student at Michigan State. Dr. Kiger is now a faculty member at the University of Wisconsin, Whitewater.

CHAPTER 1

Introduction to Motor Development

Several terms are used to refer to the study of human movement: movement science, kinesiology, human performance, and physical education. Whichever term one chooses, there are a number of subdisciplines within the general area of study. For example, exercise physiology is the study of the function of the human body during exercise or work. Biomechanics is the study of movement technique, and sport psychology ". . . is concerned with both the psychological factors that influence sport and exercise and the psychological effect derived from them" (Williams & Straub, 1993, p. 1). *Motor behavior* is the subdiscipline emphasizing the investigation of principles of human movement behavior. More specifically, it primarily ". . . stresses the principles of human skilled movement generated at a behavioral level of analysis" (Schmidt, 1988, p. 17).

MOTOR BEHAVIOR

Motor behavior can be subdivided into motor control, motor learning, and motor development. Research or study in any of these areas can therefore be considered motor behavior research. However, because each subdiscipline begins with the word "motor," there is confusion about the three areas. The descriptive word "motor" is accurate and useful for suggesting that movement is the central focus of the area of study. But research conducted in these subdisciplines is frequently interdisciplinary; that is, the research often overlaps. Also, specialists in these areas of study are often interdisciplinary in their expertise. For example, a motor learning specialist may have a strong interest or secondary specialization in motor control. To work out the differences, we now examine the focus of each motor area.

Motor control is the study of the neurophysiological factors that affect human movement. "Neurophysiological" refers to the function of the body specifically as it relates to the neurological (nervous) system. The nervous system is of particular importance in the production of human movement because the neurons (nerve cells) stimulate the muscle fibers to produce the desired human movement. Research in motor control examines questions and concepts concerning movement and the underlying neurophysiological variables. One specific topic motor control specialists study is nerve conduction velocity: Why is the speed of stimulation of a muscle fiber faster in some people or under certain circumstances?

Motor learning is the study of the processes involved in acquiring and perfecting motor skills. Because motor skills are defined as movements dependent on practice and experience for their execution (Schmidt, 1991), a motor learning specialist is especially interested in the effects of varying types of practice, experience, or learning situations on human movement. An excellent example of the type of research conducted in motor learning laboratories concerns the traditional "massed versus distributed practice" question: For optimal learning of a motor skill to occur, should the movement be practiced in long, massed sessions or in short, distributed sessions? There has been considerable research into this question.

MOTOR DEVELOPMENT

Motor development is an academic area of study. Exactly what we study in motor development is currently the source of some controversy. This controversy may have begun as early as 1974 when six motor developmentalists met to "delineate the focus of research in motor development" (Notes from Scholarly Directions Committee, 1974, p. 1). Though several attempts were required, the group eventually generated a definition of motor development as "changes in motor behavior which reflect the interaction of the maturing organism and its environment" (p. 2).

This definition, the committee believed, melded the two main opposing views of those in attendance. One group, who primarily conducted research to generate predictive data on motor skills, was most interested in the movement product. The other group, who manipulated underlying process variables to better understand movement responses, was most interested in the movement process. One member of the 1974 committee, Vern Seefeldt, believes this definition has "stood the test of time," according to his article entitled "This Is Motor Development" (1989, p. 2). As Seefeldt explains, this definition includes the phrase "changes in motor behavior" to incorporate developmental differences that occur with time. The phrase "interactions of a maturing organism and its environment" was included to recognize the contributions of genetics and the environment to the process of development. This, Seefeldt states, was important to "defuse" the historical debate over nature vs. nurture (genetics or the environment) and the magnitude of their effects on human development (1989, p. 2).

Despite Seefeldt's views, this definition is not supported by all motor developmentalists. Keogh, for example, suggested this definition in a 1977 article: [Motor development can be defined as] "changes in movement competencies from infancy to adulthood and involves many aspects of human behavior, both as they affect movement development and as movement development affects them" (p. 76). Clark and Whitall state that the "overwhelmingly" prevalent current definition of motor development is "the change in motor behavior across the lifespan" (1989, p. 183).

Clark and Whitall's definition has had considerable support. Roberton (1989) states that this is her view of motor development as well as the one proposed by the first textbook in our field, Espenschade and Eckert's *Motor Development* (1967). However, Clark and Whitall contrast that original definition with one supplied by Haywood in her text. Lifespan Motor Development (1993): "the sequential, continuous age-related process whereby an individual progresses from simple, unorganized, and unskilled movement to the achievement of highly organized, complex motor skills and finally to the adjustment of skills that accompanies aging" (p. 7).

The major difference between these last two definitions is that the former only recognizes the efforts of developmentalists to study change, the product of development, whereas the latter emphasizes the process of development. Using historical information to support their case, Clark and Whitall argue that both the product and the process of motor development have been examined throughout the history of the field of motor development and should be reflected in the definition. Therefore, they propose the following definition of motor development: "the changes in motor behavior over the lifespan and the processes which underlie these changes" (1989, p. 194).

Because a definition must be current, accurate, and relatively simple and succinct to be practical, we support Clark and Whitall in their selection of this definition as the most useful. However, we also recognize that an examination of all the definitions presented here enables a more thorough understanding of the thinking of different motor developmentalists and subsequently a more thorough understanding of the field.

With a working definition of motor development, we can now define it as a field of study: the study of the changes in motor behavior over the lifespan, the processes that underlie these changes, and the factors that affect them.

We obviously added "the study of" to our original definition of motor development. We also added "and the factors that affect them" because we believe the field of motor development encompasses more than the examination of the products and processes of motor development. It also encompasses the study of related or affecting factors. For that reason, in later chapters we will examine such topics as the effects of early motor programs on motor development, children's physical fitness, youth sports, and the effects of physical activity on the aging process.

Finally, Roberton (1988) further clarified the role of motor developmentalists by stating that we attempt to improve understanding in three general areas. First, we try to understand present motor behavior, both what is happening and why it happens. Second, we strive to understand what this behavior was like in the past and why. Finally, we seek to understand what the behavior will be like in the future and why. As we will discuss later in the chapter, motor development research is often interdisciplinary; we team with experts from other areas of study to do our research. However, what makes us unique is that we do not stop with understanding the present motor behavior; our primary interest drives us to understand what it was, what it will be, and why.

THE HISTORY OF THE FIELD OF MOTOR DEVELOPMENT

A number of brief histories of motor development have been published over the years (Clark & Whitall, 1989, Keogh, 1977; Roberton, 1988, 1989; Smoll, 1982; Thelen, 1987; Thomas, 1994; Thomas & Thomas, 1984). Keogh (1977) and Thomas and Thomas (1984) have suggested that the study of motor development began around 1920 to 1930 by physicians who were interested in creating scales to note developmental progress of infants. Roberton (1988, 1989) has indicated a much earlier starting point. She believes motor development may have begun with the work of the "baby biographers" of the late 1800s through the early 1900s. Included in this group were Darwin (1877) and Shinn (1900), who wrote "A Biographical Sketch of an Infant" and *The Biography of a Baby*, respectively. Clark and Whitall (1989) cite an even earlier starting point. They agree that Darwin and Shinn were influential but that Tiedemann's (1787, as cited by Borstelmann, 1983) observations of his son's first 2 1/2 years mark the beginning of what Clark and Whitall have named the *precursor period* of motor development, the first of their four historical periods of motor development (see Table 1-1).

TABLE 1-1   Clark and Whitall's (1989) Periods in the History of Motor Development

---

1787–1928   Precursor Period

Descriptive observation was established as a method for studying human development. The most significant influence was Darwin's "Biographical Sketch of an Infant." Early researchers were most interested in the function of the mind, though their research benefited the motor developmentalists who followed.

1928–1946   Maturational Period

Motor development as a primary interest began to emerge, and the maturational philosophy predominated. This philosophy held that the biological processes were the main influence in shaping human development. Work by Gesell and McGraw yielded valuable product and process-oriented information concerning human movement. Bayley's scales of motor development, still used today, were a product of this period. These norm-referenced scales charted motor behavior across the first three years of life.

1946–1970   Normative/Descriptive Period

In the mid 1940s interest in motor development became "dormant" (Keogh, 1977). In the early 1960s, however, a revival began. This revival was led by physical educators who were interested in children's movement and developed norm-referenced standardized tests for measuring motor performance. Kephart's publication of *The Slow Learner in the Classroom* was also an influence. Kephart maintained that certain movement activities enhanced academic performance. Though never well supported by the research, Kephart's theory still influences professional practice today.

1970–present   Process-oriented Period

The most recent period was characterized by a return to studying the processes underlying motor development rather than simply describing change. Interest grew in information processing theory which suggested that the human mind functioned much like a computer. This theory may have contributed to many psychologists returning to study motor development. A second era of this period began in the 1980s when work by Kugler, Kelso, and Turvey (1982) prompted interest in dynamical systems theory. This theory deviated substantially from information processing theory and posited that systems undergoing change are complex, coordinated, and somewhat self-organizing. Thus, a movement pattern can arise from component parts interacting among themselves and the environment though the pattern was never "coded" in the central nervous system.

The *precursor period* of motor development lasted from 1787 to 1928. That, according to Clark and Whitall, was followed by the *maturational period,* 1928–1946. The third period, the *normative/descriptive period* lasted from 1946–1970. Finally, the *process-oriented period* covered the years of 1970 to present.

In the precursor period of motor development, descriptive observation was established as a method for studying human development. As mentioned earlier, Tiedemann's observation of his young son marked the beginning of this era. Tiedemann discussed common sequences in movement behavior and the transitional period from such behaviors as the grasp reflex to eventual voluntary grasping. Over a century later, Preyer (1909, as cited by Clark & Whitall, 1989) wrote *The Mind of a Child,* which was a major impetus for the emergence of developmental psychology. However, the most significant influence of the period, according to Clark and Whitall, was such works of Darwin as "A Biographical Sketch of an Infant," which led to greater understanding of human behavior and its causes. Though these early researchers, like Darwin, were generally more interested in the function of the mind rather than motor development, motor development as a field of study benefited from their research in the years to follow.

Around 1930 motor development as a primary interest area began to emerge. Because the study of maturation was the main focus, Clark and Whitall chose to name this second historical period the maturational period. The maturational philosophy argued the significance of the biological processes on the development of the individual to the near exclusion of the effects of the environment. Clark and Whitall believed this period was initiated by the publication of Gesell's *Infancy and Human Growth* (1928). Myrtle McGraw (1935), along with Gesell, was particularly influential in espousing the maturational viewpoint. Her classic work with the twins Johnny and Jimmy and her ideas concerning critical periods are discussed in more detail in Chapter 6. While McGraw and Gesell clearly sought to determine the processes underlying changes in motor behavior, they have also become known for their descriptions of changes in motor behavior in infants and children. Thus they not only emphasized the movement process but also uncovered valuable information concerning the movement product.

Another highlight of the maturational period of motor development, according to Clark and Whitall, was the publication of Bayley's scale of motor development (1936). This scale charted normative motor behavior across the first 3 years of life and, in modified form, is still in use today.

Though this was a critical period in the history of motor development, interest in human movement began to wane in the early to mid 1940s. In fact, in his brief history of motor development, Keogh called the period from 1940 to 1960 "dormant" (1977, p. 77). Clark and Whitall suggest that a revival of motor development was occurring prior to 1960. They

state that renewed interest in motor development began toward the end of World War II and was prompted by researchers in physical education. Keogh, however, believed an increased interest in studying children with disabilities prompted the resurgence. The newly emerging interest in mind-body relationships and Kephart's *The Slow Learner in the Classroom* (1960) were specifically cited by Kephart as agents in increasing interest in motor development around 1960. Kephart's theory suggested that academic improvements could be brought about by involvement in specific types of movement activities. This theory, which was never well supported scientifically, had a substantial impact on the course of history because of its emphasis on movement activity. Many professionals still employ teaching techniques based on Kephart's theory. For that reason, it is discussed in greater detail in Chapter 4.

Despite Keogh's claim that the resurgence in motor development did not occur until around 1960, Clark and Whitall's normative/descriptive period encompasses the years 1946–1970. They specifically attribute the revival to physical education researchers such as Anna Espenschade, Ruth Glassow, and G. Lawrence Rarick whose primary interest focused on children's motor skills rather than cognitive abilities. Though there were few significant motor development studies emerging in the 1950s, an increased focus was seen on measuring children anthropometrically (bodily measures), testing their strength, measuring performance on such skills as running and jumping, and making gender comparisons on various motor performance measures (Keogh, 1977). As a result, standardized tests for evaluating children's motor performance were created. Overall, the emphasis was on developing standardized norms and describing children anthropometrically. Very little emphasis was placed on understanding the processes underlying changes in motor behavior. Thus this era derived its name, the normative/descriptive period.

According to Clark and Whitall, the 1960s brought more biomechanical analysis of movement and the emergence of *perceptual-motor theory*. Many researchers began to study the efficacy of perceptual-motor theory, which generally renewed interest in motor development. As mentioned earlier, Keogh (1977) believed that perceptual-motor theory was of greater impact historically and, perhaps, should be attributed with the "rebirth" of motor development.

The period from 1970 to present was labeled the process-oriented period as a result of the return to studying the processes underlying motor development rather than simply describing the change (products). Clark and Whitall believe this new focus was brought abut by Connolly's *Mechanisms of Motor Skill Development* (1970), which was a summation of a meeting by a small group of psychologists. This publication seemed to mark psychologists' return to the study of motor development. Many of these psychologists pursued understanding the processes of motor development by using *information processing theory*, thinking of the brain as functioning much like a computer.

Clark and Whitall also believe the increased number of published motor learning texts during this time period increased interest in information processing theory and motor development. The new interest in information processing was partially responsible for more researchers attending to the underlying processes of motor development. At the same time, however, some researchers continued to study the products of movement change as a carry-over from the previous historical period.

As we discussed earlier in this chapter, several motor developmentalists met in Seattle, Washington, in 1974 to discuss research directions in motor development. Their goal was to determine the actual focus of research in motor development (Seefeldt, 1989). Clark and Whitall believe this meeting reflected the diversity between two prevalent views of the time, process and product orientations. One view expressed was to study children's change in such underlying processes and functions as perception, memory, and attention. Much of this same type of research had already been completed using adult subjects. Others, according to Clark and Whitall, saw a need to continue the product-oriented line of investigation seeking to achieve such ends as ordering and classifying fundamental motor patterns.

The second half of Clark and Whitall's last period of motor development history began in the 1980s. This era was initiated, they say, by a paper published by Kugler, Kelso, and Turvey (1982). This publication presented an innovative theoretical perspective for the study of movement control and coordination and sharply contrasted with information processing theory. This theoretical approach, known as *dynamical systems perspective,* is an important contribution to our study of human motor development as it seeks to examine movement control and coordination as well as seeking explanations to the process of development. This perspective will be explained more thoroughly in the next section on current trends in motor development.

CURRENT TRENDS IN MOTOR DEVELOPMENT

Over the last decade or longer, two prominent trends have arisen in the study of human motor development. As we discussed in the last section, Clark and Whitall (1989) believe one of these trends to be the emergence of dynamical systems perspective. The other, despite its equally profound effect on the study of motor development, was not acknowledged by Clark and Whitall in their history of motor development. This is the trend toward studying human motor development from a lifespan perspective. Both of these trends are explained in the following sections.

Dynamical Systems Perspective

Over the years, a number of theoretical perspectives have been proposed in an attempt to explain the development of human movement. However, many of today's experts believe these theories do not adequately address the full range and complexity of human motor development. For example, the neural maturation concept dominated the thinking of motor developmentalists for years. This theory posited that the nervous system was the main control element in human movement. It was believed to be the "switch" that initiated movement. As mentioned earlier in the chapter, in more recent years, the way in which the brain organized the nervous system for movement had been compared to a computer in what is often referred to as information processing theory. Because little attention was paid to other contributing factors in these theoretical approaches, some current experts believe they were too limited to enable a complete understanding of how human movement is generated and how it evolves throughout the lifespan (Scholz, 1990).

Today, we recognize that a variety of systems interact with our nervous system to create human movement. Gravitational forces are an easy example. As we move, their impact on our neurological, muscular, and skeletal systems is constantly altered as the body or body part in question changes position. Similarly, the effect of one body part's movement alters the process of moving another. So movement is a product of an entire system comprised of numerous components or subsystems which are constantly interacting and changing. The nervous system, originally thought to be the sole determinant of movement, is a part of this system and must also dynamically change and interact with all other components if movement is to be coordinated and efficient (Kamm, Thelen, & Jensen, 1990). For example, the initial voluntary attempts at reaching and grasping are under the influence of the relevant joints, muscles, and nerves as well as the arm's weight. Gravity and numerous contextual factors like children's level of motivation, their body position, and the height and weight of the object for which they are reaching also interact. One of the main attractions of dynamical systems perspective of human movement is that it allows for explanations that include the interacting subsystems.

A major impetus in the shift to dynamical systems perspective was the work of Haken (1983). In his work, Haken discussed *synergetics,* the study of physical, chemical, and biological systems. Synergetics, according to Haken, is an attempt to establish principles governing pattern generation that would be common to a variety of systems though independent of the structure producing the behavior. In synergetics, relatively simple systems are often studied since they are easier to understand.

However, even "simple" systems can be difficult to understand. So, researchers often select *order parameters* within these systems. Order parameters are a relatively small number of carefully selected variables that have been chosen with the intention of narrowing the study of the more global system (Kamm, Thelen, & Jensen, 1990).

The work of Kugler, Kelso, and Turvey (1982) further advanced interest in dynamical systems perspective as they began to adapt the idea of synergetics to human movement. Though we discuss dynamical systems perspective for the purposes of more clearly understanding human motor development, many scientists in other disciplines are using the same theoretical approach to learn more about a variety of natural phenomena ranging from weather systems to cardiac physiology (Kamm, Thelen, & Jensen, 1990).

Regardless of the discipline in question, a number of fundamental features underlie dynamical systems theory. For example, systems are believed to be complex, multifaceted, and cooperative. No one component is thought to have priority or ultimate responsibility for the overall behavior of the system. In addition, the system is believed to be *self-organizing.* This suggests that the components cooperate and interact in an almost infinite number of ways to yield a movement whose outward appearance remains relatively stable.

So, dynamical systems perspective posits that a movement pattern can be created as a result of a near infinite combination of interactions of component parts. However, proponents of this theoretical perspective also acknowledge that one set of interactions is more easily achievable than others because it requires less energy. This particular combination of interactions of variables is called an attractor. An attractor can be relatively strong or weak depending on how readily the system returns to it. A strong attractor is said to have a deep *attractor well.* An attractor that is less commonly "sought" by the interacting system is said to have a shallow attractor well.

Another basic tenet of dynamical systems perspective is that motor development is discontinuous or constantly changing. This aspect of the "systems perspective" makes it particularly attractive to developmentalists because it offers an explanation for human motor development unlike previous theories. According to the systems perspective, motor development would occur as any one component or subsystem changes. In fact, the development or emergence of one or more new subsystems could even cause the disappearance of previously existing ones. As a subsystem changes it may alter the depth of the existing attractor well. For example, as infants increase in weight due to normal growth, their stepping rate may decrease to a point that the stepping ceases. The factor believed to be primarily responsible for the system change, in this case the weight increase, is known as a *control parameter*. During a period of change, dynamical systems perspective maintains that the whole system becomes vulnerable to more change to the point that normally insignificant factors can become control parameters. Though development usually progresses as a series of phase shifts between varying degrees of stability, an exceptionally deep attractor well can cause such phase stability that development is impeded. After several phase shifts, we may find that the contributing subsystems are almost entirely different than they were at an earlier developmental point.

Our ability to employ more complex theoretical perspectives, like dynamical systems perspective, has been facilitated by improved research technology. For example, our technology in kinematic analysis is far superior today than in years past. Improved kinematics, "the science of mechanics . . . that deals solely with describing the nature of motion" (Hay & Reid, 1988; p. 114), allows more detailed quantification and, therefore, a more complete understanding of the details of the organization and development of human movement. We can now accurately track the motion of a limb throughout its range of motion. The entire movement time can be calculated and the relative position of the component parts can be recorded repeatedly within each second of movement. Additional details like joint angles, movement accuracy, velocity, and acceleration can be determined. When combined with other advancing technologies, such as electromyographical analyses, entirely new and different views of motor development are possible. Such detailed analyses allow researchers to determine which segment of the limb may have initiated the movement and the sequence in which each became involved. Thus, enhanced scientific ability has freed researchers from their dependence on past theories that were strictly neural based and allowed greater exploration of multiple interacting factors in theories like dynamical systems (Kamm, Thelen, & Jensen, 1990).

Motor Development as a Lifespan Perspective

Over the last decade, a number of new motor development textbooks have emerged (Gabbard, 1992; Gallahue & Ozmun, 1995; Haywood, 1993; Payne & Isaacs, 1995). Unlike many of their predecessors, the authors of these books adopted a *lifespan perspective* for the study of motor development. The orientation of these texts and the increasing amount of research concerning movement in adulthood indicates a ". . . lifespan concept of motor development is emerging" (VanSant, 1990, p. 788). This was a relatively drastic deviation from earlier approaches that seemed to assume that when height growth ceased, behavior also stopped changing (Fitzgerald, 1986) or that our developmental peak was at adolescence or early adulthood (Lefrancois, 1993). The authors of the most recent motor development texts were most likely influenced by the dramatic shift occurring in our population. This shift is illustrated in Table 1-2, where the percentage of the total United States population by age group is presented by decade back to 1900. This table was created by determining the total U.S. population by decade and the total for each age group. The percent of the total population for each age group was then computed. This table clearly illustrates the rapid increase in the relative number of people over age 65 in our population. As indicated, that group increased approximately 1 percentage point each decade since 1940 except during the most recent decade, the 1980s. During those 10 years a 2 percentage point

TABLE 1-2 Percentage of U.S. Population by Age Group (Years), 1900–1990

Year	Total Population (Thousands)	< 5 years	5–14	15–24	25–34	35–44	45–54	55–64	65+↑
1990	248,710	7	14	15	17	15	10	9	13
1980	226,546	7	15	19	16	11	10	10	11
1970	204,879	8	20	19	12	11	11	9	10
1960	180,671	11	20	14	13	13	11	9	9
1950	151,684	11	16	15	16	14	11	9	8
1940	132,122	8	17	18	16	14	12	8	7
1930	123,077	9	20	18	15	14	11	7	5
1920	106,461	11	21	18	16	14	10	6	5
1910	92,407	12	21	20	17	13	9	6	4
1900	76,094	12	22	20	16	12	8	5	4

Calculations are based on Census of Population (1992), Census of Population (1983), and Historical Statistics of the United States from Colonial Times to 1970 (1975).

increase occurred. According to *Healthy People 2000* (U.S. Department of Health and Human Services, 1992), people reaching the age of 65 can expect to live well into their 80s. The growing number of older individuals in our society increases our need to study and understand this sector of the population.

Academically, adopting the lifespan approach offers the opportunity to examine a broader range of change processes as the individual is studied through both the progressive and regressive phases of development. This obviously enables the examination of many intrinsic and extrinsic factors (like a variety of cultural phenomena) which have not regularly been considered in our traditional approach to studying motor development (VanSant, 1990).

AN INTERDISCIPLINARY APPROACH TO MOTOR DEVELOPMENT

There is considerable interaction among the three subareas of motor behavior. Although we presented specific examples of topics of study within each

motor area, there is often considerable overlap. For example, the motor learning expert may seek information about the acquisition of movement skill and the differences in that acquisition as a child ages. Therefore, this effort is not simply research into motor learning but also research into motor development because a change occurring as a result of aging is also of significant concern in the investigation. Obviously, there can be similar overlap between motor development and motor control: The underlying neurophysiological factors would be examined as they change with aging. Such research could involve comparisons of children of various ages or even of children with adolescents and adults.

Motor development also interacts with many of the other subdisciplines in the study of human movement. Motor developmentalists once were satisfied to assess movement change that occurs with aging by simple visual observation, but advanced technology has made other techniques more valuable. Today, motor developmentalists often can evaluate movement more accurately by working with specialists from other fields; subtle movement differences can then be detected and analyzed using current technology from those fields. For example, in biomechanics, movement differences between various age groups can be assessed and analyzed by computer using biomechanical techniques that far surpass human capabilities to visually discern change. As in exercise physiology, accurate developmental differences in body-fat levels, lung capacity, or level of electrical stimulation in specific muscles can be determined by collaboration with exercise physiologists. As technology advances, motor development continues to increasingly depend on cooperative efforts with other related fields, making interdisciplinary efforts to enhance our knowledge increasingly common.

DESIGNING RESEARCH IN MOTOR DEVELOPMENT: CROSS SECTIONAL, LONGITUDINAL, OR . . .?

Generally, two research designs have been employed for studying motor development. In a *cross-sectional design*, subjects from the various treatment or age groups are examined on the same measure once at the same time (Baltes, 1968). For example, to examine the development of handwriting technique between childhood and adulthood, three groups of subjects might be employed. One group would include children, age 7–9. A second group would be adolescents, age 13–15, and a third would include adults, age 25–27. All subjects would be examined and measured on the specified handwriting task with the differences between groups being noted. In a *longitudinal design*, one group of subjects is observed repeatedly at different ages and different times of measurement (Baltes, 1968). So, in our hypothetical handwriting study we would now start with our child subjects and periodically examine their handwriting technique until they reach adulthood.

Commonly, researchers select a cross-sectional design because of its administrative efficiency. It offers the major advantage of time efficiency because it can be completed in a short period of time.

Despite that advantage, the cross-sectional design requires the researcher to assume change occurred because of age difference. The cross-sectional design allows age differences, but not behavior changes, to be observed. In addition, if the correct age groupings are not chosen initially for the cross-sectional design, an important part of a developmental sequence may be missed entirely (Roberton, Williams, & Langendorfer, 1980).

Though the longitudinal design requires considerably more time, the change in the subjects' motor behavior can be observed and not just assumed to have occurred. However, some problems may exist. One of the most critical is subject mortality, as subjects drop out more often than in the cross-sectional situation. This is a particular problem if subjects drop out in a nonrandom fashion, which is more likely among subjects who perform poorly on the behavior being examined. Therefore, the overall findings may be positively biased. Another potential problem with the longitudinal design is that the same subjects are retested periodically, which may also result in a more positive score on successive attempts (Baltes, 1968).

In addition to these potential problems, both designs have three components that are difficult to separate for the purposes of accurate interpretation of research findings (Thomas, 1989). The first component is simply the subjects' chronological age. The second is known as cohort, the set of experiences a group of subjects brings into the study because of the generation in which they were reared. The third component is time of measurement. This refers to the unique situation that existed at the time measurements were made. In the cross-sectional design, problems exist with confusing age and cohort (Lefrancois, 1993). For example, in the hypothetical cross-sectional handwriting study referred to earlier, the children differed from the adolescents and adults by age and by cohort. Any resultant differences in handwriting technique would likely be attributed to age but might have been due to the experiences the subjects had as a result of when they were reared. Similarly, a longitudinal design confuses age and time of measurement. Obviously, all of the subjects are similar in terms of age and cohort, but years may have passed since the last examination of their handwriting. The unique situation surrounding the previous handwriting analysis may have been sufficient to cause differences in handwriting. Unfortunately, these differences will often be attributed to age.

To help avoid some of the potential confounding of results in research, two different experimental designs are often employed, the *time-lag* and the *sequential* or *cohort* designs. In a time-lag design, different cohorts are compared at different times. For example, subjects who are 10 years old in 1995, can be compared to subjects who will be 10 in 1997, 1999, and 2001. In such a design, age remains the same while the cohort varies (Lefrancois, 1993). Thus, the potential confounding of age and cohort are reduced.

Researchers can also employ a sequential or cohort design. This design type integrates the cross-section, longitudinal, and time-lag designs within one study. In the cross-sectional portion of the study, different cohorts are tested each year. In the longitudinal portion, the same cohort is followed for an extended period of time. Meanwhile, in the time-lag portion, different cohorts are compared to each other at different times when subjects are the same age (see Figure 1-1).

Though the time-lag and the sequential designs offer resolutions to some problems inherent in cross-sectional and longitudinal testing, they also offer some unique problems. Most notably, these designs often require considerable time, effort, and money. In addition, they are very difficult to accurately analyze using current statistical techniques (see Table 1-3).

Figure 1-1 is a representation of a hypothetical study in which the effects of age on functional flexibility (neck rotation and lateral trunk and neck flexion) are examined. The effects from age 20 to age 80 are studied using a sequential design to reduce cohort effects. The sequential design includes components of time-lag, longitudinal, and cross-sectional research designs. A section of the study which examines time-lag differences (different cohorts at different times but at the same age) is indicated with a light screen. A section which examines longitudinal (same cohort at different times) differences is indicated with a medium screen. A section which examines the cross-sectional (different cohorts at the same time) differences is indicated with a dark screen.

Clearly, research design selection in motor development research is a problem. Considerable care must be taken in the design of our research because scientific progress in developmental research "is contingent largely upon the quality of its methodology"

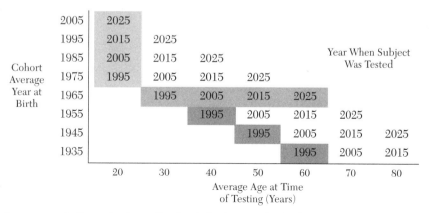

FIGURE 1-1   A representation of a hypothetical study conducted using a sequential research design.

TABLE 1-3 Pros and Cons of Various Research Designs Used in Developmental Research

	Pros	Cons
Cross-sectional	• Administratively efficient • Quickly completed • Age differences can be observed	• Cannot observe change (it must be assumed) • Premium placed on accurate determination of age groups • Age and cohort are confounded
Longitudinal	• Change can be observed across ages	• Administratively inefficient • Age and time of measurements are confounded • Subjects may be influenced by repeated testing • Subjects drop out
Sequential (Cohort)	• Accounts for generational (cohort) effects	• Administratively inefficient • Financially costly • Subjects drop out • Difficult to analyze statistically

(Baltes, 1968, p. 167). As Thomas (1989) concluded in his article on motor development research, the currently available research designs cannot completely separate chronological age, cohort, and time of measurement making valid research in motor development particularly difficult. Rarick (1989) noted, however, that cross-sectional research may be useful, within limits, as it can provide norms and predict behaviors. But a longitudinal design is more useful if the researcher is specifically interested in development and the factors affecting it.

THE DOMAINS OF HUMAN DEVELOPMENT

The study of human development can be divided into three major domains: cognitive, affective, and motor. The cognitive domain, which concerns human intellectual development, has been the primary focus of developmentalists. Intellectual development was the major interest of the most prominent of all developmentalists, Jean Piaget, who is discussed more thoroughly in Chapter 2. The affective domain is concerned primarily with the social and emotional development of the human being (thus

this domain is often called the social-emotional domain). The motor domain, concerned with human movement, is the major focus of this book.

Benjamin Bloom (1956) is generally credited with categorizing human development into the cognitive, affective, and motor domains. Bloom used his taxonomy (a method of classification) to categorize educational objectives. This approach to education has been found efficient for compartmentalizing the study of human development as well. However, although this approach facilitates the organization of our study, we must understand that such an approach is not realistic. In reality, the domains of human development are not distinct; they constantly interact with each other (see Figure 1-2). Our intellectual behavior is a function of our emotions as well as our movement, and certainly our movement is influenced by our emotions and our intellect. A student taking a written examination is an example of the interaction of the domains of behavior. Although taking a written test is generally considered a cognitive task, the student must be in an appropriate emotional state to both perform successfully on the exam and manually transcribe the answers. Emotions and movement therefore interact with the intellect as the student completes the exam.

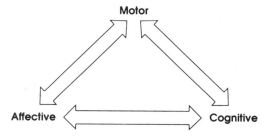

FIGURE 1-2 The three domains of human development are useful for categorizing our study of such areas as motor development. However, we must remember that these domains are not discrete; rather, they constantly interact.

THE IMPORTANCE OF MOTOR DEVELOPMENT

Human development is a diverse, complex area of study in which we cannot consider ourselves completely educated until we understand all aspects of the changes that occur throughout the lifespan. We must strive to understand both the movement changes that we commonly experience with age and the intellectual, social, and emotional changes. Our knowledge of all aspects of human development is valuable because it contributes to a general body of knowledge that enables us to better understand ourselves and the world we live in. However, although knowledge gained purely for the sake of knowledge is important, there are other, more practical applications for our knowledge of motor development.

For easy communication and more efficient organization, we divide the study of human development into the cognitive, affective, and motor domains discussed in the previous section. Because these domains of human behavior are constantly interacting, a complete understanding of any one domain requires knowledge of the domains with which it interacts. Full understanding of motor development therefore requires knowledge of the cognitive and affective domains because they so profoundly affect movement behavior. And conversely, full understanding of human development in the cognitive or affective domains requires a knowledge of

motor development. As discussed in upcoming chapters, motor development has profound effects on the development of cognitive and social behaviors throughout the lifespan.

Knowledge of motor development has other applications. For example, understanding the way people normally develop movement skills throughout the lifespan enables us to diagnose problems in those individuals who may be developing abnormally. Consider an infant who does not exhibit a particular reflex at the expected time of appearance. As discussed in greater detail in Chapter 10, certain reflexive movements normally occur at certain ages. Any significant deviations from the expected timeline may indicate the need for special treatment.

Understanding human motor development is also important for helping individuals perfect or improve their movement performance, which can yield many benefits. For example, an improved self-concept enables a person to become more emotionally stable and satisfied. Also, because there is a link between all domains of behavior, improvement in the motor

TABLE 1-4 Why Should We Study Motor Development?

1. Human development is multi-faceted. In addition to changes in human movement, intellectual, social, and emotional changes occur. Because these domains of human development are in constant interaction, we will never fully understand ourselves until we fully understand each of the domains, including the motor domain.

2. Knowledge of the way most people develop in their movement enables us to diagnose cases which are sufficiently abnormal to warrant intervention and remediation.

3. Knowledge of human motor development allows the establishment of developmentally-appropriate activities which enable optimal teaching/learning of movement skills for people of all ages and all ability levels.

domain may indirectly lead to improvements in intellectual or social development. Activities can therefore be devised to assist in the development of movement potential. To accurately create such a movement curriculum, we must have a knowledge of normal motor development. With that knowledge and the subsequent structuring of developmentally appropriate movement tasks, we can challenge individuals relative to their levels of achievement. Developmentally-appropriate movement curricula lead to more effective learning of motor tasks because the participants seldom become frustrated or bored by tasks that are too difficult or too easy.

For these reasons, knowledge of motor development is important for movement specialists working with "normal" children. This same knowledge can be applied when working with special populations. Although many disabling conditions lead to a developmental lag in an individual's movement performance, the sequence or pattern of development generally remains similar to the normal development pattern. For example, blind babies commonly lag behind sighted babies in their development of reaching behavior and independent walking. Also, Down syndrome children may take twice as long as normal children to develop early motor skills (Bower, 1977), although with proper intervention this lag can be reduced or eliminated. In both cases, the sequence for acquisitions of movement skills most likely would be normal despite the fact that the rate of development would be delayed (McClenaghan & Gallahue, 1978).

This phenomenon was well represented in a study investigating children with learning and behavior disorders and their performance on sensory perception and perceptual-motor tasks. Although these children's level of development was delayed when compared to "normal" children's level, the pattern of development was not altered (Williams, Temple, & Bateman, 1979). Wickstrom's (1983) research supported these findings; it showed that mentally retarded children also tend to be retarded in motor skill development. Some mentally retarded children, for example, may lag 2 or more years behind their

retarded peers. This lag increases in magnitude as the degree of mental retardation increases. According to Wickstrom, these individuals develop movement in a normal progression but at a much slower rate.

DEVELOPMENT, MATURATION, AND GROWTH

The movement changes throughout the lifespan are often progressive. For example, children gradually improve their walking ability until that skill becomes a smooth and efficient movement pattern. Movement patterns can also regress, as is frequently the case in later adulthood, when a person may reach the point where movements such as walking are no longer as efficient as they once were. In other words, the walking pattern of an older adult, regarding its level of perfection, may become similar to the walking pattern of a young child. There is a definite decline in ability.

Motor development thus consists of both progressions and regressions, as does development in general. The term *development* can be applied to any of the domains of human behavior. As may seem obvious after our discussions of motor development, development refers to human changes, both progressive and regressive, that occur throughout the lifespan. This simple definition varies considerably from one source to another, and the term development is often confused with two other terms that are critical to an introductory discussion of human development.

In daily conversation, the words "maturation" and "growth" can be used interchangeably. For example, a student may comment, "I really grew during last semester's course." The words "developed" or "matured" could be inserted for "grew" without changing the intended meaning. The idea is that there was a significant positive change as a result of the course.

Although the terms development, maturation, and growth used synonymously are acceptable in casual conversation, we must use them correctly and specifically within the technical areas of study and research. For the purposes of this textbook, development includes both maturation and growth. The qualitative functional changes that occur with age are collectively known as *maturation. Growth* refers to the quantitative structural changes that occur with age (see Figure 1-3). Although both terms indicate specific aspects of a metamorphosis from childhood to adulthood, maturation refers to organizational changes in the function of the organs and tissues. The individual's behavior is subsequently modified as a result of these qualitative changes. An example of maturation is the neurological organization of the brain during childhood. Virtually all anatomical parts are present from very early in childhood, but qualitative change in brain function continues to occur, enabling children to gradually achieve a higher level of cognitive ability.

Growth can be simply described as an increase in physical size. This physical transformation primarily involves hyperplasia—an increase in cell number; hypertrophy—an increase in cell size; and accretion—an increase in intercellular matter (Malina & Bouchard, 1991). Although these processes are gradual, generally imperceptible phenomena, they are increasingly evident when a human being is observed over a long time. One of the most noticeable examples of growth occurs immediately after puberty, at the onset of adolescence: Both males and females experience a growth spurt. During that time, an increase in height of several inches over a 1-year period is not unusual. That increase in height, independent of any simultaneous changes, is growth.

FIGURE 1-3 Development is a general term referring to the progressions and regressions that occur throughout the lifespan. Growth is the structural aspect of development; maturation deals with the functional changes in human development.

Maturation and growth should be separately defined for facilitating our understanding of development, but they are related aspects of the developmental process. Growth and maturation are intertwined because, as the body grows, functions improve (Stott, 1967). However, most people's rate of growth (other than increase in body fat) is often greatly reduced when they are about 20 years old. In contrast, maturation proceeds until the end of the lifespan.

GENERAL MOTOR DEVELOPMENT TERMS

As discussed earlier, there are important reasons why we need a general understanding of human motor development. Although many of us pride ourselves on the characteristics that make us unique, the general motor development of all human beings is remarkably similar. Several terms are used in motor development to depict the general growth and maturation trends that occur throughout the population.

Developmental Direction

Cephalocaudal and *proximodistal* are frequently referred to as the developmental directions because they indicate the direction in which growth and movement maturation proceeds. Cephalocaudal literally means "from the head to the tail." Specifically, this term refers to the development of the human being from the top of the body, the head, downward, toward the tail or the feet. This phenomenon is especially noticeable as it applies to growth. The head of a human fetus or infant is much larger than the head of an older child, adolescent, or adult relative to the body. The head experiences greater growth earlier than the rest of the body.

The cephalocaudal concept can also be applied to the maturation of human movement. The development of walking is an excellent example. When children first learn to walk, their legs are stiff and their feet flat. This awkward but typical walking technique is partly caused by cephalocaudal development. Control over the muscles that govern the hip joint enables the infant to swing the entire leg, but the child has not yet achieved similar ability at the knee or the ankle. With time, the child will gain comparable control at the knee and then the ankle, eventually achieving the mature walking technique.

Proximodistal, the second developmental direction, literally means "from those points close to the body's center to those points close to the periphery, or farthest from the body's center." This phenomenon is evidenced by human prenatal growth. The human evolves from the neural groove, a tiny elongated mass of cells that eventually forms the central portion of the body, the spinal column. From that central portion of the body all else will evolve until even the fingers and toes have been completed.

A similar process occurs in the acquisition of movement skill, such as an infant's early attempts at reaching and grasping (prehension). Initially, the infant's arm is controlled by the muscles that are predominantly responsible for shoulder movement. Gradually, dominance over the elbow also evolves, which allows much greater accuracy of movement. Finally, control over the wrist and then the fingers concludes the normal progression in prehension.

Interestingly, as a person ages and movement ability begins to regress, the cephalocaudal and proximodistal processes reverse themselves. The most currently acquired movements of the lower body or periphery will be the first to exhibit signs of regression. The process of movement regression slowly evolves in a "tail to head" and "outside-in" direction. However, as discussed in upcoming chapters, people can prevent or reduce such regression throughout most of their lives.

The cephalocaudal and proximodistal processes are useful tools in our efforts to gain a general understanding of motor development. The processes generally apply to human growth and motor development, but there are certain rare exceptions. For example, in the case of prehension, a child normally acquires control of the fingers before control of the thumb. This is an exception to the proximodistal rule

because the thumb is closer to the body's center than the fingers.

Differentiation and Integration

Two other terms useful for describing general motor development are *differentiation* and *integration*. Differentiation is the progression from gross, poorly controlled movement to precise, well-controlled, intentional movement. Our previous walking example also illustrates differentiation. Whereas early in the development of the walking pattern the leg swing is predominantly under the control of the large muscles surrounding the hip joint, eventually each segment of the leg becomes differentiated. That is, each segment of the leg develops a unique duty or specialization in the walking pattern, and thus the stiff, inconsistent gait that characterizes immature walking evolves into a more efficient movement pattern as the segments of the leg begin to function as individual units rather than as a unified block.

Integration is a related, similar change that occurs as an individual's movement ability gradually progresses. As just described, various muscle systems develop or change duties as movement skill improves. As the muscle systems become differentiated, they also become more capable of functioning together. For example, a young child handed one toy may hold onto it using only the hand closest to the toy. If the child is immediately handed a second toy on the same side, she will place the first toy in the other hand for safe-keeping if she is capable of integrating the use of one hand with the other (Bruner, 1970). The child incapable of such integration or coordination will simply discard the first toy in favor of the second one, freeing the receiving hand to take the new toy (see Figure 1-4). This movement may represent the hands' or arms' lack of integrative ability for this particular task.

As do the cephalocaudal and proximodistal processes, differentiation and integration reverse when movement regression occurs later in life. In other words, the improved motor ability acquired as a result of differentiation and integration gradually returns to a lower level of functioning. The coordination achieved between body parts and the parts' ability to perform highly specific duties during movement activity return to a lower level of functioning. Individuals can allay such regression, however, by maintaining certain habits and attitudes throughout life. Adulthood and movement regression is discussed in Chapter 16.

GROSS AND FINE MOVEMENT

The terms *gross* and *fine movement* are generally used to categorize types of movements; however, they can also generally describe motor development. Gross movements are primarily controlled by the large muscles or muscle groups. One relatively large muscle group, for example, is in the upper leg. These muscles are integral in producing an array of movements, such as walking, running, and skipping. These movements, primarily a function of those large muscle groups, are considered gross movements.

Fine movements are primarily governed by the small muscles or muscle groups. Many movements performed with the hands are considered fine movements because the smaller muscles of the fingers, hand, and forearm are critical to the production of finger and hand movement. Therefore, such movements as drawing, sewing, typing, or playing a musical instrument are fine movements.

Although movements are frequently categorized as gross or fine, very few are completely governed by either the small or large muscle groups. For example, handwriting is normally considered a fine movement, but as in most fine movements, there is a gross motor component: The large muscles of the shoulder are necessary for positioning the arm before the more subtle movement the smaller muscles create can be effective.

A combination of the large and small muscle groups is often responsible for the production of gross movements as well. Throwing, for example, is considered a gross movement, a logical categorization because upon casual observation the most sig-

nificant muscle involvement appears to emanate from the shoulder and the legs. A throw, however, is normally initiated with a certain degree of accuracy intended. The large muscles of the shoulder and the legs contribute greatly to the desired accuracy, but minute, subtle adjustments of the wrist and fingers are imperative for optimal precision in this movement at a high level of performance. Therefore, although throwing is considered a gross movement, an important fine motor component is critical to throwing perfection. In fact, the degree of fine motor control is a reasonably good indication of movement perfection. An individual may be capable of performing the necessary gross motor aspects of a movement, but the skill may not be honed until the person acquires the fine motor components.

The term gross and fine motor therefore can be used to categorize movement or to describe general

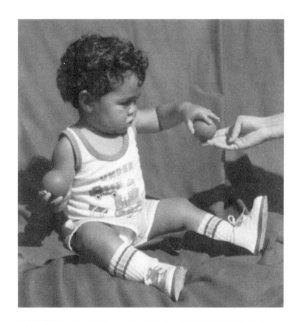

FIGURE 1-4 A young child who is handed a succession of toys may exhibit integration of the hands and arms by receiving the toy with one hand and storing it in the other. This storage process frees up the receiving hand for additional receptions.

progression or regression in motor development. As a person matures in a particular movement, the fine components of the skill become increasingly significant; the person becomes increasingly adept at both the fine and gross motor aspects of the movement. During movement regression, which often occurs from lack of activity in later life, the reverse occurs: The performer initially loses the ability to incorporate the fine motor aspects of the movement. After extreme regression, even the gross motor components of a movement begin to diminish.

THE PROCESS-PRODUCT CONTROVERSY

As described in the previous section, movements can be observed and usefully categorized by simple and general means. Often, however, movement specialists require more specific measurement. As we saw in our earlier discussion of the history of motor development, depending on the objective of their investigation and their philosophical stance, researchers generally use a *product* or a *process approach.* In the product, or task-oriented, approach (Pew, 1970, 1974) to measuring movement, the end result, the outcome, of the movement is analyzed. For example, for a child's catching performance, the product-oriented approach analyzes the child's control of the ball.

The process-oriented approach emphasizes the movement itself, with little attention to the movement outcome. In our example of catching, the researcher using the process-oriented approach focuses on the technique the child uses to attempt to accurately receive the ball rather than the amount of ball control. In some cases, the movement product and process are the same. Although the process or product can be easily distinguished in a movement like catching, the process involved in many gymnastics-related movements is also the product. In a movement like a forward roll (as in catching), the process is the technique used to perform the movement. However, in the forward roll, the technique can also be the desired end product because

in competitive situations such movements are judged on level of perfection.

The process orientation has been more popular in recent years because researchers believe that it unveils more information about the underlying processes critical to understanding human movement rather than just the outcome. However, the product orientation, criticized for its lack of concern for the underlying movement processes (Schmidt, 1988), can be valuable in movement research designed to have educational implications. For example, there has been considerable research to determine the factors that most significantly affect the outcome of certain movement skills. Children's success in movement outcome is widely accepted as an important factor in keeping children interested and motivated in the activity. Product-oriented research can determine that certain variables negatively or positively affect movement outcome, thus potentially hampering the child's likelihood of further pursuing the movement activity. Although the process approach was derived from a dissatisfaction with the product approach, both means of analyzing movement have potential value in motor development. But to fully profit from the research, the investigator must first closely examine the intent of the study and on that basis determine which approach is the most satisfactory for the specific situation (Payne, 1982).

TERMS FOR AGE PERIODS THROUGHOUT THE LIFESPAN

As depicted in Figure 1-5, specific terms are applied to the various age periods throughout the lifespan. These terms vary slightly from source to source in the ages specified but otherwise are generally accepted for use in the study of human development. These terms are *not* used to suggest that everyone in a particular age range will possess the same movement characteristics. The terms are helpful in organizing our discussion and communicating statements about persons at a particular time of life. Because these terms are frequently used throughout this

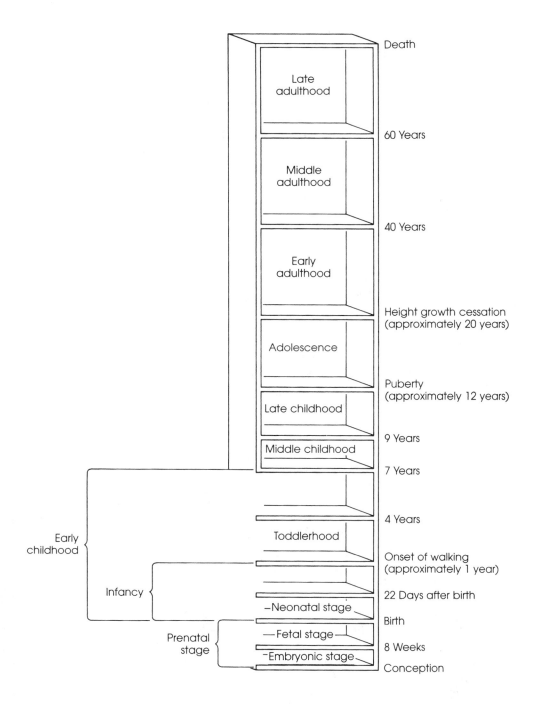

FIGURE 1-5 Age stages across the lifespan.

book, we now briefly discuss them in the order of their occurrence.

The first stage of age is the prenatal period, which spans the time from conception to birth. This period was once considered insignificant for human development but is now believed one of the most influential periods in the entire lifespan, particularly during the first 8 weeks of the prenatal period, which is known as the embryonic period. During the embryonic period, the developing human is known as an embryo. At the conclusion of the first 8 weeks of gestation, the fetal period begins. The onset of the fetal period is often described as the point at which the individual has become recognizable as a human being. Organogenesis, the formation of the vital organs, has occurred, although considerable growth and maturation have yet to take place. The individual is referred to as a fetus until the fetal period culminates at birth.

The first 22 days following birth make up the neonatal period. These 22 days are included in the period known as infancy. Therefore, a baby younger than 22 days can be called an infant or, more specifically, a neonate. Infancy lasts from birth throughout the first year of life, to the onset of independent walking.

Once children have begun to walk alone, they are considered toddlers. The approximate mean age for this landmark occurrence is 1 year; toddlerhood culminates at 4 years. This upper range for toddlerhood has been determined rather arbitrarily because no abrupt or immediate behavioral change is associated with the transformation from toddlerhood to early childhood.

Arbitrary limits have also been established to distinguish early childhood, which follows toddlerhood, from middle childhood. Early childhood spans 3 years, beginning at approximately age 4 and terminating when the child is 7 years old. Middle childhood ceases at 9 years and precedes the last preadolescent period, late childhood. Late childhood spans approximately 3 years and, as with all the periods discussed here, does not necessarily indicate an abrupt transformation to a new mode of behavior. An individual in the late childhood period is normally quite different in many respects from a person in middle childhood. However, the transformation is gradual, with the newly emerging behaviors often imperceptible. In fact, the transition from the first to the second year of late childhood may involve behavioral change as profound as that with the transition from the last year of middle childhood to the first year of late childhood.

Again, the establishment of these age periods is often arbitrary. Nevertheless, dividing the lifespan into age periods helps organize the study and promotes efficiency in examining the enormous span of time. Studying the lifespan as a whole would be exceptionally cumbersome!

The next age period, adolescence, is marked by a significant landmark of life. According to most developmentalists, the process known as puberty begins adolescence. Puberty is a time of radical hormonal releases that are directly and indirectly associated with a number of behavioral changes accompanying adolescence. This phenomenon is more thoroughly discussed in later chapters dealing with human physical changes and their effects on motor development. This important developmental landmark commonly occurs in females at approximately age 11 and in males at age 13. For this reason we should declare separate times of onset for adolescence based on gender. Although the onset of adolescence is signaled by puberty, the offset is often more arbitrarily determined. Some experts rely on such sociocultural factors as graduating from school or reaching voting age, to determine the offset. Others simply assume completion of the teen years indicates attainment of adulthood. The most common indicator, however, would be the achievement of maximal height. Adulthood is typically achieved by females at around age 19; males usually require 2 additional years (Malina & Bouchard, 1991).

Adulthood typically spans a much greater time than any of the preceding periods of life. In fact, adulthood commonly encompasses more than 60 years. To organize our discussion, we divide this lengthy block of time into early, middle, and late adulthood. Early adulthood begins at age 20 and continues until age 40. Middle adulthood encompasses the subsequent 20 years, ending at age 60.

Finally, late adulthood begins at 60 and ends at death. Because the behavioral changes in the adult are particularly gradual and subtle relative to the changes in the child or adolescent, all the adult age periods have been established arbitrarily for ease and to organize the discussion of adult motor development.

STAGES OF DEVELOPMENT

The age periods we discussed in the previous section could all be termed *stages*, or age stages. "Stage" is one of the most frequently encountered words in the study of human development, often used interchangeably with "phase," "time," or even "level." Use of the term stage implies that there is a particular time in the life of a human being that is characterized by unique behaviors. Such behaviors were not evident prior to the onset of the stage and may not be evident in the same form when the stage ends. The premise of the "terrible twos" stage, for example, is that it is common for children at or about 2 years to exhibit disruptive behavior. Furthermore, this behavior was not present before age 2 and will cease or become modified before the child passes into the next stage of behavior.

Do stages such as the terrible twos really exist? There is a major controversy among developmentalists as to whether or not such abrupt beginnings and ends of behavioral states really occur. The continuity versus discontinuity debate poses the question, Does life proceed smoothly and continuously from birth to death? Or is life discontinuous, with occasional, relatively abrupt behavioral changes occurring throughout? This debate is of considerable interest to developmentalists but remains unresolved.

Most of us find it difficult to accept the possibility that stages do not exist. Popularization of such terms as terrible twos and teenager has led us to believe that periods of unique behavior are a fact of life. Nevertheless, the existence versus nonexistence of stages is an ongoing controversy among developmentalists. There is no absolute evidence to conclusively substantiate either viewpoint.

This controversy is also prevalent in motor de- velopment. Roberton (1978) suggested that for stages to exist, a hierarchical, qualitative change must occur in the human movement behavior. In other words, one stage of behavior flows into a subsequent, qualitatively different stage. Furthermore, each stage must be unique from all others but must possess traits that link it to the preceding stage. The ordering of these behavioral states must be invariant and commonly occurring universally. Therefore, a person would not progress through the stages in reverse or mixed order, and everyone would experience these stages. There has been research to test these and other criteria to determine if stages are present in motor development. However, to this date, the research remains inconclusive regarding the existence or nonexistence of stages in human motor development.

Whether or not stages exist continues to be an important developmental concern. Even though this controversy remains unresolved, it is extremely useful to organize the study of human development into stages. Capsulizing aspects of human development into stages or manageable portions of information facilitates our attempts to study the human being. Therefore, despite a lack of documentation for the existence of stages, we refer throughout this book to stages, phases, or periods. We do not, however, suggest that these stages or periods are times of unique, hierarchical, or universal behaviors.

SUMMARY

Motor behavior is the general area of study that includes the fields of motor development, motor learning, and motor control. Motor development, the focus of this book, is the study of changes in motor behavior over the lifespan, the processes underlying these changes, and the factors affecting them.

The history of the study of motor development, according to Clark and Whitall (1989), can be divided into four periods: the precursor period, 1787–1928; the maturational period, 1928–1946; the normative/descriptive period, 1946–1970; and the process-oriented period, 1970 to present.

Two important trends that have been prevalent in recent years are the increased interest in dynamical systems perspective and the lifespan approach to studying motor development. Dynamical systems posits that a variety of systems, not just the nervous system, constantly interact and adjust to each other to create human movement. Improved kinematics, "our ability to describe the nature of motion," have facilitated the advancement of this approach. Increased interest in the entire lifespan has resulted from a rapidly aging society and the opportunity it offers for studying progression and regression as well as many new and different explanations for how we develop.

Motor development research is generally conducted using a cross-sectional or a longitudinal design. The cross-sectional design selects subjects from various age groups for observation on a given motor behavior. They are all measured or observed at approximately the same time. The longitudinal design selects only one age group of subjects and observes them for an extended period of time. While the cross-sectional design can detect differences between age groups, the longitudinal design can actually detect change. Both designs offer advantages but also have disadvantages that make research in motor development particularly difficult. Because of these disadvantages, the time-lag or sequential (cohort) designs were created. The time-lag design examines different cohorts at different times. The sequential design incorporates the time-lag, cross sectional, and longitudinal designs in one study. Thus, some of the disadvantages of the other design types are avoided, though this design is difficult to analyze statistically, less efficient administratively, and potentially costly.

Human development is often categorized into motor, cognitive, and affective domains. The cognitive domain refers to human intellectual change; the affective domain refers to social-emotional change. All of these domains are in constant interaction. Motor development strongly influences, and is strongly influenced by, cognitive and affective development.

Motor development is an important area of study because it helps us understand all aspects of human development. Practical applications from this field of study include detection of motor abnormalities, which facilitates early intervention and remediation of problems, and through our knowledge of motor development, the creation of more valid, efficient, and scientifically based programs for teaching movement skills to people of all ages.

Human development is the progressions and regressions that occur within human beings as they age. Maturation is a specific aspect of development involving the qualitative, functional changes that occur with aging. Growth, another aspect of development, concerns increases in physical size, that is, quantitative, structural increases occurring with aging.

Cephalocaudal, proximodistal, differentiation, and integration describe general motor development trends. All people follow the general progressions these terms describe but vary considerably in their rate of change.

The terms gross and fine motor refer to movements created by the large and small muscle groups, respectively. These terms are useful because they help us generally categorize movements and describe movement progressions and regressions throughout the lifespan.

Process- and product-oriented approaches are used to evaluate or measure movement performances. The process approach emphasizes the technique of the movement; the product approach examines the outcome or end product of the movement.

An age-period approach is useful for facilitating our study of motor development throughout the lifespan. We use common terms to refer to various age periods, such as infancy, toddlerhood, or early adulthood. This approach is particularly useful, but we do not suggest that these age periods are characterized by specific behavioral traits of the individuals included within the periods.

KEY TERMS

Attractor	Cohort design
Attractor well	Control parameter
Cephalocaudal	Cross-sectional design

Development
Differentiation
Dynamical systems
    perspective
Fine movement
Gross movement
Growth
Information
    processing theory

Integration
Kinematics
Lifespan perspective
Longitudinal design
Maturation
Maturational period
Motor behavior
Motor control
Motor development

Motor learning
Normative/descriptive
    period
Order parameters
Perceptual-motor
    theory
Precursor period
Process approach
Process-oriented period

Product approach
Proximodistal
Self-organizing
Sequential design
Stage
Synergetics
Time-lag design

CHAPTER 2

Cognitive and Motor Development

As mentioned in Chapter 1, the three domains of human development are the affective, cognitive, and motor. The system of categorizing human behavior into these domains evolved because it is useful for organizing and simplifying the study of human development. Although these domains of development are usually studied as individual units, we must remember that they are in constant interaction with each other. Everything we do in the motor domain is affected by our emotions, social interactions, and cognitive development; furthermore, all behavior in the affective and cognitive domains is strongly influenced by motor behavior (see Figure 2-1). This chapter examines several important specific interrelationships between the cognitive and motor domains. How does our gradually changing motor ability affect our cognitive development? How does our level of cognitive development influence our motor development? What are the significant areas of interaction?

FIGURE 2-1 Cognitive and motor development interact continually throughout the lifespan as they reciprocally inhibit or facilitate each other.

THE TERM PSYCHOMOTOR OR MOTOR?

For this book we deliberately chose to use *motor* as a general term to refer to any form of human movement behavior, rather than using the more common *psychomotor*. Psychomotor is particularly useful for referring to the domain of human development that involves human movement. Although generally used synonymously with the term motor, psychomotor actually refers to those movements initiated by an electrical impulse from the higher brain centers, for example, the motor cortex. Most human movement is the result of such stimulation. However, because there is a form of movement behavior—reflexive movement—that is initiated in the lower brain centers or the central nervous system, we use the more general term motor so as not to exclude the reflexes from the movement-related domain, the motor domain.

Nevertheless, the term psychomotor deserves special attention in this chapter. This word was created in recognition of the interaction between the mind (psycho) and human movement (motor). The mind is a critical component of the production of almost all human movement. This interactive relationship is thoroughly examined in the remainder of this chapter. We also study the equally important effects of human movement on mental or cognitive development.

JEAN PIAGET AND COGNITIVE DEVELOPMENT

Unquestionably, developmentalists have paid more attention to cognitive development than to any other domain of human behavior. And no one wrote more about cognitive development than the most famous developmentalist, Jean Piaget. Piaget is generally accepted as among the most innovative, accurate, informative, and prolific developmentalists. He wrote over 40 internationally acclaimed books and was labeled a genius by such people as Albert Einstein (Maier, 1978).

Piaget's interest in human intellectual development emerged after years of study in related fields of interest. When he was 10 years old, he published his first biology-oriented article and gradually increased his interest in biology throughout his childhood, adolescence, and early adulthood.

Eventually, Piaget became interested in examining how we "know," that is, the process of thinking. According to Piaget, this process is a critical function in life that enables us to adapt to our environment. Of particular interest to Piaget were children's incorrect responses to questions or problem-solv-

ing situations. By observing these responses, Piaget found that children demonstrated varying impressions of the world relative to each other and to adults. This system of inquiry evolved into what is now known as Piaget's *clinical method,* a system of collecting data by question-and-answer sessions to more fully understand the process of thinking (Newman & Newman, 1991). Piaget questioned many children and carefully noted their mode of approaching problems and issues. By including children from several age groups in his interviews, Piaget was able to categorize similar behaviors into the four stages of development that constitute his famous theory of cognitive development.

Piaget's Theory of Cognitive Development

Between 1925 and 1931, Piaget's wife gave birth to three children. The births were a particularly important impetus for Piaget to understand the changing cognitive processes. During those years he developed the basis of what is still the most widely accepted theory of cognitive development. In fact, Piaget's theory of cognitive development is the most detailed, systematic interpretation of any aspect of human development. This theory, although largely based on Piaget's observations of his children rather than formal scientific inquiry, is a guideline for understanding the changing thought process throughout childhood and adolescence. Furthermore, this theory has given cognitive developmentalists a specific basis from which to begin their investigating. An awareness of this theory is critical to a thorough understanding of motor development because cognitive and motor development constantly interact. Cognitive development strongly depends on the movement capabilities the individual has acquired; similarly, motor development depends on intellectual capabilities. This interactive process is apparent in Piaget's theory.

The four major stages in Piaget's theory of cognitive development are sensorimotor, preoperational, concrete operational, and formal operational (see Table 2-1). The ages Piaget cited for each stage are

TABLE 2-1   Major Stages of Piaget's Theory of Cognitive Development and Approximate Ages or Periods of Occurrence

Stage	Age/Period of Occurrence
Sensorimotor	Birth to 2 years
Preoperational	2 to 8 years
Concrete operational	8 to 11 years
Formal operational	Early to midadolescence (11 to 12 years)

only guidelines. Individual variation is expected, although it is believed that most children approximate the course of development Piaget suggested. Furthermore, not everyone achieves Piaget's highest level of cognitive development, formal thought. But children do follow the same sequence through the stages regardless of the level of cognitive ability they eventually attain. In other words, the stages are always experienced in the same order, and no stage is ever skipped, although the rate and degree of completion vary with each child. Also, each stage is increasingly more complex than its predecessor and builds on the cognitive abilities gained in the previous stage.

Adaptation   According to Piaget, cognitive development occurs through a process he called *adaptation.* Adaptation is the adjusting to the demands of the environment and the intellectualization of that adjustment through two complementary acts, assimilation and accommodation. *Assimilation* is a process by which children attempt to interpret new experiences based on their present interpretation of the world (Shaffer, 1989). This process of perceiving experiences relative to a past mode of thinking is exemplified by an infant who with one hand attempts to grasp a ball slightly too large for the small hands (Figure 2-2). The one-handed "plan" to grasp the ball was in the child's cognitive repertoire as a result of previous experience with rattles or smaller objects. Thus the infant tries to incorporate the ball, the new experience, using an already established mode of thinking.

In *accommodation,* the second facet of adaptation, the individual attempts to adjust existing thought structures to account for, or accommodate, new experiences. In the case of the infant trying to obtain the large ball, accommodation could occur when the child recognizes that the ball is larger than the more familiar rattle. The infant then modifies the approach to obtaining the ball by either adapting the one-handed grasp or by using the other hand to help. Therefore, the child has made an adjustment to accommodate the ball. A new experience or environmental event has altered the child's behavior and past understanding or interpretation of the event.

According to Piaget, assimilation and accommodation always work together. Assimilation suggests that the individual always experiences new events according to what is already known; accommodation infers that the environment always challenges the individual to modify actions relative to the specific situation (Maier, 1978). As we saw in the earlier example of the infant trying to get the large ball,

FIGURE 2-2   An example of assimilation. The infant is trying to grasp a large ball by using a one-handed reaching and grasping technique. This new experience is being incorporated into the child's cognitive repertoire by an existing mode of thinking.

both components of adaptation are highly dependent on the individual's movement, especially during Piaget's first stage of cognitive development, the sensorimotor stage. Adaptation and its two facets, assimilation and accommodation, are basic to Piaget's theory of cognitive development and emphasize the importance he placed on the role of the environment in human development.

Criticisms of Piaget's Theory Jean Piaget's theory has been amazingly well accepted by developmental experts, but some specific aspects of the theory are worth special consideration. First, although Piaget became adept at his clinical method of gathering data concerning children's thought processes, this method has been criticized for lacking scientific control during the collection process. In addition, much of Piaget's observation centered around his own children, which of course leads to concerns about his potential bias in interpreting the thought processes of people so dear to him. Nevertheless, Piaget's theory of cognitive development has withstood considerable scrutiny for many years and continues to be the most significant guide in our efforts to more fully understand human development.

Perhaps the most strongly contested aspect of Piaget's theory is his proposal that the highest level of intellectual development is formal operational, a stage he claims is often achieved by children as young as 11 years. Although Piaget stated that some children may never achieve formal operations and some may not achieve them until as late as 20 years, a significant portion of the lifespan still remains unaccounted for. Strong proponents of Piagetian theory support his notion, but increased interest in recent years in adult development has led to speculation that there be a fifth stage (Arlin, 1975; Kaluger & Kaluger, 1984). Undoubtedly, cognitive behavior continues to develop long after early adolescence, despite Piaget's relative omission of this time of life. Several of the important cognitive changes that occur during adulthood and their relationship to motor development are discussed later in the chapter.

INFANCY: THE SENSORIMOTOR STAGE AND MOTOR DEVELOPMENT

The interaction between motor and cognitive development is a lifelong process particularly evident during the first 2 years. This is acknowledged in Piaget's theory and his decision to call the first stage of cognitive development *sensorimotor.* In the sensorimotor stage, Piaget described the infant as "thinking by bodily movement" (Fein, 1978). In other words, intelligence develops as a result of movement actions and their consequences. According to Piaget, obviously movement is critical to the thought process.

The sensorimotor stage, which normally endures throughout the first 24 months of age, is a time of creating a foundation for all subsequent understanding that hinges on a child's ability to perform bodily movement. "An infant's experience of being able to grasp and hold with certainty simultaneously influences the development of cognition" (Maier, 1978, p. 3). In the sensorimotor stage, knowing and thinking emerge as a result of action that occurs via bodily movement. Of particular importance in this stage are the environment and motor development.

The sensorimotor stage is subdivided into six substages (see Table 2-2), making this stage the most detailed of any of Piaget's four major stages. The first substage is called exercise of reflexes and lasts from birth through the first month of age. This substage is characterized by the earliest form of movement behavior, the infant reflexes, and their repetition. According to Piaget, the repetition of the reflexes helps the child explore the world through movement and forms the foundation for cognitive understanding. This earliest form of movement behavior facilitates the development of intellectual behavior and may be the impetus for all future intellectual development. The infant reflexes are apparently innate forms of movement behavior that occur without stimulation from the higher centers of the brain. Reflexive movement is discussed in detail in Chapter 10; for now, we simply emphasize the role of this form of movement in the development of intellectual

TABLE 2-2 Substages of the Sensorimotor Stage of Development and Their Approximate Ages of Occurrence

Substage	Age of Occurrence
Exercise of reflexes	Birth to 1 month
Primary circular reactions	1 to 4 months
Secondary circular reactions	4 to 8 months
Secondary schemata	8 to 12 months
Tertiary circular reactions	12 to 18 months
Invention of new means through mental combinations	18 to 22 months

behavior. Reflexes help us adapt and modify our behaviors by experience. Gradually, reflexes are modified to produce a completely new behavior. For example, the nipple of the mother's breast stimulates the sucking reflex in the infant. As another example, by accident, or repetition of other reflexive movements, the child's hand may come into contact with the mouth. By trial and error and as a result of modifying existing reflexive behavior, infants may learn to find the mouth with the hand, thus becoming capable of the gratifying act of sucking the thumb: they learn a new behavior (see Figure 2-3).

The second sensorimotor substage is known as primary circular reactions. Lasting from the end of the first month until approximately 4 months, this substage is characterized by the onset of increased voluntary movement. Infants now can consciously and capably create certain movement behaviors. Whereas in the first substage repetition occurred solely by accident, now the infant makes conscious efforts to repeat desired acts. By repeating actions, infants come to realize that certain stimuli have value to them. Recognizing certain stimuli allows the child to voluntarily repeat an activity when the same stimulus is presented in the future. These repeated actions are known as circular reactions and are considered primary because they always occur in close proximity to the infant.

Movement therefore has an integral role in the development of thought processes. However, the relationship is reciprocal because the increasing cognitive abilities facilitate such movement con-

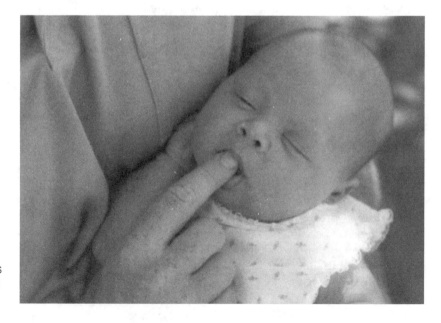

FIGURE 2-3 The sucking reflex is gradually modified to become a completely new behavior. This is an example of learning by moving.

cerns as eye-hand coordination and early reaching and grasping.

Secondary circular reactions is the third substage of the sensorimotor stage of development. Generally, this substage, which lasts from approximately 4 to 8 months, is a continuation of primary circular reactions but incorporates more enduring behaviors: movement behavior is intended to make an event lasting. The infant repeats the primary circular reactions. Examples of behaviors common in this substage are persistent shaking of a rattle and banging a toy to make noise. Such behavior familiarizes the infant with the environment and its forces.

During this substage, the infant's interaction with the environment gradually expands. In fact, two or more movement forms may be incorporated to enable more thorough interaction with and manipulation of the environment. For example, infants may make visual contact with a rattle, which stimulates them to obtain and shake the rattle. Such action is further evidence that the infant learns the stimuli and actions necessary to initiate certain behaviors through interaction with the environment via bodily movement. Furthermore, once the child can integrate vision, hearing, grasping, and certain movement behaviors, imitation, a major characteristic of secondary circular reactions, is possible. However, like most events or objects in the life of an infant of this age, there is no sense of permanency. Objects last only as long as they are viewed. Once a rattle is removed from the view of infants in this substage, they cease to seek it because they assume it no longer exists. Imitation can be performed only as long as the source of imitation is immediately present.

From approximately 8 to 12 months, the fourth substage, secondary schemata, begins. Movement is still critical in the continued development of the intellect. Past modes of movement, designed to interact with the environment, are now applied to new and unique situations, enabling many new behaviors to emerge. These new behaviors are facilitated by increasing movement capabilities such as crawling and creeping, which allow greater exploration of the environment and more contact with new objects and situations.

Particularly noteworthy in this substage are the increasing repetition of experimentation and the continued trial-and-error exploration. Through these learning processes, infants develop an ability to anticipate actions or situations that may occur in their environment. They can predict potential occurrences beyond their immediate activity. This ability, according to Piaget, is the onset of intellectual reasoning, and it allows infants to pair objects with their related activities and prepare to act on the basis of that determination. For example, when a ball is rolled to infants 8 to 12 months old, they can crudely return it. More important, the infants then prepare for their turn at receiving the ball because they realize the ball will once again be returned to them. They have associated the ball with the act of playing catch.

The secondary schemata substage is followed by the tertiary circular reactions substage. This fifth substage lasts throughout the first half of the second year and is characterized by the discovery of new ways to produce desired results through active experimentation. In fact, active experimentation now consumes a major portion of the infant's time. Results of experimentation are incorporated into existing intellectual frameworks to create entirely new knowledge. Piaget believed that reasoning is fairly well developed in this substage and is a necessary entity for the cyclical repetition of activities, characteristic of this substage, to occur.

Additionally, there is an intensified interest in the surrounding environment as well as constant attempts to understand it. Therefore, the various sensory modalities, especially vision, become extremely important in furnishing valuable information concerning the surroundings. Piaget noted that children in this substage realize that the discovery of a new object and the actual use of the object are separate entities. For example, children recognize that a ball can be thrown to create an enjoyable activity, but they know they do not have to pitch the ball at that time because they have developed the capability of delaying the act until later, with the assurance that the ball will not lose its valuable property. This ability is one of the first signs of a child being capable of visualizing an object beyond its immediate use. However, in this substage, immediate relationships are still the only relationships clearly understood.

People become increasingly important in tertiary circular reactions as they become potential sources of resolution of the child's "problems." According to Piaget, this event may be a function of children's improving ability to recognize that they are different from other people. Distinguishing the self from others facilitates the development of the ability to create action through others. For example, children can seek help for their problem-solving situations from parents or older siblings. Piaget claimed that this was a critical skill in the establishment of social development and such important human factors as emotion, competition, and rivalry. We can thus see that cognitive and motor development considerably affect development in the affective domain as well as each other.

Invention of new means through mental combinations is the last of Piaget's substages in the sensorimotor stage. Lasting from 18 to 24 months, this substage is a period of metamorphosis from active involvement in movement interactions with the environment to an increased reflection about those movements. This substage is often considered the climax of the sensorimotor stage and a transitional phase into the preoperational stage.

In this substage, children clearly recognize objects as independent from themselves and as possessing their own unique properties. Similarly, children recognize themselves as one object among the many existing in the environment. The child's interaction with environmental objects has been almost completely manifested via movement activities and has allowed an understanding of the properties of objects such as size, shape, color, texture, weight, and use to develop. However, the child may require a separate cognitive ability for each property. This fact is illustrated by children who respond to statements concerning their yellow ball but who do not understand when the ball is called the "big" ball. In fact, they may often refute such statements by noting that the ball is yellow, not big, when it is actually yellow and big.

Perhaps the most important characteristic of this substage is the development of the cognitive ability to consider the self and an object in simple situations in the past, present, and future. This cognitive skill allows contemplation of activities and may be the onset of what Piaget termed *semimental functioning*. By the end of this substage, "thinking with the body" has been gradually replaced by thinking with the mind. A new skill is made possible. Children can now recall an event without physically reenacting what happened. Furthermore, they can ponder alternatives and predict potential outcomes to situations without having to perform the acts first. The following list recaps the major developments that occur in the sensorimotor stage.

1. Increasing awareness of the difference between the self and others

2. Recognition that objects continue to exist even though they are no longer in view

3. Production of mental images that allow the contemplation of the past, present, and future

The individual, after experiencing all facets of the sensorimotor stage, now enters childhood.

CHILDHOOD: PREOPERATIONS AND MOTOR DEVELOPMENT

The *preoperational stage* begins at around 2 years and spans the next 5 years. This stage builds on the skills learned earlier in life as the child becomes more imaginative in play and recognizes that everyone views the world from a slightly different perspective. Furthermore, the child begins to more capably use symbols to represent objects in the environment. This capability enables one of the most important of all cognitive skills, verbal communication, to emerge.

Language development is the most important characteristic of preoperations and is strongly linked to rapidly improving motor abilities. The child becomes particularly adept at verbal communication very soon after learning to walk upright unassisted. Walking enables the child to more thoroughly explore and therefore understand the environment, and the rapidly expanding repertoire of new concepts gained from this increased exploration facilitates language. By the middle of the preoperational stage, most children have a highly efficient ability to communicate verbally as a result of this important interaction between motor and cognitive development.

Although Piaget generally focused on the cognitive attributes gained in each of his stages of cognitive development, in the preoperational stage he emphasized the limitations. In fact, the term preoperations was coined because at this stage children still do not have the ability to think logically or operationally. This second major stage of Piaget's theory is subdivided into two substages: preconceptual (from 2 to 4 years) and intuitive (4 to 7 years).

As mentioned, during the preconceptual substage, an ability to use symbols to represent objects in the environment emerges, for example, having a rock represent a turtle or the word "Dad" represent a certain person. Obviously, this new skill is critical to language development, but it also enables the child to more easily reconstruct past events and facilitates pretend play. During pretend play children role play; they pretend they are other individuals and use props to symbolize objects to supplement their play. This play often focuses on various movement activities and contributes significantly to all areas of child development, including motor development. It is believed that movement is enhanced by a child's pretend play, which may include such acts as imitating a parent or other role model engaged in a favorite movement activity.

Piaget believed that the preconceptual substage was characterized by a level of cognitive ability that is primitive relative to adult capabilities. Piaget said that during this stage children's thinking is flawed by their tendency to animate inanimate objects. For example, children may refer to the emotional state of a drooping flower by saying "The flower is sad!" This is a fun and interesting way to perceive the world, but it is also unrealistic and usually erroneous.

Transductive reasoning is another characteristic of the preconceptual substage. In this form of flawed reasoning, the child assumes that there is a cause and effect between two events occurring simultaneously. For example, a child who has missed breakfast may declare it cannot be morning because breakfast has not been prepared; obviously, the preparation of breakfast does not cause the onset of morning. Transductive reasoning often leads to incorrect assumptions.

Perhaps the most serious deficiency of this substage of preoperational thought is egocentrism. Children 2 to 4 years old view the world from their own narrow perspective. Not only do these youngsters have difficulty visualizing the perspective of others, they also do not adapt their rapidly developing language skills to facilitate the listener's understanding. Motor activities help in this regard because they increase a child's capability to interact socially by providing a means of locomoting to other children, thereby creating an outlet for social activity and enhanced social awareness. Increased social interaction increases the child's sensitivity to the needs and feelings of others and generally reduces the egocentrism characteristic of this stage of cognitive development.

The intuitive substage, an extension of the preconceptual substage, is characterized by reduced egocentrism and continued improvement in the use of symbols. Piaget called this substage intuitive because the child's understanding of the ways of the world are based on the appearance of objects and events that may not accurately depict reality.

As in the first substage of preoperations, Piaget continued to characterize cognitive development by the child's limitations. In both substages, the preoperational child is incapable of an ability Piaget called *conservation*. Conservation is an "ability to realize that certain properties of a substance remain unchanged when the appearance is rearranged in a superficial way" (Shaffer, 1989, p. 319). The concept of conservation is exemplified by Piaget's classic test involving a ball of clay. When the ball is manually transformed into an elongated sausage shape, the child incapable of conservation responds that the elongated clay weighs more. The child capable of conservation knows that the spatial transformation of the clay has no effect on the weight of the clay.

The inability to conserve results from the child's difficulty in attending to more than one aspect of a problem-solving situation at one time. Preoperational children cannot "decenter" their attention from one particular component of the problem. Once they attain this capability, they can concentrate on more than one aspect of that problem. In the ball of clay example, the child with conservation ability can ponder the weight, length, and even the width of the clay rather than being restricted to one aspect of the clay. Inability to decenter attention can also have significant implications in motor development. By this time in a child's life, many new motor activities, such as games, have become popular. The inability to consider simultaneously multiple aspects of a problem inhibits the child's efforts at games or activities involving complex strategies or multiple movements for each child. Consider young children involved in a game of soccer: Their attention becomes so focused on their objective of scoring a goal that they are impervious to the possibility of passing off to teammate.

LATER CHILDHOOD AND ADOLESCENCE: COGNITIVE AND MOTOR DEVELOPMENT

Toward the end of childhood, most individuals enter Piaget's third stage of cognitive development: concrete operations. First we focus on this stage, and then we examine formal operations, the last stage of cognitive development, which is considered a beginning for many young people at early adolescence.

Concrete Operational Stage

Piaget's third major stage of cognitive development, the *concrete operational*, generally spans age 7 to approximately 11 years. Many experts believe that a child attains concrete operations once the child has gained the ability to conserve. Thus a major characteristic of this stage is the enhanced ability to decenter attention from one variable in a problem-solving situation. As we mentioned earlier in our discussion of conservation, this ability to decenter attention can have important implications for motor development.

Also in this stage of development, children or young adolescents gradually attain the ability to mentally modify, organize, or even reverse their thought processes. A characteristic such as reversibility is exemplified by rolling balls A, B, and C through a small tube (Figure 2-4). We ask the child, "What order will the balls be in as they exit the other end of the tube?" Both the preoperational and the concrete operational child can correctly answer "A, B, and C," but only the child who has attained concrete operations can reverse that process. In other words, if we immediately roll the balls back through the tube without altering the order in which they exited, and ask, "What will the order of exit be this time?" only the concrete operational child can correctly respond "C, B, and A" (Fein, 1978).

Piaget used the term concrete operational because the child at this level of cognitive development faces a major limitation. Although this stage is a major advancement over the preoperational one, the concrete operational child is still limited to pondering objects, events, or situations that are real or imaginable. This of course impedes efforts to mentally examine hypothetical or abstract situations.

On the positive side, the child who has attained this level of cognitive ability is now capable of mentally representing objects or a series of actions or events. This mental capability has obvious implications for motor development. For example, the child can facilitate many movement activities by formulating strategies for or expectations about an opposing player's or team's possible intent. By being able to mentally ponder probable events or actions, the child can anticipate and, hopefully, successfully counter the opponent's tactics.

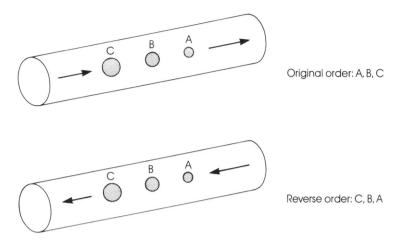

Original order: A, B, C

Reverse order: C, B, A

FIGURE 2-4 Demonstration of reversibility. The child can predict the sequence of balls A, B, and C as they exit the tube in both the original and reverse order.

Piaget considered *seriation* another characteristic common to children at this level of development. Seriation is an ability to arrange a set of variables by a certain characteristic. For example, fellow teammates can be arranged by height, and the relative relationships between these individuals can then be discerned. In other words, if a group of concrete operational children are informed that the basketball center is taller than the forward and that the forward is taller than the guard, they can determine that the center is also taller than the guard.

As emphasized throughout this chapter, there is a constant, reciprocal, mutually beneficial relationship between cognitive and motor development. Piaget indirectly referred to this phenomenon throughout his theory; the concrete operational stage is no exception. In this stage (as well as others), Piaget stressed that learning can be facilitated by doing or by actions. That is, such cognitive skills as seriation can best be taught by having children manipulate objects of various lengths and widths into series. Piaget recommended that one of the best modes of teaching such concepts as space or distance was having the child "do" by instructing the child to move through the space or the distance under consideration. In Piaget's mind, movement in the form of doing or action was a critical component in the development of cognitive ability.

Formal Operational Stage

According to Piaget, the highest level of cognitive ability begins at approximately 11 to 12 years and is known as the *formal operational stage* or, simply, formal operations. The major accomplishment in this final stage is the ability to consider ideas that are not based on reality: that is, the individual is no longer confined to observable or imaginable thoughts. Abstract ideas are possible, which enables young people to resolve problems that violate their concept about reality in the world. Children in the concrete operational stage may be completely baffled by questions concerning abstract or nonexistent events or objects. In fact, the children may respond that there is no possible response because the concept under consideration is nonexistent. Formal operators, however, are challenged and enjoy the opportunity to ponder the new concept. According to Piaget, many individuals never achieve this stage of development. In fact, people who score below average on intelligence tests most likely have not achieved formal operations (Shaffer, 1989).

Formal operators are also capable of performing what Piaget called interpropositional thought. This enhanced level of cognitive ability allows children to relate one or more parts of a proposition or a situation to another part to arrive at a solution to a problem. To illustrate, if confronted with the statement "The ball is in my left hand or it isn't in my left hand," the child in concrete operations may need to visually inspect before responding. The young adolescent in formal operations, however, can determine that the statement, although somewhat unusual, is correct. By simultaneously considering the two propositions within the statement, the formal operator determines that the ball is either in the hand or it is somewhere else, which indicates that the statement is correct.

This ability to perform interpropositional thought can be useful in many situations. In complex movement situations, this capability could enhance one's success strategically. In many team activities, the positioning of two or more players, each a "movement proposition," may indicate the onset of a particular play. A defender who can "read" the interrelationship between these movement propositions can prepare accordingly and help the team counter the play.

An additional product of formal thought is what Piaget referred to as hypothetical-deductive reasoning. This term indicates a problem-solving style in which possible solutions to a problem are generated and systematically considered. This rational, systematic, and abstract form of reasoning facilitates the selection of the correct solution. Piaget believed that this new form of reasoning, which allows consideration of the abstract, has dramatic effects on the child's emotional development, including the development of new feelings, behaviors, and goals. Newly emerging values may result from this enhanced cognitive capability. Frequently, young adolescents become increasingly idealistic as they ponder such magnanimous concepts as world peace or our search for the perfect energy source. Resolution of these problems may seem fairly simple to a young formal "operator" who can now think about what presently appear to be unrealistic situations.

The changing values that Piaget believed emerge as a result of formal operations may also affect the young adolescent's decisions concerning participation in movement endeavors. Because of increased idealism, the adolescent may decide that the competition common to many adolescent movement activities is not mutually beneficial to all involved and therefore opt to cease participation. Or the adolescent may begin to become aware of the potential benefits to be derived from participation and learn to cherish the possibility of being exceptionally fit or successful in a movement endeavor. The extent and direction of the individual's new values are also functions of the current trends among peers and society; this topic is more thoroughly discussed in Chapter 3.

ADULTHOOD: POSTFORMAL OPERATIONS

Piaget did not specifically consider adulthood in his theory of cognitive development, but many other researchers have. A number of developmentalists have proposed a fifth stage of cognitive development. One source referred to an addition to Piaget's theory as the "structural analytical stage" (Kaluger & Kaluger, 1984). This proposed fifth stage is believed to encompass a higher level of cognitive ability than does formal operations because it involves larger quantities of information.

Arlin (1975) also proposed a fifth stage, known as the problem-finding stage. As the name implies, this stage of *postformal operations* is characterized by discovering new questions to be answered instead of simply attempting to discover some logical, well-defined solution to a given problem. Rybash et al. (1986) view this form of postformal operations, though, as simply a different style of thinking rather than a definitive stage of cognitive development.

Clearly, many cognitive developmentalists believe that significant changes in cognitive ability continue well after adolescence and, most likely, throughout the remainder of the lifespan. The specifics of those changes, however, are much less clear. Nevertheless, as witnessed in infancy, childhood, and adolescence, cognitive and motor development interact reciprocally throughout adulthood. Cognitive and motor changes continue to profoundly affect each other in adulthood as they did earlier in life, although the effects appear much more gradually.

ADULTHOOD: TWO GENERAL THEORIES OF INTELLECTUAL DEVELOPMENT

As a result of the considerable research into the changing intellect during adulthood, experts generally take one of two major theoretical positions concerning this stage of cognitive abilities. The first viewpoint proposes a consistent, gradual decline in intellectual capability throughout adulthood. The second general theoretical position is considerably less severe; proponents of this more contemporarily accepted view believe some cognitive decline may occur in some areas, but certainly not all.

Total Intellectual Decline Theory

This theory is the most traditional view but is less accepted today than it was 10 to 15 years ago. Nevertheless, there is research evidence to substantiate the idea that adulthood is a time of gradual, consistent, and pervasive cognitive decline. Perhaps the most prominent evidence indicating an intellectual decline was data derived from the Wechsler Adult Intelligence Scale (WAIS) (Dacey, 1982). This scale measures 11 components of intellectual ability, 6 concerning verbal ability and 5 concerning performance ability. It has been shown that there is a decline in intellectual ability within every subtest of the WAIS. However, those who disagree with the total intellectual decline theory

respond by stating that this test does not measure all known aspects of intellectual ability. Furthermore, the WAIS has been criticized for being influenced by the test taker's socioeconomic, occupational, and educational characteristics.

Nevertheless, WAIS data have led to the controversial belief that intellect closely parallels the growth curve. An intellectual plateauing may occur as early as 15 years, followed by a consistent, gradual decline throughout the remainder of the lifespan (Savage et al., 1973).

Partial Intellectual Decline Theory

Presently the most widely accepted view is that cognitive decline occurs in some areas but not others. This theory is well substantiated by current research evidence and is generally much more emotionally satisfying because the total decline theory has been criticized for leading to a self-fulfilling prophecy; that is, if we believe that we are going to gradually lose our cognitive capabilities, we will.

Much of the research concerning cognitive change in adulthood has involved the concept of memory. Memory is a critical component to the performance of movement activities; retaining information on past performances facilitates performance on future attempts (Clark, 1978). For scientific scrutiny, memory is divided into at least three parts: primary, secondary, and tertiary. *Primary memory* is short-term, such as the ability to recall the name of a newly introduced person. In the normal adult, primary memory appears to be generally unaffected by the aging process. *Secondary memory* is exemplified by the ability to recall a newly learned list of words or the name of an individual who was introduced prior to the introduction of several other people. The efficiency of secondary memory decreases with age. *Tertiary memory* is long-term. An example of tertiary memory is the ability to recall names and locations of well-learned items, items that were learned years or even decades ago. The abundance of current research has shown no decline in tertiary memory with age, which dispels the stereotype that the old remember only idiosyncratic or generally useless information (Fozard, 1985). Furthermore, this information also adds support to the notion of a partial rather than a complete cognitive decline.

Other aspects of cognitive ability have also been examined, such as speed in information-retrieval or problem-solving tasks. It has been found that older individuals need more time to retrieve information, regardless of the kind of memory involved, than do younger adults. However, this occurrence is not believed to be a function of a less efficient retrieval system. In fact, this increased retrieval time may be a result of the more abundant knowledge acquired with age; more memory must be "scanned" to locate the pertinent information (Fozard & Poon, 1980).

Many experts believe that even in those cognitive areas where there is evidence of a decline, impaired intellectual capability may not be the cause. Rather, the motivation or personality may have changed the individual's values to the point that performing well may be less important than it was in previous years (Arenberg, 1973). Nevertheless, a person's confidence in the accuracy of response appears unaffected by age (Fozard & Poon, 1980).

Regardless of the cause of the specific forms of the cognitive decline, whenever speed is a factor, the decline increases relative to the performance of younger subjects. In fact, "one of the most pervasive manifestations for aging is slowing responses" (Ford & Plefferbaum, 1980, p. 119). This slowing of response speed that occurs with age increases as the task becomes more complex (Birren, Woods, & Williams, 1980). Interestingly, one of the most common measures of speed of response for cognitive abilities is also one commonly used for determining motor capabilities: reaction time. It is believed that this measure indicates the speed of information processing. Increased reaction time in older subjects may indicate reduced fidelity of the central nervous system.

This reduced speed in cognitive ability that frequently accompanies aging has important implications for motor development. Obviously, many movement activities require fast, even split-second, decision making. Because of many older individuals' gradually decreasing capability to efficiently make such decisions, the motor activity requiring this capability may regress with increasing age. Furthermore, as discussed earlier, secondary memory also is impaired during the normal aging process. This decline too could affect an individual's motor performance. An ability to recall, over a relatively short period of time, previous movement situations is often beneficial to performance. Decreasing cognitive capacity could potentially gradually impair motor development in specific areas.

Although such occurrences as decreasing secondary memory and decreased speed of response are currently believed common in adulthood, much can be done to delay or inhibit the onset of these factors. In fact, a lifestyle can be designed that optimizes the cognitive attributes (Jarvik & Cohen, 1973). If adults maintain use of their cognitive abilities, the decline is not likely to occur as early or as rapidly and, perhaps, can be avoided completely. In addition, movement plays an important role in this effort to maximize cognitive ability. Heart-diseased or hypertense individuals have been shown to perform more poorly on many cognitive performance tasks (Birren, Woods, & Williams, 1980); an active, movement-oriented lifestyle helps combat such conditions. Furthermore, it is believed that maintenance of an active, movement-oriented lifestyle heightens cognitive sensitivity and responsiveness because cerebral blood flow increases and neural tissues undergo positive alterations. In addition, physical activity increases the size of motor neurons while decreasing the density of the neural synapses—both factors are considered critical to inhibiting the slowdown of cognitive and motor responses that commonly occurs with old age. Reaction time and cognitive performance improve in both uninstitutionalized aged people and institutionalized geriatric patients who are placed on an exercise program (Powell & Pohndorf, 1971). Clearly, maintenance of an active, movement-oriented lifestyle into and throughout adulthood can affect cognitive as well as motor development. And, as discussed in Chapter 3, the effects are even more pervasive because social development is also strongly influenced by an individual's motor development.

KNOWLEDGE DEVELOPMENT AND SPORT PERFORMANCE

Most of the early research examining the processes that ultimately lead to skilled motor control and performance have been conducted in laboratory settings. The assigned movement task used to experimentally explore movement control and learning factors has generally involved some simple and novel movement. While such an arrangement is scientifically sound (in part this arrangement controls for differences in past experiences), it does not present problems regarding external validity. No doubt, this line of research has successfully led to better understanding of the underlying memory processes that are employed during novel skill performance. Unfortunately, we do not know whether or not these theories adequately explain performance as it is encountered in a real-world setting.

Thomas and colleagues (1988) have produced convincing evidence that improvements to the task-specific knowledge base may lead to better task-specific sport performance. It is believed that children's motor performance deficits can be attributed to their inexperience (lack of a sufficient knowledge base) and to their inefficient use of control processes. These control processes are needed to store, retrieve, and effectively use information. Indeed, some studies (Chi, 1978; Lindberg, 1980) have shown that when novice adults are compared with more experienced children, the children can perform as well as or better than the adults (cited in Thomas et al., 1988). These children probably outperformed the novice adults because of their greater depth of task-specific knowledge.

According to Anderson (1976), knowledge can be represented in two forms: *declarative knowledge* and *procedural knowledge*. Declarative knowledge can be thought of as "factual information," while procedural knowledge can be thought of as a "production system" or "how to do something." Research comparing expert and novice performers has clearly shown that the expert performer has more knowledge of task-specific concepts (Charness, 1979) and has better problem-solving abilities (Adelson, 1984).

To fully appreciate the strong relationship between cognitive abilities and sport-specific performance, it is important to realize that raw athletic ability does not necessarily ensure athletic success. Let us illustrate this point with a real-world example from the sport of basketball. There are only 7 seconds left in the game and the offensive team trails by one point. The ball is in the hands of the team's best ball handler. As time is about to expire, he looks to his right and quickly executes a perfect behind-the-back pass to a teammate located on the left side of the court. Unfortunately, this perfect pass was directed to the team's worst ball handler and worst shooter. Time expires without a final shot being attempted. This situation is unfortunate because the team's leading scorer, who was located on the right side of the court, was also open for a shot. But because the ball handler used poor judgment his superior skills did not translate into athletic success. In short, an incorrect cognitive decision was made (who best to pass the ball to), which probably cost his team the game. If successful athletic performance is to occur, then there must be a strong link between sport-specific knowledge and skilled movement execution. In our example, the ball handler should have known that the team's strategy was to get the ball into the hands of the best shooter.

French and Thomas (1987) conducted a series of two experiments that point out the strong relationship between the sport-specific knowledge base and athletic success. In their first study, these researchers studied the relationship between knowledge development, skill development, and development of expertise in basketball among children age

8 to 10 and age 11 to 12. Participants in both age-group leagues were administered a 50-item multiple-choice test to assess basketball knowledge, as well as two basketball skills tests that were adapted from the AAHPERD basketball skill test (speed shot and control dribble). An observational instrument was also developed for the purpose of assessing individual basketball performance during an actual game. This observational instrument was used to code the young participants' behaviors during one quarter of play. Behaviors were coded according to the following categories: control, decision, and execution. Control refers to the child's ability to decide what to do with the basketball once it was caught (shot, pass, dribble, etc.), while execution refers to whether or not the child performed the skill of shooting, passing, or dribbling in an appropriate manner. Coaches were also required to fill in a questionnaire for the purpose of rating their players' basketball ability. In addition, an open-ended basketball interview was conducted with the players. During this interview, players were asked questions regarding how they would respond to various basketball situations. For example, one question asked them to list appropriate offensive strategies for a two-on-one fast break.

The results from this first experiment indicated that the child experts (in both age groups) practiced longer, had more years of basketball experience, and participated in more sports than did the novices. In addition, on average the child experts made correct decisions (85 percent) more frequently than the novice performers (51 percent). Furthermore, the child experts scored higher than the novices on both skills tests and on basketball knowledge. The authors concluded that "development of sport-specific declarative knowledge is related to the development of cognitive decision-making skills or procedural knowledge, whereas development of shooting skill and dribbling skill are related to the motor execution components of control and execution" (French & Thomas, 1987, p. 24).

In their second experiment, French and Thomas (1987) wanted to determine the influence of changes in basketball skill improvement and basketball knowledge on game performance during the course of one season. Subjects were 14 child novices and 17 child experts who had participated in the first experiment. To control for maturation effects, a control group of 16 children who had no previous organized basketball experience was utilized. The basketball participants were administered the control dribble test, the speed spot-shooting test, and the basketball knowledge test at the beginning and at the end of the basketball season. The control group also was administered these same three tests two times, 7 weeks apart. Assessing playing performance involved coding behaviors during one quarter of play for each of three games. More specifically, the three games in which behaviors were coded included the first game and the last two games of the season.

In general, the findings from this second experiment found that game performance improved over the course of the season. However, this improvement was the result of being able to make more appropriate cognitive decisions during the course of a game and also being able to better catch the basketball. It was not due to improvements in basketball skill execution. In fact, during the course of this 7-week season, no significant changes were found to exist among dribbling and shooting test scores or the execution component that was coded during game performance. Thus it appears that task-specific knowledge is acquired faster than motor skill development. In other words, children in this study learned "what to do" in a given situation before they acquired the physical skills to successfully carry out their strategic plan. The researchers (French & Thomas, 1987) point out that additional research is needed before we can recommend the best combination of motor and cognitive instruction and the timing of each for the purpose of maximizing sport-specific performance.

SUMMARY

As motor and cognitive abilities develop, they facilitate and inhibit all other aspects of development.

These abilities reciprocally interact at all times throughout the lifespan, significantly affecting motor and cognitive behavior.

Jean Piaget was the most famous and prolific of all developmentalists. His theory concerning cognitive development—the most widely accepted theory in that area—is based on the sensorimotor, preoperational, concrete operational, and formal operational stages.

The interaction between motor and cognitive development is particularly evident in the sensorimotor stage, which spans the first 2 years of life. This stage is characterized by "thinking by bodily movement," which suggests that actions created by the body enhance the cognitive process.

Several major accomplishments during the sensorimotor stage are the ability to differentiate between the self and others and to recognize that objects continue to exist even though they are no longer in the visual field. Also, the child becomes capable of producing mental images that allow contemplation of the past and future as well as the present.

The major cognitive achievement during the preoperational stage is acquisition of language. This process is facilitated by rapidly improving manipulation and locomotor skills. These skills enable the child to explore more and to better understand the environment, contributing to the child's ability to express related concepts verbally.

The concrete operational stage is reached when the child has developed the ability to decenter attention from one to two or more aspects of a problem-solving situation. This decentering skill is valuable in perfecting the strategy involved in many movement activities.

Piaget believed that the formal operational stage was the highest level of cognitive ability. In formal operations, the major cognitive landmark is the acquisition of the ability to think hypothetically, that is, ponder the unreal. New cognitive abilities such as interpropositional thought may continue to enhance an individual's ability in strategic movement situations.

Many experts disagree with Piaget's view that formal operations is the highest level of cognitive ability. These experts believe that cognitive development continues throughout adulthood, although they debate the specific nature of the change. Adulthood (postformal operations) is traditionally and stereotypically viewed as a time of cognitive decline, but current evidence suggests that knowledge continues to increase and primary and tertiary memory remain relatively unimpaired. However, secondary memory and cognitive situations involving speed do decline throughout adulthood.

The decline in split-second decision making seriously impairs performance in many movement activities. However, maintenance of an active, movement-oriented lifestyle may delay the onset and slow the rate of cognitive decline because movement activity increases cerebral blood flow and causes other physiological effects.

Researchers are just beginning to examine the relationship between sport-specific knowledge and sport performance.

KEY TERMS

Accommodation

Adaptation

Assimilation

Clinical method

Concrete operational
   stage

Conservation

Declarative knowledge

Formal operational
   stage

Postformal operations

Preoperational stage

Primary memory

Procedural knowledge

Psychomotor

Secondary memory

Semimental
   functioning

Sensorimotor stage

Seriation

Tertiary memory

CHAPTER 3

Social and Motor Development

The somewhat arbitrary classifying of the human being into the cognitive, affective, and motor domains does facilitate discussion of human development, but it is not a realistic portrayal of the person. Human behavior is *not* compartmentalized; there is a complex system of constant, reciprocal exchange between an individual's cognitive, affective, and motor being. That which affects an individual in one domain is bound to have a subsequent effect in all other domains as well. For example, Chapter 2 emphasized the strong relationship between human intellectual function and movement: Any intellectual change is also accompanied by a change in motor function. Many of these changes are so slight that they are of no obvious consequence in a person's life. But other changes are of tremendous magnitude and may have lifelong implications for human

movement as well as social, emotional, and physical well-being.

This chapter examines another reciprocal relationship of particular importance to human motor development: social behavior and movement. Social behavior affects a person's movement behavior, and, conversely, there are equally strong motor effects on an individual's social development.

SOCIALIZATION

Socialization is a ". . . dual process of interaction and development through which human beings learn (1) who they are and how they are connected to the social worlds in which they live, and (2) the orientations used as a basis for the individual behaviors and group life in the same worlds" (Coakley, 1993; p. 571). Though generally associated with learning that occurs through social interactions, socialization can include any means by which a person gathers information about society and generally includes the entire process of becoming a human being. Common means of socialization include observation, inference, modeling, and trial and error, but the most important is through social interaction. The influence of others around us is extremely important in determining how and when persons acquire certain movement abilities. They are also integral in determining which movement activities we choose. The amount of social support supplied by significant others in our lives is positively associated with the extent of our participation in physical activity. Researchers have determined that parents, siblings, teachers, coaches, and friends can all have varying amounts of influence on the choices we make concerning physical activity. In turn, the movement activities we choose affect our ability to "fit in" socially based on the compatibility of our choices with the dominant social values. Our movement choices also affect our self-identity, social mobility, educational achievement, attitudes concerning masculinity and femininity, and even our moral development (e.g., attitudes about cheating and fair play) (Coakley, 1993).

Although generally associated with development during childhood, the socialization process is lifelong, facilitating a person's function within society throughout childhood, adolescence, and adulthood. Furthermore, even though the term is commonly associated with the learning that occurs through social interaction, socialization can include any means by which a person gathers information about society. Nevertheless, the most important means of learning societal rules and expectations is through social interaction, which is also true for learning human movement. The influence of others around us is extremely important in determining how and when persons acquire certain movements as well as what movements.

The process of socialization teaches the members of society their social roles. A *social role* is the behavior that members of a particular social group expect in a particular situation (Kaluger & Kaluger, 1984). There are many social roles in any society. Occupational roles of, say, a professor or a police officer are exemplified by specific expected behaviors. Family roles can be illustrated by a mother or a father, who are expected to exhibit certain behaviors relative to the rest of their family and their society. Society's role expectations tremendously influence human motor development. Movement may or may not be acquired, depending on whether individuals believe that movement to be role appropriate. In other words, is that movement one individuals assume appropriate for what they consider their role in society?

This set of expectations about behavior is formally called a *norm*. Societal norms can facilitate or inhibit people's movement development, depending on the individual's perspective of the norms. For example, in many areas of the United States, the norm is to expect less of older adults, so many older adults indeed do expect less of themselves. They are inhibited or constrained by the societal norm concerning their age group. As another example, the norm for the adolescent male regarding physical activity is vigorous involvement in movement pursuits, to the extent that his social success may depend on his athletic prowess. Both of these examples are examined more thoroughly later in the chapter.

SELF-ESTEEM DEVELOPMENT AND PHYSICAL ACTIVITY

One extremely important human characteristic affected by social interaction and physical activity is *self-esteem*, or self-worth. Self-esteem is the value we place on ourselves as persons (Gruber, 1985; Harter, 1988)(see Table 3-1). This is not to be confused with *self-concept*, which is simply our perception of self (Gruber, 1985). Self-esteem and self-concept have been widely studied, with most researchers finding

TABLE 3-1   Distinguishing Between Self-esteem (Self-worth) and Self-concept

Self-esteem (self-worth)	Self-concept
The value we place on ourselves as persons	Our perception of self

them to be significantly affected by involvement in physical activity. So much research has been done on this issue that Gruber (1985) was able to conduct a meta-analysis, a quantitative review of literature. In his review, he found 84 articles reporting studies of the effects of physical activity on self-esteem or self-concept. Of these studies, 27 offered sufficient data for use in his meta-analysis. Of those 27 studies, 18 found physical activity to significantly affect self-concept or self-esteem. Overall, Gruber determined that 66 percent of the children in physical education or directed-play situations exceeded the self-concept or self-esteem scores of the children in non-physical activity settings. Physical activity programs with physical fitness objectives were found to be particularly beneficial for the children studied.

Gruber also determined that emotionally disturbed, trainably mentally retarded, educably mentally retarded, perceptually disabled children, and economically disadvantaged child subjects who were physically active exhibited a mean self-concept score much higher than the scores of all other groups. Gruber suggested that those subjects, in particular, begin to feel important when allowed opportunities for involvement in programs of motor enrichment that are conducted by trained and supportive professionals. The greatest gain in self-esteem was, therefore, found in those who most needed it, though normal children also exhibited an improvement.

In conclusion, Gruber stated that involvement in directed play or physical education could enhance self-esteem in children though it was not clear why. Perhaps, the simple distraction is sufficient to increase self-esteem, or some have hypothesized a physiological change. The physical activity could also affect endorphins or monamine (a brain neurotransmitter) which, in turn, would alter the child's affective state. In general, Gruber (1985) believed these findings to be critical because improving one's self-image is integral to future behavior.

In more recent research, Harter (1988) has determined that self-esteem evolves developmentally in a series of somewhat predictable steps (see Table 3-2). Young children, for example, are incapable of making meaningful and consistent judgments about their *global self-worth*, the overall value that one places on the self as a person. They can, however, make reliable judgments about such elements of self-worth as cognitive and social competence and their own behavioral conduct, though they cannot accurately distinguish between these elements. Harter also contends that young children cannot distinguish between their competency in cognitive and physical skills. This does not mean that young children do not have a sense of self-worth. Rather, they simply have difficulty expressing it verbally because of their limited cognitive capabilities.

Harter believes this changes at midchildhood because of increased cognitive capabilities. At around 8 years of age children can begin to verbalize their feelings of self-worth and make judgments about their self-esteem. Furthermore, between ages 8 and 12 years, children develop the ability to distinguish between scholastic and athletic competence, peer social acceptance, physical appearance, and their own behavioral conduct.

Adolescents are capable of even greater articulation and discrimination concerning the elements of self-worth. They can distinguish all the same elements as before with the addition of close friendships, romantic appeal, and job competence. This process of development continues with college students where more distinctions are exhibited. In addition to global self-worth, Harter believes the college-age individual can differentiate and articulate 12 elements of self-worth: scholastic competence, intellectual ability, creativity, job competence, athletic competence, physical appearance, romantic appeal, peer social acceptance, close friendships, parent relationships, sense of humor, and morality. Interestingly, Harter indicates that this age group

TABLE 3-2   Self-worth Development (Harter, 1988)

Early childhood	Though young children can make reliable judgments concerning their own cognitive and social competence and behavioral conduct, they cannot distinguish between them. In addition, they cannot make judgments about their global self-worth and have difficulty in discerning between cognitive and physical skills. They also have difficulty in expressing their own sense of self-worth because of limited cognitive capabilities.
Mid–late childhood	Because of enhanced cognitive ability, children begin to verbalize self-worth and make judgments about it. Ability also begins to emerge in distinguishing between scholastic and athletic competence, peer social acceptance, physical appearance, and behavioral conduct. As in all other age groups, physical appearance and social acceptance are the most important elements contributing to global self-worth.
Adolescence	By adolescence, increased capability emerges as adolescents articulate and discern between the elements of global self-worth. In addition to the elements which they could articulate earlier, they can now distinguish feelings concerning friendship, romantic appeal, and job competence. In addition to physical appearance and social acceptance, friend and teacher support are major contributors to global self-worth.
College age	By college age, the ability to make more distinctions becomes apparent. In addition to global self-worth, the elements of scholastic competence, intellectual ability, creativity, job competence, athletic competence, physical appearance, romantic appeal, peer social acceptance, close friendships, parent relationships, sense of humor, and mortality can be articulated. In addition, clear distinctions are made between scholastic competence, intellectual ability, and creativity. Global self-worth becomes a function of the individual's perceived self-worth in the areas which have become most important personally. Intimate relationships and adequacy as a provider also become increasingly important in young adulthood.
Adulthood	By adulthood, a need has developed for further distinction between elements of self-worth including intimate relationships, nurturance, adequacy as a provider, and household management in addition to all of those mentioned earlier.

clearly distinguishes between scholastic competence, intellectual ability, and creativity.

The adult has developed a need for distinguishing additional elements of self-esteem or self-worth. Specifically, these include intimate relationships, nurturance, adequacy as a provider, and household management in addition to those mentioned for younger age groups. This need for new elements with each additional age group implies, according to Harter, a developmental change in one's self-esteem.

Harter also notes that, for each age group, certain elements of self-esteem contribute more or less to the global self-worth. Physical appearance and social acceptance, respectively, were the most important elements contributing to the global self-worth of elementary school children. Surprisingly,

these two elements of self-worth were the two most important for all age groups. For adolescents, parent and classmate support were also major contributors to global self-worth, followed by friend and teacher support. Harter expressed some surprise at the contribution of parent support in adolescents, who are generally believed to be gradually evolving to increasing reliance on peers and decreasing reliance on parents.

In college students, self-worth was a function of the individual's perceived competence in the areas that had become most important to him or her personally. As was the case with all age groups, athletic competence was not found to be a high-ranking contributor to most students' formation of global self-worth. This may seem to contradict Gruber's finding that we discussed earlier. However, we must distinguish between involvement in physical activity and athletic competence. While Gruber found physical activity to significantly improve self-esteem, Harter believes that athletic ability is a fairly low ranking influence in global self-worth. "Physical activity" as examined by Gruber implied involvement in movement, whereas "athletic competence" implies a perceived level of success in competitive sporting activities. These are clearly distinguishable and, apparently, vastly different in the effect they exert on self-esteem.

Like all other groups, the young adult's global self-worth was most affected by physical appearance and social acceptance. These elements were followed by intimate relations and sociability. Intelligence and adequacy as a provider were also found to be important contributors in young adults. The two lowest elements of self-worth were household management and athletic ability.

In general, the developmental changes noted in self-worth included an inability to express a concept of global self-worth during early childhood. This ability evolves in midchildhood, however, as we see an increasing ability to articulate global self-worth as well as differentiate some of its elements. With age, we also see the changes in the nature of social relationships being reflected in the elements influencing global self-worth. For example, while peer acceptance and romantic appeal are important to the adolescent, intimate relations and nurturance are more highly valued in the adult.

Like Gruber, Harter believes findings relative to self-worth or self-esteem to be significant. She specifically notes the pervasive effect of self-worth on one's mood or affective state. Individuals with higher levels of self-worth are more cheerful and exude higher levels of energy, whereas low self-esteem has a depressing effect on behavior. No doubt, these mood alterations could have, at least, an indirect effect on motor development. Lack of desire to participate and subsequent lack of participation would inhibit the practice necessary to develop certain movement skills. In turn, successful attainment of certain levels of motor development likely has a reciprocal effect on self-concept. The feeling of accomplishment in movement or the simple act of participation, as illustrated by Gruber's research, can positively affect the self-concept.

SOCIAL INFLUENCES DURING INFANCY

The first year of life is often considered egocentric or asocial (Kaluger & Kaluger, 1984). Although the infant becomes increasingly social through that first year and on into adulthood, the baby's first few months of life involve only limited social interaction (see Figure 3-1). Because the baby totally relies on the caregiver(s), any social interactions at this time are dependent on the caregiver's whims. There are some social ties early in infancy. One form of social attachment is the infant's attempts to maintain some form of contact with the object of the attachment, such as by visual exchange or through reciprocal touch. Another form of early attachment is the distress the baby often expresses when the object of the attachment leaves or is absent. A third form of early social attachment is the infant distinguishing and differentially responding to the caregiver.

According to Newman and Newman (1991), the formation of social attachment occurs in four stages. These stages are particularly worthy of our examination because of movement's apparent role in facilitating the social attachment. According to these researchers, initially the infant grasps, sucks, roots, and performs numerous other infant reflexes. The infant also visually tracks, gazes, cries, and smiles in an effort to initiate and maintain close social contact with the object of attachment. These behaviors are all prominently involved in the social attachment process up to the age of approximately 3 months and are critical elements in the formation of the bond between the child and the caregiver.

For the next 3 months, the baby rapidly progresses in distinguishing between strangers and familiar human figures. In the third stage, from around 7 months to 2 years, the baby becomes

FIGURE 3-1 Infants have very few social ties, but the strong family relationship created during infancy can significantly affect their motor development.

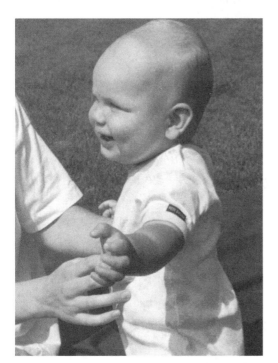

FIGURE 3-2 Gaining control of the arms and hands enables infants to manually respond to social touches.

increasingly adept at locomotion; this newfound ability enables the baby to actively seek close physical proximity with the object(s) of attachment. In the fourth stage (Figure 3-2), the baby gradually learns to control the use of the arms and hands, allowing him or her to pursue and manually respond to social touches.

Thus the newly developing movement activities facilitate and expand social interaction; the increasing social sophistication promotes and stimulates greater motor activity. The expanded social repertoire allows the baby to be more actively involved with the environment, further enhancing the motor abilities as well as the intellectual and emotional behaviors.

SOCIAL INFLUENCES DURING CHILDHOOD

Although social interrelationships during infancy are limited because babies lack social, intellectual, and motor abilities, the social influences begin to expand throughout childhood. Many specific forces contribute to the child's social development and, therefore, motor development. The family, for example, is the primary socializing agency during childhood. Although the magnitude of the family's effect may be diminishing because of present cultural trends, the family still exerts more influence on a child than does any other force. Increased television viewing and the use of babysitters and preschools at earlier ages, other important agencies of socialization (Loy & Ingham, 1973), lessen the impact of the family but have not overtaken this institution.

Play, whether done alone or in the presence of others, is also a major socializing force during childhood. Pleasurable activity is considered important to the development of such skills as problem solving, creativity, language, and many movements in general.

Another major socializing agent, although generally not a factor until the child is 4 or 5, is the school, where the teachers and coaches play an immediate role in the child's "learning of the culture." In fact, the school can overtake the family as the major socializing agency as the child approaches adolescence. The school also allows the establishment of a peer group, which can be a tremendous influence on the socialization process. Children's relationships with peer groups become increasingly important as they approach their adolescent years.

Play

The term *play* is commonly associated with children. People of all ages engage in play, but the word often inspires images of children engaged in some pleasurable, generally movement-oriented activity. Garvey (1990) described play as an activity that is always pleasurable and that the participant always positively cherishes. Furthermore, the motivation to play is intrinsic—play has no other objective. According to Garvey, play is inherently unproductive, spontaneous, and voluntary. Another important element of play is that it involves active participation by the player and "has systematic relations to what is not play." In other words, this seemingly insignificant act is actually a crucial part of learning the rules of society as well as many skills critical to functioning in that society.

Play is often based on movement. When movement, such as running, jumping, or even clapping or laughing, is involved, the pleasurable aspects of play are most clearly visible. In fact, one of children's first forms of amusement may involve being jostled or hoisted by the caregiver. Gradually, children become more involved with other children and expand their play experiences. Group play becomes particularly evident at early school age. However, play generally appears to evolve through a series of increasingly more social stages before it reaches a point of group involvement. According to Cratty (1986), play remains rather unsocial for young children even when social opportunities exist. When children are between 24 and 30 months old, their most common type of play is often solitary. Two children playing side by side pay little attention to each other and make few, if any, attempts at social interaction. They are generally so engrossed in their own activity that their companion's activity is of minimal consequence. This behavior soon evolves into what is known as parallel play. By the time children are 2 1/2 to 3 1/2 years old, they will still make few attempts to socially interact, but they may begin to display an awareness of each other and may even subtly copy each other's play behavior through observation and imitation. and imitation. Nevertheless, the children are not likely to interact to any greater extent.

Approximately 1 year later, when they are 3 1/2 to 4 1/2 years old, children will begin to display the interaction missing in their previous levels of play behavior. When involved in associative play, two or more children exhibit an awareness of each other and begin to exchange toys; however, there is no group goal. This lack of a group goal is the major difference between associative play and the final level of play during early childhood, cooperative play. Cooperative play generally occurs when children are around 4 1/2 to 5 years old and is evidenced by purposeful, group-oriented play activities involving games and even group leaders.

As a function of cooperative play, larger social units are formed. The movement activities selected for use within the larger group enable children to develop leadership skills as well as learn to compete, cooperate, and generally form a sense of need for greater social recognition. As children's social skills develop, group activities become more attractive and are more commonly sought out. Increased participation in popular group movement activities subsequently facilitates a child's motor development. Thus a positive, reciprocal relationship can develop between social and motor development; in fact, to a surprising extent, one form of development may depend on the other. Even at the young age of 5 or 6 years, group leaders are likely to be those who are superior in performing such physical activities as running, throwing, and balancing (Cratty, 1986). This is an expected phenomenon during early to late adolescence, but such a relationship between movement and social success is surprising at such a young age.

Family

As mentioned, the family is the most important socializing force in the lives of most children. The family is also the earliest and, in most cases, greatest determinant of a child's movement choices and movement success because it strongly influences the child's attitudes and expectations about movement. Furthermore, the family is largely responsible for the role that children envision for themselves. Depending on the family's views concerning physical activity, a child may or may not assume a role that is movement related. In fact, a child can even acquire a number of movement characteristics that are reminiscent of those of the parent. The parent of the same sex as the child has the greatest influence on such movement acquisition, although both parents remarkably prevail in shaping the child's movement idiosyncrasies involving, for example, gesture, gait, or posture. The child can acquire these movement habits from long-term observation of the caregiver (Birdwhistell, 1960).

The family's approval or disapproval of the child's movement endeavors is also crucial in determining future movement habits. If the child behaves motorically in a way that is rewarded, either overtly or subtly, he or she is likely to reproduce that movement behavior. However, ignoring the child's motor behavior or responding negatively may cause the behavior to subside. The family therefore can consciously or subconsciously shape their children's movement behavior, which is why Snyder and Spreitzer (1973) called the family the "most potent of socializing institutions."

In fact, Snyder and Spreitzer specifically researched the family's influence on such movement-related topics as involvement in sports. To investigate that particular question, they surveyed more than 500 people via a specially designed questionnaire. Following an examination of their results, Snyder and Spreitzer concluded that sports involvement generally begins in childhood. Furthermore, if parental interest was high, the likelihood of the child participating was much greater.

Greendorfer and Lewko (1978) conducted similar research to determine the specific role of family members in their children's sport socialization. In this research, 95 children 8 to 13 years were surveyed. Greendorfer and Lewko concluded that sport socialization begins during childhood and continues into adolescence. They further stated that the role of certain family members is significant in this socialization process. Specifically, parents were found to be a significant influence on the child's involvement in sport activities. Siblings, however, were not found to have a particularly critical effect on either boys' or girls' choices concerning involvement in sport. Also, it was determined that the father is an important predictor of sports selections for both males and females. Generally, however, boys receive greater exposure to more sport socializing agents than do girls, and such agents tend to encourage boys more than girls to participate. This fact was particularly evidenced by the finding that the father, the peers, and the teacher were all significant influences for the boys, whereas only the peers and the father were significantly influential for the girls.

More generally, this research substantiates the traditional view that boys have had more opportunity for socialization into sport and that sex differentiation does exist in this area.

The importance of the family was further reinforced by Greendorfer and Ewing's (1981) investigation. These researchers agreed with both studies cited by stating that the family can be an important predictor of involvement in sports. However, Greendorfer and Ewing also found that this process of socialization may affect children differently, depending on the children's race and gender. The researchers particularly emphasized these two factors in their paper "Race and Gender Differences in Children's Socialization into Sport" (1981). To examine these factors, Greendorfer and Ewing distributed questionnaires to hundreds of children, male and female, black and white, from 9 to 12 years old. The questionnaires were designed to determine what factors influenced children's decisions to become involved in sport activities. Based on an analysis of the results, these researchers determined that children of different genders and of different races socialized into sport differently. Among white children, boys were more influenced by their peers and their fathers; the greatest influences for girls were their teachers and their mothers. Among black children, the boys were most greatly influenced by their peers; the girls were more likely to be influenced by their teachers or sisters. These findings are somewhat contrary to Greendorfer and Lewko's findings that girls were not significantly influenced by their teachers or their sisters. That apparent contradiction may, however, add support to Greendorfer and Ewing's final conclusion that "considerable variance exists in the process by which children are initiated into games and sports."

Based on the research discussed to this point, the family is obviously integral in the sport socialization process. A child's decision to participate in movement activities and the kinds of activities selected appear to be important functions of the family. The role of the family may have other motor-related ramifications as well. Lee (1980) examined the effects of child-rearing practices on the motor performance of black and white children. Lee studied lower socioeconomic children from both races. The children ranged from slightly over 7 years to approximately 9 1/2 years and were grouped according to their mothers' attitudes concerning child rearing. The children's mothers were categorized as authoritarian or nonauthoritarian based on the results of an inventory specially designed to determine the level of parental authoritarianism. According to Lee, authoritarianism is associated with the parent's demand for obedience and the firm enforcement of the parent's expectations of the child. The nonauthoritarian mothers were more likely to exhibit permissiveness and grant their children independence. From this research, Lee determined that the children reared by the nonauthoritarian mothers had superior jumping and running skills. Lee concluded from such findings that the nonrestrictive environment may be a more ideal setting for a child's motor development because increased independence may enhance his or her opportunity to be physically active. Furthermore, Lee stated that she found the more permissive, free atmosphere more likely to be present in lower socioeconomic areas common to many black children. Lee postulated that this atmosphere and its resulting independence are why the black children in this research performed the motor tasks significantly better than the white children.

SOCIAL INFLUENCES DURING OLDER CHILDHOOD AND ADOLESCENCE

As the child approaches adolescence, the family's influence generally begins to diminish and the peer group becomes an increasingly important social force. The parent, teacher, or other adult figures in the child's life slowly lose their power of persuasion over the child as a need for peer approval becomes particularly powerful. This new social force, the *peer group*, is less structured than adult social groups but considerably more structured than the groups in the child's previous social environment. The peer group is also characterized by its transitory nature because it may vary from the neighborhood to the school as well as from day to day. It also has the capability of shaping the mode of children's dress, speech, or actions and their decisions concerning participation in movement activities. For example, members of the same peer group may often share similar gait or speech patterns (Bandura & Kupers, 1964). Furthermore, the relationships created in the peer group give the child or young adolescent friendship, support, companionship, and fun in ways that could not be achieved with the family. Peers strongly influence each other by interacting as equals, a situation unique from the family structure, which generally has a central authority figure(s). The peer group therefore often has a strong influence on decisions older children or adolescents make concerning involvement in movement activities.

This gradually evolving independence from the family enables children to shed the egocentrism so common during their earlier childhood. A person's daily interaction with peers also provides considerable learning experiences. For example, youngsters develop an increasing appreciation of many points of view because members of the same peer group often express diverse opinions. Additionally, young adolescents become increasingly aware of social norms and pressures. In fact, adolescents' social acceptability may be based on how they conform to the expectations of their social group. Two of the most common determinants of social acceptability, particularly for the male, are athletic ability and willingness to become involved in athletically oriented activities. Other determinants of social acceptability, as defined by the peer group, are appearance, academic achievement, career expectations, ethnicity, and special talents. Many of these characteristics, such as appearance and special talents, may, again, reflect the extent to which the person is involved in a movement endeavor. These characteristics are not, however, generally announced as qualifiers for status in a particular peer group, but such consistent standards are frequently used to include and exclude members.

As mentioned, movement ability partly determines peer group association but can also be molded within the group. Association with new and diverse opinions may promote participation in new versions of old games or completely new and different attempts at previously untried movement endeavors. The peer group applies pressure toward conformity, although the type of conformity varies tremendously from one peer group to another. However, if the peers consider participation in movement activities an accepted norm for their group, they pressure the members to be active in that pursuit. Gaining respect and approval becomes increasingly important to members of the peer group and depends on their adherence to the group's expectations. This often means that the peer group guides the individual into, or away from, participation, and perhaps achievement, in an athletic activity.

Team Play

During later childhood and adolescence, youngsters encounter an increasing sense of team or club participation. This factor is particularly important for influencing the types of movement activities the older children or young adolescents may select. Whereas during earlier childhood youngsters are content to play alone or in a small group, the emphasis changes as children approach adolescence. Because of increasing social capabilities and their relationship with the peer group, adolescents often actively seek group or team activities. Those who do decide to participate in a team movement experience devote much energy to trying to ensure the team's success (Newman & Newman, 1991).

Movement participation through team membership can be extremely influential in children's or adolescents' development. Through team participation, youngsters learn to work toward achieving group or team goals while subordinating personal goals, a major developmental stride for children who may still be overcoming the egocentrisms so prevalent earlier in their lives. The team concept also teaches children the importance of the division of labor. Gradually, youngsters learn that every member of the team has a duty and a responsibility and that the team's goals are most likely to be accomplished through sharing these duties and responsibilities. (See Figure 3-3.) Also, team membership often makes greater intellectual demands than the more unstructured group or individual activities of young childhood. More rules, strategies, and responsibilities are more common in team activities than in childhood group play.

In team play, the youngster also assumes greater social responsibilities. If people do not carry out their assigned duties, they may be ostracized or ridiculed. On the other hand, tremendous individual recognition is possible for those who are particularly successful in carrying out their duty to the team. Ideally, the more proficient participants should, and often do, assist the less capable, which is to the team's advantage. However, too frequently the less capable are scorned and their inability to perform blamed for the team's failure.

Although it is unpleasant to think of a child or young adolescent being scorned or ostracized in team play, in many ways the team is a model for life in general. In one respect, team participation teaches the child about failure and success as well as such common emotions as shame and embarrassment. For more successful participants, team play is an avenue for expressing humility or modesty. Experiencing these emotions personally and witnessing

them in others is an important lesson that may help youngsters deal with more difficult situations later in life.

Gender Role Identification and Movement Activity

In addition to all the functions discussed previously, the peer group serves another critical developmental purpose: It facilitates interaction with the opposite gender. During adolescence is when dating generally begins and gender roles become increasingly apparent. The degree to which adolescents associate with the role ascribed to their gender depends on several factors. The peer group influences the level at which young adolescents may identify with their gender, but *gender role identity* begins much earlier in life. The expectations for behaviors based on gender start early in childhood and often depend on the quality of a child's association with the parent of the same sex.

Even though many behaviors once commonly accepted for only one gender are now acceptable for both, many human characteristics are still considered masculine or feminine. For example, 50 percent of college students asked to describe the ideal sex role for children in their care responded

FIGURE 3-3 Team play teaches the value of cooperative efforts to achieve group goals, an important lesson for children who may still be overcoming their childhood egocentrism.

by citing dominance, aggressiveness, achievement for males, and deference, nurturance, abasement for females (Hamilton, 1977). Similarly, Michael (1970) stated that aggressive behavior is acceptable in males. In fact, males may be scorned if they are excessively dependent, whereas the opposite is true for females. This gender typing often produces rigid concepts regarding individuals' abilities and behaviors and no doubt affects decisions concerning their involvement in movement activity. Gender role conflict is often experienced by girls who seek to participate and boys who do not. Unfortunately, both cases may lead to emotional distress and limit potential by inhibiting the development of self-selected talents and skills (Oglesby & Hill, 1993).

Gender stereotypes can have major implications in an adolescent's decision to participate in a movement activity. The activity may seem enticing, but the gender role associated with that activity may conflict with the role adolescents deem appropriate for themselves. If an adolescent decides to participate anyway, a *role conflict* may be created. That is, an emotional trauma of varying proportions may evolve concerning the sex role that the adolescent considers appropriate versus the sex role that the relevant society views as appropriate.

The negative sentiment expressed by our society concerning girls and women in physical activity and sport may also affect the *attribution* of the participant. Females tend to attribute positive performances to external sources. Negative performances are attributed to internal sources. Males attribute their positive performances to internal sources demonstrating greater self-appreciation. According to Eccles and Harold (1991), these findings may be linked to the social view that females are unsuited for success in sports.

Anthrop and Allison (1983) examined this phenomenon. They assessed the level of role conflict in female high school athletes via their questionnaire that was administered to 133 female high school athletes. One half of the athletes surveyed cited little or no role conflict; 32 percent cited little problem with role conflict; 17 percent believed they had a great problem with role conflict. The authors further stated that although they believe games are critical to the total socialization process and help people learn gender roles, the games are predominantly masculine. In other words, participation for males is regarded as positive, whereas female participation can more frequently cause gender role conflict. Anthrop and Allison say this is a function of a so-called *Victorian influence*, whereby sports are perceived as potentially dangerous, particularly for the female, who is considered more delicate and thus prone to impeding her childbearing capabilities. Should the female impair her ability to bear children, she would greatly decrease her attractiveness to the male. This belief, although not as prevalent today, continues to exist, according to Anthrop and Allison.

For the male, however, from a social standpoint involvement in a movement activity is more likely to be an exclusively positive undertaking. The stereotypical male characteristics of aggression, toughness, dominance, and strength are further reinforced by a male's lively involvement in many movement activities. Thus, whereas a female's participation may cause slight to severe role conflict, a male normally avoids the emotional strife of role conflict. The female who experiences role conflict through participation in sport can attempt to ignore the expectations of others or abandon her sports-oriented role. This problem, which Anthrop and Allison described as being particularly discouraging for females involved in nonsocially accepted sports, was actually less widespread than hypothesized. Anthrop and Allison suggested the possibility, however, that the relatively low levels of "great or very great problems" with role conflict may be due to an aversion to sport by those who might have anticipated the role conflict. Or, perhaps others who had suffered role conflict had already ceased participation.

Ostrow, Jones, and Spiker (1981) performed similar research to determine if there were role expectations for 12 selected sporting activities. In this research, 93 subjects completed an Activity Appropriateness Scale and a Sex Role Inventory. From an analysis of the completed surveys, the researchers determined that boys are more easily socialized into sports activities for two reasons. First, the relatively small number of female role models is believed to reduce the number of female participants. Second, of the 12 sports examined in this research, 10 were considered to be "masculine." The authors assumed that this reduced the likelihood of female participation because the level of role conflict, discussed earlier, would likely be elevated for many female participants. Only ballet and figure skating were deemed more appropriate for female participants.

The stigma concerning the female's role in sports may be declining. Title IX, a 1972 federal mandate designed to reduce gender discrimination in education, equalized the number of athletic and physical education programs for boys and girls. This mandate has greatly increased the number and quality of programs available to female participants in this country (Anthrop & Allison, 1983). Before 1972, girls were not allowed to participate during their school years; now they are. In fact, in 1972 only 7 percent of all high school athletes were female; more recent evidence shows that number to be 35 percent. Additionally, the number of college athletic scholarships available to women athletes has increased nearly 10 times from the 1972 level of 16,000 (*NEA Today,* March 1985, p. 10). The opportunities for females to participate in a higher level of movement activity have increased, and presumably this increase has subsequently enhanced the likelihood of a female achieving a higher level of motor performance in an athletic endeavor.

SOCIAL FACTORS OF ADULTHOOD

Adulthood begins when adolescence ends. Although experts disagree about the actual time of the onset of adulthood, as discussed in Chapter 1, we are assuming that adulthood begins at age 20. Unfortunately, as we age during adulthood our involvement in movement activities or sport begins to decline. In fact, in research conducted by Rudman (1984), age was the prime determinant of sport involvement when compared to social class, level of education,

and income. This age effect was also found to be most powerful on team sports as older individuals were more likely to continue participation in individual sports.

At adulthood, three major social factors affecting human movement have their greatest negative impact on adult motor behavior, significantly affecting lifestyles and generally contributing to a tendency toward decreased participation in movement activity. These social forces are leaving school/going to work, taking a companion with the intent of a permanent relationship (usually marriage), and having children. Most people experience all of these factors early in adulthood. However, there is a trend toward postponing marriage and starting a family, or not marrying at all.

According to U.S. Department of Commerce data (1992, 1983, 1975), the number of males and females choosing to marry has decreased dramatically over the last several years. In 1960, 69 percent of males and 66 percent of females were married. That number decreased gradually through 1990 when 57 percent of males and 52 percent of females were married. As illustrated by Table 3-3, a substantial decrease in males and females choosing to marry was noted between 1970 and 1980, though the percentage has gradually declined over the last 30 years. For many, this trend will avert the negative effects marriage often has on an individual's level of physical activity and, subsequently, his or her overall motor behavior.

Once an individual begins regular employment, marries or takes a relatively permanent companion, and/or has children, the tendency for physiological

TABLE 3-3   Percentages of Married Males and Females in the United States Since 1960

	Males	Females
1990	57	52
1980	59	54
1970	66	61
1960	69	66

regression and its ensuring decline in motor performance increases greatly. For example, strength, cardiorespiratory endurance, and flexibility may all begin to decrease. This decline is much more difficult to predict than many of the motor changes that occur in children or adolescents because there is much greater interindividual variability among adults (Kausler, 1982). Thus, although there is usually a decline in motor performance when a person experiences the three major social factors, some individuals may actually improve. If an individual can overcome the normally prevailing social forces by staying involved in movement activities, the person can decrease the rate of the regression. In fact, adults can progress in movement endeavors until much later in life if they continue to regularly participate in those activities. Unfortunately, though, these social factors commonly mark the onset of a regression in motor development that will extend throughout the remainder of the lifespan.

The reasons why these factors stabilize or regress motor development are somewhat controversial. For example, although occasionally a moderately active person marries an exceptionally active person and is motivated to increase involvement in movement pursuits, this is not the norm. Typically, both partners are compelled to reduce activity levels as they become increasingly satisfied with staying at home in the company of each other. This negative effect is particularly strong between ages 18 and 34 years (Rudman, 1984). This increasing inactivity causes a decline in fitness levels and a subsequent plateauing or regression in motor development.

Many people believe that having children, for example, increases parents' overall level of activity, but generally this is not the case. Initially, having children may induce fatigue or even exhaustion because of the lack of sleep, the new responsibilities, and the rearrangement of the schedule. The children also reduce the parents' freedom or spontaneity that enabled them to more regularly participate in movement activities. Even if the parents had not been regular participants in some movement endeavor, their lifestyle becomes much more restricted and sedentary, which leads to the aforementioned

decline in the physiological abilities, causing a subsequent decline in motor ability. We must recognize, however, that having children may occasionally have the reverse effect. Having children may have a strong positive influence on parents' participation in certain sports between ages 35 and 54. This is particularly true of such sports as football, which tend to be more "family oriented" (Rudman, 1984).

For most people, beginning full-time employment, depending on the type of employment, will have similar long-term effects. Work ordinarily creates a relatively permanent lifestyle change by structuring or limiting the time a person has for participation in the activities that were once a regular source of recreational pleasure. Furthermore, the worker normally has few coworkers with similar movement interests. Unless the worker participates alone in the movement or has friends with the same interest outside the workplace, he or she may decrease or discontinue an activity. This occurrence is in considerable contrast to the school years, when a person is surrounded by same-age peers with similar interests. Leaving school therefore often decreases the number of available people with whom one can interact socially in a movement activity. A high school student can easily locate nine friends for a basketball game, but an adult may have a difficult time finding one partner for racquetball.

Social Learning and Ageism

The three major factors just discussed critically affect motor development early in adulthood. These factors, however, are not the only social elements that inhibit the level of involvement in active movement over the remainder of the lifespan. *Social learning* is the act of acquiring new behaviors by modeling the actions of others (Berger, 1994). This type of learning is important for motor development throughout the lifespan but deserves special recognition in this discussion of adulthood because it is often expected to occur only in childhood and adolescence.

Actually, social roles and expectations are learned in adulthood, just as they are in childhood and adolescence. These roles and expectations arise from the common beliefs that members of a group or a society jointly hold (Colarusso & Nemiroff, 1981). If the adult does not conform to the expectations as a result of modeling or observation, a role conflict may result. One such conflict may concern the adult's attempt at maintaining an active lifestyle. The individual may be well aware of the need to continue vigorous movement to avoid regression both motorically and physiologically, but society expects adults to become increasingly sedentary with age. In fact, society is often exceptionally protective of the older adult.

Ostrow, Jones, and Spiker (1981) addressed this issue. From their research, they determined that age barriers "blatantly exist" concerning societal expectations toward active participation in adulthood. They also found that the subjects surveyed deemed participation in the 12 sports included in the investigation decreasingly appropriate as one ages. The degree of appropriateness, as determined by the respondents, decreased as the adult aged from 20 to 80 years for such movement activities as swimming, jogging, tennis, and basketball. The only exception was bowling, which was considered as appropriate at 40 as at 20. Ostrow, Jones, and Spiker determined that this stereotyping based on age was "much more severe than sex stereotyping" concerning the appropriateness of these sports. Furthermore, this severe stereotyping no doubt contributes greatly to the "disengagement" from movement activity.

The findings of Ostrow and associates were somewhat substantiated by a recent article on "age grading" (Ostrow, Jones, & Spiker, 1981). Age grading is the idea of determining the level of perceived appropriateness of certain age groups being involved in movement activity.

Unfortunately, stereotypes concerning the aged in the United States are often negative to the extent that they can be referred to as *ageism*. Ageism is based on a person's relatively old age rather than race or gender. Like racism or sexism, ageism can lead to discrimination that can become so severe that discriminating members of society avoid or ex-

clude the older adult. This avoidance or exclusion may indicate society's aversion to the aging process and subsequent death of older adults. This form of discrimination obviously inhibits the older adult's attempts at becoming an active participant in the society. Many older adults are "forced" into a life of inactivity despite attempts to interact, and as a result, their movement capabilities as well as many other behaviors continue to regress.

Other Social Situations Likely to Affect Motor Development

Besides leaving school/going to work, marriage, and parenthood, many other social situations, usually occurring in middle to late adulthood, also significantly create a relatively permanent change in motor behavior. This change is normally a regression, but in less typical cases, depending on the individual involved, there may be a reestablishment of interest in a movement, which could lead to an improvement of the movement status. Three of the most important of these situations are the children leaving home, retirement, and death of the spouse.

When children leave home, many people think the parents are now "liberated" to pursue their own personal interests and activities, which may have been repressed in favor of the children's interests. Indeed, some parents actually do rediscover movement activity, which of course is beneficial to their movement in general. However, the norm is actually a tendency toward a more inactive lifestyle. The children's presence at home has a somewhat positive effect on the parents in that it helps keep the parents at least minimally active. In addition, a child's departure is a reminder that the parents are no longer youthful. As mentioned earlier, our society expects the older adult to generally avoid movement activity. When this expectation is coupled with the emotional crisis of a child leaving home, the likelihood of a more sedentary lifestyle is enhanced.

Retirement can have a similar effect. Today more people are living past age 65 than ever before, which means that more retirees will go through what will become a major shift in their life cycle. Retirement begins a period of leisure that has the potential for giving the retiree time to pursue movement endeavors (see Figure 3-4).

Recent research conducted by Kelly and Wescott (1991) found that most retirees were quite content with their retirement. In particular, they enjoyed their new "freedom" and leisure time. More specifically, Atchley (1989) found that a positive retirement is a function of, at least, four major conditions: the retirement was unforced, the work experience was not the most important aspect of the individual's life, the retiree's health and financial condition was sufficient to enjoy the free time, and adequate planning and preparation had occurred for and prior to the retirement.

Unfortunately retirement too frequently marks a significant decline in the standard of living, causing financial, transportation, and even nutritional problems. Retirees may also experience a loss of social status and sense of usefulness. Furthermore, retirement may be the first major realization that an individual has reached "old age," which can be an emotional trauma leading to depression and inactivity. As a result of these sentiments and social considerations related to retirement, older adults may not be sufficiently motivated or capable of seeking the movement activity that their leisure time would allow; the increased or continued inactivity in turn contributes to the individual's regression in motor development.

If they live long enough, most Americans will experience retirement and its accompanying social implications. If married, they may also experience the death of their spouse. As with all the factors mentioned to this point, this tragic experience usually causes depression and involves a long period of mourning; both factors contribute to the decrease in the overall activity level. Generally, this experience occurs during late adulthood, even after retirement. After retirement, the loss of a spouse can have a particularly grave impact because the bond between the two companions increases as they begin to spend more time together. Therefore, at a time when individuals might find the emotionally uplifting effects of movement activity especially beneficial, they are most likely to withdraw from such exploits.

Four other, more general, social problems associated with aging deserve examination because their ramifications pervade all areas of human behavior, including movement. These problems, all of which become increasingly severe with age, are income,

FIGURE 3-4 Retirement often frees individuals for active pursuit of movement activities; unfortunately, active involvement after retirement frequently decreases.

transportation, health, and nutrition. Many other considerations could be added to this list, but these factors are among the most critical for the aged, especially as related to older adults' attempts at being active participants in society.

Retirement may impede the financial status of retirees. Whereas they once had a regular income from employment, retirees now have to rely on Social Security and/or pension payments. Opponents of the Social Security program argue that it provides too little financial assistance to enable older adults to live satisfactory lifestyles. In many cases, the postretirement years are a struggle for economic survival. Minority groups suffer the consequences of poverty in old age more severely than do non-minority older adults. But no matter what the retirees' ethnic background or gender, a poor economic condition can lead to severe emotional trauma that, as discussed earlier, may indirectly affect individuals' desire or ability to become involved in movement activities. The resultant lack of movement facilitates the physiological and subsequent motor decline generally associated with aging. In other words, a vicious cycle is created: As older adults are less active, they become less able to be active.

The financial struggle that frequently accompanies retirement is the basis of a series of associated problems. Insufficient finances often impede individuals' capability to acquire transportation. If retirees have cars, maintaining the automobile in satisfactory condition becomes an additional burden. Other forms of travel, such as a taxi or a bus, may be too costly or cumbersome for an older person. Fortunately, many communities provide transportation, but where it is unavailable or unknown, the likelihood of retirees actively interacting with society decreases, which increases the level of disengagement and causes older adults to finish their lives in a sedentary, depressed, and lonely fashion.

Decreased finances and transportation may also have nutritional ramifications. Without sufficient money and transportation, older adults may find buying food a significant burden, so rather than shopping, they may attempt to go without proper nourishment. A poor diet obviously affects an individual's ability to engage with society and in fact may cause serious health problems that further devastate the older adult's attempts at staying active. The isolation that indirectly results from lack of funds, transportation, and nutrition also creates an attitude that impedes any desire on the part of the adult to participate in movement activities. The lack of participation contributes to the gradual decline in overall motor function that began at the onset of early adulthood.

THE EXERCISE-AGING CYCLE

As indicated in the last section, a number of sociocultural factors contribute to the declining levels of physical activity and fitness that often occur across adulthood. Foremost among these is the phenomenon of ageism discussed earlier in the chapter. Ageism contributes to increasingly undesirable views of people as they age. Too often older individuals are inaccurately labeled as being poor, frail, unhealthy, forgetful, and physically incapable. As illustrated by the poem," The Little Boy and the Old Man," we often treat older adults like children because of our reduced expectations for their capabilities (see Table 3-4).

Thus, the prevalent attitude that physical activity becomes less appropriate the older we become is not surprising. These attitudes commonly begin as early as preschool and continue through older adulthood. This notion, known as *age-grading* for exercise, is an obvious deterrent to exercise for adults as they begin to believe the societal attitudes leading to what may become a self-fulfilling prophecy (Berger & McInman, 1993; Berger & Hecht, 1989). When the negative attitudes concerning adulthood and involvement in physical activity are coupled with growing responsibilities and lifestyles of adulthood, the pursuit of physical activity may become a very low priority. Increasing work and family responsibilities are perceived as limiting time for "frivolous" endeavors like exercise. Particularly "at risk" are young adult working women with children who may find they have very little time to themselves. Later in adulthood, factors like retirement and the corresponding decrease in financial status and transportation inhibit efforts to be active. The combination of these factors creates a sense of diminished self-expectancy, a very low valuation of exercise, and few physically active role models. Many adults may have become so poorly skilled that physical activity is perceived as being embarrassing. Figures from *Healthy People 2000* (U.S. Department of Health and Human Services, 1992) support the notion that few adults receive adequate physical activity (see Table 3-5). Though 22 percent of the adult population receive more than 1/2 hour of light to moderate activity five or more times per week, only 10 percent exercise three or more times at a level sufficient to improve cardiovascular fitness. One fourth of adults receive no physical activity in their free time! And, a cycle of declining physical activity appears to begin as the older we get the less activity we receive.

This cycle, called the *exercise-aging cycle* (see Figure 3-5), illustrates the trend that normally occurs. Early in adulthood, in part because of the factors discussed earlier, we tend to gradually disengage from physical activities. As a result of this disengagement, physical changes become apparent. For example, our physical ability declines, fat levels increase, muscular atrophy occurs, and energy declines. We then begin to feel "old" and act "our age." Stress levels and depression increase and self-esteem declines. All of these factors further decrease one's interest and incentive to be physically active. In turn, the cycle becomes even more severe (Berger & McInman, 1993; Berger & Hecht, 1989). This is not to suggest that sociocultural phenomena are exclusively responsible for a decline in physical ability. However, according to Berger and McInman (1993), as much as 50 percent of the decline associated with aging may actually be related to a phenomenon known as *disuse atrophy* rather than the process of aging. Disuse atrophy is a wasting away of muscle mass which is the direct result of physical inactivity. See Table 3-6 for numerous examples of physiological and functional changes with age.

AVOIDING THE EXERCISE-AGING CYCLE

The exercise-aging cycle discussed in the last section is all too common in today's society. However, one's depth of involvement in this cycle is often largely a matter of lifestyle choice. Though the

TABLE 3-5   According to *Healthy People 2000* (1992)

- 22% of our population (18 years and older) receive 30 minutes or more of light to moderate physical activity 5 or more times per week.
- 12% of our population receive 30 minutes or more of light to moderate physical activity 7 or more times per week.

But . . .

- 10% exercise 3 or more times per week at a level necessary to improve cardiorespiratory fitness.
- 25% receive no leisure time physical activity.

And . . .

- physical activity declines with age!

TABLE 3-4

THE LITTLE BOY AND THE OLD MAN
By
Shel Silverstein

Said the little boy, "Sometimes I drop my spoon."
Said the little old man, "I do that too."
The little boy whispered, "I wet my pants."
"I do that too," laughed the little old man.
Said the little boy, "I often cry."
The old man nodded, "So do I."
"But worst of all," said the boy, "it seems
Grown-ups don't pay attention to me."
And he felt the warmth of a wrinkled old hand.
"I know what you mean," said the little old man.

SOURCE: Reprinted with permission from: Silverstein, S. (1981). *A light in the attic.* New York: Harper & Row.

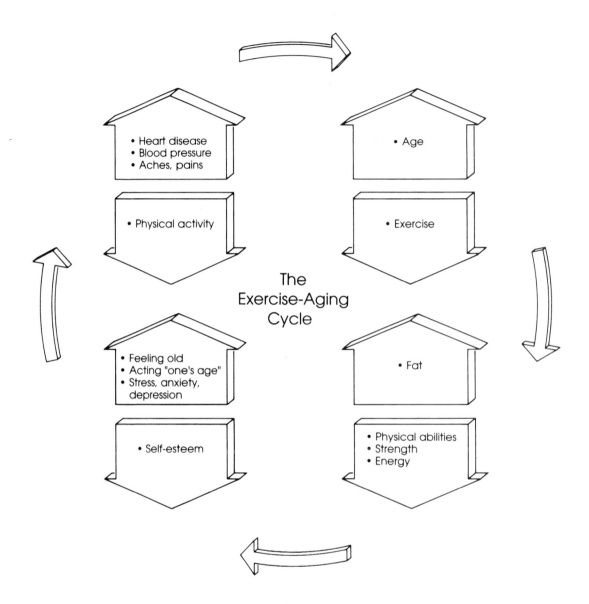

FIGURE 3-5   The Exercise Aging Cycle

Adapted from Berger and Hecht, 1989, and reprinted with permission.

effects of aging cannot be completely overcome, tremendous potential exists for lessening the regression that occurs as a result of the sociocultural effects discussed earlier in the chapter by choosing to engage in an appropriate level of physical activity.

Regression does not have to begin so early in adulthood or be so severe. Individuals who are aware of the potential that results from decreased physical activity through adulthood and who are motivated to do something about it can play an active role in

TABLE 3-6 Physiologic and Functional Changes Associated with Aging

	Decreases	Increases
Cardiovascular	Cardiac output Maximum heart rate HDL cholesterol	Systolic and diastolic blood pressures Total cholesterol Vascular resistance
Respiratory	Vital capacity Chest wall compliance Maximum ventilation Alveolar size	Functional residual capacity
Musculoskeletal	Muscle mass Elasticity in connective tissue Synovial fluid viscosity Muscle fiber length	Osteoporosis
Central Nervous System	Nerve conduction Number of neurons Motor responses Brain mass	

SOURCE: Reprinted with permission and adapted from Barry, H. C., Rich, B. S. E., and Carlson, R. T. (1993). How exercise can benefit older patients: A practical approach. *The Physician and Sports Medicine, 21*(2) 124–140.

the quality of the rest of their life. Though societal attitudes frequently suggest that, at some point, we may be too old to engage in a physical activity program ("He's too old to do aerobic dance!"), the information presented in Table 3-7 suggests otherwise. When frail, elderly patients were given appropriate levels of physical activity, remarkable results were seen. Work capacity and bone density increased. They became more flexible and improved in muscle tone and coordination. Perhaps most importantly, their mental outlook improved as anxiety and depression, the most common psychiatric disorder among older adults, declined (Barry, Rich, & Carlson, 1993). In short, a well-designed training program for any age group in adulthood can increase muscle strength and endurance, increase cardiovascular endurance, halt bone decalcification, improve joint flexibility, and generally improve level of life satisfaction enabling us to overcome, and even temporarily reverse, the exercise-aging cycle. "Exercise seems to reduce many of the ravages of older age, resulting in younger appearance, and increases in

energy, and enhanced physical capabilities" (Berger & Hecht, 1989, p. 129). Thus, the probability of a healthier, happier adulthood can increase considerably (see Figure 3-6).

SUMMARY

Socialization is one of the most dominant facilitators of movement acquisitions throughout the lifespan. Because this process of learning society's expected roles, behaviors, rules, and regulations greatly influences an individual's decisions concerning movement participation, it is a major force in human motor development.

Self-esteem, or self-worth, which is greatly affected by social interactions, was also found to be significantly influenced by involvement in physical activity. Self-esteem also follows a predictable developmental pattern evolving through increasing levels of ability to articulate and differentiate the elements of self-esteem. With age, the nature of

TABLE 3-7   Some Functional Adaptations to Exercise in Frail Elderly Patients

		Increases	Decreases
Cardiovascular		Work capacity	Resting heart rate
		HDL cholesterol	Total cholesterol
		Maximum oxygen capacity	Blood pressure
Respiratory		Minute ventilation	
		Vital capacity	
Musculoskeletal		Bone density	
		Flexibility	
		Muscle tone and strength	
		Coordination	
Miscellaneous		Mental outlook	Loneliness
		Socialization	Idle time
		Fat and carbohydrate metabolism	Anxiety
		Insulin receptor sensitivity	Symptoms and depression
		Plasma volume	Appetite
		Maintenance of lean body mass	
		Weight control	
		Metabolic rate	

Source: Reprinted with permission and adapted from Barry, H. C., Rich, B. S. E., and Carlson, R. T. (1993). How exercise can benefit older patients: A practical approach. *The Physician and Sports Medicine, 21*(2) 124–140.

social relationships and their effect on self-esteem also change as such elements of self-worth as peer acceptance and romantic appeal decline in importance. Intimate relations and nurturance increase in importance in adulthood. Interestingly, throughout the lifespan, physical appearance and social acceptance were found to be the most important elements influencing global self-worth while athletic competence was found to be one of the least influential contributors.

Infancy is a relatively asocial period of time. The interaction that does occur is greatly facilitated by the baby's movement ability. Similarly, social interaction offers the baby an opportunity to practice and expand movement opportunities.

School, television, and play are important social influences that contribute to motor development throughout childhood. Play is particularly significant because it tends to be extremely dependent on bodily movement.

During the latter part of childhood, the peer group becomes more socially important to the child and the family gradually becomes less significant. By adolescence, the peer group is generally the dominant social force and critical to the establishment of movement-related interests.

During later childhood and adolescence, team play becomes common. This type of social interaction allows the child to perfect movement skills and develop new social, cognitive, and emotional behaviors.

Of particular interest during later childhood and early adolescence is the increasing opportunity to interact with the opposite gender. This interaction assists in the creation of a gender identity. However, there can be problems if the gender role ascribed to individuals does not conform to the gender role associated with the chosen movement activity. Role conflict, which is particularly common for the female participant, can lead to emotional trauma or dropping out of an activity.

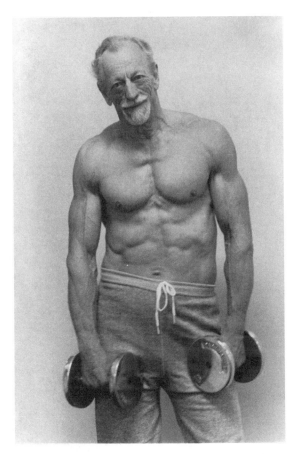

FIGURE 3-6 As illustrated by John Turner, 67, the normal movement regression through adulthood can be slowed or delayed. Turner weight lifts, jogs, and walks.

Reprinted with permission from Clark, E. (1986). *Growing old is not for sissies.* Corte Madera, CA: Pomegranate.

The three most significant social influences affecting motor development in adulthood are leaving school/going to work, marriage, and having children. All of these factors tend to increase sedentarism and inhibit the forces that facilitate motor performance. A gradual, consistent decline in motor performance often begins surprisingly early in adulthood and continues until death.

Research has shown that elementary school children through adults consider the need for physical activity to decrease in importance as people age, contributing to an exercise/aging cycle. This cycle suggests that we exercise less with increasing age, resulting in decreased physical ability and feelings of inadequacy. These feelings impair the incentive to be physically active, which further proliferates the cycle. Fortunately, with more positive attitudes and increased knowledge about aging, the negative cycle can be reduced and even reversed.

Ageism, the negative view of aging and of old people, can lead to avoidance of older adults. This attitude, common in the United States, inhibits older adults' attempts to engage with their society and impedes their efforts at maintaining an active lifestyle. Additionally, research has shown that there are stereotypes that view movement activity as increasingly inappropriate as one progresses through adulthood.

In later adulthood, a number of social forces contribute to a decreasing activity level. Children leaving home, retirement, and death of a spouse typically lead older adults away from societal interaction and movement experiences.

Despite the common social pitfalls and their effects on motor development, the early onset of movement regression can be allayed and the severity delayed if a person maintains an active lifestyle.

KEY TERMS

Age-grading	Play
Ageism	Role conflict
Attribution	Self-concept
Disuse atrophy	Self-esteem
Exercise-aging cycle	Social learning
Gender role identity	Social role
Global self-worth	Socialization
Norm	Victorian influence
Peer group	

CHAPTER 4

Perceptual-Motor Development

Perceptual-motor has become one of the most commonly used terms in motor development and education in general. Almost all motor development or elementary physical education texts contain extensive information concerning this concept. However, there is tremendous confusion about the exact meaning of the term. The perceptual-motor concept, which first began to affect education over 25 years ago, has since been misused and overused until it has been drained of much of its intended significance (Payne, 1984). More than 15 years ago, Seefeldt declared that the "term has been rendered worthless in representing specific methodology, programs, or content" (1974, p. 266). To help clear up the confusion, this chapter examines the significance of the perceptual-motor concept and several important related concepts.

WHAT IS PERCEPTUAL-MOTOR DEVELOPMENT?

Regardless of how it is specifically defined, generally the perceptual-motor concept refers to movement activities performed with the intent of improving cognitive or academic skills. The term also refers to programs involving children because most perceptual-motor development occurs during the preschool and primary school years (Gallahue, 1989). It is common practice in perceptual-motor programs to supplement or replace academic activities with movement activities to improve such academic concerns as reading, writing, and problem solving (see Figure 4-1). If the movement activities are designed specifically to improve movement ability, they do not constitute a perceptual-motor program (Seefeldt, 1974).

FIGURE 4-1 Perceptual-motor activities are designed to enhance cognitive or academic performance through the performance of movement activities.

Other Interpretations of Perceptual-Motor

Although we believe that the concept Seefeldt suggested accurately describes perceptual-motor, others have approached the concept from a different perspective. Many discussions of perceptual-motor include a statement of the movement activities considered perceptual-motor. According to the Perceptual-Motor Task Force Summary of the Perceptual-Motor Survey (Haslinger, 1971), the vast list of movements various experts claim are perceptual-motor activities leads one to believe that all human movements are perceptual-motor. This statement is supported by those who believe that all voluntary movement is perceptual-motor and all physical education programs are perceptual-motor programs (Gallahue, Werner, & Luedke, 1972). We prefer to assume that the term perceptual-motor was not created simply to replace the term physical education; perceptual-motor may be an entity encompassed within physical education, but physical education program and perceptual-motor program are not synonymous. The objectives of a physical education program can be more diverse than the relatively narrow ones of a perceptual-motor program.

Perceptual-motor is also frequently explained as concerning the relationship between human movement and the perceptions. The perceptions are the "processes by which we gain immediate awareness of what is happening outside of our bodies" (Bower, 1977, p. 1). *Perception* is a result of our ability to receive information through the senses. However, this external information is not a perception unless it is perceived. That is, there must be cognitive awareness of the reception of this information. The interrelationship between the perceptions and movement is unquestionably an important one. Without perceptions, such as those received through the senses of vision and touch, performing even the simplest movements would be difficult, if not impossible, as demonstrated in studies in which perceptually impaired children have been shown to require longer periods of time to acquire certain movement behaviors. In addition, throughout the lifespan they may lag behind children with more normally developed perceptual abilities (Adelson & Fraiberg, 1976; Williams, Temple, & Bateman, 1979).

There has also been considerable discussion about the importance of active movement for optimal development of the perceptions. Perceptual-motor programs sometimes have been justified on the basis of their value in enhancing the child's perceptual abilities. This argument is frequently substantiated by the findings of Held & Hein's 1963 study.

In their research, Held and Hein raised kittens in a completely dark environment for 8 to 12 weeks. The kittens were then separated into two groups: active and passive. A kitten from each group was attached to cartlike device that rotated around a center axis in a lighted carousel. The active kitten propelled its cart around the axis via its own leg action; the passive kitten was simply a passenger because its legs were prevented from moving. The passive kitten's cart also rotated around the center axis, but the cart was propelled by the leg movement of the active kitten because the two carts were connected (see Figure 4-2). Kittens from both groups spent up to 3 hours per day in this lighted situation. Upon being post-tested, the active kittens showed signs of having acquired normal depth perception, whereas the passive kittens exhibited impaired depth perception, which eventually improved markedly when they were exposed to light. Held and Hein concluded from this research that active movement plays a vital role in the development of visual-spatial skills such as depth perception. And, as mentioned, this research has also been used to justify perceptual-motor programs. These programs often involve children in movement activities designed to improve skills like depth perception to in turn enhance an academic ability such as reading, which normally depends on visual proficiency.

The Held and Hein research, however, has been criticized because those kittens actively involved in producing movement most likely were also required to maintain greater visual attentiveness (Shaffer, 1989). Therefore, the active kittens may have achieved better depth perception than the passive kittens because they had more visual experience and practice rather than higher levels of actively produced movement, as the original researchers suspected.

Related research by Walk (1981) supported this critical view of Held and Hein's research. Walk, on the basis of much more recent research, suggested that active movement may be an essential element in development but the movement does not need to be self-produced, only viewed. As Held and Hein did, Walk researched kittens to reach these conclusions. The kittens in Walk's research were kept in total darkness for a period of time following their birth. Then one group of kittens was removed from the darkness and allowed to actively move around the environment and examine the available visual

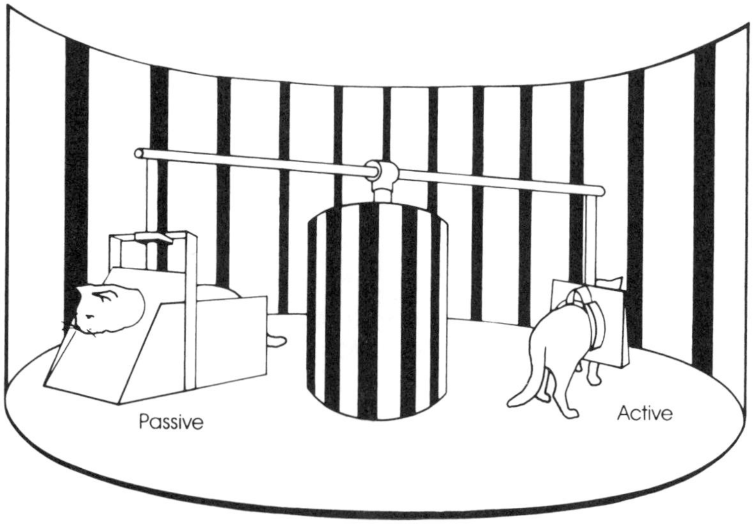

FIGURE 4-2 Held and Hein involved kittens in active and passive movement. The researchers concluded that the active movement benefited the kittens' development of depth perception, whereas the passive movement did not.

Passive   Active

stimuli. A second group of kittens was inhibited from actively moving but allowed to examine passive stimuli. A final group of kittens, also inhibited from movement, viewed active, interesting stimuli.

Following exposure to these varying situations, all kittens were tested for depth perception. The kittens that could not actively interact with the environment and watched the passive stimuli had the poorest level of depth perception. According to Walk, this was most likely due to the tendency of these kittens to become bored and fall asleep. However, the kittens that watched the active stimuli remained attentive despite their inability to actively move through their environment. As a result, these kittens developed depth perception comparable to that of the kittens that were allowed to actively move through the environment.

Walk's research and similar investigations have led to the *motion hypothesis*, which is the notion that individuals must attend to objects that move to develop a normal repertoire of visual-spatial skill (Shaffer, 1989), such as depth perception. However, contrary to early research, such as in the Held and Hein study, and considerable popular opinion, self-produced movement may not be as critical as once believed in the development of such important abilities as depth perception.

The Perceptual-Motor Process

Like Held and Hein and Walk, other authors (Werner & Rini, 1975; Williams, 1983) have theorized about the role of the perceptions in movement production and correction. However, these authors' intent was to delineate the steps in a so-called *perceptual-motor process* rather than specifically determine the role of active movement in the development of the perceptions.

Generally, the first step in the perceptual-motor process (in this case, also known as information processing) is the reception of environmental information vital to the production of the movement. Imagine a young boy who has just visually perceived a ball being tossed in his direction. By focusing on the ball, the child receives information concerning the speed, trajectory, weight, and texture of the ball that is critical to the production of a successful catching movement. The initial step in the perceptual-motor process is therefore the reception of pertinent environmental information.

Once that information has traveled to the brain via the afferent or incoming nerves, it is perceived and processed. Included in this processing is the integration of the new information with that from similar past experiences. This *sensory integration* involves a comparison of information from the present movement with that stored in the long-term memory concerning previous similar movements. This process of integrating the "new" information with the "old" enables a more accurate and complete analysis of the present movement situation and improves the chances of more successful movement production.

After information concerning the present movement has been sensory integrated with pertinent past information, the movement selection is made. The efferent, or outgoing, nerves then send a command to the muscles, creating a movement. However, the process is not yet complete because once the movement begins, information is fed back to the performer, to enable an ongoing monitoring of the movement process. This feedback is facilitated by information from the senses. Vision, hearing, touch, and proprioception play a particularly important role in the feedback process. For the young boy we mentioned earlier, seeing, hearing, or feeling the ball rebound off his own chest might cue him to modify his catching movement in future catching attempts. The sensory information therefore assists in making judgments about the movement and affects the way that movement or similar movements will be made in the future. If the information from the original motor prescription does not compare favorably with the information fed back, a correction may be made on similar movements in the future. However, if there is a close match between these two sources of information, and the movement proved successful, attempts will be made to reproduce that movement in similar movement situations in the future.

This process, although theoretical and somewhat simplistically described, appears to be generally well accepted and has no doubt led to the following related definition of *perceptual-motor development:*

> Perceptual-motor development is that part of a child's development that is concerned with changes in the movement behavior, changes that represent improvement in sensory-perceptual motor development and reafference processes that underlie such behavior (Williams, 1983, p. 9).

Therefore, perceptual-motor development, as Williams viewed it, is the child's changing, generally improving ability to utilize the perceptual-motor process that we just described and that is now summarized:

1. In the perceptual-motor process, environmental stimulation that is relevant to the movement in question is recognized.

2. The brain receives the information through the afferent (input) nervous system.

3. The information is processed at the brain by organizing and integrating the new and the old information concerning previous similar movements.

4. A decision is made to move.

5. The appropriate movement information is efferently (output) transmitted to the muscles to create the desired movement.

6. The movement is performed.

7. The movement is observed and relevant information is stored for integration with information concerning similar future movements.

Is All Movement Perceptual-Motor?

Earlier we mentioned that perceptual-motor has been considered an alternate term for physical education. We do not subscribe to this use of the term because it implies that perceptual-motor involves all the kinds of movement that one would expect to see in a physical education program. Our view is that perceptual-motor activities are movements created through the process of sensory integration that we discussed earlier; this includes all voluntary movement, such as the activities in a physical education class. However, we also stated that the intent of perceptual-motor activities is to enhance cognitive function. Although the performance of all voluntary movement activities may contribute slightly to this effort, certain movements are most commonly acclaimed for their contribution to this effort and can therefore be considered perceptual-motor activities.

In determining which movements would be considered perceptual-motor activities, an examination of the Perceptual-Motor Survey (Haslinger, 1971) was particularly useful. This survey, conducted 20 years ago, was devised by a perceptual-motor task force that was created to allay confusion surrounding the term perceptual-motor. To attain this goal, the task force solicited definitions of perceptual-motor from numerous individuals across the country who were considered experts on this topic. The task force and the experts attempted to determine the nature of perceptual-motor activities by having respondents list those movement activities they believed were perceptual-motor. An examination of the results revealed clear disagreement among the experts. No doubt there is still a comparable lack of agreement, but certain categories of movement do tend to be present on most responses to the perceptual-motor survey: balance, and spatial, temporal, body, and directional awareness, among others. These types of movement activities are also commonly cited in discussions of perceptual-motor in many current texts (Cratty, 1986; Gallahue, 1989; Williams, 1983). Also, these types of movements were among those frequently prescribed by Kephart (1964), who is regularly cited for his role in originally initiating interest in the term perceptual-motor. Kephart and his perceptual-motor theory are discussed in greater detail later in the chapter. Now we briefly discuss the movement-related concepts commonly associated with the term perceptual-motor.

BALANCE

Balance, or stability, is traditionally defined as "a state of equilibrium maintained between opposing forces" (Burton & Davis, 1992; p. 14). It is an "integral part of almost every movement task" (p. 14) and is frequently called *postural control*, which is "an ability to maintain equilibrium in a gravitational field by keeping or returning the center of body mass over its base of support" (Horak, 1987, p. 1881). In light of the contemporary emphasis placed on ecological considerations and dynamical systems, Burton and Davis (1992; p. 16) recently defined balance as being "not a state, skill, or ability but rather the aspect of a particular action involving a variety of processes that allow for the orientation of the body that is necessary to carry out the functional task at hand."

Though research is divided on the topic, balance appears to be quite task specific. It is also highly dependent upon the form and structure of one's body as factors affecting the size of the base of support, such as foot length or width, have been found to affect postural responses. Balance is also inversely proportional to the height of the body's center of mass above the base of support (Burton & Davis, 1992). Given the obvious changes in body dimensions with normal growth, balance is clearly influenced by developmental changes.

Balance, in the form of postural change, is exhibited very early in life. In fact, the fetus has been known to change position by rotating along the longitudinal axis of the body. This motion is typically initiated by a turn of the head or the hips. The fetus also changes position by alternate leg movements. This often results in a "somersault" when the legs are positioned so they can push against the uterine wall. These postural changes occur as often as 20 times per hour during the first 6 months of pregnancy and decrease in incidence during the remainder of the gestational period. This somewhat surprising decrease in the rate of postural change may be a function of the declining space available for movement as the fetus increases in size (Woollacott, Shumway-Cook, & Williams, 1989).

Following birth, babies less than 3 days old are often capable of orienting their bodies and heads relative to a visual stimulus. At 9 months of age children can activate the postural muscles in the trunk in association with reaching movements of the arms.

In general, though children from 15 months to 3 years exhibit organized leg muscle responses when balance is perturbed, the number of postural adjustments is more variable and slower than in adults. Children at this age also appear to rely primarily upon visual information in decisions concerning balance. From 4 to 6 years a slight regression in postural organization occurs and may indicate a period of time where the child is attempting to integrate various other forms of information with vision for the purposes of postural control.

By the age of 7 to 10 years, postural responses are similar to those of adults though slightly longer latency periods following a balance disruption are common compared to adults. During this portion of later childhood, the leg muscles have usually achieved adult-like balance responses though the upper body continues to improve in function (Woollacott, Shumway-Cook, & Williams, 1989).

Balance is commonly subdivided into two types: static and dynamic. *Static balance* is the ability to maintain a desired body posture or position when the body is stationary. *Dynamic balance* is also an ability to maintain a desired body posture or position when the body is moving. Both static and dynamic balances are used in many movement activities. For example, a diver uses static balance as she stands poised and relatively motionless on the tip of the diving board prior to the dive. However, once the dive has been initiated and the body is experiencing various rotations, dynamic balance helps maintain the desired body position.

Both forms of balance have been scientifically investigated to gain greater awareness of the characteristics and underlying mechanisms of balance. Clark and Watkins (1984) investigated the static balance of 6- to 9-year-old children. The children attempted balancing tasks in various body positions. While balancing, the children were asked to maintain a normal stand, stand with their hands on their hips, fold their arms across their chests, or bend over at their waists. In addition, the balance tasks were performed on both the left and right feet, with the eyes open and closed, and using a base of support of varying size. The children were timed on all balance tasks from the time their non-support foot left the floor until it returned. Developmentally, the older children in this research were not found significantly more successful on balance tasks than the younger children. However, using a larger base of support and keeping the eyes open significantly improved balance performance. Body position was also found to be a significant factor, but only when the stock used as the base of support was in a lengthwise rather than a crosswise position. Finally, the foot selected for support in the balance task was not a significant factor, although Clark and Watkins speculated that it may be critical in the way it interacts with the other variables examined. One of the most important conclusions of this research was that static balance is a multidimensional task that is affected by a multitude of variables; it therefore cannot be accurately assessed by any one test of balance.

Researchers have also studied balance by using a stabilometer. With the stabilometer, the subject must balance on a platform suspended on a single axis across its midline. The subject places one foot on each side of this axis, similar to attempting to balance on the center of a seesaw. Certain evidence implies that stabilometer performance may not increase with age, unlike most movement skills. In fact, Bachman (1961) studied males and females from 6 to 26 years old and found that there was a tendency for balance ability on the stabilometer to actually decrease with age, perhaps a function of the older performer's increasing weight, which causes faster fluctuations in the position of the base of support (Keogh & Sugden, 1985). The increasing height of the older subjects' center of gravity may also contribute to the atypical developmental trend because the height of an individual's center of gravity can increase the difficulty of this type of balance task.

Beam walking has often been the focus of research designed to investigate dynamic balance. DeOreo (1974, 1975), for example, examined the technique her 3- to 5-year-old subjects used to walk across a beam. She instructed children to cross beams of varying widths by walking forward and backward. DeOreo noticed that beam walking could

be categorized into two distinct patterns. Younger subjects tended to use a "mark time" or shuffle-step pattern in which one foot stayed in front at all times and was simply shuffled along across the beam. Older subjects seemed to have developed the more mature pattern of striding with both the left and right legs, as is common in walking. DeOreo also noted that more than 25 percent of the 3-year-old subjects were incapable of balancing well enough to cross the beam. In addition, this task became more difficult for all children as the width of the beam decreased, resulting in subjects of all ages tending to resort to the more immature shuffle-step technique. This type of research has been valuable for determining the progression children use to perform specific dynamic-balance tasks. Chapter 15 addresses several important concepts relative to balance in adulthood.

SPATIAL AWARENESS

Spatial awareness, like balance, is a movement-related concept frequently emphasized in perceptual-motor programs. As the name implies, spatial awareness is an understanding of the external spaces surrounding an individual and the individual's ability to function motorically in and through that space. Children evolve from an immature form of spatial awareness known as egocentric localization to the more advanced objective localization. Egocentric localization is an immature and limited spatial awareness in which all or most aspects of a child's understanding of the surroundings are noted in reference to one's self. Objective localization is the more advanced capability of referencing objects in space relative to objects other than the self (Gallahue, 1989).

Children often divulge their localization status when asked directions to a specific location in their surroundings. Those children who highlight landmarks other than themselves when giving the directions have developed the more advanced objective localization, whereas children who give directions with the self as the point of reference are exhibiting egocentric localization. Many experts believe that spatial awareness can be facilitated through involvement in movement activity. Unquestionably, movement often requires an acute understanding of the surroundings, such as that often exhibited by tennis players, who have developed such a high level of spatial awareness that they do not have to look at the lines surrounding the court during play to know that their opponent's shot is going to land in or out of bounds. Thus, spatial awareness is not only beneficial in many movement endeavors but can be improved by participation in the movement activity. However, numerous claims that this movement-related ability can be enhanced through movement activities in a way that will positively affect the child in academically related concerns remain unsubstantiated.

Thomas and colleagues (1983) investigated the developmental differences in a form of spatial awareness using children 4 and 9 years old. Of specific interest to these researchers were the strategies their subjects used to remember locations and distances in their environment while jogging. As we would expect, the 9-year-old children recalled both locations and distances better than did the 4-year-old youngsters. However, both groups found distances difficult to accurately recall. When subjects were assisted by various cues, they recalled locations better but still poorly remembered distance, leading to the conclusion that recalling specific distances requires a sophisticated strategy, like counting steps. This was a strategy approximately 30 percent of the 9-year-olds used; generally, the 4-year-olds did not use the technique.

Additional research by Thomas and colleagues determined that older children become increasingly likely to use a strategy to recall distances and are typically more successful than their younger counterparts in accurately remembering. However, according to this research, children 5 to 12 years old can be taught to effectively use a strategy to recall jogging distances. In fact, 5-year-olds who were taught to count steps learned to recall distance as well as 9-year-olds and slightly less effectively than 12-year-olds who were not given instruction.

TEMPORAL AWARENESS

Temporal awareness involves the gradually evolving understanding of time relationships, such as understanding the characteristics of a rapidly approaching ball. In this case, temporal awareness is an ability to predict the projectile's time of arrival, based on such characteristics as the speed, trajectory, and weight of the ball and the distance the ball has been projected across. This specific form of temporal awareness is also known as coincidence-anticipation timing and has been acclaimed as one of the most important aspects of bodily movement (Bartlett, 1958). Specifically, coincidence-anticipation timing is a person's ability to predict the arrival of a moving object to a certain point in space and to coordinate a movement with that arrival. Batting a pitched ball or attempting to intercept a soccer pass both require coincidence-anticipation timing ability. Dorfman (1977) used subjects 6 to 19 years old to investigate the development of coincidence-anticipation timing in children and young adults. To intercept an approaching target dot, subjects were instructed to move a slide to control a cursor dot appearing on a monitor. Dorfman determined a typical developmental trend: The older subjects consistently performed more proficiently and exhibited a faster rate of learning than did their younger counterparts.

In two additional studies, Haywood (1980, 1987) extended research on coincidence-anticipation timing to include adults of varying ages. Initially, Haywood examined four age groups, 7–9, 11–13, 18–32, and 60–75 years. Each group was administered 60 trials on a Bassin Anticipation Timer. This device projects a stream of lights in a predetermined direction. The subjects were required to press a button when they anticipated the light stream would reach a designated location. No gender differences were determined in coincidence-anticipation accuracy. The youngest group was the least accurate and least consistent. Accuracy was better in the older children and, according to Haywood, appeared to plateau thereafter. Older adults were highly variable in their responses and significantly less accurate than younger adults (Haywood, 1980).

In similar research using a longitudinal rather than cross-sectional design, Haywood (1987) sought to determine if coincidence-anticipation timing performance continued to decline in the later years. Using 10 older adults ranging in age from 62 to 73, Haywood repeatedly tested the subjects over a 7-year period of time. Interestingly, these subjects showed an improvement over 7 years. As the author suggested, this could have been a function of increased confidence and familiarity with the task rather than a typical age-related phenomenon.

While both of Haywood's investigations are interesting from a developmental perspective, the findings should be interpreted cautiously. Few subjects were involved, and all older adult subjects in both studies were participants in physical activity programs, which may have affected their performance on the timing task. More sedentary subjects may have performed differently.

Coincidence-anticipation timing is one particular form of temporal awareness. However, temporal awareness can occur independent of such external objects as an approaching ball. Coordination of various parts of a person's own body in a planned, synchronous fashion relative to another body part is critical to success in most movement, such as the popular jumping jack exercise. The jumping jack requires considerable temporal awareness to keep the arms and legs properly synchronized. Movement participants often become extremely adept at this form of temporal awareness.

BODY AND DIRECTIONAL AWARENESS

Body awareness, also referred to as body image, is a gradually developing ability to know and understand the names and functions of various body parts. Body awareness is the ability to understand how to produce various movements as well as the body's potential in movement performance. Body awareness is unquestionably important to optimal movement performance and has been closely linked with a related concept, directional awareness.

Directional awareness is the understanding and application of such concepts as up and down, front and back, and left and right. Directional awareness is often subdivided into laterality and directionality. Laterality is the understanding of various directional concepts; directionality is the application of that information (Cratty, 1986)). Because we constantly make directional decisions while involved in movement activities, laterality and directionality can be improved through participation in the kinds of movement activities that are commonly included in perceptual-motor programs. However, directional awareness is also important for such academically related tasks as reading. Obviously, reading depends on ability to discern letters on the basis of their direction. For example, a child with a poorly refined or underdeveloped sense of direction easily confuses a "b" and a "d." However, although directional awareness appears to be improvable as it is related to the specific movements in a perceptual-motor program, there is scant evidence as to the value of involvement in specific movement activities for improving reading achievement or other related academic concerns. Yet claims continue to be made and programs devised with the intent of involving children in specific movement activities for purposes of direct cognitive or academic gain. Some of the research that has examined the effectiveness of such programs in improving academic or cognitive ability is examined later in the chapter.

PERCEPTUAL-MOTOR THEORIES: KEPHART AND DELACATO

As mentioned, the concept of perceptual-motor has been in existence for over 30 years. Numerous programs developed by many innovators throughout these 30 years have sought to improve academic performance through involvement in some form of movement activity. However, two theorists have had particular impact on the evolution of thinking relative to the perceptual-motor concept. Kephart (1960, 1964) developed his perceptual-motor theory, in which he stated that cognitive development could be enhanced through movement. Delacato (1959, 1963) also advanced a theory about enhancing cognitive ability through movement. However, the theories are considerably different, although each has had a major impact educationally and both are the source of tremendous ongoing controversy.

Kephart's Perceptual-Motor Theory

Kephart is generally credited with initiating the emphasis that educators tend to place on movement for improving students' academic performance. Kephart believed that learning deficiencies were a result of poor sensory integration of present stimuli with the stored information concerning past stimuli. Sensory integration, discussed earlier, is a critical step in the perceptual-motor process. Kephart also believed that the feedback process, necessary for correcting errors in movement and perfecting future movements, was faulty in children with learning difficulties. Kephart therefore theorized that participation in basic forms of movement would help these integration and feedback problems and consequently improve the child's learning of such academic skills as spelling and reading. In fact, Kephart emphasized the interrelationship between the perceptions and movement by stating that we must not "think of perceptual activities and motor activities as two different items; we must think of the hyphenated term, perceptual-motor" (1960, p. 63). On the basis of Kephart's theory, children were frequently advised to actively participate in activities that involved several general areas of movement. Kephart believed that balance, eye-hand coordination, laterality, directionality, temporal and spatial awareness, and form perception enhanced cognitive as well as motor function.

Notice that the movements Kephart prescribed are similar to the movements we suggested earlier as being perceptual-motor activities. Our list is not intended to be an exhaustive inclusion of all possibilities or a replica of Kephart's recommendations; we did include the most commonly mentioned activities in response to the Perceptual-Motor Survey (Haslinger, 1971) briefly discussed earlier. This survey, which requested that experts write what they considered perceptual-motor activities, yielded a list of activities very similar to Kephart's recommendations, which had been prescribed years before the survey. Kephart's impact on movement experts throughout the country is obvious. This impact is still evident today as perceptual-motor programs continue to involve many of the kinds of movements Kephart prescribed. Kephart selected these general movement categories on the basis of his belief that children with learning difficulties frequently displayed deficiencies in these movement-related abilities. Although remnants of Kephart's ideas still pervade education today, his theory has become extremely controversial. Some educators believe that perceptual-motor programs based on Kephart's theory are educational panaceas, but others oppose the concept because there is too little substantive evidence to support such programs. The ending section of this chapter discusses some of the research into perceptual-motor programs.

Delacato and Hemispheric Dominance

Although perhaps less encompassing than Kephart's perceptual-motor theory, the theory Delacato (1959, 1963) proposed has certainly contributed to the controversy surrounding the term perceptual-motor. Like Kephart, Delacato believed that involvement in certain forms of movement behavior facilitates intellectual development. Delacato specifically believed that a critical element in optimal cognitive functioning is the development of *hemispheric dominance* (Lerch et al., 1974). In other words, one hemisphere of the brain must maintain control, or dominate the other, for certain behaviors to occur optimally. Gaining this hemispheric dominance is part of a process Delacato theorized that children who had not experienced and "perfected" certain infant movements faced an increased likelihood of intellectual problems later in life due to a lack of neurological organization. Delacato also believed that many intellectual problems could be overcome by recapitulating the early movement that was thought to be imperfect or omitted. To enable the child to experience or reexperience the infant movement, Delacato recommended a process known as patterning. Through patterning, an individual simply practiced the movement, usually crawling, to accommodate the need for the neural organization that Delacato believed was imperative to the child's enhanced cognitive functioning. Children who were incapable of actively recapitulating this movement were passively assisted through the movements. This process frequently involved numerous assistants and was often maintained for prolonged periods of time.

Although patterning has become the most widely publicized aspect of Delacato's prescription for enhanced cognitive function, other techniques are also involved. For example, reducing fluid, sugar, and salt consumption and reinspirating expired air were also believed to enhance efforts to improve the cognitive functioning of children who, according to Delacato, exhibited a lack of hemispheric dominance as a result of omitted or "improper" infant movement.

Some proponents of Delacato's theory are still around, but many experts agree that his techniques are unsubstantiated and extremely questionable (Cratty, 1986; Seefeldt, 1974; Williams, 1983). Critics of Delacato's theory cite cases of children who failed to crawl during infancy but still functioned at a normal cognitive level. The critics also noted children who were patterned, as prescribed by Delacato, yet failed to exhibit intellectual improvement. Some children, however, showed improvements when following patterning. But these cases are considered suspect since these children might have caught up because of their slower rate of maturation rather than from patterning. Intellectual improvements in children who were patterned have also been attributed to the social contact that is an inevitable part of patterning. In other words, the child was believed to benefit from the regular social interaction and attention as much as or more than from the passive or active action of the patterning.

The American Academy of Pediatrics (1993) was sufficiently opposed to Delacato's recommended treatment of neurologically impaired children that they developed and published a position statement expressing their opposition. They specifically cite several reasons for concern. For example, the AAP claims the means employed to promote the treatment made it hard for parents to reject treatment for fear of appearing inadequate as parents. In addition, the regimen of the program is extremely demanding and inflexible, which may cause the parents to feel stressed and possibly neglect other family members. Proponents also claim that rapid improvements are generally noted on the basis of assessments administered using their own development profile. Unfortunately, research validating the profile, according to he AAP, is lacking. Most important, the American Academy of Pediatrics notes that they are aware of only one scientific investigation in over 20 years that has indicated small improvements in the functioning of the patients receiving the Doman-Delacato patterning treatment. This is "cause to question the extensive claims for the patterning" (American Academy of Pediatrics, 1993).

RESEARCHING THE EFFECTIVENESS OF PERCEPTUAL-MOTOR PROGRAMS

Through a process known as *meta-analysis*, Kavale and Matson (1983) integrated the findings of over 180 scientific investigations designed to research the efficacy of perceptual-motor programs. This process of statistically integrating numerous sources examining the same topic is an intensive, scientific alternative to the more common narrative discussions of research studies. Over 60 percent of the investigations Kavale and Matson examined had been reported in research journals, with the remaining research coming from dissertations, books, and such sources as conference proceedings. The average study included in this meta-analysis involved children from the third grade at just less than 8 years of age. The average length of involvement in a perceptual-motor program was 19 weeks. It was found that, cognitively, children in this meta-analysis yielded a minimal gain. Specifically, the average subject gained 0.1 standard deviation and was performing better cognitively than only 54 percent of the control subjects, who received no perceptual-motor training. These findings support the reviews we reported earlier that stated that perceptual-motor intervention appears relatively ineffective. In fact, according to Kavale and Matson, the effects of perceptual-motor training are negligible compared to other forms of educational intervention and may even be harmful because considerable time, energy, and money frequently are wasted on these types of programs.

The authors of the meta-analysis on perceptual-motor programs were clearly opposed to intervention through perceptual-motor programs. As we mentioned throughout this chapter, many sources concur with Kavale and Matson by objectively and subjectively questioning the value of these programs. The programs Kephart and Delacato recommended received particular scrutiny. Nevertheless, we must also remember that the research that has failed to substantiate these programs has also been widely criticized. One of the most common problems encountered in investigations examining the efficacy of perceptual-motor programs is the brief period of treatment. Even programs that last nearly 5 months, which was the average time in the meta-analysis, may not be long enough. Many educators believe that a perceptual-motor program must be initiated very early in life and last for a time that may span years rather than months (Williams, 1984). In addition, although many experts agree that perceptual-motor programs are not the cure-all they once were believed to be, they may be an important indirect mode through which academic concepts can be introduced, reinforced, and developed (Gallahue, 1989). Direct improvement in academic abilities such as reading will not occur as a direct result of the kinds of perceptual-motor involvement Kephart or Delacato suggested. These programs typically do not incorporate academic concepts into the movement activity. However, when academic concepts are creatively interspersed throughout a movement activity, movement may be an excellent medium through which reading, spelling, math, social studies, or problem-solving concepts can be facilitated.

SUMMARY

Although perceptual-motor is one of the most commonly used terms in physical education, it is also one of the most confusing. Perceptual-motor refers to movement activities used to enhance academic or intellectual performance.

Perceptual-motor also implies a relationship between the perceptions and human movement. It has been purported that active participation in movement enhances such visual skills as depth perception. However, Walk's movement hypothesis states that optimal development of depth perception can occur from simply watching active, interesting stimuli.

Perceptions are important for movement to occur optimally as implied in the perceptual-motor process. This process facilitates movement behavior by accommodating the input and output of appropriate stimuli to and from the brain and includes the processing and integration of movement information while at the brain. In addition, future movement correction is possible because there is a feedback process. After the movement is completed, information about the outcome is stored for future analysis and comparison.

Although most human movement occurs via the perceptual-motor process, only certain movements are popularly believed to be perceptual-motor activities. Among the movements most often cited for value in improving cognitive or academic performance are balance and spatial, temporal, body, and directional awareness.

Kephart and Delacato proposed theories that have significantly affected education over the last 30 years. Both theorists claimed that specific movement activities can improve cognitive or academic performance. However, both theories have been heavily criticized because of a lack of scientific substantiation. Nevertheless, both theories continue to have many proponents and therefore continue to have an impact on contemporary educational theory.

Research on perceptual-motor intervention in education indicates that perceptual-motor programs may yield a negligible educational effect and actually may be harmful in some cases because they waste money, time, and energy. Kavale and Matson used meta-analysis to examine 180 studies on the effects of perceptual-motor programs. The subject receiving average treatment performed better cognitively or academically than only 54 percent of the control subjects, who had no comparable training.

A direct cognitive or academic benefit from perceptual-motor programs has not been substantiated scientifically, but the research in question has been heavily scrutinized and criticized. Many experts support the idea that perceptual-motor programs are not the panacea they were once purported to be. However, movement programs that incorporate academic concepts with the movement activities may be an excellent indirect way to supplement a childs education.

KEY TERMS

Balance
Body awareness
Directional awareness
Dynamic balance
Hemispheric
    dominance
Meta-analysis
Motion hypothesis
Perception

Perceptual-motor
Perceptual-motor
    development
Perceptual-motor
    process
Sensory integration
Spatial awareness
Static balance
Temporal awareness

CHAPTER 5

Prenatal Development Concerns

All human beings are unique, varying in appearance, personality, and movement abilities. Nevertheless, the normal growth and development process of all human beings is predictable. Although normally everyone attains the same mature human behaviors, the *rate* and ultimate *level* of achievement may vary considerably. Unfortunately, uncontrolled factors occasionally negatively influence the growth and development of the human organism. Such factors can emerge at any time throughout the lifespan; here we discuss those that are particularly influential during the prenatal state of growth and development. Because there are far more prenatal factors than we are capable of discussing in this chapter, we have limited our discussion to those that are particularly timely, devastating, or important for the study of motor development.

The negative factors influencing prenatal life are believed to be a result of genetic or environmental misfortune. An environmental agent that causes harm to the embryo or fetus is known as a *teratogen*. The extent of damage caused from a teratogen is a function of such factors as the amount of exposure, the time of exposure, and the baby's genetic makeup. Teratogens are generally most dangerous between 3 and 8 weeks of gestation. Prior to that time the placenta is not yet in place so the mother's blood supply is not being shared with the fetus. Thus, teratogens that will later be passed to the embryo or fetus from the mother are averted. So, clearly our genetic makeup (heredity) and environment can cause devastating abnormalities during the prenatal state. It is believed that most birth abnormalities, however, result from an interplay of genetic and environmental factors. For instance, Wilson (1973) estimated that approximately 10 percent of birth defects result from environmental factors and 25 percent from genetic or chromosomal defects. According to Wilson, 65 percent are caused by unknown agents.

Because there is so much uncertainty about the cause of most birth abnormalities, there has been a proliferation of research into this topic. Most of this research has been conducted since 1960, the year it was discovered that *thalidomide*, a tranquilizing drug, was the agent responsible for causing over 5000 malformed births in West Germany (Eckert, 1987). That finding dispelled the myth that the maternal environment was a protective shelter for the developing fetus.

In fact, we now know that teratogens, which are a product of the environment, exert their greatest influence during times known as *epigenetic crises* or an *epigenetic period*. An epigenetic crisis or period is a time of particular susceptibility to harm. Generally, the fetus is more susceptible to harm earlier in the pregnancy when it is growing and developing at such a rapid rate. Because of its rapid growth and development, early exposure to teratogens is likely to lead to structural and functional damage. Later exposure may cause only functional damage to the fetus (Jiminez, 1989). For that reason, the embryonic stage (the first 8 weeks of pregnancy) is often thought of as an epigenetic period. Or, the first trimester (first 3 months of pregnancy) is *generally* an epigenetic period relative to the second or third trimesters.

However, we can also use the term epigenetic period to specifically refer to the development of certain body parts. For example, thalidomide had diverse effects on babies depending on the time the mothers ingested the drug. Some babies developed malformed arms; other failed to achieve normal development of the outer ear; and some were missing a small bone in the hand. Still others were fortunate to experience no ill effects at all from the thalidomide. Clearly, the thalidomide affected the body part that was growing and developing the fastest at the time the drug was ingested. In the case of the babies who were unaffected, their mothers ingested the drug late enough in the pregnancy that the body parts typically affected were sufficiently grown and developed to avert damage. So, while earlier times in the pregnancy are *generally* a time

of increased susceptibility to harm, there are later epigenetic crises that are specific to the growth and development of *specific* body parts. Clearly, there is an epigenetic period for the development of the arms, one for the ears, and so on. Figure 5-1 presents a detailed illustration of critical periods in human development. A better understanding of the "normal" course of human development will allow you a greater appreciation for the abnormal development presented in this chapter.

This chapter presents several of the more common phenomena that have been shown to affect the developing human fetus. In addition, we emphasize the genetic and environmental phenomena that either directly or indirectly affect the attainment and refinement of motor competency. Though many of the prenatal concerns presented in this chapter are believed to exert their major effects on the cognitive development of the fetus, many others cause physical abnormalities. As we discussed in Chapter 1, because of the interaction of the domains of human development, any effect in any domain is likely to exert, at least, subtle effects on other aspects of development. Therefore, motor development is commonly affected whether it be from direct or indirect effects of the prenatal factor.

DRUGS AND MEDICATIONS

Certain drugs and medications can enter fetal circulation and therefore should be taken by a pregnant woman only under the supervision of a physician. Recreational drugs, prescriptive drugs, nonprescriptive drugs, and obstetrical medications are all chemicals that can have effects on both the mother and the developing fetus.

Recreational Drugs

These are drugs that generally serve no medical purpose. The four most widely used recreational drugs are alcohol, cocaine, tobacco, and cannabis (marijuana).

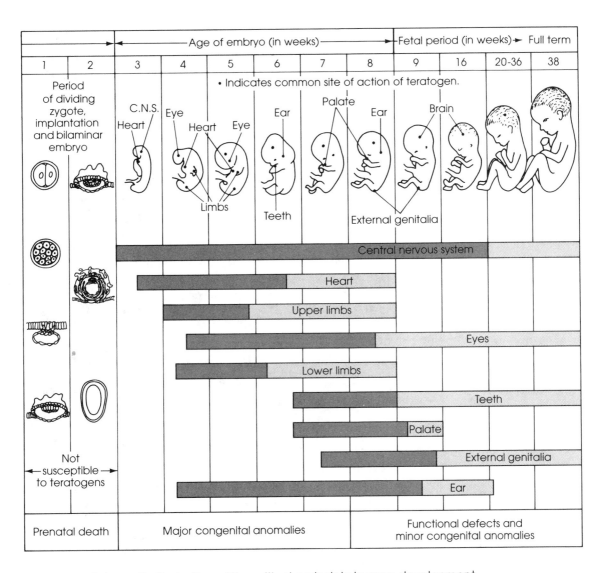

FIGURE 5-1 Schematic illustration of the critical periods in human development. During the first two weeks of development, the embryo is not usually susceptible to teratogens. During these pre-embryonic stages, a substance either damages all or most of the cells of the embryo resulting in death, or it damages only a few cells, allowing the conceptus to recover and the embryo to develop without birth defects. Light shading denotes highly sensitive periods when major defects may be produced (e.g., limb deficiencies). Darker shading indicates stages that are less sensitive to teratogens when minor defects may be induced (e.g., hypoplastic thumbs).

SOURCE: Moore and Persaud (1993). *Before We Were Born*, 4th Edition p. 130. Used with permission.

Alcohol   In the United States, on average, each consumer of alcohol ingests more than 1000 cans of beer, glasses of wine, or shots of liquor each year (Abel, 1983). Indeed the prevalence of alcohol use among women between 15 and 44 years of age is estimated to be approximately 90 percent (Mac Gregor & Chasnoff, 1993). More important, however, are findings indicating that 3.3 percent of all pregnant women can be classified as heavy drinkers (two or more drinks per occasion) during pregnancy.

Women frequently ask, "How much alcohol can I safely drink during pregnancy?" In the opinion of the American Academy of Pediatrics (1993), Committee on Substance Abuse and the Committee on Children with Disabilities, to date, "there is no established safe dose of alcohol for pregnant women" (p. 1004). In fact, the potential damage that drinking alcohol during pregnancy can have on the developing baby has led these two committees to recommend a greater societal effort to educate women of all ages to the potential dangers of drinking alcohol during pregnancy. More specifically their recommendations include: (1) the development and delivery of a mandatory curriculum for all elementary, junior high, and high school students, as well as postsecondary students attending adult education centers, (2) support of federal legislation mandating a warning label on all printed and broadcast alcohol advertisements such as, "Drinking during pregnancy may cause mental retardation and other birth defects. Avoid alcohol during pregnancy," and (3) the development of state legislation that would make available information regarding the teratogenic effects of drinking alcohol during pregnancy at marriage-licensing bureaus and other public places.

These strong recommendations are necessary since the incidence of an infant developing symptoms associated with maternal alcohol consumption is about 1 in every 300 live births. When symptoms are severe, the newborn is said to have a condition known as *fetal alcohol syndrome* (FAS). This condition (FAS), first reported by Jones and associates (1973), manifests such abnormalities as characteristic facial features, mental retardation, attention

deficit disorder with hyperactivity, and retarded physical growth in stature, weight, and head circumference. Indeed, the median birth weight of children born with FAS (2100 grams or 4 pounds, 11 ounces) is far below the median birth weight of children born without FAS (3370 grams or 7 pounds, 7 ounces) (Abel, 1990). Because of poor brain growth, FAS children attain an average IQ of only 67. Less severe symptoms are generally referred to as *fetal alcohol effects* (FAE) and include such manifestations as fine-motor dysfunction, clumsiness, delays in motor performance, and speech disorders, just to name a few.

During the neonatal period, the child may even exhibit withdrawal symptoms known as *neonatal abstinence syndrome* (NAS). Onset of NAS ranges from minutes or hours after birth to 14 days after birth, with most occurring within 72 hours (MacGregor & Chasnoff, 1993). Symptoms generally include tremulousness, hyperactivity, and irritability. In short, few organ tissues or body systems are unaffected by alcohol consumption during the prenatal period. Table 5-1 highlights selected outcomes of FAS and FAE. Note that the abnormalities associated with FAS and FAE make up three categories: growth deficiency, central nervous system dysfunctions, and craniofacial abnormalities.

Cocaine   Cocaine is the most infamous recreational drug of our time. Its use in all forms has increased dramatically in recent years. It is snorted, smoked as "crack," and injected more than ever before. Its use among pregnant women has also soared with as many as one in ten newborns being affected in some major urban areas. In any form, as little as one use of cocaine during pregnancy can have devastating consequences. Because cocaine is one of the most dangerous drugs to the unborn baby, the March of Dimes has strongly advised stopping use before pregnancy or delaying the pregnancy until the drug can be avoided. They also advise the pregnant cocaine user to reveal her cocaine use immediately to her physician so that she can receive treatment to help her stop using the drug and so that early prenatal care can begin.

TABLE 5-1   Selected Outcomes of Fetal Alcohol Syndrome/Fetal Alcohol Effects

Growth deficiency	Central nervous system dysfunctions	Craniofacial anomalies
Weight and length below 10th percentile corrected for gestational age	Weak sucking reflex	Epicanthic folds around eyes
	IQ generally less than 70	Obstruction of upper airway passages
Microcephaly	Increased reaction time	
Increased risk of congenital anomalies	Myopia (visual disorder)	
	Sensorineural hearing loss	
	Irritability (infancy)	
	Hyperactivity (childhood)	
	Hypotonic	
	Increased risk for seizures	
	Delayed motor and language development	
	Fine-motor impairment	
	Clumsiness	

One potentially devastating effect of cocaine use during pregnancy is fetal brain damage. This damage is believed to be the result of blood vessel constriction causing oxygen deprivation to the brain. Because of brain and central nervous system damage, "cocaine babies" often score low on tests of responsiveness. For example, they perform poorly on measures of infant reflexes, often having poor sucking ability. Their attention span is also reduced considerably, making them relatively unresponsive to voices or faces. In addition, they are often "jittery" and extremely irritable, as they cry with minimal provocation. This lack of responsiveness and irritability impedes the bonding process and makes the task of child rearing especially difficult for the mother and is believed to contribute to later incidence of child abuse or neglect.

Other effects from maternal cocaine use include increased occurrence of miscarriage. This is often caused by uterine contractions late in pregnancy, which can result in premature labor. Cocaine also causes extreme fluctuations in the heart rate and blood pressure of the mother and the fetus. These rapid fluctuations in blood pressure can result in ruptured blood vessels of the brain, leading to stroke and contributing to the fetal brain damage mentioned earlier. Occasionally, the blood vessels to the placenta are also affected. They can be constricted to the point that the passage of nutrients to the fetus is impeded. This causes poor prenatal nutrition and increases the likelihood of a low birth weight baby (Petitti & Coleman, 1990), who is shorter and has an abnormally small head circumference. Poor blood supply to the placenta can also cause the placenta to pull away from the uterine wall prematurely, causing extensive bleeding and potentially death to the mother and the baby.

Finally, babies born to mothers who used cocaine excessively during pregnancy are also believed to be at greater risk of sudden infant death syndrome (SIDS) and will likely exhibit a slower rate of growth compared to the norm after birth (Rist, 1990). Slow growth rate, like the effects discussed earlier, could be prevented by not using cocaine during pregnancy (Morton, 1989).

Because crack was not readily available until 1985, we are just beginning to see its effect on young children's performance as they become of school age. Initial reports suggest that many of the crack-exposed individuals are having extreme difficulty learning in the typical classroom environment. Regarding play and movement performance, Dr. Judith Howard, director of the Suspected Child Abuse and Neglect Team at the University of California, Los Angeles, writes, "Crack babies typically lack the skills and characteristics necessary for free play, self-organization, initiative, and follow-through without adult guidance. They scatter and bat toys, pick toys up and put them down, without purpose and with seeming uninvolvement" (Rist, 1990, p. 4). In short, these children need a very structured environment consisting of constant attention and guidance. The cost to public school systems to provide such a labor intensive environment will undoubtedly result in enormous expense.

Tobacco   In 1935, Sontag and Wallace (cited in Abel, 1983) first recognized the damaging effects of smoking tobacco during pregnancy. However, intensive studies investigating the effects of smoking on prenatal development did not begin until the 1950s. By 1964, the adverse effects of smoking were so well documented that the Surgeon General's Report led to warning labels being placed on cigarette packages.

During this time of intensive study, over 2200 different ingredients were found in tobacco and tobacco smoke. Many of these ingredients were believed to have deleterious effects on the developing fetus. The major defects established included decreased birth weight, higher rate of mortality at or around the time of birth, increased occurrence of miscarriage, decreased mental functioning in surviving offspring, and a twofold increase in the risk of sudden infant death syndrome. Postnatally, nicotine poisoning was a danger for the children of mothers who chose to breast-feed.

Today, the most studied pharmacological byproducts of tobacco smoke are *carbon monoxide* and *nicotine*. Carbon monoxide is known to interfere with hemoglobin's oxygen-carrying and oxygen-releasing capabilities and therefore increases the risk of fetal hypoxia (lack of oxygen to body tissues).

Nicotine also contributes to fetal hypoxia by causing the adrenals to release epinephrine, a hormone capable of constricting the placenta's blood vessels (Armitage, 1965).

Researchers speculate that approximately 40 percent of the female population smoke tobacco during pregnancy (Abel, 1983). Researchers further note that these women are more likely to experience maternal complications than are their non-smoking counterparts. Also of interest are recent findings which indicate that "second hand" smoke also leads to these same maternal complications. Researchers have only begun to examine the effects of postnatal smoking on children's health. Initial studies have found that children who live in homes where smoking is prevalent, exhibit more episodes of respiratory diseases such as bronchiolitis and pneumonia (Kandall, 1991). Table 5-2 summarizes short- and long-term risk factors associated with maternal tobacco smoking.

Cannabis   Marijuana, a mind-altering drug, is composed of more than 400 different chemicals (Turner, 1980, cited in Abel, 1983). The most active ingredient frequently discussed is *11-hydroxy-delta-9-tetrahydrocannabinal,* commonly referred to as *THC*. Some researchers have estimated that as many as 44 percent of the female population have smoked marijuana during their reproductive years (Mac Gregor & Chasnoff, 1993); those females who admitted using the drug during pregnancy do so moderately (Fried et al., 1980). There are voluminous amounts of literature associating the detrimental effects of alcohol and tobacco use with maternal and fetal complications, but as Abel wrote, "almost nothing has been reported concerning marijuana and its effects on the human embryo or fetus" (1983, p. 31). Furthermore, that research which is available is oftentimes inconclusive. For example, regular use of cannabis during pregnancy has been associated with longer gestations, shorter gestations, and normal gestational periods. Likewise, its use has also been associated with low birth weight and small-for-gestational age infants. Yet some have reported no effects at all on birth weight (MacGregor &

TABLE 5-2 Risk Factors Associated with
Maternal Tobacco Smoking

Prenatal complications

Antepartum bleeding

Premature rupture of membranes

Increased chance of miscarriage

Higher rates of stillbirth and perinatal mortality

Intrauterine growth retardation

Postnatal complications

Low birth weight

Sudden infant death syndrome (SIDS)

Long-term retardation of growth

Weight, stature, and head circumference

Respiratory disorders

Pneumonia

Bronchitis

Behavioral effects

Reduced mental alertness

Reduced visual alertness

Chasnoff, 1993). Until more conclusive evidence is available, doctors recommend that pregnant women refrain from the use of all recreational drugs.

Prescriptive Drugs

Many women have a long-term disease that must be controlled by the continuous use of prescriptive medications even during pregnancy. These women tend to give birth to malformed infants at a greater rate than women who do not use prescriptive medications. There is controversy, however, as to whether the real cause of the reported malformations is the drugs or the mother's general ill health. For instance, women who control their epilepsy by using nonbarbiturate anticonvulsants tend to increase twofold their risk of giving birth to malformed offspring (Heinonen, Slone, & Shapiro, 1977). However, when

researchers controlled for the different degrees of the disease, they found that the incidence of malformations was no greater than what would be expected in the general population. Nevertheless, caution is advised during pregnancy when prescriptive drugs are considered because they may cause damage to the fetus.

Prescriptive drugs are believed to affect the fetus in two general ways. First, they may function like thalidomide, which we discussed earlier in the chapter and which was a prescription drug. That is, they damage the body part that is growing and developing the fastest during the time of drug use. Secondly, they may adversely affect in the fetus that which was intended to be positively affected in the mother. For example, a mother taking prescriptive thyroid medication expects a positive effect on her thyroid gland. Though she may reap such benefits, the thyroid of the fetus may be damaged from the mother's prescriptive drug use.

Nonprescriptive Drugs

Nonprescriptive, or "over-the-counter," medications are generally assumed to be safe because no prescription is required for them to be dispensed. While this is generally true, many nonprescriptive drugs can have dramatic teratogenic effects on the unborn baby. For that reason, many physicians recommend not treating such illnesses as colds with nonprescriptive drugs unless absolutely necessary. If a pregnant woman feels she needs to take such a medication, she should consult her physician before taking it.

Aspirin, one of the most common over-the-counter drugs, has been linked to postterm pregnancy and prolonged labor if taken in high doses over an extended period of time. It can also cause excessive bleeding within the skull of the baby and increase the mother's bleeding during delivery. Unlike most teratogens, which are particularly dangerous early in the pregnancy, the greatest risk with aspirin occurs when taken within a few weeks of giving birth (Jiminez, 1989).

Unfortunately, many aspirin substitutes can also have adverse effects. Ibuprofen, a nonsteroidal anti-inflammatory drug, should also be avoided during the last few weeks of pregnancy. Like aspirin, it may increase the length of labor. Ibuprofen also appears to interfere with the unborn baby's breathing though minimal research is available on the prenatal effects of this drug.

Acetaminophen may be the safest substitute for aspirin as current research has shown no prenatal damage associated with this drug. However, like ibuprofen, too little research exists to allow full understanding of the effects of acetaminophen (Jimenez, 1989).

A problem with many over-the-counter medications is that they have been designed to treat an array of maladies. Such nonprescriptive medications should always be avoided during pregnancy because of increased risk of prenatal harm due to the variety of chemicals they contain. This is the case with many cold medications, which can also be potentially damaging if high in alcohol content. As discussed earlier in the chapter, ingesting alcohol during pregnancy can cause fetal alcohol syndrome or fetal alcohol effects. Avoiding cold medications can be particularly difficult during pregnancy because pregnant women tend to have lower resistance to illness and, therefore, they have more colds (University of Iowa Healthbeat, 1989).

Obstetrical Medications

Physicians prescribe and administer many drugs during pregnancy and delivery. It has been estimated that obstetrician-gynecologists prescribed 3.7 million doses of narcotic analgesics, 1.3 million doses of barbiturate sedatives, 1.1 million doses of non-narcotic analgesics, and 1.1 million doses of tranquilizers (Brackbill, 1979). Stewart, Cluff, and Philp (cited in Osofsky, 1979) reported that on the average, 7 drugs are administered during a vaginal delivery and 15.2 drugs during a Cesarean section delivery. Though health-care professionals have become more cautious concerning the effects of drugs on the unborn, just 20 years ago only 5 percent of deliveries were accomplished without anesthesia (Brackbill, 1979).

The preanesthetic medications most frequently administered to laboring women are oxytocin (initiate and aid labor), meperidine (relieve pain), and phenergan (relieve anxiety). Other forms of anesthetic agents include those for general anesthesia (loss of sensation throughout the entire body, that is, sleep) and regional anesthesia (loss of sensation in a selected area of the body).

There is controversy over the use of obstetrical medications because these agents are known to enter fetal circulation, exerting their effects on the child, within minutes after being administered to the mother. Brazelton (1961) showed that the use of preanesthetic sedatives caused depressed sucking behaviors throughout the first week of life. A longitudinal investigation by Brackbill (1976) demonstrated that infants displayed the effects of being exposed to obstetrical medications just as strongly at 8 months as during the first month of postnatal life.

MATERNAL DISEASES

There are a host of maternal diseases that can potentially exert an influence upon the developing fetus. The origin of these diseases can take many forms including the following: viral diseases (rubella, HIV), parasitic diseases (toxoplasmosis), hematologic diseases (Rh incompatibility), and endocrine diseases (diabetes mellitus). In this section we examine several of the most influential maternal diseases that can affect the outcome of pregnancy.

Rubella

Congenital rubella (German measles) reached epidemic proportions in the United States in 1964 and 1965. Vaccination programs have curtailed this infectious virus, but it is still a significant problem for those women who in their childbearing years were too old to be immunized when the vaccine was first introduced. The extent of fetal damage that may be inflicted is partly influenced by when the pregnant woman becomes infected with the virus. Offspring have an 80 percent chance of being affected when a woman contracts the virus during the first 12 weeks of gestation, a 54 percent chance between 13 and 14 weeks, and a 25 percent chance between 15 and 26 weeks (Gold, Kumar, Nankervis, & Sweet, 1991).

A broad spectrum of potential fetal defects is associated with rubella infections, including growth retardation, cataracts, bony lesions, pneumonia, hepatitis, and cardiac anomalies resulting in early heart failure. The most prevalent defect of congenital rubella is deafness (Alford, Pass, & Stagno, 1983). The incidence of congenital rubella–based defects is difficult to establish because many of the associated defects are frequently masked during infancy, surfacing only in later months (Gold, Kumar, Nankervis, & Sweet, 1991).

Human Immunodeficiency Virus

Women who carry the *human immunodeficiency virus* (HIV) are at risk of passing this deadly virus on to their offspring. The transmission rate among infected mothers ranges between 9 percent and 65 percent (Sicklick & Rubenstein, 1992). Perinatal transmission is generally accomplished in one of three ways: (1) in utero from the mother to the fetus, (2) during delivery when the fetus will come in contact with infected blood or infected vaginal secretions, and (3) through breast milk (Simonds & Rogers, 1992).

The prognosis for infants infected by HIV is not bright. In fact, the median survival time from clinical onset is only 24 months. However, there does appear to be a form of HIV (static HIV) whose course for some reason is not as rapid. Children who can survive past two years of age tend to have a better chance at prolonging life. Nevertheless, 90 percent will manifest symptoms by 4 years of age (Diamond & Cohen, 1992), and few will live past 13 years of age.

TABLE 5-3 Neurological Deterioration in HIV-Infected Children

Loss of previously acquired milestones

Failure to attain developmental milestones at the expected age

Impaired brain growth

Spasticity or rigidity

Muscle weakness

Ataxia

Seizures and extrapyramidal tract signs (tremor, athetosis)

SOURCE: Diamond & Cohen (1992)

An array of developmental disabilities are exhibited by HIV infected children. Table 5-3 lists several of the neurological complications. Many of these neurological complications were described in a case study by Diamond and Associates (1990) involving a 14-month-old white boy (J.M.) and a 6-year-old black boy (C.P.). For example, J.M. was small and exhibited noticeable muscle wasting at 4 months of age. In addition, pervasive spasticity with truncal hypotonia and poor head control was evident. He also showed no interest in playing with small toys. C.P. was also small for his age with height and weight only at the 40th percentile. He also experienced difficulty with both fine motor and visual-motor integrative tasks and used an immature pencil grip.

When the disease becomes full blown AIDS, the immune system will generally deteriorate rapidly and death is usually caused by the body's inability to fight off infection.

Toxoplasmosis

The fetus may also be infected by protozoan parasites, of which the most common is *Toxoplasma gondii*. Members of the feline (cat) family are the primary hosts for this organism. Pregnant women are frequently introduced to the organism when they are exposed to infectious oocysts present in soil contaminated by cat feces or when they ingest undercooked meats containing the active organism. This virus has been frequently called the "silent infection" because only 10 percent of the infected newborns show clinical evidence of the disease at birth (Alford, Pass, & Stagno, 1983).

In cases of acute toxoplasmosis, 85 percent of live births will experience mental retardation and convulsions; 75 percent will experience abnormalities in motor abilities. Other reported abnormalities include deafness (13 percent) and visual impairments (50 percent) that may be present at birth or take many years to become detectable (Alford, Pass, & Stagno, 1983). The incidence of acute congenital toxoplasmosis in the United States has been estimated as between 2 to 7 for every 1000 pregnancies (Chan & Sweet, 1991).

Rh Incompatibility and Erythroblastosis Fetalis

Early attempts to transfuse blood from human to human and from animal to human were not successful because people were unaware that human blood contains many different components. At the turn of the 20th century, the medical community discovered that human blood can be divided into four distinct groups (A, B, AB, O) and that attempts to cross-transfuse blood types stimulates the recipient's immune system to produce antibodies to destroy the donor's foreign cells.

We know now that in addition to the four major blood groups, the red blood cells of approximately 85 percent of the population contain an additional protein: the *Rh factor*. Individuals with the Rh factor have Rh-positive blood; those people lacking the blood protein possess Rh-negative blood. That all individuals do not possess an Rh factor on their red blood cells is of special concern for a selected group of parents. There is a potential problem when an Rh-positive man and an Rh-negative woman conceive an Rh-positive child. If during the course of gestation, the Rh-positive blood cells escape from fetal circulation to enter maternal circulation, the mother's Rh-negative blood will view the Rh-positive cells as foreign bodies. The mother's body will then be stimulated to produce antibodies against the Rh-positive cells. These antibodies may then enter fetal circulation and destroy the fetal red blood cells.

Because maternal and fetal circulation do not mix under normal circumstances, some experts suggest that fetal blood cells may enter maternal circulation by escaping from broken vessels in the placental villi. Because the placental vessels do not generally rupture until later in pregnancy, the mother develops antibodies postnatally, sparing her first offspring. However, in order for subsequent children to be protected, the mother should receive an injection of *anti-D IgG immunoglobulin* immediately after delivery. Treatment within 72 hours after delivery is adequate for protection in 98 percent of the cases. This form of treatment has been a major breakthrough in obstetrics, lowering percent of deaths from 3.9 percent in 1969 to 0.5 percent in 1986 (cited in Perry, Martin, & Morrison, 1991).

Rh-positive offspring exposed to the antibodies of their Rh-negative mother are born with a condition called *erythroblastosis fetalis*, also called congenital hemolytic disease. Characteristics of this disorder include anemia, an increased number of immature red blood cells in circulation, generalized edema, and jaundice.

The probability of a susceptible couple giving birth to an Rh-positive child depends on whether the father carries the Rh antigens on both members of his paired chromosomes (*homozygous*) or just one of the two chromosomes (*heterozygous*). If the father is a homozygous carrier, all of his children will be Rh positive; a heterozygous carrier has a 50 percent chance of producing an Rh-positive child. Approximately 12 percent of all marriages involve Rh-positive males and Rh-negative females (Eckert, 1987).

Diabetes Mellitus

Infants born to diabetic mothers remain a high-risk population in spite of improving management (insulin regulation and diet therapy). Complications during pregnancy are attributed to the fetus's exposure to a constantly altering metabolic environment. This metabolic environment can range from *normoglycemia* to *hypoglycemia* to intermittent or constant *hyperglycemia.* A particular problem is fetal hyperinsulinemia induced by maternal hyperglycemia. Pedersen and Pedersen (1971, cited in Luke, Johnson, & Petrie, 1993) have hypothesized that this condition may result in (1) *macrosomia* (birth weight above the 90th percentile for gestational age or greater than 4000 grams) making a vaginal delivery difficult; (2) inhibition of lung maturation of surfactant; (3) muscle weakness or cardiac arrhythmias as a result of decreased serum potassium; and (4) possible permanent neurologic damage brought on by neonatal hypoglycemia. Of these four outcomes, the most frequently mentioned is macrosomia. Pedersen (1977) has advanced a theory as to the cause of this condition. Namely, during the third trimester, maternal hyperglycemia leads to increases in fetal glucose. As a result, fetal secretion of insulin from the pancreas is increased causing fetal hyperinsulinemia. This increase in insulin production in turn leads to an increased level of glycogen in the fetal liver thus stimulating increased triglyceride synthesis in fat (adipose) cells. As a result, there is an increase in fetal body fat.

Of particular interest to health professionals are findings that suggest that macrosomia in infants of diabetic mothers may be an important factor in accounting for obesity in later life. More specifically, it was found that macrosomia infants at 7 years of age were classified as obese compared to only 1 in 14 appropriate-for-gestational age infants (Vohr, Lipsitt, & Oh, 1980). If hyperglycemia can be eliminated throughout the term of pregnancy, the perinatal mortality rate is similar to that seen in the general population. Table 5-4 highlights selected abnormalities of infants born to diabetic mothers.

GENETIC FACTORS

Genetic factors affecting normal prenatal growth and development can take one of two forms. That is, abnormal development can be caused by a chromosome- or gene-based disorder.

TABLE 5-4 Selected Abnormalities of Infants Born to Diabetic Mothers

Central nervous system deformities
  Spina bifida
  Hydrocephalus
Cogenital anomalies
  Heart defects
  Skeletal and central nervous system
Macrosomia
Musculoskeletal deformities
Respiratory distress syndrome
Traumatic birth injury
  Asphyxia
  Facial nerve injury
  Brachial plexus injury
  Cesarean section due to cephalopelvic disproportion

Chromosome-Based Disorders

Every normal cell within our bodies contains 46 chromosomes, with the exception of the reproductive cells (sperm and ova), which contain only 23 chromosomes. When the sperm and ova join during conception, each contributes its 23 chromosomes, to form a new individual whose cells will also contain the usual 23 pairs of genetic material. When the sex chromosomes reproduce through cell division (meiosis), there can be problems if, during the division, a pair of chromosomes does not separate properly. This lack of chromosome separation is called *meiotic nondisjunction*, the result of which is that one sperm or egg cell will contain two members of a particular numbered chromosome while the other member will contain none. If, during conception, the cell containing the extra chromosome unites with a normal sex cell, the new individual will possess 47 chromosomes. This individual is said to be trisomic, meaning that one of the chromosomes has three rather than the usual two members.

The most frequent cytogenetic defect is mongolism, commonly referred to as *Down syndrome*. The technical name for this syndrome is trisomy 21, indicating that chromosome number 21 has three chromosomes instead of the usual two. As a result of meiotic nondisjunction, Down syndrome occurs at an average rate of 1 in 600 (Valentine, 1975) to 1 in 900 births (Silver, Kempe, & Bruyn, 1977). The incidence of occurrence is greatest in children of mothers over age 35 (Fay & Smith, 1985; Redding & Hirschhorn, 1993).

The most striking behavioral outcome of this syndrome is mental retardation. This population generally obtains IQ scores between 20 and 60 and functions at a maximum average mental age of 8 years (Silver, Kempe, & Bruyn, 1977). Table 5-5 lists other prominent characteristics of this genetic defect. Pay special attention to the fact that the fundamental motor pattern, walking, is generally delayed 2 or more years and that the fine motor control associated with speech development also develops slowly.

Gene-Based Disorders

Phenylketonuria One gene-based disorder is *phenylketonuria (PKU)*. Since its discovery in 1934 by a Norwegian doctor, Asbjorn Folling, PKU has been the topic of literally thousands of research papers, mainly because the discovery led to the prevention of the mental retardation associated with PKU. Mental manifestations are the most commonly reported clinical features of the disorder, but some individuals may exhibit neurological dysfunctions and extraneural symptoms, including motor impairments, such as tight muscles and muscle tremors, to mention but two.

PKU is caused by a disturbance in amino acid metabolism, as a result of inheriting a gene that suppresses the activity of the liver enzyme phenylalanine hydroxylase. This enzyme is responsible for converting dietary L-phenylalanine to the amino acid tyrosine. If there is not enough of this conversion, the body tissues accumulate dangerous levels of L-

TABLE 5-5 Symptoms and Signs of Trisomy 21

Walking delayed 2 or more years

Speech development slow

Slow development of fine motor control

Toilet training delayed

Lower than normal birth weight

Hypotonia (too little muscle tone)

Short stature

Puberty often delayed

Prone to respiratory infections

Heart disease common

Prominent anatomical features:

    Close-setting eyes

    Short, thick neck

    Small, rather square head

phenylalanine, causing irreversible changes in the central nervous system. The estimated occurrence of the disorder is 1 in 14,000 (Evans, Subramony, Hanson, & Parker, 1991).

Unlike the other birth disorders discussed, PKU cannot be evaluated by visual inspection; blood levels of phenylalanine must be measured in the laboratory. For accurate blood level measures to be obtained, all newborns should be evaluated no sooner than 8 days after birth (Kopp & Parmelee, 1979) because the level of phenylalanine in the blood of phenylketonuric children rises after birth until the concentration reaches a dangerous level. Screening too early may result in not diagnosing 5 to 10 percent of phenylketonuric children.

As early as the mid-1950s, the medical community demonstrated that many of the symptoms of PKU could be favorably modified and even prevented by placing the child on a low phenylalanine diet. For treatment to be most effective, the disorder should be diagnosed as soon as possible. Major significant differences have been found between early- and late-treated groups of phenylketonuric children. Steinhausen (1974) found that early-treated groups maintained normal levels of development, whereas those treated after 6 months of life remained below age-level functioning in the motor and social development.

Cystic Fibrosis Another gene-based disorder is *cystic fibrosis* (CF). This devastating disease affects approximately 30,000 children and adults in the United States. Approximately 1 out of every 25 Caucasians carry the gene, and 1 in every 2500 births are affected by CF (Verp, Simpson, & Ober, 1993). One-half of the individuals with CF will expire before reaching 30 years of age, while the second half will generally live into their early 40s. Characteristically, this disease causes a thick, sticky mucus to be secreted within the lungs. This mucus causes those with CF to experience reoccurring bouts of pulmonary infections. In addition, the thick mucus will frequently clog the pancreas and interfere with normal digestion. From a movement perspective, those with CF frequently experience shortness of breath and fatigue easily. With repeated bouts of lung infections, additional scar tissue within the lungs will accumulate and worsen the condition. To date there is no cure for CF. However, in December of 1993, the U.S. Food and Drug Administration approved the first new class of CF medication in 30 years. This new drug is an enzyme that thins the CF mucus (pulmozyme). Researchers are now experimenting with gene therapy in an attempt to correct abnormalities within the gene. Within the near future, teaching hospitals around the country will begin clinical trials.

PRENATAL DIAGNOSTIC PROCEDURES

Though the list of potential teratogens seems to increase daily, most babies are born healthy. In fact, only about 4 percent will be born with abnormalities. Among those 4 percent most will have abnormalities so slight as to have minimal impact on daily function (Prenatal Health, 1989). Aiding in the battle against the small number of abnormalities that oc-

cur is an array of diagnostic tools. Though these tools are not "cures" for the prenatal abnormalities they can detect, they can alert expectant parents and health care professionals of the need to take special precautions for the remainder of the pregnancy. For some, these tools may provide valuable information to aid in deciding whether or not to continue the pregnancy.

Although medical technology is creating new diagnostic tools regularly, the four most current prenatal diagnostic tools are *ultrasound, amniocentesis, chorionic villus sampling*, and the *alphafetoprotein test*. These tools are especially important for women who are believed to be at risk for giving birth to a child with abnormalities. Characteristics that might make a woman a highrisk candidate include:

- will be over age 35 at the time of delivery
- has given birth to (or whose partner has had) previous child with a genetic disease or birth defect
- has a family history of genetic disease or birth defects
- has a medical history of certain genetic traits (e.g., sickle-cell anemia or diabetes) (Prenatal Health, 1989)

Women who are not high risk may also have these tests administered. However, these tests can be expensive and, in the case of amniocentesis and chorionic villus sampling, can pose a small risk of damaging the fetus. With the exception of the alpha-fetoprotein test, where law in some states mandates offering the test to all pregnant women, these tests should be administered judiciously.

Ultrasound Ultrasound, also referred to as a sonogram, is administered by placing a small transmitter on the abdomen of the pregnant woman. Typically, the abdomen is lubricated so the transmitter can be easily maneuvered into the position that enables the best picture of the fetus. The transmitter emits high-frequency sound waves that echo off the fetus. In turn, these sound waves are transformed into computer-enhanced images on a monitor. Though not producing a particularly clear image, a sonogram creates a clear enough picture to measure the head size of the baby to assist in determining the exact length of gestation (see Figure 5-2). It can also be used to examine the placement and structure of the placenta as well as detecting the baby's gender, multiple pregnancies, and some anatomical abnormalities. The advantages of an ultrasound test are the lack of pain, no injection is required, and it takes only about 30 minutes. While it is presumed to be a safe test, research is ongoing concerning the long-term effects of the high-frequency sound waves on the fetus (Prenatal Health, 1989).

Amniocentesis Unlike ultrasound, amniocentesis requires a needle to be inserted through the abdominal wall. This procedure, which was first used for fetal diagnosis in 1967, employs a thin needle to remove approximately 2 tablespoons of amniotic fluid drawn from the small amniotic sac around the fetus. This fluid contains fetal cells, which can be examined to determine the presence of certain abnormalities. Because amniocentesis is an intrusive test, ultrasound is used to locate the best site for puncture, to locate the placenta, and to safely guide the needle to the best pool of amniotic fluid (Bennett, 1981).

Though amniocentesis is believed to present minimum risk to the mother and fetus, the needle has been known to damage the fetus on occasion. In addition, amniocentesis has caused miscarriages in approximately 1 in 300 pregnancies (Prenatal Health, 1989). For those reasons, this test is generally only employed when the mother is at high risk for giving birth to a child with abnormalities. Amniocentesis is administered in the second trimester, usually between 15 and 17 weeks of gestation. With an increase in the resolution of ultrasound, some centers are now beginning to perform this procedure at the 13th or 14th week of gestation. Only a handful of centers are attempting the procedure prior to the 13th week of gestation (Verp, Simpson, & Ober, 1993). The process takes about 20 minutes and can detect numerous chromosomal abnormali-

ties (e.g., Down syndrome), the gender of the baby, and neural-tube defects (e.g.., spina bifida, a failure of the bony structure of the spine to close completely around the spinal cord) with a high degree of accuracy (Verp, Simpson, & Ober, 1993).

Chorionic Villus Sampling Chorionic villus sampling (CVS) is a newer technique that offers one major advantage over amniocentesis: It can be administered between 10 and 12 weeks of gestation, so that any abnormalities are detected earlier. At that time there are too few viable cells per milliliter of amniotic fluid for amniocentesis to be reliable and safe (Brambati & Oldrin, 1986). Like amniocentesis, CVS is designed to gather cell samples for examination. However, rather than sampling the amniotic fluid, CVS is intended to take samples of the small hairlike projections of the placenta (see Figure 5-3). These projections, known as villi, can reveal the same information available through amniocentesis. CVS is administered by inserting a needle through the abdomen or through the cervix of the pregnant woman. Both methods employ ultrasound to guide the needle used to take the sample.

Though CVS offers the advantage of earlier administration and thus earlier detection of abnormalities, it is also potentially more risky than amniocentesis. Three times as many miscarriages are caused by CVS than by amniocentesis, with 1 in 100 CVS administrations causing problems. Therefore, CVS is recommended for only the highest-risk pregnant women. For high-risk women, any dangers are generally believed to be outweighed by the benefit of knowing early in the pregnancy that the baby is experiencing abnormalities and may need special prenatal care (Prenatal Health, 1989).

Alpha-fetoprotein The alpha-fetoprotein test is a simple blood test performed at approximately 15 to 20 weeks into the pregnancy. This blood test measures the amount of alpha-fetoprotein (AFP) in the blood and can indicate the presence of neural-tube defects in the case of high AFP levels or such chromosomal disorders as Down syndrome when levels are low. Because the majority of women who

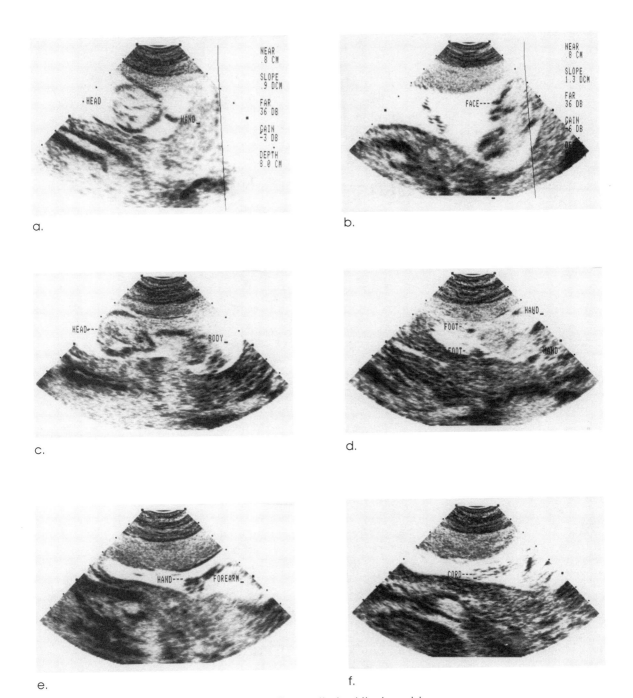

FIGURE 5-2 The sonogram is a valuable diagnostic tool that enables medical professionals to view the fetus. The head and hands (a), face (b), head and body (c), feet and hands (d), hand and forearm (e), and the umbilicus (f) are pictured above (all taken at 8 weeks of gestation).

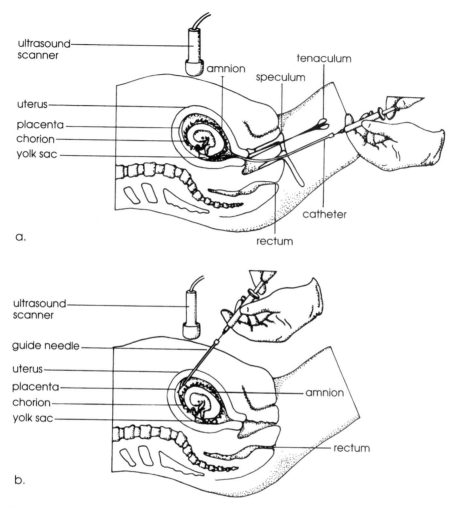

FIGURE 5-3 Several different methods are employed to gather a tissue sample in chorionic villus testing. (a) A plastic catheter is inserted through the cervix and guided by ultrasound, (b) A biopsy needle is inserted through the abdominal wall and guided by ultrasound.

have abnormal AFP levels give birth to normal babies, the AFP test is usually employed as a screening device to determine if additional prenatal diagnostic testing should be done. The presence of twins or a small miscalculation in the time of gestation can cause misinterpretation of AFP levels (Prenatal Health, 1989).

MATERNAL NUTRITION

Adequate prenatal nutrition is essential for the well being of the mother-to-be as well as the growing fetus. The prenatal diet should be sufficient in order to cover the increased metabolic load which accompanies pregnancy. These additional calories are needed to support growth of the placenta and growth of the developing fetus. Indeed, total caloric intake appears to be one of the foremost factors affecting infant birth weight (Butterfield & King, 1991). To supply the extra energy needed during pregnancy, the sedentary woman needs to increase caloric intake by approximately 300 calories per day. Women who elect to continue strenuous physical activity during pregnancy must make additional adjustments. How much of an adjustment depends on the caloric cost of the activities performed. In general, the active pregnant woman should ingest additional calories equivalent to the energy expended during physical activity plus the 300 calories per day maintenance load. If weight gain falls below expected levels during the course of pregnancy, then it may be necessary to further increase caloric intake (Butterfield & King, 1991).

How much weight should one gain over the course of pregnancy? The answer to this question is influenced by the woman's weight status prior to conception (*pregravid weight*). For example, if the woman's pregravid weight is appropriate for her height, then total gestational weight gain should be between 25–35 pounds. In contrast, if the woman is overweight (her pregravid weight 20 percent above ideal) then total gestational weight gain should be between 15–25 pounds. Last, the underweight women (more than 10 percent below ideal) should gain somewhere between 28 and 40 pounds depending upon the severity of her low pregravid weight. Table 5-6 shows the recommended distribution of this total gestational weight gain across each of the three trimesters. Ideally, these weight gains should result in an offspring weighting approximately 7.0 to 7.5 pounds (Hughes & Noppe, 1985).

The importance of receiving an adequate supply of dietary protein during pregnancy cannot be overemphasized. Research by Rosenbaum and colleagues (1973) found that 51 mothers who experienced heavy proteinuria (loss of protein in the urine) during the last 4 1/2 months of pregnancy gave birth to infants who scored significantly lower on the Bayley mental scales and the Binet IQ (at age 4) when compared to infants born to mothers without proteinuria. The appearance of this deficit suggests impaired prenatal brain growth. Thus the developing fetus must receive adequate nutrition in utero, particularly because the developing brain achieves 25 percent of its mature weight prior to birth (Chase, 1973). It is also important that the mother receive an adequate supply of vitamins and minerals, because deficiencies in these nutrients may cause physical and mental damage and in some instances fetal death. Table 5-7 is a presentation of selected nutrients based on recommended daily allowances. Pay particular attention to the recommended percent of increase in most of these nutrients as a re-

TABLE 5-6   Recommended Weight Gain During Pregnancy Based on Pregravid Weight

Pregravid Weight	1st trimester	2nd trimester	3rd trimester	Total recommended gestational weight gain
Ideal weight (Ideal weight for height)	3.5 lb	1 lb/wk	1 lb/wk	25–35 lb
Overweight (>20% above ideal)	2 lb	2/3 lb/wk	2/3 lb/wk	15–25 lb
Underweight (>10% below ideal)	5 lb	1.2 lb/wk	1.2 lb/wk	28–40 lb

SOURCE: Luke, Johnson, & Petrie (1993)

TABLE 5-7 A Comparison of Recommended Daily Allowances for Selected Nutrients Among Non-pregnant and Pregnant Women

Nutrient	Non-pregnant level	Pregnant level	Percent change
Protein	50 gm	60 gm	+20
Calcium	800 mg	1200 mg	+50
Iron	15 mg	30 mg	+100
Iodine	150 mcg	175 mcg	+17
Vitamin A	2700 IU	2700 IU	0
Vitamin D	200 IU	400 IU	+100
Vitamin E	8 mg	10 mg	+25
Vitamin C	60 mg	70 mg	+17
Folic Acid	180 mcg	400 mcg	+122

sult of pregnancy. These essential nutrients should be acquired by eating a variety of foods and every attempt must be made to avoid "empty calories." Vitamin and mineral supplements should only be taken under the watchful eye of a physician since an association has been found between selected supplements and neural tube defects including spina bifida, anencephaly, and encepholocele (Luke, Johnson, & Petrie, 1993).

Potential problems stemming from undernutrition during pregnancy are severe. We have discussed some effects that can occur to the offspring. Potentially as severe are the effects stemming from the *grandmother effect:* the second- as well as the first-generation effects of poor nutrition. From our discussion here we know that the first-generation offspring can be damaged by poor nutrition. However, a female, even if she is able to attain adequate nutrition throughout her life, has an increased chance of giving birth to an abnormal offspring if her mother was undernourished during pregnancy. This generational effect does not appear to be passed by males because it is the mother who provides the prenatal environment for the baby where the second-generation effects are believed to occur. Unfortunately, one of the repercussions of the

first-generation damage could have been the development of faulty internal organs jeopardizing the prenatal environment for the baby. Fortunately, this effect is not believed to go beyond two generations unless subsequent generations are also undernourished. The grandmother effect clearly alerts us to the perils of poor nutrition during pregnancy and the plight of the undernourished areas of the world. Poor nutrition, particularly during pregnancy, is a long-term problem.

BIRTH WEIGHT

Until fairly recently, the medical community considered any newborn weighing less than 2500 grams (5.51 pounds) premature. Today, standards classify infants weighing between 1501 grams (3.34 pounds) and 2500 grams (5.56 pounds) as low birth weight; those weighing less than 1500 grams are classified as having very low birth weight (Austin & Moawad, 1993; Moore & Resnik, 1984). However, low birth weight is not necessarily associated with premature birth. Only recently has the medical community recognized that all low birth weight newborns are not premature and that complications associated with small full-term infants are significantly different from those a premature infant experiences. Because of this distinction, gestational age and weight are no longer used independently to describe or label an infant as premature. Instead, it must be established whether the low birth weight is from a shortened gestation period or whether the growth retardation is a result of intrauterine impoverishment. This is an important distinction because the clinical outcomes of the two conditions are quite different. More specifically, low birth weight caused by intrauterine impoverishment is associated with mental retardation, whereas spastic deplegia (cerebral palsy) is more closely associated with prematurity (Churchill, 1977).

Figure 5-4 illustrates the three major diagnostic groupings of birth weight. Note that infants with a low birth weight for their gestational age can be born at either full-term (40 weeks) or preterm (37 weeks or less). These infants exhibit weights two standard

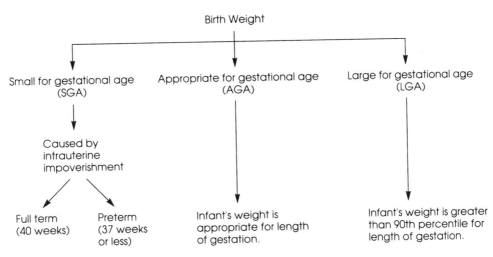

FIGURE 5-4   Birth weight classifications

deviations below their expected birth weight for their length of gestation and are generally termed *small for gestational age* (*SGA*). Excluding other congenital problems, SGA infants experience a growth retardation from inadequate nutrition in utero and are at great risk of being mentally retarded. For example, studies have shown IQ to vary as a function of birth weight, not length of pregnancy (Willerman & Churchill, 1967). The infant's inability to receive adequate nutrition in utero can have a devastating effect on brain development, particularly because brain cells have completed proliferation by 20 weeks in utero. Churchill wrote: "The infant suffering from intrauterine impoverishment is not merely small and so of small concern: it is stunted and has a permanent warp imposed within the fabric of its brain which may be expected to impede learning processes throughout its life" (1977, p. 72).

Researchers are also interested in the long-term effects of low birth weight on later motor behavior. Though we have generally assumed that SGA babies will be more likely to suffer impaired motor function later in life, few studies have been conducted on this topic. Recognizing the void in the literature, Isaacs and Pohlman (1988) recently compared 5- to 9-year-old children who were low and normal birth weight babies on fundamental motor skills and reaction time. The normal body weight group performed significantly better on locomotor and object control skills though no statistically significant differences were noted for reaction time. The researchers are careful to indicate that child-rearing attitudes of the various parents varied greatly. In fact, parents of low birth weight babies often expressed concern that their children not be involved in vigorous physical activity. This, as much as the low birth weight condition, may have accounted for the lower abilities on fundamental motor skills (Isaacs & Pohlman, 1988; Pohlman & Isaacs, 1990).

Infants born preterm but of a body weight *appropriate for gestational age* (*AGA*) tend to be at less risk than SGA infants, particularly those weighing more than 1500 grams. These children show developmental delays in weight, length, and head circumference at 1 year of age, but researchers have found that some catch-up growth occurs during the second year (Shennan & Milligan, 1980).

Another birth weight classification is *large for gestational age* (*LGA*). The birth weight of LGA infants is greater than the 90th percentile for their given gestational age. Because of the infants' large body size, birth injuries, especially brachial plexus injuries and fractures of the clavicle, are common. Respiratory distress syndrome and developmental retardation are also characteristics of this group of infants. Infants of diabetic mothers tend to be macrosomic and are, therefore, frequently LGA.

EXERCISE DURING PREGNANCY

In recent years, more and more women have sought to continue or begin exercise programs during pregnancy. This demand has led many qualified, and some unqualified, individuals to design exercise programs for the pregnant woman. These programs stem from the popular view that exercise holds beneficial effects for the pregnant woman and, possibly, her baby. However, very little research exists on the effects of exercise during pregnancy. One critical question that has yet to be scientifically answered is whether or not continuation of exercise during pregnancy affects the course of the pregnancy or the outcome of pregnancy. In an attempt to shed light on this question, Mittelmark and associates (1991) conducted an exhaustive review of the literature. Unfortunately, they concluded that a majority of the literature was plagued by design flaws making a definitive answer to the proposed question impossible. They were, however, able to uncover several consistent findings. These consistent findings included:

1. Women who exercised before pregnancy and continued to do so during pregnancy tended to weigh less, gain less weight, and deliver smaller babies than controls (by about 300–500 grams).

2. All women, regardless of initial level of physical activity, decrease their activity as pregnancy progresses.

3. No information is available to assess whether active women have better pregnancy outcomes than

their sedentary counterparts. No information is available on sedentary women.

4. Physically active women appear to tolerate labor pain better.

(Mittelmark, Dorey, & Kirschbaum, 1991, p. 228).

Injuries do occur during exercise and exercising during pregnancy is no exception (see Figure 5-5). For example, connective tissue becomes more lax and joints less stable, making the joints more susceptible to injury. The increased size of the uterus and breasts alters the center of gravity. This not only can cause a lordosis (extreme curvature of the lower back) and strain on the joints and lower back but can create balance problems as well. More falls and more back and hip pain can be expected ("Exercise During Pregnancy," 1985).

Concerning cardiovascular responses, the maternal blood volume is increased by a third or more as cardiac output is increased while at rest. These specific changes may persist for up to 4 weeks postpartum. Other cardiovascular changes include the diversion of blood away from the visceral organs to the working muscles during exercise. Though animal research indicates that up to 50 percent of the blood flow must be diverted from the viscera before the fetus is harmed, no such research has been conducted on humans. In other words, we do not know at what point exercise might begin to jeopardize the fetal oxygen supply. As a function of the cardiovascular changes discussed, the pregnant exerciser is advised to establish a target heart rate 25 to 30 percent lower than normal. Women who are high in percentage of body fat, low in activity level, or anemic should be particularly cautious when exercising during pregnancy ("Exercise During Pregnancy," 1985).

Toward the end of the pregnancy the diaphragm is elevated, which is believed to cause discomfort and dyspnea (difficult or painful breathing). This elevation does not impair the respiratory function of the lungs, because the rib cage expands to increase the overall tidal volume of the lungs. So, low levels of exercise appear to

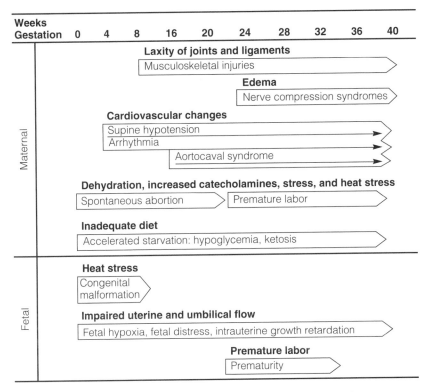

FIGURE 5-5 Potential mechanisms leading to injuries during exercise in pregnancy. The top of each box lists the etiology for potential injuries included in each box. The spacing of the boxes reflects the gestational age during which the injury is most likely to occur.

Source: Mittlemark, Wiswell, Drinkwater, & St. Jones–Repovich (1991). Used with permission.

be readily accommodated for breathing. High levels, however, tend to increase oxygen levels less than expected, indicating that, during pregnancy, the woman may not be able to maintain high activity levels as readily as normal ("Exercise During Pregnancy," 1985).

As in the nonpregnant exerciser, body temperature rises. This is particularly true if insufficient liquid is ingested, causing dehydration. In cases of dehydration, the temperature may soar to levels that are dangerous to the health of the fetus (Drinkwater & Mittlemark, 1991). The fetus, being incapable of reducing body temperature through such normal means as perspiration, may be at particular risk when

the mother's body temperature becomes too high. Though no research has been conducted on human subjects, animal research has demonstrated an increase in neural-tube defects, such as spina bifida, when the mother's body temperature is excessive over a prolonged period of time. For these reasons, moderation in exercise is advised in addition to the avoidance of exercise on very hot or humid days ("Exercise During Pregnancy," 1985).

Little has been written regarding fetal responses to maternal exercise. It does appear, however, that various fetal systems are affected. For example, fetal heart rate (FHR) increases by approximately 10–30 beats per minute as a response to maternal exercise. In addition, this elevation in FHR is sustained into recovery. In general, FHR's return to preexercise levels during the first 15 minutes of recovery in women who exercise at mild (approximately 2.5 METS) and moderate (approximately 5 METS) levels. In comparison, FHR remained elevated for at least 30 minutes in women who exercised at a strenuous level (approximately 8 METS)

TABLE 5-8 Guidelines from the American College of Obstetricians and Gynecologists Concerning Exercise During Pregnancy and Postpartum

---

1. Competitive exercise is discouraged; consistent, rather than occasional, exercise is advised.

2. Avoid: exercising on hot, humid days.

> fast, jerky movements, unstable footing, and excessive shock to the body.

> deep knee flexions, jumping causing excess jarring, and abrupt directional changes.

> arising too quickly and causing hypotension; once upright, continue to move the legs for a short time.

3. Warm up for active movement with at least 5 minutes of slow walking or stationary cycling, and warm down by stretching slowly without achieving a point of maximum stretch.

4. Carefully monitor the heart rate at times of most intense exercise and strive for a target heart rate established in consultation with your doctor.

5. Drink plenty of liquids before, during, and after the exercise.

6. Cease activity if unusual symptoms arise and seek the advice of a physician.

7. If highly inactive prior to initiation of the exercise program, begin at a very low level of intensity and increase slowly.

For pregnancy only:

1. Eat enough to ensure sufficient calories are available to meet the increased needs of exercising and pregnancy.

2. Avoid: exceeding heart rate of 140 beats per minute.

> exceeding a body temperature of 38 degrees centigrade (100 degrees Fahrenheit).

> activity for more than 15 minutes per bout.

> supine exercises.

> exercise involving the valsalva maneuver (a maneuver used in strenuous activities, creating great pressure in the thoracic area and leading to dizziness, fainting, or rarely, stroke).

3. Cease activity if pain, bleeding, dizziness, shortness of breath, heart palpitations, faintness, tachycardia (rapid heartbeat), back or pubic pain, or difficult walking occur.

SOURCE: "Exercise During Pregnancy," 1985, pp. 4–7.

(Mittlemark & Posner, 1991). For an in-depth review of maternal and fetal responses to exercise, consult the book by McMurray and colleagues (1993).

On the basis of what little is known concerning exercise during pregnancy, the American College of Obstetricians and Gynecologists (ACOG) has established exercise guidelines for pregnancy and postpartum (see Table 5-8). While some individuals may believe that these guidelines are particularly conservative, they have been created with primary concern for the safety of the mother and the baby. Because so little research has been conducted on exercise during pregnancy, any error in exercise prescription should "err on the conservative side" ("Exercise During Pregnancy," 1985, p. 3). These guidelines are also based on the premise that the exerciser's goal should be to maintain the highest fitness level possible within a maximally safe program. The ACOG also advises that "recommendations designed for a general cross-section of the population may not be appropriate for a particular individual" (p. 1).

SUMMARY

Both genetic and environmental misfortunes can alter the normal fetal growth and development process.

Drugs and medications consumed during pregnancy can affect the developing fetus. They are particularly damaging at certain times during pregnancy known as epigenetic periods.

Women should not use recreational drugs during pregnancy. Cocaine, in fact, is one of the most harmful drugs to the unborn child. The pregnant woman should also be cautious of prescriptive and nonprescriptive drugs and, when necessary, work closely with her physician in monitoring any drugs used during pregnancy as many can harm the developing fetus.

There are numerous maternal diseases that can influence the development of the fetus. The origin of these diseases can take many forms including: viral diseases, parasitic diseases, hemotologic diseases, and endocrine diseases.

Three frequent genetic abnormalities are Down syndrome, phenylketonuria, and cystic fibrosis. Down syndrome, a chromosome-based disorder, is caused by the presence of an extra chromosome on chromosome number 21. Both phenylketonuria and cystic fibrosis are gene-based disorders.

Prenatal diagnostic procedures are available to detect the presence of many fetal abnormalities. Four of the most common prenatal procedures are ultrasound, amniocentesis, chorionic villus sampling, and the alpha-fetoprotein test. These tests are particularly important for women who are believed to be at risk for fetal abnormality because of maternal age, previous child born with an abnormality, family history of abnormalities, or a medical history of certain genetic traits.

The pregnant woman must receive adequate nutrition. Maternal weight gain can be a partial indication of the nutritional state of the fetus. How much weight should be gained during the pregnancy is a function of weight status prior to conception. With adequate nutrition, maternal weight gain should produce an offspring weighting approximately 7.0 to 7.5 pounds.

Babies born to women who did not receive adequate nutrition during pregnancy score lower on mental scales and can also suffer physical impairment. In some cases, because of the grandmother effect, the damage caused from poor nutrition can be passed to a second generation. The grandmother effect can occur even when the first-generation offspring has received adequate nutrition.

There are three basic birth weight classifications: small for gestational age (SGA), appropriate for gestational age (AGA), and large for gestational age (LGA). SGA babies are particularly at risk for such associated problems as mental retardation. Recent research has also shown low birth weight babies may lag on motor skill development later in life.

KEY TERMS

Alpha-fetoprotein test   Anti-D IgG
Amniocentesis   immunoglobulin

Appropriate for gestational age (AGA)
Carbon monoxide
Chorionic villus sampling (CVS)
Congenital rubella
Cystic fibrosis (CF)
Diabetes mellitus
Down syndrome
Epigenetic period
Erythroblastosis fetalis
Fetal alcohol effect (FAE)

Fetal alcohol syndrome (FAS)
Grandmother effect
Heterozygous
Homozygous
Human immunodeficiency virus (HIV)
11-hydroxy-delta-9-tetrahydrocannabinal (THC)
Hyperglycemia
Hypoglycemia

Large for gestational age (LGA)
Macrosomia
Meiotic nondisjunction
Neonatal abstinence syndrome (NAS)
Nicotine
Normoglycemia

Phenylketonuria
Pregravid weight
Rh factor
Small for gestational age (SGA)
Teratogen
Thalidomide
Toxoplasma gondii
Ultrasound

CHAPTER 6

Effects of Early Stimulation and Deprivation

According to David Elkind (1990), the notion that "earlier is better has become an entrenched conviction among contemporary parents and educators." This trend has become so ingrained in many sectors of our society that the common philosophy now states, it is "never too early to start children in reading, math, swimming, violin, or karate lessons" (p. 3). This, according to Elkind, has resulted in a confounding of the perceived need for early education and all children's need for quality child care.

Interestingly, and perhaps logically, the general philosophical trend has been that *stimulation* is always "good" and *deprivation* is "bad." Although we admire parents who "stimulate" their child, we may scorn parents who "deprive" their child. However, can overstimulation occur? Is deprivation ever in the child's best interest? When are the best times for stimulation or the worst times for deprivation? Is stimulation worthwhile for the acquisition of all human behaviors, or are there some behaviors that cannot be facilitated by early exposure to stimulating experiences? These are all questions that researchers have considered while examining the effects of stimulation and deprivation.

EFFECTS OF EARLY STIMULATION

In recent years, parents have been involving their children more than ever in early educational programs, in everything from swimming, gymnastics, and violin lessons to the study of reading and foreign languages. The unusual aspect of these programs designed for early stimulation is that in some cases they start as early as birth. The contemporary rush to enroll children in such programs was documented in the article "Bringing Up Superbaby" (Langway et al., 1983). Many of today's babies are born to parents who are older, richer, and assured that any behavior they desire for their child can be taught. The increased knowledge concerning child development and the notion that the environment does influence human behavior have motivated parents to seek all possible advantages for their children. In fact, the belief that kindergarten is "too late" is increasingly prevalent. Burton White, author of a commercially popular book titled *The First Three Years*, states that parents are now being considered teachers, not merely the creators of the baby.

Glenn Doman wrote several books about the teaching of such skills as reading and math to babies. Although these skills are often believed to be entirely intellectual, the fine control of eye movement, for example, emphasizes the influence of motor development on one's reading or math success. For optimal success in these skills, Doman recommends initiating instruction by using flashcards during the first few days of neonatal life. Doman does not substantiate the success of this technique by scientific evidence, and there is mixed popular opinion as to the program's value. Some children have learned to respond appropriately to flashcards; others simply play with the cards. Critics of such early programs as the one Doman prescribed question the advantage of simple recognition skills enhanced by the flashcards. They further contend that such pressure to learn at an early age may actually frighten the child from future experiences of a similar nature. Child developmentalists such as Dr. Benjamin Spock have stated that children may be "overintellectualizing." This emphasis on achievement so early may hamper the emotional, physical, or creative aspects of the child's development. Wood Smethurst, Director of the Reading Center at Emory University, believes that too much early stimulation toward reading may actually cause reading difficulties later in the child's education.

Obviously, absolute evidence documenting the value or the harm of early programs has yet to be gathered. Nevertheless, in 1983, 70 percent of 4-year-olds from families with incomes higher than $25,000 per year attended preschool. Of the children from families with incomes of less than $15,000 per year, 35 percent attended (Langway et al., 1983). Parents therefore generally believe early educational stimulation is valuable, as evidenced by the quantity and popularity of the early educational programs available today. This may be the case, but no doubt such factors as the child's age and type of stimulation as well as the parental and child attitudes are critical factors in the success or failure of programs involving early stimulation.

PROGRAMS TO ENHANCE EARLY MOTOR DEVELOPMENT

As suggested in the preceding section, early stimulation programs have become extremely popular in the last several years. Because of this popularity new programs are evolving regularly by qualified or, sometimes, unqualified persons to fill the consumer demand. Despite the diversity of programs available, those that are designed to generally stimulate or optimize early motor development often fall into two categories: "*no programming*" and "*programming.*"

The no-programming category includes programs that do not emphasize the specific practice of future motor skills through developmental exercises, specialized equipment, or a motor curriculum. This mode of operation was originally advocated in Hungary at the National Institute for Infant Care and Education. The main advocate, Emmi Piker, believed in withholding instruction until an infant had learned early body control. Piker advocated avoidance of systematic practice of specific motor skills by assisting the child into certain positions or doing anything that required babies to perform a movement of which they were not yet capable. The no-programming mode suggests leaving infants on their backs until *they* are capable of changing the position. Toys are placed near the child to stimulate movement activity but are not placed too near or handed to the child. This philosophy of early stimulation also advocates against placing children in a position that they cannot attain alone. Therefore, the child would not be placed in a sitting or standing position until first capable of attaining that position alone. Furthermore, a baby who could not walk without assistance would not be given a hand or external support to enable a few extra steps. This system also advocates apparel for the baby that is highly nonrestrictive. In addition, hard-soled shoes are discouraged until the baby can walk unassisted. Even then, shoes are advised only when necessary. These measures, Piker believed, will assist the baby in the acquisition of such early movements as rolling, creeping, sitting, and standing (Ridenour, 1978).

In the programming plan for early motor programs, the parent takes an active roll in moving the baby or the baby's limbs during an activity. This plan encourages the use of infant walkers and bouncers because they are believed to facilitate posture and early locomotion. Programs in this category often employ manual manipulation of the limbs for infant fitness or flexibility. They also use special equipment—cushions, dolls, balls, rods, hoops, toys, etc.— to encourage or assist babies in movement. According to Ridenour (1978), an example of the programming plan is the Prudden Infant Fitness Program designed for parents to use at home with children from birth to 6 years. This program includes numerous activities and recommends approximately 15 minutes per day of program activity. Prudden employs manual manipulation of the baby's arms and legs and recommends new activities periodically (Ridenour, 1978).

The Krottee Curriculum also employs the programming philosophy in its series of interactive modules for babies from birth to 1 month. Each module contains activities, the expected response of the baby, an evaluation, and recommendation for a reward (usually verbal) for the baby upon completion. This curriculum, in contrast to the Prudden program, was designed for use by professionals rather than parents in the home (Ridenour, 1978).

Unfortunately, little research has been conducted to substantiate the no-programming or the programming mode of operation for early motor stimulation.

As advised by Ridenour (1978), perhaps parents should avoid programs claiming to make excessive improvements in the baby's future motor or intellectual development until more conclusive research is available. Until that time perhaps a more appropriate focus would be to educate parents on creating a stimulating home environment that may facilitate the child's natural development.

Specifically concerning infant exercise programs, the American Academy of Pediatrics (AAP) has issued a policy statement with some very clear views and recommendations. This group acknowledges an increase in the abundance of infant programs which tout massage, passive exercises, or even manipulation of the child through a variety of positions for a number of posited objectives. The AAP notes that, for infants, the "predominant" movement-related responses are reflexive and therefore, intrinsic and oriented toward "self-sufficiency." While providing stimulation whereby babies touch, play, and generally interact with their environment is important, research has not demonstrated that organized programs will improve movement skills or "provide any long-term benefit to normal infants." Furthermore, children of this young age may be more susceptible to injury when parents unintentionally exceed a safe range of motion during passive exercise. The AAP recommends that structured programs not be "promoted as being therapeutically beneficial for the development of healthy infants" and "parents be encouraged to provide a safe, nurturing, and minimally structured play environment for their infant" (American Academy of Pediatrics, 1988).

These beliefs are supported by Gardner, Karmel, and Dowd (1984), who suggest that more stimulation is not always better. In fact, they claim it may be harmful if the intensity and type of activity are not individualized to fit the infant's individual needs. Additionally, intervention may lead to false assumptions by some parents. They may think they are not offering their child enough opportunities if their child does not achieve the claims of their program. Parents not enrolled in programs may also lower their expectations of their child and create a "self-fulfilling prophecy of failure" (Gardner, Karmel, & Dowd, 1984, p. 94).

Gardner and colleagues (1984) agree that too little research has been conducted on early intervention programs. Research that has been conducted is often unsupportive of the concept of early stimulation. Though most of the best research has been conducted on animals, not humans, findings are striking. Often, a seemingly beneficial early outcome later proves to be detrimental. This has been hypothesized to be a function of the disruption of the sequencing of normal central nervous system maturation. Such may have been the case with rat pups whose eyes were opened early. Though initial signs seemed to be improved visual ability, with time, deficits emerged. This has also been noted in preterm infants who are exposed to visual stimulation earlier than full-term babies. Eventually, preterm babies may show more variable and disorganized visual responses rather than improved vision. So, clearly, additional stimulation of a specific area can be disruptive or harmful in an effort to facilitate or expedite normal function (Gardner, Karmel, & Dowd, 1984).

Though little research has been conducted on programs of early stimulation, many programs conduct self-evaluations that are intended to determine how the child's development has been enhanced. They are seldom devised to detect any detrimental effects. Furthermore, developmental gains that are noted are often those which would have occurred anyway with a normal exposure to a stimulating home environment. This is not to suggest, however, that programs should never be considered or employed. Rather, programs that make indiscriminate claims should be avoided. We must be careful consumers by seeking qualified professionals, clean and appropriate facilities, reasonable fees, and objectives that seem appropriate for the baby or child in question.

Gymboree

Though many new programs of early motor stimulation have evolved in recent years, few have gained the attention and notoriety of *Gymboree*. The first Gymboree program, designed for children from birth to 5 years, was opened in northern California in 1975 and, by 1994, had grown to over 370 franchises throughout the world. According to the founder, Joan Barnes, it was developed on the belief that the preschool years may be the most critical part of education though it is a time when parents have the least amount of outside help in educating their child. Furthermore, the gymboree philosophy assumes preschoolers need to be provided with certain types of play activities that are believed to be essential to their development but are not readily available at home, the playground, or the nursery. The environment of Gymboree is described by the developer as being safe and noncompetitive while challenging the psychomotor needs of preschoolers. Typically, a Gymboree program lasts from 9 to 13 weeks with the child attending one session per week for approximately 45 minutes. The average cost of each session was about $9 in 1994.

According to Gymboree Director of Marketing, D. Hillman (in a personal communication, February 4, 1994), Gymboree programs range from Cradlegym to Gymkids. Cradlegym is for babies as young as 1 day old. Emphasis is placed on learning beginning play ideas and on parents meeting and socializing with other parents who have similarly aged children. No equipment is used. Babygym, primarily a play program where parents continue to play a very active role, is for children 3 months to 1 year old. Children are massaged, exercised by manipulating their limbs through a range of motion, and even playfully jostled on an assortment of colorful equipment. In Gymboree, for children from 1 to 2 1/2 years, less emphasis is placed on the parent's role. Children determine what to do and little formal instruction is offered. This, according to Gymboree, enhances independence and self-confidence. In Gymgrad, for children from 2 1/2 to 4, more organized play is emphasized. Emphasis is placed on such concepts as following instructions, social interaction, imagination, and cooperation. Finally, in Gymkids, for children from 4 to 5 years old, two programs are offered, one for drama and creative movement with an emphasis on imaginative play, and one to introduce basic sports skills in a pressure free, noncompetitive environment. In both options within Gymkids direct parental involvement is eliminated so parents can drop off children or choose to stay and observe.

Most Gymboree sessions offer a variety of colorful, scaled-down equipment for children to explore with varying degrees of guidance from their parent(s). Balance beams, balls, scooters, tunnels, rollers, hoops, and ladders are a few of the many pieces of equipment that may be available for exploration during free time. Free time is one segment of each Gymboree session. A Gymboree representative is present each session to assist the children in using and enjoying the equipment. Usually, free time with the equipment is followed by group activity. These dancing, singing, or pantomine activities are said to emphasize sensory stimulation, coordination, and social interaction.

Gymboree proponents claim that parents benefit from participation by learning their child's needs and developing a better understanding of the child's growth and development. This, they say, will assist parents in accommodating their child's needs and encouraging development in an efficient, yet fun, way.

In general, Gymboree claims that its participants should show improvement in balancing, performing fundamental movements (running, jumping, throwing, catching, etc.), switching from different modes of locomotion, assuming a variety of body positions, changing directions and speeds, socializing (sharing and taking turns), and expressing the imagination freely.

To assess the outcome of their programs, Gymboree surveys parents and claims that parents report benefits for themselves and their children. Specifically, parents have cited increases in undistracted, quality time with their children. They also appear to appreciate the opportunity to meet other families and exchange ideas. They further claimed, according to Gymboree, that their children often appeared less passive and dependent, and developed better coordination and social skills, after participation in a Gymboree program (Barnes, Astor, & Tosi, 1981). However, as we mentioned

earlier, little research exists to substantiate the claims made by programs such as Gymboree. Self-evaluations must be viewed cautiously as there is an obvious bias on the part of the evaluator—Gymboree. Gymboree does make some lofty claims but generally tempers them. They are careful to point out that fun is paramount. Until controlled research is conducted we will not know whether Gymboree attains its goals or whether their participants are simply developing skills that are a normal part of the developmental process. Decisions on participating in such programs as Gymboree may need to be made on the basis of family needs, desires, and ability to pay for the sessions. As we said earlier, we need to be cautious consumers.

Swim Programs for Infants and Preschoolers

Over the last decade, one of the most common forms of early motor stimulation has been swim programs for infants and preschoolers. For infants (birth to 1 year) in particular, there may be little justification for the programs designed to teach infants to swim (American Academy of Pediatrics, 1985). However, this is not to say that slightly older preschoolers are incapable of developing swimming skills. In fact, the American Red Cross (1988) states that a child from 3 to 5 years will experience independent propulsive swimming movements. Erbaugh (1980), in her study designed to describe age-related swimming performance of 2- to 6-year-olds, found that a gradual improvement can be seen between ages 2 and 4. A more substantial improvement is then seen between ages 4 and 5. In general, the longitudinal changes that might be expected in the preschooler would include: increasing the distance traveled, improving ability to propel with the arms, improving ability to exhibit a flutter kick leg pattern, improving ability to maintain a horizontal position in the water, and improving the head position. These improvements, however, came gradually for the younger preschoolers, suggesting that even less progress would be made by an infant.

Nevertheless, the popularity of some "swim" programs for infants and preschoolers has too often been fueled by parents' visions of Olympic medals. Evidence about the success of early swim programs in facilitating the child's later level of success in swimming is contradictory. Some children have graduated from these swim programs and achieved considerable success in their later swimming endeavors, but others have left such early programs with no apparent improvement. In fact in some cases, parents claimed that their children became more fearful of the water!

Some early aquatic programs, however, may not profess to teach swimming but rather "drownproofing," "waterproofing," or simply making an infant water-safe. Most experts agree that these terms are inappropriate It is impossible to make anyone drownproof (American Academy of Pediatrics, 1985; American Red Cross, 1988; Langendorfer, 1986). The American Red Cross specifically states that "many programs make claims that drownproofing can be accomplished, but it cannot" (1988, p. 7).

Parental desire to improve the safety of their infant around water is often the impetus for involvement in infant "swimming." Interestingly, given the risks of some infant swim programs the child's overall odds of drowning could actually be increased by participating in an early swim program (American Academy of Pediatrics, 1985). In addition, the completion of a "drownproofing" program could give parents a false sense of security that could lead to tragic consequences.

Another health consideration with early aquatic programs, especially those involving infants, is the condition known as *hyponatremia*, or water intoxication. This condition was vividly described in a case study of an 11-month-old infant who swallowed more water than usual during an infant swim lesson (Bennett & Wagner, 1983). Though she experienced no problems while in the pool, 30 minutes after leaving the water she became irritable, lethargic, and disoriented. She also vomited while going to the hospital and began having seizures once she arrived. This excess water consumption is believed to reduce serum sodium levels, causing the symptoms just

described and also restlessness, weakness, and in severe cases, death. It is unknown exactly how much water must be consumed to cause hyponatremia (Bennett & Wagner, 1983) and we also have little information as to the exact number of cases of water intoxication. While hyponatremia is believed to be rare, there may be many more cases than are being reported because of the nonspecific nature of the symptoms and the fact that symptoms may not show up until hours after the water has been swallowed. Thus the relationship between the illness and exposure to the water often remains unestablished (Burd, 1986).

Hyponatremia can often be avoided by prohibiting participants from being totally submerged. Nevertheless, many local swim organizations continue to place an emphasis on the need to submerge babies during infant swim programs. Experience does indicate that the quantity of water swallowed will be increased with increased number of submersions (Bennett & Wagner, 1983). For that reason, the *YMCA Guidelines for Infant Swimming* (1984) and the "Policy Statement on Infant Swimming Programs" from the American Academy of Pediatrics (1985) advise prohibiting total submersion of infants in aquatic programs. In addition, the guidelines from the American Red Cross state that "force, prolonged or frequent submersion . . . are not acceptable techniques" in their infant and preschool aquatic program (1988, p. 4). Bennett and Wagner (1983) in their case study of an infant with hyponatremia also advise avoiding total submersion as well as stopping a lesson if a child ever swallows too much water or begins to exhibit any of the symptoms described earlier.

A more common problem with infant swim programs is *giardia*. This parasite, which develops in cysts in the intestinal tract, can cause severe diarrhea and is easily transmitted to others when the cysts circulate through the pool water. The *YMCA Guidelines for Infant Swimming* recommend certain precautions for avoiding the chance of spreading giardia, including showering after class, washing off any giardia that may have been contracted through the pool water; requiring that tight-legged diapers or pants be worn in the water; and not allowing children who have been ill, especially with diarrhea, to participate.

The American Academy of Pediatrics (AAP) also made several recommendations for infant swim programs in its 1985 policy statement (see Table 6-1). Although the AAP finds "little justification" for infant "swimming" or water-adjustment programs, it recognizes the existence of the programs and the increasing number of benefits being claimed. The AAP advises that all programs follow the *YMCA*

TABLE 6-1 Some Specific Statements or Guidelines from the American Academy of Pediatrics (1985), the YMCA (1984), and the American Red Cross (1988) on "Infant Swimming" Programs

1. For infants, "There is little justification for swimming or water adjustment programs" (AAP, 1985).

2. Avoid terms like "drownproofing" or "waterproofing" (Red Cross, 1988).

3. Avoid total submersion (AAP, 1985; YMCA, 1984) or anything that would appear to be traumatic to infants in the water since pleasure in the water should be a major objective (Red Cross, 1988).

4. Infants should have voluntary head control before starting an aquatic program (Red Cross, 1988).

5. Provide measures for avoiding fecal contamination of the pool; have participants wear tight legged diapers or pants, shower thoroughly after participation, do not allow children who have been ill, especially with diarrhea, to participate (AAP, 1985; YMCA, 1984).

6. Participants should have their own instructor, parent or responsible adult present and group lessons should be forbidden until at least 3 years of age (AAP, 1985).

7. Instructors should be qualified and certified in infant CPR (AAP, 1985).

8. Children who have been ill should be approved by a physician before participation (AAP, 1985).

9. More research is necessary on the issue of infant swim programs (AAP, 1985).

Guidelines for Infant Swimming; it strongly recommends that steps be taken to reduce fecal contamination and that total submersion be prohibited. The AAP also advises that all participants have their own instructor, parent, or responsible adult by their side and that group instruction be prohibited until the participants are at least 3 years old. All instructors should be qualified and certified in infant cardiopulmonary resuscitation techniques. All children with a history of illness or who have had recent medical problems should be approved for participation by a physician before attending infant swimming. Finally, and equally important, the AAP recommends more research into this issue.

These guidelines are somewhat similar to the more recently developed guidelines for infant and preschool aquatic programs created by the American Red Cross (1988). They advise avoiding such terminology as "drownproofing" or "waterproofing" as we discussed earlier. Like the YMCA guidelines, the Red Cross urges adult in-water supervision. It also advises avoiding any activity that would potentially traumatize a participant, as learning to experience pleasure in the water is one of its major objectives. Finally, infants must have voluntary head control prior to enrolling in a Red Cross aquatic program.

Despite the shortcomings of some early aquatic programs, exposure to the water at an early age offers many potential benefits to the participant. Though supportive data are lacking, early aquatic programs may be valuable in developing affection for the water at a young age. It may provide an excellent, unique environment for quality parent-child interactions and may be comforting to some very young children. Unfortunately, little scientific evidence exists to assist us in substantiating any of these claims or in furthering our understanding of these programs. We need much more research on the early development of swimming skill, the effects of early exposure to the water, and hyponatremia. Also, as recently recommended (Langendorfer, Bruya, & Reid, 1988), we need more substantial information concerning the effects of such factors as water condition, facility

FIGURE 6-1 Infant and preschool aquatic programs are among the most popular forms of early education.

design, and aquatic teaching methodologies to aid in the establishment of new aquatic teaching curricula. Clearly, we still have much to learn concerning infant and preschool aquatic programs.

Suzuki Method of Playing the Violin

Another of the most popular and enduring programs of early stimulation that strongly advocates the development of appropriate parent and child attitudes is the *Suzuki method* of playing the violin. This program, which is greatly dependent on the early motor and intellectual capabilities of its young students, began over 50 years ago in Japan.

Before creating this program, Suzuki pondered children's ability to speak the difficult language of Japanese at 1 or 2 years. If the children could master Japanese, why not the violin? And because children learn their language by hearing the constant chatter of those around them, would a similar process work for the violin? Thus Suzuki began the "listen and play" method of learning to play the violin.

The method is initiated by selecting a musical piece to play regularly to the child, starting as early as birth. When the child has become accustomed to or soothed by the initial selection, other musical selections can be added. However, the key to the success of this phase of the program is the tonal quality of the music played. In other words, according to Suzuki, if the parent sings offkey to the child, the effect may be negative rather than positive.

By approximately 2 to 2 1/2 years, the child begins actual violin lessons (see Figure 6-2). Attitude is particularly important in this phase of the program: This child must be motivated to request a violin, rather than making the violin and the lessons mandatory. According to the Suzuki plan, this request is developed by genuine parental interest. Suzuki believed that the child will desire that which the parents find desirable. Thus parents are encouraged to take lessons of their own. In addition, parents attend the child's lessons and learn enough to assist the child when necessary or when requested.

Also stressed in the Suzuki method is use of a properly sized violin. An oversized or undersized instrument restricts or inhibits the intricate movements required to capably play the violin. This general concept of correct size has been pondered relative to a variety of other movement activities. How is a child's catching performance, for example, influenced by the size of the ball? This and similar questions are discussed in Chapter 13, "Fundamental Locomotion Skills of Childhood."

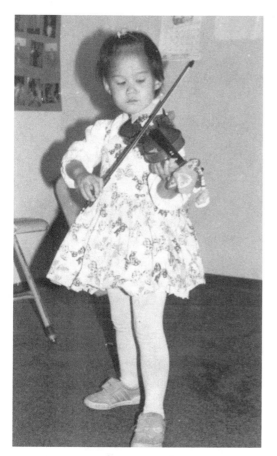

FIGURE 6-2   The Suzuki method of learning to play the violin emphasizes listening and playing.

An additional philosophy in the Suzuki method is discouraging competition between students. Children learn and play cooperatively and do not compete for "first chair." Likewise, cooperation is strongly encouraged because more experienced children are a critical component of the education of the children newer to the program (Pronko, 1969).

As is the case with most programs involving the early stimulation of children, much is unknown about the residual effects of the Suzuki method. Although some outstanding violinists began with the program, others have long since ceased their interest in the instrument. Critics of such programs con-

tend that many children have actually been discouraged from further musical involvement by being inundated with too much violin too young.

Head Start Programs

To give financially disadvantaged children a "head start" in education, the government program known as *Head Start* was started in 1965. This program, created as part of President Johnson's War on Poverty, was designed to disrupt a cycle that had become apparent in education: the disadvantaged child falling further and further behind educationally with each school year. That child, being poorly educated, would thus foster a new generation of disadvantaged children who would suffer the same plight.

The assumption underlying the Head Start idea was that a preschool program might actually boost the intellectual, social, and emotional behavior of the children involved. Experts presumed that the betterment of these components, which also strongly affect motor development, would enhance academic success. This assumption was found to be partially correct based on tracking 2100 Head Start children throughout their educational careers; the children were found to be 10 times more likely to complete a high school education without failure than were their similar socioeconomic counterparts (Begley & Carey, 1983). Although this finding appears to strongly support the idea of early education programs for children, we should be aware of the uniqueness of the group involved. Because a specific program appeared to be successful for a specific social economic group at a particular age, we cannot assume that all programs involving early education will be similarly successful. Also, although the Head Start program successfully enabled more children to complete their education without failure, Head Start children often lost any academic advantage they may have gained by as early as the fourth grade (Begley & Carey, 1983).

Additional research led to more questions concerning the effectiveness of this early educational program. For instance, to evaluate the educational value of the Head Start program, the Westinghouse report compared former Head Start students in the first, second, and third grades to children from similar socioeconomic situations who had not attended Head Start preschools. The findings were generally inconclusive. There was a significant difference regarding the learning readiness of the two groups, but no differences in language development or general achievement as measured by the Stanford achievement test (Payne et al., 1973).

Infant Walkers

Infant walkers (see Figure 6-3) have been around for centuries and have become particularly common in households with infants in the last 20 years. In fact, in 1980 an estimated 1 million infant walkers were distributed (Rieder, Schwartz, & Newman, 1986). Unfortunately, questions exist concerning the safety of infant walkers and their efficacy as a tool to promote early walking.

In 1980 over 23,900 infant-walker injuries were reported. These injuries, according to retrospective reports from hospitals, included skull fractures, abrasions, lacerations, dental injuries, burns, and trapped fingers. These figures were sufficient to prompt Rieder, Schwartz, and Newman (1986) to track walker injuries in one hospital for 1 year. During that time 139 walker-related injuries occurred (compared to 250 infants injured in auto accidents). Most of the injured babies sustained head injuries and, by far, the majority of injuries occurred as a result of falling downstairs in the walker at home. This prompted the researchers to question whether the danger is from walkers or from stairs. Clearly, if more care were taken in keeping infants in walkers away from stairs, the incidence of injury would be reduced dramatically.

Interestingly, these researchers also surveyed the parents as to the most useful function of the walker. While many responded it was a useful "baby-sitter," most said it was pleasurable for the baby because it increased mobility. Many also responded that it taught the baby to walk earlier despite the fact that research has not found that walkers are beneficial in expediting the onset of independent walking

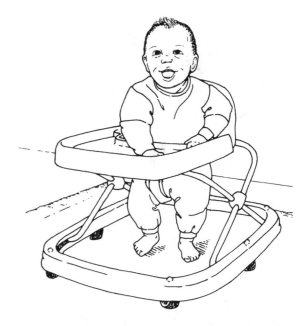

FIGURE 6-3 Infant walkers have become extremely popular in the last 20 years though research suggests some danger from their use.

(Kauffman & Ridenour. 1977; Rieder, Schwartz, & Newman, 1986). The study also found that injured babies averaged 2 hours per day in their walkers and were allowed to continue using the walker after the accident. The most common reason cited for discontinuing walker use was the onset of independent walking.

JOHNNY AND JIMMY

As long ago as 1935, Myrtle McGraw conducted what is now considered a classic investigation directly concerning motor development and the effects of early stimulation. In her research, McGraw closely monitored the twin brothers known as Johnny and Jimmy. She was particularly interested in determining if a child's normal progress in motor development could be altered by given conditions. Therefore, for the first 22 months of the twins' lives, McGraw gave Johnny toys and considerable stimulation, practice, and experience in a variety of movement activities. Jimmy, however, had few toys and minimal motor stimulation.

McGraw periodically examined the effects of the varying levels of stimulation by exposing the twins to selected movement activities. For example, Johnny was given a tricycle when he was 11 months old. He was also given considerable practice and some instruction at that time. However, McGraw noted that 8 months elapsed before Johnny showed any signs of learning on the tricycle; he then proceeded to quickly master tricycling within 2 months.

Jimmy was deprived of tricycling until he was 22 months old. However, despite his relatively low levels of stimulation, he learned tricycling much faster than Johnny. This led McGraw to conclude that a certain level of readiness is necessary for the acquisition of a motor skill. Jimmy was ready to tricycle at 22 months, but Johnny was not at 11 months. (We discuss the term *readiness* in greater detail later in this chapter.)

McGraw examined many other movement activities using the twins as her subjects. For example, Johnny was taught to roller skate at less than 1 year of age and became skillful at the task. McGraw believed that this was facilitated by his low center of gravity, which enhanced his balance. Jimmy began skating at 22 months but never became a good skater. When their skating experiences ended, both twins' ability declined rapidly. In fact, when they were 3 years old, both twins suffered from balance difficulties. Surprisingly, Johnny, the stimulated twin, was described as having more problems skating than Jimmy, which McGraw credited to attitudinal differences that were emerging: Johnny had become somewhat reckless, whereas Jimmy maintained a much more cautious approach to movement.

Johnny and Jimmy were also observed ascending and descending slopes of varying grades. Johnny exhibited better skills at ascending the slopes than Jimmy and also retained his ability better. Furthermore, Johnny appeared to be more clever at developing climbing strategies while being more graceful in the process. McGraw attributed this superior climbing ability to Johnny's early experience at a diversity of tasks, including slope climbing. When descending the slopes, Jimmy was particularly timid or cautious and occasionally uncooperative. Johnny rarely hesitated to descend and consistently maintained a higher level of ability.

Attitude similarly affected performances in jumping. For the jumping task, McGraw instructed the twins to jump down from a low pedestal. Frequently, Jimmy, who had far less early experience than his brother, could not be coaxed to jump. Johnny, however, jumped freely and with considerable skill.

McGraw also observed the twins while they were in the water. Both twins were given very early aquatic experiences that were abruptly halted when they were 17 months old, to be tested periodically in the future. Upon retesting when he was 6 years old, Johnny was found to be much more comfortable and skillful in the water. Although his brother demonstrated a normal horizontal stroking position in a well-coordinated fashion, Jimmy stayed vertical and exhibited jerky swimming actions. Johnny's advanced skill was considered rather unusual because he had never been instructed to perform the relatively sophisticated movements that he exhibited.

The contrast in levels of early stimulation for Johnny and Jimmy may have affected more than motor development. Although both Johnny and Jimmy were happy and well adjusted, Johnny was frequently favored socially. Perhaps as a result of his jealousy, Jimmy often struck Johnny and would take his toys. At other times, however, Jimmy would exhibit tremendous affection for his brother Johnny. In addition, Jimmy was more dependent on his mother and more prone to temper tantrums than was his two brother.

A Rorschach (inkblot) test divulged additional information concerning the twins' personalities. Jimmy was more immature emotionally, self-centered, and dependent; Johnny more impersonal, self-confident, too brave at times, and relatively unaggressive.

McGraw's longitudinal investigation of Johnny and Jimmy was in many respects somewhat unscientific. With only two main subjects in her investigation, we might assume that the experiences of

Johnny and Jimmy were not indicative of what would happen with other subjects of a similar age. Nevertheless, McGraw is frequently credited with having had an astute and insightful ability for determining possible explanations for the differences in movement behavior between Johnny and Jimmy.

For example, McGraw believed that the degree to which an activity maintains its state depends on its *level of fixity*. According to McGraw, the level of fixity is how well established a skill is when it is discontinued. This phenomenon may have accounted for the twins' maintenance of tricycling ability following a period of inactivity on the tricycle. The high level of skill that they developed upon initial exposure to tricycling facilitated their efforts when they were exposed to the same task at a later date.

McGraw also believed that practice and attitude were factors that greatly affected skill ability. Johnny's early practice in ascending and descending slopes and his willing attitude appeared to lead to his superior ability in this task. Jimmy had no previous experience to rely on and, perhaps as a result, was hampered by an uncooperative attitude concerning his ascension and descension of the slopes. Interestingly, though, this attitudinal difference may have had the reverse effect on roller skating. Johnny was so willing to roller skate that he became reckless and sloppy as a roller skater compared to his more conservative brother, who was extremely cautious.

Observing Johnny and Jimmy roller skating also led McGraw to conclude that growth affected the

TABLE 6-2 McGraw's Research on Twin Brothers' Motor Development

Factors Affecting Motor Development	McGraw's Explanation
Attitude	Johnny was successful in roller skating when 11 months old. He became reckless soon after, causing his performance to decline. Jimmy was frequently uncooperative, which hampered his performance in descending slopes and jumping.
Practice	Johnny descended slopes much better than his brother Jimmy and developed clever strategies in the process. Jimmy, who had minimal early practice at such skills, was much less capable and very timid in his performance.
Readiness	Johnny was introduced to tricycling when he was 11 months old. He was incapable of much success at the skill until 8 months later. Jimmy was given a tricycle when he was 22 months old and tricycled immediately, despite his lack of early stimulation. According to McGraw, Jimmy exhibited a readiness for tricycling at 22 months, which Johnny did not have at 11 months.
Growth	Johnny roller skated well when he was 11 months old but declined in his ability thereafter. This regression was attributed to his attitude and his increasing height (center of gravity), which impeded his balance.
Level of fixity	Both twins maintained their tricycling ability well despite a period of nonparticipation. McGraw attributed this to their high levels of performance (level of fixity) at the time the skill was discontinued.

facility with which the twins acquired movement ability. For example, as discussed, Johnny became relatively successful at the movement as early as 1 year of age. Jimmy was not introduced to the activity until he was 22 months old and never excelled at roller skating. McGraw believed this was because the two boys had different body sizes when they were introduced to the activity: Jimmy was much taller and therefore had a higher center of gravity, making it harder for him to maintain the balance necessary for roller skating. Johnny, although younger when he first attempted roller skating, was also shorter, which McGraw believed was an advantage for this particular movement. Table 6-2 summarizes the major factors affecting Johnny's and Jimmy's motor development.

EFFECTS OF EARLY DEPRIVATION

The effects of early forms of deprivation are important to developmentalists studying all aspects of human behavior. The type, length, time, and severity of the deprivation and its subsequent effects are all variables we strive to understand. Potentially, such information may have beneficial applications for many practical situations, including education and child rearing, although investigating the effects of deprivation is difficult. Placing a baby in an intentionally deprived environment for scientific purposes is highly unethical and inhumane, so researchers have had to rely on animal research or the unusual, sometimes tragic, human cases that have occurred "naturally" in society. Therefore, there is sparse information concerning the effects of deprivation on the human being. However, certain classic studies and cases, involving both animals and humans, have yielded important findings about the effects of various forms of deprivation early in life.

Hopi Cradleboards and Infant Development

In the 1930s Wayne Dennis extensively studied Hopi Indians. Much of this work culminated with the publication of his book *The Hopi Child* (1940). Of particular interest for motor development was Dennis' description of the use of infant cradleboards by the Hopis. As young as 1 month, and often until after the first birthday, babies were swaddled and tied to a board. While on the cradleboard the baby's arms were usually extended at the sides with only enough room for a slight bend. The legs were also placed in an extended position. Generally, according to Dennis, while on the board the Hopi infant was prevented from doing many movements that would be typical of babies who were not "cradled." For example, while in the cradleboard, babies could not touch their hands to the mouth, watch their hands, or kick their feet. Dennis also claimed that these infants were seldom taken from their home until about 4 months of age. When taken outside the home the baby was usually carried in the arms of the mother or on her back while the cradleboard was left at home. By this time babies had often become so accustomed to the board that they would cry or become restless until returned to the board. Though initially the baby was placed in the cradleboard for as much as 23 hours per day, progressively more freedom was allowed from the cradleboard starting at about 3 months of age. In addition, from 6 months the babies were not placed on their abdomens when out of the cradleboard until they were voluntarily capable of turning from a supine to a prone position. Thus, the baby was unable to practice such skills as raising the head or raising the chest off the floor when in a prone position.

As Dennis notes in his book, questions arise concerning the effect of using the cradleboard on the baby's development. Dennis maintained that, during the first few months of life, Hopi babies still assumed a flexed position when temporarily freed from the board. They also exhibited a number of other activities expected from babies not using a cradleboard. For example, they would play with their feet and hands. In fact, the sequence of acquisition of many voluntary movement skills seemed to follow the sequence which would normally occur without the "deprivation" of the cradleboard. According to Dennis, Hopi infants developed such skills as sitting, creeping, and walking in the usual sequence and at the same times as non-cradleboard, "white American children" (Dennis, 1940).

Deprivation Dwarfism

The effects of early emotional or social deprivation are much more pervasive than were once expected. For example, infants hospitalized for a long period of time frequently have been found to become listless, apathetic, and depressed. Even more surprising is that infants under extended hospital care in unstimulating environments often fail to gain weight and develop respiratory infections and fever. This condition, known as *deprivation dwarfism,* can have a permanent impact on the victim. Fortunately, in less severe cases, symptoms disappear when the child is returned home or to a more emotionally acceptable environment (Gardner, 1972).

This phenomenon was particularly well documented in Gardner's article, "Deprivation Dwarfism." Gardner described two orphanages, each directed by individuals of different temperament, one stern and uncaring, the other cheerful and loving. During one 6-month period, the relative weight gains of the children in the two orphanages were noted. The children under the care of the cheerful director at the first orphanage were larger overall relative to their respective ages. However, soon thereafter, the stern director from the second orphanage took the place of her more cheerful counterpart at the first orphanage. Ironically, this change of directors coincided with an increase of food at the first orphanage. Despite this increase in food, the emotional effect of the harsh new matron seemed to negatively influence the growth of the children: They showed reduced relative weight gain when compared to the children from the second orphanage. However, this apparent decrease in growth did not occur for all children in the first orphanage; eight children from the second orphanage who were the stern matron's favorites accompanied her to the first orphanage. They gained weight equivalently to the children in the first orphanage, the orphanage that had been directed by the more caring director. This dramatic situation illustrated the effects of ad-

verse conditions on human growth. Although the exact operative mechanism is unclear, apparently harsh early circumstances during infancy or early childhood can lead to reduced growth.

This negative influence on human growth is apparently created by serious deprivation or adverse stimulation. Deprivation dwarfism is an emotional disturbance that is registered in the higher centers of the brain and eventually conveyed to the hypothalamus, which controls the secretion of the growth hormone somatotropin. Therefore, growth is impaired, and the likelihood of other potentially serious side effects, such as sleep disruption, increases (Schiamburg, 1985). As discussed in Chapter 7, as growth is affected, motor development may also be profoundly influenced.

Gardner described another unusual case of deprivation dwarfism. This situation involved a twin brother and sister who had grown normally for their first 4 months, at which point their mother then became pregnant with another child who was unexpected and unwanted. To complicate this situation, the father lost his job and left home, leaving the mother to care for the twins. The mother became frustrated and began to focus her hostility on the male twin. By the time he was 13 months old, the male twin was approximately the size of a 7-month-old, whereas the female twin had attained normal growth. The boy was then removed from the hostile environment and medically treated, which enabled him to regain his normal size by the age of 3 1/2 years (Gardner, 1972).

Anna and a Case of Extreme Isolation

Kingsley Davis (1946) described one of the most tragic of all reported cases of early deprivation. The study involved a young girl named Anna. Anna was isolated in an atticlike room of her home with minimal stimulation of any kind for approximately 6 years. She was an illegitimate child who resided with her mother and grandfather. Anna was the unwitting victim of a family dispute because her grandfather opposed having an illegitimate child living in his home while the mother argued in favor of her staying. Unfortunately, the subsequent compromise led to Anna staying in the house but living in the attic from the age of 5 1/2 months to approximately 6 years. In the attic, Anna received minimal care, barely enough to maintain her existence. When Anna was eventually discovered, she was in terrible condition. She showed minimal signs of intelligence, could not walk or talk, and was extremely malnourished. Davis described her legs as being "skeleton-like" and her abdomen "bloated."

Upon discovery, Anna was taken to a county home. During her stay at that institution, she showed minimal signs of improvement. She had developed somewhat motorically, as she could eat by herself and was able to walk. Her speech and intellectual abilities were still severely impaired.

Approximately 2 years after being discovered in the attic, Anna was taken to a private home for retarded children. There she continued to progress, although slowly. Her prognosis was described as unfavorable because she still showed no signs of speech, other than random guttural sounds. Davis further described Anna as having an extremely poor attention span, periodically making nonpurposeful rhythmical movements, and watching her hands "as if she had seen them for the first time."

When Anna was about 8 years old, she was examined by a clinical psychologist, who found that her vision and hearing were normal and she showed progressing motor ability as she began to climb stairs. Her speech was in the babbling stage, and her mental age was determined as approximately 19 months. Her social maturity was judged roughly equivalent to a typical 23-month-old child. The examining psychologist predicted that Anna would eventually achieve the mental ability of a 6- or 7-year-old. However, he also noted that these tests were perhaps of questionable value in Anna's extreme case.

By the age of 9 years, Anna had progressed motorically. She could bounce balls and socialize somewhat. She could eat with considerable control, although her eating was confined to the use of a spoon and an eating technique typical of a much younger child. Most surprisingly, Anna had begun to speak in occasional full sentences but was still described as possessing the language abilities of a 2-year-old.

When she was 10, a final report on Anna revealed that she could string beads and build with blocks, showing evidence of progressing fine motor control. In addition, Anna walked and ran but was said to be rather clumsy. Her speech had evolved into frequent attempts at communication, although she rarely spoke in complete sentences.

Anna died at the age of 11. The case study describing Anna's conditions answered few questions concerning the effects of extreme deprivation, but it did stimulate many new thoughts and avenues of exploration concerning the effects of deprivation on the human condition. For example, how tremendous was the effect of Anna's isolation? How did Anna's actual state differ from what she would have been like in more normal circumstances? What would have happened to Anna had she been discovered earlier or later? Davis postulated that Anna's relatively early discovery may have enabled her to develop some skills that otherwise would have been impossible. Had Anna been discovered earlier, she may have had more capable communication and increased general intellectual abilities. Anna's early death was unfortunate for both humane and scientific reasons. Had she lived longer, we may have obtained partial answers to some of these questions.

The "Young Savage of Abeyron"

Throughout history stories have arisen of children being raised in the wild. According to certain versions, some of these children were even raised by wild animals, but because of lack of documentation, most of these stories are now considered myth or folklore. However, one account which has been well documented is the case of Victor, a young boy who was found in the woods of France sometime around 1799. Victor, at what was believed to be 11 to 12 years of age, was found by three "sportsmen." Victor was immediately taken to a nearby village where he was left in the care of a local widow. He remained there for as little as a week as he soon escaped back into the nearby mountains. However, occasionally he would wander near villages where he was once again captured and sent to a hospital and eventually to Paris for study. In Paris, Victor was placed under the care of a young physician by the name of Itard. Dr. Itard believed Victor's condition to be a result of "lack of experience" resulting from isolation starting as early as 4 to 5 years of age. Itard immediately attempted to provide remedial experiences to help Victor catch up.

According to reports, Victor initially appeared to be "retarded." He was also "wild and shy," very impatient, and constantly seeking an opportunity to escape. He was further described as "disgustingly dirty," very inattentive, indifferent, and possessing very little affection for those around him. In fact, he was often known to bite and scratch. He moved "spasmodically" and frequently swayed back and forth. His eyes were unsteady and expressionless and he rarely appeared to even notice loud sounds or music. Except for occasional guttural sounds, he did not speak. He appeared to have very little memory and was unable to imitate. According to Itard, "his whole life was a completely animal existence" (Itard, 1972, p. 35); he demonstrated an aversion to common foods and disliked wearing clothes and sleeping in a bed.

Victor's mode of locomotion was particularly interesting; he did not walk but tended to "trot or gallop" making walking with him very difficult. Itard also said Victor would smell anything handed to him and described Victor's chewing as being rodent-like. The rapid action of the "incisors" led Itard to the conclusion that Victor's diet had been predominantly vegetarian. Victor's body was quite scarred. Many scars appeared to be a result of animal bites while others were apparently the result of scratches acquired from years of living outdoors.

To determine Victor's level of intellectual ability, Itard placed food out of Victor's reach. Victor seemed to be intellectually incapable of using nearby chairs or other implements to assist him in reaching the food. Itard also placed bits of food beneath inverted cups to test Victor's memory of the location of the food. Again, Victor showed only a "feeble"

capacity intellectually though he finally began to track the cups with his eyes. Itard also attempted to show Victor how to use toys but Victor was said to be impatient and often simply hid or broke the toys. Finally, Itard attempted to teach him to talk, though Victor appeared to achieve little verbally beyond using certain words to express pleasure. Though Victor showed moderate overall improvement over the course of his life he never became intellectually normal. Victor died at about the age of 40 years.

CONCEPTS CONCERNING STIMULATION AND DEPRIVATION

As discussed, some fascinating and tragic situations have been studied to better understand the effects of stimulation and deprivation on human development. However, because the cases studied involved different forms of stimulation or deprivation, there are few solid conclusions. Nevertheless, many theories concerning early stimulation and deprivation have been proposed. Much of the theory to date concerns the concepts of critical periods, readiness, and catch-up (see Table 6-3). Here we define and discuss these terms and examine their relationship to early stimulation and deprivation.

TABLE 6-3 Three Important Terms in the Study of Early Stimulation and Deprivation

Critical periods: A time of particular or maximum sensitivity to environmental stimuli.

Readiness: The establishment of the minimum characteristics necessary for a particular human behavior to be acquired.

Catch-up: The human power "to stabilize and return" to a predetermined behavior or growth pattern "after being pushed off trajectory" (Tanner, 1978, p. 154).

Critical Periods

Critical periods, sometimes called sensitive periods, are times of particular sensitivity to environmental stimuli. If a child is exposed to the appropriate stimuli during this time of optimal sensitivity, a particular human behavior is likely to emerge or at least be facilitated (Newman & Newman, 1991). This term is also commonly used as a synonym for epigenic period, which is a period of time prenatally during which the individual is particularly susceptible to environmental harm (Schiamburg, 1985). The prenatal factors were discussed in Chapter 5; this discussion concentrates on our first definition of the term critical period.

There are very few known specifics concerning this type of critical period. In fact, the idea of the existence of such periods is extremely theoretical, although there is considerable evidence to suggest their presence. Evidence is scarce, however, as to exactly when critical periods last, and for which human behaviors do they function?

Also note that the notion of critical periods is that of a rather specific time in a person's life. During this time, the appropriate stimuli must be present or the potential for optimal development is lost. This concept does not indicate that total capacity for any kind of development will be squelched if the critical period is left unstimulated (Money, 1969). Therefore, even if the appropriate stimulation is not present during the critical period, mastery of a given skill may still be possible, although less than the person's genetic potential would have originally allowed.

Numerous research investigations and natural cases have led to the assumption that critical periods exist. For example, if the left hemisphere of the brain is damaged during early infancy, the right hemisphere often assumes certain functions, such as language development. However, if the left hemisphere is damaged after language has been acquired, the person may never again be capable of fluent speech, apparently because the critical period for the right hemisphere substitution has been bypassed. Perhaps the right hemisphere has been chemically or structurally altered to the point that it has become incapable of assuming left-hemisphere duties (Money, 1969).

Smiling, a fine movement, is also considered evidence that critical periods exist. A smile often occurs initially and spontaneously from approximately 5 to 14 weeks of age. At that time it can be evoked by a number of stimuli from familiar or unfamiliar individuals. For example, the sight of a human face, a touch, or a high-pitched voice frequently evokes a smile during this 9- to 10-week period early in infancy. At about 20 weeks, however, a different smiling pattern begins to emerge, in which only familiar faces elicit the smile. Children seem to lose sensitivity to the events that were once capable of causing their smiles to appear (Newman & Newman, 1991). The heightened sensitivity that existed for several weeks seems to diminish. The critical period for smiling has been further verified by studies of blind children, who smile initially at many of the same nonvisual stimuli as do sighted children but stop the behavior if it is not continually reinforced during this period of presumed sensitivity by cooing or touching (Freiberg, 1976).

Animal research has also been conducted to help fill the information void concerning critical periods. Nottebohm (1970) studied the motor task of vocalization in birds to determine if and when there was a critical period for the wild chaffinch to learn bird song. Under normal circumstances, this bird learns vocalization from adult birds and establishes a form of bird song that is basically stable after the age of 1 year. However, Nottebohm noted that when the bird was deprived of hearing normal bird song, its song became modified or abnormal. In fact, the more limited the bird's exposure to the necessary stimulus of hearing bird song, the more likely the bird was to modify the vocalization to a more rudimentary form. However, if the bird was deprived of hearing bird song after one full season of normal behavior, the deprivation seemed to have no further effect in altering the vocalization patterns. Apparently, the first 10 months to 1 year for the wild chaffinch are a critical period for the development of bird song. If the bird acquires the appropriate ability during that time, the behavior becomes fairly stable; if the behavior is not acquired, it may never optimally develop.

These examples illustrate four of the essential elements of the notion of critical periods. First, the organism must have achieved a state of readiness for the environmental stimulation to be effective. Second, there is a specific time limit. There may be multiple critical periods for any given behavior, but each behavior has a particular period when the stimulation is of optimal value. If the appropriate stimulation does not occur during this critical period, the opportunity for optimal development may be lost forever. Third, the effects of the stimulation during the critical period create a permanent and durable imprint. Therefore, even though an individual may temporarily discontinue a particular behavior, there may still be opportunity for optimal reestablishment as a result of the presence of appropriate stimuli during the critical period. Similarly, if appropriate stimuli were not present during the critical period, a permanent negative residue may remain. The individual would then be permanently incapable of optimally developing that behavior (Money, 1969). Finally, apparently there are critical periods for all aspects of human behavior. Although the critical period notion has been popularized in relation to cognitive skills, the critical period does appear extremely important in the development of social and motor skills as well as physical growth.

Many theories have been proposed to explain the phenomenon of critical periods. Bronson (1965) stated that the critical period may occur as a result of the brain's neural networks attaining an optimal level of "functional significance." According to Bronson, the termination of the critical period could be a function of the decreasing sensitivity of the neural networks. This decreasing sensitivity probably occurs toward the end of a rapid structural change that is simply an aspect of the predetermined growth pattern.

Bronson's explanation is widely accepted and forms a foundation for continued consideration, but it is not sufficiently specific to be of particular practical value. Presently there is no sufficient evidence, particularly in the area of motor development, to determine when a critical period is being experienced. Furthermore, we are not aware of the "antecedent conditions that are essential" for optimally preparing a child for movement acquisition (Seefeldt, 1982).

Readiness

The term *readiness* is often used in conjunction with the term *critical period*. Critical period is sometimes defined as "a period of maximum sensitivity or readiness for the development of a particular pattern or skill" (Schiamburg, 1985, p. 638). As this definition implies, an ultimate form of readiness can be considered a critical period. However, this may not be the case because readiness more commonly implies that the individual has become prepared, or ready, to acquire a particular behavior. In other words, the person has reached a certain point in an ongoing process that has enabled the establishment of the minimum characteristics necessary for a particular movement skill or other human behavior to be acquired. Sufficient information and ability have been accumulated and the necessary physical characteristics have been acquired so that the movement in question can be performed. Acquisition of the necessary physical characteristics infers that the person has attained a certain level of growth and that requisite neurological patterns have been created so that the new motor skill can be effectively employed. For readiness to be complete, however, the child must also be motivated to perform the behavior, implying an "internal" as well as "external" form of motivation (Kaluger & Kaluger, 1984). That is, the child must want to perform the movement skill while being appropriately encouraged from such external sources as the family.

We earlier referred to readiness in relation to McGraw's examination of the tricycling abilities of the twins Johnny and Jimmy. Johnny, who had received much stimulation and experiences early in life, was introduced to tricycling when he was 11 months old. He was incapable of performing the skill at that time and showed no signs of learning for the next 9 months. However, Jimmy, who had received minimal stimulation as an infant, tricycled almost immediately when presented with a tricycle when 22 months old. The hypothesis proposed was that Johnny, regardless of his early stimulation, was not ready to tricycle at 11 months of age. Jimmy, at 22 months, despite his relatively deprived infancy, had acquired the physiological characteristics necessary to tricycle. Despite the varying levels of stimulation the two twins experienced, Jimmy was ready to tricycle at 22 months, whereas 11 months was too early for Johnny.

As the Johnny and Jimmy example suggests, a strict interpretation of the concept of readiness implies that early experience of or instruction in a particular movement activity prior to the achievement of readiness may not be particularly valuable (Magil, 1982). The prerequisite skills must be within the child's repertoire before additional instruction is worthwhile. This belief suggests that the current trend of early educational programs may, in many cases, be fruitless.

Other researchers do not as readily accept a strict readiness theory. Bruner (1960) believed that the real burden is on the teacher or parent. Bruner stated that the child is always ready to acquire a new behavior; the key to eliciting the desired behavior from the child is determining the appropriate stimuli. Unfortunately, if Bruner's theory is accurate, the appropriate stimuli are unknown and will continue to be for years to come.

The outlook is equally disturbing for those who do subscribe to the theory of readiness, particularly regarding motor development. Currently we are unable to recognize signs that indicate that a child is ready. In fact, we really have no assurance that such signs even exist because the concept of readiness is still a theory. Therefore, we can only estimate the most appropriate time for exposing the child to movement experiences and instruction. This is unfortunate, as recognition of the signs that indicate a state of readiness would greatly facilitate our efficiency in the instruction of movement skills. This ability, however, is not presently within our understanding of human motor development.

Catch-Up

Both stimulation and deprivation can have various effects on many aspects of human development. Depending on a number of variables, many unknown, the effects vary from one situation to the next. For example, in cases of severe deprivation, one person may exhibit permanent behavioral damage while another person exhibits only temporary effects. This may be due to the phenomenon known as *catch-up*. Catch-up is the unusual power a human being displays "to stabilize and return" to a predetermined behavior or growth pattern "after being pushed off trajectory" (Tanner, 1978, p. 154). This inexplicable phenomenon occurs in response to severe deprivation or adverse treatment, such as discussed earlier in the section "Deprivation Dwarfism." Catch-up is evidence that the human being is capable of acquiring new behavior or increasing physical growth much more rapidly than normal during a period of recovery. Figure 6-4 illustrates catch-up in graph form.

The term catch-up is most frequently used in conjunction with physical growth. The term catch-up growth is common in the literature concerning human development. However, catch-up can also occur intellectually, socially, and motorically. Regardless of the domain of human development being directly affected, motor development is also modified to some degree. As discussed in Chapter 1, all domains of human development are reciprocally related. But whichever domain of human development appears most directly affected, the degree of recovery, or catch-up, appears to depend on the severity, the length, and the time of deprivation. Despite often remarkable recoveries, individuals who catch up will never fully realize their genetic potential because of the time they lost during the period of deprivation and recovery (Prader, Tanner, & Von Harnack, 1963).

Anna, the victim of severe isolation, is an excellent example of catch-up and its variability. After nearly 6 years in isolation in the atticlike room of her home, Anna was incapable of most behaviors expected of the normal 6-year-old. However, with improved care and proper treatment following her discovery, Anna caught up in many of her behav-

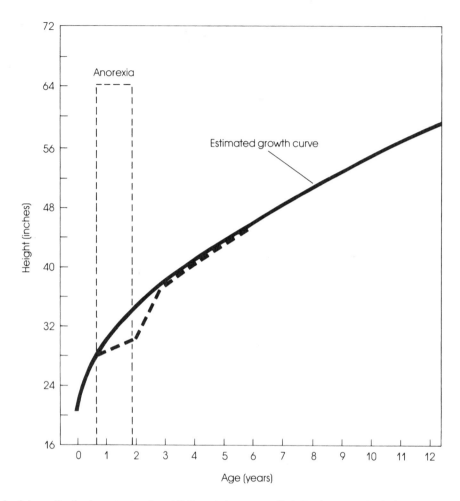

FIGURE 6-4 A hypothetical example of a child's catch-up growth following a period of anorexia, severe nutritional deprivation (adapted from Tanner, 1978).

iors, particularly physical size. Although she was extremely small and frail when discovered, Anna was actually described as "large for her age" in the years to follow (Davis, 1946). Similar catch-up occurred for certain gross motor skills. Anna could not walk when she was approximately 6 years old, but she was described as being capable at running, ball bouncing, and climbing in the years that followed. No doubt Anna had caught up physically and motorically. Unfortunately, her language and intellectual skills showed much less progress.

One of the most interesting examples of catch-up involves Harlow's studies of the rhesus monkey (Suomi & Harlow, 1978). Harlow either totally or partially isolated the monkeys from any kind of social contact for 3, 6, and 12 months. Although the total or partial isolation led to similar behavioral patterns, the longer periods of isolation created much more devastating effects. The 3-month isolates appeared to be in a state of emotional shock when allowed to interact socially. They were fearful of other monkeys and therefore avoided contact with them. This group of monkeys also exhibited the abnormal idiosyncrasies of self-clutching, self-biting, rocking, and pulling their own hair. Despite these rather unusual behaviors, the monkeys eventually recovered when allowed to play daily with a group of normal same-age monkeys.

The 6-month isolates yielded a poorer prognosis. They exhibited the same behavioral traits as were exhibited by the 3-month isolates, but this second group showed poorer ability to recover. They avoided their age-mates during play time, showing social interest only in the other isolates.

As expected, the 12-month isolates exhibited even more behavioral abnormalities. Along with exhibiting the same characteristics as the other isolates, the 12-month group revealed greater apathy and were more severely withdrawn. They were extremely passive and thus defenseless to attacks from their normal age-mates.

Follow-up investigations revealed that the monkeys that were isolated 6 months or longer exhibited continued behavioral abnormalities. Social behavior during their adolescence and adulthood was considered bizarre, as exemplified by their difficulties in sexual relationships and performance. The severity of the problem with the monkeys isolated for as much as 6 months or longer initially led Harlow to conclude that the first 6 months of social interaction may be a critical period. In other words, if social interaction were prohibited during that time of life, complete, or optimal, development of social behavior may never be possible (Suomi & Harlow, 1978).

However, in subsequent research, Suomi and Harlow found reason to doubt that initial theory. In seeking a method to rehabilitate the long-term isolates, the researchers exposed their subjects to 26 months of "therapy" with 3-month-old monkeys. Because the younger monkeys were less offensive and generally less active than the older ones, they tended to approach the isolates more cautiously. After an initial period of acquaintance, the young monkeys would even cling to the isolates. Such affection from the young "therapy monkeys" seemed to normalize the isolates' behavior to the point that

they were considered recovered by the end of the 26 weeks. Thus catch-up, although normally associated with physical growth, also appears to occur with social, emotional, intellectual, and motor development (Suomi & Harlow, 1972).

SUMMARY

Programs involving early education for children have become particularly popular in recent years. However, the value of many such programs is unsubstantiated by what little research exists on early stimulation or deprivation. In fact, some research has shown early stimulation may have long-term deleterious effects. Programs designed to stimulate or optimize early motor development have been categorized into the "no-programming" and the "programming" types. The no-programming type advocates avoidance of specific training or practice of future movements. The programming type encourages an active role in manipulating the baby in preparation for future development.

In a policy statement issued by the American Academy of Pediatrics infant exercise programs are said to be of no known benefit for the development of healthy infants. Nevertheless, the AAP encourages parents to seek "safe, nurturing, and minimally structured" play situations for their infants.

Gymboree has been one of the most popular programs designed to enhance early motor development though no research exists to support the claims made by the program. Infant and preschool aquatic programs are also extremely popular, though controversial, as they have been linked to water intoxication and giardia. Current interest in infant and preschool aquatic programs has led to the creation of guidelines by the American Academy of Pediatrics and the American Red Cross.

The Suzuki method of playing the violin is another popular early education program. This program is unique as it generally requires the parent to participate with the child. Head Start programs have also catered to the preschool-age child since 1965. Research concerning the effectiveness of this early stimulation is still inconclusive.

Infant walkers have been widely used for years though research has shown a high rate of injury from infants falling down stairs in their walkers. Research has also demonstrated that walkers do not appear to enhance walking development though parents believe they may be pleasurable for the baby.

Myrtle McGraw's research involving the twins Johnny and Jimmy yielded a number of valuable conclusions concerning the effects of early stimulation. McGraw concluded that readiness, practice, attitude, and physical growth were all particularly important factors that influence human movement at an early age.

During the 1930s, Wayne Dennis found that Hopi Indians swaddled and tied their babies to cradleboards over the first several months of life. Though this appeared to limit some forms of early stimulation, Dennis found that the Hopi babies would often cry to return to their cradleboard, and appeared to follow a developmental sequence and timeline that would be expected of non-cradleboard babies in the acquisition of sitting, creeping, and walking.

Early deprivation also has dramatic impact on early development in all domains of human behavior. Deprivation dwarfism is the retardation of physical growth following a period of severe deprivation or adverse treatment despite sufficient levels of nutrition.

Anna, the victim of severe deprivation due to isolation, was seriously impaired as a result of her mistreatment. With improved care and special treatment, she was capable of catching up motorically, although her language and intellectual skills were extremely abnormal.

One of the most interesting cases of deprivation concerned the "young savage of Abeyron." This young boy was found at an early age after having lived in the "wild" for years. He could not talk, trotted or galloped rather than walked, chewed "like a rodent," and was delayed intellectually. Despite repeated attempts at remediation, he showed little improvement in his intellectual skills and died at the young age of 40 years.

A critical period is a time of special sensitivity to environmental stimuli. If the child is appropriately stimulated during this period, the associated behavior is most likely to emerge or be facilitated.

The term readiness implies that a person has achieved a certain point in an ongoing process that has enabled the establishment of the minimum characteristics necessary for a certain behavior to be acquired. Readiness depends on an adequate level of physical growth, the requisite neurological patterns, and sufficient internal and external motivation.

Catch-up is a human being's ability to return to a predetermined pattern of behavior or growth following a severe period of deprivation or mistreatment. Although normally associated with physical growth, catch-up also appears to occur with motor development.

KEY TERMS

Catch-up

Critical periods

Deprivation

Deprivation dwarfism

Giardia

Gymboree

Head Start

Hyponatremia

Infant walkers

Level of fixity

No programming

Programming

Readiness

Stimulation

Suzuki method

CHAPTER 7

Growth and Maturation

What is the average height of a 5-year-old? How much taller will this child be in 1 year? What is this youngster's expected average body weight? What are the expected growth trends regarding height and weight during both middle and late adulthood? Which sex has longer legs, longer arms? What effect does exercise have on the dynamics of human growth? Is there a positive relationship between these physical characteristics and motor skill acquisition and motor skill performance? This chapter sheds light on these questions and explains how to measure the human body. The interrelationships between human body structure and human motor output are also discussed.

MEASURING GROWTH IN LENGTH AND STATURE

From birth to 2 years or until the child can stand without assistance, total body length (*recumbent length*) is measured while the child is supine (see Figure 7-1). A special slide ruler is used to measure the distance between the *vertex* (highest point on

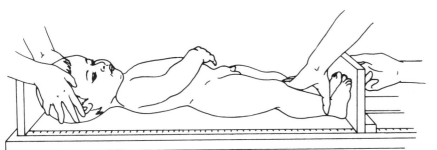

FIGURE 7-1 Measuring recumbent length

Used with permission of Ross Laboratories, Columbus, Ohio, from *Pediatric Anthropometry.* 2nd ed., © 1983, Ross Laboratories.

the skull) and the soles of the feet. The measurement should be recorded to the nearest 0.1 centimeter or 1/8 inch.

When the child is capable of standing without assistance, standing height (*stature*), the distance between the vertex and the floor, is the preferred measurement of total body length (see Figure 7-2). The child should be barefooted when the measurement is taken; this measure should be recorded to the nearest 0.1 centimeter or 1/8 inch. Note that a triangular headboard, which forms a right angle between the vertex and measurement scale, is used to increase accuracy.

Standard techniques for determining stature will not be accurate if the individual is not capable of standing erect or has severe spinal curvature. This is frequently the case when attempting to assess stature in elderly populations. However, stature can be estimated from the recumbent measure, *knee height*. Figure 7-3 illustrates the technique for measuring knee height. Note that the individual bends the left knee to a 90-degree angle. The blades of the sliding caliper are then placed under the heel and over the anterior portion of the thigh. Pressure is then applied to compress the soft tissue before a reading is taken. To ensure reliability and accuracy, two consecutive measurements should be taken and both should be within 0.5-cm agreement. The obtained knee-height value can then be substituted into one of the following equations to estimate stature:

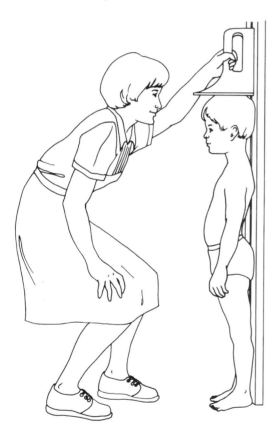

FIGURE 7-2   Measuring stature with the use of a triangular headboard

Used with permission of Ross Laboratories, Columbus, Ohio, from *Pediatric Anthropometry*, 2nd ed., © 1983, Ross Laboratories.

FIGURE 7-3   Measuring knee height

$$\text{Stature men} = 64.19 - (0.04 \times \text{age})$$
$$+ (2.02 \times \text{knee height})$$
$$\text{Stature women} = 84.88 - (0.24 \times \text{age})$$
$$+ (0.83 \times \text{knee height})$$

In solving the equation, round age to the nearest whole year and record knee height in centimeters. To convert inches to centimeters, simply multiply inches by 2.54. Conversely, if you desire to estimate stature in inches, simply divide the number derived from the equation by 2.54.

For example, if the knee height of a 75-year-old male was 50.5 cm, then his estimated stature would be calculated as follows:

$$64.19 - (0.04 \times 75) + (2.02 \times 50.5)$$
$$= 64.19 - (3) + (102.01)$$
$$= 61.19 + 102.01$$
$$= 163.2 \text{ cm or } 163.2 \text{ cm}/2.54$$
$$= 64.25 \text{ inches}$$

For a quicker but less accurate means of calculating estimated stature from knee height, the nomogram illustrated in Figure 7-4 can be used.

GROWTH IN LENGTH AND STATURE

Human prenatal life begins when the male sperm merges with the female egg, forming a zygote, which measures only 0.14 millimeter in diameter. During the next 38 to 40 weeks of intrauterine life, the fetus grows almost 5000 times longer. In fact, at no time during the human life cycle is growth in body length greater than that which occurs during the fourth prenatal month. However, growth rapidly decelerates during the remaining prenatal period. Mean body length increases approximately 90 percent between the 10th and 14th weeks of gestation, only slightly more than 10 percent during the last 4 weeks of gestation (Meridith, 1978).

Following 280 days of gestation, there is little gender difference in median birth lengths. Boys generally measure about 20 inches long (50.5 centimeters); girls generally measure about 19.75 inches long (49.9 centimeters). By the end of the first year

of infancy, boys will be approximately 30 inches long, girls approximately 29.25 inches long. Thus, during the first year of postnatal life, body length can be expected to increase approximately 50 percent.

During the second year, gains in body length average 4.75 inches (12 centimeters). After age 2, stature increases at a slower rate, until the onset of the adolescent growth spurt. This growth deceleration continues during most of the elementary school years, with one exception: Some children experience a *midgrowth spurt* in height between 6 1/2 and 8 1/2 years. This midgrowth spurt occurs more frequently in girls than in boys (Malina & Bouchard, 1991). This unexplained deviation in growth rate is less dramatic than the adolescent spurt, and little is known about it.

The many hormonal changes known to occur during adolescence cause boys and girls to rapidly grow taller. In fact, about 20 percent of the adult stature is attained during this 2 1/2- to 3-year growth spurt. The onset of this milestone usually occurs in young girls between their 10th and 11th birthdays; boys generally start their adolescent growth spurt 2 years later. However, some children will mature faster than others; the time of onset can vary by as much as 3 or more years. Because girls generally enter adolescence before boys, it is not at all uncommon for young girls to be slightly taller than young boys (average is 1 inch taller) between 11–13 years of age (Buckler, 1990). During this adolescent phase of development, boys' height increases about 4 inches (10 centimeters) per year. The female spurt is somewhat slower because girls grow about 3 inches (8 centimeters) per year. Most of the height gained during the adolescent spurt is due to a lengthening of the trunk, not a lengthening of the legs. Peak leg-length growth usually occurs 6 to 9 months earlier. "Thus a boy stops growing out of his trousers (at least in length) a year before he stops growing out of his jackets" (Tanner, 1990, p. 67).

By the time the female is 16 1/2 years old and the male nearly 18 years, 98 percent of adult height has been attained. Most authorities agree that females reach the final 2 percent of their growth by their 18th birthday and males by their 20th birthday.

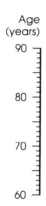

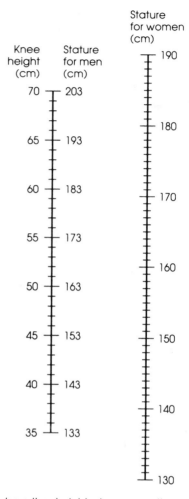

Directions

1. Locate the person's age on the column furthest to the left.
2. Locate the person's knee height on the next column.
3. Lay a ruler or straightedge so that it touches these two points—age and knee height.
4. Note where the straightedge crosses the stature column for the appropriate sex. The stature column for women is the furthest right column. The stature column for men is between that column and the knee height column. The point where the ruler crosses the appropriate column is the person's estimated stature.
5. Record the estimated stature in the person's chart.

FIGURE 7-4 Nomogram to estimate stature from knee height

Stature remains stable for 15 years after age 30. At middle age (above 40), there is an apparent decrease in height, caused by intervertebral disk degeneration and decreased thickness of joint cartilage in the lower extremities. Further reductions in height are apparent in late adulthood as the vertebral column continues to degenerate, sometimes causing abnormal spinal curvature. Table 7-1 summarizes growth for various ages. Reference data for those in late adulthood (above 60) is presented in Table 7-2.

Growth in stature can be graphically illustrated. Figure 7-5 is a typical individual *distance curve* for stature. The distance curve plots accumulative growth obtained over time. In contrast, Figure 7-6 illustrates percentile velocity curves for both boys and girls on the variable stature. The *velocity curve* plots increments of change per unit of time, making the curve useful for illustrating periods of fast and slow growth. A close examination of the velocity curves will reveal the possibility of obtaining negative values. It is incorrect to interpret these negative values as representing a decrease in stature. Instead, negative values result from measure error. For a more detailed discussion of this phenomenon, consult the work of Roche and Himes (1980).

To determine if an individual is growing normally, compare individual data to norm-referenced data. (Note: This is the most current national reference data

TABLE 7-1 Important Growth Changes in Body Length and Stature

Age	Selected Growth Information
Conception	0.14 mm in diameter
Birth (median length)	Boys: 20 in. (50.5 cm) Girls: 19.75 in. (49.9 cm)
6 months (median length)	Boys: 26.75 in. (67.8 cm) Girls: 26 in. (65.9 cm)
Year 1 (median length)	Boys: 30 in. (75 cm) Girls: 29.25 in. (73.1 cm)
	Length increases approximately 50% during the first year.
Year 2	Length increases about 4.75 in.
Years 3–5	Decelerated growth rate to about 2.75 in./yr.
Year 6–adolescence	Decelerated growth rate to about 2.25 in./yr.
Adolescence	20% of adult stature is attained during this 2 1/2- to 3-yr period.
	Approximately 4 in./yr growth for males and 3 in./yr for females.
16 1/2 years	Females attain 98% of adult stature.
18 years	Males attain 98% of adult stature.
	Average adult stature of 69 in. is roughly 3.5 times larger than that of the newborn.
	Females attain final 2% growth in stature.
20 years	Males attain final 2% growth in stature.
20–30 years	Growth of vertebral column may add another 1/8 in. (3–4 cm) to stature.
30–45 years	Stature is stable.
Above 45 years	Possible decrease in stature from disk degeneration.

TABLE 7-2   Percentiles for Stature in cm (and in.)

Age (years)	Men 95%	Men 50%	Men 5%	Age (years)	Women 95%	Women 50%	Women 5%
65	181.6 (71.5)	170.3 (67.0)	159.1 (62.6)	65	171.6 (67.6)	161.0 (63.4)	153.1 (60.3)
70	181.6 (71.5)	169.9 (66.9)	158.7 (62.5)	70	169.8 (66.9)	159.1 (62.6)	151.3 (59.6)
75	181.2 (71.3)	169.5 (66.7)	158.4 (62.4)	75	167.9 (66.1)	157.3 (61.9)	149.4 (58.8)
80	180.9 (71.2)	169.1 (66.6)	158.0 (62.2)	80	166.1 (65.4)	155.4 (61.2)	147.6 (58.1)
85	180.5 (71.1)	168.8 (66.5)	157.7 (62.1)	85	164.2 (64.6)	153.6 (60.5)	145.7 (57.4)
90	180.2 (70.9)	168.5 (66.3)	157.3 (61.9)	90	162.4 (63.9)	151.7 (59.7)	143.9 (56.6)

Used with permission of Ross Laboratories, Columbus, Ohio, from *Nutritional Assessment of the Elderly Through Anthropometry*, © 1984, Ross Laboratories.

available. A new national data set, HANES III, is scheduled to be finished in September 1995 and will likely be made available to the public over the next couple of years.) The National Center for Health Statistics (NCHS) percentile charts have been prepared for this purpose: Figures 7-7 and 7-8 are NCHS percentile charts for stature for both boys and girls (see Figure 7-6 for

NCHS velocity curves). Visual comparison of charted data to the percentile rankings can quickly alert one to growth abnormalities. Growth retardation may indicate disease, malnutrition (Martorell, Rivera, Kaplowitz, & Pollitt, 1992), child abuse (Wales & Taitz, 1992), or delayed maturation, among other conditions. If growth retardation is suspected,

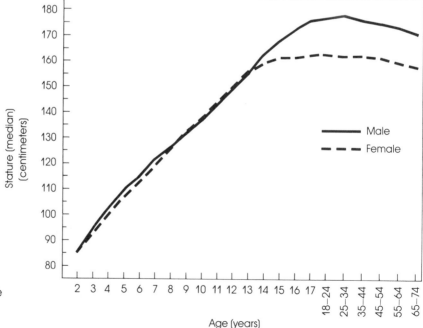

FIGURE 7-5 Typical distance curve for stature (based on NCHS data, 1973a and 1979)

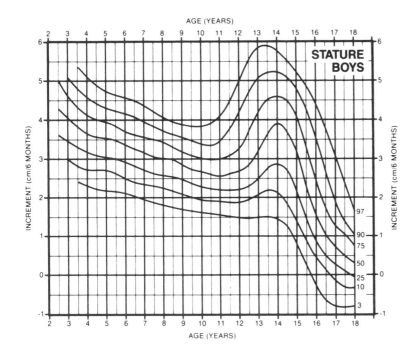

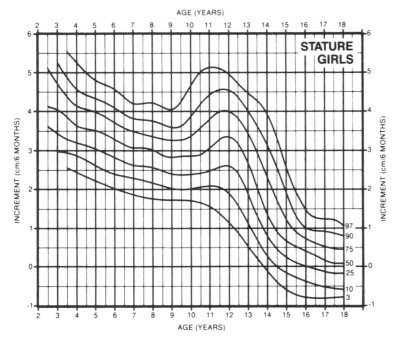

FIGURE 7-6 National Center for Health Statistics growth velocity charts for boys and girls on the variable stature

Used with permission of Ross Laboratories, Columbus, Ohio, from Ross Growth & Development Program: Incremental Growth Charts—Girls and Incremental Growth Charts—Boys, © 1981, Ross Laboratories.

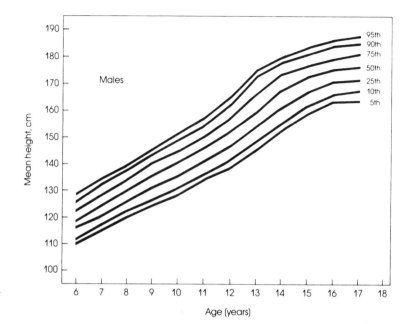

FIGURE 7-7 Percentile distribution of United States males 6–17 years of age by height in centimeters

SOURCE: National Center for Health Statistics. U.S. Department of Health, Education and Welfare, ser. 11, no. 124, January 1973.

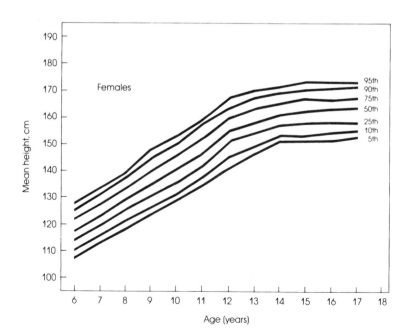

FIGURE 7-8 Percentile distribution of United States females 6–17 years of age by height in centimeters

SOURCE: National Center for Health Statistics. U.S. Department of Health, Education and Welfare, ser. 11, no. 124, January 1973.

the youngster should be referred to a physician for further screening.

MEASURING BODY WEIGHT

The instrument of choice for obtaining body weight is the *beam-type scale*. The scale should be calibrated in metric units, with a maximum capacity of at least 160 kilograms. The child stands in the middle of the scale with shoes and as much clothing as possible removed. If the child is fully clothed, make an adjustment of approximately 1 pound. A platform beam-type scale should be used to measure the body weight of infants who are not capable of standing without assistance (see Figure 7-9). In addition, other types of scales are available for bedridden individuals or adults who are not capable of standing without assistance (see Figures 7-10 and 7-11).

GROWTH IN BODY WEIGHT

At conception, the ovum weighs approximately 0.005 milligram. To place this measure in perspective, it would take over 5 million of these cells to equal just 1 ounce (Meredith, 1978). By the midpoint of the prenatal period (19 weeks), the mean body weight of a normally developing fetus is about 14 ounces (400 grams). At the end of the 34th week of gestation, the fetus is approximately 20 times heavier than it was at 14 weeks (5.5 pounds).

Median birth weights of boys and girls are 7.5 pounds (3.27 kilograms) and 7 pounds (3.23 kilograms), respectively. Only rarely does a newborn weigh more than 11 pounds. Weight at birth, however, tends to be more variable than length at birth. Apparently length, more than weight, is influenced by genetic makeup. Many extraneous factors have been shown to influence birth weight. For instance, small mothers tend to have small babies irrespective of the father's size; later-born children tend to be heavier than firstborns; mothers from low socioeconomic groups give birth to babies who are lighter than babies born to mothers from higher socioeco-

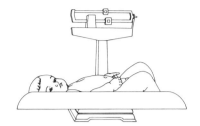

FIGURE 7-9   Platform beam-type scale

Used with permission of Ross Laboratories, Columbus, Ohio, from *Pediatric Anthropometry*, 2nd ed., © 1983, Ross Laboratories.

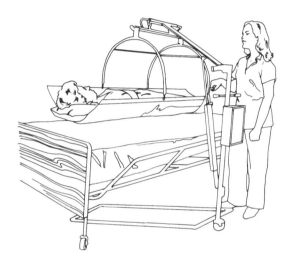

FIGURE 7-10   Bed scale

Used with permission of Ross Laboratories, Columbus, Ohio, from *Nutritional Assessment of the Elderly Through Anthropometry*, p. 4, © 1984, Ross Laboratories.

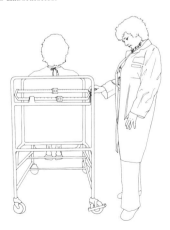

FIGURE 7-11   Chair scale

nomic groups; and twins are roughly 1.5 pounds lighter than singletons (Meredith, 1978). Thus birth weight reflects intrauterine life to a greater degree than does birth length.

During the first 6 months of postnatal life, the infant gains about 2/3 ounce (20 grams) per day. At this rate of gain, the infant will double birth weight at 5 months. This rate of weight gain slows toward the middle and later part of the first year. At the end of the first year, boys weigh about 22.5 pounds (10.15 kilograms) and girls about 21 pounds (9.53 kilograms) (Moore, 1978). Thus birth weight can be expected to triple during the first year.

Rate of weight gain continues to decelerate during the second year of life. The average child can be expected to gain about 5.5 pounds (2.5 kilograms). This rate of gain remains steady for the next 3 preschool years, with the normally developing child averaging about 4.5 pounds (2 kilograms) per year. For the next 4 to 6 years or until the onset of adolescence, annual weight gain increases slightly to 6.5 pounds (3 kilograms) per year. Nonetheless, there is a great deal of variability. One longitudinal study found that variability in body weight tripled for girls 5 to 12 1/2 years and nearly quadrupled for boys 5 to 14 1/2 years (Haubenstricker & Sapp, 1980).

Adolescence can bring about sharp increases in body weight. In fact, during this 3-year period, males add about 45 pounds (20 kilograms) to their body weight, and females add about 35 pounds (16 kilograms). Much of this added body weight is from height increases and changes in body composition. (See Chapter 8 for a discussion on the growth of adipose and muscle tissue.) Age of *peak weight velocity* (maximum rate of growth in body weight) generally occurs after peak height velocity (Beunen & Malina, 1988). Mature body weight is approximately 20 times that of birth weight.

After maturity, adults can partly control whether they add, lose, or maintain their body weight. One exception is adult weight gain following pregnancy: Women with children tend to weigh more than their childless sisters (Sinclair, 1985). Some of the weight gained during pregnancy appears to be permanent, and the amount may increase with each successive

child. After a person reaches adult weight, it is difficult to interpret changes in body weight because so much depends on the person's nutritional and exercise status. For instance, muscle and system atrophy can cause weight loss, but some sedentary but well-fed, elderly people may actually gain weight. Nonetheless, older people's body composition (fat weight versus muscle weight) is markedly different from that of young adults. Table 7-3 summarizes weight changes from conception up to adulthood. Body weight reference data for individuals in late adulthood are presented in Table 7-4.

Like stature, changes in body weight can be graphically illustrated. Figure 7-12 is a typical distance curve showing differences in body weight between males and females. In contrast, Figure 7-13 illustrates growth velocity; Figure 7-14 and 7-15 are NCHS percentile charts for the variable body weight.

STATURE AND WEIGHT: INTERRELATIONSHIP WITH MOTOR DEVELOPMENT AND PERFORMANCE

Shirley's classic study of 25 babies sparked interest in the relationship between length and weight at birth and the attainment of independent walking. In her study, Shirley concluded, "In general it may be stated that thin, muscular babies and small-boned babies walk earlier than short rotund babies and exceedingly heavy babies" (Shirley, 1931, p. 126). Norval (1947) reported similar relationships. Norval stated that "it is apparent that infants who are longer for their weight walk at an earlier age than those who are relatively short for their weight" (p. 676). Irrespective of these findings, it is difficult to imply a cause/effect relationship between length and weight at birth and the development of independent walking. Shirley recognized this possible criticism when she wrote, "Proportionate long- or short-leggedness is by no means the all-important growth factor concomitant with walking. The concomitance of the two does not imply interdependence; it may mean only mutual dependence on some third factor, such as age" (p. 120).

TABLE 7-3 Important Growth Changes in Body Weight

Age	Selected Growth Information
Conception	Ovum weighs roughly 0.005 mg.
19th week of gestation	14 oz (400 g)
34th week of gestation	Fetus is 20 times heavier than at 14 weeks (5.5 lb).
Birth (median weight)	Boys: 7.5 lb (3.27 kg) Girls: 7 lb (3.23 kg)
	Small mothers tend to have small babies.
	Later-borns are heavier than firstborns (6.8 oz).
	Twins are approximately 1.5 lb lighter than singletons.
1–3 days	Weight loss upwards of 10% of birth weight.
10 days	Weight is equal to birth weight or slightly heavier.
First 6 months	Gains about 2/3 oz (20 g)/day.
	Birth weight generally doubles at 5 months.
Last 6 months of year 1	Gains decelerate to about 1/2 oz (15 g)/day.
Year 1	Median weight of boys: 22.5 lb (10.15 kg)
	Median weight of girls: 21 lb (9.53 kg)
	Birth weight triples during first year.
Year 2	Gains about 5.5 lb (2.5 kg)
Years 3–5	Gains about 4.5 lb (2 kg)/yr
Year 6–adolescence	Slight increase in rate of weight gain to 6.5 lb (3 kg)/yr.
Adolescence	Males add about 45 lb of body weight and females about 35 lb of body weight during this 2 1/2- to 3-yr period.
Year 18 (median weight)	Males: 151 3/4 lb (68.88 kg) Females: 27 lb lighter (124 3/4 lb)
	Mature body weight is approximately 20 times greater than birth weight.
Above 19 years	Weight becomes a matter of nutritional and exercise status.
	Some weight gains during pregnancy appear permanent.

More recently, Jaffe and Kosakov (1982) attempted to relate age at walking to weight and length parameters measured at the time of walking. In their study of 135 healthy infants 6 to 18 months old, they found that overweight and obese infants as measured by Sveger's index (Sveger, 1978) demonstrated a significant delay in motor development when compared to normal-weight infants. However, 1 year later, a follow-up examination revealed that a majority (71 percent) of the motor-delayed infants were developing normally.

TABLE 7-4   Percentiles for Weight in kg (and lb)

	Men				Women		
Age (years)	95%	50%	5%	Age (years)	95%	50%	5%
65	102.0 (224.9)	79.5 (175.0)	62.6 (138.0)	65	87.1 (192.0)	66.8 (147.3)	51.2 (112.9)
70	99.1 (218.5)	76.5 (168.7)	59.7 (131.6)	70	84.9 (187.2)	64.6 (142.4)	49.0 (108.0)
75	96.3 (212.3)	73.6 (162.3)	56.8 (125.2)	75	82.8 (182.5)	62.4 (137.6)	46.8 (103.2)
80	93.4 (205.9)	70.7 (155.9)	53.9 (118.8)	80	80.6 (177.7)	60.2 (132.7)	44.7 (98.5)
85	90.5 (199.5)	67.8 (149.5)	51.0 (112.4)	85	78.4 (172.8)	58.0 (127.9)	42.5 (93.7)
90	87.6 (193.1)	64.9 (143.1)	48.1 (106.0)	90	76.2 (168.0)	55.9 (123.2)	40.3 (88.8)

During adolescence and adulthood, the interrelationship of weight and height to skilled motor performance becomes task-specific. Generally, increased body weight is an asset when an external object is propelled, such as a shot put. In contrast, lighter body weight is more advantageous when the individual's body is the object propelled. Furthermore, body weight and body fatness generally exert a negative influence on performance when the task requires the body to be supported.

ADOLESCENT AWKWARDNESS

Another issue frequently addressed in the professional literature regarding performance changes during adolescence is the concept of *adolescent awkwardness*. This term has been used to refer to a period during the growth spurt (*peak height velocity:* maximum rate of growth in height), that is accompanied by a temporary disruption in motor performance. For example, Tanner (1990) has noted

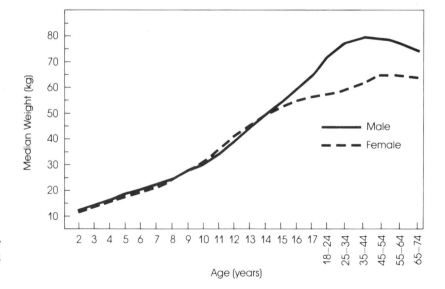

FIGURE 7-12 Typical distance curve for body weight (based on NCHS data, 1973a and 1979)

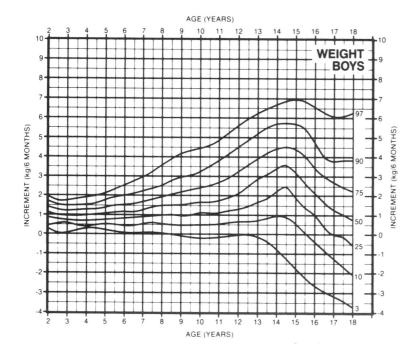

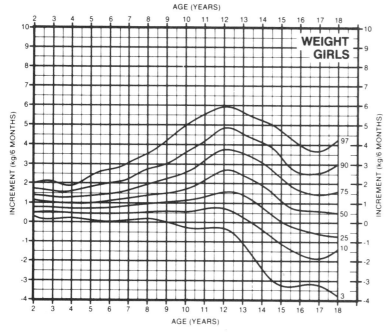

FIGURE 7-13 National Center for Health Statistics growth velocity charts for boys and girls on the variable body weight

Used with permission of Ross Laboratories, Columbus, Ohio, from Ross Growth & Development Program: Incremental Growth Charts—Boys and Incremental Growth Charts—Girls, © 1981, Ross Laboratories.

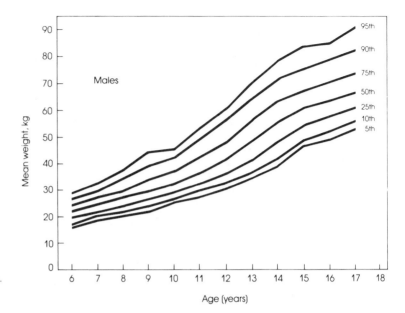

FIGURE 7-14 Percentile distribution of United States males 6–17 years of age by weight in kilograms

Source: National Center for Health Statistics. U.S. Department of Health, Education and Welfare, ser. 11, no. 124, January 1973.

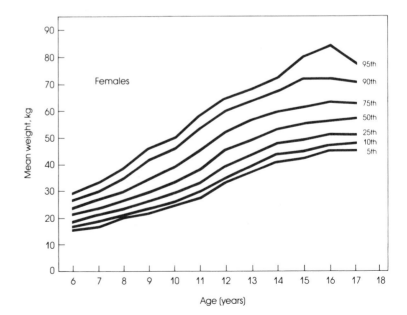

FIGURE 7-15 Percentile distribution of United States females 6–17 years of age by weight in kilograms

Source: National Center for Health Statistics. U.S. Department of Health, Education and Welfare, ser. 11, no. 124, January 1973.

a period during the growth spurt when balancing abilities may be disrupted for up to 6 months. Beunen and associates (1988) as well as Ostyn and associates (1980) also found a significant number of males, who declined in motor performance on four of seven motor tasks during peak height velocity.

Following an extensive review of the literature, Beunen and Malina (1988) concluded that this phenomenon, adolescent awkwardness, does exist, but primarily among males. However, the phenomenon is not universal. That is, not all individuals experience a disruption in motor performance during peak height velocity. These researchers report that the percentage of males exhibiting declines in performance during this growth spurt interval ranges between 1.4 percent and 33.5 percent. Table 7-5 illustrates their findings in more detail. Of particular interest is their finding that those males who exhibited a decline in performance at the time of peak height velocity were generally the best performers

TABLE 7-5   Percentage of Boys Exhibiting Declines in Motor Performance During Peak Height Velocity

Task	Number of Subjects	% Decliners
Arm pull (static strength)	444	1.4
Plate tapping (speed of limb movement)	441	7.0
Vertical jump (explosive strength)	446	9.5
Sit and reach (flexibility)	444	18.7
Leg lift (trunk strength)	444	26.1
Bent-arm hang (strength)	446	30.5
Shuttle run (agility/speed)	445	33.5

SOURCE: Based on data reported by Beunen and colleagues (1988) and Ostyn and colleagues (1980). Adapted from Beunen and Malina (1988).

at the beginning of peak height velocity. Moreover, subsequent follow-up testing during young adulthood revealed that this decline was only temporary (Beunen & Malina, 1988). For this reason, individuals responsible for motor assessments should be cautious in interpreting motor performance data that have been obtained during this critical growth period.

MEASURING CHANGES IN BODY PROPORTIONS

One body proportion measure of interest is the ratio between *sitting height* and stature (sitting height/stature × 100), which describes the contribution of the legs and trunk to total height. The person being measured should sit on a high bench so that the feet do not touch the floor; she should keep the spine erect and eyes focused straight ahead. Measure the distance between the vertex and the sitting surface.

A second measure of proportional growth is the *biacromial/bicristal ratio* (biacromial breadth/bicristal breadth × 100). Biacromial breadth, a measure of shoulder width, is the distance between the right and left acromial processes; bicristal breadth, a measure of hip width, is the distance between the right and left iliocristales (hipbones). These distances are measured with an anthropometer, a sliding caliper, or a length caliper. The person should stand erect with arms hanging naturally by the sides while being measured.

CHANGES IN BODY PROPORTIONS

Here we describe changes in sitting height as it compares with stature and contrast shoulder and hip growth. General body shape and physique are also discussed.

Changes in Sitting Height

At birth, sitting height accounts for 85 percent of total body length. By 6 years of age, sitting height's contribution to total body length has decreased to 55 percent. Typically, the sitting height's contribution to total body length in adulthood is 50 percent (Lowrey, 1986). However, there are several exceptions; for example, black children have slightly shorter sitting heights but longer lower extremities than white children at all ages (Lowrey, 1986).

Until 10 years for girls and 12 years for boys, both sexes exhibit almost the same increases in sitting height (trunk length). Given the overall stature gains during this period, it appears that 55 to 60 percent of stature gains can be attributed to leg growth in both sexes. Usually, however, boys have longer trunks than girls until they are about 12 years old. Because boys are generally taller, this means that prior to adolescence boys have relatively shorter legs than girls regarding total body length (Haubenstricker & Sapp, 1980). During adolescence and adulthood, how-ever, females have shorter legs than males of equal stature (Malina, 1975). See Figure 7-16.

Growth in Shoulder and Hip Width

Even though there are sex differences in body proportions prior to adolescence, the differences are minimal. During adolescence, however, characteristic sexual dimorphisms become apparent. Perhaps the most noticeable is the relation of shoulder width growth to hip width growth. In fact, one of the obvious characteristics of male maturity is a widening of the shoulders. In contrast, girls grow wider through the hips in relation to their shoulder development. See Figure 7-17. The bicristal/biacromial ratio is relatively constant in both boys and girls between 6 and 11 years of age. Thereafter the ratio declines in boys but continues to be relatively stable in girls (Malina & Bouchard, 1991) See Figure 7-18.

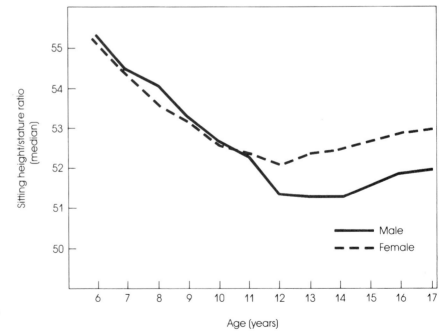

FIGURE 7-16 Sitting height/stature ratio (based on NCHS data, 1974)

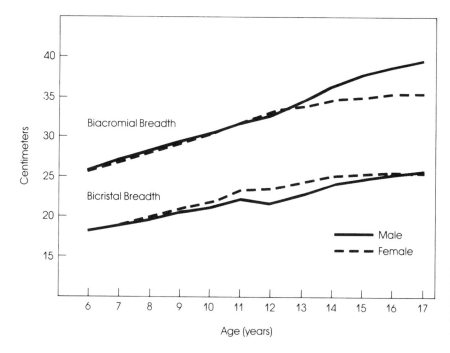

FIGURE 7-17   Mean biacromial and bicristal breadth (based on NCHS data reported in Roche & Malina, 1983)

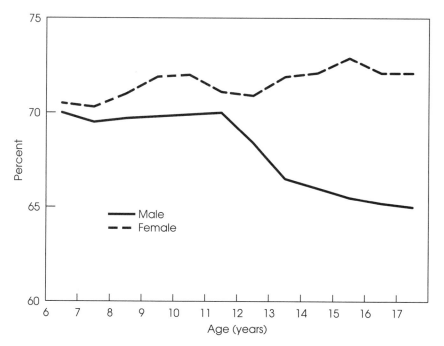

FIGURE 7-18 Bicristal/biacromial breadth × 100 (based on U.S. Health Examination data as reported by Roche and Malina, 1983)

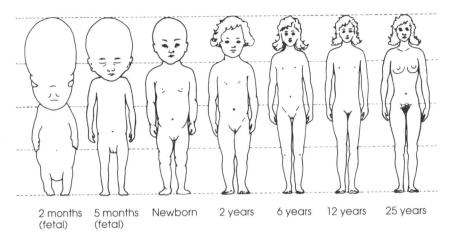

FIGURE 7-19 Changes in body proportions with age. Notice the great changes in the relative size of the head and the lower limbs.

2 months (fetal)   5 months (fetal)   Newborn   2 years   6 years   12 years   25 years

General Body Configuration

Figure 7-19 illustrates changes in body proportions with age. One of the most noticeable characteristics of the newborn is the size of the head in relation to total body length. More specifically, at birth the head contributes about 25 percent to total body length while the lower limbs contribute only 15 percent (Sinclair, 1985). Because the legs and trunk lengthen in relation to the head, the relative position of the body's midpoint descends with age. In other words, the center of gravity slowly descends through the growing years.

Changes in the Center of Gravity

As mentioned, the head, trunk, and legs do not grow proportionately; therefore, a person's center of gravity varies markedly during childhood. Although the anatomical location of the center of gravity changes with age, it remains a relatively constant proportion of total height. Most kinesiologists agree that this ratio of the center of gravity to total height is 53 to 59 percent in the adult, a range of only 6 percent. Dyson (1964) pointed out, however, that in children the ratio of the center of gravity to total height is higher because children carry a larger proportion of their weight in their upper bodies. As a general rule, the center of gravity in the male is slightly higher than that in the female.

At birth, the center of gravity is located approximately 20 centimeters above the trochanters. It slowly descends until it rests at approximately 10 centimeters above the trochanters at maturity. Although this shift of only 10 centimeters seems relatively small, there is a marked change in the center of gravity's anatomical location. In the newborn, 20 centimeters above the trochanters is an area in the lower level of the thoracic cavity at the xiphoid process; in the adult, 10 centimeters above the trochanters brings the center of gravity to the level of the iliac crest at the second or third sacral vertebra.

By the time children enter elementary school (6 years old), their center of gravity has dropped through the abdominal cavity and is located in the vicinity of the umbilicus (Palmer, 1929). The center of gravity then proceeds to descend at a uniform rate toward the proximal end of the lower extremities. This uniform rate of descent is roughly proportional to the increase in stature.

Physique

Thus far our assessment of growth across the lifespan has focused on specific body parts. However, it is important to understand overall body form (physique). The classifying of the human form dates back to Hippocrates. More recently, Sheldon (1940) popularized his method of rating physique, which was based on the premise that three components contribute to the conformation of the entire body. Sheldon described the three components as (1) *endomorphic*—roundness and softness, (2) *mesomorphic*—muscularity, and (3) *ectomorphic*—tallness and thinness. Each physique component is assessed from three standardized photographs. Each photograph is rated on a 7-point scale, with 1 representing the least expression and 7 the highest expression of the selected physique component. For instance, an endomorphic person with a 7-1-1 physique rating is high in endomorphic qualities and low in both mesomorphic and ectomorphic qualities—in other words, a very fat person.

Heath and Carter (1967) modified Sheldon's approach to include not only photographic procedures, but also anthropometric procedures. Practically speaking, this method is most frequently employed in its anthropometric form since it eliminates the moral and ethical problems associated with obtaining nude photographs.

The Heath-Carter *somatotype* is obtained as follows: The endomorphic component is derived from summing the skinfolds taken at the triceps, subscapular and suprailiac (anterior superior spine of the iliac crest). The mesomorphic component is adjusted for stature and is derived from biepicondylar breadth, bicondylar breadth, flexed-upper arm circumference and calf circumference. These latter two measurements are corrected by subtracting the skinfold measurement of the mid tricep and medial calf from their corresponding circumference measurement. According to Heath and Carter, this component represents a measure of lean body mass. The final component, the ectomorphic component, is based on stature divided by the cube root of body weight. This measure is also referred to as the *ponderal index*. One major criticism of this approach is its failure to include a trunk measure because the trunk is definitely a major component making-up ones physique.

Using data from the Harpenden Growth Study, Malina and Bouchard (1991) have concluded that changes in physique tend to appear between 3 or 4 and 8 years of age. The physique changes at these times are a result of a redistribution of subcutaneous fat, the development of lean muscle, and a lengthening of the legs relative to stature. Changes in physique are once again noticed during adolescence as sexual dimorphisms become apparent. Nevertheless, most modifications in somatotype are minor in nature.

BODY PROPORTIONS: INTERRELATIONSHIP WITH MOTOR PERFORMANCE

Because young children are top-heavy, their high center of gravity and small base of support can limit their early motor performance. Lack of balance is a major obstacle children must overcome before they are able to walk. In fact, balance is an important quality necessary for performing all fundamental motor tasks. For instance, during most physical education classes, children are required to manipulate objects, most often some type of playground ball. Whenever a child holds an object such as a playground ball, the weight of the object becomes part of the child's body weight, so the youngster's center of gravity is then further displaced in the direction of the added weight. This shift in the center of gravity can influence performance. Consider a kindergarten student who is told to catch a 13-inch playground ball. This young child, who already has a relatively high center of gravity, must now maintain control of the thrown projectile while maintaining balance. As a result of the added weight, the child is apt to lose balance in a forward direction, which is most likely why some children drop objects they momentarily have control of. They catch the object but then must release it to regain their balance. Generally, Isaacs (1976) believed that a child's high center of gravity sometimes makes it difficult for the child to come to a fast, complete stop when the activity involves a fast forward or backward movement. Furthermore, Olson (1959) suggested that this high center of gravity is why some young children have difficulty learning to perform such skills as skating and bicycling with instruction alone.

The ratio of trunk length to leg length can also potentially influence motor performance. A recent longitudinal investigation that examined the influences of physical growth on motor performance suggested that leg length in terms of total body height could have some impact on balance tasks and certain types of power events (Haubenstricker & Sapp, 1980). The female's superior balancing ability may be partly due to a combination of these factors: that is, the female's shorter legs and broader pelvis establish a lower center of gravity, hence better balancing ability (Klafs & Lyon, 1978). Although these somatic characteristics are an asset for enhancing balance, they are disadvantages in other tasks. For instance, during adolescence the general structure of the female pelvis places a girl at a disadvantage in both running and jumping events (Oxendine, 1984). In addition, Dintiman & Ward (1988) pointed out that leg length is one of three factors that can account for individual differences in sprinting speed. And as mentioned earlier, male leg length is generally greater than female leg length following adolescence.

Arm length also appears to influence motor performance. Haubenstricker and Sapp (1980) noted that the male's greater shoulder width and arm length could be an advantage to boys in throwing tasks. Oxendine supported this view when he wrote that "after age eleven boys have greater limb lengths and thus a mechanical advantage in some activities, such as throwing and striking with force" (1984, p. 213).

Haubenstricker and Sapp (1980) noted that factor analysis studies of physical growth and motor performance indicate that as much as 25 percent or more of the variance can be attributed to body size and structure. For more information regarding physical constraints and the development of motor skills, consult Newell (1984) and Kugler, Kelso, and Turvey (1982).

EXERCISE AND BONE GROWTH: INTERRELATIONSHIPS

Throughout this chapter we emphasize the role of bone growth in relation to increases in stature, sitting height, and limb length. This section sheds light on one important question: How do exercise and physical activity affect bone growth?

When studying the effects of exercise on bone growth, one must understand that bones grow three different ways: in length, width, and density. Most research examining the effects of exercise on bone length report little differences between the bone lengths of active and inactive children (Parizkova,

1968) as measured as a function of stature. The length of the weight-bearing long bones appears affected very little, if any, by exercise. In contrast, Buskirk, Andersen, and Brozek (1956) reported longer forearm bones and longer dominant hand bones in seven nationally ranked tennis players when these measures were compared with the players' nondominant side. However, note that although these bones in the upper extremities were placed under much stress, they did not perform constant weight-bearing functions.

The research examining the effects of exercise on bone density is more precise. We know that exercise increases bone density, whereas inactivity is associated with bone decalcification. Bone decalcification is readily apparent following periods of inactivity, particularly in bedridden patients or people with immobilized limbs. The Gemini astronauts experienced a bone-decalcification problem: Within 4 to 14 days they lost as much as 3 percent of their bone density from being in a weightless environment (Vose, 1974). Hence, weight-bearing activities are necessary to stimulate increases in bone density.

In general, bone tends to be deposited faster than it is broken down up to about 35 years of age for both males and females (Loucks, 1988). However, the density increases more slowly in females than males so that at its peak, the bone density of males exceeds that of females. After age 35, bone mineral is lost at a faster rate than it is deposited, particularly in inactive older adults and at the time of menopause in women. Loucks (1988) suggests that *osteoporosis* (loss of bone mineral to the point that it renders a bone susceptible to fracture) prevention programs be started before old age. More specifically, she recommends that steps be taken to increase the rate of bone deposition in adolescent girls. Furthermore, she suggests sex steroid therapy at the time of menopause, along with maintaining an active lifestyle.

The effect of exercise on bone growth is perhaps most dramatically illustrated in a case study reported by Houston and summarized by Bailey, Malina, and Rasmussen (1978). They described a young male who was born with one lower leg bone in one extremity instead of the usual two. Eighteen months after the small thin fibula was surgically relocated so it could bear weight, this bone took on the size, shape, and strength of the tibia, thus illustrating the effects of weight-bearing stress on bone growth.

Much remains to be learned about the effects of exercise on human bone growth. We know, however, that a minimal amount of physical activity is needed to sustain normal growth. Unfortunately, at this time no one has defined this minimal level.

MATURATION AND DEVELOPMENTAL AGE

The human organism spends approximately one-quarter of its lifespan in a state of physical growth. These physical changes become markedly noticeable in the developmental stage known as *adolescence*. Adolescence is characterized by rapid physical, biochemical, social, and emotional changes and involves 6 years, or approximately one-third, of a youngster's growing period. The onset of adolescence and the time necessary to advance from a state of immature to mature development varies from person to person both within and between the sexes.

Because changes during adolescence are not always discernible, *chronological age* is generally used to denote a person's level of maturity. *Developmental age,* however, is by far a better indicator of maturity than is chronological age, which simply denotes the length of time from birth but fails to address individual variation in rate of maturation. Fortunately, however, landmark parameters tied to physiological events occur in all people. These parameters share a common developmental endpoint and thus can be used for determining whether a child is lagging behind peers or springing ahead of them. Height and weight measures are inadequate because people differ in mature stature and weight. However, a set of predictable physiological parameters can be monitored in all persons. The most frequently used parameters are skeletal maturity, dental maturity, age of menarche, and genitalia maturity.

Skeletal Maturity

Skeletal age is the most widely accepted assessment procedure for determining stage of maturation. During growth, predictable changes in bone structure, observable via radiography, enable professionals to determine skeletal age. As a child matures, primary and secondary centers of bone ossify, rendering them opaque to x-ray. The progressive enlargement of these ossified bone centers can be monitored during the growth years and compared to a set of standard films in which each film in a series represents bone development of children of a similar age. The area of the body most frequently x-rayed is the left hand and wrist (see Figures 7-20 to 7-22). The first set of standardized radiographs of the hand and wrist were developed in 1937 by T. Todd and published in the same year in the now classic text *Atlas of Skeletal Maturation.* To date, the most carefully prepared atlases have been published by Todd's colleagues at Case Western Reserve University, in particular the atlas by Greulich and Pyle (1959), which is still in use today. Tanner (Tanner et al., 1975) developed a different technique of assessing skeletal maturity (Tanner-Whitehouse Method 2), but the Gruelich-Pyle standards remain the most appropriate for American children because the TW2 method was standardized with British children.

Even though the hand and wrist are the most popular assessment site, some researchers are now recommending other areas of the body, particularly the knee, using a method known as the Roche-Wainer-Thissen (RWT) technique (Roche, 1992). Which of the two sites offers the best assessment is still in question. Roche (1979), however, suggested that the choice should be guided by the purpose of the assessment. For instance, Roche believed the knee is the most appropriate site if information is being sought concerning stature. He also suggested using the knee up to 4 years of age and toward the end of maturation because during this period few maturational changes are apparent in the hand and wrist.

Dental Maturity

The development and emergence of teeth also provide important information for estimating physical maturity. There are two approaches to studying dental maturation in both deciduous (temporary) and permanent teeth. The first approach is simply counting the number of teeth that have emerged. In fact, prior to the advent of x-ray, emergence of the second molar was accepted as proof of age to work in English factories, and later, dental emergence was used for determining when a child was old enough to enter school (Demirjiam, 1979).

More recently, researchers have used radiographs to assess *dental age*. Similar to the evaluation process used for determining skeletal age, radiographs

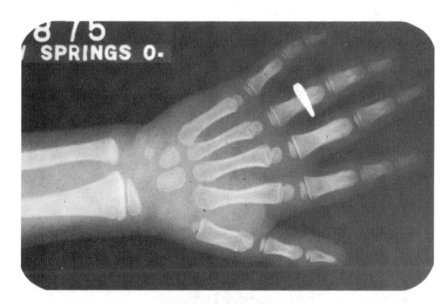

FIGURE 7-20   Hand wrist x-ray of a 3-year-old

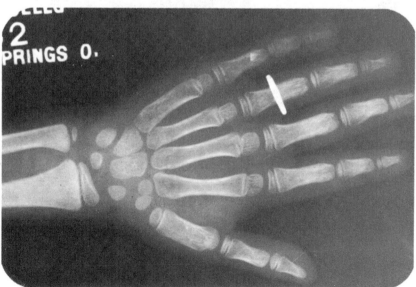

FIGURE 7-21   Hand wrist x-ray of a 5-year-old

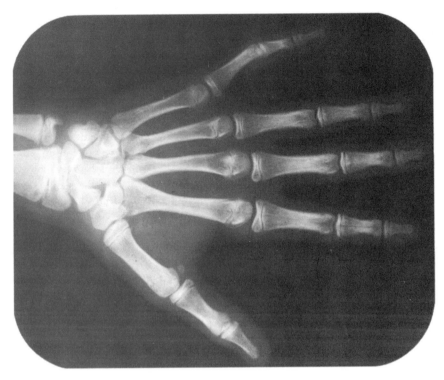

FIGURE 7-22 Hand wrist x-ray of a 14-year-old

indicate stages of calcification in both the teeth and the jaw. The use of radiographs is now considered the technique of choice because they provide a permanent record and are a way to longitudinally compare continuous sequences of development stages.

Age of Menarche

Some professionals consider the *age of menarche* an important event useful for estimating maturation (Beunen et al., 1978; Johnston, 1974), even though the event does not generally occur until relatively late in puberty. In fact, female peak growth spurt in height is over at this point, so the female is in a period of maximal growth deceleration when this milestone appears. For 95 percent of the female population, the event occurs between a chronological age of 11 and 15 ($\bar{x}$ = 12.3 – 12.8 years; Wells & Plowman, 1988). The age span, however, at which menarche occurs tends to be more closely related to skeletal maturity (12 to 14 1/2 bone-age years)

than chronological age. Even though menarche signifies the attainment of mature uterine development, it does not necessarily denote mature reproductive functioning; early menstrual cycles tend to be irregular, and often an egg is not shed from the ovary.

Researchers rely on one of the three methods for determining or estimating the date of the first menstrual flow. The most reliable and accurate technique is longitudinally following a group of females until the event occurs. Because this technique is so time-consuming, the event is most often estimated by a second technique, retrospective questioning. For instance, Beunen and colleagues (1978) asked their experimental population the following questions to determine date of onset:

1. Do you know what menstruation means?

2. Have you already menstruated?

3. Can you remember the exact date of your first menstruation?

To increase the accuracy of recall, the investigator should include questions that focus on associated events. For example, "What grade were you in?" and "Was the event close to your birthday?" The third method is statistical: calculating normative values for a large female population.

Genitalia Maturity

An ancillary method for rating maturation is evaluating by visual inspection stages of pubertal development. In the female this consists of assessing pubic hair and breast development; in the male, pubic hair as well as changes in the size of the reproductive organs are evaluated. Tables 7-6 and 7-7 describe each developmental stage. For a complete set of standardized photographs depicting each stage of development, refer to the work of Rauh and Brookman (1978).

If genitalia assessment is not feasible (because of ethical and cultural factors), a compromise is to allow the individuals to perform self-evaluation in the privacy of their own homes.

MATURATION: INTERRELATIONSHIP WITH MOTOR PERFORMANCE

Researchers recognize that physically advanced people generally perform selected motor tasks more proficiently than their less mature counterparts. For instance, it has been shown that youth baseball success is related to skeletal maturity. More specifically, data collected during the 1957 Little League World Series indicated that 71 percent of the participants had advanced skeletal ages relative to their chronological ages, while only 29 percent of the participants were delayed in skeletal age (Krogman, 1959). Hale (1956) reported somewhat similar findings when he assessed the pubic hair development of 112 participants during the 1955 Little League World Series. Not only did he find a majority of the young participants either in puberty

TABLE 7-6   Development of Pubic Hair

Female
Stage 1: There is no pubic hair.
Stage 2: There is sparse growth of long, lightly pigmented, downy hair, straight or only slightly curled, primarily along the labia.
Stage 3: The hair is considerably darker, coarser, and more curled. The hair spreads sparsely over the junction of the pubes.
Stage 4: The hair, now adult in type, covers a smaller area than in the adult.
Stage 5: The hair is adult in quantity and type.

Male
Stage 1: There is no public hair.
Stage 2: There is a sparse growth of long, slightly pigmented, downy hair, straight or only slightly curled, primarily at the base of the penis.
Stage 3: The hair is considerably darker, coarser, and more curled. The hair spreads sparsely over the junction of the pubes.
Stage 4: The hair, now adult in type, covers a smaller area than in the adult.
Stage 5: The hair is adult in quantity and type.

Used with permission of Ross Laboratories, Columbus, Ohio, from *Children Are Different*, pp. 25–29, © 1978, Ross Laboratories.

TABLE 7-7   Development of Female Breast and Male Genitalia

Female Breast

Stage 1: The breasts are preadolescent. There is elevation of the papilla only.

Stage 2: Breast bud stage. A small mound is formed by the elevation of the breast and papilla. The areolar diameter enlarges.

Stage 3: There is further enlargement of breasts and areola with no separation of their contours.

Stage 4: There is a projection of the areola and papilla to form a secondary mound above the level of the breast.

Stage 5: The breasts resemble those of a mature female as the areola has recessed to the general contour of the breast.

Male Genitalia

Stage 1: The penis, testes, and scrotum are of childhood size.

Stage 2: There is enlargement of the scrotum and testes, but the penis usually does not enlarge. The scrotal skin reddens.

Stage 3: There is further growth of the testes and scrotum and enlargement of the penis, mainly in length.

Stage 4: There is still further growth of the testes and scrotum and increased size of the penis, especially in breadth.

Stage 5: The genitalia are adult in size and shape.

Used with permission of Ross Laboratories, Columbus, Ohio, from *Children Are Different*, pp. 25–29, © 1978, Ross Laboratories.

(37.5 percent) or postpuberty (45.5 percent), he also found that the most important positions were played by postpubescent individuals; these positions were pitcher, first base, and left field. In addition, the postpubescent youngsters held the all-important fourth position in the batting order. Thus, these postpubescent athletes were bigger and stronger than their prepubescent opponents. Level of maturation as determined by pubic hair assessment has been found to correlate positively with the prediction of strength in adolescent boys (Bastos & Hegg, 1984).

In studying the young male elite athlete, Malina concluded that

early maturation, with its concomitant size and strength advantages, constitutes an asset positively associated with success in several sports. However, as adolescence approaches its termination, the maturity status of the youngsters is of less significance as the catch-up of late-maturing boys reduces the size differences so apparent in early adolescence (1984, p. 56).

This is essentially what Clark (1971) found in his now classic Medford Growth Study, namely, that the superior elementary school athlete may no longer be outstanding in junior high school and that the superior junior high school athlete may not have been outstanding in elementary school. In fact, once the late-maturing person has reached a state of post-pubescent development, he is generally larger and has more athletic success simply because he has had a longer growth period.

Although early maturation may give boys an early athletic advantage, the opposite generally is true for girls. With the exception of swimming, female athletic participation is associated with delayed biological maturation. Malina and associates (1979) first suggested that delayed biological maturation may give young girls a slight competitive edge in such Olympic events as volleyball. Beunen and colleagues (1978) also studied the relationship between age of menarche and motor performance in 398 Belgian school girls. They found the motor performances of late-maturing girls superior to the motor performances of early- and average-maturing girls on such tasks as trunk strength, functional strength, running speed, and speed of limb movement. Thus, "in general, motor performance is negatively related to biological maturity status in girls but positively related to biological maturity status in boys" (Beunen & Malina, 1988, p. 522).

Many professionals have tried to explain why this maturity-performance relationship is opposite that observed in boys. Espenschade and Eckert (cited in Beunen et al., 1978) proposed one popular hypothesis. They speculated that because menarche denotes the peak increase in motor performance, late-maturing girls have more interest in performing motor skills for a longer period of time.

SUMMARY

Growth in both stature and weight rapidly decelerates after the fourth prenatal month. Stature and weight growth remain relatively constant during the childhood years, only to accelerate again in the phase of development known as adolescence. This rapid change in body size is sometimes accompanied by a period of adolescent awkwardness, especially in boys. However, this decline in motor performance is only temporary.

During childhood, children are top-heavy; that is, they have a high center of gravity. This high center of gravity can affect children's stability.

The male's wider shoulders and longer arms give him an advantage in throwing events. On the other hand, the female is generally superior in balancing, perhaps because of her shorter legs and broader pelvis.

Growth data can be visually inspected by plotting the data on a distance curve or velocity curve. The distance curve plots accumulative growth obtained over time; a velocity curve plots the rate of change in growth per unit of time.

Physical activity affects bone density and bone width but does not influence bone length.

Developmental age is a better indicator of maturity than is chronological age. Level of maturity can be determined by skeletal maturity, dental maturity, age of menarche, and genitalia maturity.

Level of maturation can influence motor performance. In general, research indicates that postpubescent males initially outperform prepubescent males. However, once the late-maturing person reaches adolescence, this advantage is no longer evident. Nevertheless, although early maturation is associated with superior athletic performance for boys, the opposite is generally true for girls, except for female swimmers.

KEY TERMS

Adolescence	Knee height
Adolescent awkwardness	Mesomorphic
	Midgrowth spurt
Age of menarche	Osteoporosis
Beam-type scale	Peak height velocity
Biacromial/bicristal ratio	Peak weight velocity
	Ponderal index
Chronological age	Recumbent length
Dental age	Sitting height
Developmental age	Skeletal age
Distance curve	Somatotype
Ectomorphic	Stature
Endomorphic	Velocity curve
Genitalia maturity	Vertex

CHAPTER 8

Physiological Changes: Health-Related Physical Fitness

Within the last decade, the emphasis on physical fitness in both the workplace and society has shifted from motor fitness or athletic ability to what is now commonly referred to as health-related or physiological fitness. The primary thrust behind this movement is the popular notion that American children and youth are less fit today than children of 20 years ago.

The most frequently identified components that make up health-related fitness include cardiovascular endurance, body composition, flexibility, and muscular strength. Acceptable levels of fitness in each are believed, by some, to lead to a better quality of life for both children and adults.

This chapter examines each of the four components of health-related physical fitness. We look at the evolution of each component, paying particular attention to how an active lifestyle affects these components. In addition, laboratory data and field-test performance data are examined. Our field-test reference data on children and adolescents come from the National Children and Youth Fitness Studies I and II (NCYFS), which were done in 1985 and 1987. For a complete description of these two studies, refer to Chapter 17.

CARDIOVASCULAR FITNESS

Cardiovascular fitness is a special form of muscular endurance. It is the efficiency of the heart, lungs, and vascular system in delivering oxygen to the working muscle tissues so that prolonged physical work can be maintained. A person's ability to deliver oxygen to the working muscles is affected by many physiological parameters, including heart rate, stroke volume, cardiac output, and maximal oxygen consumption. Here we examine changes that occur in each parameter as a result of maturation, aging, and physical training.

Heart Rate

Heart rate (*HR*), the number of times the heart beats each minute, is a physiological parameter that undergoes much change during the lifespan. The heart rate is first evidenced about the fourth prenatal week, when the fetal heart begins to beat. Characteristically, fetal HR is rapid and frequently irregular. Immediately following birth, HR usually decreases and often is accompanied by intermittent periods of *bradycardia* (slow HR). Once independent breathing and in turn adequate blood oxygenation have been established, HR again increases but remains below fetal levels (Timiras, 1972).

At rest, children's HRs are consistently higher than adults'. In fact, the newborn infant will average about 140 beats per minute. With time (age), however, this resting heart rate will progressively decelerate. For example, by 1 year of age the average resting HR will have declined an average of 40 beats per minute. This trend is evident until late adolescence, whereupon young males will exhibit an average HR of about 57 to 60 beats per minute while the young female will average between 62 to 63 beats per minute (Malina & Bouchard, 1991). Thus resting HR can be expected to decline by about 50 percent from birth to maturity. In young adulthood the average HR among 20-year-old males and females averages 75 to 79 beats per minute, respectively. Thereafter, there is little change in resting HR until 60 years of age, when the HR again decreases slightly (Montoye, Willis, & Cunningham, 1974).

There is a linear relationship between physical work, stress, and HR. That is, up to a point, increases in workload increase HR. During labor contractions, fetal HR frequently exceeds 200 beats per minute. Furthermore, newborn crying, a form of physical work, induces rates greater than 170 beats per minute (Vaughan, 1975). In preadolescent children,

HR responses to submaximal work decline with age. Bouchard and colleagues (1977) found the submaximal HRs of 8-year-old subjects to be as much as 30 to 40 beats per minute faster in comparison to 18-year-old subjects, even though the workload was the same. Younger children most likely have higher HRs to compensate for their smaller stroke volume (Bar-Or, 1983).

Unlike submaximal HR, which declines with age, maximal HR does not decline until after maturity. The maximal HR of both children and adolescents is from 195 to 220 beats per minute. For young men and women the maximal HR generally peaks at values just under 200 beats per minute. This decline in heart rate is approximately 0.8 beats/minute/year of age (Bar-Or, 1983) and is independent of gender. Rates as high as 250 to 300 beats per minute have been reported during short bursts of activity, but when the activity is sustained, rates are significantly lower (Shephard, 1994).

The following formula provides a general estimate of maximal HR in adult populations, although it does tend to underestimate the value (Astrand & Rodahl, 1986).

$$\text{Maximal HR} = 220 - \text{age (years)}$$

To date, researchers have not been able to ascertain why HR declines with age; they suspect it is due to changes in the contractile properties of the cardiac muscle or alternations in the nervous control of the heart, which probably occur with age.

Stroke Volume

With each contraction of the heart, a certain volume of blood, called *stroke volume* (*SV*), is ejected from the left ventricle into general circulation via the aorta. In other words, stroke volume is the amount of blood pumped from the heart with each beat. The size of the stroke volume is limited by a number of factors, including heart size, contractile force of the myocardial (heart) tissue, vascular resistance to blood flow, and venous return (the rate blood is returned to the right side of the heart).

At all levels of physical work, SV is substantially lower in children than adults, most likely because of the child's smaller heart, which, as mentioned, partly explains children's need for higher HRs. At birth SV is only 3 to 4 ml per ventricular contraction. This value increases tenfold by adolescence to about 40 ml. This value remains quite stable until the adolescence growth spurt where it rapidly accelerates to about 60 ml at rest (Malina & Bouchard, 1991). In the typical untrained adult male the SV is usually between 70 and 80 milliliters per beat. This range is significantly elevated in highly trained people. Even at rest, the aerobically trained person's SV is 100 to 110 milliliters per beat (Fox, 1994).

Maximal SV is achieved during submaximal work, somewhere between 30 to 50 percent of aerobic power (cited in Shephard, 1977). A further increase in workload is not likely to significantly increase SV. During exercise, the untrained male can expect to attain an SV of 110 to 120 milliliters per beat. Conversely, the highly trained male is capable of obtaining values as high as 200 milliliters per beat, although the average values are 150 to 170 milliliters per beat (Fox, 1984). Nevertheless, at all levels of work, SV is higher in males than in females.

Like most other physiological parameters, age can affect SV. A person's SV at rest can fall as much as 30 percent between the ages of 25 and 85. During light exercise, however, elderly individuals are capable of maintaining SV slightly less than that of a young adult. But when workloads become exhausting, SV decreases 10 to 20 percent in elderly individuals (Shephard, 1981).

Cardiac Output

Cardiac output is the amount of blood that can be pumped out of the heart in 1 minute. Thus, cardiac output is the product of heart rate and stroke volume. Cardiac output is less in children than in adults, for both resting and exercising states. Although children are capable of obtaining a higher exercise HR than adults, their elevated HR is not enough to compensate for the marked difference in stroke volume.

Later in this chapter we discuss whether or not this lower cardiac output is of significance regarding maximal aerobic power.

At rest, adults have a cardiac output of approximately 5 liters per minute. With the onset of exercise, cardiac output rises in both children and adults until it reaches a new steady state. Two of the most important factors affecting ultimate maximal cardiac output are level of physical condition and age. The untrained adult generally achieves a maximal cardiac output of 20 to 25 liters per minute; a trained adult can achieve a maximal cardiac output 10 liters per minute greater than can the untrained adult.

Because both HR and SV decrease with age, so does resting cardiac output. Specifically, there is a 58 percent reduction in the amount of blood the heart can pump in a given unit of time between the ages of 25 and 85. Thus resting cardiac output, on the average, declines approximately 1 percent per year after age 25. There is a somewhat similar pattern for maximal cardiac output: Cardiac function typically declines 20 to 30 percent by age 65 (Fitzgerald, 1985).

Maximal Oxygen Consumption

An increase in the level of physical work brings a corresponding increased need for oxygen among the active muscles. Thus human beings' ability to sustain physical work for extended periods is directly related to their ability to transport oxygen to the working muscle tissue. The largest amount of oxygen that a human can consume at the tissue level is the *maximal oxygen consumption* ($\dot{V}O_2$ max). Research physiologist Herbert deVries referred to this physiological measure as "the best single measure of *physical working capacity*" (1983, p. 79).

There is abundant information about $\dot{V}O_2$ max consumption in adults and older children, but almost no data on children younger than 6 years. It is difficult to study this population because it is hard to motivate young children to an all-out maximal effort. Nevertheless, several researchers have undertaken the challenge of using subjects younger than 6 years (Mrzena & Macek, 1978). In Mrzena and Macek's study, two groups of preschool children between 3 and 5 years of age were required to walk or run on a treadmill. Group 1 performed for 5 minutes at each of the following speeds: 3, 4, and 5 kilometers per hour. In contrast, group 2 performed at 4 kilometers per hour, but instead of increasing treadmill speed, the researchers increased the treadmill's grade 5 degrees every 5 minutes until the treadmill was at a 15-degree grade. In group 1, the highest oxygen consumption value a child attained was 22.06 ± 4.7 milliliters per kilogram of body weight per minute (ml/kg/min). Oxygen consumption was higher in the second group, where the highest value attained was 28.7 ± 4.84 ml/kg/min. This study was limited by the size of the subject pool: Group 1 contained only 4 children, and group 2 had only 10 children.

Results involving children older than 6 years are fairly consistent. In developed countries, the $\dot{V}O_2$ max for boys is fairly constant during the childhood and adolescent years. Typical values for individuals 6 to 18 years old is 48 to 50 ml/kg/min (Shephard, 1978). Boys generally exhibit a spurt in maximal oxygen consumption at puberty, but it is believed that this increase is more directly related to increases in body size than to a true increase in oxygen extraction. This phenomenon raises an interesting point: Although older children obtain higher $\dot{V}O_2$ max values than do younger children, when body weight is used to standardize the measures, the discrepancy in values is no longer as great.

This point is apparent when comparing the $\dot{V}O_2$ max of young boys to that of young girls. When absolute values between the genders are compared without body weight being standardized, young boys evidence much higher values than do young girls. However, when body weight is introduced as a standardization factor, girls' working capacity is nearly as good as that of the young boys. On the average, in developed countries, young girls between 6 and 8 years of age exhibit $\dot{V}O_2$ max values of 50 ml/kg/min (Shephard, 1981). Unfortunately, girls' $\dot{V}O_2$ max declines very early in life. Shephard (1981) reported decreases in this physiological parameter in the

young female as early as 10 years. Rutenfranz and colleagues (1981) reported similar findings. In their longitudinal research, they found the decline most evident beyond 12 to 13 years of age (cited by Cunningham, Paterson, & Blimkie, 1984). Shephard speculated that this early decline is caused by the female's increase in body fat at maturation, lower blood hemoglobin concentrations at puberty, and lesser degree of large-muscle development in the lower extremities.

With age, the body's ability to acquire and deliver oxygen to the working tissue is altered, reducing physical work capacity. The rate of decline in $\dot{V}O_2$ max is between 9 and 15 percent between 45 and 55 years of age. This rate of decline accelerates in the mid 50s. For instance, a 70-year-old's physical work capacity is only one-half of what a person 50 years younger can attain (Kenney, 1982). This loss of aerobic power is caused by many factors, including increase in fat tissue and a subsequent decrease in lean muscle tissue, decreased cardiac output, and a decrease in physical activity (which so often accompanies retirement). Later in the chapter we discuss how an active lifestyle can alter or delay the decline in $\dot{V}O_2$ max.

Physical Activity and Cardiovascular Fitness in Childhood

Our understanding of the effects of physical activity on cardiovascular fitness in young children is both fragmented and limited. Also, many findings are frequently contradictory, most likely because different conditioning protocols between studies and a host of methodological factors have been used. For instance, when long-term training is used, the researcher must distinguish between training effects and those effects caused primarily by the natural growth and maturation process. Authorities have recognized that many of the reported changes following physical training occur naturally through maturation (Bar-Or, 1983); for example, lower resting and submaximal HRs are known to be by-products of physical training. But this physiological parameter naturally declines with age. Because of this predicament, Bar-Or suggested that research data must be viewed as occurring with conditioning and training, not necessarily as a *result of* conditioning or training (Bar-Or, 1983).

Rowland (1985) critically analyzed the research literature regarding aerobic responses to endurance training in preadolescent children. After reviewing 14 studies, Rowland excluded five because they had not used training regimens known to alter fitness in adult populations. Of the remaining nine studies, eight examined the influence of endurance training on $\dot{V}O_2$ max; six of these eight studies reported gains in $\dot{V}O_2$ max ranging from 7 to 26 percent, with mean gains of 14 percent. The data from these studies appear to indicate that adult training protocols are effective in improving aerobic capacity, but Rowland makes a convincing argument as to why these findings should be interpreted with caution. The limiting factors within these studies included small subject pools (6 to 16 subjects); high drop-out rates, resulting in subjects who are highly motivated toward physical activity; and the inclusion of subjects who were clearly not representative of a pediatric population.

A growing amount of evidence questions the benefit of endurance training for improving aerobic capacity in preadolescent children. This controversy is apparent in both short-term (Stewart & Gutin, 1976) and long-term (Ekblom, 1969) training studies. In the 1976 Stewart and Gutin study, 13 boys age 10 to 12 years trained 4 days per week for 8 weeks at an average intensity of 90 percent maximal HR. Following the experimental program, no significant improvement in $\dot{V}O_2$ max was noted. The researchers concluded that the already high $\dot{V}O_2$ max of children is difficult to improve, particularly in light of their already active lifestyle. Ekblom (1969) reported similar results in his longitudinal study, which required 11- to 13.6-year-old boys to train for 6 and 32 months. $\dot{V}O_2$ max rose 10 percent after 6 months and 15 and 18 percent after 32 months. However, these values were not significantly different from the values of a control group. Thus, these improvements are thought to be a result of growth, not training.

Payne and Morrow (1993) have analyzed the professional literature using a meta-analysis in an attempt to shed light on this important question regarding the effects of exercise on $\dot{V}O_2$ max in children. Their findings were based on the analysis of 28 studies resulting in 70 effect sizes. Data was also analyzed according to research design (cross-sectional and pretest/posttest). The authors concluded that findings from the cross-sectional studies must be interpreted with caution since the effect sizes calculated on these subjects may have been a reflection of "self-selection." In other words, these subjects could have been attracted to their sport because of their preexisting physiological predisposition to successful play. Those subjects who were part of a pretest/posttest design improved $\dot{V}O_2$ max by only about 2 ml/kg/min. Results indicate that changes in $\dot{V}O_2$ max in children are small to moderate and are a function of the experimental design used.

Even though mounting evidence questions the value of endurance training in preadolescent children, some experts argue that training does improve performance. Bar-Or (1983) believes that training can improve product performance by improving mechanical efficiency. For example, training can improve mechanical aspects of running style without an associated rise in aerobic capacity, with the end result being better run times.

Can endurance training improve aerobic capacity in preadolescent children? The answer remains unclear and must await the findings of better-controlled scientific research.

Cardiovascular Endurance Field-Test Data on Children and Adolescents

While a maximum treadmill test is the preferred method for determining cardiovascular efficiency ($\dot{V}O_2$ max) (Rowland, 1993), this laboratory procedure is not practical when a large number of individuals must be assessed. Instead, a more practical alternative is the use of some type of *field test*. Currently, the most popular field test of cardiovascular endurance is a timed distance run.

In the two NCYFS, two different timed distance events were used as a measure of cardiovascular endurance. Children between 6 and 7 years of age ran 1/2 mile while those between 8 and 18 years of age ran 1 mile. The average run times as reported in the NCYFS (Ross & Gilbert, 1985; Ross & Pate, 1987) are reported in Figure 8-1. With age, there is a steady improvement in run-time performance. Boys were found to peak at 16 years of age and girls at 14 years of age. Performance tends to level off after these ages with boys running the mile in slightly over 8 minutes (range: 7:44–8:20) and girls running the mile in slightly over 11 minutes (range: 10:42–11:14). On average, boys run faster than girls at all ages.

Pate and Shephard (1989) have noted that it is incorrect to assume that the yearly improvement in run-time performance is indicative of improved weight-relative $\dot{V}O_2$ max. Instead, this improvement in performance can in part be explained by a decrease in the weight-relative oxygen cost of running that results from increased leg length. Furthermore, as noted earlier, improved running technique and a better understanding of "pace" can also contribute to improved performance times.

Physical Activity and Cardiovascular Fitness in Adulthood

The effects of endurance training on the cardiovascular system of young and middle-aged adults are well documented. Authorities generally agree that to attain beneficial effects, a person must perform large-muscle activities 3 to 5 days per week for 20 to 60 minutes at an HR intensity of 60 to 85 percent of maximum. Such a program will increase physical work capacity. During submaximal work SV will increase and HR will be lower, cardiac output will increase, HR recovery following physical work will be faster, and $\dot{V}O_2$ max will increase.

Less is known about the effects of physical training in late adulthood. Frequently asked questions regarding exercise training and the elderly are: "What effect does a physical exercise training pro-

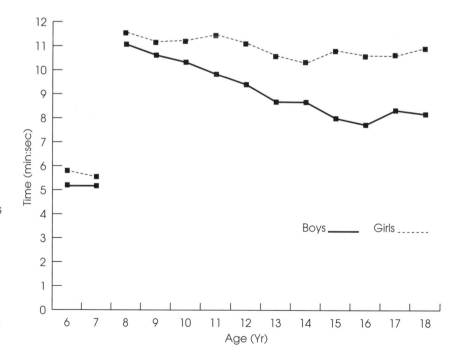

Figure 8-1 Average distance walk/run times for boys and girls based on findings of the National Children and Youth Fitness Studies I and II. Ages 6–7: 1/2 mile; ages 8–18: 1 mile.

SOURCE: As reported by Ross and Gilbert (1985) and Ross and Pate (1987).

gram have on the physical work capacities of elderly people?" "Can long-term training offset the decline in physical work capacity that sedentary people exhibit?"

After reviewing several longitudinal studies, Shephard (1978) concluded that the rate of decline in $\dot{V}O_2$ max in male athletes was about 0.60 ml/kg/min per year. The rate of decline in the general population has been established as about 1 percent per year. "In absolute terms, the rate of loss seems similar in active and in sedentary individuals, but because the athlete starts with a large working capacity, his relative loss is substantially smaller" (Shephard, 1978, p. 245).

Obviously, not all individuals age at the same rate. Take, for example, the athletic feats that are shown in Table 8-1. These performances were accomplished by individuals participating in the U.S. National Senior Sports Classic IV, which was recently held in Baton Rouge, Louisiana (U.S. National Senior Sports Organization, 1993).

What makes these individuals so different from the general population? Most authorities believe it is their active lifestyle. It has been suggested that as much as 50 percent of the functional declines that mediate physical performance are due to disuse rather than aging (deVries & Adams, 1972; Smith &

Gilligan, 1983). This becomes evident in long-term training studies. For example, in one longitudinal study spanning 13 years, the researchers found that former athletes who trained in youth but no longer maintained active lifestyles exhibited declines in aerobic capacity equal to those in the general population (Robinson et al., 1973). In this longitudinal sample, only those individuals who maintained an active lifestyle throughout middle adulthood were able to slow down the rate of deterioration of, and in some cases even improve upon, their aerobic capacity (Robinson et al., 1975). Similarly, Pollock (1974) found that endurance runners over 70 years of age had a maximum aerobic capacity that was 14 percent greater than that of their sedentary counterparts who were 20 to 30 years younger. Similar findings have been reported in short-term studies (Pollock et al., 1976), which should be of particular interest to older individuals who wonder whether it is too late for them to establish a regimen of aerobic activity. Shephard "has projected that commencement of regular fitness training at the time of retirement may delay the age at which environmental demands exceed physical capabilities (i.e., the age of dependency) by as much as 8 years" (cited in Stones & Kozma, 1985).

TABLE 8-1   Selected Winning Performances for Men and Women at the U.S. National Senior Sports Classic IV: The Senior Olympics

	Age (Yr)							
	55–59	60–64	65–69	70–74	75–79	80–84	85–89	90–94
Road Race	35:38	37:28	40:36	44:46	51:24	1:06:54		
10K	(42:24)	(49:02)	(50:08)	(56:43)	(1:02:26)	(1:30:26)	(1:21:50)	
Cycling	30:41	32:01	30:28	31:44	33:00	41:10	45:14	
20K	(32:30)	(35:17)	(37:26)	(40:44)	(44:00)	(51:40)		
1500 Meter	4:50	4:47	5:14	5:38	7:04	7:59	17:12	17:22
Run	(6:12)	(6:11)	(6:55)	(7:25)	(9:30)	(11:26)		

SOURCE: U.S. National Senior Sports Organization (1993). Scores have been rounded to the nearest second. Female performance values appear in parenthesis.

MUSCULAR STRENGTH

Minimal *muscular strength* is important because contraction of skeletal muscle makes human movement possible. We use the term minimal muscular strength, but researchers to date have not been able to qualify this term. In fact, to do so is nearly impossible because each human movement requires different degrees of strength. For instance, the 14-month-old toddler possesses enough lower-extremity strength to walk but lacks the strength needed to propel the body through space, a requirement of running. People, regardless of age, who lack the necessary strength needed to launch the body from the supporting surface are said to be *earthbound*. This inability to project the body through space limits the number of ways a person can move in the enviroment, which is why earthbound children's ability to acquire many of the fundamental movement patterns is frequently delayed. Furthermore, older children and adults whose movement freedom is restricted by inadequate levels of muscular strength generally find themselves leading a sedentary life. In brief, muscular strength is needed for the execution of all motor tasks.

Defining and Measuring Muscular Strength

Strength is the ability to exert muscular force. This muscular force, however, can be exerted under various conditions. A muscular force exerted against an immovable object, with no or very little change in the length of the exercised muscle, is called *static* or *isometric*. A muscular force exerted against a movable object, with a change in the length of the exercised muscle, is called *dynamic* or *isotonic*. Attempting to push down a wall is an example of static force; lifting a barbell is a dynamic force.

Special instruments called dynamometers and tensiometers are used to measure static muscular force. With these instruments, the variable of interest is not minimal strength but maximal strength production.

The use of these specialized instruments for mass assessment is not always feasible. Instead, when large numbers of individuals must be assessed in a short period of time the most feasible approach is to use one or more field tests. The two most frequently employed field tests of muscular strength (and endurance) are the pull-up test (upper-body strength/endurance) or chin-up test (upper-arm strength/endurance) and a modified or bent-knee sit-up test (abdominal strength/endurance).

In the next two sections, we describe in detail age-related changes in muscular strength development and performance in both laboratory and field-test situations.

Age-Related Changes in Muscular Strength Based on Laboratory Tests

Little data are available that examine strength in preschool children. However, many investigators have examined this component of fitness in populations older than 6 years. Most frequently, the dependent variable in these studies has been grip strength. This measure of static force production is used more frequently than any other test of muscular strength because it is easy to administer and is reliable (Metheny, 1941).

Studies examining changes in grip strength during the childhood and adolescent years are consistent in their findings. A review of the literature by Keogh and Sugden (1985) revealed that the grip strength in boys increased 393 percent from 7 to 17 years of age. This figure compares favorably with the values observed over 45 years ago. More specifically, Metheny found grip strength in girls increased 260 percent; Meredith reported that grip strength in males increased 359 percent between 6 and 18 years of age (cited in Metheny, 1941).

Shephard (1981) found that changes in the strength curve closely resembled changes in body weight, at least for young boys. Moreover, he stated that "the strength spurt lags at least a year behind the height spurt, and there is thus a sense in which boys outgrow their strength just prior to puberty"

(p. 219). This finding partly explains why some boys experience a brief period of clumsiness during puberty: They have not yet acquired the needed muscular strength necessary to handle their larger bodies (see discussion in Chapter 7 on adolescent awkwardness). According to Bar-Or (1989), under normal growth conditions boys' fastest increase in muscular strength occurs approximately 1 year after peak height velocity, whereas in girls the strength spurt generally occurs during the same year as peak height velocity.

Sex differences in muscular strength become most apparent after puberty. In boys, puberty is associated with the introduction of the male sex hormones, which in turn influence muscularity. During this time of development, boys become leaner and young girls begin to develop more body fat. Prior to adolescence, muscle weight is about 27 percent of total body weight, but after sexual maturity, muscle development is increased to about 40 percent of total body weight (Vrijens, 1978). In adulthood, even when body size is taken into consideration, women are only 80 percent as strong as men (Asmussen, 1973).

During early and middle adulthood, grip strength remains relatively constant. Men between 25 and 45 years exhibit an average grip strength of 54 kilograms. However, during the next 20 years, it declines by 20 percent (Shephard, 1981). In comparison, Clarke and Vaccaro (1979) found a 16 percent reduction in grip strength in a group of female master swimmers between 30–39 and 60 years of age. Precise measures are difficult to interpret since it appears that both muscular strength and muscular endurance are a function of age and activity level (Clarke, Hunt, & Dotson, 1992).

Age-Related Changes in Muscular Strength/Endurance Based on Field Tests

Popular field tests are not capable of assessing muscular strength in the absence of muscular endurance. This is because whenever repeated muscular contractions are performed under a workload that is less than maximal, an element of muscular endurance is introduced. As mentioned previously, most popular fitness batteries incorporate the use of a chin-up test (palms of hand face toward the performer) or a pull-up test (palms face away from the performer) and some type of modified sit-up test in order to assess muscular strength/endurance within a field setting. Both assessment tests require repeated muscular contractions. For example, in both National Children and Youth Fitness Studies (NCYFS), children were allowed 60 seconds to perform as many bent-knee sit-ups as possible. Likewise, both the chin-up test administered in the first NCYFS and the modified pull-up test administered in the second NCYFS required the children to perform as many repetitions as possible. Presumably, the timed bent-knee sit-up test reflects the ratio of abdominal strength/endurance to upper-body mass (Pate & Shephard, 1989), whereas the chin-up test reflects the ratio of upper-body strength/endurance to total body mass. This latter point has been confirmed in a recent investigation by Pate and colleagues (1993). This investigation sought to test the validity of five popular field tests of muscular strength and endurance (pull-ups, flexed arm/hand, push-ups New York modified pull-ups, and Vermont modified pull-ups). The researchers concluded that upper body strength and endurance as measured by these instruments were not significantly correlated with laboratory measures of absolute muscle strength and endurance in 9- to 10-year-old children. However, the test performances were moderately related to measures of muscular strength relative to body weight, indicating that body weight is a natural confounding factor in these field tests.

Figures 8-2 and 8-3 illustrate average scores for boys and girls between 6 and 18 years of age on the muscular strength/endurance items included within the NCYFS test battery. Little difference exists between boys' and girls' abdominal strength/endurance scores between 6 and 9 years of age. However, from 10 through 16 years of age the gap in performance widens, with boys always scoring higher than girls. Performance for both boys and girls tends to level off and remain constant between 16 and 18 years of age.

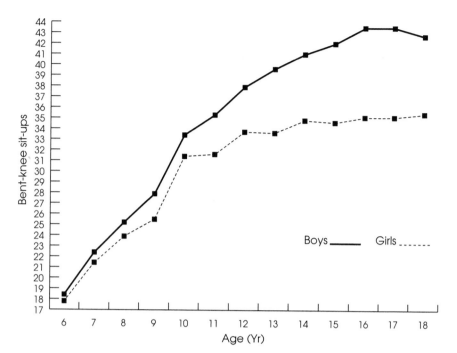

FIGURE 8-2 Average scores for boys and girls on bent-knee sit-ups (60 sec). Based on findings of the National Children and Youth Fitness Studies I and II.

SOURCE: As reported by Ross and Gilbert (1985) and Ross and Pate (1987).

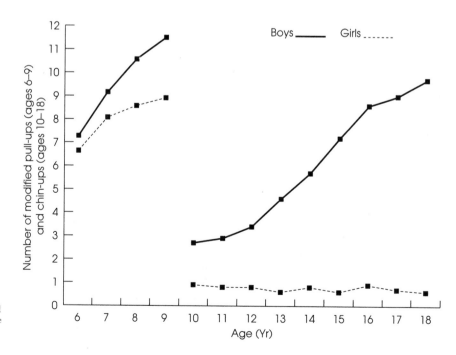

FIGURE 8-3 Average scores for boys and girls on modified pull-ups and chin-ups. Based on findings of the National Children and Youth Fitness Studies I and II.

SOURCE: As reported by Ross and Gilbert (1985) and Ross and Pate (1987).

Upper-body strength/endurance performance as reported in the first NCYFS is discouraging. Thirty percent of the boys (between 10 and 11 years) failed to perform one chin-up. For this reason, a modified pull-up test was employed in the second NCYFS to help overcome the zero performance score problem exhibited in the first NCYFS (Pate et al., 1987). Figure 8-4 depicts the special apparatus that is employed in the administration of the modified pull-up test. A complete description of this test is presented in Chapter 17. As the median scores indicate, little difference in upper-body strength exists between the genders between 6 and 9 years of age (as measured by the modified pull-up test). After 10 years of age, boys show consistent improvement in their ability to perform chin-ups, whereas on average girls were not capable of performing any chin-ups.

Muscular Strength Training

Any discussion regarding the value of resistance training on the development of muscular strength must account for the differences in training outcomes as a function of maturity level. For this rea-son, our discussion on trainability will be divided into three sections: prepubescent, adolescence/early and middle adulthood, and late adulthood.

Prepubescent Much controversy exists regarding the use of resistance training for the purpose of developing muscular strength in prepubescent populations. According to strength-training specialists (Micheli, 1988; Sale, 1989), this controversy exists in regard to three questions. First, can prepubescent children significantly increase their muscular strength through participation in a resistance-training program? Second, if gains in muscular strength are possible, does this increase in strength enhance skilled athletic performance? Lastly, does the benefit of increased strength outweigh the potential of sustaining injury during participation in a resistance-training program?

The first question is posed because popular belief has it that without a sufficient level of circulating *testosterone*, significant gains in muscular strength are not possible. This belief was reinforced when Vrijens (1978) found no significant strength gains in 16 prepubescent individuals following an 8-week training program. However, since the publication of this earlier study, most recent studies have reported significant strength gains

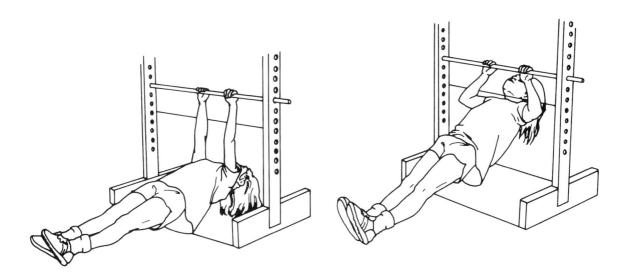

FIGURE 8-4 Modified pull-up apparatus

following participation in resistance-training programs (Faigenbaum, et al., 1993; Isaacs, Pohlman, & Craig, 1994; Ozmun, Mikesky, & Surburg, 1994; Servidio et al., 1985; Sewall & Micheli, 1986). Nevertheless, Micheli (1988) is quick to point out that other basic physiological questions regarding resistance training must be addressed before professionals are able to wholeheartedly recommend resistance training to prepubescent individuals. Namely, what is the effect of resistance training on flexibility, blood pressure, aerobic fitness, anaerobic fitness, and body composition?

Because most of the recent professional literature suggests that prepubescent individuals are capable of significantly increasing strength following resistance training, the next logical question is whether or not these strength gains are accompanied by improved athletic performance. Following an extensive review of the literature, Sale (1989) was able to uncover only two studies that addressed this question. He reports that Nielsen and colleagues (1980) and Weltman and colleagues (1986) both found that significant strength increases were accompanied by improved vertical jumping performance in their prepubescent subjects. However, Sale (1989) believes that the transfer of increased muscular strength to athletic performance depends on the nature of the sporting event. More specifically, if the athletic event does not require a lot of strategy and relies on strength, then the amount of transfer will be large. But if the athletic event is made up of "open" and complex skills, then the amount of transfer will be less. For example, Sale (1989) noted discouragement among researchers who worked with the Canadian national ski team when they found a negative correlation between strength and downhill ski times. In other words, the strongest skiers were the slowest. However, this same group of researchers have reported positive correlations between increases in muscular strength and improved time among rowers. These findings lead Sale to conclude that "with some less complex skills, one can justify the use of strength training in children in the same way one would with adolescents or adults" (1989, p. 218).

As mentioned previously, there has been much concern regarding the safety of strength training among prepubescent individuals. This concern has prompted such prestigious organizations as the American Academy of Pediatrics (AAP, 1990), the National Strength and Conditioning Association (NSCA, 1985), and the American Orthopaedic Society for Sports Medicine (AOSSM, 1985) to publish position statements regarding prepubescent strength training.

Within their position statement, the AAP (1990) makes a clear distinction among *weight training, weight lifting* or *power lifting,* and *body building.* Weight training involves the use of various resistance exercises to increase muscular strength, muscular endurance and power for sports participation, or to enhance physical fitness. In contrast, weight lifting and power lifting are considered sports that involve maximum lifts including the snatch, clean-and-jerk, squat, bench press, and the dead lifts. Body building is also considered a competitive sport where participants use resistance training to develop muscle size, symmetry, and muscle definition. All three associations now recognize that weight training can be beneficial to the prepubescent individual if conducted within the framework of other established guidelines (see Table 8-2). In addition to these guidelines, Micheli (1988) suggests that young weight trainers not be allowed to perform full squats and that no standing lifts be allowed. None of the three associations recommend prepubescent weight lifting, power lifting, or body building because of its association with injury.

An examination of Table 8-2 reveals one particular important point, namely; young children should not engage in maximum lifts. This guideline leads one to then question, "At what age is maximal lifting acceptable?" The United States Weight and Power Lifting Federations recommend maximal lifting at 14 years of age. Yet the answer to this question is not so simple since chronological age is not an acceptable indicator of biological maturity. Rather than using chronological age, it has been suggested that boys and girls not be allowed to perform maximal lifts until reaching a Tanner stage 5 level of development (see Chapter 7). At this level of devel-

TABLE 8-2 Selected Weight-Training Guidelines Taken from Position Statements of the National Strength and Conditioning Association, the American Orthopaedic Society for Sports Medicine, and the American Academy of Pediatrics, and from the work of Metcalf & Roberts (1993)

1. Before beginning a strength program, the child should have a physical examination.

2. Participant must be emotionally mature enough to follow directions from a coach.

3. Program should be supervised by someone knowledgeable in strength training.

4. Fifty to 80 percent of the child's training should be in activities other than strength training.

5. A 15-minute warm-up should precede each training session, and a 15-minute cool-down should be employed following each session.

6. The participant should be taught correct lifting techniques before resistance is added.

7. No maximum lifts are allowed. Each set should consist of 6 to 15 repetitions.

8. Weight can be increased by 1 to 3 pounds after 15 repetitions can be accomplished in good form.

9. All exercises should be carried out through the full range of motion.

10. Emphasis should be on dynamic concentric contractions.

11. The young child should use only appropriately sized equipment.

12. No competition is allowed.

13. Require 1–2 minutes rest between exercises.

14. Require at least 1 day's rest between workouts.

opmental maturity peak height velocity will have occurred and, therefore, there will be a smaller likelihood of injury to the epiphyses (growth plates).

Adolescence/Early and Middle Adulthood Less controversy surrounds the use of resistance training in adolescent and adult populations. Authorities agree that programs of progressive resistance training will result in improved muscular strength/endurance within these two populations (Fox, Kirby, & Fox, 1987). Gains in muscular strength/endurance, however, are contingent on adhering to established principles of training. The American College of Sports Medicine (ACSM, 1990) recommends that the healthy adult perform approximately 8 to 10 exercises involving the body's major muscle groups. These resistance training exercises should be performed a minimum of two times per week. Each exercise should consist of a minimum of one set with 8 to 12 repetitions being performed. According to ACSM, these minimal standards are based on two findings. First, while more intense training will result in greater strength gains, training sessions lasting longer than 1 hour per session are associated with higher drop-out rates and, second, it has been established that the extra amount of strength gained as a result of increasing frequency of training and intensity of training is relatively small. As a general rule of thumb, 60 percent of one repetition maximum is a reasonable starting intensity. Unlike cardiovascular efficiency, the length of each training session (duration) is not as important and will vary depending on the number of exercises employed and the amount of rest between exercises. Micheli's review of the literature led him to conclude that "there is good evidence that the adolescent male makes strength gains in much the same pattern as the adult male when placed on a properly designed progressive resistive strengthening program" and that "adolescent girls will also gain strength in response to progressive resistive training although the response is less dramatic than that seen in boys" (1988, p. 100).

Even though near maximal and maximal lifts are acceptable for adolescents (beyond Tanner stage 5) and young adults, there is still a need to educate these two populations about proper lifting technique. It is of particular importance that these individuals understand the importance of proper breathing during the performance of resistance training (Tanner, 1993). In short, breath holding or straining with a closed glottis (Valsalva maneuver) can cause a "blackout" and should therefore be avoided.

Late Adulthood For those in late adulthood, the paramount question is whether or not strength training is capable of altering, delaying, or even allowing one to avoid some of the physiological deterioration believed to be associated with aging. A study of female master swimmers by Dummer and associates (1985) found that although competitive swimming training positively influenced strength, there was still an age-related decline. Strength training did *not* prevent age-related declines in this parameter. Nevertheless, the physically active women in the study were able to maintain a relatively high degree of grip strength into the eighth decade of life. Dummer further noted that her subjects who were older than 60 exhibited grip strengths equivalent to those possessed by less active women in their 20s and 30s. Thus we conclude that even though decreases in muscular strength can be expected with age, the rate of decline can be significantly retarded.

In a recent review of the literature Munnings (1993) has uncovered convincing evidence that suggests that it is never too late to start a resistance-training program. Her belief is predicated on the findings of a study that reports significant gains in both strength and balance in a population of individuals between 67 and 91 years of age (Parsons et al., 1992). These senior citizens performed 15 resis-

tance exercises using free weights, three times a week for a period of 24 weeks. The fact that strength and balance was improved may not be that unusual, however; of the 17 subjects, all were taking medication for hypertension, three had undergone cancer surgery, four were diabetic, five had significant coronary artery disease, and one had undergone quadruple surgery.

Another study has demonstrated that resistance-training can benefit individuals well into the 10th decade of life (Fiatarone et al., 1990). More specifically, these frail institutionalized men and women improved quadriceps strength by 31 percent and muscle cross-sectional area by 8 percent following an 8-week resistance training program. Clinically, these individuals exhibited significant improvement in walking speed, a functional index of mobility. This and the previous study both indicate that it is the intensity of the training and not the initial level of fitness that determines the response to training (Rogers & Evans, 1993).

Mechanisms of Increasing Muscular Strength

Even though our review thus far indicates that individuals of all ages can improve strength by following a program of progressive resistance, the possibility exists that the mechanisms responsible for change differ among the various age groups. Voluntary muscular strength can be improved in several ways: by increasing the size of the muscle (*hypertrophy*) and the specific tensions that can be exerted within the muscle, and by neural adaptations that result in an increased ability of the nervous system to activate more muscle tissue. Following an extensive review of the literature, Sale concluded that the present evidence indicates that children may have more difficulty than older age groups in increasing muscle mass. On the other hand, adaptations within the nervous system are similar to or even greater in children than in older groups (1989, p. 211). Why prepubescent children have difficulty in increasing muscle mass is not clear at this time. One possible explanation is their low level of circulating *andro-*

gens (sex hormones). Indeed, with the introduction of higher levels of circulating testosterone, which occurs in boys at around 13 to 14 years of age, there is a corresponding increase in muscle hypertrophy and muscular strength, even in the absence of resistance training. Nevertheless, this circulating androgen-level theory cannot be totally accurate because young adult women (low androgen levels) can increase their muscle mass. Thus the answer to why prepubescent individuals have difficulty in increasing muscle mass must await further study.

Potential mechanisms of muscle deterioration within the elderly are many. For example, with age there is an accompanying decrease in both the size and number of muscle fibers (Isaacs, 1989). Furthermore, muscular deterioration tends to affect the *Type II*, fast-twitch, muscle fibers more than the *Type I*, slow-twitch, fibers (Rogers & Evans, 1993). Because of this reduction in fast-twitch fibers, elderly individuals frequently experience a reduction in speed of muscular contractions. This may in part help explain why falls are so frequently incurred by elderly individuals. Even when a loss of postural balance is recognized, it may be of little value if muscles in the lower extremity are not capable of contracting quickly and with sufficient force to regain postural stability (Mortimer, Pirozzolo, & Maletta, 1982). Furthermore, those fibers that are not lost and do not atrophy tend to fatigue more quickly. This is believed to be caused by degenerative changes involving energy metabolism.

FLEXIBILITY

The abilities to ambulate and perform such daily tasks as bending over to pick up an object, tying shoes, rising up out of a chair, and even eating all have one thing in common: Each task requires bending of various parts of the body. Smooth functioning of the body's joints makes these bending movements possible. The range of movement within these joints, *flexibility,* is regionally specific. In other words, there is little relationship between the flexibility of each of the body's joints. For example, a person with flexible shoulders does not necessarily have a flexible back. Thus, few physical-fitness test batteries include flexibility among the test items because it is impossible to determine the one best flexibility test that would estimate total body flexibility. Nevertheless, when a flexibility test is included, it is generally a test of hamstring, back, and hip flexibility—the *sit-and-reach test* (see Figure 8-5). Our study of flexibility is further complicated because researchers, to date, have not been able to determine how much flexibility is needed for optimal health. The next section examines the general course of flexibility across the lifespan.

Flexibility: Performance Trends

Surprisingly, there is little empirical information on flexibility and joint mobility. However, what literature there is is consistent in its findings. More specifically, when the sit-and-reach test is used to measure hamstring, hip, and back flexibility, the data illustrate that peak flexibility is achieved in the late teens or early 20s. Thereafter, range of motion decreases. This trend is most apparent in the recent large-scale studies called National Children and Youth Fitness Studies I and II (Ross et al., 1985, 1987). In these studies, norms were established for a nationally represented sample of youngsters 6 through 18 years of age (see Figure 8-6). Generally, the data from these studies show a yearly increase in range of motion during these childhood and adolescent years. Furthermore, gender differences were apparent in that girls attained better scores than boys across all ages and across all percentile ranges. This finding is also consistent with the sit-and-reach data obtained from studies of Canadian children (Docherty & Bell, 1985). Docherty and Bell also noted that across the four age groups examined (6, 9, 12, and 15 years), the relative difference in flexibility between the genders widened with age.

Using 378 sedentary females between age 14 and 76, Alexander, Ready, and Fougere-Mailey (1985) also reported decreases in sit-and-reach performance with age. However, decreases in flexibility

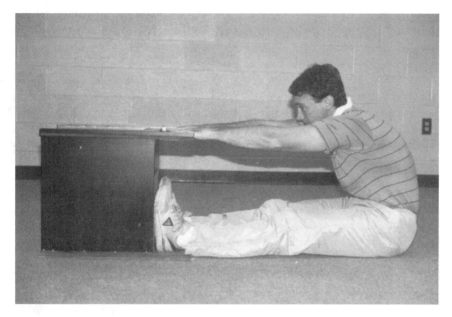

FIGURE 8-5   Sit-and-reach test

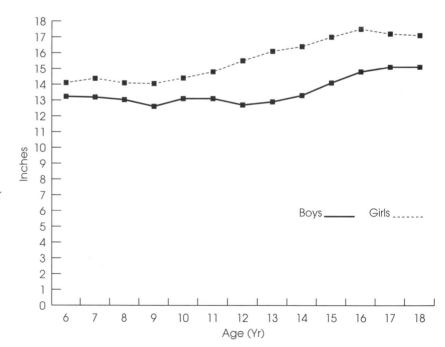

FIGURE 8-6 Average sit and reach scores for boys and girls based on findings of the National Children and Youth Fitness Studies I and II

The zero point was located at 12 inches.

SOURCE: As reported by Ross and Gilbert (1985) and Ross and Pate (1987).

were gradual up to age 49, whereupon significant drops occur with age.

Declining Flexibility and Aging: Causes and Therapy

Because flexibility is known to decrease with age, we wonder what causes this decline in our range of motion. This decrease in joint mobility is partly caused by physiological changes to the structures that make up the joint: tendons, ligaments, muscle, synovial fluid, and cartilage. With age, the joint's connective structures become less resilient and crack and fray. Synovial fluid becomes less viscous, and cartilage is frequently damaged from both injury and everyday wear and tear. Degenerative joint disease such as osteoarthrosis also contributes to loss of joint functioning. Adrian's (1981) review of the literature revealed that about 80 percent of the population between 55 and 64 years have signs of osteoarthrosis in at least one joint. Furthermore, although joint degeneration is usually associated with aged populations, the degenerative process actually begins prior to skeletal maturity (Whitbourne, 1985). Further research is needed to separate those processes that are age-related and those that are pathological.

Even though researchers have not been able to ascertain to what extent joint changes are caused by age-related processes or by pathological changes, one fact is clear: Physical activity is necessary to maintain joint mobility. Moreover, joint flexibility can be improved with moderate to light activity. This finding was illustrated in Munns's study (1981), in which 20 experimental and 20 control subjects between 65 and 88 years of age volunteered to take part in a 12-week exercise and dance program to determine its effect on joint flexibility. At the conclusion of the experiment, subjects in the experimental group showed significant improvement in all six joints measured: neck, shoulder, wrist, hip and back, knee, and ankle. Range of motion improved from a low of 8.3 percent in the shoulder to a high of 48.3 percent in the ankle. In contrast, control subjects showed decreased flexibility in the same

six joints, from 2.7 percent in the knee to 5.1 percent in both the shoulder and ankle.

Controlling for level of activity, Germain and Blair (1983) found that shoulder flexibility decreases after 10 years of age. However, this decrease was minimal in people who were active.

BODY COMPOSITION

We live in a technological society—a society that is relying increasingly more on special machinery to perform many of our daily tasks. The use of robotics in the work force has improved productivity, but we are paying a price for this technology. Some experts believe that this price is an increased sedentary lifestyle. Accompanying this sedentary lifestyle is a corresponding increase in the number of overweight and overfat people. Adipose (fat) tissue does serve many useful and important functions: It insulates the body, it can be a source of energy reserve, and it is also a protective cushion for internal organs. Unfortunately, mounting evidence suggests that excess fat in relation to total body composition may have serious health consequences. The obese subjects in the long-term Framingham cohort study (Kannel & Gordon, 1977) were found to have high blood lipid levels, elevated blood pressure, and many other physiological parameters associated with cardiovascular disease. Despite this evidence that points to a strong association between overfatness and cardiovascular disease, scientists have not been able to absolutely ascertain the ideal level of body fat a person should possess.

Defining Obesity

The term *obesity* is difficult to precisely define because so many different definitions have been offered, which partly explains why scientists have difficulty establishing an ideal level of fatty tissue. An acceptable level as defined by one definition may describe an unacceptable level according to another. Three popular definitions take a social, statistical, and operational approach (Sims, 1977). The major thesis of the social definition is appearance. If a person looks as if he is extremely overweight, then he is considered obese, even though no sophisticated measurements are taken. The statistical definition is based on estimates established from normative studies. For instance, a person weighing 50 to 100 pounds above her desired weight is classified as extremely obese. Or a man falling above the 80th to 95th percentile on whatever criteria is being used may be classified as obese. The operational definition "estimates a level of overweight based on various criteria below which there is no improvement in mortality and morbidity" (Sims, 1977, p. 21).

Researchers subscribe to the statistical definition, where norms for proposed ideal body fat are based on descriptive data. Nevertheless, descriptive data are population-specific. That is, observed levels of body fat will differ, depending on many factors. For instance, sex, race, lifestyle and many geographical factors can all influence *body composition.* In other words, how much of our body is made up of fat and how much is composed of *lean body tissue* such as muscle and bone?

Because of these apparent problems, during the Sixth Ross Conference on Medical Research (Newman, 1985), Roche suggested that we no longer use the terms "standard" or "ideal" to describe body composition. He stated that "standard and ideal imply values that are fixed for all time, with biologic interpretations of what ought to be. However, these reference data change from one survey to the next" (p. 4). Therefore, in the following section, when we describe changes in body composition across the lifespan, keep in mind that we are simply highlighting general trends and that these trends are population-specific. This helps explain the wide range of values reported in different studies.

General Growth Trends of Adipose Tissue

Subcutaneous adipose tissue first appears toward the end of the second trimester and rapidly accelerates during the last 2 months of gestation. Fomon and colleagues estimated that at birth the amount of fat present is about 13 percent in boys and 15 percent in girls. This fat is stored in about 5 billion adipocytes (fat cells). The number of fat cells continues to increase during childhood. For example, during the next 11 months, the percentage of body fat can rise to 20 to 25 percent in boys and 21 to 26 percent in girls (cited in Newman, 1985). This increase in fat tissue during the first year of life is one of the two rapid growth spurts of adipose tissue. The second spurt occurs during puberty in boys and during both prepuberty and puberty in girls (Bonnet & Rocour-Brumioul, 1981). The result of this second spurt is a greater fat mass in girls than in boys. On the average, the young but mature female can have a body-fat content 50 percent greater than that of her male counterpart of the same age (Bonnet & Rocour-Brumioul, 1981). Authorities believe there is no further increase in the number of adipocytes following puberty. Instead, changes in fat's contribution to overall body composition depend on the size of each fat cell, not the number of fat cells.

There appears to be one period in the lifespan when body fat declines: at the onset of independent walking. It ends somewhere between 6 and 8 years of age; at this time, body fat is about one-half of what it was at 1 year of age (Sinclair, 1985).

A person whose body-fat content is 1 or 2 standard deviations above the mean is believed outside the normal range recommended for optimal health. Lohman (1982) believed that body-fat content should be 15 and 25 percent, respectively, in the male and female. He noted, however, that a satisfactory range for health is 10 to 22 percent in men and 20 to 32 percent in women. (These values are significantly lower in athletes.) On the other side of the coin, minimal fat content should be 3 to 7 percent in men and 10 to 20 percent in women (Lohman, 1982).

Body weight per se is not an appropriate indicator of body composition. Body weight tends to reach its peak at abut 45 years of age, and during the next 20 years, body weight generally decreases or remains constant. A decrease in body weight implies a reduction in adipose tissue, but generally this is not the case. For instance, skinfold thicknesses do not change during this period of time, so this reduction in body weight is due to a reduction in lean body mass, not fat mass (Shephard, 1978). The increasingly sedentary lifestyle that generally accompanies aging partly explains this reduction in lean body mass.

Field-Test Measures of Body Fat

While *hydrostatic weighing* (weighing a person underwater in order to determine body density) is currently the preferred method for estimating percent body fat, this laboratory procedure is not always practical. Instead, a more practical alternative is the use of *skinfold calipers.* Calipers are used to indirectly estimate body composition. While numerous companies manufacture skinfold calipers, the caliper of choice is manufactured by Harpenden. An appropriate, yet less expensive substitute is the caliper produced by Lange. One should shy away from cheap plastic calipers, which have scales that are difficult to read and are not spring loaded. Using calipers that are spring loaded ensures that a constant calibrated pressure is applied to the double fold of skin and fat tissue.

Skinfold calipers were used in both NCYFS to estimate body fat in children between 6 and 18 years of age. Table 8-3 presents the findings of this study. The values reported on the 6- through 9-years-olds were obtained by summing the skinfold thicknesses for the tricep, subscapular, and medial calf. In contrast, reported values for the 10- through 18-year-olds were obtained by summing only the tricep and subscapular skinfolds. It is difficult to compare trends between these two age groups because of the inclusion of the medial calf measure in the younger group. In order to make comparisons across ages easier, Figure 8-7 is a graphic illustration of changes in only the sum of tricep and subscapular skinfolds across both age groups (the medial calf measure has been removed from the younger age group). It is clearly evident that girls possess more body fat than boys at all ages. In general, body fat appears to steadily increase in girls until 15 years of age. In contrast, boys exhibit a steady increase in body fat until about 10 years; thereafter, it remains relatively constant through 18 years of age. One should also note that the magnitude of difference between the genders widens significantly after 11 years of age, and this widening trend continues until about age 15. At this time the average sum of tricep and subscapular skinfolds is nearly 10 mm greater in girls.

When the NCYFS data are compared with the 1960s data reported by the National Center for Health Statistics, it becomes apparent that today's

TABLE 8-3   Average Sum of Skinfolds (mm) for Boys and Girls Based on Findings of the National Children and Youth Fitness Studies I and II

	Age (years)												
	6	7	8	9	10	11	12	13	14	15	16	17	18
	Sum of Tricep, Subscapular, and Medial Calf Skinfolds												
Boys	24.56	26.36	28.91	32.07									
Girls	30.55	32.25	36.11	39.16									
	Sum of Tricep and Subscapular Skinfolds												
Boys					20.90	21.20	21.60	20.10	20.10	20.10	19.40	20.10	20.20
Girls					22.60	24.80	25.30	26.80	27.90	30.00	28.70	30.20	28.90

SOURCE: As reported by Ross and Gilbert (1985) and Ross and Pate (1987).

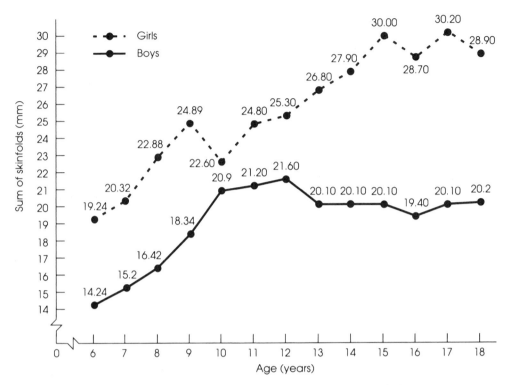

FIGURE 8-7   Average sum of tricep and subscapular skinfold thicknesses in boys and girls based on findings of the National Children and Youth Fitness Studies I and II (as reported by Ross and Gilbert, 1985, and Ross et al., 1987).

youth possess more body fat than do children of about 20 years ago. More specifically, the median sum of the tricep and subscapular skinfold measures of the children who participated in the two NCYFS were about 2 to 3 mm greater in the 10- to 18-year-olds and 2 to 4 mm greater in the 6- to 9-year-olds (Ross & Pate, 1987). Nevertheless, authorities are unclear at this time as to whether this increase in body fat among youth will have any long-term negative consequences on adult well-being (Raithel, 1988).

Skinfold thickness remains relatively constant between 45 and 65 years of age (Shephard, 1978) although its value can be greatly affected by both nutritional and exercise status. The data presented in Tables 8-4 and 8-5 show a definite decrease in both tricep and subscapular skinfold thickness in men and women between 65 and 90 years of age

(Chumlea, Roche, & Mukherjee, 1984). Chumlea and colleagues (1984) have recognized that both obesity and malnutrition are common occurrences in late adulthood. For this reason, they recommend that body-fat changes be closely monitored in elderly individuals. Obesity tends to be the most common reason elderly individuals approach the 95th percentile in measures of body fat, whereas malnutrition and serious illness may cause a significant drop in body fat.

Relationship of Obesity to Motor Development and Performance

As early as 1931, Shirley (1931) noted that of the 25 babies in her study, the heavy ones evidenced more delays in walking than did the lighter ba-

TABLE 8-4   Percentiles for Triceps Skinfold Thickness in mm

	Men				Women		
Age (years)	95%	50%	5%	Age (years)	95%	50%	5%
65	27.0	13.8	8.6	65	33.0	21.6	13.5
70	26.1	12.9	7.7	70	32.0	20.6	12.5
75	25.2	12.0	6.8	75	31.0	19.6	11.5
80	24.3	11.2	6.0	80	30.0	18.6	10.5
85	23.4	10.3	5.1	85	29.0	17.6	9.5
90	22.6	9.4	4.2	90	28.0	16.6	8.5

Used with permission of Ross Laboratories, Columbus, Ohio, from *Nutritional Assessment of the Elderly Through Anthropometry* ©1984, Ross Laboratories.

bies. More recently, Jaffe and Kosakov (1982) echoed this finding in their study of the motor development of fat babies. The authors used the Sveger's index of body weight to categorize 135 babies as being either of normal weight or fat. The fat babies were further classified as either overweight or obese; 29 percent of the overweight babies and 36 percent of the obese babies evidenced motor delays as measured by the Sheridan Stycar Developmental Assessment Schedules. In comparison, only 9 percent of the normal-weight babies showed any delay in their motor development. Although this study showed a relationship between body weight and motor performance, it is important to note that the Sveger index does not require measurement of subcutaneous fat. Instead, the index is calculated as a ratio between actual weight and height to expected weight and height for age. Thus we must cautiously interpret the result because body composition was not measured.

TABLE 8-5   Percentiles for Subscapular Skinfold Thickness in mm

	Men				Women		
Age (years)	95%	50%	5%	Age (years)	95%	50%	5%
65	35.7	20.0	11.2	65	33.1	16.4	8.5
70	34.0	18.2	9.4	70	32.5	15.8	7.9
75	32.2	16.4	7.7	75	31.9	15.2	7.3
80	30.4	14.7	5.9	80	31.3	14.6	6.7
85	28.7	12.9	4.1	85	30.7	14.0	6.1
90	26.9	11.2	2.4	90	30.1	13.5	5.5

Used with permission of Ross Laboratories, Columbus, Ohio, from *Nutritional Assessment of the Elderly Through Anthropometry* © 1984, Ross Laboratories.

This was not the case in a recent study by Pissanos and colleagues (1983), who used the Sum of Skinfold Fat Test to study the influence of age, sex, and body composition on predicting children's performance on basic motor abilities and on health-related physical fitness. Subjects were 80 boys and girls 6 years 8 months to 10 years 3 months old. This study found that body composition was the best predictor of cardiovascular performance, as measured by a step test, and power, as measured by the standing long jump. Thus the authors concluded that "large amounts of subcutaneous fat is negatively related to activities in which the body is projected through space" (p. 76). Slaughter, Lohman, and Misner (1977) also reported that the 7- to 12-year-old subjects in their study who had large amounts of body fat ran slower in the mile and 600-yard run than did the leaner subjects.

GENDER DIFFERENCES IN HEALTH-RELATED PHYSICAL FITNESS

Uncovering gender differences in health-related physical fitness was the subject of an investigation by Thomas, Nelson, and Church (1991). The study involved a secondary analysis of the physical and environmental variables measured in the National Children and Youth Fitness Study I and II. Across all ages examined (6–18 years), boys outperformed girls in three (distance run, chin-up, and sit-up) of the four health-related fitness components. The only event where girls consistently outperformed boys was the sit-and-reach test. The pattern of difference between the genders was similar for all three events. Namely, a gradual increase during the elementary school years followed by a more rapid acceleration in differences after puberty in favor of the boys. Gender differences were then adjusted for physical and environmental factors. This analysis found the most important factors prior to puberty to be predominately skinfolds, while after puberty the major factors to reduce the gender differences were both

skinfolds and the amount of exercise outside of school time. In fact, compared to the girls, boys consistently reported involvement in higher intensity activities from about 9 or 10 years of age.

FACTORS ASSOCIATED WITH PHYSIOLOGICAL FITNESS IN CHILDREN AND ADOLESCENTS

One of the major objectives of both NCYFS was to attempt to uncover factors that may influence a child's performance on physiological-fitness test items. In general, children who performed best on tests of physiological fitness tended to participate in more community-based activities, watch less television, receive their physical education instruction from a specialist, experience more activities over the course of a year, and come from a family which was more active and willing to spend more time exercising with its children (Dotson & Ross, 1985; Pate & Ross, 1987).

Do the preceding factors cause higher fitness? At this point, it is difficult to say because these associated factors were analyzed with correlational statistics and utilized cross-sectional data. In order to specifically answer our question, we must await the result of more sophisticated analysis of longitudinal data (Pate & Ross, 1987).

Regarding exercise intensity, approximately 59 percent of the subjects reported participating in moderate to high intensity physical activity. Blair and associates (1989) have recommended that physical activity be of such an intensity to result in an energy expenditure of 12.6 kJ/kg/day in order to derive health benefits. Over 75 percent of the children surveyed in the NCYFS exceeded this standard (very active: >16.8 kJ/kg/day). This is an important finding since some suggest that activity levels exhibited during childhood may influence adult level of activity (Armstrong, 1992; Dennison et al., 1988). If future research were to support this finding, it would represent an additional reason to encourage active lifestyles during childhood.

POINTS OF CONTROVERSY AND CONCERN

As mentioned at the beginning of this chapter, the primary thrust behind the health-related physical fitness movement is the notion that American children and youth are less fit today than children of 20 years ago. While this notion has been perpetuated in the popular press, when we analyze the performance of the 37,454 children and youth who participated in the FITNESSGRAM program (Weber et al., 1986), our analysis would suggest otherwise. In brief, it was determined that most U.S. boys and girls who took this fitness test obtained acceptable scores (Blair et al., 1989).

It is important to remember that one reason so much importance has been placed on the attainment of acceptable levels of physiological fitness is because of its alleged association with optimal health. That is, we assume that children who obtain acceptable fitness standards will evade serious health problems. Unfortunately, researchers have not been able to support this assumption with empirical evidence. According to Blair and associates, "childhood exercise habits are probably not associated with adult health status. . . . Thus, adult exercise has a much greater beneficial effect on adult health status than does childhood exercise" (1989, p. 402). This point of view has been substantiated by Brill and colleagues who reported that "athletic participation in youth is not associated with coronary risk factor status in middle age in Cooper Clinic patients" (cited in Blair et al., 1989).

Yes, it is true that children today possess more body fat than did children of years past; and yes, many children today find it difficult to do even one chin-up or one pull-up. But the point is this: Most health-related fitness tests judge individual performance against norm-referenced standards. In other words, where does a given individual fall in reference to his or her peers? Unfortunately, at this point in time, researchers are unable to identify, for example, just how much body fat is acceptable and how many chin-ups one must be capable of doing in order to be deemed physiologi-

cally physically fit. Until we are able to do so, this controversy will remain an item of much debate.

Moreover, because of this debate, motor developmentalists, physical educators, and curriculum specialists are currently debating the issue of what should be emphasized in today's curriculum: motor skill development or physiological fitness. Once again, the debate will continue until we are able to obtain an acceptable answer to our original question: What are the exact performance standards needed in order to obtain optimal health?

At the other end of the age continuum is our concern regarding the maintenance of an active lifestyle throughout the entire lifespan. While it is true that life expectancy is improving, one must also consider the quality of these additional years. For example, Barry and colleagues (1993) have noted that while life expectancy in Quebec has increased to 70.3 years in men and 78.2 years in women, that disability-free life expectancies are only 59 and 60 years, respectively. In other words, we may be living longer but it is important that we find ways to remain independently functional during the latter years of life. As should be evident from the information presented in this chapter, physical activity can make an important contribution toward maintaining functional independence.

SUMMARY

Cardiovascular fitness is the ability to deliver oxygen to the working muscle tissues. Increased workloads involve a corresponding increase in cardiac output, the amount of blood pumped through the heart in 1 minute. This increased blood flow is made possible by an increase in the heart's rate of contraction and the amount of blood ejected with each beat. Aging affects each of these parameters; for instance, HR, SV, and cardiac output all decrease with age.

The largest amount of oxygen the body can consume at the tissue level is called $\dot{V}O_2$ max. Generally $\dot{V}O_2$ max remains fairly constant during the childhood and adolescent years. Boys may exhibit greater values than girls, but the differences are not as great when differences in body size are considered. The influence of aging on this parameter first becomes evident at about 12 to 13 years, when girls experience a reduction in $\dot{V}O_2$ max. In general, rate of decline is between 9 and 15 percent between 45 and 55 years of age; thereafter, the rate of decline accelerates. Furthermore, individuals with anorexia nervosa experience a reduction in physical work capacity greater than what can be explained by the corresponding reduction in the various physiological parameters that influence $\dot{V}O_2$ max.

A growing amount of evidence questions the benefit of aerobic training for improving aerobic capacity in preadolescent children.

Strength is the ability to exert force. Static force is produced when there is no change in the length of the exercised muscle; dynamic force is produced when the exercised muscle does change its length. Most studies examining strength changes across the lifespan use grip strength as the dependent variable. Boys increase their grip strength by 393 percent between the ages of 7 and 17. Girls improve their grip strength about 260 percent between the ages of 6 and 18. Between 25 and 45 years, men lose about 20 percent of their grip strength, and active women between 30–39 and 60 years of age lose about 16 percent of their grip strength.

Most authorities now agree that resistance training can improve muscular strength in prepubescent individuals, especially if approved guidelines are followed. To date, the American Academy of Pediatrics, the National Strength and Conditioning Association, and the American Orthopaedic Society for Sports Medicine have published position statements and guidelines for prepubescent resistance training.

Flexibility is the range of motion of a joint. yearly increases in sit-and-reach flexibility are apparent during childhood and adolescence. Thereafter, decreases in joint mobility become evident. Girls are usually more flexible than boys, and this gender difference widens with age.

Body composition is the ratio of fat tissue to lean muscle mass. We focused our attention on the development of fat tissue. There are two growth spurts of fat tissue, the first during the first year of life and the second during puberty in boys and both prepuberty and puberty in girls. Following this second spurt, girls possess more body fat than boys throughout the lifespan.

Large amounts of body fat are negatively related to activities in which the body is projected through space.

KEY TERMS

Androgens
Body building (sport)
Body composition
Bradycardia
Cardiac output
Cardiovascular fitness
Dynamic, or isotonic, force
Earthbound
Field test
Flexibility
Heart rate (HR)
Hydrostatic weighing
Hypertrophy
Lean body tissue
Maximal oxygen consumption

Muscular strength
Obesity
Physical working capacity
Power lifting (sport)
Sit-and-reach test
Skinfold calipers
Static, or isometric, force
Stroke volume (SV)
Subcutaneous adipose tissue
Testosterone
Type I muscle fibers
Type II muscle fibers
Weight lifting (sport)
Weight training

CHAPTER 9

Movement and the Changing Senses

The human organism is composed of many complicated communication channels that allow us to respond to the multitude of stimuli we encounter, primarily during our waking hours. This communicative link between the human organism and the environment is in part made possible by a group of senses: vision, proprioception, touch, taste, smell, and hearing. Information we receive from these senses enables us to describe our environment.

Without doubt, we rely on vision more than on any other sense to describe our environment and to react to environmental stimuli. In fact, most movement tasks are initiated as a result of receiving visual information. Vision provides the needed information for us to adjust our bodies to intercept moving objects. Furthermore, we rely on vision not only to emulate the movements of others but also to find our way around our visually oriented world.

Even though vision is the sensory modality of choice, nonvisual sensory modalities are also known

to influence motor development and motor performance. Therefore, this chapter will end with a brief discussion of the nonvisual sensory modalities and the role they play in both directly and indirectly influencing both motor development and motor performance.

UNDERSTANDING THE MECHANICS OF VISION

The photographic camera and the human eye share many common structural features. For a sharp photograph to be obtained, the lens of the camera must be focused so that light rays converge on its light-sensitive material, the photographic film. Likewise, for a clear visual image, light entering the eye must converge on the eye's light-sensitive tissue, the *retina*.

The retina is composed of two types of photoreceptors: *rods*, which make colorless night vision possible, and *cones*, which make color vision and acuity possible. Cones are predominantly concentrated in a region of the retina known as the *macula*; the rod cells are located in the periphery and thus make peripheral vision possible.

Exactly how does varying light enter the eye and then focus on the retina? Again, we will contrast the similarities between a camera and the human eye to illustrate this point. At one time or another you took a photograph that came out blurred, perhaps because light entering the camera did not properly converge onto the camera's film, causing the image to be out of focus. You should have changed the refractory power of the camera's lens by rotating it either clockwise or counterclockwise. Similarly, the ocular refractory power of the human eye can be adjusted by changing the shape of the eye's lens. The lens of the human eye changes shape whenever the *ciliary muscle* is contracted. This process that enables a clear retinal image to be maintained in the presence of varying light conditions is called *accommodation*. Sharp vision is possible whenever light properly converges on the macula.

PHYSICAL DEVELOPMENT OF THE EYE

The eye develops as an outgrowth of the forebrain and is an inseparable component of the central nervous system. Of the 12 cranial nerves, 6 play a role in vision. The eye, like the brain, achieves most of its growth prior to birth. For instance, at birth the anteroposterior diameter of the eye is 17 millimeters; 3 years later it measures about 22.5 millimeters—just 1.5 millimeters short of adult size. Because the eye is shorter at birth than it will be at maturity, the infant's eye is *hyperopic;* that is, light entering the eye focuses behind the retina (see Figure 9-1). Nevertheless, sharp vision is possible because of accommodation.

The eye's cornea also increases its diameter 2 millimeters during the first year of life and at adulthood measures 12 millimeters. Thereafter, the cornea does not grow in size but does change its curvature, to become less spherical.

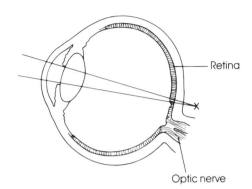

FIGURE 9-1 A hyperopic eye: Light enters the eye and focuses behind the retina.

The retina is also fairly well developed at birth, even though it is thicker than an adult retina and contains mostly rod cells (Whipple, 1966). During the first postnatal month, as the retina thins and cone cells begin to squeeze between the rod cells, the macula becomes more differentiated. By 8 months of age, the macula is histologically mature.

The muscles that control eye movements and the dilator muscles of the pupil are perhaps the slowest structures to develop. Ciliary muscle cells are first present in the eye at about the fifth prenatal month (Smith, Gallie, & Morin, 1983). Thus, except for the macular and dilator muscles of the pupil, by the end of the sixth prenatal month all eye parts are present and presumably able to function (Smith, Gallie, & Morin, 1983).

DEVELOPMENT OF SELECTED VISUAL TRAITS AND SKILLED MOTOR PERFORMANCE

Despite the relative advanced size of the eye in utero, the eye is still immature at birth because optimal vision requires good central and peripheral function of the retina, the ability to appreciate depth, and the ability to track moving objects. Here we describe postnatal changes within these selected visual attributes, paying special attention to the influence of these changes on skilled motor performance.

Visual Acuity

Visual acuity is the degree of detail that can be seen in an object. The fine details of objects are blurred for a person with poor visual acuity.

To better appreciate changes in visual acuity across the lifespan, we must first describe how this measure of visual sharpness is determined. With the most common technique, a person resolves the smallest letters possible on the *Snellen eye chart* (see Figures 9-2 and 9-3). Visual acuity determined by the Snellen eye chart is called *static visual acuity* because both the target and the performer are stationary. Normal distance visual acuity is expressed in fractional notation. Thus, a person with 20/20 vision can clearly see an object placed 20 feet away in the same manner that other people with normal vision can see objects placed 20 feet away. An example of less-than-normal static acuity is a person with 20/100 vision: this person can clearly see objects placed 20 feet away, whereas people with normal vision can see the same objects 100 feet away. Use of the Snellen eye chart is not recommended before 3 years of age.

Developmentally, improvement in static visual acuity occurs during the first 4 to 5 years of life. However, there is much variability in reported acuity measures both within and across different ages. For instance, at birth, visual acuity has been estimated as between 20/300 (Andrew, 1978) and 20/800 (Atkinson & Braddick, 1974), and 1 month, estimates are 20/600 to 20/300 (Atkinson & Braddick, 1974). By the end of the first year, the infant's visual acuity is probably between 20/100 (Andrew, 1978) and 20/200 (Atkinson & Braddick, 1974). Normal static distance acuity (20/20) is generally attained sometime during the fourth or fifth year (Lowrey, 1978). At first glance, it may appear that the infant has very low-quality functional vision. In reality, however, infants are capable of handling most of the static visual tasks they confront. For example, the acuity level of a 1-month-old infant is adequate for resolving facial expressions when the baby is held close to a person. Similarly, the acuity level of a 6-month-old infant is adequate for stimulating

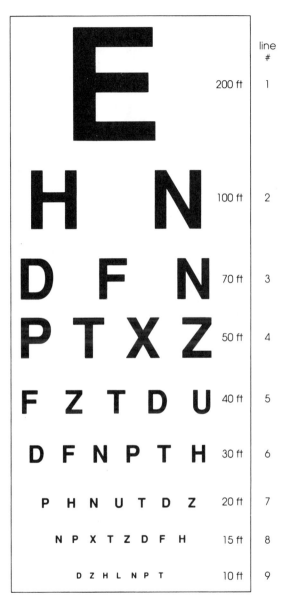

FIGURE 9-2 This Snellen eye chart is used to determine static visual acuity for individuals who are old enough to recognize letters.

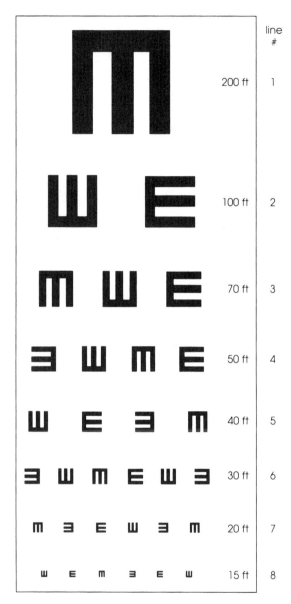

	line #
200 ft	1
100 ft	2
70 ft	3
50 ft	4
40 ft	5
30 ft	6
20 ft	7
15 ft	8

FIGURE 9-3 This Snellen eye chart is used with children in grades K–1 who may not be capable of letter recognition. The child must point in the direction that the **"E"** symbol faces or state that the symbol faces up, down, right, or left.

the visual curiosity that is needed to elicit reaching for small objects as grasping skills begin to develop. In other words, static acuity is adequate for the major visual tasks that an infant confronts.

A second type of visual acuity is called *dynamic visual acuity,* which is the ability to see the detail in moving objects. According to Miller and Ludvigh (1953), dynamic visual acuity reflects the ability of the central nervous system to estimate an object's direction and velocity and the ability of the ocular-motor system "to catch" and "to hold" an object's image on the eye's fovea (center posterior part of the retina) long enough to permit resolution of the object's detail.

According to Morris (1977), dynamic visual acuity improves between 6 and 20 years of age. Therefore, static visual acuity matures before dynamic visual acuity. The most significant changes in dynamic visual acuity occur between 5 and 7 years, 9 and 10 years, and 11 and 12 years (Williams, 1983). Decreases in this visual attribute start at about 25 years. In general, dynamic visual efficiency decreases as the object of interest increases speed (Morris, 1980).

Visual Acuity and Motor Performance Both static and dynamic visual acuity correlate with specific motor performance tasks. Thus this visual attribute may play a key role in motor task performance. For example, correlations as high as 0.76 have been found between measures of dynamic visual acuity and basketball field-goal shooting percentage during a competitive season (Beals et al., 1971). Similar results were reported by Morris and Kreighbaum (1977), who found that high-percentage basketball field-goal shooters showed less variability in selected dynamic visual acuity scores than did a group of low-percentage field-goal shooters. Results from these two investigations suggest that shooting from the field in basketball may be highly dependent on dynamic visual acuity. Studies by Sanderson and Whiting (1974, 1978) also suggest a possible relationship between dynamic visual acuity and task performance. Sanderson and Whiting found a significant relationship between dynamic visual acuity and performance on a ball-catching task. This explains why people with less than desirable degrees of dynamic visual acuity may have to use special equipment when playing ball skill activities. For instance, fleece balls and whiffle balls travel through space slower than baseballs, thus giving participants more time to process visual information.

Visual Acuity and Exercise Exercise generally influences visual acuity. Russian physiologists have reported as much as 45 percent visual acuity improvement in 73 percent of the participants following a 1000-meter race (Graybiel, Jokl, & Trapp, 1955). Vlahov also noted improved visual acuity following both bicycle ergometer exercise bouts (1977a) and participation in the Harvard Step Test (1977b). Even participation in the recreational activity of table tennis for 10 minutes can temporarily improve visual acuity (Whiting & Sanderson, 1972). Improvements in acuity have lasted as long as 2 hours after the exercise ended (Graybiel, Jokl, & Trapp, 1955). This increase in acuity is probably caused by the increased blood flow in and subsequent oxygenation of the eye.

Effects of Aging on Visual Acuity *Senile macular degeneration (SMD)* is one of the most prevalent causes of loss of visual acuity in the elderly. This serious condition is the result of many anatomical changes that occur in the retina with age, including a reduction in the number of photoreceptors, reduced blood supply to the retina caused by vascular sclerosis, and loss of ocular reflexes. Visual acuity in people afflicted with SMD is from 20/50 to 20/100. Most of the changes associated with SMD occur within the macula, so SMD usually only affects central vision, leaving peripheral vision unchanged. Therefore, although the elderly with SMD are not capable of driving and may find reading difficult, they are still capable of general mobility.

A person's ability to make out the fine details of an object can also be caused by optical factors. For example, two optical factors that can influence the brightness of the image focused on the retina are the size of the pupil and the condition of the eyes' lenses. With advancing age, some people may experience a reduction in their pupils' resting diameter, which decreases the amount of light reaching the retina. This condition is called *senile miosis*. A clouding of the crystalline lens, called *cataracts*, can also be the culprit. Typically, there is a linear decline in the amount of light reaching the retina between 30 and 60 years. In fact, the amount of light that reaches the retina at age 60 is only one third the amount of light that reached the retina 40 years earlier (Weale, 1963).

By approximately 40 years of age we begin to lose the ability to accommodate near objects. For instance, print can be brought into focus from 10 centimeters at age 20, 18 centimeters at age 40, 50 centimeters at age 50, and 100 centimeters by 70 years (Shephard, 1978). This inability to clearly focus near objects is clinically known as *presbyopia*. Because presbyopia does not affect distance vision, some of its symptoms can be overcome by wearing bifocal lenses. These special lenses contain the person's normal prescription in the top half of the eyeglasses, and the bottom half is of a different prescription that allows for more normal near vision.

Binocular Vision and Depth Perception

As mentioned, the ocular muscles that control eye movements are not fully developed at birth. As a result, the newborn frequently moves each eye at random; the newborn has *strabismus*, or cross-eyes. Strabismus is common at birth but should not persist beyond the first year. Usually the degree of strabismus greatly diminishes during the first week of life, and by the end of the third month, most normal infants move both eyes in a coordinated manner, even though they may occasionally squint until they are 8 months old (Whipple, 1966).

Coordinated eye movements are important because they are the basis of *binocular vision*, which occurs when both eyes move in unison so that each eye focuses the desired image on its macula. Because each eye views the object from a different angle, there is a slight disparity between the two macula images. The human brain is capable of fusing and comparing this disparity and using this information as a primary cue for judging depth. Thus, although binocular vision is contingent on a properly functioning visual system, depth perception is a cerebral function.

Gibson and Walk's (1960) classic *visual cliff* study (see Figure 9-4) was one of the first to demonstrate that infants are capable of organizing depth clues during the first year of life. The researchers constructed a platform that was raised several feet off the ground. They laid plastic glass across a checkerboard pattern; on one side the pattern was directly under the glass, and on the other side the pattern was on the floor, thus creating a visual drop-off or cliff. Infants 6 to 14 months old were placed in the middle of the platform. When mothers called their infants from the side of the visual cliff, nearly all the babies backed off and cried, refusing to cross the apparent cliff. However, when mothers coaxed their infants from the other side, all ventured over the apparent shallow area. This finding implied that in-

fants could detect the differences in depth between the two sides.

One question that has interested researchers for many years is whether depth perception is innate or develops with time. There are arguments for both positions, but mounting evidence indicates that some form of depth recognition is possible early in life. Nevertheless, even though depth perception begins to develop early in life, it is slow to mature, as evidenced by toddlers frequently bumping into things that they apparently see. In any case, depth perception is usually mature by 6 years of age.

The accurate judgment of depth is an important visual attribute for skilled motor performance. Nevertheless, the research literature presents conflicting viewpoints regarding the relationship between depth perception and sporting success. Attempts at correlating measures of depth perception with both basketball shooting from the field (Beals et al., 1971;

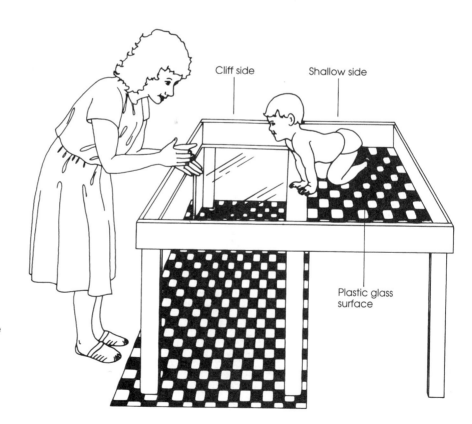

FIGURE 9-4 An illustration of the visual cliff. Note the mother attempting to coax the infant into crossing the apparent deep (cliff) side.

Cliff side   Shallow side

Plastic glass surface

Shick, 1971) and from the freethrow line failed to produce high-positive correlations. Conversely, earlier studies reported that 30 tennis players perceived depth better than 122 football players and that the more skillful athlete perceived depth better than the average athlete (Graybiel, Jokl, & Trapp, 1955). One might speculate on the basis of these findings that accurate depth perception is task-specific. In addition, most likely the central nervous system uses secondary cues (shadows, ball texture, projectile size) to perceive depth, which explains how some athletes maintain a high level of performance without the aid of stereo vision.

Field of Vision

According to Sage, "field of vision refers to the entire extent of the environment that can be seen without a change in fixation of the eye" (1984, p. 133). Two frequently studied aspects of field of vision are lateral and vertical *peripheral vision*. Normal adult lateral peripheral vision is usually just over 90 degrees from straight ahead, resulting in a visual field slightly over 180 degrees (Atkinson & Braddick, 1974). In contrast, normal adult vertical peripheral vision is approximately 47 degrees above the visual midlines and approximately 65 degrees below the visual midline (Sage, 1984). Consequently, adults are capable of detecting movements that significantly deviate from central vision.

In comparison, the infant's field of vision is extremely limited. For example, when fixating on a light located in their central field of vision, infants younger than 2 months will not refixate on a second light introduced until it is within 15 degrees laterally. When the second light is allowed to blink, the neonate's lateral peripheral vision enlarges to 25 degrees, and at 7 weeks of age to 35 degrees (Macfarlane, Harris, & Barnes, 1976).

Davids (1987) has expressed concern that reported functional peripheral vision values have predominantly been collected in laboratory situations and as a result lack ecological validity. He believes it is important to measure the development of peripheral vision in more ecologically valid settings because it may influence our expectations of children's performance in ball games in which peripheral vision is used. According to Davids, the problem with laboratory assessments is their failure to include an appropriate central task during the peripheral vision assessment. Indeed, earlier work has noted that the presence of a central task can significantly affect peripheral vision performance (Ikeda & Takevchi, 1975).

Davids (1987) examined peripheral vision processing capabilities in both children and adults (age groups: 9-, 12-, 15-year-olds and adults). The uniqueness of his study was that peripheral vision processing was assessed not only by itself (single task similar to most laboratory tasks) but also in ecologically valid settings where subjects were presented peripheral information during the performance of a ball-catching task (dual task performance; see Figure 9-5). An analysis of the data revealed that during the dual task 9-year-old subjects made significantly more catching errors than did subjects in the other three age groups. This finding is particularly interesting when one considers that during the single task performance, there was no difference in peripheral visual sensitivity between the 9-year-olds and the adults.

Davids's findings suggest that earlier laboratory estimates regarding the size of the functional visual field have been overestimated in children. Only the adult subjects (over 18 years) were capable of effectively coping with the dual processing demands presented in this study. It therefore appears that the size of the functional peripheral visual field is reduced when the child performer is confronted with a real-world central task such as catching a ball. According to Davids, "The implications for teachers and coaches of ball games are that due consideration must be given to the central task when instructing young athletes to respond to peripheral visual cues such as gaps in the field, positioning of players, and location of boundaries and targets" (1987, p. 283).

The role of peripheral vision in monitoring limb movements in infancy and childhood is not clear. However, a group of studies that Graybiel, Jokl, and

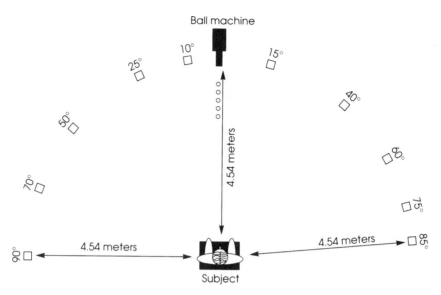

FIGURE 9-5 Davids's 1987 experiment examining peripheral vision processing during the performance of a catching task.

Trapp (1955) reported illustrate the importance of peripheral vision to skilled motor performance in an adult population. Central and peripheral vision were systematically occluded during performance in various track and field events and in gymnastics and skiing events. In all cases the championship athletes reported that the elimination of peripheral vision affected their performance more than did the exclusion of central vision. Common complaints included a loss of precision and timing, difficulty in judging distances, and clumsiness of movements. It appears that when carrying out skills at high speeds, performers have to rely on peripheral vision for essential spatial orientation cues.

Obviously, performers in some sport activities rely on peripheral vision to deceive opponents. Without doubt, basketball is one activity in which an increased field of vision is an asset. Most people would agree that a ball handler must utilize peripheral vision to avoid the mistake of "telegraphing" the pass. This assumption is supported by the work of Hobson and Henderson (1941), who found that a group of proficient basketball passers had a lateral visual perception 15 degrees greater than that of other ball

players. Furthermore, the team's two best shooters had a vertical visual field that was 10 degrees greater than normal.

Effects of Aging on Depth Perception and Field of Vision

Many of the changes associated with SMD also affect the size of a person's field of vision. Not only are retinal cells lost in the area of the macula, there is also an accompanying loss of photoreceptors in the retina's periphery. Burg (1968) found that a person's lateral field of vision is at its greatest at about age 35; thereafter, the size of the functional field of vision gradually decreases until about age 60, whereupon changes occur more rapidly (Wolf & Nadroski, 1971). Anatomical and physiological changes within the visual system itself are not the only causes of decreased field of vision. Changes in facial structure can also help reduce the size of the visual field. For instance, with age the upper eyelid may droop, a clinical condition known as *senile ptosis*. This condition can significantly limit vertical peripheral vision. Furthermore, loss of fat tissue around the orbital sockets can make the eyeball sink, restricting vision in all directions (Shephard, 1978).

Eye Dominance

It is well known that humans show a dominance for handedness, and within the last decade much has been written about right versus left hemispherical brain dominance. A lesser-known fact regarding human makeup is *eye dominance,* which refers to the ability of one eye to lead the other in tasks involving visual tracking and visual fixation.

The development of eye dominance is believed to be established early in life. About 75 percent of children will develop a dominant eye by 3 years of age and by 5 years the percentage of children who develop a dominant eye will increase to about 95 percent (cited in Whiting, 1971).

The most frequently used test to determine eye dominance is the "hole-in-card" test. To administer this test, simply cut a 1/4-inch (diameter) hole in the middle of a sheet of cardboard measuring 11 inches square. Standing 7 feet from a blackboard, instruct the individual to hold the cardboard at arm's length and, while keeping both eyes open, to look through the hole and locate a 1/2-inch (diameter) dot that is drawn on the blackboard. Now instruct the individual to close one eye. If the dot remains in view, then the open eye is the dominant eye. If the dot disappears, then the eye that was closed is the dominant eye.

Most studies examining the association between eye dominance and motor performance have included handedness as an additional variable. Individuals who are right-eyed and right-handed or left-eyed and left-handed are said to possess *unilateral dominance,* which means their dominant eye is on the same side of the body as their dominant hand. In contrast, *cross-laterals* are either right-eyed and left-handed or left-eyed and right-handed.

A majority of the studies investigating this topic have found unilaterals to be superior to crossed-laterals in a variety of tasks (Adams, 1965; Christina et al., 1981; Payne, 1988). Nevertheless, Adams (1965) has noted that a great deal of speculation exists among baseball coaches, suggesting that the crossed-lateral performer may have a distinct advantage in such tasks as batting. It is believed, among baseball coaches, that this purported advantage is due to the fact that the dominant eye of the crossed-lateral hitter is closer to the pitcher. Moreover, this lead eye is not restricted by having to view across the bridge of the batter's nose. Indeed, it appears that crossed-lateral dominance is a trait that is represented to a greater degree among baseball players as compared to the general population. Teig, an optometrist, found more than half of the 250 major league baseball players he examined to exhibit crossed-lateral dominance. By contrast, only 20 percent of the general population exhibit this trait (cited in Oxendine, 1984).

While an overwhelming majority of the research has reported superior performance among unilaterals, Sage (1984) cautions that crossed-laterals also perform well in a variety of activities and therefore recommends that no attempts be made to switch a performer from a crossed-lateral to a unilateral technique.

Tracking and Object Interception

To successfully gain control over a projectile, the performer must visually track the object to be intercepted. The primary purpose of *tracking* the object is to gain important information regarding the object's flight. Thus, a properly functioning ocular-motor system is needed to track the object and a properly functioning motor system is needed to act on the object.

The ocular-motor system is composed of two eye-movement systems. First, the smooth pursuit system is capable of matching eye-movement speed with the speed of the projectile, to maintain a stable retinal image. Second, the saccadic eye-movement system detects and corrects differences between projectile location and eye fixation. When objects are traveling faster than 24.70 to 33.54 meters per second, the saccadic system is primarily used (Yarbas, 1967).

Developmentally, the infant is not capable of freely moving the eyes across an arc of 180 degrees until sometime between 40 and 52 weeks of age (Corbin, 1980), which explains why tracking is first accomplished primarily by head movements and then through a series of eye-head movements. By 5 or 6 years of age, children can efficiently track objects moving in the horizontal plane. When children are between 8 and 9 years of age, they can track balls that travel in an arc (Morris, 1980). As dynamic visual acuity improves, so does the ability to track fast-moving objects because whenever an object is moving at an angular velocity at which smooth eye movements are no longer possible, the pursuit task becomes a function of dynamic visual acuity (Sanderson, 1972).

The coordinated interception of a moving object is a task frequently studied in research laboratories. This process involving object interception is commonly referred to as *coincidence-anticipation*. Most frequently, the Bassin anticipation timer (Lafayette Instrument Company, Model 50-575) has been selected as the instrument of choice to measure coincidence-anticipation (see Figure 9-6). The apparatus consists of one yellow warning light and two runways attached end-to-end. Each runway consists of 16 red LEDs that are 0.6 cm in diameter and spaced 4.5 cm apart. The sequentially lighted LED (Light Emitting Diode) lamps are designed to give the appearance of a moving stimulus. Most often the objective of the task is to depress a button placed at the end of the runway so that one's response coincides with the lighting of the last runway lamp. In order to be successful at this task, you must initiate the response one reaction time and one movement time before the lighting of the target lamp.

Many factors can influence how well a person can make a motor response coincide with the arrival of an external object, including object speed, object predictability, viewing time, and gender and age (Magill, 1985). Briefly, coincidence-anticipation improves with age (up to a point that has yet to be determined) and is greatly influenced by practice (Dorfman, 1977). It also appears that boys perform more accurately than girls (Isaacs, 1983) and that both very slow- and very fast-moving objects cause greater performance error. This finding led Wade (1980) to speculate that both children and adults may respond most accurately to speeds that they confront in their everyday world.

Based on these findings, one can speculate that a slowly projected ball may not necessarily always be the easiest to catch. Furthermore, when a child is first learning to catch, the teacher should consistently toss the ball directly toward the child instead of using an arced delivery. This may explain why

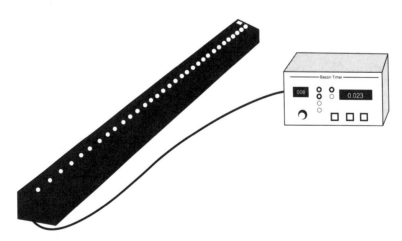

FIGURE 9-6   The Bassin anticipation timer

Isaacs (1984) found that young T-baseball players missed 85 percent of all fly balls.

More recently, Isaacs (1987) has described a procedure whereby two independent Bassin anticipation timers are interfaced, making it capable of measuring a type of coincidence-anticipation involving the estimation of intersection of two converging targets. Developmental data generated on this modified apparatus will be available in the near future.

Teachers of motor skills should also be aware that each visual trait described in this chapter may be improved with visual training. Dr. Arthur Seiderman and Steven Schneider's (1983) book *The Athletic Eye* describes in detail a visual-training program.

MOTOR DEVELOPMENT OF BLIND CHILDREN

Chapters 10 through 14 discuss at length the acquisition of selected reflexes and motor skills. This section describes the development of selected motor acts in blind children.

The general public considers *blindness* a total loss of vision, but this is a misconception. The official definition of blindness is based on distance vision as measured by the Snellen eye chart and does not take into consideration near vision. Thus a legally blind person may be capable of considerable vision when objects are placed close to the eyes. In general, residual vision in legally blind people can range from total blindness, where light is not perceived, to a Snellen distance vision of 20/200, which is the equivalent of an 80 percent loss of vision. Therefore, whenever we speak of blindness, we also should specify the degrees of residual vision remaining, if any.

The effects of blindness on a person's motor development also depend on the age of onset. Those people who are congenitally blind or who become blind before they are 5 years old do not retain a workable visual imagery (Lowenfeld, 1981). Thus the congenitally blind must adjust to our visual world without the advantage of working from an established visual reference point. Conversely, those individuals who lose their sight later in life are more capable of dealing with life's demands because they have experienced vision and are capable of remembering it. Obviously, blindness exerts its most devastating effects on motor development and motor performance when the newborn experiences total blindness (that is, 0 percent residual vision). The following sections discuss the specific influence of congenital blindness on early motor development.

Head and Trunk Control

Several weeks after birth, sighted infants attempt to raise their head off the crib mattress; soon thereafter the back is arched and the chest elevates. Because of visual curiosity, the infant elevates the trunk for increasingly longer periods of time. Thus, for the sighted infant, visual curiosity elicits the movements that aid in the development of head, neck, and trunk control. Blind infants, however, tend to cry and fuss in the prone position. Parents often then place them on their back, in an attempt to pacify, but this position does not help the development of head and upper body control because the practice environment is not conducive. And even when blind infants stay in the prone position, they arch the head and neck less frequently than sighted infants because there is no vision to initiate purposeful movement at this young age.

Independent Sitting

Somewhere between 4 and 8 months of age, most sighted infants are capable of sitting alone. Blind infants are also capable of sitting alone at this time if their parents have adequately prepared them for this milestone. However, if the blind infants have spent prolonged periods of time supine, they will not have had the opportunity to develop the necessary head, neck, and trunk control to sit alone.

Creeping

By approximately 10 months of age, sighted infants are capable of supporting themselves on their hands and knees, thus making creeping possible. Visual curiosity entices the sighted infant to creep toward objects that are in sight but out of reach. Obviously, such visual curiosity is absent in the blind infant. If the unsighted infant is to develop normally, a sensory modality other than vision must be used to instigate infant creeping and exploration of the unseen environment. Parents of blind infants should stimulate children's curiosity by enticing them to move toward noise-making toys; this audiomotor coordination ability is conceptualized by about 1 year of age (Jan, Freeman, & Scott, 1977).

Independent Walking

Both sighted and blind children are capable of standing and walking with support at approximately the same time. Nevertheless, the achievement of independent walking is significantly delayed in blind children (Adelson & Fraiberg, 1976). In fact, children with partial vision tend to walk sooner than totally blind children or those who possess only light perception. When independent walking is achieved, the blind child characteristically exhibits an insecure gait consisting of a wide base of support, flat-footed contact with the supporting surface, and toeing out. These characteristics describe the expected sequence of events in sighted children, but some unsighted individuals exhibit these immature characteristics throughout the lifespan.

Prehension

Prehension, the ability to grasp and seize objects with the hands, is an important aspect of a child's motor development. Prehensile abilities enable a child to gather information about the environment in new ways. Increased and varied exploration is possible because of the child's ability to seize and manipulate objects with the hands. This new mode of exploration lets the child discover properties of objects and allows the child to use objects as implements in achieving goals (Bower, 1982).

Vision is important for the development of prehension for three reasons. First, the initial phase of self-directed reaching is visually evoked; that is, the child reaches upon viewing some object in the environment. This form of reaching is an improvement over the random grasping that occurs earlier in the child's life. Second, vision is used to facilitate hand closure around an object once the child has manual contact with the desired object. Third, during the act of visually guided reaching, vision enables the child to correct errors throughout the reach.

Thus, for the blind child the primary modality for stimulating prehensile skills is absent (Troster & Brambring, 1993). Because reaching for sound-producing objects generally will not occur until the last quarter of the first year of life, it is important that parents encourage their blind child to manipulate objects that have been placed in her or his hand. In addition, manual guidance by the parents is also important; it is imperative that finger dexterity and sensitivity be acquired early in development because it establishes a readiness for Braille instruction at school age (Jan, Fremand, & Scott, 1977).

An investigation by Adelson & Fraiberg (1976) compared the gross motor achievements of 10 congenitally blind infants to normally sighted peers. The children were observed for 2 years, and comparisons were made in reference to selected items from the Bayley Scales of Infant Development. Table 9-1 has the median age comparisons for the sighted and blind children on selected Bayley Scale items. Note that nearly all the blind infants were found to be on schedule when compared to their sighted counterparts on items requiring postural control. These items include: sits alone momentarily, makes stepping movements when hands are held, and stands alone. Attaining these items on schedule suggests normal development of trunk control and the ability to bear weight and perform stepping movements with support.

However, there were five items in which the blind subjects showed significant delays. With the exception of elevates self by arms when prone, the remaining four items—raises self to sitting position, stands up using furniture (pulls to stand), walks alone (three steps), and walks alone across room—all involve self-initiated mobility. Thus the authors con-

TABLE 9-1 Comparison of Sighted and Unsighted Children on Selected Bayley Scale Items

Item	Median Age (months)	
	Sighted	Unsighted
Elevates self by arms, prone	2.1	8.75
Sits alone momentarily	5.3	6.75
Rolls from back to stomach	6.4	7.25
Sits alone steadily	6.6	8.00
Raises self to sitting position	8.3	11.00
Stands up using furniture (pulls up to stand)	8.6	13.00
Makes stepping movements (walks with hands held)	8.8	10.75
Stands alone	11.0	13.00
Walks alone, 3 steps	11.7	15.25
Walks alone across room	12.1	19.25°

°One child had not achieved this task by age 2 years.
Source: Adapted from E. Adelson and S. Fraiberg (1976), Sensory Deficit and Motor Development in Infants Blind from Birth," in Z. S. Jastrzembska (ed.), *The Effects of Blindness and Other Impairments on Early Development* (New York: The American Foundation for the Blind).

cluded that if blind children are to develop within the normal limits of their sighted peers in self-initiated mobility, they need sound as an adaptive substitute for sight; this substitution should occur toward the end of the first year of life.

Play Behavior of Blind Children

For the sighted child, play is a spontaneous and creative act carried out for its own sake and usually consisting of self-imposed games where new movement skills are learned and old movement skills are defined. New movement ideas are picked up from imitating the movements of other children. Thus play is an important learning medium. In contrast, blind children tend to be inactive and show little drive to explore their unseen environment. If left on their own, many engage in physical activity involving little more than body rocking, eye pressing, and finger tapping (Jan, Freeman, & Scott, 1977). Therefore, it is important—within reason—not to overprotect the blind child. Blind children should

be given the opportunity to engage in numerous movement experiences and should be encouraged to explore their unseen world.

THE NONVISUAL SENSES

While the visual system is the predominant system of choice, it is by no means the only sensory modality that can exert an influence on motor development and motor performance. Unfortunately, compared to the visual system, little information is available on the other sensory modalities that are known to influence motor development and motor performance. This lack of information relating to the nonvisual senses was recognized by Reisman (1987) when she wrote, "To be able to consider five sensory modalities in one chapter is actually a statement about the need for further research in this area. Not only is there much work to be done in understanding changing sensitivities with age, especially in the cutaneous senses, but very little attention has been paid to the normal range of individual differences to be found in infant sensory functioning" (p. 295). Nevertheless, in this section we will briefly describe the proprioceptive system and its accompanying vestibular apparatus as well as the cutaneous system. The auditory system can also indirectly affect motor development and motor performance, as has been addressed earlier in this chapter in the motor development of blind children.

The Proprioceptive System

The proprioceptive system makes it possible for an individual to be aware of his or her movements as well as the ability to perceive the location of one's body parts in space without visual reference to them. This feat is made possible by a group of sensory receptors located in the body's joints, muscles, tendons, and the labyrinth of the inner ear. These specialized receptors are the *muscle spindles, Golgi tendon organs, joint receptors,* and the *vestibular apparatus.* These sensory receptors respond to changes in joint angles, changes in the length and tension relationship of muscles and to movements of the head. Since these receptor cells are activated by mechanical deformation, they are frequently referred to as *mechanoreceptors.* Let's briefly examine the function of each.

The muscle spindle receptors are oval shaped (cigar-shaped) structures that are attached in parallel with the muscles' largest fibers, known as the extrafusal muscle fibers. Contained within the spindle itself is a smaller muscle fiber known as an intrafusal muscle fiber. Because the fibers lie parallel to one another and are attached to the sheath of the extrafusal fibers, it is possible for the muscle spindle to gauge the amount of tension within the muscle itself. For instance, when the larger extrafusal muscle fibers are stretched, they, in turn, stretch the smaller intrafusal fibers of the muscle spindle. This stretch will cause activation of the spindle, resulting in afferent discharge. The effect of an afferent discharge is to stimulate the skeletomotor neurons, which, in turn, will cause a

contraction of the muscle's larger extrafusal fibers, thus reducing the stretch on the intrafusal muscle fibers. The classical knee jerk is an example of this phenomenon.

The Golgi tendon organs are small stretch receptors which are located near the junction of the muscle and the muscle's tendon (musculo-tendinous junction). Their primary role is to detect tension in the muscle's tendon and, in fact, provide the central nervous system with continuous information regarding force development in both static and dynamic conditions. These highly sensitive organs play a major role in maintaining muscle tone.

Joint receptors are located throughout the body and, as the name implies, are located in the body's joints. More specifically, these receptors are located in the joint's capsule in those areas that are most responsive to stretch. While some joint receptors fire at specific joint angles, most fire at the joint's extreme range of motion. This has lead researchers to question the early belief that these receptors were responsible for providing precise information about movement (Schmidt, 1988). Instead, some now believe that these receptors could be acting as "limit detectors." For example, "joint receptors in the hip could signal the end of the flexion phase of the step cycle; their reflex effect might help to terminate activity in the appropriate flexion muscles, and contribute to the initiation of the extension phase of the step cycle" (Tracey 1980, cited in Sage, 1984).

The vestibular apparatus which is located in the inner ear is responsible for registering head motion as well as accompanying body motion. Anytime the head is turned or moved through space, the vestibular receptors will be stimulated. As illustrated in Figure 9-7, the vestibular system is actually composed of two subsystems, the *semicircular canals* and the *otolith organs* (utricle and saccule). The semicircular canals are fluid-filled ducts that lie at right angles to one another. Because they are capable of registering changes in head motion they are sometimes referred to as angular accelerometers. Unlike the semicircular canals that primarily detect rotational motion, the otolith organs are primarily responsible for detecting linear acceleration as they

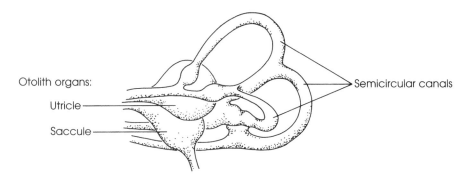

Otolith organs:

Utricle

Saccule

Semicircular canals

FIGURE 9-7   The vestibular system is composed of two subsystems, the semicircular canals and the otolith organs.

provide information concerning the body's position in relation to the force of gravity (Sage, 1984). This system is also important in some reflexive behaviors (righting reflex) and the coordination of visual fixation.

The proprioceptive system plays an important role in motor development and skilled motor performance. Briefly, proprioception is a factor contributing to the development of body awareness, spatial awareness, and directional awareness. In addition, the vestibular apparatus is critical in the development of both static and dynamic balance, a topic which is discussed at some length in Chapter 4 and Chapter 16.

The Cutaneous System

The *cutaneous system,* also known as *tactile* sensitivity, receives its information from sensory receptors located at the body's surface, the skin. Once thought of as just the sense of touch, we now know that the cutaneous system consists of at least four skin senses: pressure, coldness, warmth, and pain. Because of its sensitivity to temperature and pain it is this sensory system that alerts us to potential adverse environmental conditions.

When studying the development of the cutaneous system, researchers typically look for one of three possible responses to tactile stimulation. These three possible responses include reflex, withdrawal, or approach responses. For example, the reflex behaviors known as the sucking reflex, the searching reflex, the Babkin reflex, the Babinski reflex, as well as the palmar grasp and plantar grasp reflex are all normally elicited by tactile stimulation (see Chapter 10). Withdrawal responses generally manifest themselves when the infant or child attempts to turn the head or move a limb away from the source of stimulation and may sometimes be accompanied by a facial grimace. Lastly, approach behaviors are generally exhibited by children when they show responsiveness to kisses, hugs, and playful tickling. In fact, these approach behaviors are essential for the human attachment-bonding process early in life and are also important later in life when intimacy and human sexual interactions become evident.

Which of these three possible reactions to tactile stimulation will be exhibited depends upon many factors. Some of these factors include mood state (awake or sleeping), area of stimulation (body area), gender, and level of maturity. For example, an absence of the palmar, plantar, and Babkin reflexes has been noted during periods of quiet sleep, but sometimes observed during active sleep, and nearly always when the infants were quietly awake. Regarding gender, females have been found to habituate to vibrotactile stimulation at an earlier age than males (Leader et al., 1982). This is believed to be a result of the female's greater level of nervous system maturity.

The cutaneous system is believed by many to be the first functional sensory system to develop. For example, Humphrey (1964) has demonstrated the functional capacity of this system's receptors as early as 7.5 weeks fetal age. More specifically, Humphrey noted that light stroking of the perioral area would elicit a neck flexion causing the head to move away from the stimulus. Approximately 1 week later, however, the same stimulus would on occasions result in the fetus turning the head toward the stimulus, accompanied by opening the mouth and swallowing. This is believed to be the precursor to the feeding reflex seen at birth (Humphrey, 1970).

Initially, sensitivity to tactile stimulation is greatest in those parts of the body that are used to explore the child's ever changing world. These body regions of greatest sensitivity include the mouth, lips, and tongue. One only has to observe a newborn infant for a short period of time to witness this fact. As soon as the child comes in contact with an object, it is generally placed into the mouth for exploration. This point is best highlighted by Lippsitt's (1978) observation: "The importance of such tactual stimulation, and the low threshold of the newborn for response to it, can be demonstrated by rotating the finger completely around the lips in a circle, and noting the precise following of such stimulation which many newborns can demonstrate" (p. 499).

The cutaneous receptors play an important role in both motor development and motor control. For example, as mentioned previously, this sense is initially used by the infant to explore objects within its new world. Nevertheless, perhaps its importance is best illustrated by persons with *Romberg's sign* disease. Individuals with this disease have varying degrees of damage to the sensory receptors, usually those in the soles of their feet. As a result, they experience difficulty in maintaining balance, especially if their eyes are closed. Furthermore, if the sensory receptors are damaged in the hands, fine motor manipulations with the hand or fingers are extremely difficult when vision is not available, and even impossible if the receptors are completely destroyed. Just think how often you have held an object in your

hand only to have it start to slip. In this scenario, most individuals will be capable of quickly grasping the slipping object to keep it from falling. In fact, Johansson and Westling (1989) report that our ability to recognize that an object is slipping from our grasp and then to quickly tighten our grasp, only takes about 80 msec. This research indicates the rapidity with which individuals can respond to cutaneous stimulation.

SUMMARY

A sharp visual image is possible whenever light entering the eye converges on the aspect of the retina called the macula. Varying light entering the eye comes to rest on the macula through the process of accommodation.

The eye develops as an outgrowth of the forebrain and remains an inseparable component of the central nervous system throughout the lifespan. Like the brain, the eye achieves most of its growth prior to birth.

The eye is functionally immature at birth. For instance, visual acuity steadily improves during the first 4 to 5 years, as do depth perception and field of vision. Furthermore, these visual attributes correlate positively with selected motor tasks.

After about 40 years of age, there are changes in functional vision. These changes become noticeable because the amount of light reaching the eye's retina is reduced and there is frequent difficulty in focusing near objects.

Because with age less light reaches the retina, it is important that elderly people perform physical tasks in well-illuminated activity areas. In addition, activity supervisors should be aware that bifocal wearers frequently experience difficulty in both tracking and judging the speed of moving objects.

The effects of blindness on motor development depend on the age of onset and the degree of residual vision remaining, if any. Blindness exerts its most devastating effects on motor development and motor performance when the newborn is totally blind. Because visual curiosity elicits movement, the unsighted child is not visually motivated to explore the unseen world. If the unsighted infant is to develop normally, another sensory modality (usually sound) must be substituted for vision.

Vision is not the only sensory modality known to influence motor development and motor performance. Two other important sensory systems are the proprioceptive system and the cutaneous system. The proprioceptive system receives sensory input from joint receptors, muscle spindles, and the Golgi tendon organs. Each of these specialized receptors monitors the stretch and/or force being placed upon the muscle and its tendons. Additionally, the vestibular system, an element of the proprioceptive system, provides information regarding changes in the body's position in space and the location of the body's limbs in space without visual reference to them. The primary components of the vestibular system include the semicircular canals and the otolith organs. Lastly, the cutaneous system, also known as tactile sensitivity, is a specialized system that receives information regarding pressure, temperature, and pain.

KEY TERMS

Accommodation
Binocular vision
Blindness
Cataracts
Ciliary muscle
Coincidence-
    anticipation
Cones
Crossed-laterals
Cutaneous system
Dynamic visual acuity
Eye dominance
Golgi tendon organs
Hyperopic
Joint receptors
Macula
Mechanoreceptors
Muscle spindles
Otolith organs

Peripheral vision
Presbyopia
Proprioceptive system
Retina
Rods
Semicircular canals
Senile macular
    degeneration (SMD)
Senile miosis
Senile ptosis
Snellen eye chart
Static visual acuity
Strabismus
Tracking
Unilateral dominance
Vestibular apparatus
Visual acuity
Visual cliff

CHAPTER 10

Infant Reflexes and Stereotypies

Infancy is one of the most interesting of all periods of life to study. This time is particularly fascinating because of the two types of movements characteristic of the first several months of life: infant reflexes and stereotypies. This chapter describes these movements and their importance in the developmental process.

IMPORTANCE OF THE INFANT REFLEXES

During the last 4 months of prenatal life and the first 4 months after birth, a human being's movement repertoire is composed largely of movements that are reflexive; that is, each movement is an involuntary, stereotyped response to a particular stimulus. As an example, when a stimulus, such as touching the palm of the infant's hand, is applied, the stimulated hand closes in a routine or stereo-

typical response—each time the appropriate stimulus is applied, the same, or a highly similar, response occurs. Perhaps even more interesting is the fact that the reflexes are involuntary; these movements are a result of an unconscious effort by a person, unlike later, more familiar voluntary movements. Most reflexes also occur *subcortically*, which literally means "below the level of the cortex of the brain." A more understandable description is "below the level of the higher brain centers," because some reflexes are processed in such lower brain areas as the brain stem (Fiorentino, 1963). Reflexive movements are therefore produced without direct involvement of the higher brain centers. The electrical impulse the stimulus creates travels to the central nervous system. From there, the information is integrated and the appropriate movement message is issued to the muscles involved in the response. This simple method of movement production seems appropriate for producing certain reflexes such as the palmar grasp. However, the production of the more involved reflexes (discussed later) is one of the many phenomena of human motor development.

Infant versus Lifespan Reflexes

In normal, healthy infants, the infant reflexes typically do not last much beyond the first birthday (the downward, sideward, and backward parachuting reflexes are exceptions, see Table 10-1). However, some reflexes persevere much longer. In fact, in normal, healthy individuals, several reflexes last throughout the lifespan. For example, most of us have personally experienced the knee-jerk reflex; while seated the physician taps our patellar tendon directly below the patella and our lower leg "jerks" creating a rapid, partial extension. The flexor withdrawal reflex is another example. It exists during infancy yet does not typically cease at the end of the first year of life. In the flexor withdrawal reflex our arm abruptly flexes upon touching a sharp or hot object. Obviously this reflex is often quite useful in protecting us from injury. All reflexes which endure throughout the lifespan in normal healthy individuals are called *lifespan reflexes*. Because this chapter emphasizes the infant reflexes, the lifespan reflexes will not be discussed.

Role of the Reflexes in Survival

The infant reflexes are not only an interesting aspect of human development but are extremely important as well (see Table 10-2). A human being is born with few voluntary capabilities and limited mobility. Human neonates are basically helpless and therefore highly dependent on their caretakers and their reflexes for their protection and survival. The infant reflexes predominantly used for protection, nutrition, or survival are the *primitive reflexes*. The primitive reflexes are those that appear during gestation or at birth and have become suppressed by 6 months of age. They occur in all normal newborns (Barnes, Crutchfield, & Heriza, 1984).

The sucking reflex is one of the best-known primitive reflexes; it is characterized by an oral sucking action when the lips are stimulated. A neonate is born without the voluntary capacity to ingest food, so the sucking reflex enables the baby to ingest by involuntary means, taking in the nutrients essential for survival. This reflex is discussed in greater detail later in the chapter.

Also important in maintaining sufficient nourishment for the infant is the search or rooting reflex, which functions in conjunction with the sucking reflex. The search reflex is elicited when the area of the cheek close to the lips is stimulated. The infant's head turns in the direction of the stimulation. This reflex enables the immobile newborn baby to seek nourishment the mother provides when stimulated by the mother's breast.

The labyrinthine reflex is a slightly different protective reflex that is also crucial for survival. If an infant is placed in a prone position, breathing may be inhibited to the point of suffocation. The helpless neonate has insufficient voluntary capabilities to raise or turn the head to improve breathing. However, the involuntary labyrinthine reflex enables the infant to "right" or elevate the head, thus restoring the head to a position more conducive to breathing and allowing the baby to survive. But although the labyrinthine reflex is a protective function, it is best known for its relationship to the development of upright posture, as discussed in more detail later in the chapter.

Role of the Reflexes in Developing Future Movement

Reflexes related to the development of later voluntary movement are known as *postural reflexes*. Postural reflexes are thought to be a basis for future movements that, unlike the reflexes, emanate from a stimulation initiated by the higher brain centers. Some reflexes are believed to be directly integrated, modified, and incorporated into more complex patterns to form voluntary movements (Fiorentino, 1981). The walking reflex is one of the most obvious

TABLE 10-1 Expected Time of Occurrence of Selected Infant Reflexes (Months)

	Age (Years)												
	B	1	2	3	4	5	6	7	8	9	10	11	12
Primitive													
Palmar grasp													
Sucking													
Search													
Moro													
Startle													
Asymmetric tonic neck													
Symmetric tonic neck													
Plantar grasp													
Babinski													
Palmar mandibular													
Palmar mental													
Postural													
Stepping													
Crawling													
Swimming	2 weeks												
Head righting													
Body righting													
Parachuting down													+
side													+
back													+
Labyrinthine													
Pull-up													

° Also thought to exist for some weeks prenatally

examples of a postural reflex facilitating later voluntary movement. If an infant 1 or 2 months old is held upright with the feet touching a supporting surface, the pressure on the feet stimulates the legs to perform a walking action. This movement is, of course, reflexive; the infant makes no conscious effort to produce this movement—the movement occurs involuntarily and subcortically. This early, involuntary, walkinglike movement is a critical antecedent to optimal development of voluntary walking, which appears in the months to follow.

The purported link between certain infant reflexes and later voluntary movement is questionable. As Bower (1976) described in an article, "Repetitive Processes in Child Development," these reflexes, believed to be linked to voluntary behavior, often disappear before the onset of the "related" voluntary movement. This is what happens with the

TABLE 10-2   Why Study the Infant Reflexes?

1. During the last four months prenatally and the first four months postnatally, reflexive movement is such a dominant form of movement that the human being has been labeled a "reflex machine" (Wyke, 1975; p. 27).

2. By nourishing and protecting, the primitive reflexes are critical for human survival.

3. The postural reflexes are believed to be basic to more complex, voluntary movement of later infancy.

4. Though the age of appearance and disappearance of infant reflexes is somewhat variable, reflexes can be an important step in diagnosing infant health and neurological maturation.

walking reflex. The walking reflex is noticeable soon after birth, but around the sixth month of life the reflex ceases. Application of the appropriate stimulus no longer evokes the walkinglike actions in the legs; 4 to 8 months may then elapse before the child can walk voluntarily. "How can something that disappears be critical for subsequent development?" (Bower, p. 39). Because there is a rather long time between the offset of the reflex and the onset of the related voluntary movement, the role of the infant reflexes in the development of later voluntary movements is in question.

The overwhelmingly prevalent view, however, is that the reflexes "provide automatic movement that is a form of practice for aiding in the attainment of future movements" (Coley, 1978, p. 43). They "blend into voluntary patterns of movement . . . and are necessary for beginning movement and the development of muscle tone" (Lord, 1977, p. 89). Furthermore, the reflexes "play a dominant role in the regulation of degree, strength, balance, and distribution of muscular tone" (Fiorentino, 1981, p. 26). This muscular tone is critical to performance of future voluntary movements.

Specific and supporting research has been conducted to gain more scientific insight into this controversy. Infants whose walking reflex was regularly stimulated began to walk at an earlier age than their nonstimulated counterparts (Zelazo, 1976). This research was undertaken with the assumption that if stimulation of the walking reflex preceding the disappearance phase affects the rate of emergence of voluntary walking, there must be a link between the pre- and postdisappearance movements. Bower (1976) conducted a similar study in which infants were subjected to "intensive practice" in reaching movements during the involuntary phase of reaching behavior. As in the Zelazo study, Bower found that the predisappearance stimulation expedited the emergence of the postdisappearance voluntary movement. In fact, in some cases, those children who were given practice experienced no disappearance phase whatsoever (Bower, 1976). "Such results pointed to the possibility that the reason abilities disappear is that they are not exercised" (p. 40). More importantly, these results can be interpreted as demonstrating a link between the predisappearance involuntary reaching and grasping and the postdisappearance voluntary reaching and grasping movements.

The Reflexes as Diagnostic Tools

The infant reflexes are crucial for the infant's survival and for the development of future voluntary movements. These early, involuntary forms of movement behavior are also important in determining the infant's level of neurological maturation. Pediatricians commonly use many reflexes as diagnostic tools. Although the age at which each infant reflex emerges and disappears varies with each individual child, knowledge of the normal timeline can help in diagnosing problems. Severe deviations from the normal time frame may indicate neurological immaturity or dysfunction. If the reflex in question is lacking, excessively weak, asymmetrical, or persisting past the normal age of offset, the examining health professional is alerted to a need for additional testing or to intervention to correct the dysfunction.

Reflexes should be carefully tested only by trained professionals. Some parents become frantic when they cannot elicit a particular reflex, assuming that their child has an impaired neurological system when, in fact, the parents' incorrect application of the stimulus or the baby's temporary behavioral state is causing the difficulty in eliciting the expected response. Normally, for any infant reflex to be elicited, there must be a state of quiet. If the baby is restless, crying, sleepy, or distracted, she may not respond to the applied stimulus; this lack of response certainly should not be considered an indication of a neurological aberration.

Many infant reflexes are tested during normal physical examinations of the baby. One of the most commonly used to detect neurological dysfunction is the Moro reflex, which may signify a cerebral birth injury if it is lacking or asymmetrical (appearing more forcefully on one side of the body than the other). The asymmetric tonic neck reflex is another common infant diagnostic tool. If this reflex perseveres past the normal time of disappearance, cerebral palsy or other neural damage could be indicated (Lorton & Lorton, 1984). These reflexes, described in more detail later, are two examples of the many infant reflexes that help health-care professionals determine the infant's neurological state.

The Milani Comparetti Neuromotor Developmental Examination is an evaluation instrument that uses a number of infant reflexes. This test was designed to evaluate neurological maturity of children from birth to 24 months of age. This standardized method of examining reflexive movement presents an opportunity to visually inspect children's motor patterns and the patterns' appropriateness for the children's age. The overall objective of the test is to develop a profile of children's movement in relation to what is normally expected for children of a specific age. This examination is useful in monitoring motor function during normal checkups and is especially valuable for use with children suspected of a motor delay (Frankenburg, Thornton, & Cohrs, 1981).

A more recent tool designed to examine the status of the infant reflexes is the *Primitive Reflex Profile* (Capute et al., 1984). This scale was developed to enable quantification of the level of presence or strength of primitive reflexes such as the asymmetric tonic neck, symmetric tonic neck, and the Moro reflexes. The authors of this profile believed that this tool was necessary because all previous reflex

evaluation systems noted only the presence or absence of the reflex, not the degree of strength. This system was also believed to enable a uniform grading system that would assist in charting findings and facilitate communication of the results. Primitive reflexes were emphasized because of the major role they play in enabling normal motor function as they become suppressed throughout the first year of life. In fact, according to the authors of the profile, the primitive reflexes may be the most sensitive indicators of early motor abnormality. As we mentioned earlier, if these reflexes persist past their expected time of occurrence, some dysfunction may be indicated.

To enable quantification of the reflexes, the Primitive Reflex Profile employs a five-point classification system. A 0 is assigned when a reflex is totally absent. A 1 indicates a reflex that is only sufficiently present to create a small change in muscle tone. A 2 is assigned when the reflex is physically present and readily visible, while a 3 indicates the same but with more noticeable strength or force. A 4 is assigned when the reflex is so strong that it dominates the individual.

PINPOINTING THE NUMBER OF INFANT REFLEXES

Although the total number of infant reflexes has been estimated at 27 (Lorton & Lorton, 1984), it is difficult to determine an accurate count, for several reasons. First, various experts use different terminology to refer to the same reflex because there is more than one term for many of the reflexes. For example, the rooting reflex is also called the search reflex or the cardinal points reflex because stimulation of the cardinal points—the four quadrants of the mouth—elicits a searching response.

Furthermore, the reflexes themselves are often poorly defined. The components, as well as the name, of a certain infant reflex may vary, depending on the source, such as with the palmar grasp reflex. The palmar grasp generally is considered as consisting of the four fingers closing when the palm is stimulated. Twitchell (1970) proposed that this reflex may in fact be much more complex. According to Twitchell, there are multiple stimuli and multiple responses involved in the reflexive grasping. Along with the familiar closing of the four fingers, Twitchell described a "synergistic flexion" response of the fingers as well as every joint of the arm when the appropriate muscles of the shoulders are stretched. This stretching, often referred to as a traction response, may occur when the palm of the hand is stimulated or even when there is a slight tug on the arm. In addition, Twitchell described what he called "local reactions." If specific areas of the hand are stimulated, there may be specific responses, depending on the infant's age or neurological maturity. For example, between the ages of 4 and 8 weeks, said Twitchell, a stimulation between the thumb and forefinger elicits a flexion of just those two digits. During the following weeks, a similar response can be elicited for each finger individually if the surface of the palm near the base of that finger is stimulated. Are these local reactions distinct infant reflexes, or are they all part of the palmar grasp? Twitchell inferred that these specific stimuli and responses are all a part of the development of the palmar grasp and eventually voluntary reaching and grasping behavior. Some sources differentiate between the palmar grasp reflex and the traction response; others cite only the palmar grasp. There is such confusion with other reflexes as well, complicating attempts to accurately number and organize the infant reflexes.

PRIMITIVE REFLEXES

Here we discuss the stimulus, response, approximate age of emergence and disappearance, and various points of interest concerning many infant primitive reflexes. This section is not an all-inclusive list of the infant reflexes; it discusses those reflexes considered the most interesting, important, or exemplary of important points.

Palmar Grasp

The *palmar grasp reflex*, one of the most well known of all infant reflexes, may also be one of the first to emerge (see Figure 10-1). The palmar grasp reflex normally appears in utero, as early as the fifth month of gestation. As mentioned earlier, there is evidence indicating that this reflex may be much

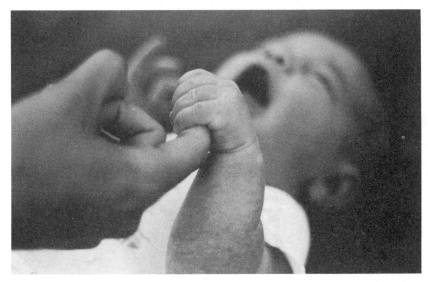

FIGURE 10-1 The palmar grasp reflex is one of the most noticeable reflexes to emerge.

more complex than generally believed. However, the basic palmar grasp reflex is a response to tactile stimulation of the palm of the hand. When the palm is stimulated, all four fingers of the stimulated hand flex or close. Although the thumb does not respond to this stimulus, the grasping response of the palmar grasp reflex can be surprisingly forceful. For example, if an adult simultaneously stimulates both of an infant's palms, the infant may respond with a grasp sufficiently forceful to enable the adult to lift the infant completely off the supporting surface. The palmar grasp reflex normally endures through the fourth month. A grasping action of the hand will likely persist past that time, but it will be voluntary, not reflexive. In fact, the palmar grasp reflex is believed to play an important role in the acquisition of early forms of voluntary reaching and grasping (Twitchell, 1970).

Sucking Reflex

Another reflex that appears very early in life is the *sucking reflex,* which is normally present prenatally. In fact, babies are occasionally born with "sucking blisters" on their lips, created by sucking actions during the prenatal state (Payne, 1985). The sucking response is elicited by the lips being stimulated, such as by the touch of the mother's breast. This stimulation actually evokes two sucking-related responses. See Figure 10-2. The first and most obvious response is the creation of a negative intraoral pressure as the sucking occurs. Second, the tongue applies a positive pressure; it presses upward and slightly forward with each sucking action. Thus, following the appropriate stimulation, there is a series of sucking movements, each movement consisting of the simultaneous application of negative and positive pressure. This movement normally remains a reflex through the third month of infancy; thereafter, it will be voluntary.

Search Reflex

The *search reflex* is often considered in conjunction with the sucking reflex, a logical approach because both reflexes are functionally linked to obtaining

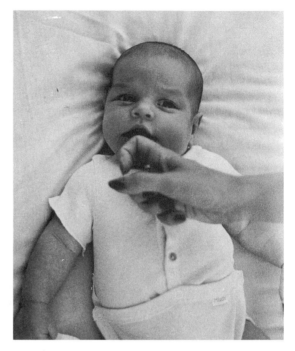

FIGURE 10-2 The sucking reflex occurs pre- and postnatally.

food. The search reflex helps the infant locate the source of nourishment, and then the sucking reflex enables the baby to ingest the food. This reflex, however, contributes to more than the baby's nourishment as the rotation of the neck often elicits other reflexes including the head- and body-righting reflexes. Also, failure or persistence of this reflex may be a sign of central nervous system or sensorimotor dysfunction. Asymmetrical appearance may mean an injury has occurred in a facial nerve or muscle, or one side of the brain (Barnes, Crutchfield, & Heriza, 1984).

Like the sucking reflex, the search reflex is believed to exist for some weeks prenatally and persist through the third month of infancy in most instances. The search reflex normally can be elicited by softly stroking the area of the face surrounding the mouth. The corresponding response is the infant's head turning in the direction of the stimulus (see Figure 10-3). The sensitive area surrounding the mouth is sometimes referred to as the cardinal point, so the

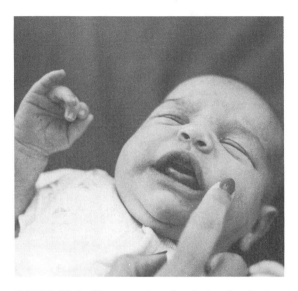

FIGURE 10-3 The search reflex helps the baby locate nourishment. It turns the head toward the food source when part of the cheek near the mouth is gently stimulated.

search reflex is also called the cardinal points reflex (and as mentioned earlier, the rooting reflex).

Moro Reflex

As mentioned, the *Moro reflex* is one of the most useful for diagnosing the infant's neurological maturation (see Figure 10-4). This reflex often exists at birth and endures until the infant is approximately 4 to 6 months old.

The Moro reflex can be elicited in a number of ways. One stimulus is to place the palm of the hand under the baby's head and then suddenly but gently lower the head a few inches. This stimulus causes the baby's arms, fingers, and legs to extend. The same response occurs if the entire baby is held and suddenly lowered 3 or 4 inches. Also, if the surface on which the baby is lying is struck with the palm of the hand, normally the Moro reflex will occur. There is, however, some disagreement concerning the role

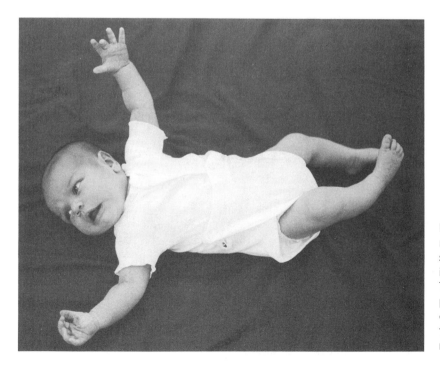

FIGURE 10-4 The Motor reflex is elicited by the same stimuli that will induce the startle reflex. The Moro, however, precedes the startle and causes the arms and legs to immediately extend rather than flex.

of the legs in the Moro reflex. Most experts agree that the legs extend unless they were already extended. Then they flex. Both of these situations may lead to a slight tremor or shaking of the legs (Barnes, Crutchfield, & Heriza, 1984). Interestingly, the disappearance of this reflex depends on the type of stimulus used; the "head drop" Moro disappears sooner than the other two types.

Failure to acquire the Moro reflex by birth may indicate a central nervous system dysfunction. Persisting past the expected time of suppression may indicate a sensorimotor problem. In addition, persistence will delay voluntary sitting, head control, and other motor milestones. Asymmetry of the Moro, as we have seen with other reflexes, may indicate an injury to one side of the brain (Barnes, Crutchfield, & Heriza, 1984).

Startle Reflex

The *startle reflex* is similar in many ways to the Moro reflex. The startle reflex can also be elicited by a rapid change of head position or striking the surface that supports the baby. The response these stimuli generate, however, is different than the Moro response. Whereas the Moro causes the limbs to immediately extend, the startle reflex causes the arms and legs to immediately flex. Furthermore, the Moro normally disappears at 4 to 6 months of age, but the startle may not appear until 2 to 3 months after the Moro disappears. The startle reflex in this form is normally suppressed by 1 year of age, although less severe startle responses are elicited throughout the lifespan.

Asymmetric Tonic Neck Reflex

The *asymmetric tonic neck reflex*, sometimes referred to as the bow and arrow or fencer's position, is commonly seen in premature babies but may not be noticeable in full-term infants. This reflex can be elicited when the baby is prone or supine. When the head is turned to one side or the other, the limbs on the face side extend while the limbs on the op-

posite side flex (see Figure 10-5). The asymmetric tonic neck reflex is generally strongest at approximately 2 months but occasionally can be elicited in infants up to 3 months old. This reflex is believed to facilitate the development of an awareness of both sides of the body as well as help develop eye-hand coordination (Lord, 1977).

Symmetric Tonic Neck Reflex

In the asymmetric tonic neck reflex, the right-side limbs respond differently than the left-side limbs, but this is not the case in the *symmetric tonic neck reflex*. As the term implies, the limbs in this reflex move symmetrically. This symmetrical response can be elicited by placing the baby in a supported sitting position. If the infant is tipped backward far enough, the neck eventually extends, which is the stimulus for a corresponding extension of the arms and flexion of the legs. However, if the baby is tipped forward until the neck is fully flexed, the arms flex, and the legs extend (see Figure 10-6).

This reflex is particularly critical in that its persistence may impede voluntary head raising when the infant is in a prone or supine position. It will also inhibit reaching and grasping, unsupported sitting, balance for walking, and virtually all major motor milestones (Barnes, Crutchfield, & Heriza, 1984).

Like the asymmetric tonic neck reflex, the symmetric tonic neck reflex is often noticeable from birth through approximately 3 months of age. Also like the asymmetric tonic neck reflex, persistence in this reflex can cause serious problems. For example, spinal flexion deformities may occur as well as difficulty in walking, standing, and sitting (Barnes, Crutchfield, & Heriza, 1984).

Plantar Grasp Reflex

From birth through the first year of infancy, the *plantar grasp reflex* normally can be elicited. This reflex is evoked by applying slight pressure, usually with the fingertip, to the ball of the foot, causing all the

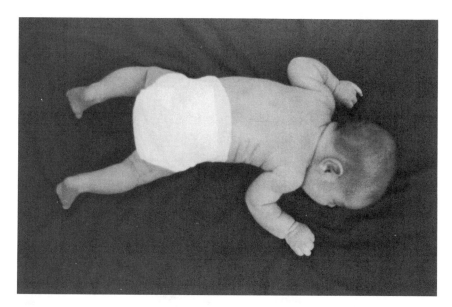

FIGURE 10-5 The asymmetric tonic neck reflex causes flexion on one side and extension on the other.

FIGURE 10-6 The symmetric tonic neck reflex is often observable during the first few months of life.

toes of that foot to flex. The toes curl around the stimulating object as if attempting to grasp, as in the palmar grasp reflex of the hand (see Figure 10-7).

The plantar grasp must be suppressed before the child can stand erect, stand alone, or walk. Parents will also have difficulty in putting on shoes for a child who still exhibits an active plantar grasp reflex (Barnes, Crutchfield, & Heriza, 1984).

Babinski Reflex

Like the plantar grasp reflex, the *Babinski reflex* is normally evidenced from birth. The bottom of the foot is stroked the entire length, from the heel to the toes, causing all toes of that foot to fan out and extend (see Figure 10-8).

Palmar Mandibular Reflex

The *palmar mandibular reflex*, or Babkin reflex, is another infant reflex normally present at birth. The Babkin is elicited by applying pressure simultaneously to the palm of each hand, eliciting all or one of the following responses: the mouth opens, the eyes close, and the neck flexes, tilting the head forward (see Figure 10-9). The Babkin response also

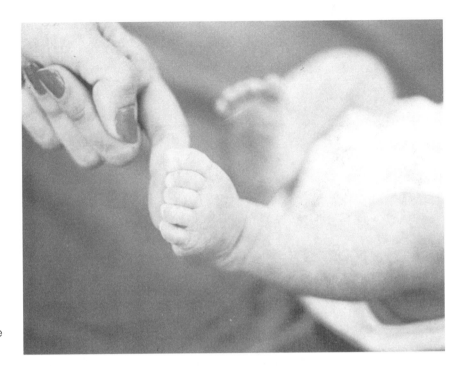

FIGURE 10-7 In the plantar grasp reflex, the toes appear to be attempting to grasp.

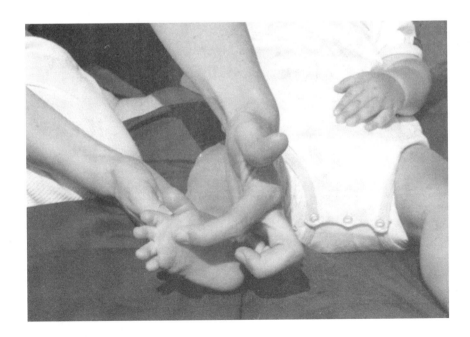

FIGURE 10-8 The Babinski reflex is elicited by a stimulus somewhat similar to that of the plantar grasp reflex, but the response is different.

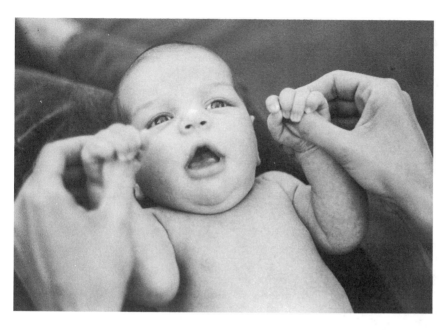

FIGURE 10-9 The palmar mandibular reflex is one of the most unusual reflexes because it makes the eyes close, the mouth open, and the head tilt forward.

occurs if the hand of a human neonate is lightly stimulated by hair. The Babkin reflex normally disappears by age 3 months. Interestingly, some experts believe that this reflex links the human to animals lower on the phylogenetic scale because it often helps young animals cling to their mothers when feeding.

Palmar Mental Reflex

The *palmar mental reflex,* like the Babkin, elicits a facial response when the base of the palm of either hand is scratched; this scratching causes the lower jaw to open and close (see Figure 10-10). The actual response is thus a series of contractions of the jaw muscles. Like the Babkin, the palmar mental reflex is first observable at birth and normally ceases by the third month.

POSTURAL REFLEXES

As with the primitive reflexes, here we discuss the details of the postural reflexes. Again, the discus-

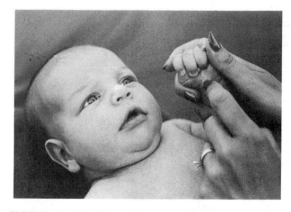

FIGURE 10-10 The palmar mental reflex is elicited by scratching the base of either palm.

sion is not meant to be comprehensive, but it does highlight important points about these reflexes.

Stepping Reflex

The *stepping,* or walking, *reflex,* is an essential forerunner to an important voluntary movement, walking. The stepping reflex is elicited by holding the infant upright with the feet touching a supporting surface; the pressure on the bottom of the feet causes the legs to lift and then descend (see Figure 10-11). This leg action often occurs alternately and therefore resembles a crude form of walking. Although this reflex is also called the walking reflex, there is none of the hip stability or accompanying arm movement that occurs with voluntary walking. The stepping—or walking—reflex generally can be elicited within the first few weeks following birth and persists through the fifth or sixth month.

Crawling Reflex

The *crawling reflex* is another example of an infant reflex considered a precursor to later voluntary movement. This reflex can be observed from birth through the first 3 to 4 months. To elicit this reflex, the baby is placed prone on the floor or table. The soles of the feet are stroked alternately, causing the legs and arms to move in a crawlinglike action (see Figure 10-12). The crawling reflex disappears about 3 months before more voluntary creeping begins. This reflex is believed essential for furthering development of sufficient muscular tone for future voluntary creeping.

Swimming Reflex

One of the most unusual infant reflexes is the *swimming reflex*. Involuntary swimminglike movements can be elicited days after birth. The baby is held horizontally over a solid surface, such as a tabletop or a floor, over the surface of water, or in the water. The response to the stimulus is the arms and legs moving in a well-coordinated swimming-type action (see Figure 10-13). These movements are observable as early as the second neonatal week and normally endure through the fifth month of infancy. Recognition of this reflex has contributed substantially to the popularity of infant swim programs. Proponents of such programs assume that early stimulation of this reflex will positively affect voluntary swimming later in life. Presently, as discussed

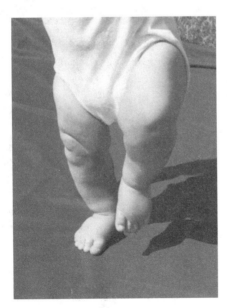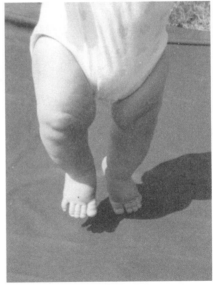

FIGURE 10-11   The stepping reflex can be elicited within the first few weeks following birth, even though unassisted voluntary walking may not occur until the first birthday.

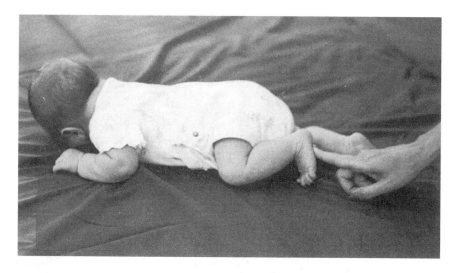

FIGURE 10-12 The crawling reflex is believed essential to the development of future voluntary creeping.

FIGURE 10-13 The swimming reflex is characterized by the baby's swiminglike movements when held in a horizontal position.

in Chapter 6, there is no scientific evidence to support this view.

Head- and Body-Righting Reflexes

The *head- and body-righting reflexes* are two similar infant reflexes believed related to the attainment of voluntary rolling movements. The head-righting reflex can be observed as early as the first month of infancy. This reflex is elicited by turning the baby's body in either direction when the infant is supine. The head responds by "righting" itself with the body; in other words, the head returns to a front-facing position relative to the

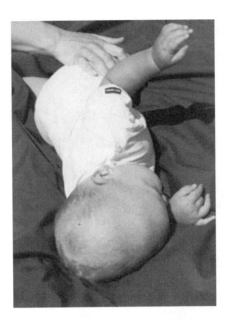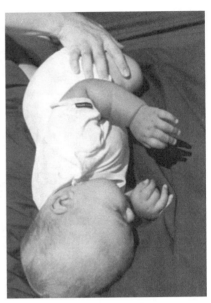

FIGURE 10-14   In the head-righting reflex, the head "rights" itself with the body when the body is turned to one side.

shoulders (see Figure 10-14). This reflex normally disappears by the age of 6 months.

In contrast to the head-righting reflex, the body-righting reflex involves the head turning and the body "righting" itself. If the infant is placed supine and the head gently turned to one side or the other, the body follows. That is, the body rotates in the direction the head is turned to regain the front-facing relationship between the head and the shoulders. This rotation of the body is not segmental; the body responds by rotating as a single unit (Fiorentino, 1963). Unlike the head-righting reflex, the body-righting reflex may not be evident until the fifth month of infancy. It frequently lasts throughout the first year of life.

Parachuting Reflexes

The *parachuting,* or propping, *reflexes* appear related to the attainment of upright posture. These reflexes occur when the infant is tipped off balance in any direction. Being off balance when in an upright position stimulates a protective movement in the direction of the potential fall. For example, when the infant is tilted forward, the arms make a prop-

ping movement, extending toward the front as the fingers extend and separate. This reflex occurs as early as 4 months of age. These propping movements appear to be conscious attempts to break a fall, but like all infant reflexes, they are involuntary. See Figure 10-15.

These propping movements can also occur downward, sideward, and backward. The downward parachuting reaction can be elicited as early as 4 months if the child is suddenly lowered 2 to 3 feet when held upright. The infant's legs suddenly extend and spread, and the feet rotate slightly outward. The sideward propping movements are observable after approximately 6 months of age and are most easily elicited by placing the infant in a sitting position and then gently tilting him to either side. As in the forward parachuting reflex, the arms and fingers extend, in this case toward the side of the potential fall. The backward propping may not occur until 10 months of age, and like the other parachuting reflexes, normally causes a propping movement in the direction of the fall. However, the backward propping reflex may also cause the body to rotate, apparently to avoid falling backward. All the propping reflexes frequently persist past the first year of life.

FIGURE 10-15 Parachuting reflexes appear to occur consciously in an effort to break a potential fall, but like all reflexes, they are really subcortical.

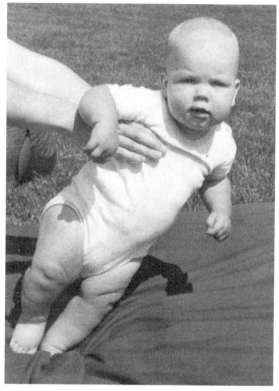

FIGURE 10-16 The labyrinthine reflex endures throughout most of the first year and apparently is related to the attainment of upright posture.

Labyrinthine Reflex

The *labyrinthine reflex* generally appears at approximately 2 to 3 months of age and lasts throughout the first year of life. This reflex, like the parachuting reflexes, may be critical to the attainment of upright posture. The labyrinthine is characterized by the head tilting in a direction opposite the direction the body is tilted (see Figure 10-16). For example, if the infant is held at the waist and tilted forward, the neck extends to enable the head to maintain its original upright position. If the baby is tilted backward, the neck extends to enable the head to maintain the upright position. A similar response occurs when the baby is tilted to either side.

Pull-Up Reflex

The *pull-up reflex* may also be related to the attainment of upright posture. Furthermore, like the labyrinthine reflex, the pull-up reflex may not be observable until the third month of infancy. This reflex is most easily elicited by placing the infant in a supported standing position. Holding the baby's hands, carefully tip her in any direction; this stimulus makes the supporting arm(s) flex or extend in an apparent effort to maintain the upright position (see Figure 10-17). For example, if the baby is tipped backward, the arms flex to pull her toward the supporting person and back into an upright position. If the infant is topped forward, the arms extend to push

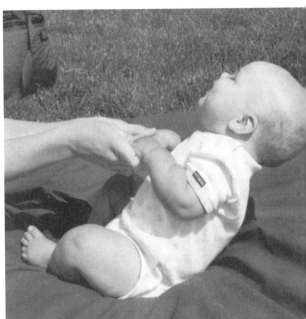

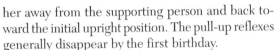

her away from the supporting person and back toward the initial upright position. The pull-up reflexes generally disappear by the first birthday.

STEREOTYPIES

The infant reflexes are the most studied form of human movement during the first few months of life. Much less attention has been paid to another group of movements also characteristic of infancy. These movements, carefully described by Thelen in a 1979 article, are rhythmical, patterned, seemingly centrally controlled and known as *stereotypies*. Stereotypies are believed to be relatively intrinsic because they do not appear to be behaviors infants learn by imitation. In addition, these stereotyped movements do not seem to serve a purpose, as they are not regulated by the sensory system. They generally represent movement that is one of the most simple, patterned actions for the muscle group involved. Stereotypies are often simple flexions, extensions, or

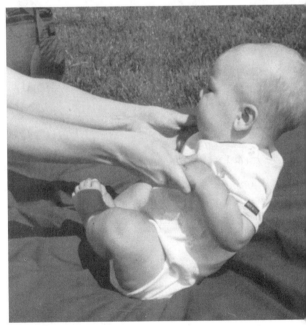

FIGURE 10-17 In the pull-up reflex, when the baby is tipped backward, an arm flexes in an effort to maintain the upright position.

rotations that are repeated in nearly identical, often alternating, fashion.

Interestingly, this type of movement is common among insects, birds, and fish. Among primates, such as zoo animals, repetitive, patterned movements are often considered pathological. Even for the human being, during any other time of life such movement would be considered abnormal; indeed, such behavior is often seen in people with mental or emotional problems. In the human infant, however, stereotypies are considered normal behavior that is evidence of functional maturation of the neurological system. However, they are not a sign of voluntary, goal-oriented movement behavior.

In her research, Thelen (1979) observed many different stereotypies. She also found that all the 20 infants she observed exhibited stereotypies. In fact, during the periods when stereotyping behavior was most common, the infants often spent as much as 40 percent of each hour exhibiting stereotypies.

Stereotypies of the legs and feet were one of the most common and first forms of rhythmical and patterned behavior Thelen observed. Rhythmical kicking was the first noticed and was evident for months to follow. These stereotypies of the legs and feet most commonly occurred when the babies were prone or supine. Examples of the leg and feet stereotypies Thelen observed were simultaneous leg kicking, alternate leg kicking, feet rubbing together, single leg kicks of various kinds, and a sharp flexing of the backs of the legs. Stereotypies of the legs were the most common form of stereotyped movement noted. They also began earlier than the other types, as early as 4 weeks of age. These rhythmical, patterned movements of the legs and feet seem to reach their peak occurrence at around 24 to 32 weeks of age, becoming much less common by 44 to 52 weeks.

Thelen found that the legs and feet were not the only parts of the body to become involved in stereotyped movement. She categorized other stereotypies by their location of occurrence: Several stereotypies occurred in the region of the hands and arms, including arm waving while holding an object, and one arm, as well as two arms, banging against a surface. Thelen also noted several patterned, repetitive hand movements such as total hand flexion and rotation as well as individual finger flexion. The peak occurrence for arm and hand stereotypies was 34 to 42 weeks. However, the arm stereotypies generally appeared as early as 4 to 12 weeks, whereas the hand movements typically were not evident until 14 to 22 weeks. The finger stereotypies, like the movements of the arms, occurred as early as 4 to 12 weeks but reached their peak at 24 to 32 weeks.

Thelen placed another group of stereotypies into what she termed the "torso" category. Included were such movements as arching the back and rocking when in an "all fours" or creepinglike position, rocking and bouncing when in an unsupported sitting position, and bouncing while standing. In general, these movements often reached their peak later than the movements of the legs and feet and the arms and hands, although they first appeared as early as 14 to 22 months of age.

Thelen's final category of stereotyped movement of infancy was the head and face. This grouping included some of the most interesting stereotypies. Compared to the other stereotyped movements, the stereotypies in this category were considered somewhat rare. Examples of head and face stereotypies were head nodding, head shaking as if indicating "no," in and out tongue protrusions, and nonnutritive sucking. Thelen also noted small rhythmical mouthing movements.

The most common stereotypies were the single leg kick, two-leg kick, alternate leg kick, arm wave, arm wave with an object, arm banging against a surface with and without an object, and finger flexion. Thelen concluded that these, as well as the other stereotyped forms of behavior she noted, are apparently developmentally significant. She reached this conclusion upon noticing that, for example, stereotyped kicking precedes voluntary use of the legs and stereotyped finger flexion precedes voluntary attempts at grasping. However, stereotypes have not been absolutely determined to be precursors of more mature motor behavior.

The number of different stereotypies increases throughout the first year. The frequency of occurrence also increases throughout the first year, peaking at approximately 24 to 42 weeks of age. Throughout the first year, many stereotypies cease and new ones emerge. There is then a major decline in the occurrence of stereotypies during the last two to three months of the first year.

SUMMARY

During the last 4 months in utero and the first 4 months of postnatal life, infant reflexes and stereotypies are the dominant form of human movement. An infant reflex is an involuntary and routine response to a particular stimulus.

The infant reflexes are extremely important to human development for a number of reasons. Many of the reflexes are protective; the sucking reflex, for example, enables babies to ingest food. Other reflexes help the baby avoid injury.

The infant reflexes are considered crucial for the development of subsequent voluntary movements. Reflexes such as crawling, labyrinthine, palmar grasp, and stepping are essential to the normal attainment of voluntary crawling, upright posture, voluntary grasping, and voluntary walking, respectively.

Other infant reflexes are important for neurologically examining the infant and diagnosing any abnormality. The ages of onset and offset of the infant reflexes normally follow a predictable timeline. Deviations from that timeline sometimes indicate neural damage. Also, an excessively weak, lacking, asymmetrical, or persistent reflex can indicate a variety of neural problems.

Stereotypies are another form of movement observable during infancy. These movements are characterized by patterned, stereotyped, highly intrinsic, and apparently involuntary movements of the legs and feet; arms, hands, and fingers; torso; and head and face. Like reflexes, stereotypies are believed important in the development of more advanced voluntary movements in later life.

KEY TERMS

Asymmetric tonic neck reflex
Babinski reflex
Crawling reflex
Head- and body-righting reflexes
Labyrinthine reflex
Lifespan reflexes
Moro reflex
Palmar grasp reflex
Palmar mandibular reflex
Palmar mental reflex
Parachuting reflexes
Plantar grasp reflex
Postural reflexes
Primitive reflex profile
Primitive reflexes
Pull-up reflex
Search reflex
Startle reflex
Stepping reflex
Stereotypies
Subcortical
Sucking reflex
Swimming reflex
Symmetric tonic neck reflex

CHAPTER 11

Voluntary Movements of Infancy

As discussed in Chapter 10, reflexive movement is the first dominant form of human movement. The reflex is a unique form of movement that is involuntary and subcortical; it is performed without conscious effort and without stimulation from the higher brain centers. At about the fourth week of life, however, cortically controlled *voluntary movement* begins to appear (Wyke, 1975). The first signs of voluntary movement are slight, including only movements of the head, neck, and eyes. Nevertheless, after these first cortically controlled movements appear, the voluntary movements become increasingly prevalent and instrumental in enabling children to move in their environment. A child during the first year of life has been described as a "reflex machine" (Wyke, 1975, p. 27), but cerebral cortical control slowly assumes command of movement production as the subcortically produced reflexes gradually disappear. The diameters of the nerve dendrites, which carry the electrical stimulation to induce movement, slowly increase, accelerating the velocity of the stimulation and thus more efficiently facilitating the motor nerve cell activity necessary for producing voluntary movement.

The process of the higher brain center slowly assuming command is gradual, but by the end of the first year of life, there is almost complete voluntary control of movement. A few of the infant reflexes discussed in Chapter 10 may endure past the first year of life, but most disappear. Voluntary movement "the ultimate expression in the striated muscle of the integrated effects of a host of cortical and subcortical facilitory and inhibitory influences" (Wyke, 1975, p. 27), becomes the dominant source of human movement midway through the first year of life.

The voluntary movements of infancy are commonly called rudimentary movements (Gallahue, 1989; Zaichowsky, Zaichowsky, & Martinek, 1980) because they are the "rudiments" of future, more advanced movement forms. These early voluntary movements are the first, slight beginnings of the more advanced movements that normally follow.

Through a sequential, predictable, generally universal sequence of movement acquisition, the early voluntary movements gradually progress into the more readily recognizable movements of later life. For example, during the first year there are major changes in a baby's ability to position the body. This new ability eventually frees the hands to enhance voluntary reaching and grasping movements. Another example is the achievement of upright posture, which enables the child to accomplish the most popular motor landmark of early life: walking. These progressions are discussed in greater depth throughout this chapter.

CATEGORIZING THE VOLUNTARY MOVEMENTS OF INFANCY

For ease of organization and discussion, the voluntary movements of infancy are often grouped into three major categories. Depending on the source, the terminology for the three categories varies somewhat. According to Gallahue (1989), the three major categories of early voluntary movement are *stability, locomotion,* and *manipulation.* Another text, however (Keogh & Sugden, 1985), uses the terms *postural control, locomotion,* and *manual control.* Although the terms for the categories vary slightly, the movements are the same. For example, stability or postural control includes a wide range of voluntary movements, from head control to the eventual attainment of upright posture. Locomotion, a common category in both classification systems, includes such movements as creeping and crawling and all their variations. Finally, manipulation or manual control involves the voluntary use of the hands, such as the entire progression of movements leading to the attainment of a mature reaching, grasping, and releasing ability. All these movements and all other important voluntary movements of infancy are discussed on the following pages, in order of their appearance when possible. This pattern can-

not be followed absolutely, however, because often the infant acquires more than one motor ability simultaneously.

HEAD CONTROL

Because the human being typically develops movement ability cephalocaudally, acquisition of the ability to make voluntary movements begins at the head. When born, a baby has virtually no voluntary control over the head or neck, although reflexive movement may be evident, as in the head-righting reflex discussed in Chapter 10 (when the body is turned to one side or the other, the head rights itself with the shoulders). Conscious, cortical, or voluntary control over the head or neck may gradually become apparent by the end of the first month of life (Hottinger, 1973). This progression continues until 5 months, at which time the child normally exhibits relatively good muscular control over this region of the body. Figure 11-1 depicts this general sequence of head movements, which is initiated by the child elevating the head when placed prone. This seemingly simple act is often evident at approximately 2 months of age. Soon thereafter, at 2 to 3 months of age, the child can position the head from left to right or right to left when prone. When 3 months old, a child normally is capable of maintaining the head erect and upright when held in an upright sitting or standing position. Finally, at approximately 5 months of age, the child can raise the head when supine. This movement, as well as those described earlier, may seem insignificant, but vision is initially the only means of exploring the environment. Control of the head enables infants to thoroughly scan their surroundings while initiating the complex process of attaining upright posture.

BODY CONTROL

In the cephalocaudal pattern of development, control of the uppermost areas of the body follows

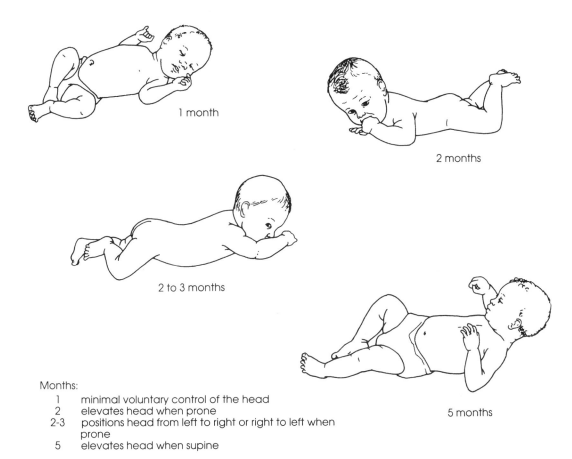

1 month

2 months

2 to 3 months

5 months

Months:
1	minimal voluntary control of the head
2	elevates head when prone
2-3	positions head from left to right or right to left when prone
5	elevates head when supine

FIGURE 11-1   Voluntary control of the head

attainment of head control. Then gradually, lower areas of the body also gain voluntary control. This cephalocaudal progression in body control begins at about 2 months of age, when the child gains the ability to elevate not only the head but the chest as well. The infant executes this maneuver by applying pressure to the supporting surface with the upper arms. This does not indicate particularly useful control of the arms, however, because the forearms and hands play a minimal role in this effort. Control of the arms, hands, and fingers is more thoroughly discussed later in the chapter.

Gaining voluntary control of body movement is particularly important during the first few months of life because these early forms of movement are crucial for attaining more advanced movements. For example, one of the most important forms of body control evident after chest elevation is the child's attempt to roll from a supine to a prone position. The acquisition of this movement skill at approximately 6 months enables the child to attain the proper position for crawling. A form of rolling generally is noticeable earlier in life, but that movement is reflexive, not voluntary. The voluntary back-to-front rolling action is initially rigid, but gradually the movement becomes "segmented," with the head turning first, followed by the shoulders, trunk, and hips (Zaichowsky, Zaichowsky, & Martinek, 1980). By approximately 8 months, the infant can roll from front to back as well as back to front.

Another important voluntary movement that indicates children's constantly expanding repertoire of movement is the attainment of upright posture. Upright posture is important because it frees the hands for more selective reaching, grasping, and releasing (see Figure 11-2). While supine or prone, the child has limited use of the arms and hands. In fact, these body parts are often occupied with maintaining or changing the horizontal body position and therefore are unavailable for selective attempts to obtain or manipulate objects in the child's environment. If assisted, infants can sit as early as 3 months of age. Because infants have very little lumbar control at that time, a helpful hand is necessary for supporting the lower back and abdomen. This sitting skill evolves into the ability to sit without such support by 5 months of age because lumbar control has increased substantially. Nevertheless, the child may not have complete control of the lower back and abdomen, so the sitting position is characterized by an acute forward lean. Furthermore, the child's ability to balance is still inadequate, so infants at 5

months need to stabilize themselves by holding an external object, such as a piece of furniture. By 7 months, the child has gained sufficient movement ability to attain this self-supported sitting position from either a prone or a supine position. Finally, by approximately 8 months, most children can sit without assistance or support.

Attainment of upright body posture, like sitting, is clearly a major achievement of early development. Sitting alone offers many benefits to the infant; however, it may have many other consequences for the achievement of other abilities. For example, Rochat (1992) studied the impact of an infant's ability to "self-sit" on the development of early eye-hand coordination. Rochat's subjects were two groups of infants 5–8 months old. Half were able and half were unable to sit on their own. Each infant was presented with a variety of displays while in four different positions: seated, reclined, prone (75 degrees to the floor), and supine. Overall, nonsitters contacted the objects in the display 89 percent of the time, while sitters made contact 98 percent of the time. All infants were found to have the least amount of success while in the supine position. Furthermore, nonsitters exhibited significantly more two-handed reaches overall. However, when seated, the nonsitters' incidence of two-handed responses decreased compared to other positions. Overall, sitters tended to reach more with one hand in all positions, while the nonsitters only tended to use one hand when seated. Rochat believes these findings demonstrate the importance of self-sitting on early eye-hand coordination. Specifically, infants' ability to sit appears to be linked to the use of the two hands in reaching activities (Rochat, 1992).

The progression in attaining upright posture does not end with sitting. One of the most popular movement landmarks is achieving complete upright posture, an unsupported standing position. This movement ability, like the others discussed earlier, is critical to future development. An upright posture enables children to walk; walking lets children expand their exploratory range and therefore facilitates cognitive, social, and motor development. The

FIGURE 11-2 Ability to maintain upright posture frees the hands and arms for reaching and grasping.

onset of the standing progression generally occurs at about 9 months, when the child begins to exhibit an ability to pull from a sitting to a standing position. For the child to attain the standing position, an external object such as a piece of furniture is required for support. Following a period of experimentation to "test" the balance, the child can stand beside furniture, occasionally reaching out for support. This standing position is characterized by a wide base of support and a "high guard" arm position. In other words, the feet generally are a considerable distance apart and the hands held high. By the age of 1 year, the child is often successful at standing unassisted. See Figure 11-3. Walking, which soon follows in the motor development progression, is discussed in Chapter 13.

PRONE LOCOMOTION

As mentioned, the acquisition of body control during infancy facilitates the development of other movements. Locomotion evolves from children gaining the ability to position their bodies for movement from one location in space to another. Initially children position themselves prone. From the onset of voluntary attainment of the prone position to the end of the first year of life, there are a number of transformations in a child's prone locomotion. There are semblances of crawling prior to 7 months of age, but these movements are reflexively rather than voluntarily controlled. The next 6 months of life are the main concern in voluntary locomotion because during this time the child becomes adept at movements in the prone position (Keogh & Sugden, 1985). This is a valuable movement acquisition because locomotion, even in the prone position, enables the child to more thoroughly explore the surrounding environment.

Like all the voluntary movements of infancy, locomotion develops in a predictable progression. However, although the progression generally is similar for all children, the rate at which these movement skills are acquired may vary considerably. The rate of acquisition for *all* voluntary movements during infancy may vary, but there is an even greater difference among children for attaining prone locomotor movements.

Creeping and *crawling* are the two locomotion movements that have received the most notoriety among both the general populace and motor developmentalists. Unfortunately, there is some confusion as to the specific meaning of the two terms. To many parents and lay people, creeping denotes a precrawling movement consisting of inefficient, highly variable arm and leg movements intended to propel the body forward. According to many contemporary references, however, that description is more accurate for crawling. Crawling actually precedes creeping in the progression of movement acquisition for prone locomotion (Gallahue, 1989: Keogh & Sugden, 1985; Zaichowsky, Zaichowsky, & Martinek, 1980). Although some experts disagree with this terminology (Cratty, 1986), most current texts involving motor development cite crawling as the antecedent to creeping. For our purposes here, crawling is considered the less mature of the two forms of locomotion, regardless of the popular use of the term.

Creeping normally begins from approximately 7 to 9 months of age (this rate may vary considerably, depending on the child and the environment). In the first attempts at locomotion, the trunk is minimally elevated off the supporting surface. The infant tries to travel by thrusting the arms forward and then subsequently flexing them. The flexion of the arms may eventually lead to a slight forward thrust. Initially the legs are minimally involved, although eventually they play an extremely important role in the more advanced forms of prone locomotion. Soon after the initial attempts at forward progress, a leg(s) may be flexed up to or under the body. This flexion may cause the body to move toward the rear, a backward crawling (Gesell & Ames, 1940). This somewhat counterproductive form of locomotion is short-term, however, because the child soon begins to use the legs more efficiently to help move forward. The child flexes the legs and then reextends them for propulsion. This action may initially involve both legs simultaneously extended in a vigorous

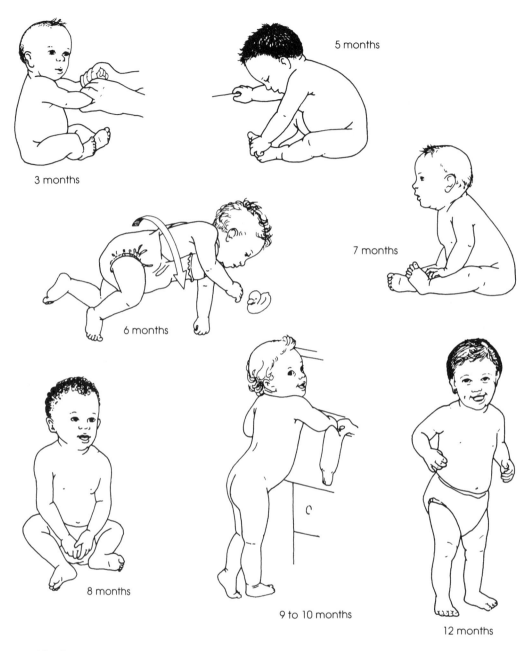

Months:
   3   tries to roll from supine to prone position; maintains sitting position when assisted
   5   sits when holding external supporting object
   6   rolls from supine to prone position; maintains standing position when assisted
   7   achieves sitting position from prone or supine position
   8   sits alone; rolls from prone to supine position
   9-10   pulls self to standing position, briefly maintains stand while holding
          external supporting object
   12   stands unassisted

FIGURE 11-3   Voluntary control of the body

motion that causes the body to move forward in short and abrupt actions.

Gradually, the infant's body is elevated from the supporting surface. As the elevation of the body increases, the legs can be flexed into a position beneath the body, increasing the infant's ability to locomote and leading to the more sophisticated movement form known as creeping. Crawling is a form of locomotion in which the body is, in a sense, dragged or "slid" along the supporting surface, but creeping is an elevated, highly efficient form of locomotion. In fact, many children who have learned to walk often revert to creeping when they have a desire to make speedy progress. Once the body is elevated from the supporting surface, a variety of limb movements are evident in creeping. Initially, the child will move only one limb at a time (Eckert, 1973), which is obviously an inefficient, slow form of beginning creeping that has yet to be perfected.

Eventually, the child develops a *contralateral* or a *homolateral* creeping pattern. The homolateral pattern is characterized by the limbs on the same side simultaneously moving forward and backward; for example, as the right leg goes forward, so does the right arm. Most children crawl in this fashion (Gallahue, Werner, & Luedke, 1975). In some cases, however, children develop a contralateral creeping pattern in which the movements of the limbs oppose each other. For example, in the contralateral pattern, as the right leg moves forward, the right arm moves back. Rather than the arm and leg on the same side being coordinated to move simultaneously, the arm and leg on opposite body sides work together.

An efficient form of creeping, contralateral or homolateral, may begin to appear as early as 9 months of age. However, as indicated in Figure 11-4, most children do not creep efficiently until the first year of age. Once children begin to creep, they rapidly become so efficient that they can creep up stairs. This form of creeping is almost identical to creeping on a flat surface (Eckert, 1973) but initially may lead to frustration because most likely the child will be unable to descend the stairs.

UPRIGHT LOCOMOTION

Many experts consider upright locomotion, which includes walking, the culmination of the acquisition of a series of infant voluntary movements. Walking is of obvious importance to the human being and is the result of the progression of movement skills described to this point. Although there is no question of the value of upright locomotion, many parents place too much significance on the age at which their offspring start walking. The acquisition of any skill—motor, cognitive, or social—is enough to excite many parents, but often there is extreme emphasis on the rate of acquisition of unassisted walking. Contrary to the beliefs of many parents, there is little evidence proving that early walking accelerates or refines skill performance later in life.

Regardless of when a child begins to walk independently, the initial upright locomotion is far from a mature walking pattern. (The more advanced forms of walking are discussed in more depth in Chapter 13.) Before a child walks unassisted, a predictable movement progression generally occurs. If assisted by considerable support, a child can walk as early as 8 months of age, although this varies considerably. In fact, children occasionally walk independently at 8 months of age, but this rarely occurs. At approximately 10 months, a child can walk with much less support. Generally, by this time a strong handhold is enough to enable the child to "cruise" laterally around furniture or other supporting objects. By 11 months, children have normally progressed to a level of proficiency enabling them to walk when led by another person. Finally, by 12 months of age, the child normally walks unassisted. See Figure 11-5.

Each step in the progression to a mature walking pattern is characterized by many extremely immature walking techniques. For example, the infant often assumes a wide stance. The knees maintain a flexed position, and the toes point out slightly. The length of the steps is highly inconsistent.

Interestingly, children with smaller bones (Shirley, 1931) or linear frames (Norval, 1947) are believed to walk somewhat earlier than larger-boned

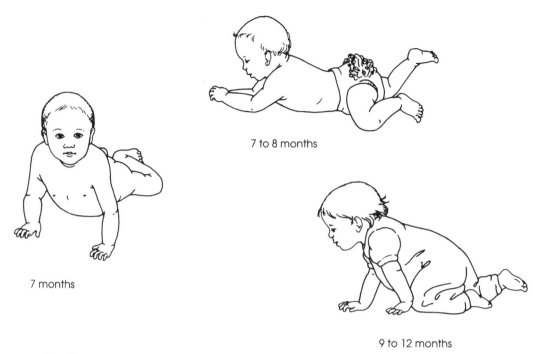

7 to 8 months

7 months

9 to 12 months

Months:
  7   elevates trunk slightly; forward arm extension and flexion creates occasional forward movement; leg flexion occasionally creates backward crawling
  7-8 initial crawling
  9-12 creeping; creeping up stairs

FIGURE 11-4   Prone locomotion

or larger-framed children. According to Garn, larger muscle mass delays the attainment of walking skill. In fact, the child's muscle mass at 6 months of age is believed to relatively accurately predict the onset of independent walking (Garn, 1966).

REACHING, GRASPING, AND RELEASING

Parents and others are familiar with many of the voluntary movements of infancy discussed so far. The date of the child's first successful and unsupported stand is frequently a highlight of infancy eagerly anticipated by parents. Creeping, and especially walking, are similarly awaited. But early voluntary use of the hands generally is not as awaited as other voluntary infant movements. Parents readily cite the date of the child's first unassisted walk, but generally they are much less aware of the baby's initial attempts to reach, grasp, and manipulate a nearby object, even though prehension is an extremely important aspect of the child's motor development. Use of the hands enables children to gather information about their environment in a new way. Manipulation enables increased and varied exploration; this new mode of exploration lets the child discover properties of objects and use the objects as implements in achieving goals (Bower, 1982).

Months:
    8   walks with assistance of considerable support
  10   walks laterally around furniture using handhold for support
  11   walks when led with slight handhold to maintain balance
  12   walks unassisted

FIGURE 11-5 Upright locomotion

Although popular awareness concerning prehension appears lacking, much has been written about this early form of manipulation. The first forms of manipulation, like many other voluntary movements discussed earlier, are reflexive. The palmar grasp reflex discussed in Chapter 10 is not intentional manipulation, but it does give the child an involuntary means of grasping an object during the first few months of life. Surprisingly, a voluntary form of reaching has also been reported as present in the newborn (Bower, 1982). The newborn reaching behaviors quickly vanish, however, as higher brain centers become more dominant in controlling movement. This initially inhibits the newborn reaching behavior until new "connections" are formed, which allow the movement to reappear (Humphrey, 1969).

This reappearance, often cited as the "first" successful reach and grasp, generally appears around 4 months of age. At this time the movement behavior is similar in technique to that present in the newborn. In fact, the newborn reaching behavior, which lasts for about 4 weeks, and the reaching that reappears at 4 months are called *phase I reaching* (Bower, 1977).

This phase I reaching and *grasping* is characterized by a number of specific qualities. First, the reach and grasp occur simultaneously. As the child reaches, the hand may open and close repeatedly rather than open upon attaining the desired object. This inability to grasp accurately is indicative of the phase I imperfect abilities of reaching and grasping relative to the more advanced *phase II*. Also characteristic of phase I reaching and grasping is one-handed reaching, if the desired object is not too heavy. This is generally a mature reaching technique among older children. However, Bower believed that during early infancy this technique allows minimal success in actually attaining control of the desired object and is therefore indicative of the immature reaching characteristics of phase I.

Phase I reaching is also visually initiated. That is, children reach when they see something in their environment. This form of reaching is an improvement over the random groping that occurs earlier

in the child's life. But, because the reach is only visually initiated and not controlled, the 5-month-old child may frequently fail to achieve the desired goal. At this age, the child retracts the hand upon an initial failure and completely reattempts the reach. The child is not yet capable of correcting the error during the reach.

Vision also plays an important role in the phase I grasp. Once the child makes manual contact with the desired object, vision facilitates hand closure. In other words, children decide when to grasp based on what they visually perceive to be necessary. Visually monitoring the hand upon contact enables children to determine exactly when they should close the hand around the desired object.

Phase II reaching and grasping is considerably advanced over that of phase I. Phase II generally becomes apparent by the sixth to seventh month of life. Unlike phase I behavior, the more advanced phase II behavior is characterized by a differentiated reach and grasp. Once the reach has been completed, the child attempts the grasp. This is a considerable advancement over the random, repeated grasping seen throughout the reach in phase I. Furthermore, in phase II, the infant uses two hands when attempting to contact and acquire an external object. Although this is not typically the mature technique an older child would select, this method is the most successful for an infant with more inaccurate manual control. Also, whereas in phase I the reach was visually initiated, in phase II the reach is visually initiated *and* visually controlled, which is why this newly acquired, more efficient movement form is often called visually guided reaching. This term emphasizes the important role of vision in enabling the child to correct errors throughout the reach. Children in phase II can actually visually monitor the reach to ensure that they achieve the proper destination. Table 11-1 summarizes phases I and II.

Vision is also a critical part of the grasp in phase I. As described earlier, the infant's vision is integral in determining exactly when to close the hand in phase I reaching and grasping. Although vision becomes prominent in guiding the reach in phase II,

TABLE 11-1   Bower's (1977) Phase I and II Reaching and Grasping
Behavior Characteristics

Phase I	Phase II
1. Simultaneous reaching and grasping	**1.** Differentiated reaching and grasping
2. One-handed reaching	**2.** Two-handed reaching
3. Visual initiation of the reach	**3.** Visual initiation and guidance of the reach
4. Visual control of the grasp	**4.** Tactile control of the grasp

the role of vision in the grasp diminishes. For phase II infants, the grasp is controlled by tactile stimulation. The touch or feel that they perceive via their hands or fingers becomes the dominant force in making decisions concerning the grasp.

Despite Bower's claims concerning the importance of vision in early reaching and grasping behavior, recent evidence suggests that it may not be necessary. Traditionally, as Bower has suggested, we have believed that the earliest accurate forms of reaching are visually guided and, though highly variable, appear within the first few months of life. A number of studies in recent years have sought to eliminate infants' view of their hands to determine the effects on the incidence and accuracy of reaching behavior (Perris & Clifton, 1988; Stack, Muir, Sherriff, & Roman, 1989). If reaching in dark (where infants can see glowing objects but not their hands) and light situations begin around the same time, we would assume that proprioceptive cues are apparently providing valuable information to infants. Clifton, Muir, Ashmead, and Clarkson (1993) recently investigated this issue. Seven infants from 6 to 25 weeks of age were videotaped reaching in light and dark situations for objects that made a sound, glowed in the dark, made a sound and glowed, and were "in conflict" as a rattle was presented on one side while a glowing object was presented on the other. The researchers found considerable individual differences among the infants. The onset of touching ranged from 7 to 16 weeks while the onset for

grasping ranged from 11 to 19 weeks. Despite a relatively wide range of individual differences, touching and grasping objects in the light and dark situations emerged at the same age for individual infants. For both light and dark situations the first signs of touching began about 12 weeks and stabilized by 16 weeks. Grasping began at about 16 weeks and stabilized at about 20 weeks. This led to the conclusion that the development of manual contact with objects is similar when the hand and target are sighted versus when only the target is sighted. In short, according to this research, infants do not appear to need to see their hands to reach. They can reach for objects which they hear but not see and see but not hear. In addition, they can do both of these with or without seeing their own hands. These relatively recent findings are in conflict with traditional beliefs that reaching is dependent on viewing the hand and the target in early reaching and grasping activities. However, as these abilities become refined, viewing one's own hand may become more important. On the basis of these findings, Clifton and associates stated that the "emphasis on visual guidance of the hands . . . needs to be revised" (p. 1109). Furthermore, in future theories governing the study of infant reaching, greater emphasis needs to be placed on the role of proprioception (Clifton, Muir, Ashmead, & Clarkson, 1993).

The metamorphosis of reaching and grasping behavior from phase I and phase II as described by

Bower follows the general proximodistal rule of motor development. Proximodistal is the development of movement ability from the points close to the center of the body or the midline to the distal or extreme points. Reaching and grasping behavior does exactly that. In fact, at about 4 months of life, reaching is predominantly controlled by the shoulder and elbow. These first attempts at purposeful reaching are slow and awkward but soon develop into accurate, efficient movements. By as early as 5 to 6 months, the child has developed greater wrist, hand, and finger control and can use the thumb in opposition to the other fingers. By 9 to 10 months, the child can use the thumb to oppose one finger, to enable more precise "pincerlike" control (Keogh & Sugden, 1985). However, despite the considerable improvement in reaching and grasping ability over a relatively short time span, the child may not be able to easily release an object until 18 months of age. Relaxing the muscles in the arm sufficiently to facilitate the release of an object is one of the final acquisitions in the infant reaching, grasping, and *releasing* progression.

Anticipation and Object Control in Reaching and Grasping

To fully achieve adultlike reaching and grasping capabilities, the child must master the skills described and be able to adjust for the varying sizes, shapes, and weights of objects, which requires different reaching and grasping techniques. Mounoud and Bower (1974) carefully studied infants' awareness of the properties of objects and the effect on their reaching and grasping behavior. As is the case with many movement behaviors, there appeared to be a distinct progression. Through their research, Mounoud and Bower determined that prior to 9 months of age, the application of force in the reach was unrelated to the weight of an object. Therefore, regardless of an object's weight, the child applied the same force in both the arm movement and the subsequent grasp. The researchers determined this re-

action as they observed the arms of their subjects suddenly raise or lower when presented with a series of objects of varying weights. Mounoud and Bower gained additional information by placing force transducers on the objects the infants were receiving; the transducers indicated the magnitude of the force being applied during the grasp.

By 9 months of age, most of the subjects had developed the ability to adjust to the weight of the object after they had grasped it. However, limited anticipatory abilities were evident. This inadequacy diminished by 1 year of age as the infants developed skill in adjusting their arm and hand tension when they were repeatedly presented with the same object. Errors were initially made, but if the same object was presented to the children, errors were eliminated. However, this was true only for familiar objects—the knowledge the infants gained from the repeated application of one object did not positively affect their performance on the first few trials with new objects.

By the age of 18 months, the children exhibited anticipation. Upon repeated presentations, they displayed an awareness that the same object weighs the same. Furthermore, the subjects seemed to follow the "rule" that similar objects weigh more or less than the familiar object based on length. Therefore, although anticipation was evident, it was not always accurate because longer objects are not always heavier. Nevertheless, Mounoud and Bower concluded that by the age of 18 months, their subjects had developed an ability to perform two critical skills: anticipate and differentiate their reaching and grasping responses (see Table 11-2).

Bimanual Control

Many cognitive and psychomotor skills are necessary for optimal manual control. So far we have dealt predominantly with one-handed reaching. However, in many practical instances movement from both arms and hands must be integrated. Bruner (1970) examined a number of specific manipulative circumstances, including complementary use of the hands.

TABLE 11-2   Approximate Occurrence and Highlights of Reaching Grasping, and Releasing

Age	Characteristics
Birth	Phase I reaching
1 month	Phase I reaching disappears
4 months	Phase I reaching reappears
4 to 5 months	Unable to receive multiple toys
5 to 6 months	Thumb used to oppose fingers in grasping
6 months	Phase II reaching appears
6 to 8 months	Receives two toys while storing one toy in opposite hand
9 months	Adjusts arm and hand tension to object's weight after grasping the object
9 to 10 months	Thumb can oppose one finger in grasping
9 to 11 months	Receives three toys; stores first two toys on lap or chair
12 months	Adjusts arm and hand tension upon repeatedly receiving the same object
12 to 14 months	Receives three or more toys and crosses midline to hand toys to other person
18 months	Releases objects with relative ease; anticipates arm and hand tension for repeated presentation of same object: expects unknown long objects to weigh more than short objects

In examining the progression of reaching and grasping behavior, Bruner specifically investigated infants' control of several objects simultaneously. Subjects were 4 to 17 months old. The infants were handed a second toy immediately after receiving a first toy. The second toy was handed to the side of the body that was already occupied by the first toy. If the infant did not take the toy within 15 to 20 seconds, the second toy was moved to the infant's midline. If the child took the toy at any time, he was handed a third toy (and a fourth one, if necessary).

The 4- to 5-month-old infants in the Bruner research exhibited varying abilities. Some could not reach and grasp any of the toys; others could reach and grasp the toys but were unable to maintain control thereafter. None of the subjects in this youngest of age groups was able to deal with more than one toy at a time.

The 6- to 8-month-old subjects displayed a more highly developed reaching and grasping ability. They easily grasped the first toy and generally received a second. To facilitate this process, they transferred the first toy to the opposite hand for storage while receiving the second toy on the side to which it was offered. Three objects, however, appeared beyond the ability level of the infants in this group.

The 9- to 11-month-old group exhibited another new skill. Most subjects at this age could receive three objects, although this task was troublesome initially. To manipulate three objects, the child frequently positioned the initial toy(s) in the lap or on a nearby chair to free the hand for receiving the next toy. By 12 months of age, the infant often handed the initial toys to an experimenter or nearby parent for safekeeping. By this age, Bruner noted, subjects could cross the midline in handing the toy to a nearby person, a skill usually not exhibited in younger age groups. In addition, the two oldest age groups, the 12- to 14-month-olds and the 15- to 17-month-olds, could all handle three or more objects successfully. However, the oldest subjects consistently used a storage method, whereas the 12- to 14-month-old group used a variety of techniques. But even among these two older groups of subjects, toys were stored on the lap, in the chair, or handed to a nearby person rather than being stored in the other arm. A major point of importance in this research was that complementary use of the two hands to achieve a purposeful goal was evident as early as 6 to 8 months by infants storing a toy in one hand to free the receiving hand for a second toy.

Bruner performed additional research to more specifically examine bimanual control. In this research, a child was exposed to a box with a visible toy inside. To obtain the toy, the child had to slide open a wooden lid, keep the lid open, and grasp and withdraw the toy with the other hand. For this research, Bruner used the same subjects who were studied in the previous investigation, with the exception of the 4- to 5-month-old group. Bruner fund that although the younger groups were successful in this endeavor only approximately 20 percent of the time, the older age groups were successful 90 percent of the time. A common progression was also noted. Younger subjects often simply struck the box. A second strategy that was also unsatisfactory was closing the door immediately after opening. A successful but still single-handed approach was then used: The lid was opened and released, to free the hand for grabbing the toy. Once the lid was released, the hand was slowly slipped into the box to grasp the toy. This technique was commonly used by the subjects in the 12- to 14-month-old group and occasionally by older subjects. In approximately 16 to 17 percent of all trials, the subjects in the 12- to 14-month-old group used two hands. However, as described by Bruner, these movements were not efficient and were characterized by poor timing.

The complementary use of two hands increased in the two older age groups. In fact, two hands were used over 30 percent of the time. Bruner concluded from this research that the bimanual control necessary for success in this task was well structured and differentiated by 18 months of age but still could not be considered mastered.

SUMMARY

By the end of the first few months of life, infant reflexes have begun to be replaced by the cortically controlled voluntary movements. These voluntary movements develop in a fairly predictable sequence, although the rate of acquisition of the movement skill may vary considerably from child to child.

Voluntary movement follows a cephalocaudal pattern of development: The head is the first body part to be voluntarily controlled. This is an important movement acquisition because it enables the child to more completely visually scan the environment.

Body control is gained soon after control of the head. The upper body gains control first, with lower portions gradually acquiring voluntary movement. Control of the body enables appropriate positioning for the eventual acquisition of locomotion and allows the child to position the body in such a way as to free the hands for reaching and grasping.

Locomotion is an important contributor to the child's cognitive development because many new environments can be experienced. Initial crawling is slow, inefficient, awkward, and characterized by an extremely low-to-the-ground prone position. Soon the child develops a more elevated and efficient form of locomotion known as creeping.

Independent walking is preceded by a number of assisted forms of upright locomotion. Cruising laterally around furniture while maintaining a handhold for balance and assisted walking are both significant forms of locomotion because they contribute to emergence of independent walking and running in the locomotor progression.

Reaching and grasping abilities are facilitated by the emergence of upright posture and locomotion.

Upright positioning frees the hands for more frequent use; locomotion enables the child to move to
objects of interest for purposes of manipulation.

Reaching and grasping, according to Bower,
emerge in two phases. Increasing control of the arms
and hands is particularly important because it allows increased manual exploration and facilitates
daily routine activities.

KEY TERMS

Contralateral	Manipulation
Crawling	Phase I reaching
Creeping	Phase II reaching
Grasping	Releasing
Homolateral	Stability
Locomotion	Voluntary movement

CHAPTER 12

Fine Motor Development

The term *fine motor* generally refers to those movements predominantly produced by the smaller muscles or muscle groups of the body. As discussed in Chapter 1, the terms *fine* and *gross motor* can be generally used to categorize types of movements. Running and walking are predominantly functions of the efforts of the larger muscle groups of the body, so we usually think of these movements as gross motor. However, manual activity such as sewing, sculpting, drawing, and playing most musical instruments involves smaller muscle groups of the body, so such movements are therefore considered fine motor. Fine movements usually involve the use of the hands. Williams (1983) confined her definition of fine movement to just the movements of the hands and the eyes. Fine movement, she said, is "the ability to coordinate or regulate the use of the eyes and the hands together in precise and adaptive movement patterns" (p. 188). Although this definition

accurately notes the "precise and adaptive" nature of fine movement, it also implies that fine movement must involve the hands and the eyes. This is generally the case, but it might not be true for a visually impaired individual who, despite no involvement of the eyes, still develops fine motor control. This definition also fails to encompass those who have developed fine motor control of another body part. A soccer player, for example, often develops exceptional fine motor control of the foot for precisely manipulating the ball around defenders.

There is little information concerning these nonhand types of fine movement, and only slightly more information about fine movement of the hands. Because the most practical information concerning fine movement involves the hand, this chapter emphasizes the development of fine hand movements critical to daily activities and to the attainment of high-level performance in many movement endeavors.

ASSESSING FINE MOVEMENT

Though many tools exist for assessing both gross and fine movement, many of these instruments do not establish clear performance criteria or maintain complete or contemporary norms. Furthermore, some assessment tools employ norms that are incomplete or were devised from multiple sources, making review of the original sources difficult. For these reasons, norms developed by several of these instruments are often discrepant, which may indicate a need for research into the establishment of a new protocol for assessment (Noller & Ingrisano (1984). With that in mind Noller and Ingrisano (1984) examined nearly 200 healthy birth to 6-year-old subjects on 37 motor tasks. They selected these test items on the basis of which items appeared most frequently in other assessment batteries. The time of emergence and achievement on these tasks were determined by Noller and Ingrisano. Emergence of a task was considered to have occurred when 68 percent of the subjects within a 6-month interval performed the task independently. Achievement was considered to have occurred when 95 percent of the subjects within a 6-month interval were capable of independent performance. These particular levels were selected because of their similarity to standard deviations in population statistics and the ease of comparison to other assessment tools.

The findings concerning time of emergence and achievement, as well as the norm from other popular assessment tools, are presented in Table 12-1. According to Noller and Ingrisano, the emergence times appear to be fairly similar to established norms though achievement times were found to vary considerably from other published norms. While all of these figures are worthwhile for roughly indicating the times of attainment of certain fine motor tasks, sufficient discrepancies exist to suggest that more research is necessary concerning fine motor assessment.

CATEGORIZING MANIPULATION

Use of the hands, or *manipulation,* is an ability most people take for granted, even though there is a need for manipulation hundreds of times a day. Because of the critical nature of hand movement, there have been efforts to categorize the many types of daily hand movements, to facilitate discussion and study. Traditionally, hand movement involves intrinsic and extrinsic movements. *Intrinsic movements* are coordinated movements of the individual digits used to manage an object already in the hand. *Extrinsic movements* displace both the hand and the in-hand object through movements of the upper limb (Elliott & Connolly, 1984).

Intrinsic and extrinsic are useful terms for organizing the movements of the hand, but Elliott and Connolly (1984) found these terms somewhat general, so they created a slightly more detailed system of categorizing the "bewildering number of hand movements." In their system, there are three categories of hand movements: *simple synergies, reciprocal synergies,* and *sequential patterns.* Although these three general categories are believed to encompass most types of hand movements, the authors state that movements involving flexion-extension movements, such as typing or piano playing, have not been categorized.

The simple synergy category involves all hand movements in which the action of all the digits, including the thumb, is similar. The digits converge on an object and sometimes alternately flex and extend. Examples of simple synergies include the action of squeezing a rubber ball, most pinching and squeezing movements, and the formation of the dynamic tripod, the grip most people use when holding a writing implement or when handwriting.

Reciprocal synergies are combinations of movements involving the thumb and other involved digits reciprocally and simultaneously interacting to produce relatively dissimilar movements. Reciprocal synergies might involve the flexion of the fingers as the thumb adducts or extends. Elliott and Connolly noted that the thumb's capacity for movement, which is independent of the fingers, is often

TABLE 12-1 Comparison of the Norms for the Attainment (in months of age) of Various Fine Motor Skills as Determined by Several Popular Assessment instruments and Noller and Ingrisano's 1984 Study

				Sources			Noller/Ingrisano	
Task	Peabody	DPIYC	Bayley	Gesell	DDST	Erhardt	Emergence	Achievement
Tracking across midline								
toward right	2–3			2	2.5		Bᵃ–5	6–11
toward left	2–3			2	2.5		B–5	6–11
Tracking 180°								
toward right	2–3			4	4			6–11
toward left	2–3			4	4			6–11
Turns to sound								
turns right			3.8	6–7			6–11	
turns left			3.8	6–7			6–11	
Reach and grasp of 1-in. cube	4–5		4.6	5				6–11
Radial digital grasp of cube						8	12–17	48–53
Transfers cube	6–7	3–5	5.5	7	7.5		6–11	
Stacks a tower of cubes								
2	12–15	12–15	13.8	15	20	15	12–17	18–23
3	16–18	16–19	16.7	15				18–23
4	16–18			18	26			18–23
5	19–24			21			18–23	24–29
6	19–24	20–23	28	21			18–23	30–35
7	19–24			24				24–29
8	25–30	28–31	30	30	38			30–35
9	31–36			30			30–35	48–53
10	31–36			36			36–41	54–59
Copies cube bridge	37–48						36–41	54–59
Copies cube gate				54			30–35	54–59
Pincer grasp raisin	10–11	9–11		11	14.7			
Pincer grasp rice							18–23	36–41
Copies drawing square	37–48				60	54	54–59	
Static tripod grasp on crayon								
when copying square						36–48	42–47	
Formboard								
places round shape	12–15	16–19	16.8	15			12–17	18–23
places square shape	16–18	20–23	21.2	21			18–23	30–35
places triangular shape	31–36	20–23	21.2	36			18–23	24–29
Finger opposition		61–72					48–53	66–71

ᵃB stands for birth.

Source: Adapted from Noller and Ingrisano and reprinted with the permission of the American Physical Therapy Association.

used in the production of reciprocal synergies. This category of hand movement includes many intrinsic movements such as twiddling of the thumbs or rolling a pencil back and forth between the thumb and forefinger.

A major difference between sequential patterns and the other two categories is that sequential patterns are indeed sequential, not simultaneous. A systematic sequence of hand movements contributes to the attainment of a specific goal. Included in this category of movements are tying a knot, unscrewing a lid, or squeezing a tube of toothpaste until toothpaste flows from the opening.

This system of categorizing hand movement is still relatively new but helpful for communicating or describing information concerning hand movement. It also alerts us to the extremely wide range of movement the broad term *manipulation* encompasses.

THE DEVELOPMENT OF PREHENSION

Manipulation is a general term referring to hand use and movement at any time throughout the lifespan. *Prehension* applies specifically to the act of grasping. Prehension is critical to the development of a multitude of hand movements used throughout the lifespan.

One of the most frequently cited studies in this area of prehension was completed over 60 years ago. Though the findings of this research have recently been called into question, the work of Halverson (1931) is often considered a classic study in the area of early manipulation because of the depth of the conclusions and the critical nature of the subject under investigation.

The purpose of the Halverson study was to examine the development of prehension, particularly the grasp, in children 16 to 52 weeks old. To examine the children's grasping ability, Halverson presented each child with a 1-inch red cube, filmed the response, and then attempted to describe the developmental progression for the grasp of the cube. Generally, Halverson noted that the total process of

prehension, early reaching, grasping, and releasing behavior involved four steps: (1) the object is visually located; (2) the object is approached; (3) the object is grasped; (4) the child disposes of the object by releasing it.

More specifically, Halverson noted that there appeared to be three basic methods of reaching. The most immature method involved sweeping the hand and arm in a backhand manner toward the object. Eventually, this mode of reaching evolved into a more mature sweeping or scooping approach. Despite the advanced nature of this method relative to the backhand style, this second method was indirect or "circuitous" and involved approaches from a variety of angles. Finally, the children in the study developed a direct reach that is common in slightly older, more motorically advanced children.

The brunt of Halverson's investigation concerned the actual grasp of the object. Overall, Halverson noted that younger children had not yet developed the ability to oppose the fingers with the thumb. He noted that when children reached for red cube, the position of the thumb during the reach often indicated the likelihood of the thumb being used in opposition to the fingers. If the thumb was inward when the hand approached the cube, thumb opposition was likely to occur. However, a thumb positioned downward or curled under the hand indicated an upcoming grasp that was less mature than the thumb-opposition grasp.

Halverson also found a relatively specific progressive sequence of grasping behavior in his 4- to 13-month-old subjects. Initially, at 4 months of age, the child was totally incapable of making contact with the object. This initial step in the progression was followed, at 5 months, by an ability to crudely make contact but an inability to actually acquire the object. The third step in the developmental sequence of grasping was known as the "primitive squeeze," also characteristic of children very near 5 months of age. In this case, the hand was generally thrust beyond the desired object and then scooped or corralled inward until the object was actually squeezed against the body or the other hand. The hand performed no real grasping action. In the fourth step, at approximately 6 months of age, a grasp of sorts did occur. This "squeeze grasp" was made possible by the hand approaching the object laterally until contact was made—then the fingers closed around the object and pressed it against the palm of the hand. This system of acquiring the cube was the first sign of an actual grasp and was typically clumsy and unsuccessful.

The fifth type of grasping, the "hand grasp," occurred at approximately 7 months and was somewhat similar to the squeeze grasp except that the child bridged the hand down over the cube. The child maintained the thumb in a position parallel to the fingers, which had curled down over the side of the cube. Once that position was attained, the fingers pressed the cube against the heel of the hand. This form of grasp was similar to the sixth level of grasping ability Halverson noted. In the "palm grasp," the hand was again placed down over the cube. However, as the fingers curled down over the side of the cube, so did the thumb. This appeared to be an initial sign of the thumb's ability to oppose the movement of the fingers and was also common in infants at approximately 7 months.

The opposition of the thumb became increasingly apparent in the seventh level of grasping. For example, at approximately 8 months, the "superior palm grasp" was facilitated by placing the hand, radial side down, on the cube. The thumb then pressed on the near side of the cube as the first two fingers curled down onto the far side and applied opposing pressure. This system was similar to the grasp observed in level 8 at 9 months, the "inferior forefinger grasp." The thumb and forefinger opposition noted in level 8 once again was evident but was initiated by the fingers wrapping around the cube and pointing medially rather than downward. As in the seventh level, once acquired, the cube was controlled and maintained near the palm area of the hand.

At 13 months of age, in the next to the last level of grasping that Halverson observed, the cube was finally controlled and maintained by the fingertips of the first three fingers, which were opposed by the thumb. To attain this control, Halverson noted

that the hand was stabilized by the tabletop during the initial contact and grasp of the cube. This characteristic differentiates level 9, the "forefinger grasp," from level 10, the "superior forefinger grasp," which also becomes common among infants at approximately 13 months of age. Otherwise, the superior forefinger grasp was similar to the level 9 grasp. Table 12-2 summarizes the 10 stages of grasping development.

Generally, Halverson noted a progression that clearly evidenced the proximodistal pattern of development discussed in Chapter 1. Movement ability progressed in a direction away from the body. Although the initial efforts at obtaining an object through reaching and grasping were crude shoulder and elbow movements, the finer movements of the hand, and eventually the fingertips, attained eventual control. In addition, Halverson noted a gradual increase in the movements' speed and efficiency as these children aged from 16 to 52 weeks. More recent research confirmed that the progression Halverson originally observed has endured throughout the years. However, these various movement abilities are likely to emerge earlier today than in previous years as a result of enhanced standards of living, improved nutrition, and greater awareness of the importance of early motor experiences (Hohlstein, 1974). The specific time the various grasping-related skills emerge continues to be extremely variable.

A NEW VIEW OF THE DEVELOPMENT OF PREHENSION

As we discussed in the last section, the development of prehension as seen by Halverson (1931) has been viewed as an ordered, relatively fixed, sequence of grip patterns predictably evolving with increasing age. However, according to more recent research (Newell et al., 1989), this view may be a function of the narrow range of constraints imposed in Halverson's research. In that study, young subjects were offered cubes of only one size to grasp. Newell and his associates sought to examine the effects of

TABLE 12-2 Halverson's 10 Stages of Grasping Development in Children 16 to 52 Weeks Old

Grasping Characteristic	Approximate Age of Occurrence (months)
Failure to make contact.	4
Crude contact but failure to obtain the object.	5
Object is scooped toward the body and squeezed against the body or opposite hand.	5
Following a lateral approach of the hand, the fingers close around the object and press it against the palm of the hand, the first sign of an actual grasp.	6
Hand is bridged down over the object, with the thumb parallel to the fingers; then the fingers press the object against the palm of the hand.	7
Hand is bridged down over the object, with the fingers and the thumb curling over the object, an initial sign of thumb opposition.	7
Hand is placed, radial side down, on the object; the thumb presses the near side of the object while the fingers apply pressure opposite the far side.	8
Fingers wrap around the object by pointing medially rather than down; once acquired, the object is maintained in the palm area.	9
Fingertips of the first three fingers opposite the action of the thumb in the grasp while the hand is stabilized on the supporting surface.	13
Fingertips oppose the action of the thumb without the hand being stabilized, as in the previous stage.	13

using various sizes of objects that had been scaled to the hand size of the preschool-age and adult subjects. Ten cube sizes were used to examine which hand was employed, the number of fingers used with the thumb in contacting objects, depth of finger contact or grip (side, top, etc.). Some differences were noted. For example, adults used one hand 60 percent of the time (two hands 40 percent of the time) while children used one hand 38.6 percent of the time. The object-to-hand-size ratio was found to be a significant factor related to the subject's use of one or two hands. Older subjects were also found to demonstrate slightly more use of the right hand, indicating that hand dominance may not yet be firmly established by the age of 4 years. When objects were scaled to the subject's hand size, the overall trend for grasping was quite similar for adult and child subjects. One finger and the thumb were used for small objects. Two to three fingers were used with the thumb for intermediate sized objects and four fingers and the thumb were used for larger objects. The size of the object that seemed to create a shift to a new pattern of grasping differed between age groups. However, when the object was scaled to the subject's hand size, the "shifting point" was quite similar.

According to Newell and associates, over 1000 combinations of finger/thumb grips are possible, but subjects tend to use only a fraction of those. Adult subjects regularly employed 14 combinations, while children used 22. Even within preferred grips, certain choices appeared to dominate. Five grips accounted for 62 percent of the grips used by children and 89 percent of the grips used by adults (see Figure 12-1). The authors noted that eliminating the "playful behavior" of the child subjects would have increased the number of times that children use the five most common grips.

Based on the results of their research, Newell and his associates concluded that task constraints, in this case object size, play a major role in grip patterns for children and adults. Furthermore, contrary to traditional views of grip pattern development, children and adults use similar patterns for similarly sized objects relative to their hand size. In short, developmental progressions may be considerably

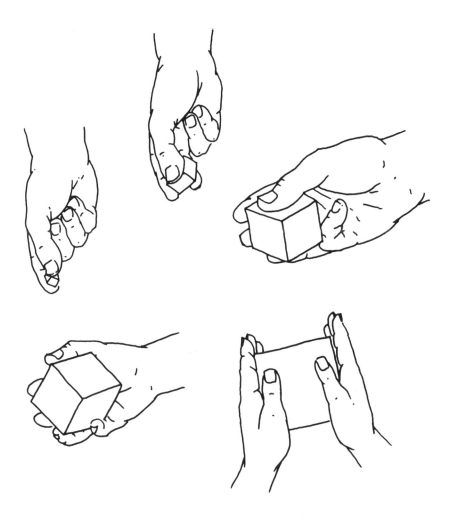

FIGURE 12-1   The five most common grip patterns encountered by Newell, Scully, Tenenbaum, and Hardiman (1989) in their research on child and adult grip patterns

more "flexible" than those previously described by Halverson (Newellet al., 1989). In fact, Halverson's work may be ". . . a reflection of the narrow range of constraints tested rather than a rigid sequence of biological or cognitive prescriptions for action" (Newell, Scully, & McDonald, 1989; p. 819).

To gain further insight into the development of prehension, Newell and colleagues compared grasping in 4- to 8-month-old infants using objects of varying sizes and shapes (Newell, Scully, & McDonald, 1989). Subjects were generally found to use two hands more commonly with larger objects. According to the authors, this indicated an ability to differentiate one- and two-hand grasps and object size as young as 4 months old. In addition, the number of fingers used to grasp increased as the size of the object increased. The number of fingers employed was also influenced by object shape. Of all the one-hand grasps, approximately 50 percent occurred with the right hand (or the left hand). Apparently hand dominance had not yet begun to evolve in children this young. All subjects in this study, even the 4-month-olds, exhibited an ability to differentiate finger use based on object size. However, the younger subjects exhibited more variability in finger combinations.

As in Newell's previous research, five-finger configurations accounted for most grips. And, as we might expect from the research cited earlier, minimal age differences were noted in the grasping of 4- to 8-month-olds, though the younger subjects required more haptic information to differentiate grip configurations, while 8-month-olds were more likely to use visual information (Newell, Scully, & McDonald, 1989). *Haptic perception* is the "ability to acquire information about objects with the hands, to discriminate and recognize objects from handling them as opposed to looking at them" (Bushnell & Boudreau, 1993; p. 1008).

EXPLORATORY PROCEDURES AND HAPTIC PERCEPTION

As discussed, haptic perception is the ability to glean information from objects by manipulation. Properties that we can haptically perceive include tempera-

ture, size, texture, hardness, weight, and shape (Bushnell & Boudreau, 1993). Haptic sensitivity seems to emerge in a predictable sequence. The majority of research on haptic perception has involved texture or shape distinction and older infants (over 6 months of age). However, evidence exists that suggests that haptic perception may evolve as early as the first few months of life. Only infants over 6 months old have been studied concerning haptic perception of temperature; however, children much younger than 6 months withdraw their hands from heat or cold. Children over 6 months can perceive and discriminate hardness, but little is known considering younger children. Children under six months are not believed to possess the ability to perceive texture, though during the last half of the first year, texture can be perceived. Similar findings exist for weight, though it begins a few months later, at around 9 months. Shape perception evolves later yet, around 12 to 15 months. In short, a consistent order of emergence for haptic perception appears to exist (Bushnell & Boudreau, 1993).

The emergence of haptic perception appears to be closely linked to one's ability to perform certain types of hand movements. These hand movements, called *exploratory procedures,* are exemplified by lateral, alternate rubbing motions across an object's surface to detect texture (Lederman & Kaltzky, 1987). Another example is "unsupported holding." In this case, an in-hand object is alternately raised and lowered to assist in the perception of weight. These and other exploratory procedures are illustrated in Figure 12-2. Any restriction of these hand movements may inhibit a child's ability to learn about the object. Thus, an inability in any of the exploratory procedures may reduce certain forms of haptic sensitivity.

According to Bushnell and Boudreau (1993), infant object manipulation evolves through three phases. From birth to 3 months, babies simply clutch objects in the fist. This is largely influenced by the palmar grasp reflex discussed in Chapter 10. At this age the object is held with one hand, occasionally brought to the mouth or brought to the body's midline and held with both hands. Fingers may not open and close much while holding the object, but, if they

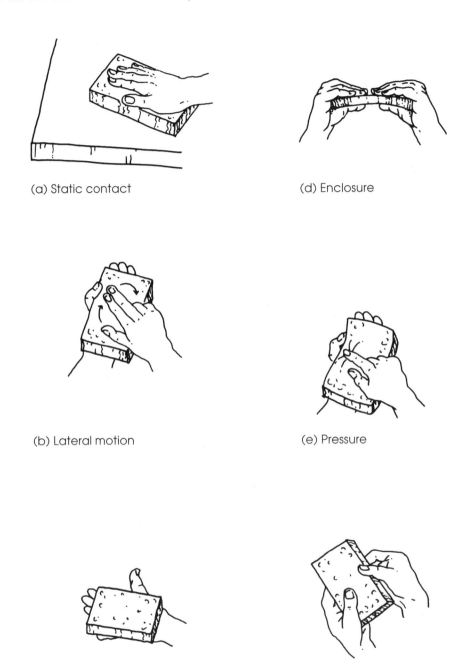

(a) Static contact

(d) Enclosure

(b) Lateral motion

(e) Pressure

(c) Unsupported holding

(f) Contour following

FIGURE 12-2 The optimal hand movement patterns for acquiring the object properties of temperature (a), texture (b), weight (c), volume/size (d), hardness (e), and shape (f) according to Lederman and Klatzky (1987).

do, the fingers create a kneading-like motion. Exploratory procedures at this age may be sufficient to detect haptic properties of temperature, size, and possible hardness. Interestingly, according to Bushnell and Boudreau (1993), the available research suggests that this is the order in which the ability to detect haptic properties typically emerges.

The second phase begins at approximately 4 months of age, when a wider variety of hand movements is evidenced. Visual control of manipulation and more varied and differentiated finger movements are noticeable. This includes poking, scratching, rubbing, waving, and banging objects. Infants also exchange the objects from hand to hand and perform some "unsupported holding" (see Figure 12-2). As indicated by Bushnell and Boudreau (1993), once these manipulatory capabilities are exhibited, the manipulatory capabilities again seem to govern haptic abilities as haptic sensitivity to hardness emerges around 6 to 7 months of age. Haptic sensitivity to texture typically emerges around 6 months, while sensitivity to weight may not occur until after 9 months. In short, throughout the middle of the first year, a number of manipulatory capabilities emerge that appear to be similar to those necessary to perceive related haptic properties.

By 9 to 10 months a third phase emerges when infants' ability to sit makes two-handed manipulation easier. Through "complimentary bimanual activities," one hand can position an object while the other manipulates and explores. Around this time, "contour-following" is exhibited. One hand maintains the object while the other smoothly passes over the object's outline. This gradually evolving manipulatory ability appears to contribute to the infant's ability to perceive configurational shape, which, according to Bushnell and Boudreau (1993), emerges around 12 to 15 months in most infants.

Generally, manipulatory capabilities seem to determine the order in which haptic perceptions emerge. One possible exception may be weight perception, which appears to emerge several months after the ability to perform unsupported holding (around 4 months of age). Though research is contradictory as to when the haptic ability to perceive weight emerges, Bushnell and Boudreau (1993) believe it may not be until around 9 months of age. Nevertheless, manipulation appears to be integral to the emergence of haptic ability since object properties that correspond to exploratory procedures that have not yet evolved cannot be discriminated. Thus, an infant's manipulatory ability appears to be a constraint to the perception of certain object properties (Bushnell & Boudreau, 1993).

HOLDING A WRITING IMPLEMENT

Although fine movement has been relatively underresearched compared to other forms of movement, one aspect of fine movement that has received considerable attention is the development of technique, or the movement process, involved in handwriting or drawing. The mature grasp of the pencil or crayon is referred to as the *dynamic tripod*, a finger posture in which the thumb, middle finger, and index finger function as a tripod for the writing implement, enabling a child to perform small, highly coordinated finger movement. Figure 12-3 illustrates the dynamic tripod. This writing or drawing hand position normally develops from the simple tripod, in which the correct hand positioning is evident but the small coordinated movements common to the more mature dynamic tripod are lacking (Rosenbloom & Horton, 1971). The dynamic tripod is usually present by 7 years of age (Ziviani, 1983). Prior to the development of the dynamic tripod, the child passes through a series of rather predictable stages of handwriting technique.

In examining children who were 1 1/2 to 7 years old, Rosenbloom and Horton determined that the earliest grasp of a writing implement usually involved the entire hand. The *supinate grasp* involved all four fingers and the thumb wrapped around the pencil to form a fist. This crude grasp, pictured in Figure 12-4, was normally replaced by the *pronate grasp*, which involved a palm-down hand position (Figure 12-5).

Once the child uses the pronate grasp, the thumb and fingers begin to play an increasingly important role in the development of the handwriting or drawing technique. For example, very young children

FIGURE 12-3 The dynamic tripod, the third and final stage of holding a writing or drawing implement. The thumb, middle finger, and index finger form a base for the implement.

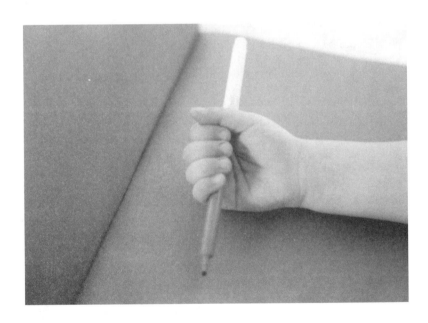

FIGURE 12-4 The supinate grasp, the first stage in holding a writing or drawing implement.

often use their nonwriting hand to adjust the writing implement. However, as increased finger and thumb control emerge, that action becomes less important because the children can make adjustments by using the fingers and thumb of the writing hand.

Generally, from 2 to 6 years, as children's writing ability develops, the hand moves closer to the tip of the pencil. Initially, children hold the pencil a considerable distance from the tip as the movements emanate from the shoulder. Later, the elbow pro-

FIGURE 12-5 The pronate grasp: The hand is held with the palm down.

duces the movement necessary to propel the pencil. Finally, moving in proximodistal fashion, the fingers and thumb gain sufficient control to enable improved pencil control. This improved level of movement technique, characterized by minute flexion and extension of the hand joints involved in forming the tripod, emerges in most children when they are 4 to 6 years old. In most cases, this enables the child to have developed a rather mature dynamic tripod by 7 years of age (Rosenbloom & Horton, 1971).

De Ajuriaguerra and associates (1979; cited in Blote, 1988) further determined that young children show clear developmental trends in handwriting. For example, posture becomes more upright while the position of the trunk becomes more stable. This creates less need for support by distal body parts, which frees those parts for more mature writing-related movements. The hand also becomes more stable and is more commonly held below the line of writing instead of on the line as is the case with younger writers. Also increasingly prevalent is positioning the hand in line with the forearm. Generally, children were found to become more economic in their writing

styles and displayed a visible proximodistal trend. In other words, movements close to the body decreased in number as those movements farther from the body became more common.

Additional research on writing posture and writing movement of children from 5 1/2 to approximately 7 1/2 years of age found considerable, nongender-related variations in children's writing development. However, as they aged, children generally tended to more commonly exhibit a mature arm and hand position. Percentages of children exhibiting specific handwriting characteristics are presented in Table 12-3. Interestingly, children were also found to increase the amount of muscle tension in writing from about 6 1/2 to 7 1/2 years. An extreme low, forward-leaning position also became prominent in many children. This position may be for improved visual inspection of the writing product and was believed to be related to increased effort to improve the writing. Only one characteristic was found to be significantly gender related. Excessive flexion of the index finger was more common among boys than girls (Blote & van Der Heijden, 1988; Blote, Zielstra, & Zoetewey, 1987).

TABLE 12-3 Percentages of 5 1/2- to 6 1/2-year-old Children Performing Certain Handwriting Characteristics

Characteristic	Percentage
Whole forearm on table	75
Upright body	81
Body not turned	80
Shoulders horizontal	85
Wrist in line with forearm	52
Wrist slightly extended	41
Paper perpendicular	51
Paper turned counterclockwise	30
Very low grip on pencil	53
Tripod grip	56
Proximal joint of index finger less than 90 degrees	53
Thumb opposing index finger	82
Pencil rests on:	
Third phalanx of middle finger	91
Second phalanx of middle finger	9
Tip of middle finger does not rest on shaft of pencil	87
No recurrent lifting of hand	90
No recurrent lifting of forearm	80

Source: Blote, Zielstra, and Zoetewey (1987).

CROSS-CULTURAL COMPARISON OF DEVELOPMENT OF THE DYNAMIC TRIPOD

The Rosenbloom and Horton (1971) research was conducted using British children as subjects. Saida and Miyashita (1979) similarly investigated the development of pencil manipulation among Japanese children. The purpose of this research was to examine the development of Japanese children and to perform a cross-cultural comparison by contrasting the results with Rosenbloom and Horton's earlier findings.

The developmental sequence of the dynamic tripod was found to be similar in the Japanese children. For example, the Japanese children evolved through four stages of finger posture. Stage 1 was a palmar grasp of the pencil, with control of the movement emanating from the shoulder and elbow. This was similar to the supinate grasp Rosenbloom and Horton described. Stage 2 was an incomplete tripod, a transition from and a combination of the palmar grasp of the pencil and the dynamic tripod. Stage 3 involved a tripod positioning of the hand with noticeable wrist movement, although the small coordinated movements of the fingers were absent. Stage 4 was the dynamic tripod, including the highly coordinated finger movements. Over 50 percent of the Japanese boys achieved this final stage by the age of just past 48 months. The girls were even more advanced, with over 50 percent achieving stage 4 by as much as a year earlier. Saida and Miyashita also noted that although some generalizations could be proposed relative to age, there were marked individual differences as to when the pencil-manipulation technique was attained. One female subject first exhibited the dynamic tripod at 35 months, one male at 63 months.

In general, the Japanese children exhibited a developmental finger posture sequence much like the British children. They also tended to gradually move their hand closer to the pencil tip as they aged. Furthermore, the average age for attaining the simple tripod was similar, with the British and Japanese children exhibiting this finger posture at 31 and 29 months, respectively.

There was a major difference between the two groups regarding the age at which the dynamic tripod emerged. The Japanese children attained it at the average age of 35 months, the British children 13 months later, at age 48 months. The authors speculated that this difference most likely occurred because of certain cultural factors. Particularly noteworthy is the fact that Japanese children often learn to use chopsticks early in life, which may enable them to develop more advanced manipulative skills at an early age. Saida and Miyashita also speculated that any differences that do exist may begin to diminish with the continued and increased availability of convenient devices that minimize the practice of manipulative skills, such as push-button appliances like electric toothbrushes or pencil sharpeners.

THE DYNAMIC TRIPOD FROM 6 TO 14 YEARS

Studies such as Rosenbloom and Horton's and Saida and Miyashita's provided information about fine movement during childhood, but there have been few investigations into any aspect of fine motor development beyond childhood, including the study of the development of the dynamic tripod. Ziviani (1983), however, noting the void of information following the achievement of the dynamic tripod, examined the refinement of this technique in children 6 to 14 years old. Subjects in this research were photographed while writing and then rated by the researchers on four characteristics. The degree of flexion of the interphalangeal joint (large knuckle) of the writing forefinger was noted—if the flexion exceeded 90 degrees, the subject was assigned a score of 1; if the angle was less than 90 degrees, a score of 2 was assigned. The angle of forearm pronation/supination was also deemed a critical factor. If the writing forearm was supinated at less than 45 degrees, the subject was assigned a 1; 2 was assigned for any other condition. Third, if more than the index finger was used on the shaft of the pencil, the subject received a 1. If the thumb and index finger gripped the pencil and the pencil rested on the radial aspect (thumb side) of the middle finger, the subject was assigned a 2. Finally, if the fingers were not a pad-to-pad opposition around the pencil, a 1 was assigned; if they were, a 2 was assigned.

Using this method, Ziviani was able to determine that for both index finger flexion and forearm pronation/supination there was a significantly greater likelihood of the younger subjects scoring a 1. In other words, the younger subjects would be more likely to flex the index finger and supinate the forearm excessively. The age of changing from the immature to mature characteristics on both the finger flexion and the forearm positioning was found to be approximately 10 years. The number of fingers used on the pencil and the pad-to-pad opposition were not found to be characteristics that were significantly age-related in this investigation. In general, Ziviani concluded that the dynamic tripod does continue to be refined between the ages of 6 and 14 years.

DRAWING AND WRITING: MOVEMENT PRODUCTS

As determined earlier in the chapter, there is a sequential development of movement technique for the manipulation of a pencil or any writing or drawing implement. This development is universal; only the rate of acquisition of the stages of movement ability varies. This movement ability is called the movement process. This section examines the development of the result of the movement process, the movement product.

Drawing: The Product

Children typically "draw" before they attempt to form the specific letters necessary for handwriting. Drawing ability has been deemed partly a function of the child's mental age. There are exceptions to this general statement, but there is some supportive evidence. For example, brain-injured children who function at a lower mental age than their peers of the same chronological age often have significantly greater difficulties drawing. These difficulties are manifested by an immature, exceptionally general way of mentally representing a figure. A second problem inhibiting drawing ability in children of lower mental age is their attempts at transcribing the desired image onto paper. Often the brain issues conflicting stimuli to the hand, resulting in an exceptionally immature drawing (Abercrombie, 1970).

Most children initiate their drawing development as early as 15 to 20 months by producing scribbles that have no apparent organization or intended goal. In fact, the first attempt at scribbling may occur by accident. Upon being reinforced by the resulting scribbles, the child usually does additional scribbling but often shows signs of hesitancy. Those scribbles soon become bolder as the child gains confidence.

They also become less spontaneous and are drawn slower as children attempt to control the movement of the hand with their eyes while actually pondering exactly what to create.

Following a collection and in-depth study of millions of children's paintings, Kellogg (1969) proposed that drawing is a four-step process. The *scribbling stage* is the first step to acquisition of the necessary hand-eye coordination for drawing (see Figure 12-6). Step 2, according to Kellogg is the creation of diagrams and combinations of diagrams. This *combine stage* begins with the construction of basic geometric figures such as spirals and simple crosses (see Figure 12-7). An example of the combine stage is the 2-year-old who draws a series of spiral figures or spirals and circles. The child then slowly develops sufficient understanding and motor control to create more precise figures, such as squares, rectangles, and triangles. Furthermore, the child becomes capable of drawing these shapes in combination with other shapes to form such things as simple houses or other familiar objects.

Step 3 in the development of the drawing product is what Kellogg referred to as the *aggregate stage* (see Figure 12-8). The child not only combines diagrams and figures but does so in combinations of three or more. Of course, the increasing number of combinations of figures enables the child to create more complex drawings. This increasing ability is culminated in the *pictorial stage* (see Figure 12-9),

which is characterized by pictures drawn with increasing precision and complexity. An example of this increasing complexity is the 8- or 9-year-old child who has learned to draw the human figure with depth rather than the stick figure that characterized earlier artwork.

As described by Kellogg, these four major stages create a progression that most children follow, but the specific age norms for drawing are difficult to determine because a multitude of variables tremendously affect drawing. One of the most important factors affecting the level of drawing development is the home environment: Children with a home environment conducive to drawing develop skills at an earlier age. Particularly notable components of the positive home environment are opportunities to observe other people drawing and the availability of the necessary writing implements.

Children's drawing development has been extensively examined, and there has been considerable research into the development of a specific type of drawing by children: design copying. Typically, this type of research requires children to reproduce a particular design. For example, Birch and Lefford (1967), in one of the most comprehensive examinations of design copying, asked children 5 to 11 years old to reproduce triangles and diamonds by tracing them, drawing them on a line grid, or drawing them freehand. In each case, children improved and became more consistent with age. There was a particularly dramatic increase in ability from 5 to 6 years of age; the magnitude of improvement equaled that which occurs in most children between 6 and 11 years.

Generally, children involved in this research were able to trace with the least difficulty. Following in order of increasing difficulty were drawing with the line grid and then freehand drawing. The tracing of triangles and diamonds was concluded to be "mature" at 6 years of age for most subjects. Maturity in the line-grid tasks occurred at 9 years of age, and freehand drawing of the triangle continued to improve through the age of 9. Freehand drawing of the diamond continued to improve through age 11, which was the highest age in the research.

FIGURE 12-6   Scribbling stage, the first stage of drawing

FIGURE 12-7   Combine stage: The child combines diagrams of figures and shapes.

These age-related findings were similar to those Ayres (1978) found. Ayres studied 4- to 11-year-old children in similar design-copying research. Ayres determined that ability to design copying improved through 9 years and then plateaued because by that age children were near the mature level. The most dramatic improvement noted, similar to Birch and Lefford's finding, was between the ages of 5 and 7 years.

Children also display a marked sequential pattern in the way they copy and trace designs of geometric shapes. Normally, they begin at the lower left of the design and start with a vertical stroke, followed by progress to the right. In fact, children who are simply asked to point to the beginning of a letter or shape most commonly indicate the lower left aspect of the figure.

This early method of design reproduction has been hypothesized as a possible cause for children's tendencies to reverse the letter d more frequently than the letter b. This is a logical explanation because the letter d requires that children reverse their usual tendency and progress to the left rather than to the right. The cause of this tendency has not been determined; however, speculation has centered on the relationship of design copying to handedness and the structure of manuscript letters (Bernbaum & Goodnow, 1974).

Handwriting: The Product

Handwriting is generally preceded by the initial attempts at drawing. These initial efforts familiarize the child with the writing implement and are critical for sufficiently improving fine motor ability so that the child is able to form letters. Several researchers (Reimer et al., 1975; Stennet, Smythe, &

FIGURE 12-8
Aggregate stage: The child continues to combine, but in increasing numbers of combinations.

FIGURE 12-9 Pictorial stage, the last stage of drawing: The child draws with more precision and complexity.

Hardy, 1972) examined the development of the ability to print letters. Through this research, experts determined that children at 4 years of age are usually capable of printing recognizable numbers or letters but often fail to organize them purposefully on the page (see Figure 12-10). Typically, the letters or numbers are randomly scattered over the page; they may also be written sideways or extremely slanted.

By 5 or 6 years, however, the child has generally mastered name printing. The 5-year-old normally writes in large, irregularly shaped uppercase letters that become larger toward the end of the name. The letters of 5-year-old children generally are 1/2 to 2 inches high. The 6-year-old may include the surname or pertinent initials but still write in uneven uppercase letters that are occasionally reversed. The letters the 6-year-old produces continue to be large, although smaller than those most 5-year-olds produce. By age 7, the height of the letter typically has decreased to approximately 1/4 inch. Children in the second grade generally master the production of uppercase letters and name printing, but the smaller lowercase letters continue to be difficult for many third graders. Children through third grade normally find single-stroke letters, such as I, c, and s, easier to form than multiple-stroke letters, such as f, k, or

t. Also, letters with horizontal and vertical strokes, such as E, T, and H, are easier to write than letters with slants or combined slants with vertical or horizontal strokes, such as K, B, and Z. Finally, most children also find spacing letters a difficult task that often remains unmastered until they are approximately 9 years old (Cratty, 1986).

FINGER TAPPING

Most of the research on fine motor development has centered on handwriting and drawing changes during childhood. Other areas of research, however, have contributed considerably to our general knowledge of fine movement. Finger tapping, for example, is an important indicator of fine motor coordination and is often used to diagnose neurological difficulty. From research on finger tapping, investigators have determined that the increased coordination occurring over the first several years of life is highly correlated with an increase in the performance speed of the movement task. In addition, this increase in coordination and speed of movement typically plateaus at approximately 8 to 10 years on most finger-tapping tasks (Denckla, 1974).

Finger-tapping tasks are often categorized into repetitive and successive movements. Repetitive tasks are repetitions of the same movement, such as tapping the thumb and forefinger together as rapidly as possible. Successive movements are a series of similar movements performed in rapid succession. For example, a successive task that has been examined in research involving kindergarten through second-grade children is the rapid tapping of the thumb successively with each samehand finger. In performing these kinds of tasks, young children were found to improve consistently with age. Also, girls performed better than boys at all three grades involved in the research. Interestingly, right-hand superiority was noted in these right-hand-dominant children for the repetitive but not the successive tasks; according to the author, this was an unexpected finding (Denckla, 1973).

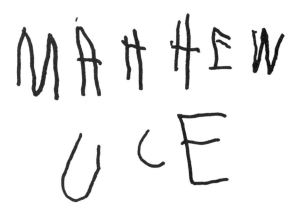

FIGURE 12-10 The letters a child forms when approximately 4 years old are often uppercase, large, and unorganized on the page.

FINE MOTOR SLOWING IN LATE ADULTHOOD

As noted in the discussion of such fine movements as handwriting and finger tapping, most individuals' coordination and speed of performance plateau fairly early in life. From then on, few obvious changes are noticeable until regression begins late in life. Whereas the first few years of life are characterized by the central nervous system's increasing capacity and improved movement capability in a proximodistal direction, later life often involves a reversal of that process. The degeneration of neurons is a phenomenon associated with aging (Bondareff, 1985). This degeneration, in conjunction with higher incidence of such chronic diseases as arthritis and osteoporosis, can reverse the proximodistal progression that occurred earlier in life. The fine motor development that was developed at the distal portions of the body, such as the fingertips, regresses. Movement can become less refined as arm and shoulder control regains control over movements that were once precisely coordinated by wrist and finger action.

Fine motor behavior may also slow as a result of the neurological degeneration associated with aging. In fact, Salthouse (1985) reviewed many movement-related studies that examined the phenomenon of slowing with age. This process of becoming slower in movement is well established. In fact, Salthouse used terms such as "least disputed" and "most pervasive" to describe the slowing process. However, he also noted that this slowing trend is much more common in some types of movements than others. For example, the slowing in handwriting is much more evident than that noticed in finger-tapping research.

An interesting way to express the association of age and reduced speed for a given movement activity is with a correlation coefficient. A higher correlation coefficient indicates a higher relationship between age and time to perform the movement in question. Although Salthouse admitted that this technique may occasionally be misleading, generally the coefficient gives a useful rough estimate of the magnitude of the age/speed relationship. In reviewing the research examining a variety of kinds of movement, Salthouse found the mean and median coefficients for 11 reaction-time studies to be .32 and .31, respectively. Those values can be compared with the results from six movement-time studies in which the mean and median coefficients were .49 and .545. Examples of other analyzed movements were card sorting, .54; dialing a telephone, .64; zipping a garment, .64; unwrapping a Band-Aid, .48; squeezing toothpaste, .55; and using a fork, .33.

Slowing with age is believed to occur in many fine and gross movements, but Salthouse stated that there are three major areas of exceptions to this general rule. First, he noted that physically fit or exceptionally healthy individuals maintain their speed quite well relative to younger healthy adults. Physical activity is a means of allaying the slowing process. Second, practice also inhibits the slowing process. Older adults who consistently and regularly repeat or practice the activity in question generally show considerably less slowing than young adults who have been uninvolved in the activity for long periods. Finally, Salthouse found that movement involved in the creation of vocal responses shows fewer signs of slowing than manipulatory movement.

In research specifically designed to examine the effects of physical activity and aging on fine motor performance, Normand, Kerr, and Metiviei (1987) noted that slowing in movement behavior is especially common with complex movements. This is particularly true of many fine movements and, as Salthouse suggested earlier, is generally believed to be strongly related to an individual's health, personal habits (e.g., physical activity), and the nature of the task. Also, while it was once believed that slowing with age was a function of decline in muscles, joints, or organs specifically related to the movement, many experts now believe that the slowing may be a function of deterioration in the central nervous system. This, of course, means that slowing could happen in cognitive processes as well as human movement. Also, because the central nervous system governs both mental and motor capacities, information gathered concerning psychomotor changes in speed may contribute to the body of knowledge concerning the central nervous system and cognitive slowing with age. Slowing reaction time, according to Normand, Kerr, and Metiviei (1987), could be a function of loss of brain cells, reduction of cerebral blood flow, or the presence of disease (e.g., atherosclerosis), which may disrupt the central nervous system. They further claim, as Salthouse suggested earlier in this section, that declining physical fitness may be a contributor to slowing with age.

To test their hypothesis, Normand, Kerr, and Metiviei (1987) studied the effects of short-term increases in physical activity level on performance of a fine motor task. The task was to rapidly and repeatedly align a steering wheel with specified target areas. Both accuracy and speed of response were important factors in the study. All of the subjects, averaging over 65 years of age, were tested before and after participating in a 10-week exercise program. Contrary to the original hypothesis and the research of others, Normand, Kerr, and Metiviei did not find an improved level of fine motor performance on the posttest. However, periodic, informal assessments of physiological change revealed that these subjects, originally believed to be sedentary, also failed to show a physiological improvement. Perhaps, as the authors suggest, the subjects were not sedentary as originally believed. Though none were actively engaged in a physical activity program, their daily routines of walking while shopping or doing yardwork may have been sufficient to make an improvement in physiological parameters, and therefore fine motor ability, more difficult.

This research is in contrast to other investigations, which have shown physical activity to enhance other forms of motor performance (Clarkson & Kroll, 1978; Spirduso, 1977). Of particular interest was the reaction- and movement-time research conducted by Spirduso (1977). In her investigation, 50- to 70-year-old active and inactive subjects were compared to their 20- to 30-year old counterparts on simple and discriminant reaction and movement time. Though the younger adults performed better overall on these measures, activity level was a significant factor. This prompted Spirduso to conclude that "a life of physical activity appeared to play a more dominant role in simple and discriminant reaction time and movement time and age" (p. 435).

SUMMARY

Fine movement refers to those movements that are predominantly produced by the small muscles or muscle groups of the body.

Manipulation, or use of the hands, is one of the most critical of the fine movements because hundreds of manipulative movements are performed each day. Manipulation has been categorized into intrinsic movements involving coordinated movements of the individual digits and extrinsic movements, which involve the management of an object that is already in hand. A more specific system of categorization includes simple synergies, reciprocal synergies, and sequential patterns.

In a frequently cited study conducted over 60 years ago, Halverson (1931) described the early reaching and grasping of 4- to 13-month-old infants. Three basic stages of development were determined for reaching, whereas grasping evolved through a 10-stage progression. Generally, a proximodistal progression was noted.

More recent research by Newell and associates has led to the questioning of the "classic" work of Halverson. This research examined adult and child reaching and grasping when the object size was scaled to the size of the subject's hand. Though some differences were noted, the overall trend for grasping was quite similar for adult and child subjects. Object size was found to play a major role in grip patterns employed by children and adults.

Recent work by Bushnell and Boudreau (1993) examined the haptic perception or the ability to glean information from objects via the hands; they found haptic perception to be an apparent function of early ability in manipulation. The emergence of exploratory procedures, like poking or unsupported "holding of an object," were found to be linked to the emergence of haptic properties of objects. Thus, any early restriction of hand movements may restrict an infant's ability to learn about an object's properties.

The development of the hand position for holding a writing implement has been one of the most widely researched areas of fine movement. The first hand position used for grasping a pencil or crayon is usually a supinate grasp: a fist around the pencil. This typically evolves into a pronate grasp, which is a palm-down position characterized by the fingers curled around the pencil, with the index finger extending the length of the pencil and pointing toward the point. Finally, usually by 7 years of age the dynamic tripod is developed, a hand position that enables highly coordinated finger movement to occur.

Other notable developmental handwriting trends seen in young children include an increase in upright posture, a more stable trunk and hand, and an increase in the likelihood of holding the hand below the line of writing and in line with the forearm. Children were also found to increase in forward lean and muscle tension at around 7 years of age.

Extensive studies by Kellogg led to the formulation of four major stages of drawing development as determined by the product of the act of drawing. Initially, children go through the scribbling stage, in which they simply scribble with no apparent objective in mind. In the combine stage, children create diagrams and combinations of diagrams. The third stage, the aggregate stage, is characterized by combinations of three or more diagrams or figures. Stage 4, the pictorial stage, is typified by pictures drawn with continued complexity and precision.

Like drawing, handwriting can also be described developmentally by the product of the action. Researchers in this area have noted that recognizable letter writing is generally evident by 4 years of age, although there is little organization of the letters. By 5 or 6 years, children can print their names using large uppercase letters. By 7 years, children write letters much smaller and can effectively print lowercase letters.

Finger tapping is another area of fine movement that has been of interest to fine motor researchers.

Through finger-tapping tests, investigators have determined that increased coordination and speed of performance occur over the first several years of life. For most finger-tapping tasks, this improvement typically plateaus at approximately 8 to 10 years.

The speed and coordination of many forms of fine movement plateau fairly early in life. No major fine-motor changes are noted until the later stages of life, when a regression may occur, a reversal of the proximodistal trend in development. Fine movement may become less precise as the elbow and shoulder begin to guide the hand through movements once led by fingertip control. Slowing and decreased coordination may also occur as a result of the neural degeneration that often accompanies aging. Although slowing with age is a well-substantiated fact and inevitable for many people, physical activity and practice attenuate or even eliminate the slowing process in later adulthood.

In research designed to examine the effects of short-term increases in physical activity and aging on fine motor performance, researchers administered a rapid and repetitive fine motor task to subjects who were over 65 years of age and involved in a 10-week physical activity program. Though this investigation did not show an improved level of performance in fine movement, similar reaction- and movement-time research has shown that physical activity through adulthood may be a more important factor in reaction and movement time than age is.

KEY TERMS

Aggregate stage	Manipulation
Combine stage	Pictorial stage
Dynamic tripod	Prehension
Exploratory procedures	Pronate grasp
Extrinsic movements	Reciprocal synergies
Fine motor	Scribbling stage
Haptic perception	Sequential patterns
Intrinsic movements	Simple synergies
	Supinate grasp

CHAPTER **13**

Fundamental Locomotion Skills of Childhood

Children's motor repertoires greatly expand during the second year of life. At this time, children no longer have to rely on rudimentary motor behaviors to locomote, explore, and manipulate their environment. They begin to develop and use fundamental skills of locomotion that include walking, running, jumping, and hopping. In addition, when several of these skills are combined, galloping, sliding, and skipping emerge. These fundamental locomotor skills can be thought of as the building blocks of the more specific skills developed later in childhood.

At the end of the first year or at the beginning of the second year, children are capable of walking without support, and soon thereafter running is evident. In turn, as soon as children are capable of momentarily propelling themselves through space, as is required in running, they will also be capable of performing some type of jumping and hopping maneuver. As strength, balance, and motor coordination improves, combination patterns will appear.

These combination patterns include galloping, sliding, and skipping.

This chapter reviews the professional literature regarding the development of these fundamental skills of locomotion and explores factors that may affect their development.

WALKING

The onset of independent *walking* or *upright bipedal locomotion* is truly a glorious occasion in the lives of both infants and parents. Shortly after the birth of their offspring, many parents await the onset of this milestone with great interest and enthusiasm. However, this important event has more far-reaching ramifications for the infant. Up to this point, the infant has had to rely on the prewalking movement patterns of crawling, creeping, and locomoting with handholds. Each movement pattern is useful for getting the child from point A to point B, but they all have one major limitation: Each requires the use of the hands to perform the movement. Thus, while the child is locomoting, the hands are not free to explore the changing environment. In contrast, as soon as the infant is capable of walking alone, his hands are no longer tied up in performing the movement but are free to more fully explore the ever-changing environment.

This form of locomotion is characterized by a progressive alternation of leading legs and continuous contact with the supporting surface. The walking cycle or *gait* cycle is the distance covered by two heel strikes of the same foot and consists of two distinct phases: a *swing phase* and a stance or *support phase* (Burnett & Johnson, 1971). The swing phase begins when the foot or toes of one leg leave the supporting surface and ends when the heel or foot of the same leg recontacts the ground. The time when balance is maintained on only one foot is the support phase. Thus, while the right foot is in the swing phase, the left foot is in the support phase. When both feet are in contact with the supporting surface, the walker is in a *double support phase*.

Even though Bernstein (1967) recognized that walking is one of the most highly automatized motor acts that adults perform, the same is not true for the walking infant. An infant's initial attempt at unsupported walking has little in common with normal adult walking because to achieve independent walking, the infant must overcome two major obstacles. Not only must the infant have sufficient leg strength to support the body weight, she must also be capable of maintaining a state of equilibrium. Subsequently, many of the observable characteristics of initial walking are designed to foster stability. For example, the initial movement pattern of independent walking is characterized by short, quick, rigid steps; the toes point outward, and the infant assumes a wide base of support. In addition, the infant makes a flat-footed contact with the ground instead of the heel-toe contact of an adult gait. Further attempts to maintain stability are implemented by carrying the arms in a high guard position. Also, the infant keeps the arms rigid; they do not swing

freely in opposition to the legs. This independent walking pattern is apparent in most children by 12 months of age, even though the normal range is considered from 9 to 17 months. Table 13-1 summarizes certain walking characteristics. During the next 2 to 6 years, many gradual changes occur within each gait parameter, enabling the child to progressively assume a more adultlike style of walking.

Dynamic Base

To maintain balance during initial walking attempts, the infant places the feet apart, to widen the base of support (see Figure 13-1). As balance improves, the child brings the feet closer together. This base of support is brought within the lateral dimensions of the trunk by 17.5 weeks after the onset of independent walking (Burnett & Johnson, 1971). Scrutton (1969) reported little variation in the width of the base between 1- and 4-year-old children. Of the 97 children examined, only 6 had a dynamic base of less than 2 inches and only 2 had a dynamic base greater than 5 inches.

Foot Angle

Foot angle is the amount of toeing-out or toeing-in. In general, the degree of toeing-out decreases during the first 4 years of life and then remains fairly

TABLE 13-1   Selected Walking Characteristics

Characteristic	Appearance*	Range*
Heel strike	22.6	3–50
Base within lateral dimensions of trunk	17.5	5–43
Synchronous movement of upper extremities	21.6	6–43
Double knee lock	27.2	8–55

*Weeks after the onset of independent walking.
SOURCE: Based on the data from Burnett and Johnson (1971).

Note the high guard-arm position, wide base of support, flat-footed contact and toeing-out in this immature walker.

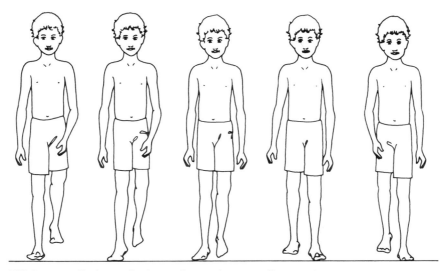

With improved balance, the base of support narrows, the arms are lowered and work in opposition to the legs, and the toes point more in a forward direction.

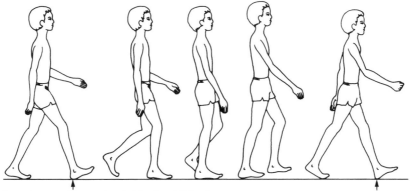

In mature walking, a heel strike is exhibited.

FIGURE 13-1 An illustration of selected improvements in walking

stable during the teens (Engel & Staheli, 1974), although some researchers have documented increasingly narrow bases of support up to 45 years of age (Murray, Drought, & Kory, 1964). In contrast, Engel & Staheli (1974) found toeing-in to be rare and consider this gait pattern abnormal. More specifically, they found only 6 of 130 (4.6 percent) children from 1 day to 14 years old exhibiting toeing-in gaits.

Walking Speed

Walking speed, another gait parameter, is determined by the length of the stride and the speed of the stepping movements. Each measure differs, depending on whether the walking movements are performed with or without support. Statham & Murray (1971) found both step frequency and walking speed greatest in independent walking as compared to supported walking, although there was much variability among the seven children studied. Statham and Murray found that children who were capable of walking 6 feet without support had a stepping rate of 158 steps per minute, whereas infants who walked with support attained only 107 steps per minute. More recent work reported the average footfalls per minute for babies as 180 to 200 per minute, in contrast to the average adult step frequency of 140 footfalls per minute (Keogh & Sugden, 1985). In short, step frequency decreases with advancing age during the childhood years.

Scrutton (1969) studied the other component of walking speed, step length. He found that the average step length of 97 "normal" children younger than 5 years old increased from 1.5 to 2 inches annually. More specifically, the average step length of the 1-, 2-, 3-, and 4-year-old children was 10, 11.5, 13, and 15 inches, respectively. In adult populations, step length is related to stature: Taller people generally have a longer step length (Murray, Drought, & Kory, 1964).

Until the infant gains sufficient neuromuscular control, the baby must take more steps per unit of time to increase walking speed. This lack of neuromuscular control precludes any successful attempt at increasing walking speed by increasing step length (Sutherland, 1984). With age, gains in neuromuscular control partly contribute to longer steps.

One study that illustrated differences in step length, stride length, step frequency, and walking speed was conducted at San Diego Children's Hospital (Sutherland, 1984). Table 13-2 summarizes the findings, which were based on a subject population of 464 "normal" children 1 to 7 years old and a comparative sample of 15 adults 19 to 40 years old.

Briefly, the researchers concluded that most observable gait changes occur by 3 years of age. In fact, they found little difference between the walking patterns of 3- and 7-year-old children, with the exception of diminished stride length and a fairly high step frequency for younger children. In addition, the average 3-year-old child displayed adultlike joint-rotation characteristics.

TABLE 13-2 Selected Walking Parameters with Advancing Age

Age (years)	Gait Parameter			
	Step Length (cm)	Stride Length (cm)	Steps/ Minute	Walking Speed (cm/s)
1	21.6	43.0	175.7	63.7
2	27.5	54.9	155.8	71.8
3	32.9	67.7	153.5	85.5
7	47.9	96.5	143.5	114.3
Adult	65.5	129.4	114.0	121.6

SOURCE: Based on data from Sutherland (1984).

RUNNING

Running is sometimes referred to as a natural extension of walking. This form of human locomotion is characterized by an alternate support phase and an airborne or *flight phase*. This flight phase is what most readily distinguishes the walk from the run. See Figure 13-2.

As with walking, children must overcome several obstacles before they will be capable of exhibiting characteristics associated with minimal running form. First, and perhaps most important, children need enough lower-limb strength to both propel themselves through the air and handle the additional force encountered when the airborne foot strikes the supporting surface. The magnitude of this impact can exceed three times the child's body weight. Second, the child needs improved motor coordination to control the rapidly moving legs.

At first, running takes on many characteristics of an immature walk: a wide base of support, arms held in a high guard position, and flat-footed contact with the supporting surface. Reverting back to this immature pattern is the child's way of temporarily improving balance while gaining confidence in performing this new movement.

On the average, most children exhibit minimal running form somewhere between 6 to 12 months after the onset of independent walking, in other words, between the 18th and 24th months of life.

As children acquire increased lower-limb strength, improved balance, and finally improved motor control, their running pattern will look more adultlike.

Selected Improvements in the Running Pattern

A close examination of the running pattern reveals that each running cycle consists of three phases: the support phase, the flight phase, and the recovery phase. The arms also play an important role. This section examines in greater detail certain developmental changes that occur during the running cycle.

Support Phase and Flight Phase The support phase absorbs the impact of the striking foot, supports the body, and maintains forward motion while accelerating the body's center of gravity as the support leg provides thrust to propel the body forward. The inexperienced runner performs the foot strike with the full sole. As running form improves, the runner tends to contact the ground closer toward the ball of the foot. Data that Fortney (1983) collected support this finding. In her study, the 2-year-old subjects' support ankle formed an angle slightly less than 90 degrees at contact with the ground. In contrast, her 4- and 6-year-old subjects attained 98 degrees ankle plantar flexion (toes pointing toward ground) at contact.

At first, the inexperienced runner is incapable of projecting the body through space for any significant distance because the runner does not effectively use the thrust leg. The progressive developmental trend of the thrust leg calls for more involvement of the hip, knee, and ankle to provide full extension to generate maximum thrust. This increased extension of the segments of the thrust leg becomes more evident with increasing age. This was particularly apparent in Fortney's (1983) research; she noted increasing degrees of support-knee extension at takeoff between the 2- (33.67 degrees), 4- (19.25 degrees), and 6-year-old children (15.20 degrees). She also reported similar trends across ages in relation to both ankle and hip extension.

FIGURE 13-2 Running—the flight phase.

Recovery Phase Once the body has been thrust into the air by the vigorous extension of the support leg, the support leg enters a phase of recovery. The leg that has been projected backward must be quickly brought forward to once again repeat its function in the next running cycle. There are obvious developmental trends in how the recovery leg is brought forward.

The experienced runner flexes the knee so the heel of the foot of the recovery leg comes very close to making contact with the buttock. The knee and thigh are then swung forward until the thigh is practically parallel with the running surface. This thigh position is usually reached the moment the support foot leaves the supporting surface (James, & Brubaker, 1973). While the body is airborne, the knee of the forward leg is extended, thus allowing the foot to descend toward the running surface. The experienced runner does not place the foot so far in front of his or her center of gravity as to produce a braking effect.

In contrast, the inexperienced runner does not achieve a degree of knee flexion sufficient to bring the heel close to the buttock. Similarly, insufficient hip flexion keeps the thigh from forming a right angle with the body's trunk. In fact, because of this insufficient knee and hip flexion, the inexperienced runner frequently stumbles because there is not adequate clearance between the foot and ground during the recovery phase. Frequently, the inexperienced runner resorts to turning the toes inward or outward to create sufficient foot-ground clearance during the forward swing of the recovery leg.

Arm Actions The arms also play an important role in contributing to running form and running performance. During the child's first attempts at running, the arms are flexed in the high guard position to aid balance and do not work in opposition to the legs. In a slightly more adultlike pattern, the arms are lowered and generally hang free but still do not help running speed by working in opposition to the legs. Furthermore, when the beginning runner is observed from the front, it is evident that the arms

hook or swing across the body's midline, causing undesired trunk rotation (Payne, 1985).

In contrast, the experienced runner is capable of using the arms in opposition to the legs. The elbows are flexed at 90 degrees, and a vigorous pumping action of the arms toward but not across the body's midline fosters forward momentum.

Developmental Sequences for Running

Researchers have hypothesized developmental sequences for the fundamental motor skill of running. Table 13-3 presents Roberton and Halverson's component approach analysis. Note that this approach describes changes that are expected to occur within each body segment. In contrast, Figure 13-3 illustrates the total body approach for describing the developmental sequences of running. In this approach, the "total body configuration" during performance is described. Also included in this figure is a horizontal bar graph that denotes when 60 percent of boys and girls can perform at a specific developmental level. (These values will undoubtedly change as data sets are continually updated and new data sets analyzed.) This graphed information can be useful to movement specialists when confronted with such questions as "How close to maturity is my child's performance?" or "At what age should my child be expected to perform at a specific level of competence?" (Branta, Haubenstricker, & Seefeldt, 1984). Furthermore, this information is also useful for comparing the "relative difficulty in achieving the various stages [developmental levels] by noting the time-span between their attainment" (Seefeldt & Haubenstricker, 1982, p. 314).

Developmental Performance Trends for Running

Few investigators have studied the kinetics and kinematics of a developmental running pattern in young children. In fact, Fortney (1983) uncovered

TABLE 13-3 Developmental Sequences for Running: Component Approach

Leg Action Component

Step 1: The run is flat-footed with minimal flight. The swing leg is slightly abducted as it comes forward. When seen from overhead, the path of the swing leg curves out to the side during its movement forward. Foot eversion gives a toeing-out appearance to the swinging leg. The angle of the knee of the swing leg is greater than 90° during forward motion.

Step 2: The swing thigh moves forward with greater acceleration, causing 90° of maximal flexion in the knee. From the rear, the foot is no longer toed-out nor is the thigh abducted. The sideward swing of the thigh continues, however, causing the foot to cross the body midline when viewed from the rear. Flight time increases. After contact, which may still be flat-footed, the support knee flexes more as the child's weight rides over the foot.

Step 3: Foot contact is with the heel or the ball of the foot. The forward movement of the swing leg is primarily in the sagittal plane. Flexion of the thigh at the hip carries the knee higher at the end of the forward swing. The support leg moves from flexion to complete extension by takeoff.

Arm Action Component

Step 1: The arms do not participate in the running action. They are sometimes held in high guard or, more frequently, middle guard position. In high guard, the hands are held about shoulder high. Sometimes they ride even higher if the laterally rotated arms are abducted at the shoulder and the elbows flexed. In middle guard, the lateral rotation decreases, allowing the hands to be held waist high. They remain motionless, except in reaction to shifts in equilibrium.

Step 2: Spinal rotation swings the arms bilaterally to counterbalance rotation of the pelvis and swing leg. The frequently oblique plane of motion plus continual balancing adjustments give a flailing appearance to the arm action.

Step 3: Spinal rotation continues to be the prime mover of the arms. Now the elbow of the arm swinging forward begins to flex, then extend during the backward swing. The combination of rotation and elbow flexion causes the arm rotating forward to cross the body midline and the arm rotating back to abduct, swinging obliquely outward from the body.

Step 4: The humerus (upper arm) begins to drive forward and back in the sagittal plane independent of spinal rotation. The movement is in opposition to the other arm and to the leg on the same side. Elbow flexion is maintained, oscillating about a 90° angle during the forward and backward arm swings.

Note: These sequences have not been validated. They were hypothesized by Roberton (1983) from the work of Wickstrom (1983) and Seefeldt, Reuschlein, and Vogel (1972).
Source: Roberton and Halverson (1984).

FIGURE 13-3 Developmental sequences for running: total body approach

SOURCE: Fountain et al. (1981); Seefeldt and Haubenstricker (1982); Seefeldt, Reuschlein, and Vogel (1972). All material used with permission.

Stage 1 The arms are extended sideward at shoulder height (high guard position). The stride is short and of shoulder width. The surface contact is made with the entire foot, striking simultaneously. Little knee flexion is seen. The feet remain near the surface

Stage 2 Arms are carried at middle guard position (waist height). The stride is longer and approaches the midsaggital line. The surface contact is usually made with the entire foot, striking simultaneously. Greater knee flexion is noted in the restraining phase. The swing leg is flexed, and the movement of the legs becomes anterior-posterior.

Stage 3 The arms are no longer used primarily for balance but rather are carried below waist level and may flex and assume a counterrotary action. The foot contact is heel-toe. Stride length increases, and both feet move along a midsaggital line. The swing-leg flexion may be as great as 90°.

(continued)

FIGURE 13-3 *(continued)*

Stage 4 Foot contact is heel-toe at slow or modest velocities but may be entirely on the metatarsal arch while sprinting. Arm action is in direct opposition to leg action. Knee flexion is used to maintain the momentum during the support phase. The swing leg may flex until it is nearly in contact with the buttocks during its recovery phase.

Insufficient movements common to running patterns are: inversion or eversion of the foot during the support phase. Inversion results in a medial rotation of the leg and thigh during the support phase and is characterized by an oblique rather than an anterior-posterior pattern as the leg is brought forward in the swing phase.

Eversion of the foot during the support phase results in lateral rotation of the leg and thigh. This pattern is often accompanied by an exaggerated counterrotary action of the arms in an attempt to maintain a uniform direction.

Age at which 60 percent of the boys and girls were able to perform at a specific developmental level for the fundamental motor skill of running.

only six studies. There is, however, no lack of product performance data related to children's running speed. Unfortunately, these data are often difficult to compare because of the different distances the children were required to run and the different types of starts that were used (stationary or running), as illustrated in Table 13-4. Nevertheless, a comparison of the data suggests overall developmental performance trends. Generally, the data indicate a fairly consistent year-to-year improvement in running speed for both boys and girls with boys running faster than girls at all ages.

On average, girls' running speed peaks at about 14 to 15 years of age, whereas boys' running speed continues to improve beyond 17 years. This represents nearly a 20 percent improvement in running speed for boys between 9 and 17 years of age. Girls improved only about 8 percent during this time (based on average AAHPER data, 1976). Branta, Haubenstricker, and Seefeldt (1984) have reported an approximate 30 percent increase in running speed in both boys and girls from 5 to 10 years of age. This finding was based on a 30-yard dash in which a 5-yard running start was allowed.

TABLE 13-4 Developmental Performance Trends for Running

Age (years)	Run Distance	Average Run Times (seconds)	Study
2.5	30 yd°	11.50 male 12.20 female	Fountain et al., 1981
3	40 ft†	3.54 male 3.96 female	Morris et al., 1982
3	30 yd°	10.20 male 10.90 female	Fountain et al., 1981
3.5	20 yd	12.07 male 13.97 female	Frederick, 1977
3.5	30 yd°	9.70 male 9.70 female	Fountain et al., 1981
4	40 ft†	3.26 male 3.35 female	Morris et al., 1982
4	20 yd	12.11 male 11.62 female	Frederick, 1977
4	30 yd°	8.60 male 8.80 female	Fountain et al., 1981
4.5	20 yd	11.23 male 11.35 female	Frederick, 1977
4.5	30 yd°	8.30 male 8.80 female	Fountain et al., 1981
5	40 ft†	2.74 male 2.88 female	Morris et al., 1982
5	20 yd	11.35 male 10.91 female	Frederick, 1977
5	30 yd	6.29 male 6.82 female	Milne, Seefeldt, & Reuschlein, 1976
5	30 yd‡	6.77 male 6.81 female	Branta, Haubenstricker, & Seefeldt, 1984
5	30 yd°	7.20 male 7.40 female	Fountain et al., 1981
5.5	20 yd	9.52 male 10.20 female	Frederick, 1977
6	40 ft†	2.62 male 2.76 female	Morris et al., 1982
6	10 yd	3.34	DiNucci, 1976
6	30 yd	5.54 male 5.85 female	Milne, Seefeldt, & Reuschlein, 1976
6	30 yd‡	6.02 male 6.20 female	Branta, Haubenstricker, & Seefeldt, 1984

TABLE 13-4 *(continued)*

Age (years)	Run Distance	Average Run Times (seconds)	Study
7	10 yd	3.15	DiNucci, 1976
7	30 yd‡	5.54 male 5.61 female	Branta, Haubenstricker, & Seefeldt, 1984
7	50 yd	10.31	DiNucci, 1976
8	10 yd	2.98	DiNucci, 1976
8	30 yd‡	5.23 male 5.31 female	Branta, Haubenstricker, & Seefeldt, 1984
8	50 yd	9.66	DiNucci, 1976
9	30 yd‡	4.98 male 5.08 female	Branta, Haubenstricker, & Seefeldt, 1984
9–10	50 yd	8.20 male 8.60 female	AAHPER, 1976
11	50 yd	8.00 male 8.30 female	AAHPER, 1976
12	50 yd	7.80 male 8.10 female	AAHPER, 1976
13	50 yd	7.50 male 8.00 female	AAHPER, 1976
14	50 yd	7.20 male 7.80 female	AAHPER, 1976
15	50 yd	6.90 male 7.80 female	AAHPER, 1976
16	50 yd	6.70 male 7.90 female	AAHPER, 1976
17+	50 yd	6.60 male 7.90 female	AAHPER, 1976

*Subjects were allowed a 3-foot running start.   †Subjects were allowed a 12-foot running start.
‡Subjects were allowed a 15-foot running start.

A unique approach for studying running speed in young children was conducted by Fountain and colleagues (1981). More specifically, these researchers were in part interested in studying the relationship between developmental stage and running velocity. Data were collected over a 3-year period on a mixed longitudinal sample. Running speed was measured during a 30-yard dash in which a running start was employed (approximately 3 feet). Developmental running stage was assessed by the total body approach as suggested by Seefeldt, Reuschlein, and Vogel (1972). Total run times for 153 boys and 106 girls were correlated with developmental stage and yielded correlation coefficients of –.44 and –.54 for the boys and girls, respectively. Developmental stage thus accounted for 19 percent of the variance in total run times for the boys and about 29 percent of the variance in total run times for the girls. In general, the more immature the running pattern, the longer it took the children to complete the 30-yard dash.

When run times were converted to yards/second, it was found that each sex improved by 1.6 yards/second over the age range studied. By 5 years of age, the boys were running 4.2 yards/second while the girls were running 4.0 yards/second.

JUMPING

Jumping is a fundamental movement that occurs when the body is projected into the air by force generated in one or both legs and the body lands on one or both feet. Jumping can be accomplished in several ways. For example, *hopping* is a form of jumping in which the propelling force is generated in one leg and the landing is accomplished on the same leg. But if the landing occurs on the nonpropelling leg, the movement is called a *leap*.

Researchers speculate that the downward leap while descending a step is the child's first experience with jumping (Hellebrandt et al., 1961). Keogh and Sugden (1985), however, suggested that a more sensible way to consider the beginning of jumping development is to examine jumping patterns that involve a two-footed takeoff. The two-footed jumping patterns that have received the most attention are the vertical jump and the horizontal or standing long jump. In the vertical jump, the body is thrust upward; in the horizontal jump, the body is propelled both upward and outward. Irrespective of the direction the body is propelled, both two-footed jumping patterns have similar phases, including a preparatory, a takeoff, a flight, and a landing phase.

Preparatory Phase

A great deal of preparatory movement is associated with experienced two-footed jumping. Preparatory movements are necessary to ready the body to spring into action; such movements include a crouch or flexion of the hips, knees, and ankles, and a backward swing of the arms. Many of these preparatory movements are absent in the inexperienced jumper. For instance, very little if any crouch precedes the jump, and a corresponding arm swing is also absent or minimized (Payne, 1985).

Takeoff and Flight Phases

Once the preparatory movements have been accomplished, a rapid and vigorous extension of the hips, knees, and ankles along with a vigorous swing of the arms in the direction of desired travel provide the impetus for the body to become airborne. See Figure 13-4. Because the inexperienced jumper does not properly crouch, there is very little extension of the body segments. Furthermore, the inexperienced jumper is not able to integrate the arms with the lower extremities to increase the momentum of the jump (Hellebrandt et al., 1961). Consequently, only a short distance or height is traversed.

Angle of takeoff is also an important factor to consider. The most effective angle of takeoff in horizontal jumping is 45 degrees. In comparing good and poor jumpers, Zimmerman (1956) found that good jumpers used lower takeoff angles than did poor jumpers.

Landing Phase

During the airborne phase of the horizontal jump, the extended legs are brought forward and ahead of the body's center of gravity as the landing is anticipated. When studying college women. Felton (1960; cited in Atwater, 1973) reported that the most successful horizontal jumpers landed with their heels

FIGURE 13-4   The advanced jumper fully extends the body during the takeoff phase.

5.56 inches ahead of their center of gravity; the heels of the poorest jumpers were only 3.60 inches ahead of their center of gravity. Because inexperienced jumpers are unable to gain adequate height and forward momentum, they do not have enough time to get their feet ahead of their center of gravity.

Another obvious characteristic of the inexperienced jumper is the inability to flex the hips, knees, and ankles upon landing. This stiff-legged landing makes the landing look rigid and jolts the jumper. In contrast, the experienced jumper slowly flexes the hips, knees, and ankles to gradually absorb the force of the jump (Figure 13-5).

FIGURE 13-5 The advanced jumper absorbs the landing forces by flexing the knees, hips, and ankles at impact.

Developmental Sequences for the Standing Long Jump

Table 13-5 presents a hypothesized developmental sequence (component approach) for the fundamental motor skill—the standing long jump. An alternative developmental sequence (total body approach) is illustrated in Figure 13-6. This latter developmental sequence has withstood preliminary validation on a mixed longitudinal sample (Haubenstricker, Seefeldt, & Branta, 1983). This preliminary validation study included 430 preschool children (30–65 months) and 1986 primary-grade children (72–107 months) as subjects. As depicted in the horizontal bar graph at the end of Figure 13-6, a developmental stage 1 pattern was found to be most prominent in children under 42 months of age (3 1/2 years). In contrast, a stage 2 jumping pattern was found to be most prevalent between 48 and 84 months of age (4 and 7 years), whereas a stage 3 jumping pattern was dominant by 96 months of age (8 years). Only about 10 percent of the older subjects (102–107 months) were found to exhibit the most mature stage 4 pattern of jumping.

A Variation of Jumping: Hopping

Hopping is a form of jumping in which one foot is used to project the body into space and the subsequent landing is on the same propelling foot. This fundamental movement is considered more difficult than the two-footed jump because it requires additional strength and better balance.

Using a prelongitudinal screening technique, Halverson and Williams (1985) provided evidence for the existence of developmental steps within both the leg and arm components of hopping. The purpose of a prelongitudinal screening is to initially determine if the hypothesized components contain all observable behaviors and whether the steps within each component are arranged correctly (Roberton, Williams, & Langendorfer, 1980). After making some changes, the researchers were able to describe four steps within the leg component of the hop and five steps within the arm component. Table

TABLE 13-5 Developmental Sequences for the Standing Long Jump: Component Approach

Takeoff Phase
Leg Action Component

Step 1: Fall and catch. The weight is shifted forward. The knee and ankle are held in flexion or extend slightly as gravity rotates the body over the balls of the feet. Takeoff occurs when the toes are pulled from the surface in preparation for the landing "catch."

Step 2: Two-footed takeoff; partial extension. Both feet leave the ground symmetrically, but the hips, knees, and/or ankles do not reach full extension by takeoff.

Step 3: Two-footed takeoff; full extension. Both feet leave the ground symmetrically, with hips, knees, and ankles fully extended by takeoff.

Trunk Action Component

Step 1: Slight lean; head back. The trunk leans forward less than 30° from the vertical. The neck is hyperextended.

Step 2: Slight lean; head aligned. The trunk leans forward less than 30°, with the neck flexed or aligned with the trunk at takeoff.

Step 3: Forward lean; chin tucked. The trunk is inclined forward 30° or more (with the vertical) at takeoff, with the neck flexed.

Step 4: Forward lean; head aligned. The trunk is inclined forward 30° or more. The neck is aligned with the trunk or slightly extended.

Arm Action Component

Step 1: Arms inactive. The arms are held at the side with the elbows flexed. Arm movement, if any, is inconsistent and random.

Step 2: Winging arms. The arms extend backward in a winging posture at takeoff.

Step 3: Arms abducted. The arms are abducted about 90°, with the elbows often flexed, in a high or middle guard position.

Step 4: Arms forward; partial stretch. The arms flex forward and upward with minimal abduction, reaching incomplete extension overhead by takeoff.

Step 5: Arms forward; full stretch. The arms flex forward, reaching full extension overhead by takeoff.

Flight and Landing Phase
Leg Action Component

Step 1: Minimal tuck. The thigh is carried in flight more than 45° below the horizontal. The legs may assume either symmetrical or asymmetrical configurations during flight, resulting on one- or two-footed landings.

Step 2: Partial tuck. During flight, the hips and knees flex synchronously. The thigh approaches a 20–35° angle below the horizontal. The knees then extend for a two-footed landing.

TABLE 13-5 (*continued*)

Step 3: Full tuck. During flight, flexion of both knees precedes hip flexion. The hips then flex, bringing the thighs to the horizontal. The knees then extend, reaching forward to a two-footed landing.

Trunk Action Component

Step 1: Slight lean. During flight, the trunk maintains its forward inclination of less than 30°, then flexes for landing.

Step 2: Corrected lean. The trunk corrects its forward lean of 30° or more by hyperextending. It then flexes forward for landing.

Step 3: Maintained lean. The trunk maintains the forward lean of 30° or more from takeoff to midflight, then flexes forward for landing.

Arm Action Component

Step 1: Arms winging. In two-footed takeoff jumps, the shoulders may retract while the arms extend backward (winging) during flight. They move forward (parachuting) during landing.

Step 2: Arms abducted; lateral rotation. During flight, the arms hold a high guard position and continue lateral rotation. They parachute for landing.

Step 3: Arms abducted; medial rotation. During flight, the arms assume high or middle guard positions but medially rotate early in the flight. They parachute for landing.

Step 4: Arms overhead. During flight, the arms are held overhead. In middle flight, the arms lower (extend) from their overhead flexed position, reaching forward at landing.

Note: These developmental steps have not been validated. They have been modified by Halverson from the work of Van Sant (in progress).
Source: Roberton and Halverson (1984).

13-6 describes each hypothesized step. There is greater extension of the propelling leg and greater involvement of the nonsupport or swing leg to assist projection. The arms are initially inactive but soon become involved by assisting the hop and by working in opposition to the legs.

Halverson and Williams concluded that 5-year-old children were at predominantly low and intermediate developmental levels and that girls were more developmentally advanced than boys. In addition, most children used less advanced developmental patterns when hopping on their nonpreferred foot.

Using the total body approach (see Figure 13-7), Haubenstricker and colleagues (1989) have produced data that agree with these earlier findings. Namely, hopping is performed better on the preferred foot as opposed to the nonpreferred foot, girls are more developmentally advanced than boys, and most 5-year-old boys and girls have not developed a mature hopping pattern. More specifically, these researchers found only 3 percent of the 5-year-old boys and 6 percent of the 5-year-old girls to exhibit a stage 4 hopping pattern (most mature stage). Furthermore, over 60 percent of these 5-year-olds were found to exhibit a stage 2 developmental level of

FIGURE 13-6   Developmental sequences for the standing long jump: total body approach
SOURCE: Haubenstricker, Seefeldt, and Branta (1983); Seefeldt and Haubenstricker (1982); Seefeldt, Reuschlein, and Vogel (1972). All material used with permission.

Stage 1   Vertical component of force may be greater than horizontal; resulting jump is then upward rather than forward. Arms move backward, acting as brakes to stop the momentum of the trunk as the legs extend in front of the center of mass.

Stage 2   The arms move in an anterior-posterior direction during the preparatory phase but move sideward (winging action) during the in-flight phase. The knees and hips flex and extend more fully than in stage 1. The angle of takeoff is still markedly above 45°. The landing is made with the center of gravity above the base of support, with the thighs perpendicular to the surface rather than parallel as in the reaching position of stage 4.

Stage 3   The arms swing backward and then forward during the preparatory phase. The knees and hips flex fully prior to takeoff. Upon takeoff the arms extend and move forward but do not exceed the height of the head. The knee extension may be complete, but the takeoff angle is still greater than 45°. Upon landing, the thigh is still less than parallel to the surface and the center of gravity is near the base of support when viewed from the frontal plane.

FIGURE 13-6 *(continued)*

Stage 4 The arms extend vigorously forward and upward upon takeoff, reaching full extension above the head at "lift-off." The hips and knees are extended fully with the takeoff angle at 45° or less. In preparation for landing, the arms are brought downward and the legs are thrust forward until the thigh is parallel to the surface. The center of gravity is far behind the base of support upon foot contact, but at the moment of contact the knees are flexed and the arms are thrust forward in order to maintain the momentum to carry the center of gravity beyond the feet.

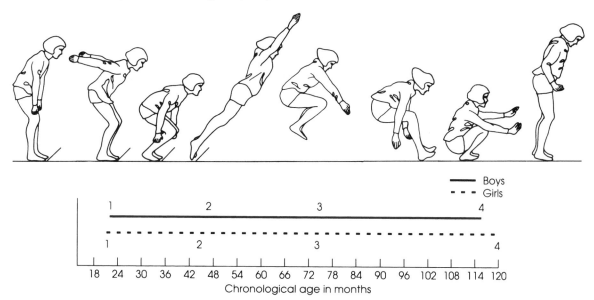

Age at which 60 percent of the boys and girls were able to perform at a specific developmental level for the fundamental motor skill, the standing long jump.

hopping. Moreover, 10 percent of the boys and 6 percent of the girls still could not hop by 4 years of age.

In general, girls were approximately 6 months more advanced than boys. For example, the stage 1 pattern of hopping was most prevalent in 3-year-old girls, but it was not until 3 1/2 years of age that it became the most dominant pattern in boys. Likewise, girls predominantly exhibited stage 2 characteristics by age 4, whereas boys were generally delayed until 4 1/2 years of age (Haubenstricker et al., 1989).

COMBINING FUNDAMENTAL MOVEMENTS: THE GALLOP, SLIDE, AND SKIP

Fundamental motor patterns can be combined to elicit new movement patterns. The three most often described patterns include the *gallop*, the *slide*, and the *skip*. As would be expected, these more complex motor patterns do not emerge until sometime after the development of their single motor pattern counterparts.

TABLE 13-6 Developmental Steps within Two Components of Hopping: Component Approach

<table>
<tr><td align="center">Leg Action</td></tr>
</table>

Step 1: Momentary flight. The support knee and hip quickly flex, pulling (instead of projecting) the foot from the floor. The flight is momentary. Only one or two hops can be achieved. The swing leg is lifted high and held in an inactive position to the side or in front of the body.

Step 2: Fall and catch; swing leg inactive. Forward lean allows minimal knee and ankle extension to help the body "fall" forward of the support foot and then quickly catch itself again. The swing leg is inactive. Repeated hops are achieved.

Step 3: Projected takeoff; swing leg assists. Perceptible pretakeoff extension occurs in the support leg, hip, knee, and ankle. There is little delay in changing from knee and ankle flexion on landing to takeoff extension. The swing leg now pumps up and down to assist in projection, but range is insufficient to carry it behind the support leg.

Step 4: Projection delay; swing leg leads. The child's weight on landing is smoothly transferred along the foot to the ball before the knee and ankle extend to take off. The range of the pumping action in the swing leg increases so that it passes behind the support leg when viewed from the side.

<table>
<tr><td align="center">Revised Developmental Sequence for Arm Action in Hopping</td></tr>
</table>

Step 1: Bilateral inactive. The arms are held bilaterally, usually high and out to the side, although other positions behind or in front of the body may occur. Any arm action is usually slight and not consistent.

Step 2: Bilateral reactive. Arms swing upward briefly and then are medially rotated at the shoulder in a winging movement prior to takeoff. This movement appears to occur in reaction to loss of balance.

Step 3: Bilateral assist. The arms pump up and down together, usually in front of the line of the trunk. Any downward and backward motion of the arms occurs after takeoff. The arms may move parallel to each other or be held at different levels as they move up and down.

Step 4: Semi-opposition. The arm on the side opposite the swing leg swings forward with that leg and back as the leg moves down. The position of the other arm is variable, often staying in front of the body or to the side.

Step 5: Opposing assist. The arm opposite the swing leg moves forward and upward in synchrony with the forward and upward movement of that leg. The other arm moves in the direction opposite the action of the swing leg. The range of movement in the arm action may be minimal unless the task requires speed or distance.

SOURCE: Halverson and Williams (1985).

FIGURE 13-7 Developmental sequences for hopping: total body approach.

Source: Haubenstricker, Henn, and Seefeldt (1975); Haubenstricker et al. (1989); Seefeldt and Haubenstricker (1974, 1982). All material used with permission.

Stage 1   The nonsupport knee is flexed at 90° or less with the nonsupport thigh parallel to the surface. This position places the nonsupport foot in front of the body so that it may be used for support if balance is lost. The body is held in an upright position with the arms flexed at the elbows. The hands are held near shoulder height and slightly to the side in a stabilizing position. Force production is generally limited so that little height or distance is achieved in a single hop.

Stage 2   The nonsupport knee is fully flexed so that the foot is near the buttocks. The thigh of the nonsupport leg is nearly parallel to the surface. The trunk is flexed at the hip, resulting in a slight forward lean. The performer gains considerable height by flexing and extending the joints of the supporting leg and by extending at the hip joint. In addition, the thigh of the nonsupport leg aids in force production by flexing at the hip joint. Upon landing, the force is absorbed by flexion at the hips and the supporting knee. The arms participate vigorously in force production as they move up and down in a bilateral manner. Due to the vigorous action and precarious balance of performers at this stage, the number of hops generally ranges from two to four.

(continued)

FIGURE 13-7 *(continued)*

Stage 3 The thigh of the nonsupport leg is in a vertical position with the knee flexed at 90° or less. Performers exhibit greater body lean forward than in stage 1 or 2, with the result that the hips are farther in front of the support leg upon takeoff. This forward lean of the trunk results in greater distance in relation to the height of the hop.

The knee of the nonsupport leg remains near the vertical (frontal) plane, but knee flexion may vary as the body is projected and received by the supporting leg. The arms are used in force production, moving bilaterally upward during the force production phase.

Stage 4 The knee of the nonsupport leg is flexed at 90° or less, but the entire leg swings back and forth like a pendulum as it aids in force production. The arms are carried close to the sides of the body, with elbow flexion at 90°. As the nonsupport leg increases its force production, that of the arms seems to diminish.

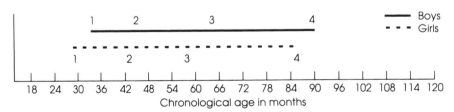

Age at which 60 percent of the boys and girls were able to perform at a specific developmental level for the fundamental motor skill of hopping.

FIGURE 13-8 Developmental sequences for galloping: total body approach

Source: Sapp (1980). All materials used with permission.

Stage 1 The pattern resembles a rhythmically uneven run with the performer often reverting to the traditional running pattern. The tempo tends to be relatively fast and the rhythm inconsistent. The trail leg crosses in front of the lead leg during the airbone phase and remains in front at contact. The trail leg is flexed at ≤45° during the airborne phase. Both feet generally contact the floor in a heel-toe pattern although either foot may strike the surface flat-footed.

Stage 2 The pattern is executed at a slow to moderate tempo with the rhythm often appearing choppy. The trail leg moves in front of, adjacent to, or behind the lead leg during the airborne phase, but is always adjacent to or behind the lead leg at contact. The trail leg is extended during the airborne phase, often causing the trail foot to turn out and the lead leg to flex at ≤45°. The feet usually contact the floor in a heel-toe/heel-toe or toe/toe combination. The transfer of weight may appear stiff and exaggerated. The vertical component is often exaggerated as the trunk extends to lift the body up.

(continued)

FIGURE 13-8 (*continued*)

Step 3 The pattern is smooth, rhythmical, and executed at a moderate tempo. The trail leg may cross in front of or move adjacent to the lead leg during the airborne phase but is placed adjacent to or behind the lead leg at contact. Both the lead and trail legs are flexed at ≤45° with the feet carried close to the surface during the airborne phase. The lead foot meets the surface with a heel-toe pattern followed by a transfer of weight to the ball of the trail foot.

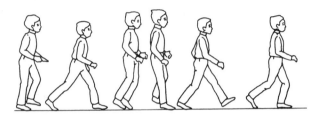

Of these three motor patterns, the gallop is the first to be exhibited. The two basic fundamental motor patterns which make-up the gallop are: (1) a forward step, followed by a (2) leap onto the trailing foot. By definition, this pattern must be performed in a forward front-facing direction whereby the same leg always leads. The gallop will frequently begin to emerge shortly after running has been accomplished (about 2 years of age). At this time, however, the child will be capable of leading with the preferred leg. Galloping with the non-preferred leg as the lead, is not accomplished until several years later. Figure 13-8 illustrates and describes the developmental sequences for galloping (total body approach).

The slide is essentially the same as a gallop with one exception. Whereas the gallop is performed in a forward direction, the slide is performed in a sideward direction. The child's difficulty in performing this more complicated motor pattern arises because the child is required to face a different direction from the line of intended movement. More specifically, the child must face straight ahead while moving in a sideward direction. As a result, early attempts at sliding will frequently start off correctly, but eventually, the child will begin to point the toe of the leading leg toward the direction of movement, and shortly thereafter the trunk will rotate as well.

At this point the initial slide is converted into the easier motor pattern of galloping. Sliding is an extremely important motor skill to acquire since it is used in many types of sporting activities. For example, moving along the baseline in tennis, taking a lead off of a base, and guarding an opponent in basketball, all require a sliding movement.

Of the three motor patterns described, skipping is by far the most difficult. The skip consists of a forward step followed by a hop on the same foot (uneven rhythmical pattern). In addition, there is alternation of the leading leg. Unlike the gallop and slide, when skipping, both motor tasks (step and hop) must be accomplished on the same foot before the body's weight is transferred onto the other foot. Obviously, being required to perform dual tasks on a single leg is more difficult than performing a single task per leg as is required in both galloping and sliding. The child may experience difficulty in maintaining balance when first attempting to skip. If this balance problem is severe, the child should skip in place while holding onto the back of a chair. With this arrangement, the child can maintain balance while still being afforded the opportunity to learn this more complex motor pattern. Table 13-7 describes both the leg action and the arm action component of the skip as presented from the component approach

TABLE 13-7 Developmental Sequences for Skipping: Component Approach

Leg action component

Step 1. One-footed skip. One foot completes a step and hop before the weight is transferred to the other foot. The other foot just steps.

Step 2. Two-footed skip; Flat-footed landing. Each foot completes a step and a hop before the weight is transferred to the other foot. Landing from the hop is on the total foot, or on the ball of the foot, with the heel touching down before the weight is transferred (flat-footed landing).

Step 3. Two-footed skip; Ball of the foot landing. Landing from the hop is on the ball of the foot. The heel does not touch down before the weight is transferred to the other foot. Body lean increases over that found in Step 2.

Arm action component

Step 1. Bilateral assist. The arms pump bilaterally up as the weight is shifted from the hopping to the stepping foot and down during the hop takeoff and flight.

Step 2. Semi-opposition. The arms first swing up bilaterally. During the hop on the right foot, the right arm moves down and back only slightly while the left arm continues to move backward until the step on the left foot. Then, both arms again move forward and upward in a new bilateral pumping action. Now, however, the left arm moves back only slightly while the right arm moves backward until the step on the right foot. Although the arm action has the beginnings of opposition, at some time in the arm cycle both hands are in front of the body.

Step 3. Opposition. The arm opposite the stepping leg swings upward and forward in synchrony with that leg and reverses direction when the stepping leg touches the floor. The arm on the same side as the stepping leg moves backward and down in opposition to the stepping leg. At no time are both hands in front of the body.

Note: These sequences, hypothesized by Halverson, have not been validated.
SOURCE: Roberton and Halverson (1984).

perspective. In contrast, Figure 13-9 illustrates and describes the developmental sequences for skipping from the total body approach perspective. As indicated by the bar graph which accompanies Figure 13-9, girls are generally more advanced than boys. In fact, girls were found to exhibit the more mature developmental level (Stage 3) about 6 to 7 months before young boys. On average, young boys and girls generally start to skip sometime between their sixth and seventh birthdays.

SUMMARY

Walking is a fundamental movement in which there is an alternation of leading legs and continuous contact with the ground. To maintain balance during initial walking attempts, the child spreads the feet, points the toes outward, and carries the arms in a high guard position. Most children are capable of independent walking by 12 months, although the normal range is from 9 to 17 months.

FIGURE 13-9 Developmental sequences for skipping: total body approach
SOURCE: Sapp (1980) Seefeldt and Haubenstricker (1974, 1982). All material used with permission.

Stage 1 A deliberate step-hop pattern is employed, an occasional double hop is present, there is little effective use of the arms to provide momentum, an exaggerated step or leap is present during the transfer of weight from one suuporting limb to the other, and the total action appears segmented.

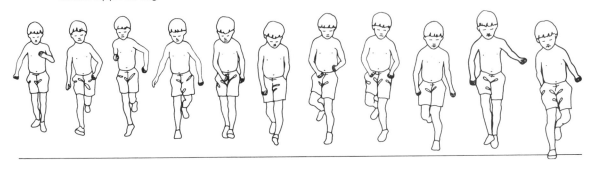

Step 2 There is rhythmical transfer of weight during the step phase, increased use of arms in providing forward and upward momentum, and exaggeration of vertical component during the airborne phase, that is, while executing the hop.

(continued)

FIGURE 13-9   *(continued)*

Stage 3 There is rhythmical transfer of weight during all phases and reduced arm action during the transfer of weight phase. The foot of the supporting limb is carried near the surface during the hopping phase.

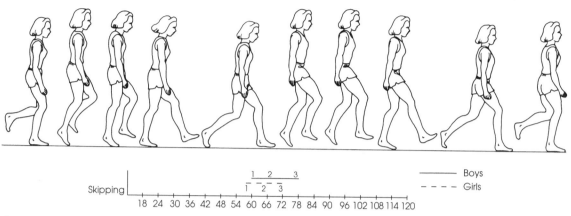

Age at which 60 percent of the boys and girls were able to perform at a specific developmental level for the fundamental motor skill of skipping.

Running is different than walking in that there is a momentary phase of suspension during which neither foot is in contact with the ground. Most children exhibit minimal running form between 18 and 24 months of age.

Jumping is propelling the body into the air from force generated in one or both legs and landing on one or both feet. Hopping, vertical jumping, horizontal or long jumping, and leaping are all variations of jumping. Each jumping variation consists of four phases: preparatory, takeoff, flight, and landing phases. Most children are capable of some form of jumping shortly after acquiring the ability to run.

After learning to walk, run, jump, and hop children begin to perform several of these skills in combination. As a result, new movement skills emerge; namely, the gallop, slide, and skip. The gallop is a front-facing movement where a step is taken onto the forward leg followed by a leap onto the rear foot. In galloping the same leg always leads. Sliding is similar to galloping with one exception: the movement is performed sideways. This skill is more difficult than the gallop because, when sliding, the child must face in one direction (front-facing) while mov-

ing in a different direction (sideways). Once again the same leg always leads. The most difficult of the three combination skills is the skip. The skip is a step-hop combination where both movements are performed on the same leg before the body's weight is transferred onto the other leg. This dual movement results in an alternation of leading legs. The skipping pattern is generally exhibited in both boys and girls sometimes between their sixth and seventh birthday. However, girls are more advanced than boys by about 6 or 7 months.

KEY TERMS

Double support phase	Skip
Flight phase	Slide
Gait	Support phase
Gallop	Swing phase
Hop	Upright bipedal
Jump	locomotion
Leap	Walking
Run	

CHAPTER 14

Fundamental Object-Control Skills of Childhood

As soon as the child is capable of ambulating without assistance, the hands become free to explore the ever-changing environment more effectively. With time, experience, and practice, both eye-hand and eye-foot coordination dramatically improve. At this time the child will begin to exhibit a category of skills commonly referred to as *object-control skills.* These skills include: overarm throwing, both one- and two-handed catching, and striking both with and without an implement. Implements that might be used with these object control skills are racquets and bats. Sports actions that employ these skills without the use of an implement are those such as dribbling, place kicking, and punting.

OVERARM THROWING

Of the fundamental movements discussed in this chapter, *throwing* is perhaps the most complex. There are many different throwing patterns (under-

arm, sidearm, overarm), but this discussion is limited to one of the most common forms, the one-handed overarm throw. The one-handed overarm throw can be conveniently divided into three phases: (1) The preparatory phase consists of all movements directed away from the intended line of projection. (2) The execution phase consists of all movements performed in the direction of the throw. (3) The follow-through phase consists of all movements performed following the release of the projectile (Langendorfer, 1980). Understanding these three phases will facilitate your understanding of the following information.

Developmental Stages of Throwing

Monica Wild (1938) is generally credited with setting the standards for the study of developmental throwing stages. Her classic study over a half-century ago in part attempted to uncover age and sex characteristics of throwing in 32 boys and girls 2 to 12 years old. As a result of this research, Wild described four developmental overarm throwing stages; Table 14-1 summarizes each stage.

Within these four developmental stages, two developmental trends are evident. First, movement progresses from an anterior-posterior plane to a horizontal plane, and second, the base of support changes from a stationary to a shifting position (McClenaghan & Gallahue, 1978).

Researchers from the University of Wisconsin–Madison attempted to improve upon Wilds's pioneering work. Langendorfer (1980), for example, studied age-related changes in the arm action components during the preparatory phase of a forceful overarm throw. Using over 1000 trials recorded on 16mm film from both cross-sectional and longitudinal data, he proposed a motor development sequence consisting of four hypothesized steps.

Step 1 is best described as a lack of any preparatory backswing. Once the ball is grasped it is moved directly forward. In step 2, the ball is brought up beside the head by upward humerus flexion and exaggerated elbow flexion. Step 3 is subdivided into one of three options. Option 1 is a circular overhead preparatory movement with the elbow extended. Option 2 is a preparatory movement characterized by a lateral swing backward. Option 3 is a simple vertical lift of the throwing arm. Step 4, the most advanced preparatory sequence, is a circular arm action in which the arm moves down and back. Figure 14-1 depicts each step.

To test this hypothesized sequence, Langendorfer (1980) analyzed 228 throwing trials of children followed from grades 1–6. When the data were analyzed by observing each child's progression through the hypothesized order, it was found that of the 65 subjects analyzed, only one omitted step 3 and only four transposed the hypothesized order. Even stronger support for this hypothesized sequence was obtained when the data were analyzed according to group rather than individual progress through the entire sequence. In short, with advancing age, an increased percentage of the sample used more advanced preparatory movements. There were drastic differences, however, between the two sexes. By the second grade, boys predominantly used step 4 characteristics, whereas girls had just begun to exhibit this most advanced movement pattern.

Roberton (1978) studied other components related to the forceful overarm throw. She presented longitudinal evidence for developmental stages within the humerus, the forearm, and the trunk components of the forceful overarm throw. Of particular interest is Roberton's finding that

> development within component parts may proceed at different rates in the same individual or at different rates in different individuals. For instance, one child might move ahead a stage in his trunk action while another child moved ahead a stage in his arm action. Thus two individuals going through the same stages within each component could look quite different at any one time (1977, p. 55).

Table 14-2 presents Roberton's developmental sequences.

Seefeldt, Reuschlein, and Vogel (1972) have also hypothesized a developmental sequence for the fundamental motor skill of throwing. Their developmental sequence, which appears in Figure 14-2, has withstood preliminary validation with the use of a mixed longitudinal sample (Haubenstricker, Branta, & Seefeldt, 1983). A close examination of the horizontal bar graph accompanying Figure 14-2 makes apparent the large sex difference in throwing development (Seefeldt & Haubenstricker, 1982). More specifically, note that the age at which 60 percent of the boys exhibited a stage 5 throwing pattern (most mature) was 63 months (slightly past 5 years of age). In contrast, 60 percent of the girls studied were not capable of exhibiting stage 5 characteristics until 102 months of age (about 8 1/2 years). It is important to point out that the data used to construct the horizontal bar graph were collected in the latter half of the 1970s. More recent data collected and analyzed by the same group of researchers have yielded somewhat different findings. More specifically, 58 percent of the boys age 90 to 95 months were found to exhibit a stage 5 developmental level of throwing, but only 12.4 percent of the girls in this same age

TABLE 14-1 Wild's Four Developmental Stages of Throwing

Stage 1 (2- and 3-year-olds)	Stage 2 (3 1/2- to 5-year-olds)	Stage 3 (5- and 6-year-olds)	Stage 4 (6 1/2 years and older)
Throw is arm dominated. Preparatory arm movements involve bringing the arm sideways-upward or forward-upward.	Body moves in horizontal plane instead of anterior-posterior plane.	Forward step is unilateral to the throwing arm.	Forward step is taken with the contralateral leg.
Thrower faces the direction of intended throw at all times.	Throwing arm moves in a high oblique plane or horizontal plane above the shoulder.	Arm is prepared by swinging it obliquely upward over the shoulder with a large degree of elbow flexion.	Trunk rotation is clearly evident. Arm is horizontally adducted in the forward swing.
No rotation of trunk and hips is evident.	Throwing is initiated predominantly by arm and elbow extension. Feet remain stationary, but rotary movement of the trunk is observable.	Arm follows through forward and downward and is accompanied by forward flexion of the trunk.	
Feet remain stationary during the entire throwing act.			

Source: Based on findings from Wild (1938).

FIGURE 14-1 The four steps of Langendorfer's hypothesized developmental sequence of the preparatory arm action of the overarm throw. Read all steps from left to right.

Step 1

Step 2

Step 3
Option 1

Option 2

(continued)

FIGURE 14-1   *(continued)*

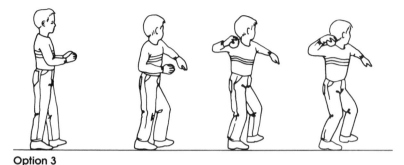

Option 3

Step 4

group exhibited stage 5 throwing characteristics. In fact, only 24.4 percent of the girls in the oldest age group studied (102–107 months) exhibited the most mature pattern of throwing, whereas 77.3 percent of the boys in this oldest age group exhibited a stage 5 developmental level of performance (Haubenstricker, Branta, & Seefeldt, 1983).

Developmental Performance Trends for Overarm Throwing

Three techniques have been used to study changes in children's throwing performance. The most frequently used technique is the throw for distance, followed by the throw for accuracy and the measure of the velocity of the throw. Irrespective of the technique, there is annual improvement in both sexes; in addition, males perform more successfully than females at all ages (Butterfield & Loovis, 1993; Frederick, 1977; Halverson, Roberton, & Langendorfer, 1982; Nelson, Thomas, & Nelson, 1991; Roberton et al., 1979; Van Slooten, 1973).

Most throwing studies that have used throwing distance or throwing accuracy as a criterion have collected the data cross-sectionally. One exception is the Wisconsin studies, which have longitudinally examined changes in children's overarm ball-throwing velocities. For example, Roberton et al. (1979) studied changes in ball-throwing velocities of 54 children from kindergarten through second grade. The researchers found that the boys' throwing velocities on the average increased 5.04 feet per second per year (ft/s/yr) (range: 5–8 ft/s/yr), whereas the girls' throwing velocities on the average increased only 2.94 ft/s/yr (range: 2–3 ft/s/yr). In a follow-up study, 22 boys and 17 girls of the original 54 subjects were reassessed when they had reached seventh grade. One purpose of this second study was to determine how well the predicted longitudinal units of change would hold up over time. The results supported the earlier prediction regarding annual units of change for the boys' ball-throwing velocities, but the girls' unit of change had to be increased to 2–4.5 ft/s/yr.

TABLE 14-2   Roberton's Developmental Sequence for the Trunk, Backswing, Humerus, Forearm, and Foot Action in the Overarm Throw for Force*: Component Approach

Trunk Action

Step 1: No trunk action or forward-backward movements. Only the arm is active in force production. Sometimes, the forward thrust of the arm pulls the trunk into a passive left rotation (assuming a right-handed throw), but no twist-up precedes that action. If trunk action occurs, it accompanies the forward thrust of the arm by flexing forward at the hips. Preparatory extension sometimes precedes forward hip flexion.

Step 2: Upper trunk rotation or total trunk "block" rotation. The spine and pelvis both rotate away from the intended line of flight and then simultaneously begin forward rotation, acting as a unit or "block." Occasionally, only the upper spine twists away, then toward the direction of force. The pelvis then remains fixed, facing the line of flight, or joins the rotary movement after forward spinal rotation has begun.

Step 3: Differentiated rotation. The pelvis precedes the upper spine in initiating forward rotation. The child twists away from the intended line of ball flight and then begins forward rotation with the pelvis while the upper spine is still twisting away.

Preparatory Arm-Backswing Component

Step 1: No backswing. The ball in the hand moves directly forward to release from the arm's original position when the hand first grasped the ball.

Step 2: Elbow and humeral flexion. The ball moves away from the intended line of flight to a position behind or alongside the head by upward flexion of the humerus and concomitant elbow flexion.

Step 3: Circular, upward backswing. The ball moves away from the intended line of flight to a position behind the head via a circular overhead movement with elbow extended, or an oblique swing back, or a vertical lift from the hip.

Step 4: Circular, downward backswing. The ball moves away from the intended line of flight to a position behind the head via a circular, down, and back motion, which carries the hand below the waist.

Humerus (Upper Arm) Action Component During Forward Swing

Step 1: Humerus oblique. The humerus moves forward to ball release in a plane that intersects the trunk obliquely above or below the horizontal line of the shoulders. Occasionally, during the backswing, the humerus is placed at a right angle to the trunk, with the elbow pointing toward the target. It maintains this fixed position during the throw.

Step 2: Humerus aligned but independent. The humerus moves forward to ball release in a plane horizontally aligned with the shoulder, forming a right angle between humerus and trunk. By the time the shoulders (upper spine) reach front facing, the humerus (elbow) has moved independently ahead of the outline of the body (as seen from the side) via horizontal adduction at the shoulder.

(continued)

TABLE 14-2 (*continued*)

Step 3: Humerus lags. The humerus moves forward to ball release horizontally aligned, but at the moment the shoulders (upper spine) reach front facing, the humerus remains within the outline of the body (as seen from the side). No horizontal adduction of the humerus occurs before front facing.

Forearm Action Component During Forward Swing

Step 1: No forearm lag. The forearm and ball move steadily forward to ball release throughout the throwing action.

Step 2: Forearm lag. The forearm and ball appear to "lag," i.e., to remain stationary behind the child or to move down or back in relation to the child. The lagging forearm reaches its farthest point back, deepest point down, or last stationary point *before* the shoulders (upper spine) reach front facing.

Step 3: Delayed forearm lag. The lagging forearm delays reaching its final point of lag until the moment of front facing.

Action of the Feet†

Step 1: No step. The child throws from the initial foot position.

Step 2: Homolateral step. The child steps with the foot on the same side as the throwing hand.

Step 3: Contralateral, short step. The child steps with the foot on the opposite side from the throwing hand.

Step 4: Contralateral, long step. The child steps with the opposite foot a distance of over half the child's standing height.

*Validation studies (Halverson, Roberton, & Langendorfer, 1982; Roberton, 1977, 1978; Roberton & DiRocco, 1981; Roberton & Langendorfer, 1980) support these sequences for the overarm throw, with the exception of the preparatory arm backswing sequence that Roberton (1983) hypothesized from the work of Langendorfer (1980). Langendorfer (1982) felt that the humerus and forearm components are appropriate for overarm striking.
†This sequence was hypothesized by Roberton (1983) from the work of Leme and Shambes (1978); Seefeldt, Reuschlein, & Vogel (1972); and Wild (1938).
Source: Roberton and Halverson (1984).

Factors that Influence Overarm Throwing Performance

In this section we describe two factors that have been found to influence throwing performance: the influence of instruction and the influence of ball size. Accounting for gender differences in overarm throwing will be addressed in the following section.

Instruction A basic question in recent years has been whether instruction can facilitate developmental changes or whether the year-to-year improvement in many fundamental skills is due more to age than to instruction. To investigate this question, Halverson and associates (1977) administered a movement program that included 120 minutes of guided practice in overarm throwing to 24 kindergarten students. A second group of 24 kindergarten students received the same movement program but no exposure to throwing instruction. A third group received neither program. Following the 8-week instructional program, no significant changes were found in the children's ball-throwing velocities. In a follow-up study, Halverson and Roberton (1979) used the same research design but measured devel-

FIGURE 14-2 Developmental sequences for throwing: total body approach
Source: Haubenstricker, Branta, and Seefeldt (1983); Seefeldt and Haubenstricker (1976, 1982); Seefeldt, Reuschlein, and Vogel (1972). All material used with permission.

Stage 1 The throwing motion is essentially posterior-anterior in direction. The feet usually remain stationary during the throw. Infrequently, the performer may step or walk just prior to moving the ball into position for throwing. There is little or no trunk rotation in the most rudimentary pattern at this stage, but children at the point of transition between stages 1 and 2 may evoke slight trunk rotation in preparation for the throw and extensive hip and trunk rotation in the follow-through phase. In the typical stage 1, the force for projecting the ball comes from hip flexion, shoulder protraction, and elbow extension.

Stage 2 The distinctive feature of this stage is the rotation of the body about an imaginary vertical axis, with the hips, spine, and shoulders rotating as one unit. The performer may step forward with either an ipsilateral or contralateral pattern, but the arm is brought forward in a transverse plane. The motion may resemble a "sling" rather than a throw due to the extended arm position during the course of the throw.

(continued)

FIGURE 14-2   *(continued)*

Stage 3   The distinctive pattern in stage 3 is the ipsilateral arm-leg action. The ball is placed into a throwing position above the shoulder by a vertical and posterior motion of the arm at the time that the ipsilateral leg is moving forward. This stage involves little or no rotation of the spine and hips in preparation for the throw. The follow-through phase includes flexion at the hip joint and some trunk rotation toward the side opposite the throwing arm.

Stage 4   The movement is contralateral, with the leg opposite the throwing arm striding forward as the throwing arm is moved in a vertical and posterior direction during the wind-up phase. There is little or no rotation of the hips and spine during the wind-up phase; thus, the motion of the trunk and arm closely resembles the motions of stages 1 and 3. The stride forward with the contralateral leg provides for a wide base of support and greater stability during the force production phase of the throw.

(continued)

FIGURE 14-2 (*continued*)

Stage 5 The wind-up phase begins with the throwing hand moving in a downward arc and then backward as the opposite leg moves forward. This concurrent action rotates the hip and spine into position for forceful derotation. As the contralateral foot strikes the surface, the hips, spine, and shoulder begin derotating in sequence. The contralateral leg begins to extend at the knee, providing an equal and opposite reaction to the throwing arm. The arm opposite the throwing limb also moves forcefully toward the body to assist in the equal and opposite reaction.

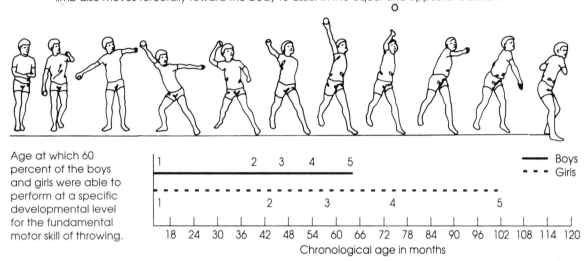

Age at which 60 percent of the boys and girls were able to perform at a specific developmental level for the fundamental motor skill of throwing.

Chronological age in months

opmental changes in movement components instead of developmental changes in ball-throwing velocity. An analysis of the data indicated that instruction significantly influenced throwing technique. Of the seven movement components examined, the experimental subjects used more advanced form in forearm lag, trunk action, stepping action, and range of spinal rotation. From these two studies, the researchers concluded that instruction significantly affected changes in throwing technique but not greater horizontal ball velocities. Halverson and Roberton recommended that ball-throwing velocity not be used as the sole index when investigating overarm throwing development in children.

In work similar to that of the preceding studies, Luedke (1980) administered a specially designed throwing instructional program to 144 second- and fourth-grade boys. This special program focused on increasing the range of motion in each of the following throwing components: stride length, arm retraction, side facing, trunk rotation, preparatory leg recoil, arm patterns, and stride opposition. Following the 6-week experimental program, "increased range of motion instruction" was found to have a significant effect on the throwing patterns of both the second- and fourth-grade boys. This form of instruction was most effective in increasing the stride length component of the overarm throw.

Ball Size   As will be described later in this chapter, numerous studies have examined the influence of ball size on young children's catching ability, but only recently have researchers begun to examine its influence on throwing performance. Burton and colleagues (1992) examined the influence of ball size on the throwing performances of 40 children (5–6 yr, 7–8 yr, 9–10 yr) and 20 adults (19–33 yr). The subjects were required to throw six different sized (1.9, 4.1, 5.8, 7.8, 9.6, and 11.6 inches in diameter) styrofoam balls as hard as possible toward a wall that was 6.7 meters away. Styrofoam was chosen to minimize the effect that ball weight may have on throwing performance. Each throwing trial was evaluated using Roberton's component approach model, which was described earlier in this chapter. This study found throwing technique to be quite stable. More specifically, stable patterns of performance were exhibited 88.4 percent of the time within a selected ball diameter. When patterns of throwing performance became unstable, it marked the beginning of a transition to a new component level 70.6 percent of the time. In addition, the researchers hypothesized that whenever the ball diameter was scaled-up, there would reach a transitional point were performers would resort to a less mature throwing pattern. This hypothesis was supported, but only for the backswing (53.3 percent) and forearm (61.3 percent) components. No significant differences were found among the other three components (humerus, 25 percent; trunk, 0 percent; and feet, 2.5 percent).

In a second study, Burton and colleagues (1993) sought to examine the influence of ball size on grasping patterns as well as throwing patterns among 104 subjects who were equally distributed between five age categories (5–6 yr, 7–8 yr, 9–10 yr, 13–14 yr, 19–33 yr). The performance task was essentially identical to that reported in the first study. The researchers witnessed a transition from one-handed grasping to two-handed grasping as the diameter of the ball increased, with adults switching at a significantly larger diameter compared to younger subjects. However, when hand size was taken into consideration younger subjects switched from a two-handed grasping pattern to a one-handed grasping pattern significantly later than adults. Furthermore, there was no significant difference in the relative ball diameter at which boys and girls switched from a one- to a two-handed grasp. Regarding throwing pattern, two-handed throwing was exhibited less than 25 percent of the time and was mostly found among the five- and six-year-old females. These two studies point out the importance of considering both ball size and the relationship between ball size and hand width when assessing throwing performance.

Accounting for Gender Differences in Overarm Throwing

Anyone who works regularly with young children will tell you that there is a vast difference between the overarm throwing abilities of young boys and young girls. In fact, using meta-analysis to examine gender differences among 20 motor performance tasks, Thomas and French (1985) found the greatest gender differences among the skills examined to be for throwing. This finding has lead researchers to develop a series of studies designed to uncover why such gender differences exist. Researchers have speculated that such differences could be accounted for by heredity and sociocultural factors. This view was supported when Nelson and colleagues (1986) found that the throwing performance of 5-year-old girls was just 57 percent of that of similar age boys. However, when the scores were adjusted for joint diameters, shoulder/hip ratio, forearm length, as well as for arm and leg muscle mass, the throwing performance of girls improved to 69 percent of that found for boys. In a 3-year follow-up study involving 26 of the original 100 children (Nelson, Thomas, & Nelson, 1991), boy's throwing distance was positively associated with a heredity factor (arm muscle mass) and one sociocultural factor: the presence of an adult male in the home. In contrast, girls who weighed more and had more body fat along with greater joint diameters and more estimated arm and leg muscle mass threw further than their smaller and weaker female counterparts. Nevertheless, the performance of these larger and stronger girls still lagged behind their male peers. It was specifically noted that over this 3-year period boys had improved their throwing distance by 11 meters while girls improved by only 4.6 meters. Thus, by 9 years of age, girls threw only 49 percent as far as boys. Furthermore, when using "throwing technique" as the variable of interest, it was noted that over this period, girl's trunk rotation and foot action did not improve as much as the boys. In fact, by third grade most boys exhibited mature throwing form, while the girls were still using block rotation and failed to take a long-vigorous step on the contralateral foot. The authors speculated that sociocultural factors such as lack of encouragement and therefore lack of practice time for the young girls may be contributing factors as to why the developmental level of their movement pattern did not significantly change during this 3-year period.

In a study designed to specifically examine the effects of selected sociocultural factors upon the overarm throwing performance of children in kindergarten through grade 3, the authors concluded that, ". . . the orderly development of fundamental movement patterns is essential and is predicated to a large extent upon appropriate nurture experiences provided within the sociocultural milieu of the child" (East & Hensley, 1985, p. 126). This conclusion was based on their finding that as much as 25 percent of the variance could be contributed to the stereotyped father-figure who directed the daughter's play experiences away from sports and physically competitive situations. It was also noted that in every instance, amount of time spent watching television was negatively correlated with throwing performance. In other words, those children who watched the most television, tended to exhibit poorer throwing performance than those children who watched less television.

Recently Thomas and colleagues (1992) have posed an interesting question, "Can gender differences in throwing be accounted for by factors involving human evolution?" The authors build their argument around an examination of throwing behaviors believed to be exhibited in early humans and chimpanzees. It is believed that throwing was more prevalent among males and was probably used during defensive encounters and for hunting. The authors write, "Circumstantial evidence from antiquity suggests a potential connection" (p. 73).

CATCHING

Catching is the action of bringing an airborne object under control by using the hands and arms. Unlike throwing, there has been little process-oriented research into developmental stages associated with this important fundamental movement pattern. In fact, none of the process-oriented studies conducted have validated its hypothesized stages through longitudinal study (Deach, 1950; Gutteridge, 1939; Wellman, 1937). Nevertheless, these studies do allow us to make several generalizations concerning the development of catching.

Developmental Aspects: Two-Handed Catching

Usually children's first attempts at stopping or controlling a moving object occur when they are seated on the floor with their legs spread apart. At first a child will be successful in stopping a rolled ball by trapping the ball against the legs. With practice, the child will soon be able to trap the ball against the floor by using only the hands, with the palms facing down toward the floor.

A child's first attempts at catching an aerial ball are generally passive. That is, the child stands facing the tosser, who attempts to project the ball into the child's outstretched arms so he can trap the ball against his body. The palms of the hands face upward, and the child makes no attempt to adjust his body or arms to the oncoming ball.

As children's visuoperceptual systems improve, they attempt to adjust their hands and arms to the ball's changing flight characteristics. The palms of the hands are now adjusted to face one another instead of upward, and the elbows are slightly bent so that the hands are in front of the face. Still, in most instances the ball will make initial contact with the arms or body as the arms are brought up toward the face. When the ball is retained, it is done so by being hugged or trapped against the body. At this stage of development, some children may exhibit fear when the projected ball approaches them (see Figure 14-3). Negative reactions to the tossed ball include turning the head away from the ball; leaning backward, away from the ball; and closing the eyes (Deach, 1950). Seefeldt (1972a) noted these fear reactions in children 4 through 6 years of age but found no such negative reactions to a projectile in children between 1 1/2 and 3 years. Based on this finding, Seefeldt speculated that fear of the projectile may be a conditioned response from earlier failures at the task, not a natural phenomenon.

At the most advanced level of catching development, the performer adjusts the entire body so as to control the projectile with only the hands. In addition, the mature catcher "gives with the catch"; the momentum of the projectile is absorbed by flexing the elbows at the moment of hand-ball contact—the elbows act as shock absorbers.

FIGURE 14-3   This 6-year-old child is showing fear in reaction to the thrown ball.

These developmental characteristics are evident in Kay's (1970) comparative film analysis of the catching styles of 2-, 5-, and 15-year-old children. Kay described the 2-year-old child as approaching the task without any general strategy. The child tended to maintain a static position throughout the entire task and focused her eyes on the tosser, not the ball. In short, this young child reacted too late. As Kay stated, "For the most part she is doing something after it has happened, often very long after, as when she eventually turns to fetch the ball that has fallen" (p. 144).

In contrast, the 5-year-old child was able to anticipate some of the ball's changing flight characteristics and focused her eyes on the thrower, the ball,

and even her own hands. This child's poor timing and coordination limited her ability to retain the ball. Her movements were correct but appeared to be carried out in slow motion.

Finally, the 15-year-old child was capable of predicting the ball's flight characteristics, and he carried out preparatory responses well in advance of the ball's arrival. "The overall impression is one of smoothness and ease. The eyes are concentrated upon the ball; they do not watch the hands, which are controlled entirely from the boy's own awareness of the position of his limbs" (Kay, 1970, p. 145).

Developmental Sequences for Two-Handed Catching

Table 14-3 presents Roberton and Halverson's component analysis for the fundamental motor skill of catching. In contrast, Figure 14-4 illustrates the developmental sequences for catching based on the total body approach. This latter approach has withstood preliminary validation within a mixed longitudinal sample (Haubenstricker, Branta, & Seefeldt, 1983).

A close inspection of the horizontal bar graph at the end of Figure 14-4 indicates that there is little difference in the developmental level of catching between boys and girls prior to 48 months of age (4 years). However, 1 year later, 60 percent of the girls exhibited a stage 4 developmental level of performance whereas a majority (60 percent) of the boys did not achieve this level of development until approximately 6 years of age. Also note that according to this data, which were collected in the latter half of the 1970s (but reported by Seefeldt and Haubenstricker in 1982), girls obtained the most mature level of performance several months before boys did. An analysis of a more recent data set has yielded different findings (Haubenstricker, Seefeldt, & Branta, 1983). More specifically, using a mixed longitudinal sample, Haubenstricker, Seefeldt, & Branta (1983) found that approximately 60 percent of the males exhibited the most mature catching pattern (stage 5) somewhere between 90 (n = 174) and 96 (n = 210) months of age. In contrast, the number of girls exhibiting stage 5 catching characteristics was only about 40 percent (90 months, n =

TABLE 14-3 Developmental Sequences for Catching: Component Approach

Preparation: Arm Component

Step 1: The arms are outstretched with elbows extended, awaiting the tossed ball.

Step 2: The arms await the ball toss with some shoulder flexion still apparent, but flexion now appears in the elbows.

Step 3: The arms await the ball in a relaxed posture at the sides of the body or slightly ahead of the body. The elbows may be flexed.

Reception: Arm Component

Step 1: The arms remain outstretched and the elbows rigid. There is little to no "give," so the ball bounces off the arms.

Step 2: The elbows flex to carry the hands upward toward the face. Initially, ball contact is primarily with the arms, and the object is trapped against the body.

Step 3: Initial contact is with the hands. If unsuccessful in using the fingers, the child may still trap the ball against the chest. The hands still move upward toward the face.

Step 4: Ball contact is made with the hands. The elbows still flex but the shoulders extend, bringing the ball down and toward the body rather than up toward the face.

Hand Component

Step 1: The palms of the hands face upward. (Rolling balls elicit a palms-down, trapping action.)

Step 2: The palms of the hands face each other.

Step 3: The palms of the hands are adjusted to the flight and size of the oncoming object. Thumbs or little fingers are placed close together, depending on the height of the flight path.

Body Component

Step 1: There is no adjustment of the body in response to the flight path of the ball.

Step 2: The arms and trunk begin to move in relation to the ball's flight path.

Step 3: The feet, trunk, and arms all move to adjust to the path of the oncoming ball.

Note: These sequences have not been validated. They were hypothesized by Harper (1979).
Source: Roberton and Halverson (1984).

177; 96 months, n = 175). Furthermore, approximately 70 percent of the male subjects within the oldest age group studied (102–107 months) exhibited a stage 5 developmental level of catching, whereas only about 49 percent of the girls in this oldest age group performed at the highest level. These more recent data suggest that boys reach the most mature level of catching development before girls do.

Developmental Aspects: One-Handed Catching

While there is a wealth of information regarding the development of two-handed catching in young boys and girls, little scientific evidence exists regarding children's ability to catch with one hand. One of the first studies to examine one-handed catching in

FIGURE 14-4   Developmental sequences for catching: total body approach

Source: Haubenstricker, Branta, and Seefeldt (1983); Seefeldt (1972a); Seefeldt and Haubenstricker (1982); All material used with permission.

Stage 1   The child presents his arms directly in front of him, with the elbows extended and the palms facing upward or inward toward the midsaggital plane. As the ball contacts the hands or arms, the elbows are flexed and the arms and hands attempt to secure the ball by holding it against the chest.

Stage 2   The child prepares to receive the object with the arms in front of the body, the elbows extended or slightly flexed. Upon presentation of the ball, the arms begin an encircling motion that culminates by securing the ball against the chest. Stage 2 also differs from stage 1 in that the receiver initiates the arm action prior to ball-arm contact in stage 2.

(continued)

FIGURE 14-4 *(continued)*

Stage 3 The child prepares to receive the ball with arms that are slightly flexed and extended forward at the shoulder. Many children also receive the ball with arms that are flexed at the elbow, with the elbow ahead of a frontal plane.

> *Substage 1:* The child uses his chest as the first contact point of the ball and attempts to secure the ball by holding it to his chest with the hands and arms.
>
> *Substage 2:* The child attempts to catch the ball with his hands. Upon his failure to hold it securely he maneuvers it to his chest, where it is controlled by hands and arms.

Stage 4 The child prepares to receive the ball by flexing the elbows and presenting the arms ahead of the frontal plane. Skillful performers may keep the elbows at the sides and flex the arms simultaneously as they bring them forward to meet the ball. The ball is caught with the hands, without making contact with any other body parts.

(continued)

FIGURE 14-4 *(continued)*

Stage 5 The same upper segmental action is identical to stage 4. In addition, the child is required to change his stationary base in order to receive the ball. Stage 5 is included because of the apparent difficulty that many children encounter when they are required to move in relation to an approaching object.

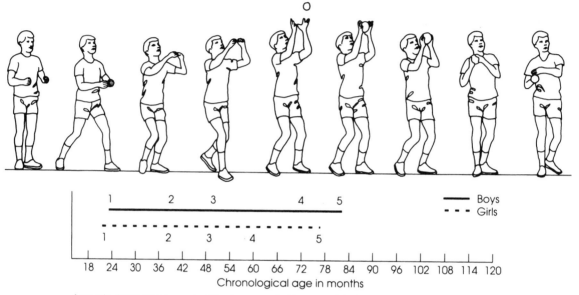

Age at which 60 percent of the boys and girls were able to perform at a specific developmental level for the fundamental motor skill of catching.

young children was conducted by Fischman and colleagues (1992). The authors were interested in determining performance trends and gender differences in the one-handed catching ability of 240 children between the ages of 5 and 12 years of age. In addition, they were also interested in studying how the location of the ball toss affected hand orientation. A tennis ball was tossed from a distance of 9 feet to one of four locations: waist height, shoulder height, above-the-head, and out to the side at waist level. Similar to two-handed catching, performance improved with age for both boys and girls. Success rate among the boys ranged from 17.2 percent at 5 years of age to 95.8 percent at 12 years of age. Girls were less proficient with success ranging from 4.2 percent to 92.2 percent at 5 and 12 years

of age respectively. While the authors concluded that by 12 years of age the skill appeared to be essentially mastered, one could offer an alternate hypothesis; namely, the task may have been too easy for the older children. This was not the case for the younger children. Of the 294 "no-contacts" (no part of the body contacted the ball), 269 occurred among the 5- to 8-year-old children. One could speculate that such poor performance is caused by immature temporal and spatial organization.

Ball location was also found to be an important factor. Balls tossed above-the-head and out to the side elicited the use of correct hand orientation. Even though the fewest number of balls was caught when the ball was tossed toward the waist, appropriate hand orientation was nevertheless exhibited.

This finding suggests that even the youngest children may be capable of perceptually orienting the hand in line with the oncoming ball but experienced difficulty in executing the closure of the fingers around the ball.

Williams (1992b) compared the one-handed and two-handed catching performances of young children between 4 and 10 years of age. Catching attempts were classified as being a "cradle" (hand is flexed to form a cradle into which the ball will passively fall and is then trapped against the body), a clamp (hand moves toward the ball, palm facing inward, but as the ball approaches the hand moves underneath the falling ball and is grasped with the palm of the hand), or a grasp (hand reaches for oncoming ball with the palm facing the ball allowing the flexed fingers to grasp the ball well in front of the body). Success with one-handed catching was only one-half as successful as two-handed catching. While grasping (the most mature technique) was the prominent movement strategy for catching with two hands, the prominent movement strategy for catching with one hand was the least-mature cradling technique. In fact, grasping declined from 66 percent to 26 percent when one-handed catching was required. This is further evidence that environmental constraints can contribute to changes in movement patterns. To date, developmental sequences have not been hypothesized for one-handed catching.

Factors That Influence Catching Performance

There has been no shortage of studies designed to examine factors that may influence catching performance. Unfortunately, it is difficult to compare and contrast these studies because they vary as to type of ball used; distance of projection; speed, color, and angle of projection; and the type of evaluation system used. Nevertheless, an awareness of these findings can aid future investigative research.

Ball Size The effects of ball size on an individual's catching ability have received much research attention (Isaacs, 1980; McCaskill & Wellman, 1938; Payne, 1985a; Payne & Koslow, 1981; Strohmeyer, Williams, & Schaub-George, 1991; Victors, 1961; Warner, 1952; Wickstrom, 1983). Initial studies consistently concluded that larger balls improve young children's catching performance. These conclusions were often based on the premise that young children are far-sighted and would thus profit from using the larger ball, which would be easier to visually track (Smith, 1970). Also, based on neurological considerations, the young child was assumed to have insufficient fine motor control for grasping the smaller object. Most early studies, however, evaluated the child's catching attempts on a pass-fail basis: The child either did or did not retain control of the ball. Human error was a major consideration because balls were often simply tossed to the subject by the experimenter, allowing for considerable variability of tosses.

More recently, researchers have attempted to eliminate some of the shortcomings of the earlier research by implementing more sophisticated statistical analyses, mechanically projecting ball tosses to reduce human error, and using weighted rating scales to evaluate catching performance beyond the simple pass-fail. These recent investigations, however, have led to a sharp dissimilarity in findings.

Some research has found small balls to be more conducive to successful catching (Isaacs, 1980). Such research employed a rating scale designed to evaluate the maturation level children displayed in their catching technique. As discussed in Chapter 1, this is a process-oriented means of evaluation. Table 14-3, Figure 14-4, and the scale below are all examples of process-oriented ratings for the skill of catching.

0. Initial body contact; subject makes no attempt to contact the ball.

1. Arm and/or body contact, miss: initial attempt to contact is made on the arms and/or body, and the ball is missed.

2. Arm and/or body contact, save: initial contact is on the arms and/or body, and the ball is retained.

3. Hand contact, miss: initial contact is made by the hands, but ball is then dropped immediately or dropped following arm or body contact.

4. Hand contact, assisted catch: initial contact is made by the hands. The ball is juggled but retained by using arms and/or body for assistance.

5. Hand contact, clean catch: the ball is contacted and retained by the hands only. The ball may be brought into the body on the follow-through after control is gained by the hands.

(Hellweg, 1972; Isaacs, 1980)

Research employing this scale was based on the premise that future success in catching depends on the early development of a mature technique. Generally, a smaller ball tended to elicit a more mature hand catch rather than an arm/chest trap. This research also determined that as the ball size increased, the maturity level in the catching technique regressed. In other words, the child would be more likely to resort to the more immature chest-trap method of catching (Isaacs, 1980; Victors, 1961; Wickstrom, 1983).

Studies finding children to be more successful using larger balls generally employed rating scales designed to evaluate the level of control that the child maintained over the ball, regardless of the maturity of the catching technique, a product-oriented evaluation. An example of a product-oriented rating scale is as follows:

1. failure to react
2. one hand contacts, ball dropped
3. two hands contact, ball dropped
4. uncontrolled catch (bobbled)
5. controlled catch

(Payne, 1985a; Payne & Koslow, 1981)

This research was based on the premise that children's ability to control the ball, regardless of the maturity of their technique, would make them feel successful in the movement and inspire them to try again (Payne, 1985a; Payne & Koslow, 1981).

Clearly, we need more information on this topic. In particular, we need to know what is the critical issue in teaching a motor skill. Should we place the premium on early acquisition of a mature technique or on early success in terms of simply controlling the ball (Payne, 1982)? Unfortunately, little scientific information is presently available to answer this question, which is so critical to the optimal teaching of motor skills to children.

Ball and Background Color   Manipulation of both ball color and background color may be another way to improve catching performance (Gavnishy, 1970; Ghosh, 1973). In studying the effects of ball and background color on young children's catching performances, Morris (1976) found that blue and yellow balls were caught significantly better than white balls. Furthermore, children attained their highest catching scores when blue balls were projected against a white background.

Data that Isaacs (1980) obtained indicated that a child's preferred color may also be influential in catching performances. Before being administered a criterion catch test, subjects were required to choose their favorite colored ball. Results of this study indicated that irrespective of ball color, both the boys and the girls tended to catch their preferred-color ball significantly better than their nonpreferred-color balls. Isaacs speculated that because the children in this study focused their selective attention on the ball for a longer time when catching their preferred-color ball, they were therefore able to obtain more critical information concerning the ball's flight.

Ball Velocity   Ridenour (1974) determined that ball speed is also an influential factor in children's ability to accurately predict the direction in which a projectile is moving. Subjects in Ridenour's study were not required to catch the ball, but it can be generalized that prediction of an object's direction is necessary in a catching task. This was evident in Bruce's (1966) investigation. With 7-, 9-, and 11-year-old subjects, he found that the catching performances of the 7- and 9-year-old children declined as ball speed increased from 25 to 33 feet per second.

Trajectory Angle   Variations in trajectory angles were also a major feature in Bruce's (1966) investigation. The balls were projected at either a

30- or 60-degree angle. An analysis of the data indicated that angle of projection did not significantly affect a child's catching ability. On the other hand, Williams (1968) used nine skilled and nine unskilled catchers in an attempt to determine the effects of trajectory angle on judging speed and accuracy of a moving object. Results of Williams's study indicated that the unskilled catchers performed better when balls were projected at a 34-degree angle, whereas the group as a whole performed better when the balls were projected at a 44-degree angle.

Vision and Viewing Time   Without a doubt, the catcher must rely on visual information to form a strategy that will lead to a successful catch. Research indicates that as viewing time decreases, so does proficiency in retaining the projectile (Nessler, 1973; Whiting, Gill, & Stephenson, 1970). Thus the teacher should use a ball that moves slowly through space (e.g., beach ball, whiffle ball, sponge ball) when working with inexperienced catchers.

Instruction   To date, only one study has examined the influence of catching instruction on children's one-handed catching ability. Using a single subject design, Williams (1992a) trained an 8-year-old boy. Training consisted of four assessment sessions and three instruction plus practice sessions administered alternately on 7 successive days. Each instruction and practice session lasted 30 minutes. Following the third instruction and practice session, significant changes were observed in both percent of successful catches and level of maturity (technique) used to retain the projected ball. Williams noted that by the end of the study, this 8-year-old boy's catching ability had progressed from that of a typical 8-year-old to that of subjects who were 2 years older.

STRIKING

Striking is a fundamental movement in which a designated body part or some implement is used to project an object. Propulsion skills are necessary in many sport activities and can occur in a variety of forms. For example, the bare hand is used as the striking implement in volleyball. The striking pattern can be underhanded, as in serving the volleyball, or overhanded, as in spiking the volleyball. When an implement is used, such as a racquet or bat, the striking pattern is accomplished with either one or two hands. Regardless of the movement pattern employed, certain characteristics are readily observable. This section describes the development of striking an object with both a body part (hand and/or foot) and an implement (racquet or bat).

Developmental Aspects of One- and Two-Handed Striking

The child's initial attempt at striking an object with either the bare hand or some implement is very similar to the overarm throwing pattern young children exhibit. Briefly, at an inexperienced level of development, a child uses an overarm pattern that is predominantly flexion and extension of the forearm. The child usually directly faces the object to be struck and may or may not take a forward step. If the child does take a forward step, it is with the *homolateral* leg, the leg on the same side of the body as the striking arm. Thus all the striking movements are accomplished in the anterior-posterior plane.

The child's upward-downward swing pattern gradually "flattens out." Flattening out the swing facilitates the child's ability to contact the ball. In most instances this sidearm striking pattern becomes well defined by approximately 36 months (Espenschade & Eckert, 1980). Nevertheless, Espenschade and Eckert noted that when children are under stress to successfully strike a ball, they generally resort to an inexperienced overarm striking pattern.

Harper and Struna (1973) studied longitudinal changes in the one-handed striking pattern of two children filmed over 1 year. Both the 40-month-old girl and the 43-month-old boy were asked to strike a suspended ball as hard as possible toward a wall. Initially, the young girl's swing consisted purely of horizontal adduction of the striking arm. She took little backswing and did not take a forward step.

Spinal or pelvic rotation was not evident. However, 3 months later, she had made much progress toward a more advanced sidearm striking pattern. The girl now took a forward step with the *contralateral* leg (the leg opposite the striking arm), and there was simultaneous spinal and pelvic rotation. Because the young boy already exhibited many advanced characteristics of the one-handed sidearm swing at the first filming, observable changes in his striking pattern were more subtle. Over the 1-year period, the most noticeable changes in his striking pattern were a longer stride into the ball and an increase in the preparatory backswing.

In another study, Wickstrom (1968; cited in Wickstrom, 1983) examined the sidearm striking patterns of 33 preschool children 21 to 60 months old. His data revealed that children younger than 30 months used the overarm striking pattern when attempting to contact the suspended ball with either a bat or paddle. Children older than 30 months also used an overarm striking pattern, but they responded favorably when encouraged to use a sidearm striking pattern. Finally, Wickstrom was amazed at how close the 4-year-olds' striking pattern was to an adult pattern. Table 14-4 summarizes the major

characteristics of striking development while Figure 14-5 describes and illustrates a total body approach to the analysis of striking with a bat.

Stationary Ball Bouncing

Bouncing a ball is a fundamental movement used in many childhood and adult activities. At an advanced level of development, a person bounces or *dribbles* a ball by using the hand to repeatedly push the ball downward. At inexperienced levels of performance, a person uses one or two hands to strike instead of push the ball. Thus, striking is one of the developmental stages of ball bouncing.

Initially, the striking pattern resembles a spanking or slapping motion of the hand and wrist (see Figure 14-6). Wickstrom (1980), one of the few researchers to study the acquisition of ball-handling skills in young children, filmed 115 children in kindergarten through second grade to study developmental characteristics within this fundamental movement pattern. He noted that the inexperienced dribbler held the fingers of the striking hand close together and sometimes slightly hyperextended the fingers at contact. Following contact with the ball, the child

TABLE 14-4 Major Characteristics of General Striking Development

Inexperienced Striker	Advanced Striker
1. Striker usually takes no step, but if the striker does, it is with the homolateral leg.	1. Striker takes a forward step with the foot opposite the striking arm or striking side.
2. Child uses an up-down striking motion.	2. Child uses a full backswing.
3. Striker takes little backswing with the striking arm or implement.	3. Child swings the striking implement horizontally.
4. The striker's trunk and hips do not rotate and there is no block rotation.	4. Differentiated trunk and hip rotation is present.
5. Striker holds the arms rigid with little, if any, wrist snap when swinging a paddle or bat.	5. In the two-handed striking pattern, the striker's arms are relaxed and there is a noticeable coordinated wrist snap when swinging a bat.

SOURCE: Payne (1985b).

FIGURE 14-5   Developmental sequences for striking with a bat: total body approach
Source: Seefeldt and Haubenstricker (1974b, 1982). All material used with permission.

Stage 1   The motion is primarily posterior-anterior in direction. The movement begins with hip extension and slight spinal extension and retraction of the shoulder on the striking side of the body. The elbows flex fully. The feet remain stationary throughout the movement with the primary force coming from extension of the flexed joints.

Stage 2   The feet remain stationary or either the right or left foot may receive the weight as the body moves toward the approaching ball. The primary pattern is the unitary rotation of the hip-spinal linkage about an imaginary vertical axis. The forward movement of the bat is in a transverse plane.

Stage 3   The shift of weight to the front-supporting foot occurs in an ipsilateral pattern. The trunk rotation-derotation is decreased markedly in comparison to stage 2, and the movement of the bat is in an oblique-vertical plane instead of the transverse path as seen in stage 2.

(continued)

FIGURE 14-5 (*continued*)

Stage 4 The transfer of weight in rotation-derotation is in a contralateral pattern. The shift of weight to the forward foot occurs while the bat is still moving backward as the hips, spine, and shoulder girdle assume their force-producing positions. At the initiation of the forward movement the bat is kept near the body. Elbow extension and the supination-pronation of the hands do not occur until the arms and hands are well forward and ready to extend the lever in preparation to meet the ball. At contact the weight is on the forward foot.

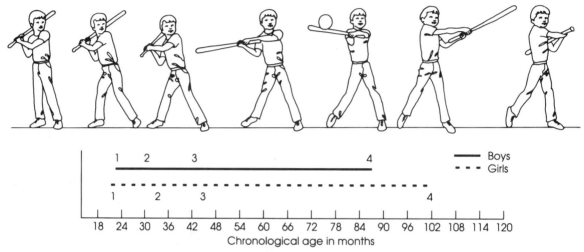

Age at which 60 percent of the boys and girls were able to perform at a specific developmental level for the fundamental motor skill of striking with a bat.

quickly retracted the arm and there was little extension of the elbow. Because their eye-hand coordination was poor, the young performers struck the ball in an inconsistent manner. As would be expected, these children had difficulty controlling the direction in which the ball was hit. Timing hand-ball contact was also difficult for the inexperienced performers. It is common to observe an inexperienced performer slapping at the ball when the ball is traveling down and quickly retracting the arm when the ball is rebounding up, thus never making contact with the ball.

In contrast, the experienced dribbler pushes the ball toward the floor so that the elbow is nearly fully extended. The dribbling arm stays extended and recontacts the ball when it bounces approximately two-thirds of the way up. Once hand-ball contact has been made, the hand retracts slowly, thus enabling the hand to maintain contact with the ball. The fingers are spread apart and the ball

is once again pushed downward to start another dribbling cycle.

The transition from inexperienced to experienced performance becomes evident as the individual gradually extends the elbow and delays retracting the forearm. Meeting the ball before it has reached its peak height and "giving" with the ball enable the hand to maintain contact with the ball, so the ball is pushed rather than struck toward the floor.

Kicking

Kicking is another form of striking; the foot is used to give impetus to a ball. The style of kicking that we describe in this section is called *place kicking*. In place kicking, the ball is placed either on the ground or on a kicking tee. In its most mature form, the advanced place kicker will approach the ball from a running start. The last step taken prior

FIGURE 14-6   An illustration of inexperienced and mature dribbling

The inexperienced dribbler slaps at the ball.

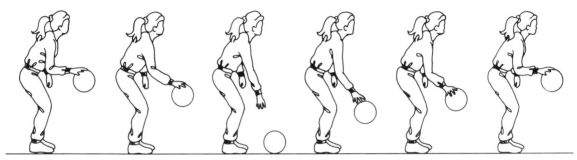

The mature dribbler fully extends the arm and when ball-hand contact is made, the arm retracts and the hand maintains contact with the ball.

to ball-foot contact involves a leap step onto the plant or support foot. Simultaneously, the kicking leg is prepared by flexing the knee and hyperextending the hip. This preparatory backswing will enable the leg to be thrust forward vigorously and subsequently powerfully project the ball. After kicking the ball, the kicking leg continues to travel upward—the leg is allowed to follow through. The follow-through should be vigorous enough to cause the support leg to leave the ground. Simply put, a hop is performed on the support leg. During this kicking sequence, the kicker's center of gravity is displaced. To subsequently maintain balance, the advanced place kicker positions the trunk so it leans slightly backward and the arms oppose the action of the legs.

In contrast, the inexperienced place kicker lacks many of these preparatory movements. The child

simply pushes the ball away with the foot. In fact, the foot barely leaves the floor, there is no attempted backswing of the kicking leg, the leg remains straight throughout the kicking motion, and there is no follow-through. In addition, the child holds the arms straight by the side of the body rather than using them to maintain body balance.

At an intermediate level of place kicking development, preparatory movements are noticeable. There is less flexion of the knee and hip than in an advanced pattern, but some preparation is evident. The arms are elevated to help maintain balance but still do not work in opposition to the legs. The follow-through of the kicking leg is evident after the kick but is less than what is expected at an advanced level of kicking development. These developmental changes in place kicking are illustrated and presented in more detail in Figure 14-7.

FIGURE 14-7   Developmental sequences for kicking: total body approach

Source: Haubenstricker et al. (1981); Seefeldt (1972b); Seefeldt and Haubenstricker (1975a, 1982). All material used with permission.

Stage 1   *Preparatory phase:* The performer is usually stationary and positioned near the ball. If the performer moves prior to kicking, the steps are short and concerned with spatial relationships rather than attaining momentum for the kick.

Force production: The thigh of the kicking leg moves forward with the knee flexed and is nearly parallel to the surface by the time the foot contacts the ball. Knee-joint extension occurs after contact, resulting in a pushing rather than a striking action. Upper extremity action is usually bilateral but may show some opposition in older performers. (If the performer is too far from the ball as the extremity moves to meet the ball, the knee flexes only slightly and the leg swings forward from the hip in a pushing action.)

Follow-through phase: The knee of the kicking leg continues to extend until it approaches 180°. If the trunk is inclined forward following contact with the ball, the performer will step forward to regain balance. If the trunk is leaning backward, the kicking leg will move backward after ball contact to achieve body balance.

Stage 2   *Preparatory phase:* The performer is stationary. Initial action involves hyperextension at the hips and flexion at the knee so that the thigh of the kicking leg is behind the midfrontal plane. The arms may move into a position of opposition in situations of extreme hyperextension at the hips.

Force production: The kicking leg moves forward with the knee joint in a flexed position. Knee-joint extension begins just prior to foot contact with the ball. Arm-leg opposition occurs during the kick.

Follow-through phase: Knee extension continues after the ball leaves the foot, but the force of the kick usually is not sufficient to move the body forward. Instead, the performer usually steps sideward or backward.

(continued)

FIGURE 14-7   (*continued*)

Stage 3   *Preparatory phase:* The performer takes one or more deliberate steps to approach the ball. The support leg is placed near the ball and slightly to the side of it.

Force production: The kicking foot stays near the surface as it approaches the ball, resulting in less flexion than in stage 2. The trunk remains nearly upright, thereby preventing maximum force production. The knee begins to extend prior to contact. Arm-leg opposition is evident.

Follow-through phase: The force of the kick may carry the performer past the point of contact if the approach was vigorous. Otherwise, the performer may remain near the point of contact.

Stage 4   *Preparatory phase:* The approach involves one or more steps with the final "step" being an airborne run or leap. This permits hyperextension of the hip and flexion of the knee as in stage 2.

Force production: The shoulders are retracted and the trunk is inclined backward as the supporting leg makes contact with the surface and the kicking leg begins to move forward. The movement of the thigh nearly stops as the knee joint begins to extend rapidly just prior to contact with the ball. Arm-leg opposition is present as in the previous two stages.

Follow-through phase: If the forward momentum of the kick is sufficient, the performer either hops on the support leg or scissors the legs while airborne in order to land on the kicking foot. If the kicking foot is not vigorous, the performer may merely step in the direction of the kick.

(*continued*)

FIGURE 14-7 (*continued*)

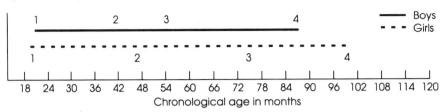

Age at which 60 percent of the boys and girls were able to perform at a specific developmental level for the fundamental motor skill of kicking.

Punting

Unlike place kicking, which requires one to kick a stationary ball, *punting* involves striking an airborne ball with the foot. Obviously, the complexity of punting greatly exceeds that of place kicking. Table 14-5 describes the hypothesized developmental sequences for punting based on the component approach (Roberton & Halverson, 1984) while Figure 14-8 describes and illustrates this same task from the perspective of the total body approach. Many of the changing developmental characteristics used in describing the place kick are also evident in punting. Namely, the immature punter is generally stationary, fails to properly prepare the kicking leg, and also fails to follow through with sufficient force. With this technique, there is obviously no leap step prior to ball-foot contact and no hop on the supporting foot following ball-foot contact. In addition, the ball is held with both hands and is generally presented by tossing it upward and slightly forward.

In contrast, the mature punter will move forward rapidly, leaping onto the support foot prior to ball-foot contact. The kicking leg is prepared by hyperextending the hip and flexing the knee. Following ball-foot contact, a vigorous follow-through generally causes a forward hop on the support leg.

SUMMARY

This chapter describes the development of a group of motor skills collectively referred to as *object-control skills*. The specific skills described in this chap-

ter included: overarm throwing, both one- and two-handed catching, striking with an implement (racquet or bat), and striking with a body part (place kicking and punting).

One-handed overarm throwing consists of a preparatory phase, an execution phase, and a follow-through phase. Initially, throwing is arm dominated; in contrast, advanced throwing involves trunk rotation and a forward step with the contralateral leg. Thus, movement progresses from an anterior-posterior plane to a horizontal plane and the base of support changes from a stationary to a shifting position. Gender differences in overarm throwing favor the male. In fact, one study that examined gender performance differences found that of the 20 skills examined, the greatest difference in performance was for throwing. It appears that both biological and sociocultural factors contribute to these performance differences between the genders.

Adultlike catching involves using only the hands to bring a moving object under control. The infant's first attempt at stopping a moving object occurs when the child is seated and traps a rolled ball against the body. Next, the child stands and attempts to trap a rolled ball against the floor. When first attempting to catch a thrown ball, some children may exhibit fear. Factors such as ball size, ball and background color, ball velocity, trajectory angle, and viewing time can all influence children's catching performance.

Researchers are just beginning to examine the development of one-handed catching in young children. Based on the very limited amount of research available, it appears that children are only about one-

TABLE 14-5   Developmental Sequences for Punting: Component Approach

Ball Release: Arm Component

Step 1: Hands are on the sides of the ball. The ball is tossed upward from both hands after the support foot has landed (if a step was taken).

Step 2: Hands are on the sides of the ball. The ball is dropped from chest height after the support foot has landed (if a step was taken).

Step 3: Hands are on the sides of the ball. The ball is lifted upward and forward from waist level. It is released at the time of or just prior to the landing of the support foot.

Step 4: One hand is rotated to the side and under the ball. The other hand is rotated to the side and top of the ball. The hands carry the ball on a forward and upward path during the approach. It is released at chest level as the final approach stride begins.

Ball Contact: Arm Component

Step 1: Arms drop bilaterally from ball release to a position on each side of the hips at ball contact.

Step 2: Arms bilaterally abduct after ball release. The arm on the side of the kicking leg may pull back as that leg swings forward.

Step 3: After ball release, the arms bilaterally abduct during flight. At contact the arm opposite the kicking leg has swung forward with that leg. The arm on the side of the kicking leg remains abducted and to the rear.

Leg Action Component

Step 1: No step or one short step is taken. The kicking leg swings forward from a position parallel to or slightly behind the support foot. The knee may be totally extended by contact or, more frequently, still flexed 90° with contact above or below the knee joint. The thigh is still moving upward at contact. The ankle tends to be flexed.

Step 2: Several steps may be taken. The last step onto the support leg is a long stride. The thigh of the kicking leg has slowed or stopped forward motion at contact. The ankle is extended. The knee has 20–30° of extension still possible by contact.

Step 3: The child may take several steps, but the last is actually a leap onto the support foot. After contact, the momentum of the kicking leg pulls the child off the ground in a hop.

Note: These sequences, hypothesized by Roberton (1983), have not been validated.
SOURCE: Roberton and Halverson (1984).

half as successful when attempting to catch with one hand as compared with two-handed catching. There is a regression in the technique used when attempting to catch one-handed. Similar to two-handed catching, boys' one-handed catching performance is generally superior to that of girls. It appears that the major difficulty factor for these young children is not hand orientation, but instead the ability to correctly time the closure of the fingers around the approaching ball (grasping). One study has found that instruction and practice in catching can improve one-handed catching performance.

FIGURE 14-8 Developmental sequences for punting: total body approach

Source: Seefeldt and Haubenstricker (1975b). All material used with permission.

Stage 1 The performer is stationary as the hands and foot prepare for the punting action. The ball is held with both hands at waist height or higher prior to placing it in position for punting. The ball may be manipulated in a variety of ways for punting: (1) It may be held in both hands as the punting foot is lifted forward and upward with hip and knee flexion. The punting force in this situation represents a push as the ball is contacted by the plantar side of the foot when the knee extends. (2) The ball may be tossed up and forward into the air. The performer then must move forward to get the body into punting position. (3) The performer may bounce the ball and attempt to punt it as it rebounds from the surface. Whatever the mode of placing the ball into a punting position, the primary characteristics of stage 1 are a stationary preparatory position and flexion at the hip and knee of the punting leg, placing these segments in front of the midfrontal plane.

Stage 2 the performer is stationary during the preparatory phase. The ball is held in both hands and may be dropped or tossed forward or upward in preparation for punting it with the foot. The nonsupport leg is flexed at the knee, and the thigh is perpendicular to the surface or behind the midfrontal plane as the leg is placed into punting position. As the punting leg moves forward, its momentum may carry the performer forward for a step, but generally the force is upward, causing the punter to step backward after striking the ball.

(continued)

FIGURE 14-8 (*continued*)

Stage 3 The performer moves forward deliberately for one or more steps in preparation for punting the ball. The ball is generally released in a forward and downward direction. The knee is flexed at 90° or less, but the thigh is farther behind the midfrontal plane than in stage 2, due to the stepping action. The follow-through of the striking leg will generally carry the punter ahead of the point where the ball was contacted.

Stage 4 The punter's approach is rapid, usually comprising one or more steps, culminating in a leap just prior to contacting the ball. If the leap does not precede the punt, the forward momentum may be enhanced by taking a large step. The ball is contacted at or below knee height as a result of the ball having been released in a forward and downward direction. The momentum of the swinging leg carries the punter off of the surface in an upward and forward direction after the punt.

Striking is a fundamental movement in which a designated body part or implement is used to project an object. When an implement is used, the inexperienced striker swings the implement up and down, similar to an overarm throwing pattern. In contrast, the experienced striker's swinging motion is side-arm or horizontal. Ball bouncing, place kicking, and punting are examples of fundamental movements in which a body part is used to strike a ball.

KEY TERMS

Catching
Contralateral
Dribbling
Homolateral
Kicking

Object-control skills
Place kicking
Punting
Striking
Throwing

CHAPTER 15

Youth Sports

Researchers estimate that there are more than 30 million children between 6 and 16 years of age who now participate in nonschool sports programs (Martens, 1978). The number continues to increase, for various reasons. First, there is a trend toward earlier participation. Just a few years ago, growth and development specialists shuddered to think that children as young as 5 or 6 years were participating in team activities such as T-baseball and youth football. Today, a 4-year-old holds an age-group record for running a marathon—over 26 miles—in 6 hours and 3 seconds (Jeffers, 1980). In fact, there has been an attempt to conduct an "infant olympics" (*Richard Times Dispatch*, 1979). Thus in the near future there may be international and national records for crawling and creeping speeds!

Why is there a trend toward earlier involvement? One reason is the rule changes within selected sports. For example, in T-baseball, even the youngest child can perform because the rules allow children to strike a stationary ball instead of one delivered by a pitcher. Conversely, defensive performance is no longer required, as rule changes limit the number of players who can bat per inning. Therefore, when the defensive team is unable to get anyone out, sides at bat change simply because all offensive players have had a turn at bat.

A second factor affecting the number of participants is an increase in female involvement. In 1971, the National Federation identified only 14 interscholastic sports for girls; by 1974 the number had risen to 25 sports involving 1.3 million participants, an increase of 350 percent in just 3 years (cited in Shaffer, 1982). More recently, the National Federation (1993) has reported a continued increase in female interscholastic sports involvement. For example, in 1979 the number of females participating in interscholastic soccer was 23,475; in 1992 participation had increased to 149,053.

Third, American children are beginning to get involved in what used to be considered nontraditional sports activities. Without doubt, American children have become infatuated with baseball, football, basketball, swimming, and soccer. However, the availability of agency- and community-sponsored programs in such activities as tennis, cycling, bowling, ice hockey, gymnastics, volley-ball, track and field, cross-country, figure skating, downhill and cross-country skiing, and many other sports has opened the door to participation for those children not interested in the more traditional sports.

Finally, there has been a dramatic increase in the number of disabled children who now actively participate in sports. This increase is directly linked to an increase in agency- and community-sponsored programs that serve people with various degrees of disabilities, including American Wheelchair Bowling Association, Amputee Sports Association, Handicapped Scuba Association, National Foundation of Wheelchair Tennis, National Wheelchair Softball Association, United States Quad Rugby Association, and the Special Olympics. Additionally, special equipment is now available for the disabled, further encouraging participation in sports.

Nearly everyone is pleased to see so many children become involved in youth sport activities. Researchers have surveyed the professional literature and have found 20 objectives as to why so many agencies sponsor youth sports programs (cited in Seefeldt, 1987). A sampling of these objectives include: the development of motoric competencies, the development of both health-related as well as motor-related physical fitness, to learn how to compete, to allow children to sense a feeling of belonging to a group, and to learn socially acceptable values and behaviors, just to name a few. In the minds of children, however, are these objectives being met? In this chapter we examine these and other important questions pertaining to children's involvement in youth sports.

WHERE CHILDREN PARTICIPATE IN SPORTS

As mentioned previously, the number of youth participating in organized sports programs continues to increase. A recent national survey (National Federation, 1993) of interscholastic sports has revealed that participation has increased to over 5.4 million. Table 15-1 lists the 10 most popular interscholastic sports and their numbers of participants.

This national survey now recognizes soccer as the fifth most popular sport for both boys and girls. In fact, much of the increase seen in this years survey is directly due to an increase in girls participation in both soccer and volleyball.

WHY CHILDREN PARTICIPATE IN SPORTS

Often-cited reasons for children's participation in sports include: to improve skills, to have fun, to be

TABLE 15-1   Ten Most Popular Interscholastic Sports for Boys and Girls

Sport	Rank	Number of Participants
BOYS		
Football	1	910,407
Basketball	2	521,023
Baseball	3	430,401
Outdoor track & field	4	412,638
Soccer	5	242,095
Wrestling	6	222,025
Cross country	7	159,536
Tennis	8	138,177
Golf	9	129,001
Swimming & diving	10	78,474
GIRLS		
Basketball	1	397,586
Outdoor track & field	2	334,942
Volleyball	3	313,055
Fast pitch softball	4	225,638
Soccer	5	149,053
Tennis	6	136,919
Cross country	7	116,221
Swimming & diving	8	93,545
Field hockey	9	51,092
Slow pitch softball	10	42,884

SOURCE: National Federation (1993).

with friends, to be part of a team, to experience excitement, to receive awards, to win, and to become more physically fit. Of these reasons, "to have fun" appears to be the most predominant reason children want to be involved in sport (Gill, Gross, & Huddleston, 1983; Sapp & Haubenstricker, 1978). Nevertheless, the idea of having fun can mean different things to different individuals. Said differently, what is enjoyable for one may not be enjoyable to another. For this reason, researchers have begun to study the underlying factors that affect enjoyment of sport.

Take, for example, a large-scale study conducted by Wankel and Kreisel (1985). In their study, 822 soccer, baseball, and hockey participants between 7 and 14 years of age were surveyed (10-item inventory) to determine why they enjoyed sports. Three sports groupings were employed because another purpose was to determine if reasons for enjoyment differed across sports. Results indicated that the top four enjoyment factors (improving skills, testing abilities against others, excitement of the game, and personal accomplishment—i.e., intrinsic factors) were consistent across all three sports groups. Of moderate importance were the social factors regarding "being on a team" and "being with friends." The extrinsic factors, which included "getting awards" and "pleasing others," were consistently selected as the least important factors for sports enjoyment. Also of interest was the finding that "winning the game" was ranked eighth in the list of ten factors.

Based on these findings, Wankel and Kreisel offer the following suggestions:

> Emphasis should be on involvement, skill development, and enjoyment of doing the skills. Winning and receiving rewards for playing, aspects that are frequently given considerable emphasis by parents, coaches, and the media, are of secondary importance to the participant's enjoyment and accordingly should not be heavily emphasized. The establishment of rigid schedules and elimination play-offs to declare winners is a questionable practice if the criterion is to provide enjoyment to all participants. . . . Each child should be provided an opportunity to develop his or her skills, be provided with a reasonable challenge, and be afforded an opportunity for personal accomplishment and satisfaction (1985, pp. 62–63).

The most comprehensive findings to date are from a study sponsored by the Athletic Footwear Association and conducted through the Youth Sports Institute at Michigan State University under the direction of Martha Ewing and Vern Seefeldt (Athletic Footwear Association, 1990). This survey sampled more than 10,000 youth in 11 American cities. Table 15-2 shows the 10 most important reasons a child chose to participate in their favorite sport. The data taken along with earlier findings consistently show that children want to participate to have "fun" and that "winning" ranks last or very near.

PARTICIPATION: COMPETENCE MOTIVATION THEORY

Other researchers have made convincing arguments that participation motivation can be linked to existing theoretical models. One model that is frequently mentioned is Harter's model of perceived competence (Harter, 1978, 1982). According to her theory, individuals are motivated to be successful in various achievement areas such as sports (physical), academics (cognitive), or human relationships (social). When performance attempts are successful, the in-

TABLE 15-2 The 10 Most Important Reasons I Play My Best School Sport

1. To have fun
2. To improve my skills
3. To stay in shape
4. To do something I'm good at
5. For the excitement of competition
6. To get exercise
7. To play as part of a team
8. For the challenge of competition
9. To learn new skills
10. To win

Sample: 2,000 boys and 1,900 girls, grade 7–12, who identified a "best" school sport. Answers above were among 25 responses rated on a 5-point scale.
SOURCE: Athletic Footwear Association (1990).

dividual experiences a positive effect. This perception of successful competence motivates the individual to continue participation. Likewise, the theory predicts that individuals low in perceived competence will discontinue participation.

Scientific studies designed to test Harter's theory within a sport context have been fairly successful. For example, Roberts, Kleiber, and Duda (1981) found that youth sport participants scored higher in both perceived cognitive and perceived physical competence than did nonparticipants. Likewise, Feltz and Petlichkoff (1983) reported that current sport participants scored higher on perceived physical competence than did dropouts. However, more recent work (Ulrich, 1987) failed to find a significant relationship between children in grades K–4 and perceived physical competence as measured by Harter's Perceived Competence Scale for Children (1982). Nevertheless, motor competence (as measured by the broad jump, flexed-arm hang, sit-ups, side-step test, 60-yard shuttle run, playground ball dribble, soccer ball dribble, softball repeated throw test, and soccer ball throw) was found to significantly relate to participation in organized sports programs. Furthermore, the children's perceptions of physical competence were also significantly related to their performance on the motor-competence test battery (Ulrich, 1987).

In summary, we can conclude that children participate in organized sport for a multitude of reasons. Unfortunately, children's most often stated reasons for participation (intrinsic reasons) do not always coincide with the program goals established by the adult leadership.

WHY CHILDREN DROP OUT OF SPORTS

Gould (1987) has estimated that about 35 percent of the millions of children who participate in a youth sport will withdraw from the program within any given year. However, contradictory to popular belief, most children do not drop out of a sport because of excessive stress. Instead, empirical evidence suggests that most sports drop-outs do so because

of interpersonal problems (e.g., dislike the coach) or to pursue other leisure activities (Dishman, 1989). Most often the other activity is another sport. For example, when interviewing swimming drop-outs, Gould and colleagues (1982) reported that 80 percent of the youngsters had either reentered or planned to reenter a sport activity. Likewise, Klint and Weiss (1986) found that of 37 gymnasts who dropped out of participation, 35 reentered gymnastics or another sport (cited in Gould & Petlichkoff, 1988). For this reason, sports psychologists recommend that we use caution in interpreting the term "sport dropout" (Gould & Petlichkoff, 1988). Obviously, there is a vast difference between children who withdraw from sports permanently and those who withdraw from one sport activity only to become involved in a different one. In fact, regarding the youngest competitors, frequent withdrawal from sports may signify nothing more than the child's attempt to sample many different sports before selecting the few that best meet his or her needs.

As we mentioned earlier, when sports participation is not fun, then there is a greater tendency for children to drop-out (see Table 15-3). When children were asked what changes would need to be

TABLE 15-3 The 11 Most Important Reasons Children Stopped Playing a Sport

1. I lost interest.
2. I was not having fun.
3. It took too much time.
4. Coach was a poor teacher.
5. There was too much pressure (worry).
6. I wanted non-sport activity.
7. I was tired of it.
8. Needed more study time.
9. Coach played favorites.
10. The sport was boring.
11. There was an over-emphasis on winning.

Sample: 2,700 boys and 3,100 girls who said they had recently stopped playing a school or non-school sport. Answers above were among 30 responses rated on a 5-point scale.
SOURCE: Athletic Footwear Association (1990).

TABLE 15-4 The 6 Most Important Changes Children Would Make in a Sport that Was Previously Dropped

---

"I would play again if . . ."

BOYS

1. Practices were more fun.
2. I could play more.
3. Coaches understood players better.
4. There was no conflict with studies.
5. Coaches were better teachers.
6. There was no conflict with social life.

GIRLS

1. Practices were more fun.
2. There was no conflict with studies.
3. Coaches understood players better.
4. There was no conflict with social life.
5. I could play more.
6. Coaches were better teachers.

Sample: 2,700 boys, 3,100 girls, grades 7–12, who said they had recently stopped playing a school or non-school sport. They rated 21 different responses on a five-point scale.
SOURCE: Athletic Footwear Association (1990).

made before they would once again reenter their sport, both the boys and the girls ranked as most important the need to "make practices more fun" (Athletic Footwear Association, 1990). Table 15-4 presents the six most important changes that these boys and girls would make before they are willing to reenter a sport that they had earlier dropped.

SPORT PARTICIPATION: CONTROVERSIES

Participation in sports during the childhood and adolescent years has become an American way of life. Involvement in both recreational and competitive athletics contributes significantly to the young participants' physical, social, emotional, and cognitive development. But sports participation, whether competitive or recreational, is sometimes clouded by controversial issues. This section examines several of the most frequently mentioned issues. For

ease of discussion, these controversial issues have been divided into two categories: medical and psychological.

Medical Issues

Potential physical danger is a major criticism of youth sport participation (see Table 15-5). But is this criticism warranted? And if so, are some activities more dangerous than others? Furthermore, are the injuries incurred avoidable? To help answer these important questions, we first examine injury rates of selected sports and then discuss whether the number of injuries can be reduced.

Football The American Academy of Pediatrics Committee on Sports Medicine has classified football as a *contact/collision sport*. In general, collision sports have become synonymous with physical injury. Obviously, whenever people are repeatedly running into one another, injuries will occur. But is this true for all ages and levels of play? Silverstein (1979) observed three games per week for two youth football league seasons. He found that the average overall injury rate was 15 percent. Most interesting, however, was his finding which showed that both age and weight influenced rate of injury. For instance, the 8- to 11-year-old participants who weighed no more than 90 pounds experienced an overall injury rate of only 10 percent in 1977 and 14.4 percent in the following season. In contrast, the 12- and 13-year-old players who weighed up to 110 pounds experienced an injury rate of 28.3 percent in the first season studied and 13 percent in the next season. The high rate of injury experienced in 1977 was attributed to having only 12 players on the team most of the season. Nevertheless, average rate of injury was greater in this older group of children. The 14-year-old participants who weighed up to 130 pounds exhibited an average rate of 20.6 percent in 1977 (once again attributed to a small number of players on the team) and 11 percent in 1978. Rate of injury in youth tackle football is therefore relatively low in comparison to that in professional football. More specifically, the National Football

TABLE 15-5 Highlights of Common Sports Injuries in Children and Adolescents

Baseball

1. Elbow and shoulder overuse injuries are the most frequent.
2. Chronic pathologic changes in the elbow and shoulder are very uncommon before adolescence.
3. Contact and collision injuries are infrequent.
4. Deaths have resulted from cardiac damage secondary to nonpenetrating chest trauma.

Football

1. At the youth level, significant injury occurs in 10 percent of participants. The hand or wrist and knee are the most common injury sites. Fractures and sprains are the most common types of injury, and surgery is rarely required.
2. At the high school level, significant injury occurs in 12 percent to 17 percent of participants. The knee and ankle are the most common injury sites. Sprains and strains are the most common types of injury, and surgery is required for 4 percent of players.

Basketball

1. The ankle is most commonly injured.
2. Female basketball players appear to be at greater risk of developing significant knee injuries.

Wrestling

1. The preadolescent injury experience is different from that of older wrestlers.
2. High school wrestlers are most likely to sustain knee sprains, back strains, and shoulder injuries.
3. "Cauliflower ears" are decreasing in frequency.
4. Surgical correction is frequently required for injuries that are sustained.

Soccer

1. Youth soccer is associated with a low rate of injury (2 percent–5 percent).
2. Adolescent players have a higher rate injury (6 percent–9 percent).
3. The ankle, knee, and forefoot are most often injured.
4. Significant knee sprains are not uncommon.
5. Repeated heading of the soccer ball may cause brain injury.

Skiing

1. Children incur 22–23 percent of the total skiing injuries.
2. Metatarsal fractures, foot and ankle sprains, and lateral malleolar fractures have decreased in frequency.
3. Spiral and transverse boot top fractures are now more prevalent.
4. Significant knee injuries occur with increasing frequency as children get older.
5. Ulnar collateral ligament sprains of the thumb are common.

(continued)

TABLE 15-5 *(continued)*

Gymnastics

1. Injury rates are between 12–22 percent.
2. The lower extremity is most often injured.
3. Half the injuries are macrotraumatic and half are due to overuse syndromes.
4. Spondylolysis occurs four times more often than in the general population.

Hockey

1. Youth hockey injury rates are 2–3 percent; high school rates are 25 percent.
2. Lacerations and contusions are the most common injury.
3. Facial injuries have been significantly reduced since the use of the face mask was mandated.
4. Cervical spine injuries may be increasing.

SOURCE: Dyment (1991). Used with permission.

League has reported an average injury rate of 90 percent per year (Galton, 1980). Furthermore, this study and others (Dyment, 1991) suggest that the preadolescent athlete is at less risk for injury than is the high school, college, or professional football player.

As mentioned, these prior studies have been limited by their small sample size. More recently, however, many of the findings reported in those earlier studies have been substantiated in a large-scale study by Goldberg and colleagues (1988), who studied the injury experiences of 5128 boys between 8 and 15 years of age. Only significant injuries were studied (those restricting participation for more than 7 days). Table 15-6 highlights their findings. As in previous small-scale studies, overall injury rate was rather low (5 percent) with most injuries occurring among older and heavier participants. Unlike higher levels of play (college and professional), most significant injuries in youth football involved the upper extremity, particularly the hand and wrist. Because a significant number of major injuries (those restricting participation for more than 21 days) occurred to members of kickoff and punt-return teams, the researchers suggested that youth football administrators consider modifying the sport to eliminate this dangerous aspect of the game. They also recommended that steps be taken to reduce the number of injuries caused by direct impact with the football helmet (18.4 percent). Their recommendations include requiring participants to wear helmets constructed with a soft padded top and having coaches reevaluate the instructional methods used to teach blocking and tackling. This latter recommendation was offered earlier by Silverstein (1979), who found that *spearing*, an outlawed tackling technique in which the helmet is used as a weapon, accounted for approximately 30 percent of the injuries reported in his study. Indeed, since spearing was outlawed in 1976, the number of catastrophic injuries has been greatly reduced. In fact, the number of high school fatalities as a result of football injury has decreased from 20 in 1965 to 4 in 1985 (Mueller & Blyth, 1986). This finding emphasizes the need for coaches to teach their players the correct technique for executing sport skills.

Soccer Soccer is one of America's fastest-growing sports. In the United States the U.S. Soccer Federation has reported that 1.5 million youth under 17 years of age played in their league in 1989. From a more global perspective, the Soccer Industry Council's 1990 estimates suggest a soccer participation rate of more than 6 million youth under 12 years of age (cited in Kibler, 1993). Like football, soccer is also classified as a *contact/collision sport*. (American Academy of Pediatrics, 1988). Even

TABLE 15-6   Injuries in Youth Football

Injury Rate by Weight (kg)/(years):	N	% Injury Rate	No. of Injuries
49.5–67.5/12–15	177	9.6	(17)
40.5–60.8/11–14	1,160	8.4	(97)
36–51.8/10–13	1,489	5.8	(86)
29.3–45/9–12	1,610	2.7	(44)
22.5–38.3/8–11	692	1.9	(13)
Overall injury rate	5,128	5.0	(257)
Most-prone injury sites:			
Hand/wrist		27.6	
Knee		18.7	
Shoulder/humerus		11.3	
Most common injuries:			
Fractures		35.0	(90)
Epiphyseal fractures		5.1	(13)
Sprains		24.5	(63)
Contusions		16.7	(43)
Strains		7.0	(18)
Injury rates by position:			
Quarterbacks/running backs		30.4	
Defensive linemen		22.2	
Offensive linemen		12.8	
Linebackers		10.9	
Kickoff/punt-return team members		7.4	
Defensive backs		5.8	
Receivers		2.7	
Occurrence of major injuries (players restricted for more than 21 days):			
Kickoff/punt-return team members		63.2	
Quarterback/running backs		44.9	
Causes of injuries:			
No unusual occurrence		58.6	(150)
Helmet		18.4	(47)
Contact after ball whistled dead		8.6	(22)
Contact during conditioning drills		8.2	(21)

Source: Goldberg et al. (1988).

though we know that the overall injury rate among professional soccer players is about one injury per season, less is known about the injury rate and type of injuries to young children and adolescents. Nilsson and Roaas (1978) examined all injuries that occurred during the 1975 and 1977 Norway Cup. During these two tournaments, 25,000 players between 11 and 18 years competed in 2987 matches. The medical personnel on duty at the tournaments saw a total of 1343 injuries including cases of illnesses not directly related to soccer participation. An analysis of data revealed that girls were twice as likely to be injured as boys. Additionally, Nilsson and Roaas noted that injury rates per 1000 hours of play were greater in the final rounds of play than during the qualifying rounds. For instance, during qualifying rounds the rate of injury for boys and girls was 21.5 and 39.5, respectively. However, during the final rounds of play, rate of injury increased to 27.5 for boys and 53.5 for girls. Nilsson and Roaas suspect that the girls' higher rate of injury was partly caused by their lower level of skill and training. Fortunately, most injuries were minor. Contusions (36 percent), sprains and strains (20 percent), and skin abrasions (39 percent) made up a majority of the reported injuries. Only 3.5 percent of the injuries were fractures. Because 9 out of every 10 injured players missed less than 1 day of play, the authors believe that young soccer players are participating in a fairly safe activity. American studies support this contention. Shively, Grana, and Ellis (1981) reported an injury rate of only 8.5 per 1000 participants among high school boys and 20 per 1000 participants among high school girls.

In a most recent study, Kibler (1993) examined injuries to both preadolescent and adolescent boys and girls between 12–19 years of age who participated in soccer. Injury data were gathered over a 4-year period from individuals participating in the Bluegrass Invitational Soccer Tournament (1987–1990). An injury was defined as any condition that required a player to be removed from the game or miss a game or anyone who received treatment at the tournament's medical facility. Table 15-7 summaries the findings that represent data collected over 480 games, resulting in 74,000 player hours. Over

TABLE 15-7 Injuries in Youth Soccer

Site of Injury	
Thigh	21.0%
Knee	15.8%
Ankle	13.0%
Foot	12.8%
Torso	10.9%
Head & Neck	8.05

Type of Injury	
Contusions	32.0%
Muscle strains	24.5%
Sprains	21.8%
Fractures	9.0%
Heat illness	4.5%
Concussions	1.5%

Cause of Injury	
Person-to-person contact	43.0%
Repetitive overload	20.4%
Contact with ground	17.5%
Contact with objects (goal posts, etc.)	6.5%

Effect of Injury on Playing Status	
Missed one game	38.5%
Missed remaining games	19.3%

Source: Kibler (1993).

this course there were 179 injuries reported. This number of injuries represents an injury rate of just 23.8 for every 10,000 player hours.

These results support findings from other studies that suggest that youth soccer is a relatively safe activity. In fact, 37 percent of the reported injuries required no major treatment while 43.7 percent of injuries did require medical treatment. Only 11.8 percent of the injuries required hospital evaluation.

These results lend insight into ways in which soccer injuries could possibly be reduced. Since most injuries were caused by person to person contact, closer officiating, pregame warnings regarding inappropriate playing tactics (take downs, hacking, etc.), and coaching within the spirit of the rules should all be emphasized. Furthermore, protective padding on goal posts and the removal of all sideline objects (chairs, benches, water coolers) should further reduce soccer injuries.

Downhill Skiing Even though skiing injuries are generally not the result of making contact with another person, this activity has still been classified by the American Academy of Pediatrics (1988) as a *limited contact/impact sport*. With skiing, injuries generally result when contact is made with the ground or some stationary object. To make matters worse, this contact frequently occurs at a high rate of speed. A 6-year study that Johnson and colleagues (1980) conducted suggests that there are approximately 500,000 skiing injuries per year in the United States (cited in Blitzer et al., 1984). These injuries, however, are not equally distributed across either age or gender. For example, when Garrick and Requa (1979) studied injury patterns in children and adolescent skiers, they found girls more prone to injury than boys. Furthermore, injury rate increased steadily with an increase in age up to 13 years. The lowest rate of injury was for children younger than 10 years. Rate of injury leveled off between 13 and 15 years of age and declined slightly through age 17. Of the 423 injuries reported among the 3456 participants, 51 percent of the injuries were sprains; 47 fractures (11.1 percent) were observed, and most were sustained by the 12- and 13-year-olds.

A more recent longitudinal study covering 9 years reported somewhat different findings (Blitzer et al., 1984). In this study, children younger than 11 years experienced the same rate of injury as adults. More specifically, adults obtained one injury for every 254 skier days, whereas children 10 and under obtained one injury every 253 skier days. Children between 11 and 13 years experienced the highest rate of injury: one every 151 skier days. Although these rates of injury may initially appear excessive, they are actually not when you consider that the average number of ski days per year is only 14.

Overuse Injuries *Overuse injuries* are becoming more prevalent among America's young athletes. This should come as no surprise in the light of the fact that young athletes are specializing in sports at earlier ages. Specialization generally entails intense year-round involvement. In fact, it is not uncommon for young athletes to attend sport camps that require them to train from 4 to 6 hours per day. It has also been reported that in order to become a top junior tennis player, the young athlete must practice a minimum of 8 to 15 hours per week (Wild, 1992). Perhaps even more discouraging are reports that runners as young as 4 (Jeffers, 1980) and 6 years of age (cited in Kozar & Lord, 1988) are successfully completing marathons.

Overuse injuries occur as a result of placing the child's muscular and skeletal system under repeated stress over long periods of time. This class of injury should not be taken lightly because if activity is not curtailed, permanent injury could result. In adults, overuse injuries generally involve bone (stress fractures), tendon (Achilles tendinitis), and fascia (plantar fasciitis). In children and adolescents, however, additional prone structures include physes (growth plates), cartilage of the apophyses (a site where the tendon unites with the bone), and articular cartilage (Clain & Hershman, 1989). The two most prevalent traction apophyses include Osgood-Schlatter disease (insertion of the patellar tendon at the tibial tubercle) and Sever's disease (insertion of the Achilles tendon into the calcaneous). Both diseases are most prevalent in adolescence when skeletal growth exceeds soft-tissue elongation thus causing muscle tightness about the prone site (Clain & Hershman, 1989). For these reason, young athletes should be encouraged to stretch both before and after physical activity.

Overuse injuries involving bone can result in stress fractures. The offending culprit is often the result of an abrupt change in exercise frequency and intensity. Most often the injury site is either the lower extremity or the hip. This type of injury is frequently difficult to diagnose without the use of sophisticated imagery (bone scan, etc.).

"Little League elbow" refers to a class of overuse injuries resulting from repeated forces being applied to the medial and lateral structures of the elbow. Most often the pain will occur on the elbow's medial side. As the name implies, this overuse injury is most prevalent in baseball pitchers (Gugenheim et al., 1976; Larson et al., 1976). This medical condition has led youth sport administrators to change and modify baseball rules in an attempt to protect the young athlete. Among the more important changes and modifications are the following: T-baseball, where the pitcher does not deliver the ball to the batter, is becoming more popular; some leagues no longer allow the pitcher to throw a curve ball; and most youth leagues now limit the number of innings per week that a youngster can pitch.

Because stress injuries are caused by patterns of overuse, young children should be discouraged from specializing in a particular sport during the childhood years. Instead, they should be encouraged to play several sports and even different positions within a selected sport. This way, the child is less likely to overuse a specific body part.

Are Youth Sport Injuries Avoidable? A major challenge for organizers of youth programs is to devise methods and procedures that will curtail the number of youth sport injuries. Organizers of children's sports programs need to answer two major questions: (1) Are children's sport injuries avoidable? If they are, (2) What steps can be taken to ensure a safer and healthier environment?

Although research on children's sport-related injuries is in its infancy, initial findings suggest that many injuries are avoidable. In one study, Goldberg and colleagues (1979) found that 32 of 51 sport-related injuries could have been avoided if proper precautions had been taken. These precautions included (1) wearing properly fitting safety equipment, (2) avoiding play on wet fields where footing is poor, and (3) avoiding excessive repeated movements such as those described in the section on stress injuries. Other experts believe that the number of injuries can be reduced if coaches are more attuned to the youngsters' physical and emotional state. For example, Williams (1980) found that children forced to participate in sports experience a higher rate of

injury when compared to children who want to participate. Furthermore, because many injuries occur late in a game or practice session, coaches should be aware of their players' state of fatigue.

Our search of the literature also suggests that special precautions should be taken when working with young girls of all ages and young boys 11 to 13 years old because these two populations appear to be at the greatest risk for injury. The American Academy of Pediatrics (Dyment, 1991) recommends the 10 factors listed in Table 15-8 as a means of injury prevention.

Young Athletes' Nutritional Requirements
The young athlete's nutritional requirements are essentially the same as those of any active child. The child's appetite should dictate caloric need. In general, parents should provide well-balanced meals, being sure to serve portions from each of the four basic food groups. Unfortunately, there is a problem when parents alter children's diets in an attempt to give their child a competitive edge. For example, because certain sports are organized according to weight, such as wrestling and youth football, some children have been placed on diets, even periods of fasting, so that they can compete in a lower weight class. This practice should be avoided for reasons described shortly.

TABLE 15-8 Factors to Be Considered in the Prevention of Injuries

1. Proper conditioning
2. Avoidance of excesses in training
3. Appropriate competitive environment
4. Complete resolution of a prior injury
5. Appropriate supervision
6. Rule changes
7. Instruction in correct biomechanics
8. Appropriate equipment
9. Complete preparticipation physical assessment
10. Appropriate matching of competitors

SOURCE: Dyment (1991). Used with permission.

Another nutritional concern is the use of dietary supplements, especially vitamins. Generally the body excretes any excess vitamins, but some vitamins are not readily excreted and can accumulate in toxic levels; vitamins A and E are two vitamins that can be harmful when taken in very large doses. Dr. Nathan Smith, a well-noted pediatrician, recently reported five cases of vitamin A poisoning. In one case, parents of a young tennis player who had experienced vitamin A poisoning repeatedly kept putting the child back on the vitamin (Barnes, 1979), believing that large doses of this vitamin would give their child a competitive advantage. Vitamin supplements are *not* necessary when the young athlete is eating balanced meals.

Making Weight Several youth sports match teams for competition on the basis of body weight. The primary intent of using this method is to better ensure the safety of those involved and provide a well-balanced competitive athletic contest. The intent is positive, but some adults have used unacceptable practices to give their child a competitive edge. One such negative practice is using unacceptable means to reduce the child's body weight so the child can compete in a lower weight class. The most widely used approach is depleting the body of its water content by having the child exercise in a sauna; not letting the young athlete drink water, even to the extent of requiring the child to spit into a cup instead of swallowing; administering diuretics; and requiring the child to exercise while wearing a rubber suit. Reducing body weight through rapid dehydration is extremely dangerous and should never be done. Without adequate body fluids (water), the cells, urine output, blood volume, and sweating mechanisms cannot function properly. A 3 percent weight loss of body fluids can decrease physical performance; a 5 percent loss can cause apparent signs of heat exhaustion; a 7 percent loss can cause hallucinations; a 10 percent loss can lead to heat stroke and circulatory collapse.

The young athlete also should not be encouraged to fast. Fasting withholds the vital food substances needed to ensure proper growth during these formative years. In addition, bulimic behaviors are now being uncovered as a means of further reducing body weight (Oppliger, Landry, Foster, & Lambrecht, 1993).

Psychological Issues

Critics of youth sports frequently express concern regarding the young athlete's ability to handle stressful situations. Limited amounts of stress have been shown to improve motor performance, but critics believe that too much competitive stress can lead to a multitude of negative behavioral, psychological, and even health-related outcomes. Are our young athletes being exposed to too much competitive stress? If so, what are the outcomes of this competitive stress? Furthermore, if too much stress is present, how can it be reduced?

Before answering these important questions, we first define what we mean by the term *stress*. Stress is generally viewed as an unpleasant emotional state. Passer (1982) developed a four-stage model that precisely illustrates how this unpleasant state is evoked. The four stages are situation, appraisal, emotional response, and consequences. First, the stress process is evoked whenever a person is placed in a demanding situation and the person views the outcome of the situation as being important. The person then appraises the situation in an attempt to determine if he or she can meet its demands. A young boy may become threatened and feel anxious before the start of an athletic contest because he wants to perform well but is not sure that he has the motor skills necessary for success. Whenever a person is threatened, emotional responses become evident. According to Passer these emotional responses are made up of not only physiological components but also cognitive-attentional components. For instance, the boy may become so preoccupied with worrying about the outcome of performance that he does not pay attention to important task-related cues that are necessary for successful performance. Passer's fourth and final stage, consequences, brings us back to one of our original questions, namely, "What are the outcomes of competitive stress?" As mentioned previously, when sport participation loses its appeal children will frequently either withdraw from the disliked activity to pursue a more enjoyable activity or, in some cases, withdraw permanently from sport.

Stress—Another Viewpoint   Proponents of youth sports programs do not argue with the fact that excessive stress is not beneficial. However, they do argue that youth sport participation is by no means the only stressful situation young people encounter in their lives. The proponents' view is best supported by Simon and Martens's work (1979). These two researchers examined the level of precompetitive *state anxiety* among 468 boys who took part in various youth sport programs and 281 boys who competed in other achievement-oriented activities, including a softball game played in a physical education class, a general school test, group competition within a band, and a band solo competition. As illustrated in Figure 15-1, the researchers found

the greatest amount of precompetitive state anxiety among the band solo contestants. Furthermore, among the 11 sport and nonsport activities examined in the study, state anxiety was greatest in the individual activities. Passer wrote, "This is somewhat ironic because the popular media and youth sport critics typically focus on team sports when discussing or illustrating the stressful nature of athletic competition" (Simon & Martens, 1982, p. 167). In fact, on average participating in team sports was no more stressful than taking a paper and pencil test.

Reducing Competitive Stress   Undoubtedly, children will experience varying degrees of stress from participation in sports. However, steps can be taken to reduce the likelihood of this stress becoming excessive. One key is to change something about the sport so that success will occur more frequently than failure. For example, in T-baseball, the offensive demand requiring that the baseball be struck off a stationary batting tee obviously increases the

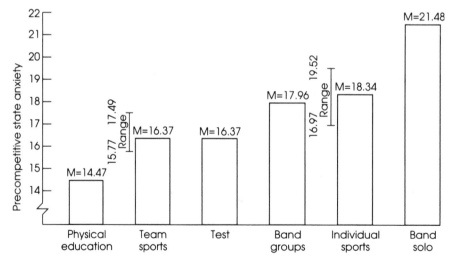

FIGURE 15-1   Children's precompetitive state anxiety in 11 sport and nonsport activities. The precompetitive state anxiety scale ranges from 10 to 30. The category labeled team sport includes football, hockey, baseball, and basketball while the category labeled individual sports includes swimming, gymnastics, and wrestling.

Source: Adapted from Simon and Martens (1979).

probability that the young athlete will not strike out. In fact, an investigation by Isaacs (1984) found a strikeout rate of only 4 percent among young T-baseball players. Furthermore, according to Isaacs (1981), children's basketball shooting performance can be improved by lowering the basketball goal and by using a smaller basketball. In short, when children experience a fair amount of success, they will develop more self-confidence about their ability to meet the demands of their sport, and in turn they will feel less threatened when confronted with the demands.

A second way to instill self-confidence and thus reduce stress is by skill training. Youth sport personnel, particularly coaches, should spend more of their practice time teaching motor skills and less time scrimmaging. Furthermore, when scrimmaging is incorporated, the focus should be to reduce performance uncertainty by practicing potential situations that may arise during a competitive contest. Coaches who adhere to these two practices are helping their young players develop self-confidence in their ability not only to meet the physical demands of the sport but also to handle efficiently most situations that may occur during competitive play. Anxiety is reduced whenever the uncertainty surrounding an event is removed or reduced. Furthermore, research indicates that children who perceive themselves as competent are less threatened and actually perform better during the contest (Feltz, 1984). Thus, it is essential that the coach help the players develop an attitude of "I can do it."

To further reduce competitive stress, the outcome of the contest (winning or losing) should be placed into perspective. There should not be too much emphasis on winning the game. Recall that the stress process is evoked when the participant views the outcome of the situation as important. To a degree, when there is an increase in the importance of the outcome, there is also an accompanying increase in stress. Thus, other influential people can help young athletes by not overemphasizing winning. For instance, some young children may feel that they have disappointed their parents or coach if they have not played well. This is wrong. Parents and coaches should make it clear that the outcome of an athletic contest in no way changes their attitude of love toward the child.

Finally, self-imposed stress can be reduced by helping each child set realistic goals. Realistic goals are those that motivate the young athlete to do his or her personal best and to recognize self-limitations (Martens et al., 1981). Some children set their performance goals so high that they are impossible to achieve. To keep this from happening, Paulson (1980) suggested that before the season begins, each participant writes out what she or he wants to accomplish in the upcoming season. These objectives should focus primarily on individual improvement, not team performance. For example, one child may want to improve his batting average by 20 points over last year's average or perhaps commit five fewer errors. If team objectives are established, they should be very general, such as "We will score 15 more runs this season than we did last season." When realistic goals are established at the beginning of the season, children can still feel like winners regardless of their team's win/loss record. According to Paulson, the term "winning" needs to be redefined. "Instead of requiring that it involve beating someone else, the new definition of winning focuses on the learning and improvement an individual or team experiences in a season" (1980, p. 25).

YOUTH SPORT COACHING

Without a doubt, a youth sport program is only as good as its adult leaders. With appropriate leadership, the youth sport experience can significantly foster young children's growth and development. In this section, we examine more closely the coaching profession, paying particular attention to volunteer coaches. In addition, we will address the controversial issue regarding the education and certification of coaches. Finally, guidelines for effective coaching will be explored.

Who's Coaching Our Children?

Of the approximate 3.5 million coaches in the United States, about 2.5 million are serving as volunteers (Martens, 1988). A logical question is "What motivates so many individuals to give of their valuable time and energy to serve in this voluntary role?" Researchers from the United States and Canada have attempted to design studies that may shed light on this question. For example, in one Canadian study volunteer coaches indicated that the most important reasons for their involvement included personal enjoyment, skill development of players, character development of players, and personal challenge (Hansen & Gauthier, 1988). However, some individuals involved with this Canadian study believe that an even stronger motivator was the involvement of the coach's child in the league. Indeed, 54 percent of the Canadian coaches surveyed had one or two children participating in the hockey league in which they coached. Similar trends have been reported in the United States.

A Need for Educating Coaches

Even though most youth sport coaches have children's best interests in mind, the sad fact is that most coaches do not have the training necessary for providing an optimal youth sport experience. For instance, a 1978 Joint Legislative Study Committee from the state of Michigan found that only 11 percent of the youth sport coaches surveyed had a degree in physical education or recreation and that only 9 percent called coaching their main occupation (cited in Brown, 1982). More recent estimates suggest that less than 20 percent of all coaches have received any formal training in coaching (Kimiecik, 1988). Conn and Razor (1989) argue that school and youth organization administrators have both a legal and moral responsibility to ensure that those individuals who work with our youth are qualified to serve in such a capacity. When unqualified individuals are awarded coaching responsibilities, the likelihood of litigation significantly increases. Only in those states that have established criteria for coaches has the number of injuries and subsequent lawsuits decreased (Conn & Razor, 1989).

Current Coaching Certification Requirements

At present, national standards for the certification of coaches do not exist within the United States. Instead, in those states where some sort of certifi-

cation is required it is frequently left up to individual school districts or youth organizations. These organizations will usually provide only minimal in-service training. A recent exception to this rule is the state of Florida. More specifically, the Florida Department of Education has mandated that a coaching certification plan be in effect in all school districts by 1989 (Kimiecik, 1988). This bold effort is obviously needed in more states. Take, for example, a recent national survey that revealed that only 35 percent of the states have any required certification standards for coaches (Sabock & Chandler-Garvin, 1986). Furthermore, often these standards are less than comprehensive. In Connecticut and Rhode Island, for example, teachers must simply possess a valid first-aid certificate in order to receive coaching certification (Sisley & Wiese, 1987). This finding is particularly disheartening when one considers that game officials of interscholastic contests are required to be certified but the coaches who work with the children on a daily basis are not.

Arguments Against Mandatory Coaching Certification

As mentioned earlier, there has been a large increase in the number of children participating in both interscholastic and community/agency-sponsored youth sport programs. Unfortunately, this positive trend in participation is not without a downside. With increased participation comes a need to increase sport offerings. This in turn creates a greater demand for additional coaches. In short, the demand for coaches now exceeds supply. Those who argue against mandatory coaching certification express concern that making certification mandatory would subsequently cause many volunteers to withdraw their service, thus creating a further shortage of coaches. Consequently, many youth sport programs may have to be eliminated. Others argue that to require coaching certification would be too expensive. In turn, this financial burden may force some youth sport leagues to fold. Lopiano (1986) argues that this view is short sighted and analogous to saying that one technique of reducing the high cost of medical care would be to eliminate certification of doctors and hospitals.

Fred Engh, president of the National Youth Sports Coaches Association, believes mandatory coaching certification would have a positive effect on the number of individuals willing to volunteer to coach our children. He believes that there are many citizens who would be willing to coach but choose not to because they do not feel qualified to coach (cited in Kimiecik, 1988). Making coaching certification mandatory would require the availability of coaching education, which should increase the pool of individuals willing to serve the youth sport community.

Current Coaching Certification Programs

Within recent years a growing number of organizations have been developed for the purpose of providing educational programs to prospective coaches. Graduates of these educational programs learn how to teach motor skills to children, organize a practice, physically train children, prevent and recognize sport injuries, and communicate with and motivate young athletes. Educational information is generally conveyed through videotapes, printed materials, and small-group discussions. The names and addresses of seven of these organizations are presented in Table 15-9.

Evaluating Coaching Effectiveness

Player-coach interactions can significantly influence the lives of children. In essence, the coach serves as a role model affecting not only the child's skill development but also his or her attitudes and values. For this reason, it is important for youth sport coaches to have a better understanding of their impact on the young athlete. To this end, researchers from the University of Washington, Seattle, developed the *Coaching Behavioral Assessment System* (*CBAS*) (Smith, Smoll, & Hunt, 1977). This behavioral assessment instrument is designed to evaluate the behaviors of coaches in an actual game setting. Briefly, the instrument is used to assess two classes

of behaviors: reactive behaviors and spontaneous behaviors. As illustrated in Table 15-10 (page 338), reactive behaviors refer to the coach's reactions to player behaviors such as desirable performance, mistakes, and misbehaviors, while spontaneous behaviors refer to game-related or game-irrelevant behaviors initiated by the coach.

TABLE 15-9 Organizations Dedicated to the Advancement of Knowledge Through Coaching Certification

American Sport Education Program
    National Center
    Box 5076
    Champaign, IL 61820
    (800) 342-5457

National Youth Sports Coaches Association
    2611 Old Okeechobee Road
    West Palm Beach, FL 33409
    (407) 684-1141

North American Youth Sport Institute
    Jack Hutslar, Executive Director
    4985 Oak Garden Drive
    Kernersville, NC 27284
    (910) 784-4926

National Association for Sports and Physical Education
    1900 Association Drive
    Reston, VA 22091
    (703) 476-3410

National High School Athletic Coaches Association
    Box 1808
    Ocala, FL 32678
    (904) 622-3660

National Federation of Interscholastic Coaches
        Association
    11724 Plaza Circle
    Kansas City, MO 64195
    (816) 464-5400

Canada's National Coaching Certification Program
    333 River Road
    Ottawa, Ontario
    Canada
    (416) 495-3427

To use the CBAS, unannounced observers using a time sampling procedure code the behaviors of the coach being observed. Analysis of raw data can include percentage of behaviors across all game observations or the rate of behaviors falling in each category per unit of time. The developers of the instrument suggest using the percentage measure when studying baseball coaches and the rate per unit of time measure when studying basketball coaches (Smoll & Smith, 1984).

Guidelines for Effective Coaching

Research results acquired through studies using the Coaching Behavioral Assessment System have proven instrumental in the development of behavioral guidelines for coaches' interactions with players. Not only are these guidelines useful to the coach, but parents of prospective young athletes can also use these guidelines as a screening device in order to select the best coach to work with their child. These behavioral guidelines are presented in Table 15-11.

RIGHTS OF YOUNG ATHLETES

Throughout this chapter we have described and recommended various ways in which the youth sport experience can be enhanced in order that all involved may experience the joy of sport to its fullest. To this end, we recommend that all youth sport leaders ascribe and uphold the principles outlined in Table 15-12. This document *Bill of Rights for Young Athletes*, was written to protect young athletes from adult exploitation (Thomas, 1977).

In a further attempt to protect young athletes, various organizations have developed position statements regarding recommended practices for children's athletic endeavors. One of the most prestigious organizations, American Academy of Pediatrics (AAP), has been very active and vocal in its quest to improve the youth sport experience. Table 15-13 lists the titles of policy statements pertinent to children in sport. To obtain copies of these policy statements, write the AAP at the address given at the bottom of the table.

SUMMARY

The number of young athletes participating in organized youth sport programs continues to grow. Researchers estimate that more than 30 million children between 6 and 16 years old now participate in nonschool sports programs, for several reasons: greater participation at younger ages, greater female involvement, greater involvement in nontraditional activities, and greater participation by disabled individuals.

Children participate in sport for a number of reasons, but the most often cited reason is "to have fun." Researchers consistently find that children participate for intrinsic reasons (fun, to be part of a group, etc.) not extrinsic reasons (e.g., trophies).

Contrary to popular belief, most youth sport injuries are minor, primarily simple contusions, sprains, and strains. In general, girls tend to be at greater risk of injury than boys; this difference in rate of injury has been attributed to the young girls' lower level of skill and training. In an attempt to reduce the number of youth sport injuries, authorities agree that young children should be encouraged to play many different sports during their formative years. Children who do specialize in one activity year-round tend to be at greater risk for obtaining a stress or overuse injury. When special precautions are taken, many sport injuries are avoidable.

The nutritional requirements for a young athlete are the same as for any active child. Furthermore, dietary supplements such as vitamins do not give the young athlete a competitive edge.

Some experts believe that competitive stress is the agent that causes children to discontinue sport participation at an increasingly early age. However, proponents of youth sport programs point out that activities other than sports produce stress in the lives of young children. Nevertheless, both critics and proponents of youth sport programs agree that steps can be taken to ensure that the amount of stress

TABLE 15-10 Response Categories for the Coaching Behavioral Assessment

Reactive Behaviors	
Category	Explanation
1. Desirable performance	
a. Positive reinforcement (R)	Coach gives a verbal or nonverbal sign of approval to a desired behavior.
b. Nonreinforcement (NR)	Coach exhibits no reaction to desired behavior.
2. Mistakes or errors	
a. Mistake-contingent encouragement (EM)	Coach encourages player following a mistake or error.
b. Mistake-contingent technical instruction (TIM)	Coach shows the player how the play should have been performed.
c. Punishment (P)	Coach exhibits a verbal or nonverbal negative reaction to a mistake.
d. Punitive technical instruction (TIM + P)	Coach administers TIM in a hostile manner.
e. Ignoring mistakes (IM)	Coach gives neither a positive nor a negative response to a player mistake.
3. Misbehaviors	
a. Keeping control (KC)	Coach responds to a player in order to maintain order.

Spontaneous Behaviors	
Category	Explanation
1. Game-related	
a. General technical instruction (GTI)	Coach-initiated behavior not following a mistake designed to instruct in the technique and strategies of the sport.
b. General encouragement (GE)	Spontaneous encouragement given by the coach that does not follow a mistake.
c. Organization (O)	Administrative behavior directed toward players. Example: telling players what the batting order is.
2. Game-irrelevant	
a. General communication (GC)	General interaction with players that is not related to the game.

SOURCE: Adapted from Smith, Smoll, and Hunt (1977) and Smoll and Smith (1984).

TABLE 15-11   Guidelines to Enhance the Youth Sport Experience

1. Coach should have a healthy philosophy of winning.

    a. Winning is not everything, nor the only thing.

    b. Losing a game should not be viewed as failing.

    c. Winning is not synonymous with success.

    d. Children should understand that success is found in the striving to do one's best.

2. Coaches' reactions to desirable behaviors:

    a. Be generous with positive reinforcement.

    b. Have realistic expectations of performance.

    c. Reinforce desired behaviors as quickly as possible.

    d. Reinforce effort as frequently as performance results.

3. Coaches' reactions to mistakes:

    a. Give encouragement.

    b. Give corrective instruction in a positive manner—but only if you suspect the player is not aware of the corrective information.

    c. Never punish a child for making a technical mistake.

    d. Never administer corrective instruction in a hostile manner.

4. Coaches' reactions to misbehaviors, lack of attention, and maintaining discipline:

    a. Establish team rules that are clearly understood by all.

    b. Allow player involvement in the establishment and enforcement of team rules.

    c. During the game, players should understand that all members are a part of the team, even those on the bench.

5. Coaches should initiate these behaviors:

    a. Set a good example as an adult role model.

    b. Encourage and reinforce both effort and progress.

    c. Encourage players to be supportive of one another and reinforce such behaviors.

    d. Always convey instruction in a positive manner.

    e. Always be patient and never expect more than a maximum effort from his or her athletes.

    f. Be an effective communicator.

Source: Adapted from Smoll and Smith (1984).

TABLE 15-12   Bill of Rights for Young Athletes

1. Right of the opportunity to participate in sports regardless of ability level
2. Right to participate at a level that is commensurate with each child's developmental level
3. Right to have qualified adult leadership
4. Right to participate in safe and healthy environments
5. Right of each child to share in the leadership and decision making of their sport participation
6. Right to play as a child and not as an adult
7. Right to proper preparation for participation in the sport
8. Right to an equal opportunity to strive for success
9. Right to be treated with dignity by all involved
10. Right to have fun through sport

SOURCE: Thomas (1977).

young children encounter during sport participation is reduced. Each revolves around one central theme: Improve the child's self-confidence concerning ability to meet the demands of the selected sport.

Most youth sport coaches are in a program because of their son's or daughter's involvement in the same program. Unfortunately, most of these coaches do not have the appropriate training to foster an optimal youth sports experience. Within recent years, several organizations have been formed to provide coaching education for volunteer coaches.

TABLE 15-13   American Academy of Pediatrics: Policy Statements

Risks in long-distance running for children

Competitive athletics for children of elementary school age

Sports and the child with epilepsy

Weight training and weight lifting: information for the pediatrician

Recommendations for participation in competitive sports

Infant exercise programs

Trampolines II

Physical fitness and the schools

Exercise for mentally retarded children

The asthmatic child's participation in sports and physical education

Swimming instruction for infants

Health-appraisal guidelines for day camps and residence camps

Dimethyl Sulfoxide (DMSO)

Anabolic steroids and the adolescent athlete

Atlantoaxial instability in Down syndrome

Climatic heat stress and the exercising child

Participation in boxing among children and young adults

To obtain copies, write to American Academy of Pediatrics, Publications Dept., 141 Northwest Point Blvd., Elk Grove Village, IL 60009.

KEY TERMS

Bill of Rights for Young Athletes
Coaching Behavioral Assessment System
Competence motivation theory
Contact/collision sport

Limited contact/ impact sport
Overuse injuries
Spearing
State anxiety
Stress

CHAPTER 16

MOVEMENT IN ADULTHOOD

As discussed in Chapter 1, motor development is the study of the changes in motor behavior over the lifespan, the processes that underlie these changes, and the factors that affect them. Although this definition is widely accepted, generally it is not practically applied. Motor development traditionally has been a field of study in which childhood is the major emphasis. Adolescence occasionally has been examined; movement in adulthood, seldom. Most motor developmentalists readily admit to an expertise in childhood movement but relative ignorance about the motor changes and related factors of adulthood.

The overall omission of adulthood in the study of human development has not been confined to motor development. In fact, developmentalists in general have tended to primarily investigate children and adolescents, studying adulthood only minimally or not at all. Occasional references are made to the cessation of development once adulthood is attained. And, as discussed in Chapter 2, Piaget, perhaps the most famous of all developmentalists, terminated his theory of cognitive development well before the onset of adulthood.

Adulthood has also been excluded from discussion in many motor development textbooks (Corbin, 1980; Cratty, 1986; Gallahue, 1989; Keogh & Sugden, 1985; Thomas, 1984; Williams, 1983; Zaichowsky, Zaichowsky, & Martinek, 1980). These are unfortunate trends because, as we clearly saw in preceding chapters, development does not cease once people attain adulthood.

The traditional infatuation with the study of childhood is somewhat understandable, however. From a researcher's point of view, examining a child's rapidly changing behavior is much more immediately gratifying than observing the slower process of change that accompanies adult behavior. Additionally, although children's relatively short attention spans sometime make them less than desirable subjects, there is much more positive popular reinforcement for the child developmentalists versus those who study adulthood, no doubt partially due to ageism. As discussed in Chapter 3, ageism is the negative view many people have concerning advancing age and the elderly in general. Our own fear of the aging process may become so severe that we reject or avoid everything associated with aging, including old people and information concerning old people.

Another reason for the infatuation with the study of childhood rather than the latter periods of the lifespan is the presumption that research findings concerning children will be more practical and important than findings from the study of adult development. Many child development findings are believed to have direct practical implications for such critical areas as childrearing practice or educational curriculum or methodology. The findings from the study of adulthood, however, have traditionally lacked such obvious potential for much practical application.

However, in recent years the awareness of the public and researchers concerning adulthood has changed drastically. The potential societal problems that "baby boomers" have created have become a public issue. Because such a large segment of the population of the United States was born between 1948 and 1964 we must prepare ourselves for the potential societal dilemma when the baby boomers reach late adulthood.

Experts estimate that approximately 10 percent of Americans were 65 year old and over in 1980. That number rose to 12.5 percent in 1986 and is expected to be 16.5 percent by the year 2020. Compared to the current percentages, the number will have nearly doubled by 2040 when the percentage will be approximately 20-25 percent (Hagberg, 1994). As indicated in Chapter 1, the over-65 age group is the only group to have shown a consistent increase in their percentage (census figures were not reported for older age groups). However, as indicated by the figures provided by Ubell (1984), it is expected that the over-85 age group will have increased by almost six times by the year 2010.

In fact, as Table 16-1 reveals, in 2040 there will be almost as many women over 85 as there are presently men over 65. Our preparation for this inevitable occurrence should be a logical approach to ensure older adults every possible chance of maintaining a quality life through their old age. Equally important, however, is our need to advance our knowledge concerning adulthood to learn to reduce

TABLE 16-1   Projected increase of Older Americans Through the Year 2040

Year	Millions of Americans Over 65		
	All	Women	Men
1980	26.3	15.8	10.5
2000	36.1	21.8	14.3
2040	68.4	39.9	28.5

Year	Millions of Americans Over 85		
	All	Women	Men
1980	2.3	1.6	0.7
2000	5.1	3.7	1.4
2040	13.3	9.1	4.2

Source: Ubell (1984).

both the older adult's unnecessary dependence on society and the financial drain that could be a result of that dependence. No doubt this vital and practical application of our knowledge of adulthood will also lead to an improved quality (and perhaps quantity) of life for us all. Increased knowledge in all areas of development, including motor development, will help us enhance the quality of life for all ages of adults.

This chapter discusses the trends in movement behavior in adulthood. Those areas of movement in adulthood that have been investigated in some depth are emphasized. As mentioned, there is much less information about adults than children. However, one area of motor development in adults that has been examined extensively is balance, postural sway, and the incidence of falls.

BALANCE, POSTURAL SWAY, AND FALLS

Because many investigators believe that the incidence of falls increases with age, *balance* in adulthood has been studied considerably to determine its role in the etiology of falling among older adults. Balance, which is essential for daily tasks and most movement pursuits, gradually becomes centrally controlled during childhood. In other words, many balance behaviors become somewhat automatic as a child becomes an adult. However, this process reverses itself in late adulthood as balance gradually begins to require greater conscious effort than it had previously in life (Woollacott, Shumway-Cook, & Nasher, 1982).

Research on adults, especially older adults, and postural control are often complicated by the researcher's definition of "elderly" and the failure of researchers to adequately separate healthy older subjects from those with a pathological condition (Woollacott, 1989). This may explain why research in this area often yields contradictory findings. For example, some studies have shown minimal change in the function of the neural substructure of postural control; others show a severe decline. Balance differences are less likely to be seen between young and older adults in research that has controlled for subjects' pathological conditions (Woollacott, 1989).

From late childhood or early adolescence through approximately 60 years of age static control of posture improves. After age 60 decrements generally appear to the point that people over 80 may exhibit postural control like children from 6 to 9 years old. Nevertheless, older and younger adults tend to have similar automatic postural muscle responses when their balance is perturbed, though the efficiency of activating the system of older adults may decline. Further decrements are noted when older adults are deprived of certain forms of sensory information. For example, when somatosensory and visual information is incongruent with postural sway, older adults may lose balance completely. This may be a function of declining sensory systems in some older adults. Research has shown that many balance related systems like vision, joint position, and vestibular senses decline with age (Woollacott, 1989). However, as we noted earlier, this research must be interpreted cautiously because of potential confounding of factors.

In the study of balance in adulthood, the magnitude of a person's body sway while standing is often used to indicate balance ability (Shephard, 1978). Overstall and associates (1977) examined the body sway of subjects 60 to 96 years old. These researchers also gathered information about the frequency and type of falls the subjects experienced, for comparison with similar information gathered about younger adult subjects. *Postural sway* was determined to increase with age and was found to be higher in female subjects of all ages. This finding as supported by Hasselkus and Shambes's earlier research (1975). They examined women in early and late adulthood in an upright stance and an upright forward-leaning position. According to this 1975 research, balance control probably declines as the central nervous system's capacity to control movement diminishes. Specifically, the control of balance may be impeded by the reduction of the number of cells in the cerebellum and the brain stem and a decreased capacity for using proprioceptive information. In other words, the information received about the position of various body parts is less accurate, inhibiting the ability for precise body control (Shephard, 1978). The large amount of postural sway in female subjects has been attributed to their reduced muscle mass per body weight relative to the males'. The decreasing balance ability was believed to contribute to the increasing number of falls as well as the older adults' increased inability to avoid the fall once the fall started (Overstall et al., 1977). Balance is recovered with less speed and efficiency in later adulthood than in earlier periods of the lifespan (Woollacott, Shumway-Cook, & Nasher, 1982).

In Overstall's research, the number of people claiming to be plagued by falls increased throughout adulthood, to a high of 43 percent of the women and 21 percent of the men in late adulthood. Poorer eyesight, increased medication, and changing walking patterns have also been cited as potential contributors to the increasing rate of falling. The specific walking characteristic believed to contribute to falling was older adults' tendency to gradually decrease the height of the foot raise during walking. As discussed in the following section, reduced foot raise has been noted in research on the walking patterns of older adults. Table 16-2 summarizes adult balance, sway, and falling characteristics.

Table 16-2 Important Findings for Balance, Postural Sway, and Falling in Adulthood

- Postural sway increases with age (Overstall et al., 1977).
- Postural sway is higher in females throughout adulthood (Hasselkus & Shambes, 1975; Overstall et al., 1977).
- With increasing age, the adult receives less accurate information concerning positions of the body parts because the number of cells in the cerebellum and brain stem decreases (Shephard, 1978).
- The number of falls increases with age (Overstall et al., 1977).
- Balance is recovered with less speed and adroitness as a person ages (Woollacott, Shumway-Cook, & Nasher, 1982).
- Reduced visual capability, increased medication, and lower foot raise during walking also contribute to the increased number of falls in adulthood.

WALKING PATTERNS OF ADULTHOOD

Although there has been very little research into typical adult trends for most movement patterns, the walking pattern or *gait* has been considerably investigated. For example, Aniansson (1980) determined that the norm for adult walking speed in Sweden was approximately 1.4 meters per second. However, when specifically examining adults older than 70, she noted a walking speed of 1.2 meters per second for males and 1.1 meters per second for females, an indication that older adults walk much slower than the norm. Step height, as mentioned earlier relative to increased rate of falling, also decreased in these older adult subjects. The women in particular had difficulty executing a 40-centimeter step; this difficulty was even more prominent when a 50-centimeter step was used.

To develop a simple, inexpensive, and reliable means of analyzing gait, Murray, Drought, and Kory (1964) conducted a more detailed investigation into the gait of adults 20 to 65 years old. Murray and associates also hoped that the establishment of normal ranges for several components of walking would enable future investigators to determine abnormalities in individual gait patterns.

Murray, Drought, and Kory photographed their subjects using a speed graphic camera, which takes a series of photos in a predetermined short period of time. Measurements were then taken that enabled the investigators to determine such factors as:

- duration of entire walking cycle
- duration of stance and leg swing
- length and width of strides and foot angles
- amount of pelvic tipping
- amount of hip flexion
- amount of ankle extension

All of these characteristics were used to compare subjects by age and height. The cycle duration—the time between successive strikes of the left heel—did not vary significantly as a function of age or height, as was also true for the duration of the stance, the time each foot is in contact with the floor. However, the duration of the stance increased significantly as the overall duration of the cycle increased. The duration of the stance also seemed to relate highly to the duration of the swing, the time the foot is entirely off the floor while the opposite foot remains in contact with the supporting surface. The magnitude of the swing duration increased with the duration of the stance but was not significantly affected by age or height.

Unlike the other characteristics, *step* and *stride length* did show a significant difference according to age and height. The stride length was described as "the linear distance in the plane of progression between successive points of foot to floor contact of the same foot" (Murray, Drought, and Kory, 1964, p. 341). The step length was defined as "the distance between successive point of floor to floor contact of alternate feet" (p. 341). Both of these characteristics differed significantly between the youngest group of adults (20 to 25 years) and the oldest group (60 to 65 years). The authors speculated that this decreasing step and stride length reflects a restraint among older walkers that is common in much younger walkers when walking on a slippery surface. The taller subjects in this research also tended to take longer steps and strides compared to the shorter subjects. Foot angle, the amount of in- or out-toeing, was another significant factor. No significant differences were determined according to height, but older subjects exhibited a significantly greater tendency to out-toe. Interestingly, this is a characteristic very common among immature walkers early in life. The *out-toeing* is a technique used to improve lateral stability as the ability to control balance declines in the later adult years.

Murray, Drought, and Kory (1964) also examined the amount of pelvic tipping, the forward and backward movement of the top of the pelvis (iliac crest). Although this characteristic did not vary systematically with height or age, hip flexion did. Older and shorter subjects exhibited slightly greater flexion in

the hip when taking a stride. In addition, older subjects showed less ankle extension at the end of the stance, a condition that most likely contributed to the older subjects' reduced stride length.

Khattab (1980) also examined a variety of gait parameters. However, rather than using adults of varying ages, she compared adults to children. Specifically, Khattab selected subjects 4 to 25 years old. Subjects were instructed to walk across a force platform designed to determine the magnitude of the various forces as the foot struck the platform. Subjects were filmed, to help describe walking techniques. Generally, Khattab found that the children in her research exhibited many adult-like walking characteristics. However, her young adult subjects had considerably fewer balance problems because their center of gravity was relatively lower. Also, adults were more efficient, although less energetic walkers, with longer strides. Adults displayed less flexion and extension of the hip joint in striding and required less backward force to slow their forward momentum following a heel strike. No significant differences were noted between child and adult walkers in peak vertical forces relative to body weight or in the swing/stance ratio, the length of time the leg was swinging relative to the amount of time the foot was in contact with the floor. Table 16-3 summarizes major findings from all of the gait research discussed.

TABLE 16-3 Important Findings Concerning Adult Walking Patterns

Early vs. Late Adulthood	Children vs. Young Adults (Khattab, 1980)
• Walking speed decreased (Aniansson, 1980).	• Adults had considerably fewer balance problems because their center of gravity was lower relative to their total height.
• Step height decreased (Aniansson, 1980).	
• Step and stride length significantly shorter among older walkers (Murray, Drought, & Kory, 1964).	• Adults were more efficient, less energetic walkers.
• Older subjects had significantly greater tendency to out-toe (Murray, Drought, & Kory, 1964).	• Adults took longer strides because of their longer leg length.
• Older adults had greater hip extension during the stride (Murray, Drought, & Kory, 1964).	• Adults displayed reduced hip flexion and extension during striding.
• Older subjects' ankle extension was reduced at the end of the stance (Murray, Drought, & Kory, 1964).	• Adults required less rearward force to slow the forward momentum following a heel strike.

ADULT PERFORMANCE ON SELECTED MOTOR ACTIVITIES

As stated earlier, with the exception of specific areas, there has been minimal research into the movement technique of adult performers. However, Klinger (1980) studied 60-year-old women who professed to be regular exercisers and reached some interesting conclusions. These women's vertical jump pattern generally was similar to the pattern that a comparison group of college-aged women used. There were major differences, however, in the older subjects' ability to achieve as much leg extension or velocity and, therefore, impulse. These women were also tested on such activities as the tennis backhand, throwing, batting, and the overhand backhand stroke. In each case, the angular velocity the college-aged subject attained was greater than that of the older adults. However, note that in many cases the older subjects had no athletic background and had gone years without performing any of the tested movement skills. When the older subjects were subdivided into a high and a low movement ability group, the high group moved faster and with greater coordination, displayed a greater range of motion, transferred their weight more easily, and generally had a more erect posture.

Aniansson (1980) examined the functional capacity of 70-year-old men and women performing routing daily activities: Seven percent of the subjects exhibited difficulties in such routine activities as dressing and maintaining hygiene. Particularly noteworthy were decreases in flexibility, which impeded such necessary movements as touching the hand to the foot for putting on socks or tying shoes. The subjects also had problems rising from a sitting position and performing the supination and pronation required in daily reaching activities.

Unquestionably, these kinds of declines are related to the increased inactivity that is common for most people as they age. Several investigations have been undertaken to describe the regularity with which most adults participate in leisure-time movement activity; the percentage of participants normally decreases with age. Cunningham et al. (1968) found the number of subjects involved in "very little" activity increased considerably from 40 to 69 years of age. Sidney and Shephard (1977) also found elderly men and women highly inactive, although many consider themselves just the opposite. These researchers also noted that their volunteer subjects, although inactive, were probably more active than the "normal" person of comparable age.

AGE OF PEAK PROFICIENCY

In 1953 Harvey Lehman wrote *Age and Achievement.* In this publication Lehman sought to "set forth the relationship between chronological age and outstanding performances" (Lehman, 1953, p. vii). His work consisted of extensive tables detailing the ages of attainment of outstanding performances in music, art, literature, leadership, and, of course, "physical skills." Lehman carefully noted that his work was not intended to determine the rate at which abilities "decay," nor were the ages designated for peak achievement indicative of biological factors alone. Clearly, many sociological factors contribute, and Lehman explained that simply noting the ages of peak achievement would not in any way explain the interaction of the many factors involved in the attainment of peak achievement.

Lehman's work on peak achievement in "physical skills" has been widely reprinted (see Table 16-4). In fact, his table denoting ages of peak achievement in a number of "physical skills" has appeared in many other motor development books (Eckert, 1987; Haywood, 1993) indicating considerable interest in his work. An examination of Lehman's original table explains why he concluded that more vigorous skills like "boxing, football, ice hockey, and tennis tend to deteriorate relatively early" with peak performances generally occurring before the age of 30. "Other skills, such as rifle and pistol shooting, bowling, duck-pin bowling, and billiards, which require less explosive outbursts of speed and energy . . . deteriorate more slowly" (p. 253). Interestingly, Lehman also noted the possibility that "more recently born athletes have learned to better preserve themselves and maintain their physical

Table 16-4   Ages at Which Individuals Have Exhibited Peak Proficiency at "Physical" Skills

Type of skill	No. of cases	Median age	Mean age
U.S.A. outdoor tennis champions	89	26.35	27.12
Runs batted in: annual champions of the two major baseball leagues	49	27.10	27.97
U.S.A. indoor tennis champions	64	28.00	27.45
World champion heavy-weight pugilists	77	29.19	29.51
Base stealers: annual champions of the two major baseball leagues	31	29.21	28.85
Indianapolis-Speedway racers and national auto-racing champions	82	29.56	30.18
Best hitters: annual champions of the two major baseball leagues	53	29.70	29.56
Best pitchers: annual champions of the two major baseball leagues	51	30.10	30.03
Open golf champions of England and of the U.S.A.	127	30.72	31.29
National individual rifle-shooting champions	84	31.33	31.45
State corn-husking champions of the U.S.A.	103	31.50	30.66
World, national, and state pistol-shooting champions	47	31.90	30.63
National amateur bowling champions	58	32.33	32.78
National amateur duck-pin bowling champions	91	32.35	32.19
Professional golf champions of England and of the U.S.A.	53	32.44	32.14
World record-breakers at billiards	42	35.00	35.67
World champion billiardists	74	35.75	34.38

SOURCE: Adapted and printed with permission of Princeton University Press.

fitness." Thus we might expect athletes in more recent years to be achieving peak performances later than they did prior to 1953. Unfortunately, Lehman's work culminated with the publication of his book in 1953 and by today's standards his "more recently born athletes" are not at all recent.

Recognizing that changes may have occurred in the intervening 40-plus years since Lehman's work, Degnan and Payne (1994) updated, and in some areas expanded, the work of Lehman (see Table 16-5). While information on such activities as duck-pin bowling was unavailable, Degnan and Payne were able to accumulate data on most other "physical skills" studied by Lehman. Starting in 1953, the last year of Lehman's work, Degnan and Payne more precisely subdivided many of the original "physical skills" and, in many cases, added values for female performers. As illustrated in Table 16-5, we can see that performers in the "more vigorous skills" still achieve peak performance earlier than those in ac-

tivities requiring "less explosive outbursts of speed and energy." For example, in recent years, median and mean ages of peak performance for tennis ranged from approximately 24 to 26 years of age for both men and women. Baseball players, as determined by Degnan and Payne, achieved peak performance closer to 30 years of age, while golf and auto racing performances were achieved in the early to mid-thirties, respectively. Perhaps most interesting, and somewhat surprising, Lehman's contention that "more recently born athletes" would benefit from more advanced training and "preservation" techniques to maintain their physical fitness is not generally upheld by the recent data. Both median and mean ages of peak performances are less in many athletes charted from 1953 to 1993 than those reported in Lehman's work. For example, Lehman's tennis champions were achieving peak performances between the ages of 26 to 28. In more recent years peak performances for both male and female tennis

Table 16-5   Ages At Which Individuals Have Exhibited Proficiency at "Physical" Skill

Type of Skill	Years of Inclusion	No. of Cases	Median Age	Mean Age
Tennis: Men				
U.S. Open	1956–92	29	25	25.6
Wimbledon	1961–90	27	24	24.48
French Open	1969–88	15	24	23.4
Australian Open	1969–91	16	27	26.88
Tennis: Women				
U.S. Open	1962–93	34	26	25.11
Wimbledon	1953–93	35	24	25.14
French Open	1969–93	22	25	24.5
Australian Open	1969–93	22	25	25.2
Baseball				
MVP	1953-88	73	29	28.79
Batting Average	1953–91	78	28	28.5
Home runs	1953–91	89	29	28.97
Stolen bases	1953–91	77	28	27.86
RBI	1953–91	82	29.5	29.14
Cy Young Award	1956–92	64	29	29.43
Boxing				
Heavyweight	1952–92	31	26	26.68
Middleweight	1953–88	39	30	30.3
Auto Racing				
Indianapolis 500	1953–93	39	35	35.59
Daytona 500	1960–94	28	36	36
Winston Cup	1964–91	25	35	34.36
Golf: Men				
U.S. Open	1953-92	32	33	33.28
PGA	1961–93	29	33	33.83
Masters	1953–93	36	32	32.5
British Open	1953–93	38	31	30.86
PGA Leading Money	1955–92	34	32	31.5
Golf: Women				
U.S. Women's Open	1958–92	33	29.455	29.46
LPGA Championship	1957–87	22	28.5	29.68
LPGA Leading Money	1954–91	33	32	31.79
Bowling				
American Bowling Congress: Men's Singles Champions	1959–93	36	28	30.56
Basketball				
National Basketball Association: League Leaders				
Rebounds	1953–89	37	26	27
Assists	1953–89	37	26	26.27
Scoring	1954–93	26	26.5	26.62
MVP	1956–89	34	27	26.56
Free Throw %	1953–89	36	29	29.36

<small>Source: Degnan and Payne (1994).</small>

players have been achieved from 24 to 26 years of age. Peak performances in golf seem to have stayed about the same, while auto-racing ages have increased considerably. One group that does seem to add credence to Lehman's theory is speedway and auto-racing champions, who where achieving peak performances around age 30 prior to 1953. In the last 40 years mean and median performances have occurred in the mid-30s.

As mentioned, these figures do not explain the underlying sociological or biological factors leading to peak performance. However, they do provide interesting bases for future research, which may someday provide some answers concerning the impact and relationship of biological and sociological factors on potential for peak performances.

ADULT PERFORMANCE DURING HIGH AROUSAL

Considerable research has been conducted on adult motor behavior during times of high arousal. In a series of studies conducted on older versus younger adults playing miniature golf, an age-related decline appeared to occur in situations of high arousal and high cognitive demand. This finding has been consistent in research with large numbers of subjects of varying skill levels and in competitions of varying levels of importance. It has also been detected in miniature golf competitions at varying locations and has been reproduced in field and laboratory settings. In every case, young adults performed better when a need arose for compensating for nonoptimal levels of arousal or increased competitive distraction. Researchers have suggested this phenomenon may be a function of an age-related decline in ability to deal with the increased cognitive demands of high-arousal movement situations. Furthermore, they speculate that it could be related to a combination of physiological factors. The neuroendocrine system, for example, may affect the action of the endocrine glands on the metabolic rate. Or, specific "target tissues" may begin to respond differently to hormonal

actions as we age. If any of these hypotheses are correct, a decline in movement ability during times of high arousal would be extremely pervasive and affect many more movement activities than just miniature golf (Backman and Molander, 1989).

Fortunately, this apparent decline in motor performance during times of high arousal appears to be somewhat reversible. Drug therapy (beta andrenergic blocks) has been recommended as one source of reversal. However, the best ways for older adults to avoid performance decrements during times of high arousal would be relaxation training and refocusing the attention during the high-arousal periods of competition (Backman & Molander, 1989).

MOVEMENT SPEED IN ADULTHOOD

Although human beings display "incredible individual differences in many motor performances as they age" (Spirduso, 1985, p. 89), a number of norms have been noted concerning the speed of various adult movements. As discussed earlier, walking speed generally decreases with age, particularly in late adulthood. The speed of many other kinds of movements, such as running, also appears to be affected.

Running Speed

The maintenance of running records and the advent of masters-age-group running programs throughout the world have facilitated examinations of running speed and age. By comparing the published records of runners from various age groups, researchers have found that the long-distance running times of the best 40-year-old runners are similar to those of world-class runners. However, by the age of 70, top runners may be only 70 percent as fast as the world-class long-distance runners. Also, for older men, the relative running speed increases as the distance increases (see Figure 16-1). Therefore, the relative sprint speed for the older person does not compare as favorably as longer distance

FIGURE 16-1 Running speed at short distances normally declines considerably with age, but the relative running speed for longer distances is often well preserved.

speeds to world-class efforts, most likely a result of a general decrease in running speed with age because such techniques as interval training for speed maintenance are fairly uncommon among older runners. Also, older runners may have increasing responsibilities in nonrunning activities, which impairs their efforts to train. Finally, older runners may not have the peak levels of motivation that many younger runners maintain; unquestionably, such motivation is critical for optimal performance (Riegel, 1981).

Reaction and Response Time

Two measures that researchers interested in the effects of aging on movement have extensively examined are *reaction time* and *movement time.* Reaction time has been the most studied factor. As discussed in Chapter 2, reaction time has also been used to determine the status of the central nervous system for cognitive function. Specifically, reaction time is "the interval from presentation of an unanticipated stimulus until the beginning of the response" (Schmidt, 1991; p. 286). Movement time is the "interval from the initiation of the movement until its termination" (Schmidt, 1991; p. 285). The movement may be short and simple, such as pressing a button, or longer and more sophisticated, such as running.

According to some investigators, reaction time and movement time decline systematically in adults. In an investigation of subjects 6 to 84 years old, speed increased up to 19 years of age but decreased systematically thereafter (Hodgkins, 1962). Researchers such as Jarvik and Cohen (1973) substantiated these claims when they determined that some of the greatest declines with aging may be in the performance of speeded movement tasks. In particular, Jarvik and Cohen found that reaction time was longer and more variable in older subjects, which, they stated, indicated reduced functional capability of the central nervous system, cell loss, and decreased nerve conductivity.

Considerable evidence exists indicating that activities requiring more complex processing of information will lead to a greater rate of slowing (Hertzog, 1991). In fact, Welford (1982) believed that the amount of decline in reaction time is related to how complicated the task is. According to Welford, there are slight changes from 20 to 60 years in repetitive and simple movements. These movements include many reaction-time tasks, such as lifting a finger off a button when presented with a certain stimulus. Slightly more complicated tasks, such as alternately tapping the hand or a pencil between two targets located next to each other, also minimally decline with age. However, there is more significant change in the rate of slowing when the task becomes increasingly complex. For example, rapidly pressing a series of buttons in varied order on successive trials is more complicated and more likely to cause slower performances in older subjects.

Welford categorized the complications that typically have been most involved in research in this area as *spatial transpositions* and *symbolic translations*. Spatial transpositions are usually the simpler of the two complications because they involve relating one signal at one position to a response at another position. For example, releasing a button when a light stimulus appears is a spatial transposition. The symbolic translation requires the subject to respond to a signal by a predetermined number or code. For example, if a blue stimulus light appears, the subject must press the first in a series of buttons: if the yellow light appears, the second button in the series must be pressed. Symbolic translations generally cause disproportionate slowing in older subjects. In research combining both types of complications, older subjects' response speed has been determined to be further hampered because response becomes increasingly inaccurate as it slows.

The phenomenon of slowing with age for relatively simple versus more complex movements generally has been explained by the *last-in-first-out hypothesis*. This hypothesis suggests that the neural and muscular capability to perform simple movement acts, such as reflexive movements or other integrated movements that fall into the category of spatial transpositions, is developed early in life and appears to somewhat resist decline with aging. However, more coordinated, goal-oriented, or complicated movements, such as the symbolic translations discussed earlier, are not developed until later in life and begin to decline in people as young as 30 (Spirduso, 1985).

Physiologically, a number of more specific factors are also believed to contribute to the slowing that occurs with age. The number of functional neurons and the muscle fibers they stimulate (motor units) decreases with age. At the same time, more intense neural stimulations are required because the threshold of excitation of the muscles generally declines as much as 15 to 35 percent between ages 20 and 60 years (Welford, 1982). Although more intense and "clear" neural stimulation may be required, the signal may actually decline in quality. The clarity of the signal appears to be a function of the ratio between the impulse of the neural stimulation and the extraneous "noise" or interference. With age, the decreasing capacity of the sense organs and the loss of brain cells cause reduced signal levels as noise levels increase. Therefore, a lower signal-to-noise ratio results, requiring the person to respond with slower motor movements (Birren, Woods, & Williams, 1980).

In addition to these common physiological changes, older people also approach movement performance with a different strategy: They are willing to sacrifice speed of movement for increased accuracy, leading to the *speed/accuracy tradeoff*, which may be a function of the older person's more cautious approach to movement (Schmidt, 1988). The speed/accuracy tradeoff is discussed in more detail later in the chapter.

Rabitt and Rogers's (1965) research lends additional support to the theory that adults are somewhat more cautious in their approach to movement. A comparison of the speed of movement of young and old adult subjects to one of two alternative endpoints yielded interesting findings. The young adults were capable of pondering which was their assigned endpoint during the initial phase of the movement; the older subjects were incapable of such simultaneous activity because they intently focused their attention on monitoring their movement. Rabitt and Rogers believed that this research demonstrated older adult subjects' inability to suppress the monitoring of their movement. The increased monitoring may have occurred as a result of the muscles receiving slower neural stimulation, which may have caused the subjects to become aware of the stimulus and excessively focus their attention on the movement activity. Also, the monitoring may be suppressed when the subject is assured or confident of the outcome. Rabitt and Rogers speculated that the adult subjects in their research may have lacked the assurance or confidence necessary for suppressing the monitoring.

Stones and Kozma (1981) proposed additional theories to account for the age effects that exist in many movement activities. For example, movements requiring maximal, or near-maximal, energy expenditure decline faster than those that require lesser levels of energy. Second, Stones and Kozma speculated that activities requiring explosive muscular contraction and rapid power production tend to decrease in popularity with age. To support this hypothesis, they cited decreasing numbers of older runners who interval train and the reduced popularity of power lifting among older adults. This idea is no doubt strongly related to their third hypothesis, which states that as people age, they are less motivated to train or practice activities that require a repetition of near-maximal explosive efforts. The resulting lack of training or practice causes an obvious decline in function at a faster rate than would be common in a younger performer.

IS A MOVEMENT DECLINE INEVITABLE WITH AGE?

Most adults show considerable decline in movement ability as they age. However, this decline, although inevitable for most people, does not have to begin as early or as abruptly as it does for many adults. Clearly, by taking an active role in daily habits, the evident movement regression or decline can be delayed, postponed, or possibly prevented. The decline in movement performance can be avoided by certain compensatory strategies, exercise, and practice.

Compensation for the Movement Decline

Although there is a certain amount of movement decline with age, there are a number of ways older adults can compensate for such phenomena as reduced speed, strength, or endurance and maintain extremely high levels of performance. For example, in longer activities where fatigue might be a factor, the older adult can learn to conserve energy by pac-

ing: doling out energy more cautiously and avoiding unnecessary expenditures of effort. Many performers, such as distance runners, cyclists, or swimmers, consciously practice pacing, but in some older adults a certain amount of pacing occurs subconsciously as they moderate performance through a constant concern for preserving their energy. See Figure 16–2.

The older adult may practice other subconscious or automatic compensatory tendencies. For example, an adult may apply more effort than a younger person. However, this mode of compensation does not work

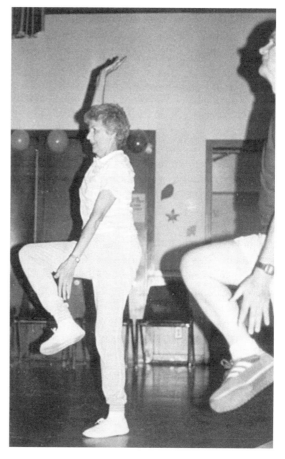

FIGURE 16-2 For the older adult, pacing is often an effective way to compensate for loss of speed.

for extended periods of time because fatigue occurs more readily than with pacing. Furthermore, the long-term application of this form of compensation could lead to increased incidences of stress, ulcers, or heart problems. Experts differ as to whether or not older adults use this tactic more than their younger counterparts (Welford, 1982).

Some older adults may compensate for movement deficits by long- and short-term anticipation of movement. Short-term anticipation is, for example, the racquetball player focusing on her opponent's movement so as to gain insight into proper positioning on the court. Long-term anticipation can also be useful for providing preparation through practice or for securing sufficient rest and might increase the success of performance in an upcoming movement activity. However, although some older adults effectively use compensation, they do not seem to do so any more frequently than younger adults.

As mentioned earlier, older adults often sacrifice speed for accuracy in movement activities and occasionally may use the tactic as a form of compensation. For example, the speed/accuracy tradeoff is particularly common and useful among skilled adults. However, this form of compensation, although useful in many situations, cannot fully overcome movement deficits because the additional time the older adults gain is often insufficient to overcome the accuracy of the more youthful performers (Salthouse, 1979).

Finally, older performers may be able to compensate somewhat as a result of higher criteria or greater expectations concerning their performances. This has been found particularly true in certain memory tasks as well as tests involving sensory discrimination (Hutman & Sekuler, 1980; Potash & Jones, 1977). No doubt, having greater expectations of performance often overcomes some of the resulting movement deficit from such factors as the decrease in movement speed (Welford, 1982).

Effects of Exercise on the Movement Decline

A decline in movement performance is common as adults age, but there are means for avoiding the decline. Movement can even be maintained and improved well into late adulthood by continuing active involvement in movement participation. The continuation of participation in movement activity is so influential that active older adults are more similar to young active adults than to old inactive adults in performance on reaction time, choice reaction time, and response time tasks (Aniansson, 1980). The body build is also more likely to look youthful; this is simply determined by examining elderly athletes, who often have a body type similar to that of younger people (Shephard, 1978). Unfortunately, our culture often views adulthood, especially late adulthood, as a time to slow down. Adults also may be plagued by the idea that the need for exercise diminishes or that their ability is too limited for participation. In some cases older adults experience *dyspnea,* painful or difficult breathing, which can lead to a fear of overexertion. No doubt, all of these factors contribute to the increasing inactivity that often accompanies aging.

Those who do continue a regular regimen of physical activity can avoid the extremely negative cycle that frequently engulfs the aging. This cycle generally begins as activity decreases with age. As people become increasingly inactive, the biological factors that regulate the system decline, impairing the ability to engage in movement activity. However, an active regimen of movement yields beneficial effects and breaks the cycle. In addition, even movements that seem unrelated to the experienced activity may improve (Spirduso, 1982). See Figure 16–3.

As noted earlier, reaction time has been the primary focus of researchers concerned with movement changes and aging. Those investigators who examine the effects of movement activity or exercise on movement through adulthood also have focused on reaction time. Such research has shown that exercise reduces reaction time in adult subjects, as a result of many positive biological changes that accompany chronic exercise.

Among the positive changes that accompany cardiovascular activity is increased blood flow, which may actually improve the brain's function. Exercise

FIGURE 16-3 By maintaining an active, exercising lifestyle, most adults can postpone or avoid many forms of movement decline. In fact, improvements in motor performance can frequently be elicited throughout the lifespan.

also tends to have an arousing effect, which may improve adults' speed of performance. However, the overall benefit from this factor is somewhat disputed because some experts believe that the additional arousal, although benefiting speed, may decrease the accuracy of performance. Another possible explanation for the beneficial effects of exercise on reaction time is that the active muscles positively influence the neural connections and the neurons that stimulate the muscle (Welford, 1982).

A multitude of other biological changes also accompany a regular exercise regimen. These factors, many of which were discussed more thoroughly in Chapter 8, include increasing work capacity, bone density, flexibility, muscle strength, coordination, and weight control. Reductions are seen in such factors as resting heart rate, total cholesterol, and blood pressure. These biological changes are accompanied by improved mental outlook and self-esteem and reduced idle time, anxiety, and loneliness (Barry, Rich, and Carlson, 1993). All of these factors greatly contribute to the quality of life and our ability to stay active. Thus, the vicious cycle created by inactivity can be slowed and, many times, even reversed.

Effects of Practice on the Movement Decline

Like regular physical exercise, practice of a specific movement activity is an effective way for an adult to postpone or avoid movement regression or, in many cases, improve specific movement endeavors. In fact, in examining the performance of adult subjects on reaction-time tasks, researchers have determined that practice facilitates improvement through late adulthood. Older adult subjects often show greater improvement with practice than do younger adult subjects, even though overall performance levels between the two groups may initially vary considerably (Salthouse & Somberg, 1982).

Pursuit rotor research has yielded similar findings. With the pursuit rotor device, the subject must keep a wand in contact with a moving light target as the target moves through various configurations,

such as a circle. When old and young subjects were tested, there was minimal difference in the performance levels when both groups were allowed to practice before testing. The prepractice performance levels of the young surpassed those of the old, so the practice was considered more beneficial to the older than the younger adult subjects (Surburg, 1976). In general, there is little evidence to support the notion that older subjects improve differently in movement tasks following practice than do younger subjects. Despite considerable popular opinion to the contrary, adults do benefit from practice throughout life.

Physical Activity Trends in Adulthood

As indicated in the previous section, the contributions of an active lifestyle are becoming increasingly clear. Nevertheless, surveys indicate that most adults do not choose to participate in physical activity. Recent survey information from Australia, Canada, England, and the United States revealed that approximately 10 percent of the adult populations were "aerobically active." "Aerobically active" meant that one "engaged in vigorous activities during leisure time on an average of at least three occasions weekly for 20-30 minutes or more per occasion" (Stephens & Caspersen, 1994; p. 204). Clearly, sedentarism appears to be the lifestyle of choice. The number of people falling into the sedentary category (even less than moderately active) appears to range from about 25 to 33 percent in most countries surveyed. England and Finland seem to be somewhat exceptional in that their percentage of sedentary people is somewhat less. In Finland, as many as 15 percent of the 30- to 59- year-olds were believed to be highly active (Stephens & Caspersen, 1994).

Fortunately, the incidence of sedentarism appears to be declining in many countries. The number of people exercising in the United States increased slightly from 1980 to 1990, though no change was noted in Australia and a slight decrease in the number of physically active people was noted in Canada. This increase in leisure-time physical activity is believed to be mostly sedentary people becoming moderately active rather than moderately active people becoming vigorously active. In addition, in most countries studied, males were 80 percent more likely to be vigorously active than females (Stephens & Caspersen, 1994).

In examining developmental trends and activity levels, older adults have generally been found to be less active than younger adults. In addition, when active, older adults often choose activities that require less energy expenditure. A slight exception to the overall general trend was noted at the end of high school, where an extreme reduction in physical activity level appears suddenly. In Canada, for example, 20- to 24-year-old subjects were found to be two times less likely to be physically active than 10-to 14-year-olds. Further into adulthood, if the intensity of the activity is considered relative to age, the expected decline across adulthood diminishes, and people at 65 years or slightly younger actually show a slight increase in activity level. In addition, in the United States, older adults increased their involvement in physical activity more than younger adults during the 1980s, a trend which appears to be continuing. Furthermore, American males and females, 18 to 29 and 30 to 44, were the only groups not increasing their leisure time involvement in physical activity, while 20-to 24-year-olds were the only age group not showing a similar increase in Canada. So, despite the relatively high numbers of sedentary people in many of the countries studied, some positive trends appear to exist (Stephens & Caspersen. 1994).

TEACHING MOVEMENT SKILL TO THE OLDER ADULT

Due to an increasing number of older adults and heightened awareness of the benefits of physical activity, many new programs emphasizing motor skill instruction for older adults have evolved. No doubt, many more will be created to meet an increased need in the years to come. Unfortunately, many of these programs will not be designed and directed by experts specifically trained for teaching move-

ment skill to the older adult. Through the early 1980s existing programs were most often led by volunteers or others without specific training or professional education in exercise, movement, or recreation (Heitmann, 1982). This trend has continued into the 1990s. Additionally, little research exists to assist trained professionals in designing and implementing older-adult movement instruction programs. While considerable research has been done on the adult physiological system, very little has been done on psychomotor performance. This makes it more difficult to establish a program that is congruent with the needs and objectives of the older adult.

However, according to Heitmann (1982), we do know that certain steps should be taken in formulating a program of movement instruction for the older adult. First, the existing research should be examined to increase awareness of the older adult's specific needs concerning physiological rehabilitation or maintenance. Second, the research should be used to establish a viable instructional process. Third, a program of preparation of professionals in instructing and directing programs for older adults should be implemented. According to Heitmann (1982), professionals should be well trained in the scientific bases of physical education with specific emphasis on the older adult. They must know how to implement teaching methodologies that are specific to the elderly, thus enabling the older adult to acquire skill in the most efficient manner. These professionals also must be prepared in fitness and motor skill rehabilitation and maintenance procedures that are specific to the elderly. Heitmann (1982) suggests that training of these professionals might parallel university teacher-credential programs. Following a 4-year specialized course of study, an internship would be prescribed. Upon successful completion of the curriculum and the internship, a specialized credential could be awarded.

Heitmann further suggests that, in designing the motor skill program for the older adult, the individual's hierarchy of needs should be heeded. The first need is physiological. Older adults may have had health problems or been sedentary for an extended period of time. As a result they might be poorly motivated. A major emphasis must, therefore, be placed on appropriately motivating the participants. A second need is for the safety and security of the participants. Because some may have impaired vision or hearing, particular care must be taken in giving instructions. Hearing, in particular, often becomes distorted or difficult because of the echo or noise associated with a gymnasium or similar movement setting. Furthermore, Heitmann cautions against creating excess physiological and emotional stress in the participants.

Other needs that should be considered are those for belonging, affection, and identification. To assist in fulfilling these needs, Heitmann recommends the creation of a caring environment where participants feel comfortable, feel they belong, and feel they can communicate. Establishing this type of environment will also assist in meeting this last group of needs that Heitmann mentions—the need for self-esteem, success, and self-respect—which can be met by delivering positive reinforcement to the participants. When all of these needs are attained, Heitmann claims, the participant can achieve the highest level of fulfillment in the program of motor skill instruction.

Following Heitmann's advice, Anshel (1989) examined the research specifically related to information processing theory to establish guidelines for motor skill instruction of the older adult. Information processing is a theory we discussed briefly in Chapters 1 and 4. This theory suggests that the human being functions much like a computer in the performance of a movement skill. According to information processing theory, we first receive environmental stimulation suggesting that a movement is impending through the brain's afferent (input) system. This information is organized and integrated (i.e., compared to old information about similar situations) by the brain and a decision to move is made. Then this information is sent via the efferent (output) system to the muscles to create the desired moment. The movement occurs and is observed so relevant information can be stored for future attempts at similar movements.

Using this theory and current research, Anshel (1989) created a series of recommendations for teaching older adults movement skill. First, to enhance the psychological readiness of the learner, a proper level of arousal must be achieved. This can be attained, according to Anshel, in several ways. Maintain good eye contact, speak sufficiently loud, keep a fairly close distance to participants when communicating, and address the participants by name. Finally, but equally important, inform the participants of the importance of learning the skill.

Anshel also recommends reducing verbal input to a minimum because it can slow the information processing system. So, articulate clearly, be concise, and reduce the speed of delivery slightly. To further assist the older participant, make the environment conducive to learning motor skills by, for example, trying to eliminate all extraneous interference that could inhibit the participant's reception of information. Also, make sure lighting is adequate and the room temperature is appropriate for all.

Anshel also recommends teaching the participants appropriate attentional strategies. Help them learn where to focus their attention. This requires instruction in what input they should look and listen for—and what input they should ignore. In addition, teach the participants what sensations should accompany the movement they are learning.

Anshel believes that several strategies will facilitate older adults' perception and, therefore, skill acquisition. First, they must develop the proper sensory and motor "set." A set is the participant's readiness to employ the senses to receive relevant information. A racquetball player, for example, may watch the front wall for the positioning of the ball while listening to gain information concerning the ball's velocity. Anshel claims that these cues may be internal rather than external as they were in the racquetball example. Imagine a diver who may need to focus on internal sensations to monitor progress during a dive. The focus of attention, whether internal or external, is the set. Second, participants must be prepared with anticipatory strategies; that is, they must know the demands of the upcoming task in advance. An ability to correctly predict what movements might be required is particularly helpful for the elderly, who may gain speed of response or greater accuracy by their accurate anticipation.

A third strategy, according to Anshel, is that skill practice should be taught in the actual sequence in which it will happen and under circumstances that realistically simulate the task demands. At the same time, the instructor must be aware of the limitations of many older adults. For example, because they may require more time to react, allow participants more time to receive the necessary stimulation prior to responding. And reduce the speed and complexity of the incoming information while allowing more time for movement alterations if necessary. During this process also try to "attach old learning." In other words, try to help the participant integrate the upcoming task with previous similar tasks. Then, once the movement has occurred, allow more time than usual for the participant to observe what transpired so that this information will be available for integration on future attempts.

Anshel also notes that short-term memory deficits have been evidenced in the elderly. Recognition of this fact may also be beneficial in teaching situations. To assist older adults with any short-term memory deficits, encourage them to talk themselves through the task at a self-paced speed. This, Anshel believes, will reinforce short-term memory. Also, assist them in selecting the most meaningful movement cues that should be recognized and remembered. This might be further facilitated by the use of mental imagery or visualization. Encourage participants to picture themselves performing the skill.

Older adults have also been known to display somewhat slower recall than their younger counterparts. Recognizing this, allow participants more time to respond to stimuli, ponder their response, and store the relevant information about the movement. Situations where the older adult is rushed or extremely rapid recall is required may be discouraging. Anshel recommends establishing a slower, more constant pace initially. The pace can then be gradually speeded up.

Older performers are also characterized by checking their actions more frequently than do younger adults. They also monitor longer after the response, which sometimes results in overanticipation on the subsequent response. This simply means that older adults should be given more time to reorganize their thoughts after performing a movement. They are frequently less capable of programming a rapid series of movements in a short period of time. For those reasons, Anshel (1989) offers several instructional strategies. First, as mentioned earlier, follow the actual sequence of events so the participant learns the correct sequence. Later, more speed can be added. Second, have the participants focus on specific body parts or environmental information immediately before, during, and after the movement. Ask them about the sensations associated with the movement. Third, provide feedback immediately following a movement because the older performer relies heavily on it for future performances. Feedback should be precise, positive, and quantitative ("drop your racket head about 4 inches").

SUMMARY

Traditionally, the study of adult development has been overshadowed by the study of children and adolescents. However, because of the rapidly increasing number of individuals approaching middle and late adulthood, this trend is ending as many developmentalists now focus their attention on the adult years.

As people age, balance often requires greater conscious awareness, which leads to increased body sway and an increased number of falls among older adults.

Although there is a paucity of research into the movement behavior of adult subjects, one area that has been studied in depth is the adult walking pattern. Such research has determined that even though many similar walking characteristics are retained through adulthood, there is also considerable change. Compared to younger adults, older adult walkers show decreased step and stride length and decreased flexion and extension of the hip joint.

Perhaps as a subconscious attempt to improve stability, the amount of out-toeing increases with age.

When a number of selected movement activities were examined, it was found that angular velocities of body parts during movement generally decreased for 60-year-old women compared to college-aged women. In addition, a small percentage of 70-year-olds exhibited difficulty in certain daily dressing and hygiene activities. Decreased flexibility was thought to be a major source of problems for these people.

An interesting way of examining motor performance in adulthood is to determine age of "peak performance." Work conducted prior to 1953 found ages for peak performances in more "vigorous skills" to be occurring before peak performances in activities requiring "less explosive outbursts of speed and energy." While that trend continues today, more recent research determined that peak performance in many activities is occurring earlier today than 40 years ago.

Older adults appear to exhibit performance decrements during times of high arousal. This has been hypothesized to be a function of decreasing ability to deal with the increased cognitive demands of high-arousal movement situations. Or, it may be related to changes in the neuroendocrine system and its indirect effects on movement behavior. To some extent this decline can be reversed by drug therapy, relaxation training, or refocusing the attention during performance.

Speed of movement typically declines with age, not only walking and running but also the more subtle kinds of movements measured in reaction-time research. Although a general slowing with age is common, the decrease is particularly pronounced in the more complicated movements known as symbolic translations. There is less decline, if any, in the simpler spatial transpositions.

The decrease in speed with age is caused by several critical factors: reduction in functional motor units, need for more intense neural stimulation, and increased caution in performance.

Declines in movement ability are extremely common for most aging people, but the decline can be postponed or, in some cases, avoided. To help maintain movement ability, a number of strategies may compensate. More important, regular practice and exercise are extremely effective in maintaining or even improving movement ability in adulthood.

Though physical activity during adulthood appears to be beneficial, trends in physical activity indicate that most adults choose to maintain a relatively inactive lifestyle. As many as a third of all people surveyed fell into the "sedentary" category. Fortunately, this number may be decreasing in many countries. In addition, men appear to be more vigorously active than females, and older adults have been increasing their activity levels more than younger adults in recent years.

A growing population of older adults and greater interest in movement are increasing the need for quality movement-instruction programs for adults. Unfortunately, too few quality programs exist. Steps need to be taken to increase the number of professionals qualified to teach movement skills to older adults. Furthermore, these individuals need to focus on the research to ascertain the most efficient means of teaching movement skills to their clients.

KEY TERMS

Balance	Reaction time
Dyspnea	Spatial transpositions
Gait	Speed/accuracy
Last-in-first-out	tradeoff
hypothesis	Step length
Movement time	Stride length
Out-toeing	Symbolic translations
Postural sway	

CHAPTER **17**

Assessment

Certain studies suggest that many physical educators fail to properly assess their students' motor behaviors (Safrit 1990). In fact, one study that Haubenstricker conducted (1984) found that physical educators devote very little time to assessment, and when assessment does occur, it most frequently takes the form of a teacher-made test. Why is there this dilemma? Many teachers complain that tests are too difficult, too time-consuming, and too expensive to administer, but there are many valid assessment instruments that teachers in school and nonschool settings can feasibly administer. We believe the primary culprit is a lack of teacher training—many teachers simply do not fully understand the role of assessment and do not know how to select and administer tests. This chapter has been designed to help teachers and others overcome this deficiency. It describes why teachers should assess, what they should assess, how to prepare students for assessment, and how to select the assessment instrument that best meets personal needs. Various assessment instruments are also reviewed.

GUIDELINES FOR ASSESSMENT

The assessment process should not be approached haphazardly; it should be planned systematically. Following are seven important questions to consider before beginning to assess students:

1. Why do you want to assess your students?

2. What variables do you plan to assess?

3. Which tests purport to assess the important variables that you have identified?

4. How will you prepare yourself for collecting the data?

5. Do you have the statistical skills to interpret the assessment data?

6. Will you be conducting an informal or formal assessment?

7. How, and with whom, will you share the assessment results?

Why Assess?

Many professionals assess student performance as a simple matter of course, probably because when they were in school their instructor periodically assessed their performance. But assessment of student performance should be carried out with a specific purpose in mind, such as one of the following:

1. *Screening.* Screening is a process whereby people are assessed to determine if they should be referred for further testing or whether they need a special program of instruction. Practically speaking, a physical education instructor may want to screen students at the beginning of the school year, to identify children who have special needs.

2. *Program content.* Assessment results can be used to help plan the content of your program. By assessing students' incoming ability, you will be able to write program objectives that challenge students.

3. *Student progress.* Assessment can also be used to determine how well students are proceeding toward course objectives.

4. *Program evaluation.* You can assess your students' performance to determine whether a specific program of instruction is fostering their skill development.

5. *Classification.* Through assessment, it is possible to place students in homogeneous or heterogeneous groups. For example, when equating teams for competition, it is best if the two teams competing against each other have similar skills.

What Variables to Assess

Once you have determined why you need to assess, you will want to determine which variables to assess. Instructional units that are tied to specific course objectives generally indicate which variables need to be assessed; for example, in a gymnastics unit, you may want to assess balance and upper-body strength. In short, assess those variables that are part of your course objectives.

Selecting the Best Test

To select the best test, you will want to review all available tests that purport to assess the variables in question. Popular physical education measurement textbooks contain descriptions of available tests (Safrit, 1990; Strand & Wilson, 1993), as does the classic *Mental Measurements Yearbook* (Conoley & Kramer, 1989).

After consulting these references, you should be able to identify several tests that assess the variables in which you are interested. Now you must decide which test instrument best meets your needs. To help you make this decision, consider each of the following questions:

1. Is the test statistically valid, reliable, and objective?

2. If the test is norm-referenced, are the norms established on a population similar to the one you plan to assess?

3. Is the test instrument feasible to administer?

4. Do you have the training and expertise to administer the test as well as interpret the results?

Characteristics of Ideal Tests Acceptable test instruments should be valid, reliable, and objective. A valid test measures what it claims to measure. One type of validity frequently used in motor development and physical education is *content validity:* The instrument contains tasks that measure specific content of interest. This type of validity is often logically determined by a panel of experts. For example, experts have determined that the 50-yard dash is a valid indicator of running speed because it measures how fast a person runs. Other types of validity are statistically determined, and a detailed discussion of them is beyond the scope of this text. Consistency of test results is another important characteristic of a good test. A test is reliable if student scores do not significantly vary from day to day, assuming that the students have not received additional instruction. Thus *test reliability* is the test score's freedom from error.

The third characteristic of an ideal test is *objectivity* (sometimes called *interrater reliability*), which is the degree of accuracy to which a test is scored. Content validity is frequently determined subjectively, but both reliability and objectivity are determined statistically. Statistical determination is possible by computing a correlation coefficient for two sets of scores. For example, to determine objectivity, a set of ratings compiled by one scorer is correlated with the scores obtained by a second scorer. Because the resulting correlation coefficient can never be greater than 1.00, a correlation of 0.80 or 0.90 is generally deemed acceptable.

Caution: Norms Are Population-Specific
Norms describe how large groups of people score in regard to selected variables. Because one large group can differ from another large group in regard to a variable of interest, norms are population-specific. An example is norms for height. Because American children are generally taller than Japanese children, it would be inappropriate to interchange normative values within these two populations. The same holds true regarding tests of motor proficiency and tests of physical fitness.

Therefore, if you decide to use a norm-referenced test, make certain that the norms were established on a population similar to the one you intend to assess.

Test Feasibility You may find several tests that meet all of the selection criteria, so the next step is to determine which of these tests are more feasible to administer. Consider the following points:

1. Which test can be administered in the least amount of time?

2. Must you administer the test individually, or can it be administered to groups?

3. Do you have the training and expertise to administer the test (some tests require extensive training)?

4. Do you have all of the supplies and equipment needed for test administration? Some tests must be purchased as part of a test kit that may cost several hundred dollars.

5. Do you have the training and expertise to interpret the test results?

Besides referring to the publications mentioned earlier in this section, consult the test manual that accompanies most tests. Generally, the manual describes in detail how the test was developed and how it should be administered.

Preparing Students for Assessment

Without a doubt, requiring people to perform strange motor tasks, in unfamiliar surroundings, in front of strangers, while sometimes using strange looking equipment, can produce a great deal of test anxiety. However, there are several steps that should help reduce this uneasy feeling that frequently accompanies the administration of an assessment instrument. Werder and Kalakian (1985) suggested that, before assessing, give consideration to the test environment and the participants' physical and psychological needs.

Test Environment   The room where the assessment is to be administered should be as comfortable as possible, and the room's temperature and lighting should be ideal. The testing area should be free of unnecessary furniture and free from distractions, such as high noise levels. Above all, the area should be free from potential hazards.

Meeting Physical Needs   Also consider the participants' physical needs. For example, thirsty participants or those who must use the restroom will have their attention distracted from the assessment situation. Establish a procedure whereby you ask before assessment begins whether or not the participant needs to be excused.

Meeting Psychological Needs   The following procedures help reduce test anxiety:

1. When participants arrive, do not rush into the assessment: engage them in informal conversation for a couple of minutes. Introduce yourself, and get the participants to talk about themselves. Ask a question such as "What are some of your favorite activities?" This technique relaxes the participants by making them focus their attention on themselves instead of the assessment.

2. Tell the participants what they will be doing during the assessment. In other words, reveal the unexpected.

3. When talking with the participants, try not to use the word "test," which can make many people nervous.

4. If equipment is to be used during the assessment, give participants an opportunity to explore it before assessment begins. For example, before requiring participants to catch a ball, let them informally play with the ball, so they can experience for themselves that the ball is soft and will not harm them.

Instructor Preparation and Data Collection

After selecting an assessment instrument and preparing your students for assessment, there is still one additional preparation—you must now be certain that you are adequately prepared to administer the assessment. To help prepare yourself, ask the following questions: Do I have the necessary equipment needed to administer the assessment? If administering a standardized assessment, can I deliver the standardized directions to students taking the assessment? Do I have an appropriate score sheet with extra pencils on hand? Am I adequately prepared to administer the assessment without constantly referring to the test manual? In short, you must think through and even pilot (test run) your assessment procedures prior to administering to your target population.

If your assessment requires you to observe and then rate developmental movement performance, do you possess valid observational skills? In other words, do you have a complete understanding of the developmental milestones being assessed? Are you

able to recognize deviations from the norm? And of utmost importance, have you thought through observational vantage points for each skill being assessed? For example, say that you are planning on observing an individual's stage of maturity for the fundamental locomotor skill, running. As the student performs, from what angle will you be observing. Will the runner be coming directly toward you, or running away from you, or will you be observing the runner from a profile view? Obviously the answer depends upon which component of the skill is being evaluated. If you are assessing the relationship of the heel to the buttock, then a profile view would be most appropriate. However, if you were observing the runner to determine whether or not the hands were crossing the body's midline, then requiring the runner to run directly toward you would be most appropriate. As should now be evident, you should plot observational vantage points for each skill being assessed prior to assessment.

Interpreting the Assessment Data

The most frequently asked question following data collection is, "How well did the student perform in accordance with accepted criteria or norms?" To answer this question you will need to have at least an introductory understanding of two measurement concepts: measures of central tendency and measures of variability.

Measures of central tendency include the mean, the median, and the mode. The mean is simply the arithmetic average. To calculate, add all the raw scores and divide by the number of students who took part in the assessment. The median is actually the 50th percentile, the exact midpoint of a distribution of scores. The mode, the most crude measure of central tendency, is the score that appears most frequently within the distribution.

While the mean score describes the average performance within a distribution of scores, measures of variability describe the spread of the scores. The most frequently used measure of variability is the *standard deviation*. The standard deviation describes the degree to which the scores vary about the mean of the distribution. The concept of standard deviation can be best illustrated by its relationship to the normal bell-shaped curve shown in Figure 17–1. This curve is a theoretical model based on laws of chance that describe the phenomenon which is observed when large groups of individuals are tested. Notice that the curve consists of three positive and three negative standard deviation (σ) units. The area under the curve represents performance occurrences. That is, 68 percent of a normally distributed population will score somewhere between +1 σ and –1 σ, while 95 percent will be represented somewhere between +2 σ and –2 σ units. Likewise, 99.7 percent of the population tested will fall somewhere between +3 σ and –3 σ units.

When analyzing assessment data, you will be interested in determining whether the raw score of interest falls above or below the mean and how far the score deviates away from the mean score. When real data is involved, σ units are transformed into actual scores. Let an example illustrate the point. Billy's mother is interested in how her son performed on a test measuring abdominal strength/endurance (sit-up test). Billy was able to perform 35 sit-ups. How does Billy's performance rank among his classmates or among students in a standardized population? To answer this question you need to know the mean and σ of the distribution of scores of which Billy is a member. To complete our example, we will say that the mean of the distribution of sit-up scores is 45 and its σ is 10. With this information we can now say that Billy's score was below the average score. Not only was his score below average, but it is –1 σ below the mean. Therefore, we can say that 84 percent of the individuals within this distribution performed better than Billy and conversely, Billy performed better than 16 percent of the individuals within this distribution.

Formal Versus Informal Assessment

We generally think of assessment as being a very detailed formal process. This formal process has been described as any situation in which the student is aware that he or she is being observed and evaluated (Sherrill, 1993). Unfortunately, many individuals become anxious and "tighten up" in these formal settings. As a result, a true performance score is probably not being obtained. For this reason, you may choose on occasion to engage in an informal assessment. When assessment is performed in an informal manner, the student is not generally aware that an observation is being made.

Linder (1993a; 1993b) has described a type of informal assessment known as, *transdisciplinary*

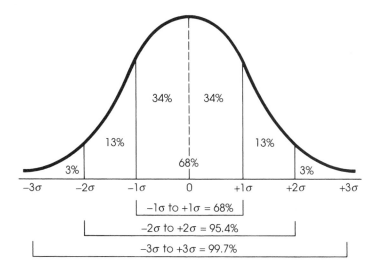

FIGURE 17-1 The normal curve

play-based assessment. One aspect of this type of informal assessment involves both unstructured and structured motor play. The play-based assessment is accomplished by allowing the child free play within an approved area but in the presence of an adult facilitator. At first the facilitator simply plays along and models the child's play behavior. However, later on, the facilitator will coax the child into exhibiting new movement tasks that the child did not spontaneously initiate. During this time, but unbeknown to the child, an evaluation is being conducted. In fact, videotaping the play session is recommended.

Physical educators and other professionals are often confronted with a situation whereby they must evaluate a large group of students within a short period of time. If this is to be accomplished, it is important to select an assessment instrument that lends itself to this function. For example, two assessment instruments that lend themselves to assessing large groups of students are the Test of Gross Motor Development as well as the "total body approach" of assessing the basic fundamental motor skills. More will be said about these two useful assessment tools later in the chapter. The point that we are making here is that all assessments need not be carried out in a formal manner. The nature and purpose of the assessment will, in part, dictate which instrument or method is the most appropriate to employ and, as pointed out earlier, you must decide upon the nature and purpose of the assessment before selecting an assessment instrument.

Sharing Assessment Results

Once test results have been analyzed and interpreted, the information should be shared with the appropriate people. Depending on the circumstances, these appropriate people are the parents, fellow teachers, the school nurse, and a host of other professionals. This information can be shared through written communication, but we know from experience that individual face-to-face communication is best for reviewing the written assessment. Realistically, however, we are aware that individual conferences are not always possible when large

groups of people are involved. Nevertheless, whether you convey assessment results individually or through written communication, the goal of the communication is the same: an explanation of why you assessed, what you assessed, and what the assessment revealed. Be careful to use terminology that the layperson will understand; especially avoid using complicated statistical terms. Remember that parents are going to be interested in knowing what they can do to improve their child's motor or fitness abilities, so be prepared to offer program suggestions. Also have references available to which you can refer the parents for additional program information.

TYPES OF ASSESSMENT INSTRUMENTS

After realistically considering the questions mentioned earlier, you will be in a better position to choose the type of test that will best meet your needs. This section examines the advantages and disadvantages of several assessment tools.

Norm-Referenced

Norm-referenced (NR) assessment instruments are basically *quantitative evaluations* designed to compare a person's skills and abilities with those of others from similar age, sex, and socioeconomic categories. Because the normative scales are derived from statistical procedures, these types of instruments are sometimes referred to as *psychometric.* Currently popular NR tests are the Bayley Scales of Infant Development (Bayley, 1969), the Gesell Developmental Schedules (Gesell & Ames, 1940), Bruininks-Oseretsky Test of Motor Proficiency (Bruininks, 1978), AAHPERD Health-Related Fitness Test (AAHPERD, 1980), and the Test of Gross Motor Development (Ulrich, 1985a).

Advantages   Norm-referenced tests are popular because most (but not all) are easy to administer. The examiner needs minimal training to administer the test, and scoring procedures generally are simple. The assessment score provides information as to where a person stands in relation to peers at a given point in time.

Disadvantages Because NR scales provide information concerning a person's "average" functioning, they are not precise and cannot pinpoint the cause of skill or developmental deficits. They simply supply information as to where a given person stands in comparison to people from similar backgrounds. Scores obtained from NR tests offer little insight into programming considerations.

Criterion-Referenced

Criterion-referenced (CR) assessment instruments evaluate the "quality" of a person's performance. Because development proceeds along a predictable sequence of milestones, it is possible to determine where a person lies within this continuum. Thus, one major difference between NR and CR assessments is that the latter compare people to themselves over time, whereas the former compare people to a standardized population at a given point in time. With CR tests, the examiner's primary interest, for example, is not how far a person can throw a ball but rather the technique (form) the person uses when projecting the ball. Motor development professionals frequently refer to this type of assessment as "process-oriented," which is discussed later in this chapter.

Advantages Results from CR assessment instruments lend more insight into programming considerations than do results from NR tests. The CR test also provides for true developmental assessment, that is, comparing a person to self-performance along a continuum from immature to mature performance styles.

Disadvantages CR tests are more complicated to administer than NR tests, so much more training is needed. Frequently, the examiner must learn many functional definitions for intraskill components, which often causes scoring difficulties.

Product-Oriented Assessment

Motor development researchers in the first half of the century relied heavily on the use of *product-oriented assessment* techniques. When employing this approach, the examiner is more interested in performance outcomes than the technique used to perform the task, for instance, how far or how fast a person can throw a ball. The form or technique used to throw the ball is generally of little interest to the product-oriented assessment examiner. Thus product-oriented assessments are similar to NR assessments because both measure quantitative performance outcomes. They differ in that with NR assessments, normative data have been established for the quantitative measures. The advantages and disadvantages of product-oriented assessments are similar to those for NR assessments.

PRODUCT-ORIENTED VS. PROCESS-ORIENTED ASSESSMENT: A COMPARATIVE EXAMPLE

Pretend that you are to assess the catching ability of a 7-year-old girl. The following examples illustrate major differences between product-and process-oriented assessment.

Product-Oriented Assessment

Without a doubt, the simplest product-oriented assessment to evaluate catching performance is the pass-fail system. The girl's performance is assessed by determining the number of thrown balls that she retained versus the number of balls she dropped. To score, 1 point is awarded for each ball retained; dropped balls are recorded as 0 points.

Process-Oriented Assessment

Within the discipline of motor development, the most widely discussed *process-oriented assessment techniques* are those Roberton and colleagues at the

University of Wisconsin, Madison, described. Their technique is based on the idea that because development occurs at different times within different body components, assessment of motor behavior should involve a segmental or component approach. This component approach requires "the identification of developmental characteristics of body parts within a task" (Safrit, 1990, p. 199). Refer to Table 14-3 which illustrates the hypothesized developmental sequence for catching. Note that the emphasis in this type of evaluation is how each body component reacts to the oncoming projectile.

In addition refer to Chapters 13 and 14, where we present in detail the component approach for assessing running, jumping, hopping, galloping, sliding, skipping, throwing, catching, and kicking.

Roberton and Halverson, both noted for their use of process-oriented assessment, pointed out several major drawbacks of the component approach. They felt that a comprehensive understanding of developmental steps and a prolonged period of study and practice of the techniques are required:

> . . . pre-observation study of the definitions of each developmental step and the decision rules for identifying that step is always necessary. . . . The ease with which successful coaches and teachers seem to spot the movement characteristics of their athletes and stu-

dents comes from years of hard work (Roberton & Halverson, 1984, pp. 53–54).

The feasibility of incorporating such an assessment approach within a large-scale school setting is questionable. Take, for example, the findings of a doctoral dissertation (Jenkot, 1986). Jenkot (1986 used 206 male and female students in grades K–3 in an attempt to study the feasibility of using Roberton and Halverson's component approach to assess both hopping and skipping. Table 17-1 describes the time commitment needed to train evaluators and to collect and record the data. While Jenkot concluded that the component approach was feasible to use in a large-scale setting, we take issue with this conclusion. Given that most elementary physical-education classes meet with the physical education specialist once or twice per week in 30-minute sessions, it would have taken nearly seven class periods to simply videotape these two simple skills. Furthermore, we believe that few physical educators are willing to devote so much "out of class" time to assess student performance. It is our belief, however, that the component approach is feasible in small-scale clinical and research settings. As mentioned earlier, assessment instruments, such as Ulrich's Test of Gross Motor Development (1985a)

TABLE 17-1 Findings from Jenkot's 1986 Study on the Feasibility of Large-Scale Implementation of the component Approach for Assessing Fundamental Motor Skills in Grades K–3

Task	Time Commitment
Amount of time needed to train two teachers to code with .80 criterion agreement the two tasks of hopping and skipping:	
Coder #1	9 hours 40 minutes
Coder #2	5 hours 45 minutes
Time needed to videotape 206 students performing the hop and the skip	3 hours 17 minutes
Time needed to code children's performances from the video recording	18 hours 46 minutes

Source: Jenkot (1986).

and the Michigan State University "total body approach" assessments, are far less time-consuming and easier to administer and therefore are more feasible to use in large-scale settings.

SELECTED NORM-REFERENCED INSTRUMENTS

This section briefly describes four popular norm-referenced assessment instruments. In addition to Bayley Scales of Infant Development, the Bruininks-Oseretsky Test of Motor Proficiency, and the Basic Motor Ability Test–Revised, we also describe the Denver II.

Bayley Scales of Infant Development

The Bayley Scales of Infant Development (BSID) (Bayley, 1969) is a norm-referenced instrument consisting of three scales and comparative indices: (1) a mental scale—Mental Development Index (MDI) of 163 items; it measures responses to visual and auditory stimuli and object manipulation; (2) motor scale—Psychomotor Development Index (PDI) of 81 items; it measures fine and gross motor coordination; (3) an infant behavior record that is an interview rating scale used to measure such factors as attention span and social behavior. Although the BSID is generally administered to "normal" infants and toddlers between 2 months and 30 months of age, Jansma (1981) pointed out its usefulness with seriously disabled children who may be older chronologically but delayed developmentally. A modified version of the BSID, *Modification for Youngsters with Handicapping Conditions* (Hoffman, 1975), is also available.

Scoring is determined by a pass-fail format, with the total number of items passed a basis for determining the PDI and MDI quotients, which are computed from a normed table. The mental and motor scales take trained personnel approximately 45 minutes to administer. Norms were established on 1262 normal children. Split-half reliability coefficients range from .81 to .93 and .68 to .92 for the MDI

and PDI, respectively. The BSID is one of the best norm-referenced instruments available for use with infants.

Bruininks-Oseretsky Test of Motor Proficiency

The Bruininks-Oseretsky Test of Motor Proficiency (BOTMP) is a norm-referenced *test battery* of eight subtests comprising 46 items. A short form, which comprises 14 items from the complete battery, can be used as a quick screening device. The battery provides both a comprehensive index of motor proficiency and individual measures of fine and gross motor skills for children 4 1/2 to 14 1/2 years old. The complete battery can be administered in 45 to 60 minutes; the short form takes approximately 15 to 20 minutes.

Test administration does require various pieces of equipment. The required equipment can be made, or it can be bought for about $250 (it comes in a well-designed, well-packaged carrying case). The $250 price includes score sheets, equipment needed to administer the complete battery, and the examiner's manual, which contains all the standardized tables needed to score the test.

The standardization procedures included a sampling of 765 children selected on the basis of age, sex, race, community size, and geographic region in accordance with the 1970 census (Bruininks, 1978). Average test-retest reliability coefficients for the complete battery and short form are 0.87 and 0.86 respectively. Haubenstricker and associates (1981) found the BOTMP useful for discriminating between "normal" children and those with gross motor dysfunction.

Basic Motor Ability Test–Revised

The Basic Motor Ability Test–Revised (BMAT–R) is a norm-based test used to assess selected large- and small-muscle control responses. The original test was constructed in 1974 and revised in 1978 by Arnheim and Sinclair (1979). The battery of tests can be administered to children 4 to 12 years old. One advantage of the test is that it can be administered to a group of five children in approximately 30 minutes. Test norms were established on 1563 children of various backgrounds. The reliability for the entire test is .93. Table 17-2 shows the various test items.

Denver II

The Denver II (Frankenburg, Dodds, & Archer, 1990) represents a major revision and restandardization of the original Denver Development screening Test (Frankenburg, & Dodds, 1967), which was first developed nearly 27 years ago. The test is designed to screen children between birth and 6 years of age for developmental delays in four aspects of the child's development: (1) personal-social—the ability to perform such tasks as drinking from a cup, removing own garments, and washing and drying the hands; (2) fine motor adaptive—the ability to perform such tasks as passing a block from hand to hand and stacking blocks; (3) language—the ability to imitate sounds, name body parts, define words, etc, and (4) gross motor—the ability to sit, walk, jump, throw, etc. The entire test consists of 125 items and takes no longer to administer than the original 105 item test. The Denver II score sheet

is uniquely laid out as illustrated in Figure 17-2. Each test item is represented by a bar positioned between two age scales, one at the top and one at the bottom of the score sheet. Each bar is scaled to show when 25, 50, 75, and 90 percent of the "normal" children can accomplish a particular item. To determine which test items would be administered, you simply locate the child's age on the age scales and draw a vertical line from the top to the bottom scale. The number of test items that you will administer varies with age. You should administer all items through which the age line passes. In addition, three items to the left of the age line should also be examined.

Each item is graded as pass, fail, refusal, or no opportunity to observe. Whenever possible, an interview with the parents should be obtained in order to determine how the child is performing within the home environment. For decision-making purposes, individual item performance is classified as either a delay, a caution, or normal. A delay represents a failure of an item that 90 percent of age group peers have passed. A caution is denoted if a child fails an item that 75 percent up to and including 90 percent of age group peers have passed. The test is suspect if a child exhibits one or more delays and/or two or more cautions.

TABLE 17-2   BMAT–R Test Items

Item	Purpose
Bead stringing	Eye-hand coordination and dexterity
Target throwing	Eye-hand coordination as related to throwing
Marble transfer	Finger dexterity and speed of hand movement
Back and hamstring stretch	Flexibility
Standing long jump	Strength and power of lower leg and thigh
Face down to standing	Speed and agility
Static balance	Stationary balance with eyes open and eyes closed
Basketball throw	Explosive arm and shoulder strength
Ball striking	Striking coordination
Target kicking	Eye-foot coordination
Agility run	Test ability to change directions quickly

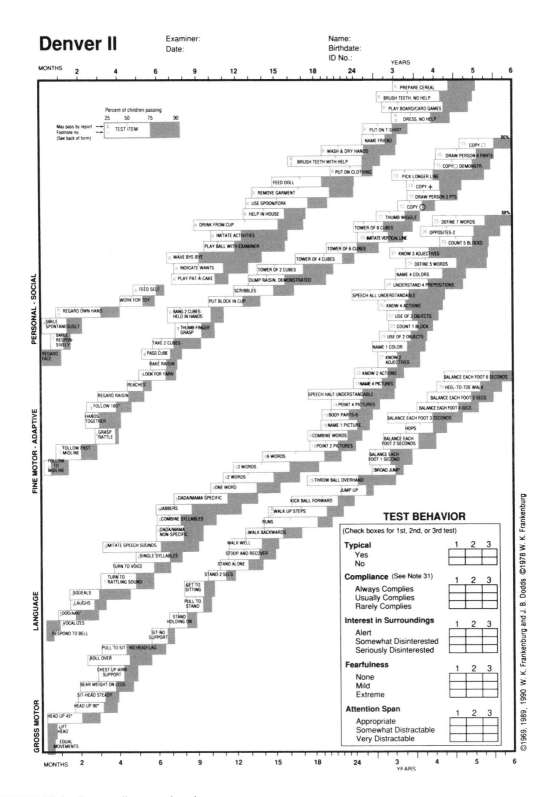

FIGURE 17-2 Denver II score sheet

The standardization procedures included a sampling of 2096 children from Colorado. Four types of item reliability were assessed: (1) interrater, (2) 5- to 10-minute test-retest, (3) 7- to 10-day test-retest using the same examiner and same observer, and (4) 7- to 10-day test-retest using an inter-examiner and inter-observer format. The mean percentage of agreement for each of the four types of reliability was high, ranging from 99.7 percent to 87.5 percent (Frankenburg et al., 1992).

For those interested in learning to administer this test, several training aids are now available. The aids include a self-evaluation with answers within the Denver II Training Manual, a technical manual, video instructional programs, a proficiency test, and master instructor training. The manuals, videotapes, and proficiency tests can be obtained from Denver Development Materials, Inc.; P.O. Box 6919, Denver, CO 80206-0917; (303) 355–4729. Master instructor training is provided by the Denver II office at Community Child Development; 1056 East 19th Avenue, Box B215, Denver, CO 80118; (303) 831-8559 (Frankenburg, et al., 1992).

SELECTED PROCESS-ORIENTED ASSESSMENT INSTRUMENTS

This section describes four popular process-oriented assessment instruments: the Ohio State University Scale of Intra-Gross Motor Assessment, the Developmental Sequence of Motor Skills Inventory, the Fundamental Motor Pattern Assessment Instrument, and the Test of Gross Motor Development.

SIGMA

The Ohio State University Scale of Intra-Gross Motor Assessment (SIGMA) (Loovis & Ersing, 1979) is a criterion-referenced assessment tool designed to evaluate the motor behavior of normal preschool and elementary school children as well as the young mentally retarded child. Each of the 11 fundamental motor skills examined (walking, stair climbing, running, throwing, catching, jumping, hopping, skipping, striking, kicking, ladder climb-

ing) is presented in four developmental levels. The authors state that SIGMA is unique from other tests in that it can be administered in formal testing situations or in an informal free-play setting. Ease of test administration is simplified because of a skill format sheet. Each sheet contains five sources of information to help the examiner: (1) equipment needed to administer the test, (2) directions about the test conditions, (3) criterion test performance, (4) references from which more information about the skill can be obtained, and (5) summative terms/phrases that best describe the child's performance.

SIGMA's content validity was determined by a panel of 11 experts who used a five-point Likert-type scale to rate the test for understandability and usefulness and by documentary analysis of the literature (Sherrill, 1986). Reliability of student performance was not reported. However, 13 judges were required to rate the performance of 12 children who had been videotaped. The tape was viewed two times, 1 week apart and the data were analyzed by Scott's *pi* statistic. Interjudge agreement ranged from 0.50 to 1.00; intrajudge agreement ranged from 0.67 to 1.00.

One unique aspect of the SIGMA is its accompanying program, the Performance Base Curriculum (PBC). The PBC is essentially an instructional program that states objectives and activities for each developmental level within each skill. The PBC is directly related to the SIGMA in that it provides a critical link between assessment and program intervention.

Developmental Sequence of Motor Skills Inventory

Unlike the component analysis Roberton and colleagues used, other professionals prefer to use a more global analysis based on the configuration of the total body during performance of a task. This assessment technique evolved from identification of developmental sequences within selected skills. Each sequence consists of three to five stages stated in terms of observable behaviors. The teacher's task is to observe children performing the skills and then to classify them according to their level of development. To date, the developmental sequences that have been studied are running, hopping, skipping, galloping, long jumping, throwing, catching, striking, kicking, and punting. Table 17-3 highlights the stage characteristics for each of these fundamental motor skills. These developmental sequences are the outgrowth of data collected at the Michigan State University Motor Performance Study. Remember, these skills have been presented in detail in Chapters 13 and 14.

Fundamental Motor Pattern Assessment Instrument

The Fundamental Motor Pattern Assessment Instrument was developed as an outgrowth of a 1976 doctoral dissertation by McClenaghan and later published by McClenaghan and Gallahue (1978). This observational instrument can be used to assess developmental changes over time for the following fundamental patterns: Walking, running, jumping, throwing overhand, catching, and kicking. The performer's quality of movement is scored as being in one of three stages of development: (1) initial stage—first observable attempt at performing the movement pattern; (2) elementary stage—improved coordination and the addition of more mature patterns being integrated into the movement; (3) mature stage—skilled, coordinated, adultlike performance.

Stage descriptions are accompanied by well-illustrated visuals that serve as scoring aids. The authors report test-retest reliability performance of 88.6 percent, with interrater objectivity ranging form 80 to 95 percent (McClenaghan & Gallahue, 1978).

Test of Gross Motor Development

Published in 1985, the Test of Gross Motor Development was designed to assess selected motor skills in children 3 to 10 years old (Ulrich, 1985a). The 12 motor skills that are assessed are divided into two subtests: locomotor skills and object control skills. The run, gallop, hop, skip, horizontal jump, leap, and slide are the locomotor skills measured; object control skills include the two-hand strike, stationary ball bounce, catch, kick, and overhand throw.

The test is designed to be individually administered in approximately 15 minutes. The test manual is well written and easy to understand. The test was standardized on a normative sample of 908 children in eight states. Content validity was established by unanimous agreement among three experts. Split-half reliability coefficients of 0.85 and 0.78 were recorded for the locomotor subtest and object control subtest, respectively. There is an extensive review of this assessment instrument in Langendorfer's (1986) work.

ASSESSING THE DISABLED

Comparative studies of disabled and nondisabled populations support the contention that although individuals with selected special needs perform behind their "normal" peers, both may follow similar patterns of development (DiRocco, 1979). Unfortunately, many assessment instruments, both norm- and criterion-referenced, are geared toward the so-called normal population and so cannot be appropriately used with special populations. For instance, a child with spina bifida who is confined to a wheelchair may have normal motor ability in the upper extremities, but the inability to use the legs while throwing a ball makes normative performance data comparisons inappropriate (DiRooco, 1979).

Special populations pose other potential problems concerning assessment instruments geared to "normal" populations. Frequently, the developmental starting points for special children are so low that their scores are not included in the assessment materials. Clearly, there is a need for the development of more valid test instruments to assess the motor development of those with disabling conditions. Perhaps the passage of the Education for All Handicapped Children Act (PL 94–142) will ensure more emphasis on the development of such assessment instruments.

Instruments Used by Adapted Specialists

Results from a recent national survey identified 31 standardized motor assessment instruments that are

TABLE 17-3 Summary of Fundamental Motor Skill Stage Characteristics—MSU Motor Performance Study: Total Body Approach

Fundamental Motor Skill	Stage 1	Stage 2	Stage 3	Stage 4	Stage 5
Throw	Vertical wind-up "Chop throw" Feet stationary No spinal rotation	Horizontal wind-up "Sling throw" Block rotation Follow-through across body	High wind-up Ipsilateral step Little spinal rotation Follow-through across body	High wind-up Contralateral step Little spinal rotation Follow-through across body	Downward arc wind-up Contralateral step Segmented body rotation Arm-leg follow-through
Catch	Delayed arm action Arms straight in front until ball contact, then scooping action to chest Feet stationary	Arms encircle ball as it approaches Ball is "hugged" to chest Feet stationary or may take one step	"To chest" catch Arms "scoop" under ball to trap it to chest Single step may be used to approach ball	Catch with hands only Feet stationary or limited to one step	Catch with hands only Whole body moves through space
Kick	Little/no leg wind-up Stationary position Foot "pushes" ball Step backward after kick (usually)	Leg wind-up to the rear Stationary position Opposition of arms and legs	Moving approach Foot travels in a low arc Arm/leg opposition Forward or sideward step on follow-through	Rapid approach Backward trunk lean during wind-up Leap before kick Hop after kick	
Punt	No leg wind-up Ball toss erratic Body stationary Push ball/step back	Leg wind-up to the rear Ball toss still erratic Body stationary Forceful kick attempt	Preparatory step(s) Some arm/leg yoking Ball toss or drop	Rapid approach Controlled drop Leap before ball contact Hop after ball contact	
Strike	"Chop" strike Feet stationary	Horizontal push/swing Block rotation Feet stationary/stepping	Ipsilateral step Diagonal downward swing	Contralateral step Segmented body rotation Wrist rollover on follow-through	

(continued)

TABLE 17-3 (*continued*)

Fundamental Motor Skill	Stage 1	Stage 2	Stage 3	Stage 4	Stage 5
Long Jump	Arms act as "brakes" Large vertical component Legs not extended	Arms act as "wings" Vertical component still great Legs near full extension	Arms move forward/ elbows in front of trunk at takeoff Hands to head height Takeoff angle still above 45° Legs often fully extended	Complete arm and leg extension at takeoff Takeoff near 45° angle Thighs parallel to surface when feet contact for landing	
Run	Arms-high guard Flat-footed contact Short stride Wide stride, shoulder width	Arms at middle guard position Vertical component still great Legs near full extension	Arms at low guard position Arm opposition—elbows nearly extended Heel-toe contact	Heel-toe contact (toe-heel when sprinting) Arm-leg opposition High heel recovery Elbow flexion	
Hop	Nonsupport foot in front with thigh parallel to floor Body erect Hands shoulder height	Nonsupport knee flexed with knee in front and foot behind support leg Slight body lean forward Bilateral arm action	Nonsupport thigh vertical with foot behind support leg—knee flexed More body lean forward Bilateral arm action	Pendular action on nonsupport leg Forward body lean Arm opposition with swing leg	
Gallop	Resembles rhythmically uneven run Trail leg crosses in front of lead leg during airborne phase, remains in front at contact	Slow-moderate tempo, choppy rhythm Trail leg stiff Hips often oriented sideways Vertical component exaggerated	Smooth, rhythmical pattern, moderate tempo Feet remain close to ground Hips oriented forward		
Skip	Broken skip pattern or irregular rhythm Slow, deliberate movement Ineffective arm action	Rhythmical skip pattern Arms provide body lift Excessive vertical component	Arm action reduced/hands below shoulders Easy, rhythmical movement Support foot near surface on hop		

SOURCE: Haubenstricker, 1990. Used with permission

frequently used by adapted physical education specialists (Ulrich, 1985b). Of these instruments, 69 percent of the respondents used the 11 tests listed in Table 17-4. While several of these instruments have already been described earlier in the chapter, the remainder of this section will be devoted to a brief description of several more of these instruments with particular attention to those that were developed specifically for the assessment of individuals with special needs. For a comparative analysis of these 11 tests, the reader is encouraged to consult the work of Miles, Nierengarten, and Nearing (1988).

Brigance Diagnostic Inventory of Early Development

The Brigance Diagnostic Inventory of Early Development (BDIED) (Brigance, 1978) is a criterion-referenced test with norms. The BDIED assesses behaviors that are divided into the 11 domains illustrated in Table 17-5. Of the 11 domains, the first 4 are generally considered the most relevant for pro-

TABLE 17-4 Motor Assessment Tests Frequently used by Adapted Physical Educators

Rank	Test
1.	Bruininks-Oseretsky Test of Motor Proficiency
2.	AAHPERD Special Fitness Test for Mildly Mentally Retarded Persons
3.	Brigance Diagnostic Inventory of Early Development
4.	Hughes Basic Gross Motor Assessment
5.	Project A.C.T.I.V.E. Motor Ability Test
6.	Purdue Perceptual-Motor Survey
7.	AAHPERD Health Related Fitness Test
8.	I CAN Project—Fundamental Skills
9.	Ohio State University Scale of Intra-Gross Motor Assessment (SIGMA)
10.	AAHPERD Youth Fitness Test
11.	Denver Development Screening Test

Source: As reported by Ulrich (1985b).

fessionals working in the discipline of motor behavior (preambulatory motor skills and behaviors, gross motor skills and behaviors, fine motor skills and behaviors, and self-help skills). This multidomain test is designed for use with individuals between birth and 6 years of age. The test is easy to administer, and interpretation of test results is, in part, simplified by the developmental age levels accompanying each skill sequence. These developmental age levels are used to roughly indicate when a certain behavior should start to be exhibited and when that same behavior is typically mastered. Because of the wide range of skills assessed and the flexible test format, the BDIED is very useful for assessing young individuals with severely disabling conditions (Bagnato & Neisworth, 1981).

Purdue Perceptual-Motor Survey

The Purdue Perceptual-Motor Survey was constructed on the idea that perceptual-motor abilities are necessary for the acquisition of academic skills. More specifically, if certain motor generalizations are not obtained it may be manifested in slow academic learning. This survey, which was developed by Roach and Kephart, is "not designed for diagno-

TABLE 17-5 Brigance Diagnostic Inventory of Early Development: Assessment Categories

Preambulatory motor skills and behaviors

Gross motor skills and behaviors

Fine motor skills and behaviors

Self-help skills

Prespeech behaviors

Speech and language skills

General knowledge and comprehension

Readiness skills

Basic reading skills

Writing skills

Math skills

sis, per se, but to allow the clinician to observe perceptual-motor behavior in a series of behavioral performances" (Roach & Kephart, 1966, p. 11). As such, this survey should be used only as a screening device. If suspect performance is observed, further investigation would be needed before a diagnosis could be made. The survey was designed to be used with children between 6 and 10 years of age. The survey consists of 22 items subdivided into the following five categories:

1. balance and posture
2. body image and differentiation
3. perceptual-motor match
4. ocular control
5. form perception

Each survey item is evaluated on a scale of 1 to 4. Table 17-6 lists the 22 survey items according to category. Test-retest reliability estimates and objectivity estimates have been reported in the range of 0.95. Nevertheless, standardization procedures are suspect because only 200 children from one school were used in the validation process.

I CAN

Improving the quality of physical education instruction for all students is one of the primary goals of the I CAN project. This project, originally funded by the Bureau of Education for the Handicapped, is under the direction of Janet A. Wessel, Ph.D.

The target population is "children whose overall developmental growth is slower than the average, as well as for children with specific learning disabilities, social or emotional adjustment difficulties, and/or economic or language disadvantages" (Wessel, 1976, p. ix). Furthermore, the curriculum is designed for individuals between 3 and 25 years of age.

Currently, I CAN consists of three curricula programs, each of which is subdivided into several instructional modules. Each module consists of a curriculum guide, assessment records, game cards,

TABLE 17-6   The Purdue Perceptual-Motor Survey

Survey Category	Survey Item
Balance and posture	Walking board
	forward
	backward
	sidewise
	Jumping
Body image and differentiation	Identification of body parts
	Imitation of movement
	Obstacle course
	Kraus-Weber (strength)
	Angels-in-the-snow
Perceptual-motor match	Chalkboard drawing
	circle
	double circle
	lateral line
	vertical line
	Rhythmic writing
	rhythm
	reproduction
	orientation
Ocular control	Ocular pursuits
	both eyes
	right eye
	left eye
	convergence
Form perception	Visual achievement forms
	forms
	organization

and an implementation guide. Table 17-7 illustrates the modules currently available and their cost.

Assessment is accomplished through a criterion-referenced approach. Each curriculum kit is neatly packaged and easy to administer. Once the curriculum kits have been purchased, there is no additional expense because the assessment forms are not copyrighted and therefore may be reproduced.

Test reliability was calculated on only three skills and on the basis of percent agreement (run = 95%; overhand throw = 89%; catch = 90%). According to the test developers, it was assumed that other test items would probably have similar reliability estimates because they were all developed using the same instructional model. Content validity has not been established and is deferred to the user (Wessel, 1976).

AIDS IN ASSESSING MOTOR SKILLS

As mentioned, one disadvantage of many tests is the need for the test examiner to learn many functional definitions describing the criterion behavior associated with each developmental level within a given skill. Checklists or reminder sheets that list key descriptive terms for each developmental level can jog the examiner's memory. Regardless of a person's expertise with the developmental stages of selected tasks, it is still an excellent idea to have such a checklist at hand, to ensure consistent scoring.

Videotaping individual performance is another way to assess motor skills. Certain motor skills must be executed at high rates of speed, so even the experienced examiner may have difficulty denoting exactly what took place within each body segment during the performance of the task. Today's video units are capable of slow-motion playback, thus af-

fording more precise analysis of most motor skills. However, one motor skill that does not totally lend itself to video analysis is the overarm throw for force because the video unit's framing rate is not fast enough to freeze the ballistic movement of the throwing arm. As a result, the throwing arm is likely to be blurred.

Another advantage of videotaping is that it decreases the number of times a child must perform a task so the examiner can evaluate the developmental level of each body segment. Within a given test session, for example, a very young child may become fatigued if required to perform a forward roll 20 times. With videotaping or filming, the child need perform only a few trials. The examiner at a later time can play back the tape or film many times while evaluating each body segment.

ASSESSING PHYSICAL FITNESS

To this point, we have focused our attention on the assessment of motor skills. There is, however, a rapidly growing body of knowledge regarding the assessment of components of physical fitness. In the sections to follow, we describe several of the most

TABLE 17-7 I CAN: Programs and Modules

Program	Module	Cost
Preprimary motor and play skills	Locomotor Object control Body control Health fitness Play equipment Play participation	$32
Primary skills	Fundamental skills Body management Health/fitness Aquatics	$495
Sport, leisure, and recreation skills	Team sports Dance and individual sports Outdoor activities Backyard/neighborhood activities	$414

frequently used physical-fitness test batteries. More specifically, we describe the four batteries produced by the American Alliance for Health, Physical Education, Recreation, and Dance as well as the two batteries of tests known as the National Children and Youth Fitness Study.

AAHPERD Youth Fitness Test

The American Alliance for Health, Physical Education, Recreation, and Dance Youth Fitness Test was first published in 1958 in response to a study that found European children to be in better physical condition than American children (Kraus & Hirschland, 1954). The test was revised in both 1975 and 1976. The current revision (AAHPERD, 1976) consists of six items. Table 17-8 lists the six test items and identifies which fitness component each measures.

While the original version was developed by a group of physical educators who logically selected the test items, the 1976 version was developed by a national normative survey. Norms are available for ages 9 through 17+ years. The major criticism of this test battery is that it does not emphasize health-related fitness; instead, motor fitness is stressed. Some experts have questioned the test's validation procedures and reliability estimates, as neither are reported in the test manual (Safrit, 1990)

AAHPERD Health-Related Physical Fitness Test

As the name implies, this test was designed to emphasize what is commonly referred to as physiological fitness. The following three criteria were used to select the test items:

1. The test should measure a range that extends from severely limited dysfunction to high levels of functional capacity.

2. The test should be composed of items that can be improved with physical activity.

3. The test should accurately reflect an individual's physical fitness status and changes in functional capacity.

TABLE 17-8   AAHPERD Youth Fitness Test

Test Item	Fitness Component Measured
Pull-ups (males only)	Arm and shoulder girdle strength and endurance
Flexed-arm hang (females only)	Arm and shoulder girdle strength and endurance
Shuttle run	Agility: the ability to change directions quickly and in a coordinated manner
Standing long jump	Leg power
50-yard dash	Speed
600-yard run°	Cardiovascular endurance
Sit-ups (bent knee) (1-min time limit)	Abdominal strength and endurance

°Optional distance runs include a 1-mile run or 9-minute run for ages 10 to 12 years and a 1 1/2-mile run or a 12-minute run for those 13 years of age and older. Norms for these optional runs are taken from the Texas test (1973).

The test battery consists of components that measure cardiovascular endurance and body composition as well as abdominal and low-back hamstring musculoskeletal function. The test manual (1980) describes each of the tests and contains test norms for children in grades 1–12. Norms for college students have been developed by Pate (1985).

Physical Best

Physical Best is the most recent AAHPERD health-related physical fitness package (AAHPERD, 1988). It contains three components:

1. an instrument designed for the assessment of health-related physical fitness

2. an education component

3. an awards program

The assessment instrument evaluates the five health-related physical fitness components: aerobic endurance, body composition, flexibility, muscular strength, and muscular endurance. Validity coefficients range from 0.60 to 0.98, and most reliability estimates exceed 0.80 (Hastad & Lacy, 1994). Health fitness standards for children between 5 and 18 years of age are contained in the test manual.

The educational component is designed to integrate knowledge regarding the five health-related physical fitness areas. The educational kit contains lesson plans, individualized contracts used for goal setting, report cards, and letters to parents.

The Physical Best awards program is designed to motivate all students to do their personal best and to encourage participants to compete against themselves instead of other individuals. Table 17-9 illustrates this three-tier awards program.

National Children and Youth Fitness Studies I and II

The National Children and Youth Fitness Study (NCYFS) was undertaken in 1985 by the Department of Health and Human Services for the purpose of describing the current fitness status of

American children and youth. The first of the two fitness studies utilized items from the AAHPERD Health-Related Physical Fitness Test along with a chin-up test. Norms were developed on a national sample of 8800 participants between 10 and 17 years of age. These norms are published in the January 1985 edition of the *Journal of Physical Education, Recreation, and Dance* (Ross et al., 1985).

As an outgrowth of the first NCYFS, a second study was undertaken to describe the current fitness status of American children younger than 10 years of age. Norms were developed and broken down by age/sex (6–9 years of age) and grade/sex (grade 1–4) for each of the five fitness tests administered. The NCYFS–II differed from the first test in two ways. First, cardiovascular endurance was measured by a 1-mile run for children who were 8 or 9 years of age while a 1/2–mile run was employed for children under 8 years of age. Second, instead of using a chin-up test to assess upper-body strength, a modified pull-up test was used, which required the construction of a special apparatus (Pate et al., 1987). Like the NCYFS–I, the NCYFS–II was also

TABLE 17-9 American Alliance Physical Best Awards Program

Award	Purpose	Criteria
Fitness activity award	To recognize participation in appropriate physical activity beyond that which is experienced in required physical education class.	Student must maintain an activity log that details involvement in appropriate activity outside the required physical education class.
Fitness goals award	To recognize the attainment of an individual fitness goal.	Student must successfully attain an individualized fitness goal that was written in a contract constructed by both the student and teacher
Health fitness award	To recognize mastery of the health fitness standards as published in the test manual.	Student must obtain the minimum level of health-related fitness on all test items contained in the Physical Best fitness battery.

developed with the use of a national sample. Norms for the NCYFS–II are published in the November/December 1987 edition of the *Journal of Physical Education, Recreation, and Dance* (Ross et al., 1987).

AAHPERD Functional Fitness Test for Older Adults

The AAHPERD Functional Fitness Test for Older Adults test is designed to be used with individuals 60+ years of age. The phrase "functional fitness" in the test's name is defined as "the physical capacity of the individual to meet ordinary and unexpected demands of daily life safely and effectively" (Osness, 1989, p. 65). In accordance with that definition, the test contains items that are closely related to the types of normal activities generally encountered by individuals 60+ years of age.

This field test for older adults consists of five test items: a test of agility/dynamic balance, a 1/2-mile walk (endurance), a test of trunk/leg flexibility (a sit-and-reach test), a test of muscular strength/endurance, and a "soda pop" coordination test. All that is needed to administer these tests is: floor tape, stop watch, two traffic cone markers, a chair without arms, three soda pop cans, and a 4- and an 8-pound weight, which can be easily made by putting sand into 1-gallon plastic milk jugs.

SUMMARY

Psychomotor assessment should be systematically, not haphazardly approached and based on a plan that links assessment with curricular programming.

It is difficult to select an appropriate test instrument. The instrument should be valid, reliable, and objective, and feasible to administer and interpret. However, the most important characteristic is test validity. If the test fails to assess what it purports to assess, the instrument is of no value.

Norm-referenced test instruments are popular because most (but not all) are easy to administer and usually require minimal examiner training. This type of assessment provides information about a person's average functioning. On the other hand, criterion-referenced assessment instruments evaluate quality of individual performance or set a level for mastery learning.

The following are norm-referenced assessment instruments: the Bayley Scales of Infant Development, the Bruininks-Oseretsky Test of Motor Proficiency, the Basic Motor Ability Test–Revised, and the Denver II.

Popular process-oriented assessment instruments include the Ohio State University Scale of Intra-Gross Motor Assessment (SIGMA), the Developmental Sequence of Motor Skills Inventory, the Fundamental Motor Pattern Assessment Instrument, and the Test of Gross Motor Development.

It is important not to use an assessment instrument geared to a "normal" population when assessing disabled people. At present, there is a need for more assessment instruments to be validated with disabled populations.

Another area of interest to motor behavior specialists is the assessment of physical fitness. Within the past 10 years the American Alliance for Health, Physical Education, Recreation, and Dance has produced several instruments geared toward both the young and the elderly. Two other fitness test batteries gaining in popularity are the National Children and Youth Fitness Study, I and II.

KEY TERMS

Content validity
Correlation coefficient
Criterion-referenced (CR) assessment instruments
Interrater reliability
Norm-referenced (NR) assessment instruments
Objectivity

Play-based assessment
Process-oriented assessments
Product-oriented assessments
Psychometric
Quantitative evaluations
Test battery
Test reliability

CHAPTER 18

Planning and Conducting Developmental Movement Programs

There is much more to organizing and conducting a developmental movement program than just having a thorough understanding of motor development principles and theories. You also need exceptional organizational and communicative skills and the ability to work well with people—these all-important satellite skills can make or break a program. This chapter presents a systematic approach for planning and implementing this special type of program. Planning and implementing the program is a monumental task, one that takes much time, consideration, and effort.

For ease of presentation, our systematic approach is divided into three phases. In phase 1 you determine whether you have the resources to implement a quality program. For instance, can the program's aims and goals be met given the existing facilities, equipment, and personnel? Phase 2 concerns selected administrative concerns: how to advertise the

program, how to register participants, and many other important procedures. Phase 3 is devoted to certain curricular issues, such as how to organize the participation aspect of the program.

PREPROGRAM CONSIDERATIONS

Before implementing a developmental movement program, you must first determine whether there is a need for such a program. If there is a need, do you have the necessary facilities, equipment, and personnel for implementing the program? This section shows you how to answer these vital questions.

Philosophy

The first step in planning an effective and efficient developmental movement program is to consider two very important elements of any program. First, what will be the *philosophy* governing the operation of the program? What do you hope to accomplish by implementing a program? Is your objective to give the so-called normal child movement experiences necessary to foster optimal development, or is the program being designed to help children remediate existing motor problems? Do you intend to cater to the highly skilled person who wants to become even more proficient in specific sport skills? In any case, you must determine the program's aims and objectives.

Second, you must consider the *scope* of the program. Even though most developmental movement programs are designed with young children in mind, remember that motor development and motor refinement are lifelong processes. As such, will your program cater to preschool children, elementary school children, adolescents, younger adults, or older adults? Furthermore, do you plan to include people from special populations? In other words, will you offer an *adapted program*? If so, what will be the emphasis of this program? Will it be designed for the mentally retarded, the orthopedically disabled, or for individuals with some other disabling condition?

Figure 18-1 illustrates areas that could be included in a developmental movement program. Initially, you should not attempt to implement more than one area. Be patient, take your time; be certain that you can successfully implement one of these programs before you attempt to branch out into other program areas.

Facilities and Equipment

Once you have established a philosophy and defined the population you want to serve, determine whether you have the facilities and equipment needed to implement the program. The amount and type of equipment needed will depend on the scope of the program and the age groups to be served. Therefore, equipment and apparatus needs differ from program to program. This section does not list the numerous pieces of available play apparatus and equipment; it describes the differences in various types of equipment and apparatus and offers general guidelines that should help you select the most appropriate material.

Types of Indoor and Outdoor Play Apparatus

There are two types of play apparatus: developmental and nondevelopmental. *Developmental apparatus* foster both organic and skill development, two objectives of most motor development programs. For example, developmental apparatus that contribute to strength development include horizontal ladder, jungle gym, chinning bar, climbing pole, and parallel bars.

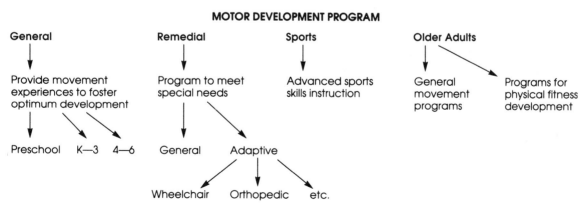

MOTOR DEVELOPMENT PROGRAM

FIGURE 18-1 Potential areas of emphasis in a motor development program

Young children especially enjoy playing on *nondevelopmental apparatus,* but this type of apparatus contributes little to the physical objectives of a developmental movement program. Nondevelopmental apparatus include sliding boards, swings, merry-go-rounds, seesaws, and spring animals. Also be aware that nondevelopmental equipment is frequently misused in such a manner as to cause bodily injury.

Developmentally Appropriate Equipment

Any time a person is required to perform a motor task with equipment that is not *developmentally appropriate,* performance suffers (see Figure 18-2). For example, a young child who is required to shoot a regulation-size basketball toward a 10-foot basketball goal faces a predicament. In most instances, the youngster is not capable of using the correct technique to project the ball toward the basket because the ball is too big and too heavy and the basketball goal too high. As a result, the child uses an inappropriate shooting technique, such as an over-the-shoulder shot or an underhanded between-the-legs shot to propel the ball toward the basket. An experimental investigation that Isaacs and Karpman (1981) conducted revealed just how unsuccessful 8- and 9-year-old children could be when required to use inappropriate equipment. In this investigation, 30 boys and 30 girls were required to shoot regulation-size basketballs, junior-size basketballs, and an even smaller and lighter Nerf basketball (soft rubber) toward 8- and 10-foot basketball goals. These young children were five times more likely to make the shot when the basketball goal was 8 feet rather than the standard 10 feet. In addition, their likelihood of missing the shot was less when they used the junior-size basketball. These findings were also supported by Haywood (1978) and Wright (1967), who found that letting children use smaller and lighter basketballs improved achievement scores on a basketball-shooting accuracy task. Also, as discussed in Chapter 14, the size of the ball influences children's throwing performance. Burton and colleagues (1992, 1993) found a critical transitional point when ball size would begin to interfere with throwing tech-

FIGURE 18-2 Failure is inevitable whenever appropriate equipment and facilities are not utilized.

nique and the manner in which the ball is grasped. All of these studies suggest that we should take into consideration the size of the performer when recommending play equipment. In other words, the play equipment should be appropriately scaled to the size of the child.

How can you be certain that your equipment is developmentally appropriate? Furthermore, does your equipment take into consideration individual differences in skill ability? Little research is available to help us answer these two important questions. However, Herkowitz (1978, 1984) offered three suggestions. First, group together equipment with similar functions but of different sizes. For instance, set chinning bars at different heights and be sure the diameters of the bars are different, to take into consideration differences in hand size. Similarly, construct vertical and horizontal ladders with different spacing between rungs. Second, use adjustable equipment to accommodate differences in developmental levels, such as jumping hurdles, batting tees, and basketball goals, all of which can be adjusted to different heights. Last, Herkowitz suggested using a single piece of equipment constructed in such a manner that it can accommodate different developmental levels, for example, a specially constructed balance beam that is very wide at one end but progressively narrow toward the other end. These three guidelines should help you select the most appropriate equipment for your program.

Playgrounds A properly equipped and designed playground can help foster motor development. According to Siedentop and coauthors, "the use of playspace over time is related to the complexity and novelty of the playspace" (1984, p. 184). For this reason, they discourage incorporating large play apparatus that by design are unchangeable, such as the nondevelopmental apparatus mentioned earlier. They recommend incorporating apparatus that can take on many different shapes. For instance, a basic piece of equipment can be embedded into the playground to which portable attachments such as ladders, stairs, and horizontal bars can be attached in different configurations. When not in use, the attachments can be kept in a storage unit located on the playground. A play environment that is capable of taking on many different looks helps eliminate boredom and encourages creative movement.

Only within recent years have we become more concerned about the number of children who sustain injury while participating on playgrounds. National surveys indicated that nearly a quarter of a million children under 15 years of age are treated in hospital emergency rooms because of injuries related to playground equipment (Bruya & Langendorfer, 1988; Frost, 1990; American Academy of Orthopedic Surgeons, 1991). As indicated in Table 18-1, the vast majority of playground injuries are caused by falling from play apparatus onto a hard surface or onto other parts of the apparatus. In fact, yard surfacing was found to be inadequate in 114 of 130 playgrounds surveyed in 11 states and the District of Columbia (Duston, 1992). Inappropriate surfaces include concrete, hard-packed dirt, asphalt, and even grass. More appropriate surfaces would include sand, loosely packed pea gravel, mulch, and rubber padding. Table 18-2 presents several steps that can be taken to reduce the number of playground injuries.

If you would like additional information on playground safety you can obtain a free copy of a handbook by contacting: *Playground Equipment Handbook,* U. S. Consumer Product Safety Commission, Washington, DC 20207. In addition, a free copy of *Play It Safe, A Guide to Playground Safety,* the American Academy of Orthopedic Surgeons brochure, can be obtained by calling 800-824-BONES.

TABLE 18-1 Public Playground Equipment Injury Rates and Their Causes

Primary Cause of Injury	Percentage
Falls resulting in contact with the underlying surface	58
Striking the equipment while falling	14
Falls resulting in contact with other equipment	2
Impact with moving equipment	13.1
Impact with stationary equipment	5.4
Contacting protrusions, pinch points, sharp edges, and sharp points	6.9

SOURCE: Adapted from American Academy of Orthopedic Surgeons (1991). Based on data from the National Electronic Injury Surveillance System (NEISS) special study, April–December 1988, U.S. Consumer Product Safety Commission, Directorate Epidemiology, Division of Hazard Analysis, Washington, DC.

TABLE 18-2 Factors to Consider for the Reduction of Playground Injuries

Surfaces Under Playground Apparatus

Sand surfacing should be 8 to 10 inches deep.

Fine pea gravel (1/4 inch) surfacing should be 10–12 inches deep.

Organic materials such as mulch or shredded wood should be 10–12 inches deep.

As a general rule of thumb, the surfacing under playground apparatus should be loose and deep enough to make walking on the material difficult. In other words, if you can easily walk on the material, it probably is not deep enough or loose enough to adequately absorb the body's impact.

Playground Design Considerations

Establish a "use zone" around all equipment with adequate space for entering and exiting the play area.

Physically separate the most popular playground equipment to help avoid overcrowding.

Establish separate play areas for younger and older children.

Install guardrails on elevated platforms.

Use developmentally appropriate equipment to ensure proper hand-grip size when grasping.

Separate playgrounds from streets by a fence, shrubs, or other physical barriers.

Apparatus should be accessible to wheelchair traffic.

Playground Maintenance

Inspect playground equipment regularly for rust, sharp edges, wood rot, loose bolts, bent parts, and bearing wear.

Inspect supporting surfaces and replace materials that do not meet the specifications outlined in the section titled, "Surfaces under playground apparatus."

Inspect playground for and remove broken glass, sharp objects, and holes.

Equipment Storage and Transport When acquiring equipment, give special consideration to storing and transporting it. Is there enough room for storing such apparatus as balance beams, parallel bars, and other large pieces of equipment? If so, is the storage area conveniently located in regard to the activity area? Are these large and heavy pieces of equipment easy to assemble and disassemble? If not, chances are they will not be used frequently in the program. Ideally, the storage area should be located as close as possible to the activity area, even within the same area if possible.

Smaller pieces of equipment, such as balls, hoops, and racquets, also require much storage space. To facilitate the storage and transport of this type of small equipment, buy or make several bins to which you can attach wheels. With such a setup you simply roll out the equipment for a given instructional station, making only one trip, which is certainly more efficient than carrying two or three balls to a station and having to make several trips before the station is totally assembled. If you cannot construct these bins, buy large rubber trash cans that have been attached to dollies. Not only does this arrangement facilitate the speed at which a station can be set up, but it is also a valuable organizational tool because we no longer have to frantically look for equipment—we always know in which can the equipment is located.

Personnel

A motor development program accompanied by the most elaborate, versatile, and expensive equipment is not necessarily guaranteed success, because the success of any program is directly dependent on the personnel available to implement the program. You must assemble an instructional staff—a team of individuals committed to working toward the common aims and goals of the program.

University- or College-Based Programs If the program is being conducted in conjunction with a local college or university, it may be feasible to put together an instructional team of undergraduate and graduate students who want the experience of working with people in a movement environment. This arrangement is particularly attractive because most college students who elect to take part in the program may be available for several years, which helps eliminate the need to retrain a new instructional team every few months. Nevertheless, you should expect an influx of different personnel because inevitably members of your instructional team graduate or leave the program for some reason.

To combat this dilemma, establish some type of hierarchical arrangement or ranking among instructional personnel. For example, people who have completed a series of courses in motor development and those who have had prior work experience in a clinic are assigned the position of *station leader*. Station leaders are responsible for a variety of tasks, including (1) directing assigned activities and instruction in a given area of expertise, (2) training less experienced staff members, and (3) perhaps being assigned supervisory duties. The less-experienced people are *assistant instructors* or *general assistants*. Assistant instructors are usually physical

education majors who have acquired some area of expertise but have not taken a sequence of course work in motor development. Furthermore, they generally do not have any prior teaching experience with the population involved. General assistants, an entry level position, have neither experience in teaching nor an area of expertise. The primary duties of assistant instructors are to help carry out the directives of the station leaders and to serve as partners to the participants in the clinic. This partner or friend relationship between participant and clinician fosters a more social and relaxed atmosphere in which learning new skills can take place. Furthermore, because both participant and clinician are actively involved in participating in assigned activities under the direction of both assistant instructors and station leaders, the general assistant gains valuable experience in learning how to teach in a movement environment while slowly acquiring an area of expertise. Thus, both the motor development participant and the general assistant learn through direct participation in the program.

Public School–Based Programs Not all motor programs can be developed around college students. In fact, most programs conducted in public schools are developed, organized, and carried out by one person, usually the physical education teacher. Unfortunately, one person is not usually capable of offering the one-to-one attention so often necessary when working with the people who typically attend these special programs. Thus, the physical educator's challenge is to recruit additional help, in most cases *volunteers*. Frequently, volunteers are viewed as more trouble than they are worth, but this is unfortunate because volunteers, even volunteers with little or no teaching experience, can perform valuable duties, enabling those with teaching experience to spend more time with program participants.

If the use of volunteers is to be successful, Dunn, Morehouse, and Fredericks (1985) recommend that you consider their rules for the use of volunteers:

1. Take the time to train your volunteers. Be sure they understand their role in your program.

2. If volunteers are to be involved in teaching, be sure they are assigned teaching duties compatible to their level of training.

3. Establish a system whereby constructive feedback can be given to volunteers. Faulty performance should be corrected tactfully and proper performance praised.

4. Because there may be so little time to communicate with your volunteers, you will need to establish a simplified system of communication. Volunteers need to know what to do with given individuals, and you need to obtain from the volunteers information concerning given student performances.

5. Maintain a system of flexible scheduling.

Volunteers can be enlisted by consulting teachers, your parent-teacher association, local civic groups, private agencies, and local recreational departments. Also, do not overlook the possibility of using older students who attend neighboring schools.

ADMINISTRATIVE CONSIDERATIONS

As the director of a motor development program, you probably envision yourself spending most of your time working directly with program participants. Unfortunately, if your goal is to run a trouble-free program, you will probably be spending more time than you ever imagined handling administrative responsibilities. This section discusses the administrative tasks you are likely to confront. By following our suggestions, you should save time in handling these important duties.

Advertising the Program

Once you decide to implement a motor development program, you must then determine if there will be enough interest in the program to justify its existence. You can use one of two approaches. First, conduct a local survey to get a feel for the community's acceptance of the program. Or skip this process and go directly to advertising the program and accepting applications. We recommend the latter approach—our experience has been that although the community may support the program in theory, when it comes to actually registering, the percentage of affirmative responses is often lower.

Depending on the scope of the program, there are different forms of advertising. If the scope of the program is limited to just one school, a simple announcement sent home in the school's newsletter suffices. In some special instances you may want to send a personal letter to the parents of children you know will benefit from participation in the program. On the other hand, if the scope of the program is to be extended into the community, then you must establish a broader advertising base. Develop program flyers and place them in various community establishments or send them to local civic organizations. Furthermore, most local newspapers seek community-interest stories; we have found local papers an excellent way to get in-depth coverage at no expense. Simply call the local newspaper and tell them about your program. Usually, they will be glad to send someone out to interview you.

Certain essential information should be included in your advertising, whether it is in the form of a flyer or newspaper interview:

1. Tell the public the purpose of the program and how it can help them or their child.

2. Identify the age range of the participants.

3. State meeting times, meeting place, and length of program. For instance, the program will be held in Torrence Elementary School Gymnasium from 9:00 a.m. to 11:30 a.m. for eight consecutive Saturdays starting October 7, 1995.

4. Outline the registration procedures.

5. Is there a registration fee; if so, how much?

6. Include a telephone number where you can be reached if anyone has any further questions.

Remember, advertising is crucial because the best-designed program is of no value if it has no participants.

Registration

In most instances, the registration form can be a part of the advertisement flyer. Figure 18-3 is an example of a registration form. Note that the form is divided into two distinct sections. The first section contains information pertinent to the motor development program; the second section is an application for enrollment. This form serves two purposes. The bottom section, which is to be filled in by a parent or participant, is used for administrative purposes because it contains personal information about the applicant. And because the form is signed, it shows approval or consent for participation in the program. The applicant retains the top half of the form; this part contains most of the important information about the program, such as dates, meeting times, and meeting place.

When applications are received in the mail, you should get into the habit of processing each one immediately. Initially screen each application to determine if the applicant conforms to the program's philosophy and scope. For example, is the applicant within the appropriate age range that the program is to serve? In addition, does the applicant have any physical limitations that would preclude participation in the program? If the answers to these two questions are satisfactory, then place the person's name on an official enrollment list.

Next, send the applicant a letter or postcard confirming acceptance into the program. On this letter or postcard remind the applicant about the program's starting date, starting time, and meeting location. In addition, inform the applicant of any special first-day procedures, such as what to wear.

Orientation Meeting

If the program includes young children, you have an obligation to keep all parents well informed. An *orientation meeting* can partly serve this purpose. More specifically, at the orientation meeting you disseminate important information about the operation as well as the purpose of the program. During this meeting, address each of the following issues:

1. Explain the philosophy of the program and what you hope to accomplish.

2. Explain drop-off and pick-up procedures and stress the importance of being prompt.

3. Explain cancellation procedures in the event of inclement weather.

4. Urge all participants to carry health insurance in case of an accident. If appropriate, also describe supplemental accident insurance that can be acquired.

5. Briefly preview the upcoming *parents' workshop* at which parents can learn how to teach movement skills to their children.

6. Explain your policy concerning parents' observation of their children during clinical sessions.

7. Have individuals fill in any consent forms.

8. Conduct an open question-answer discussion.

Send an agenda to all participants approximately 10 days before the meeting. You may want to include this agenda in your letter confirming enrollment.

First-Aid and Emergency Procedures

Motor development participants have a right to learn and play in a safe physical environment. In general, a well thought out and well-organized program will produce such an environment. Nevertheless, whenever people engage in movement tasks, accidents can occur. Fortunately, most accidents will be minor scrapes and bruises. However, there is a potential for more serious injury. But whether injuries are minor or serious, organizers of developmental movement programs must be prepared to handle both.

Who should be contacted when injuries occur? Who should administer first aid? What is the telephone number of the nearest rescue squad? In short, how should emergencies be handled? To provide a clear directive for all involved, these questions can best be addressed by establishing a set of first-aid and emergency procedures. Above all, remember that for these procedures to be effective, all person-

CLINE ELEMENTARY SCHOOL
DEVELOPMENTAL MOVEMENT PROGRAM

What   During Fall 1995, the Cline Elementary School Motor Development Clinic will again be offered to the general public. The purpose of the clinic is to improve the motor skill development and sport skills of elementary school children (Grades K–6).

How   Participants will receive individualized instruction in physical fitness, gymnastics, perceptual-motor activities, and various sport skills to include soccer, basketball, tennis, racquetball, and other individual preferences. A periodic evaluation will be performed, and parents will be provided with a written progress report. The clinic will give consideration to the first 60 applications received before September 14, 1995.

When   The clinic will be held on Saturday mornings:

Session I :   9:00–10:30 A.M.   Grades 4–6

Session II: 10:30–12:00 noon   Grades K–3

The clinic will start October 7, 1995. The fee will be $40 per child. Sessions will be held in the Cline Elementary School gym at 1704 Virginia Avenue, Centerville, OH 45458. Enrollment will be limited to foster a low student-teacher ratio. For additional information call 873-3222.

To apply for enrollment, please complete the following by September 14, 1995, and mail to Cline Elementary School, 1704 Virginia Avenue, Centerville, OH 45458.

Payment must accompany application. Check only—made payable to:

Cline Elementary—Motor Development Clinic

Child's name _____

Address _____

Phone _____ Sex _____ Grade _____

Parent's signature _____

Does your child have any physical limitations that require special considerations? If

so, please describe. _____

_____

FIGURE 18-3 Sample registration form

nel should be required to demonstrate their understanding of the hierarchical steps to be taken when an accident occurs.

Of particular concern in recent years is the establishment of blood management procedures. This has become a special concern because of the recent epidemic in the spread of HIV and AIDS. Table 18-3 provides general guidelines for handling an accident where any amount of blood is present.

Cancellation Procedures

Uncontrollable circumstances, such as inclement weather, may occasionally require you to postpone a clinical session. Regardless of the reason for the postponement, you have an obligation to notify all personnel and participants as soon as possible. How would you handle the following situation?

On Saturday mornings during the winter months you conduct your motor development program from 10:00 to 11:30 a.m. One Saturday, at approximately 8:00 a.m., a light snow begins to fall and the temperature falls

well below freezing. You are concerned about the deteriorating weather conditions but by 8:30 a.m. you feel that weather conditions do not warrant canceling the day's program. However, during the next 15 minutes the conditions rapidly worsen. By 9:00 a.m. you decide to cancel the Saturday program. However, because of the distance that your 60 participants must travel to get to the program, you need to get the cancellation information to them within the next 15 to 20 minutes. How can you do this?

Obviously there is not enough time for you to individually contact 60 families by telephone. The task is impossible unless you previously thought through such a situation and developed as well as conveyed to all participants a procedure to follow when threatening weather hits or is approaching.

The solution is simple. Because the program is being conducted in the winter months, you should have recognized the potential for inclement weather. Consequently, you need to contact a radio station that routinely announces cancellations caused by inclement weather conditions. You will not be able to simply call the radio station when you decide to can-

TABLE 18-3 Blood Management Procedures

1. All activity must stop at the first sight of blood.

2. Whenever possible, the injured party should be responsible for cleaning his or her own wound.

3. Rubber gloves should always be worn when handling blood directly from an open wound or indirectly (bloody towels, clothing, etc.). The hands must be washed immediately after glove removal.

4. Anyone with blood on their clothing must be removed from the activity. This is not restricted to the injured party but also to anyone else who may have blood on their clothing.

5. The participant must change clothing before being allowed to return to the activity or the bloody portion of the clothing must be cleaned and then treated with a fresh 1:100 dilution (1/4 cup sodium hypochlorite to gallon water) of sodium hypochlorite (bleach).

6. Blood contaminated surfaces must also be cleaned with a 1:100 dilution of sodium hypochlorite before activity is allowed to continue.

7. Any contaminated materials must be kept in separate biohazard containers, cleaned separately, or properly disposed.

Source: Adapted from Rasor (1994).

cel the day's program because the telephone operator at the station has no way of knowing whether you are the person with the authority to make such decisions. Instead, visit the radio station well in advance. The station manager will probably require you to fill in a special form and produce positive identification. You will then be assigned an individual password. Whenever you decide to cancel the program, simply call the radio station, give them your special password, and they will make the announcement over the airwaves. Remember to discuss these procedures with the parents during the parent orientation meeting. Above all, make sure that everyone knows which stations will be making the announcement.

Drop-Off and Pick-Up Procedures

One way to increase enrollment is to make program attendance as trouble-free as possible, particularly when participants are children because there is an extra burden on parents. The most troublesome aspect of the program, according to parents, occurs in having to transport their child to and from the program. Furthermore, because most clinical sessions seldom last longer than 1 or 1 1/2 hours, parents frequently complain that by the time they return home it is time to return to pick up their child.

To combat these problems, during the orientation meeting we suggest to the parents two possible solutions. First, parents can plan to do their grocery shopping while their child attends the program. To ensure that the parents have enough time, we have implemented an efficient drop-off and pick-up procedure. Parents of participants are given a large sign that has their child's name printed on it. Up to 15 minutes before the start of the program, parents can drive to a designated drop-off location, flash their name plate, and immediately the child's instructor comes to the car and walks the child to the activity area. Time is saved because parents never have to leave their cars. Parents especially like this procedure during inclement weather. The same procedure is followed for picking up participants. Not only

is this technique efficient, but it also makes a potentially dangerous aspect of the program safer because the children no longer have to walk to a parking lot, darting between cars.

A second solution is to provide activities for the parents while their child takes part in the movement program. A survey of parents whose children attend the Wright State University Motor Development Program resulted in the following activities: an exercise class, a television room, a quiet room reserved for reading, and a room where video movies are shown. These activities are scheduled to end approximately 15 minutes before the movement program. Parents then go to a predetermined location just outside the activity area and pick up their child.

Positive responses to these two drop-off and pick-up procedures have been overwhelming. Parents no longer feel that they waste the entire day or evening transporting their child to extracurricular activities.

Computer-Assisted Organization

As should be evident by now, organizing and conducting a motor development program can be time-consuming. You have to send out applications, advertise the program, handle registration and confirmation letters, maintain files on all participants, and perform many other administrative duties. Do not get discouraged—in this age of technology, help is available: the microcomputer. Most teachers now have access to microcomputers in their own school, and computer programs (software) are now available to handle all of the administrative activities. Visit a local microcomputer store and tell them your needs. Using a microcomputer to handle administrative tasks will save you time so you can get on with the task you enjoy the most: working with people in a movement environment.

CURRICULAR CONSIDERATIONS

The two previous sections showed you how to overcome many of the pitfalls frequently encountered when initially setting up a motor development program. For the most part, the discussion focused on philosophical and administrative considerations. One vital consideration that still needs to be addressed is how to plan and organize the participation aspect of the program. Briefly, you must become aware of each participant's level of functioning, organize a learning environment conducive to optimal learning, and devise a means of disseminating program results.

Preprogram Assessments

During the first one or two clinical sessions you must assess each participant's incoming ability. Abilities to be assessed will differ, depending on the program philosophy and the scope of the program. For example, if the program is designed for preschool children and children in the first and second grades, you will assess children's abilities in the fundamental movement skills. But if your program philosophy is to improve adolescents' sport skills ability, your assessment will include a specific sport skills test and perhaps a measure of motor and physiological fitness. A program designed for the elderly may include a wide range of movement assessments and measures of motor and physiological fitness.

Regardless of what is assessed, keep in mind that the purpose of a preprogram assessment is to establish a baseline to which comparisons can be made in the future. And above all, these initial assessments must be linked to program content. That is, once weaknesses are evident, you must implement an individualized program designed to remediate these deficiencies. This concept was stressed in Chapter 17; refer to that chapter for ideas concerning assessment and the administration of various assessment instruments.

Instructional Organization

When designing lessons in the motor domain, participation is essential to the learning process. Although some researchers have found that mental rather than physical practice improves skill perfor-

mance, the best way to learn new skills and refine old skills is through participation. In other words, people of all ages learn best by doing.

How you structure the learning environment can influence whether or not there will be maximum participation. Also keep in mind that your instructional organization must provide for both maximum and individualized instruction. We have found the *stations approach* most effective for organizing instruction. In fact, some of the potential problems presented earlier can be overcome if the stations approach to instruction is used. For instance, maximum participation requires, in most instances, that each person has a piece of equipment and that waiting time for a turn to use equipment is at an absolute minimum. By dividing the number of people who need to use a specific type of equipment, say basketballs, there will obviously be less waiting for a turn.

Another advantage of the stations approach is that it allows for ability grouping or mainstreaming. Not all participants in the program will be functioning at the same skill level. Therefore, based on preprogram assessments, an individualized program is written for each participant. Participants who possess similar degrees of proficiency in a given skill area can be easily grouped together for instruction. In our program, the general assistants are responsible for transporting participants to their individually assigned stations.

The amount of time that a participant should spend at any one station depends on age, interest, and attention span. In general, you can reasonably expect elementary school children to spend approximately 15 to 20 minutes at each of four stations during any clinical session. A 10-minute juice break between the second and third stations can do wonders for rejuvenating the child's level of interest.

Instructional Delivery Considerations

The best movement curriculum is of little value if the instructor is unable to effectively convey information to the program participants. In this section we address instructional points to consider and their implications. Adhering to these instructional delivery considerations should help foster your ability to teach motor skills.

Demonstrations The demonstration presents to the participants a picture of the skill to be learned, thus lending them a sense of direction. The old saying "A picture is worth a thousand words" appears to be especially true when teaching motor skills.

Because the primary purpose of utilizing a demonstration is to present to the learners a visual illustration of the task, care must be taken in selecting demonstrators. Ideally, the individual who is the most proficient at performing the selected task should be selected to demonstrate; however, many instructors feel an obligation to perform all demonstrations themselves. One advantage of the teacher demonstration appears to be the earning of students' respect. There are inherent disadvantages, however, to teacher-performed demonstrations. Students who experience difficulty in performing the selected task generally give up too early, and when reminded of the teacher demonstration, they will frequently alibi, "Sure you can do it because you are the teacher." Such problems can be avoided by utilizing student demonstrations. The added peer influence from these demonstrations encourages more desire and determination in practice sessions.

To find a suitable student demonstrator, you can simply ask the students, for example, to find the best method to dribble a basketball. While the children are participating in this self-discovery process, be on the lookout for students who utilize acceptable techniques. After a short period of time, you will be able to point out those who are utilizing the best methods so that other participants may watch their performance.

A word of caution: While demonstrations may be an influential factor in skill development, their use does not guarantee improved rates of learning. For demonstrations to be effective, the teacher needs to have the student's attention and in most instances should use multiple demonstrations. Remember the following two conditions for developing effective demonstrations:

1. Condition: The learner must be attentive to the demonstration.

Implication: Before allowing the demonstrator to perform, care must be taken to ensure student attention. Eliminate all external distractions. If distractions occur during the demonstration, wait until the disturbances have passed.

2. Condition: The learner must know in advance the key elements to look for during the demonstration.

Implication: Because most skills contain more than one key element, the ability to model behavior can be facilitated through multiple demonstrations. During each demonstration, direct the participant's attention (precue) to different aspects of the task (one cue at a time). In demonstrating the forward roll, for example, direct the participants' attention toward the initial hand position. During the second demonstration, tell the participants to focus their attention on the position of the chin during performance. Following three to five demonstration trials, students will have been exposed to the key components. Thus, multiple demonstrations tend to be more effective than a single demonstration.

Visual Aids Recall that the purpose of a demonstration is to present to the learners a visual representation of expert performance in hope that they will in turn model the behavior. With this in mind it should be clear that any type of visual media may be utilized to visually represent the task. Common sources of visual media that may be effective include filmloops, videotapes, flow charts, and slides and pictures.

For example, the teacher wants students to view the positioning of the legs and ankles during the execution of a cartwheel roundoff. Nature, however, requires that this task be performed at a high rate of speed—a speed so fast that the novice performer is not likely to see clearly the body regions specified by the instructor. In this case, it would be more appropriate to utilize a filmloop or motion picture showing someone performing this task. These media can then be shown in slow-motion and stop-action replay, which will allow the learner to follow the desired regions of observation through the entire range of the activity. For schools with budgets that do not support an extensive film library, a viable alternative is to either make or purchase a series of inexpensive flow charts, which are actually frame-by-frame pictures or illustrations of someone performing a specific task. Figure 18–4 is an example of a flow chart depicting the cartwheel roundoff.

Attention   During task performance we must direct our attention to the most important elements of the task while ignoring those elements that are of little importance to task performance (background noise). This concept is sometimes referred to as selective attention. As mentioned earlier, precuing, or telling performers where to focus their attention prior to task execution, is one technique that can be used to help ensure that students attend to the important elements of a specified task. The importance of attending to visual demonstrations has already been addressed.

Many theories exist that try to explain why we tend to lose attention. One theory suggests that we lose our ability to attend when we are required to perform in monotonous surrounds while another theory suggests that attention is lost when we are required to respond to very infrequent signals. Thus, teachers of motor skills should make frequent changes in the physical teaching environment. For example, classes should not always be held at the same location each day, drills and activities should be limited in duration to avoid boredom, and class

routines should be frequently changed. Above all, avoid teaching formations that require students to wait in long lines before getting a turn to perform.

Memory   The terms *memory* and *forgetting* go hand in hand. Memory can be thought of as information that can be retrieved when needed, whereas forgetting generally is referred to as information that cannot be retrieved from memory. For ease of discussion, think of the structure of memory as being composed of two structures: short-term memory (STM) and long-term memory (LTM). Unlike LTM, STM is limited in both capacity, the number of items we can recall, and in duration, the length of time we can recall the items. Thus, when teaching motor skills, you must be careful not to overload the participants' memory capacity by giving them more information or instructions to attend to than is necessary. Furthermore, once information is conveyed to participants, you must organize the learning environment so that practice can begin immediately; otherwise the students may forget what they are supposed to do. Information in STM must be acted upon within 20 to 30 seconds or it will be forgotten.

Levels of Processing   Whenever the teacher presents new information to students, it will reside in STM, provided that the students were paying attention. The job of the teacher, however, is to get the students to move this information from STM

FIGURE 18-4   Flow chart depicting cartwheel roundoff

into LTM, which can be accomplished if they act upon the new information. An example illustrates the point. You call the information operator to obtain a telephone number, but unfortunately you do not have a pencil to write this number down onto paper. In all likelihood, as soon as you get the number from the operator you start to repeat it to yourself over and over again until you have successfully dialed the number. This action plan is referred to as a control process known as *rehearsal.* In other words, you have acted upon the information (new telephone number) in an attempt to move it from STM to LTM. The same idea can be used in the learning of new motor skills. That is why it is so important to let participants begin practicing within 20 to 30 seconds following a demonstration.

Attaching Verbal Labels to Movement
Memory can also be facilitated if meaningful labels are attached to physical movements. One verbal label frequently used in physical education is the clock face. For example, instead of just demonstrating a movement such as hitting a tennis ball with a racquet, tell the student to swing the racquet from 6 o'clock to 12 o'clock. If the student is capable of telling time, then this verbal label will probably help her establish the correct vertical swing technique needed to correctly hit the tennis ball. Above all, the label must be meaningful to the student; obviously, the preceding example would be of little value to a student who could not tell time.

Feedback and Knowledge of Results Sometimes the two terms "feedback" and "knowledge of results" (KOR) are used interchangeably. This is unfortunate because the two terms do have different definitions. Feedback refers to information that the performer receives through the performer's own senses (e.g., eyes, ears), whereas *knowledge of results* refers to information that the performer receives from an external source—generally the teacher. Both feedback and KOR are useful for error correction. KOR tends to be very important during the early stages of learning a new motor skill because at this stage of learning novice performers are not capable of knowing what feedback information they should be attending to. As a result, the teacher must point out to the student aspects of performance that need to be corrected. Once the performer is able to establish a "model of correct performance," then feedback becomes more important. A model of correct performance is essentially an abstract representation in the performer's mind as to what correct performance should look and feel like. This abstract representation is compared with actual performance on each performance trial and when the two do not match up, then corrections in performance need to be made.

When KOR is conveyed to a performer, the teacher must be sure that the information is meaningful. For instance, a first grader can probably understand the direction "Move a little faster" but probably would not be able to derive much useful meaning out of the direction "You need to move 600 milliseconds faster." Thus, for KOR to be useful the information given must be meaningful.

A final point regarding KOR is that it should not be given after every performance trial. This is because the performer needs time to process (think about) the KOR information. Furthermore, recall that the teacher is giving KOR in an attempt to help the performer develop a model of correct performance. When KOR is given after every performance trial, the student begins to ignore internal feedback and uses KOR as a crutch.

Primacy-Recency Theory This theory suggests that we remember the first and the most recent information that is presented. Thus, during any class the student is likely to have the most difficulty recalling the middle portion of the lesson. For this reason, the teacher should spend the last couple of minutes reviewing the lesson, paying particular attention to the middle portion of the lesson.

Many other effective points to consider can be found in any applied textbook on motor learning. We suggest that you consult the one written by Magill (1989).

Postprogram Discussions

Following each clinical session, all personnel should gather for a brief period to discuss the day's program. During this time, encourage people to discuss and impart information that may be helpful to others. For example, someone may wish to tell the group how she successfully handled a particular discipline problem. Or perhaps someone wants additional information regarding the instructional procedures for teaching a particular skill. Or someone may have a particular problem for which he wants the advice of the entire group. In short, this concluding activity is a time when all personnel can gather to discuss problems and share ideas and other types of general information. Furthermore, now is the time to update any records.

Parents' Workshop

As mentioned, the director of the program should keep parents informed of their child's progress. We recommend a workshop for parents. During this workshop, all parents receive a copy of their child's motor development assessment and an explanation of how to interpret the assessment scores.

The parents' workshop can also be used for two other purposes. First, you receive feedback from the parents regarding their likes and dislikes about the program. We have found this information very helpful over the years for improving the service provided. Second, this time can be used to instruct parents on how to work with their child's movement needs in the home environment.

SUMMARY

Before implementing a motor development program, you must develop a program philosophy. This philosophy partly describes what you hope the program will accomplish. Once you determine a philosophy, the next step is to decide whether the goals and objectives of the program can be met given the existing resources. Do you have the facilities, equipment, and personnel needed to run a quality program?

To run a trouble-free program, expect to spend much time with administrative responsibilities. In particular, you will need to develop a multitude of operational procedures, such as first aid and emergencies, cancellations, advertising and registration, and general operations. Carrying out these administrative duties can be simplified by using a microcomputer.

Also give consideration to instructional organization. You must plan and organize the participation aspect of the program. We suggest using the stations approach. Furthermore, consider program assessment and the dissemination of this information; this information can be shared with the parents in a parents' workshop.

KEY TERMS

Adaptive program	Nondevelopmental
Assistant instructors	apparatus
Developmental	Orientation meeting
apparatus	Parents' workshop
Developmentally	Program philosophy
appropriate	Program scope
equipment	Rehearsal
Feedback	Stations approach
General assistants	Station leaders
Knowledge of results	Volunteers
Microcomputer	

References

CHAPTER 1

Baltes, P. B. (1968). Longitudinal and cross sectional sequences in the study of age and generation effects. *Human Development, 11,* 145–171.

Bayley, N. (1936). *The California infant scale of motor development.* Berkeley: University of California Press.

Bloom, B. S. (1956). *Taxonomy of educational objectives: Handbook I: Cognitive domain.* New York: McKay.

Borstelmann, L. J. (1983). Children before psychology. In W. Kessen (Ed.), *Handbook of child psychology: Volume 1. History, theory, and methods,* 4th ed. New York: Wiley.

Bower, T. G. R. (1977). *A primer of infant development.* San Francisco: W. H. Freeman.

Bruner, J. S. (1970). The growth and structure of skill. In K. J. Connolly (Ed.), *Mechanisms of motor skill development.* London: Academic Press.

Chu, D. (1982). *Dimensions of sport studies.* New York: Wiley.

Clark, J. E., & Whitall, J. (1989). What is motor development: The lessons of history. *Quest, 41,* 183–202.

Connolly, K. J. (1970). *Mechanisms of motor skill development.* London: Academic Press.

Darwin, C. (1877). A biographical sketch of an infant. *Mind, 2,* 285–294.

Espenschade, A., & Eckert, H. (1967). *Motor development.* Columbus, OH: Merrill.

Fitzgerald, J. M. (1986). *Lifespan human development.* Belmont, CA: Wadsworth.

Gabbard, C. (1992). *Lifelong motor development.* Dubuque, IA: Brown.

Gallahue, D. L., & Ozmun, J. C. (1995). *Understanding motor development: Infants, children, adolescents, adults* (3rd ed.). Indianapolis: Benchmark.

Gesell, A. (1928). *Infancy and human growth.* New York: Macmillan.

Haken, H. (1983). *Synergetics, an introduction: Nonequilibrium phase transitions and self-organization in physics, chemistry, and biology.* New York: Springer-Verlag.

Hay, J. G., & Reid, J. G. (1988). *Anatomy, mechanics, and human motion,* 2nd ed. Englewood Cliffs, NJ: Prentice Hall.

Haywood, K. M. (1993). *Lifespan motor development,* 2nd ed. Champaign, IL: Human Kinetics.

Kamm, K., Thelen, E., & Jensen, J. L. (1990). A dynamical systems approach to motor development. *Physical Therapy, 70(12),* 763–775.

Keogh, J. F. (1977). The study of movement skill development. *Quest, 28,* 76–88.

Kephart, N. C. (1960). *The slow learner in the classroom.* Columbus, OH: Merrill.

Kugler, P. N., Kelso, J. A. S., & Turvey, M. T. (1982). On the control and co-ordination of naturally developing systems. In J. A. S. Kelso & J. E. Clark (Eds.), *The development of movement control and co-ordination.* New York: Wiley.

Lefrancois, G. (1993). *The lifespan.* Belmont, CA: Wadsworth.

Malina, R. M., & Bouchard, C. (1991). *Growth, maturation, and physical activity.* Champaign, IL: Human Kinetics.

McClenaghan, B. A., & Gallahue, D. L. (1978). *Fundamental movement: A developmental and remedial approach.* Philadelphia: Saunders.

McGraw, M. (1935). *Growth: A study of Johnny and Jimmy.* New York: Appleton-Century-Crofts.

Notes from Scholarly Directions Committee of NCPEAM and NAPECW (1974, Nov.). Seattle, Wash.

Payne, V. G. (1982). Current status of research on object reception as a function of ball size. *Perceptual and Motor Skills, 55,* 953–954.

Pew, R. W. (1970). Toward a process-oriented theory of human skilled performance. *Journal of Motor Behavior, 2,* 8–24.

———. (1974). Human perceptual motor performance. In B. H. Kantowitz (Ed.), *Human information processing: Tutorials in performance and cognition.* New York: Erlbaum.

Rarick, G. L. (1989). Motor development: A commentary. In J. S. Skinner, C. B. Corbin, D. M. Landers,

P. E. Martin, & C. L. Wells (Eds.), *Future directions in exercise and sport science research,* 383–391. Champaign, IL: Human Kinetics.

Roberton, M. A. (1978). Stages of motor development. In M. V. Ridenour (Ed.), *Motor development: Issues and applications.* Princeton, NJ: Princeton Book Company.

———. (1988). The weaver's loom: A developmental metaphor. In J. E. Clark & J. H. Humphrey (Eds.), *Advances in motor development research 2.* New York: AMS Press.

———. (1989). Motor development: Recognizing our roots, charting our future. *Quest, 41,* 213–223.

Roberton, M., Williams, K., & Langendorfer, S. (1980). Prelongitudinal screening of motor development sequences. *Research Quarterly for Exercise and Sport, 51*(4), 724–731.

Schaie, K. W. (1965). A general model for the study of developmental problems. *Psychological Bulletin, 64,* 92–107.

Schmidt, R. A. (1991). *Motor learning and performance: From principles to practice.* Champaign, IL: Human Kinetics.

———. (1988). *Motor control and learning: A behavioral emphasis* (2nd ed.). Champaign, IL: Human Kinetics.

Scholz, J. P. (1990). Dynamic pattern theory—Some implications. *Physical Therapy, 70*(12), 827–843.

Seefeldt, V. (1989). This is motor development. *Motor Development Academy Newsletter, 10,* 2–5.

Shinn, M. (1900). *The biography of a baby.* Boston: Houghton Mifflin.

Smoll, F. L. (1982). Developmental kinesiology: Toward a subdiscipline focusing on motor development. In J. S. Kelso & J. E. Clark (Eds.), *The development of movement control and coordination.* New York: Wiley.

Stott, L. H. (1967). *Child development: An individual longitudinal approach.* New York: Holt, Rinehart and Winston.

Thelen, E. (1987). The role of motor development in developmental psychology: A view of the past and an agenda for the future. In N. Eisenberg (Ed.), *Contemporary topics in developmental psychology.* New York: Wiley.

Thomas, J. R. (1994). History of motor behavior (in press). In J. D. Massengale and R. A. Swanson (Eds.), *History of Exercise and Sport Sciences.* Champaign, IL: Human Kinetics.

Thomas, J. R. (1989). Naturalistic research can drive motor development theory. In J. S. Skinner, C. B. Corbin, D. M. Landers, P. E. Martin, & C. L. Wells (Eds.), *Future directions in exercise and sport science research,* 349–367. Champaign, IL: Human Kinetics.

Thomas, J. R., & Thomas, K. (1984). Planning kiddie research: Little kids but big problems, In J. R. Thomas (Ed.) *Motor development during childhood and adolescence.* Minneapolis: Burgess.

United States Department of Commerce: Bureau of the Census. (1992). *1990 Census of the population: General population characteristics.* Washington, DC: U.S. Government Printing Office.

United States Department of Commerce: Bureau of the Census. (1983). *1980 Census of the population: General population characteristics.* Washington, DC: U.S. Government Printing Office.

United States Department of Commerce: Bureaus of the Census. (1975). *Historical Statistics of the United States: Colonial times to 1970.* Washington, DC: U. S. Government Printing Office.

United States Department of Health and Human Services: Public Health Service, (1992). *Healthy People 2000: National health promotion and disease prevention objectives.* Boston: Jones and Bartlett.

VanSant, A. F. (1990). Life-span development in functional tasks. *Physical Therapy, 70*(12), 788–798.

Wickstrom, R. L. (1983). *Fundamental movement patterns.* Philadelphia: Lea & Febiger.

Williams, H., Temple, I., & Bateman, J. (1979). A test battery to assess intrasensory and intersensory development of young children. *Perceptual and Motor Skills, 48,* 643–659.

Williams, J. M., & Straub, W. F. (1993). Sport psychology: Past, present, and future. In J. M. Williams (Ed.), *Applied sport psychology: Personal growth to peak performance,* Mountain View, CA: Mayfield.

CHAPTER 2

Adelson, B. (1984). When novices surpass experts: The difficulty of a task may increase with expertise. *Journal of Experimental Psychology: Learning, Memory, and Cognition, 10,* 483–495.

Anderson, J. R. (1976). *Language, memory, and thought.* Hillsdale, NJ: Erlbaum.

Arenberg, D. (1973). Cognition and aging: Verbal learning, memory, and problem solving. In C. Eisdorfer & M.

P. Lawton (Eds.), *The psychology of adult development and aging.* Washington, DC: American Psychological Association.

Arlin, P. K. (1975). Cognitive development in adulthood: A fifth stage? *Developmental Psychology, 11,* 602–606.

Birren, J. E., Woods, A. M., & Williams, M. V. (1980). Behavioral slowing with age: Causes, organization and consequences. In L. W. Poon (Ed.), *Aging in the 80's: Psychological issues.* Washington, DC: American Psychological Association.

Charness, N. (1979). Components of skill in bridge. *Canadian Journal of Psychology, 33,* 1–16.

Chi, M. T. H. (1978). Knowledge structures and memory development. In R. S. Siegler (Ed.), *Children's thinking: What develops?* Hillsdale, NJ: Erlbaum.

Clark, J. E. (1978). Memory processes in the early acquisition of motor skills. In M. V. Ridenour (Ed.), *Motor development: Issues and applications.* Princeton, NJ: Princeton Book Company.

Dacey, J. S. (1982). *Adult development.* Glenview, IL: Scott, Foresman.

Fein, G. (1978). *Child development.* Englewood Cliffs, NJ: Prentice-Hall.

Ford, J. M., & Plefferbaum, A. (1980). The utility of brain potentials in determining age-related changes in the central nervous system and cognitive function. In L. W. Poon (Ed.), *Aging in the 80's: Psychological issues.* Washington, DC: American Psychological Association.

Fozard, J. L. (1985). Memory changes in aging. In H. K. Ulatowska (Ed.), *The aging brain: Communication in the elderly.* San Diego: College-Hill Press.

Fozard, J. L., & Poon, L. W. (1980). The time for remembering. In L. W. Poon (Ed.), *Aging in the 80's: Psychological issues.* Washington DC: American Psychological Association.

French, K. E., & Thomas, J. R. (1987). The relation of knowledge development to children's basketball performance. *Journal of Sport Psychology, 9,* 15–32.

Jarvik, L. F., & Cohen, D. (1973). A biobehavioral approach to internal changes with aging. In C. Eisdorfer & M. P. Lawton (Eds.). *The psychology of adult development and aging.* Washington, DC: American Psychological Association.

Kaluger, G., & Kaluger, M. F. (1984). *Human development: The span of life.* St. Louis: Times Mirror/Mosby.

Lindberg, M. A. (1980). Is the knowledge base development a necessary and sufficient condition for memory development? *Journal of Experimental Child Psychology, 30,* 401–410.

Maier, H. W. (1978). *Three theories of child development.* New York: Harper & Row.

Newman, B. M., & Newman, P. R. (1991). *Development through life: A psychosocial approach,* 5th ed. Pacific Grove, CA: Brooks/Cole.

Powell, R. R., & Pohndorf, R. H. (1971). Comparison of adult exercisers and nonexercisers on fluid intelligence and physiological variables. *Research Quarterly, 23,* 70–71.

Rybash, J. M., Hoyer, W. J., & Roodin, P. A. (1986). *Adult cognition and aging.* New York: Pergamon Press.

Savage, R. D., Britton, P. G., Bolton, N., & Hall, E. H. (1973). *Intellectual functioning in the aged.* London: Methuen & Co.

Shaffer, D. R. (1989). *Developmental psychology: Childhood and adolescence.* Pacific Grove, CA: Brooks/Cole.

Thomas, J. R., French, K. E., Thomas, K. T., & Gallagher, J. D. (1988). Children's knowledge development and sport performance. In F. L. Smoll, R. A. Magill, & M. J. Ash (Eds.), *Children in sport,* 3rd ed. Champaign, IL: Human Kinetics.

CHAPTER 3

Atchley, R. C. (1989). A continuity theory of aging. *Gerontologist, 29,* 183–190.

Anthrop, J., & Allison, M. T. (1983). Role conflict and the high school female athlete. *Research Quarterly for Exercise and Sport, 54,* 104–111.

Bandura, A., & Kupers, C. J. (1964). Transmission of patterns of self-reinforcement through modeling. *Journal of Abnormal Psychology, 69,* 1–9.

Barry, H. C., Rich, B. S. E., & Carlson, R. T. (1993). How exercise can benefit older patients: A practical approach. *The physician and sports medicine, 21*(2), 124–140.

Berger, K. S. (1994). *The developing person through the lifespan,* 3rd ed. New York: Worth.

Berger, B. G., & McInman, A. (1993). Exercise and the quality of life. In R. N. Singer, M. Murphey, & L. K. Tennant (Eds.), *Handbook of research on sport psychology.* New York: Macmillan.

Berger, B. G., & Hecht, L. M. (1989). Exercise, aging, and psychological well-being: The mind-body question. In A. C. Ostrow (Ed.), *Aging and motor behavior.* Indianapolis: Benchmark.

Birdwhistell, R. L. (1960). *Kinesics and communication: Explorations in communication.* Boston: Beacon Press.

Clark, E. (1986). *Growing old is not for sissies.* Corte Madera, CA: Pomegranate.

Coakley, J. (1993). Socialization and sport. In R. N. Singer, M. Murphey, and L. K. Tennant (Eds.), *Handbook of research on sport psychology.* New York: Macmillan.

Colarusso, C. A., & Nemiroff, R. A. (1981). *Adult development.* New York: Plenum Press.

Cratty, B. J. (1986). *Perceptual and motor development in infants and children,* 3rd ed. Englewood Cliffs: NJ: Prentice Hall.

Eccles, J., & Harold, R. (1991). Gender differences in sport involvement: Applying the Eccles expectancy value model. *Journal of Applied Sport Psychology, 3,* 7–35.

Garvey, K. (1990). *Play.* Cambridge, Mass.: Harvard University Press.

Greendorfer, S. L., & Ewing, M. E. (1981). Race and gender differences in children's socialization into sport. *Research Quarterly for Exercise and Sport, 52,* 301–310.

Greendorfer, S. L., & Lewko, J. H. (1978). Role of the family members in sport socialization of children. *Research Quarterly, 49,* 146–152.

Gruber, J. J. (1985). Physical activity and self-esteem development in children: A meta-analysis. *The Academy Papers, 19,* 30–48.

Hamilton, M. L. (1977). Ideal sex roles for children and acceptance of variation from stereotypic sex roles. *Adolescence, 12,* 89–96.

Harter, S. (1988). Causes, correlates, and the functional role of global self-worth: A life-span perspective. In J. Killigian & R. Sternberg (Eds.), *Perceptions of competence and incompetence across the life-span.* New Haven, CN: Yale University Press.

Kaluger, G., & Kaluger, M. F. (1984). *Human development: The span of life.* St. Louis: Times Mirror/Mosby.

Kausler, D. H. (1982). *Experimental psychology and aging.* New York: Wiley.

Kelly, J. R., & Wescott, G. (1991). *International Journal of Aging and Human Development, 32,* 81–89.

Kenyon, G. S., & McPherson, B. D. (1973). Becoming involved in physical activity and sport: A process of socialization. In G. L. Rarick (Ed.), *Physical activity: Human growth and development.* New York: Academic Press.

Lee, A. M. (1980). Child rearing practices and motor performance of black and white children. *Research Quarterly for Exercise and Sport, 51,* 494–500.

Loy, J. L., & Ingham, A. G. (1973). Play, games and sports in psychosocial development of children and youth. In G. L. Rarick (Ed.), *Physical activity: Human growth and development.* New York: Academic Press.

Michael, M. (1970). Sex typing and socialization. In P. H. Mussen (Ed.), *Carmichael's manual of child psychology,* vol. 2. New York: Wiley.

NEA Today (1985). School yard . . . daring to be great, Mar. 10.

Newman, B. M., & Newman, P. R. (1991). *Development through life: A Psychosocial approach,* 5th ed. Pacific Grove, CA: Brooks/Cole.

Oglesby, C. A., & Hill, K. L. (1993). Gender and sport. In R. N. Singer, M. Murphey, & L. K. Tennant (Eds.), *Handbook of research on sport psychology.* New York: Macmillan.

Ostrow, A. C., Jones, D. C., & Spiker, D. D. (1981). Age role expectations and sex role expectations for selected sport activities. *Research Quarterly for Exercise and Sport, 52,* 216–227.

Rudman, W. J. (1984). Life course socioeconomic transitions and sport involvement: A theory of restricted opportunity. In B.D. McPherson (Ed.). *The 1984 Olympic scientific congress proceedings, Volume 5: Sport and aging.* Champaign, IL: Human Kinetics.

Silverstein, S. (1981). *A light in the attic.* New York: Harper & Row.

Snyder, E. E., & Spreitzer, E. A. (1973). Family influence and involvement in sports. *Research Quarterly, 44,* 249–255.

United States Department of Commerce: Bureau of the Census. (1992). *1990 Census of the population: General population characteristics.* Washington, DC: U. S. Government Printing Office.

United States Department of Commerce: Bureau of the Census. (1983). *1980 Census of the population: General population characteristics.* Washington, DC: U. S. Government Printing Office.

United States Department of Commerce: Bureau of the Census. (1975). *Historical Statistics of the United States: Colonial times to 1970.* Washington, DC: U.S. Government Printing Office.

U.S. Department of Health and Human Services: Public Health Service. (1992). *Healthy people 2000: National health and disease prevention objectives.* Boston: Jones and Bartlett.

CHAPTER 4

Adelson, E., & Fraiberg, S. (1976). Sensory deficit and motor development in infants blind from birth. In Z. S. Jastrzembska (Ed.), *The effects of blindness and other impairments on early development.* New York: The American Foundation for the Blind.

American Academy of Pediatrics (1993). Policy statement: The Doman-Delacato treatment of neurologically handicapped children. Elk Grove Village, IL: AAP.

Bachman, J. C. (1961). Motor learning and performance as related to age and sex in two measures of balance coordination. *Research Quarterly, 32,* 123–137.

Bartlett, F. C. (1958). *Thinking.* New York: Basic Books.

Bower, T. G. R. (1977). *Perceptual world of children.* Cambridge, MA: Harvard University Press.

Burton, A. W., & Davis, W. E. (1992). Assessing balance in adapted physical education: Fundamental concepts and applications. *Adapted Physical Activity Quarterly, 9,* 14–46.

Clark, J. E., & Watkins, D. L. (1984). Static balance in young children. *Child Development, 55,* 854–857.

Cratty, B. J. (1986). *Perceptual and motor development in infants and children,* 3rd edition. Englewood Cliffs, NJ: Prentice-Hall.

Delacato, C. H. (1959). *Treatment and prevention of reading problems.* Springfield, IL: Thomas.

———. (1963). *The diagnosis and treatment of speech and reading problems.* Springfield, IL: Thomas.

DeOreo, K. O. (1974). The performance and development of fundamental motor skills in preschool children. In M. Wade & R. Martens (Eds.), *Psychology of motor behavior and sport.* Urbana, IL: Human Kinetics.

———. (1975). Dynamic balance in preschool children: Process and product. In D. Landers (Ed.), *Psychology of sport and motor behavior II,* Proceedings of NASPSPA, Pennsylvania State University.

Dorfman, P. W. (1977). Timing and anticipation: A developmental perspective. *Journal of Motor Behavior, 9,* 67–79.

Gallahue, D. L. (1989). *Understanding motor development in children,* 2nd ed. Indianapolis: Benchmark.

Gallahue, D. L., Werner, P. H., & Luedke, G. C. (1972). *A conceptual approach to moving and learning.* New York: Wiley.

Haslinger, L. W. (1971). Perceptual-motor task force summary of perceptual-motor survey. In American Association of Health, Physical Education, Recreation, and Dance (Ed.), *Foundations and practices in perceptual-motor learning: A quest for learning.* Washington, DC.

Haywood, K. M. (1980). Coincidence-anticipation accuracy across the lifespan. *Experimental Aging Research, 6*(5), 451–462.

———. (1987). A longitudinal analysis of anticipatory judgment in older adult motor performance. In A. C. Ostrow (Ed.), *Aging and motor behavior.* Indianapolis: Benchmark.

Held, R., & Hein, A. (1963). Movement-produced stimulation in the development of visually guided behavior. *Journal of Comparative and Physiological Psychology, 56,* 872–876.

Horak, F. B. (1987). Clinical measures of postural control in adults. *Physical Therapy, 67,* 1881–1885.

Kavale, K., & Matson, P. D. (1983). One jumped off the balance beam: Meta-analysis of perceptual-motor training. *Journal of Learning Disabilities, 16,* 165–173.

Keogh, J., & Sugden, D. (1985). *Movement skill development.* New York: Macmillan.

Kephart, N. (1960). *The slow learner in the classroom.* Columbus, OH: Merrill.

———. (1964). Perceptual-motor aspects of learning disabilities. *Exceptional Child, 31,* 201–206.

Lerch, H. A., Becker, J. E., Ward, B. M., & Nelson, J. A. (1974). *Perceptual-motor learning: Theory and practice.* Palo Alto, CA: Peek Publications.

Payne, V. G. (1984). Perceptual-motor, what does it really mean? Anaheim, Calif., Presentation at the National Conference of the American Alliance for Health, Physical Education, Recreation, and Dance.

Seefeldt, V. (1974). Perceptual-motor programs. In J. H. Wilmore (Ed.), *Exercise and sports sciences reviews,* vol. 2. New York: Academic Press.

Shaffer, D. R. (1989). *Developmental Psychology: Childhood and adolescence,* 2nd ed., Pacific Grove, CA: Brooks/Cole.

Thomas, J. R., Thomas, K. T., Lee, A. M., Testerman, E., & Ashby, M. (1983). Age differences in use of strategy for recall of movement in a large-scale environment. *Research Quarterly for Exercise and Sport, 54*(3), 264–272.

Walk, R. D. (1981). *Perceptual development.* Monterey, CA: Brooks/Cole.

Werner, P., & Rini, L. (1975). *Perceptual motor development equipment.* New York: Wiley.

Williams, H. G. (1983). *Perceptual and motor development.* Englewood Cliffs, NJ: Prentice-Hall.

———. (1984). Problems in research in perceptual-motor development. Anaheim, Calif., Presentation at the National Conference of the American Alliance for Health, Physical Education, Recreation, and Dance.

Williams, H. G., Temple, I., & Bateman, J. (1979). A test battery to assess intrasensory and intersensory development of young children. *Perceptual and Motor Skills, 48,* 643–659.

Woollacott, M. H., Shumway-Cook, A., & Williams, H. (1989). The development of posture and balance control in children. In M. H. Woollacott and A. Shumway-Cook (Eds.), *Development of posture and gait across the lifespan.* Columbia, SC: University of South Carolina Press.

CHAPTER 5

Abel, E. L. (1983). *Marihuana, tobacco, alcohol and reproduction.* Boca Ratan, FL: CRC Press.

Abel, E. L. (1990). *Fetal alcohol syndrome.* Oradel, NJ: Medical Economics Books.

Alford, C. A., Pass, R. F., & Stagno, S. (1983). Chronic congenital infections and common environmental causes for severe and subtle birth defects. In S. C. Finley, W. H. Finley, & C. E. Flowers, Jr. (Eds.), *Birth defects: Clinical and ethical considerations.* New York: Alan R. Liss.

American Academy of Pediatrics (1993). Fetal alcohol syndrome and fetal alcohol effects. *Pediatrics, 91,* 1004–1006.

Armitage, A. K. (1965). Effects of nicotine and tobacco smoke on blood pressure and release of catecholamines from the adrenal glands. *British Journal of Pharmacology, 25,* 515.

Austin, R. J., & Moawad, A. H. (1993). The very low birth weight fetus. In C. C. Lin, M. S. Verp, and R. E. Sabbagha (Eds.), *The high-risk fetus: Pathophysiology, diagnosis, and management.* New York: Springer-Verlag.

Bennett, M. J. (1981). Amniocentesis. In M. Sanders (Ed.), *Amniotic fluid and its clinical significance.* New York: Marcel Drekker.

Brackbill, Y. (1976). Long-term effects of obstetrical anesthesis on infant autonomic function. *Developmental Psychobiology, 9,* 353–358.

———. (1979). Obstetrical medication and infant behavior. In J. D. Osofsky (Ed.), *Handbook of infant development.* New York: Wiley.

Brambati, B., & Oldrin, A. (1986). Methods of chorionic villus sampling. In B. Brambati, G. Simoni, & S. Fabio (Eds.), *Chorionic villus sampling.* New York: Marcel Drekker.

Brazelton, T. B. (1961). Effects of maternal medications on the neonate and his behavior. *Journal of Pediatrics, 58,* 513–518.

Butterfield, G., & King, F. C. (1991). Nutritional needs of physically active pregnant women. In R. A. Mittlemark, R. A. Wiswell, and B. L. Drinkwater (Eds.), *Exercise in pregnancy,* 2nd ed. Baltimore: Williams & Wilkins.

Chan, M. C. K., & Sweet, A. Y. (1991). Parasitic diseases. In A. Y. Sweet and E. G. Brown (Eds.), *Fetal and neonatal effects of maternal disease.* St. Louis, MO: Mosby-Year Book, Inc.

Chase, H. (1973). The effects of intrauterine and postnatal undernutrition on normal brain development. *Annals of New York Academy of Science, 205,* 231–244.

Churchill, J. A. (1977). Factors in intrauterine impoverishment. In K. S. Moghissi & T. N. Evans (Eds.), *Nutritional impacts on women throughout life with emphasis on reproduction.* New York: Harper & Row.

Diamond, G. W., & Cohen, H. J. (1992). Developmental disabilities in children with HIV infection. In A. C. Croker, H. J. Cohen, and T. A. Kastner (Eds.), *HIV infection and developmental disabilities: A resource for service providers.* Baltimore: Paul H. Brookes Publishing.

Diamond, G. W., Gurdin, P., Wiznia, A. A., Belman, A. L., Rubinstein, A., & Cohen, H. J. (1990). Effects of congenital HIV infection on neurodevelopmental status of babies in foster care. *Developmental Medicine and Child Neurology, 32,* 999–1005.

Drinkwater, B. L., Wiswell, R. A., & Mittlemark, R. A. (1991). Heat stress and pregnancy. In R. A. Mittlemark, R. A. Wiswell, and B. L. Drinkwater (Eds.), *Exercise in pregnancy,* 2nd ed. Baltimore: Williams & Wilkins.

Eckert, H. M. (1987). *Motor development,* 3rd ed. Indianapolis: Benchmark.

Evans, O. B., Subramony, S. H., Hanson, R. R., & Parker, C. C. (1991). Neurologic diseases. In A. Y. Sweet and E. G. Brown (Eds.), *Fetal and neonatal effects of maternal disease.* St. Louis, MO: Mosby-Year Book, Inc.

Exercise during pregnancy and the postnatal period (1985). American College of Obstetricians and Gynecologists.

Fay, F. C., Smith K. S., (1985). *Childbearing after 35: The risk and rewards.* New York: Balsam Press.

Fried, P. A., Watkinson, B, Grant, A., & Knights, R. M. (1980). Changing patterns of soft drug use prior to and during pregnancy: A prospective study. *Drug Alcohol Dependency, 6,* 323–343.

Gold, E., Kumar, M. L., Nankervis, G. A., & Sweet, A. Y. (1991). Viral infections. In A. Y. Sweet and E. G. Brown (Eds.), *Fetal and neonatal effects of maternal disease.* St. Louis, MO: Mosby-Year Book, Inc.

Heinonen, O. P. Slone, D., & Shapiro, S. (1977). *Birth defects and drugs in pregnancy.* Littleton, Mass.: Publishing Sciences Group.

Hughes, F. P., & Noppe, L. D. (1985). *Human development across the lifespan.* St. Paul: West.

Isaacs, L. D., & Pohlman, R. (1988, Oct.). Motor development and performance concerns regarding individuals of low birth weight. Paper presented at the meeting of the Motor Development Research Consortium, University of Illinois, Urbana, IL.

Jiminez, L. M. (1989). Will it hurt my baby? *American Baby,* Sept. 92–104.

Jones, K. L., Smith D. W., Ulleland, C. N., & Streissguth, A. P. (1973). Pattern of malformation in offspring of chronic alcoholic mothers. *Lancet, 1,* 1267–1271.

Kandall, S. R. (1991). Drug abuse. In A. Y. Sweet and E. G. Brown (Eds.), *Fetal and neonatal effects of maternal disease.* St. Louis, MO: Mosby-Year Book, Inc.

Kopp, C. B., & Parmelee, A. H. (1979). Prenatal and perinatal influences on infant behavior. In J. D. Osofsky (Ed.), *Handbook of infant development.* New York: Wiley.

Little, R. (1977). Alcohol consumption during pregnancy and decreased birthweight. *American Journal of Public Health, 67,* 1154–1156.

Luke, B., Johnson, T. R., & Petrie, R. H. (1993). *Clinical maternal-fetal nutrition.* Boston: Little, Brown and Company.

MacGregor, S. N., & Chasnoff, I. F. (1993). Substance abuse in pregnancy. In C. C. Lin, M. S. Verp, and R. E. Sabbagha (Eds.), *The high-risk fetus: Pathophysiology, diagnosis, and management.* New York: Springer-Verlag.

McMurray, R. G., Mottola, M. F., Wolfe, L. A., Artal, R., Millar, L., & Pivarnik, J. M. (1993). Recent advances in understanding maternal and fetal responses to exercise. *Medicine & Science in Sports & Exercise, 25,* 1305–1321.

Mittlemark, R. A., Dorey, F. J., & Kirschbaum, T. H. (1991). Effect of maternal exercise on pregnancy outcome. In R. A. Mittlemark, R. A. Wiswell, and B. L. Drinkwater (Eds.), *Exercise in pregnancy,* 2nd ed. Baltimore: Williams and Wilkins.

Mittlemark, R. A. & Posner, M. D. (1991). Fetal responses to maternal exercise. In R. A. Mittlemark, R. A. Wiswell, and B. L. Drinkwater (Eds.), *Exercise in pregnancy,* 2nd ed. Baltimore: Williams & Wilkins.

Mittlemark, R. A., Wiswell, R. A., Drinkwater, B. L., & St. Jones-Repovich, W. W. (1991). Exercise guidelines for pregnancy. In R. A. Mittlemark, R. A. Wiswell, and B. L. Drinkwater (Eds.), *Exercise in Pregnancy,* 2nd ed. Baltimore: Williams & Wilkins.

Moore, K. L. & Persaud, T. V. N. (1993). *Before we are born: Essentials of embryology and birth defects,* 4th ed. Philadelphia: Saunders.

Moore, T. R., & Resnik, R. (1984). Special problems of VLBW infants. *Contemporary OB/GYN,* 174–190.

Morton, R. F. (1989). Cocaine and pregnancy. *American Baby,* Sept., 10.

Osofsky, J. D. (Ed.). (1979). *Handbook of infant development.* New York: Wiley.

Pederson, J. (1977). *The pregnant diabetic and her newborn,* 2nd ed. Baltimore: Williams & Wilkins.

Pedersen, J., & Pedersen, L. M. (1971). Diabetes mellitus and pregnancy: The hyperglycemia, hyperinsulinemia theory and the weight of the newborn baby. In R. Rodriguez and J. Vallance-Owens (Eds.), Proceeding of the 7th Congress of the International Diabetes Federation. Amsterdam: *Excerta Medica, 97,* 678–685.

Perry, K. G, Martin, J. N., & Morrison, J. C. (1991). Hematologic and hemorrhagic disease. In A. Y. Sweet and E. G. Brown (Eds.), *Fetal and neonatal effects of maternal disease.* St. Louis, MO: Mosby-Year Book, Inc.

Petitti, D. B., & Coleman, C. (1990). Cocaine and the risk of low birth weight. *American Journal of Public Health, 80,* 25–28.

Pohlman, R. L., & Isaacs, L. D. (1990). The previously low birth weight infant: Fundamental motor skill outcomes in the 5- to 9-year-old. *Pediatric Exercise Science, 2,* 263–271.

Prenatal health (1989, Summer). *Planning for health.* Oakland, Calif.: Kaiser Permanente.

Redding, H., & Hirschhorn, K. (1993). *Guide to human chromosome defects.* New York: The National Foundation—March of Dimes.

Rist, M. C. (1990). The shadow children: Preparing for the arrival of crack babies in school. *Research Bulletin, 9,* 1–6.

Rosenbaum, A. L., Churchill, J. A., Shakhashiri, A. A., & Moody, R. L. (1973). Neuropsychologic outcome of children whose mothers had proteinuria during pregnancy: A report from the collaborative study of cerebral palsy. In L. J. Stone, H. T. Smith, & L. B. Murphy (Eds.), *The competent infant: Research and commentary.* New York: Basic Books.

Shennan, A. T., & Milligan, J. E. (1980). The growth and development of infants weighing 1000 to 2000 grams at birth and delivery in a perinatal unit. *American Journal of Obstetrics and Gynecology, 136,* 273–275.

Sicklick, M. J., & Rubinstein, A. (1992). Types of HIV infection and the course of the disease. In A. C. Crocker, H. J. Cohen, and T. A. Kastner (Eds.). *HIV infection and developmental disabilities: A resource for service providers.* Baltimore: Paul H. Brookes Publishing.

Silver, H. K., Kempe, C. K., & Bruyn, H. B. (1977). *Handbook of pediatrics,* 12th ed. Los Altos, CA: Lange Medical Publications.

Simonds, R. J., & Rogers, M. F. (1992). Epidemiology of HIV in children and other populations. In A. C. Crocker, H. J. Cohen, and T. A. Kastner (Eds.), *HIV infection and developmental disabilities: A resource for service providers.* Baltimore: Paul H. Brookes Publishing.

Steinhausen, H. C. (1974). Psychological evaluation of treatment in phenylketonuria: Intellectual, motor, and social development. *Neuropaediatrie, 5,* 146–156.

Stewart, R. B., Cluff, L. E., & Philip, R. (1977). *Drug monitoring: A requirement for responsible drug use.* Baltimore: Williams & Wilkins.

Turner, C. E. (1980). Marijuana research and problems: An Overview, *Pharm. Int., 7,* 93.

University of Iowa healthbeat (1989). *Iowa Alumni Review, 42*(4), 13.

Valentine, G. H. (1975). *The chromosome disorders: An introduction for clinicians,* 3rd ed. Philadelphia: Lippincott.

Verp, M. S., Simpson, J. L., & Ober, C. (1993). Prenatal diagnosis of genetic disorders. In C. C. Lin, M. S. Verp, and R. E. Sabbagha (Eds.), *The high-risk fetus: Pathophysiology, diagnosis, and management.* New York: Springer-Verlag.

Vohr, B. R., Lipsitt, L. P., & Oh, W. (1980). Somatic growth of children of diabetic mothers with reference to birth size, *Journal of Pediatrics, 97,* 196–199.

Willerman, L., & Churchill, J. (1967). Intelligence and birthweight in identical twins. *Child Development, 12,* 623–629.

Wilson, J. G. (1973). *Environmental and birth defects.* New York: Academic Press.

CHAPTER 6

American Academy of Pediatrics (1988). Policy statement: Infant exercise programs. *Pediatrics, 82*(5), 800.

———— (1985). Policy statement: Infant swim programs. *American Academy of Pediatrics News, 1*(15).

American Red Cross (1988). *American Red Cross infant and preschool aquatic programs: Parent's guide.*

Barnes, J., Astor, S. D., & Tosi, U. (1981). *Gymboree: Giving your child physical, mental, and social confidence through play.* Garden City, N.Y.: Doubleday.

Begley, S., & Carey, J. (1983). How far does Head Start go? *Newsweek,* Mar. 28, 65.

Bennett, H. J., & Wagner, T. (1983). Acute hyponatremia and seizures in an infant after a swim lesson. *Pediatrics, 72*(1), 125–127.

Bronson, G. (1965). The hierarchy of the central nervous system: Implications for learning processes and critical periods in early development. *Behavioral Sciences, 10,* 7–25.

Bruner, J. (1960). *The process of education.* Cambridge, MA: Harvard University Press.

Burd, B. (1986). Infant swimming: Immersed in controversy. *Physician and Sportsmedicine, 14*(3), 239–244.

Davis, K. (1946). A final note on a case of extreme isolation. *American Journal of Sociology, 52,* 432–437.

Dennis, W. (1940). *The Hopi child.* New York: Appleton-Century Company.

Elkind, D. (1990). Academic pressures—Too much, too soon: The demise of play. In E. Klugman and S. Smilanky (Eds.), *Children's play and learning: Perspectives and policy implications.* New York: Teachers College Press.

Erbaugh, S. J. (1980). The development of swimming skills of preschool children. In C. H. Nadeau, W. R. Halliwell, and K. M. Newell (Eds.), *Psychology of motor behavior and sport—1979.* Champaign, IL: Human Kinetics.

Freiberg, S. (1976). *Insights from the blind: Developmental studies of blind children.* New York: Basic Books.

Gardner, J. M., Karmel, B. Z., & Dowd, J. M. (1984). Relationship of infant psychobiological development to infant intervention programs. *Journal of the Child in Contemporary Society, 17,* 93–108.

Gardner, L. I. (1972). Deprivation dwarfism. *Scientific American*, July, 76–82.

Itard, J. M. G. (1972). First development of the young savage of Abeyron. In W. Dennis (Ed.), *Historical readings in developmental psychology.* New York: Appleton-Century Crofts.

Kaluger, G., & Kaluger, M. F. (1984). *Human development: The span of life.* St. Louis: Times Mirror/Mosby.

Kauffman, I., & Ridenour, M. (1977). Influence of an infant walker on onset and quality of walking pattern of locomotion. *Perceptual and Motor Skills, 45,* 1323–1329.

Langendorfer, S. (1986). Aquatics for the young child: Facts and myths. *Journal of Physical Education and Recreation, 57*(Aug.), 61–66.

Langendorfer, S., Bruya, L. D., & Reid, A. (1988). Facilitating aquatic motor development: A review of developmental and environmental variables. In J. Clark and J. H. Humphrey (Eds.), *Advances in motor development research, vol. 2.* New York: AMS Press.

Langway, L., Jackson, T., Zabarsky, M., Shirely, D., & Whitmore, J. (1983). Bringing up superbaby. *Newsweek,* Mar. 28, 60–66.

Magill, R. A. (1982). Critical periods: Relation to youth sport. In R. A. Magil, M. J. Ash, & F. L. Smoll (Eds.), *Children in sport.* Champaign, IL: Human Kinetics.

McGraw, M. (1935). *Growth: A study of Johnny and Jimmy.* New York: Appleton-Century Crofts. (Reprinted in 1975 by Arno Press.)

Money, J. (1969). Physical, mental, and critical periods. *Journal of Learning Disabilities, 2,* 28–29.

Newman, B. M., & Newman, P. R. (1991). *Development through life: A psychosocial approach,* 5th ed. Pacific Grove, CA: Brooks/Cole.

Nottebohm, F. (1970). Ontogeny of bird song. *Science, 167,* 950–956.

Payne, J. S., Mercer, C. D., Payne, R. A., & Davison, R. G. (1973). *Head Start: A tragicomedy with epilogue.* New York: Behavioral Publications.

Prader, A., Tanner, J., & Von Harnack, G. (1963). Catch-up growth following illness or starvation. *Journal of Pediatrics, 62,* 654–659.

Pronko, N. H. (1969). On learning to play the violin at the age of four without tears. *Psychology Today, 2,* 52.

Ridenour, M. V. (1978). Programs to optimize infant motor development. In M. V. Ridenour, J. Herkowitz, J. Clark, J. Teeple, and M. A. Roberton (Eds), *Motor development: Issues and applications.* Princeton, NJ: Princeton Book Company.

Rieder, M. J., Schwartz, C., & Newman, J. (1986). Pattern of walker use and walker injury. *Pediatrics, 78*(3), 488–493.

Schiamburg, L. B. (1985). *Human development.* New York: Macmillan.

Seefeldt, V. (1982). The concept of readiness applied to motor skill acquisition. In R. A. Magill, M. J. Ash, & F. L. Smoll (Eds.), *Children in sport.* Champaign, IL: Human Kinetics.

Suomi, S. J., & Harlow, H. F. (1972). Social rehabilitation of isolate-reared monkeys. *Developmental Psychology, 6,* 487–496.

———(1978). Early experience and social development in rhesus monkeys. In M. E. Lamb (Ed.). *Social and personality development.* New York: Holt, Rinehart and Winston.

Tanner, J. M. (1978). *Fetus into man: Physical growth from conception to maturity.* Cambridge, MA: Harvard University Press.

White, B. L. (1975). *The First Three Years of Life.* Englewood Cliffs, NJ: Prentice-Hall.

YMCA Division of Aquatics (1984). *YMCA Guidelines for Infant Swimming.* Chicago: YMCA of the USA.

CHAPTER 7

Bailey, D. A., Malina, R. M., & Rasmussen, R. L. (1978). The influence of exercise, physical activity, and athletic performance on the dynamics of human growth. In F. Falkner & J. M. Tanner (Eds.), *Human growth: Postnatal growth.* New York: Plenum Press.

Bastos, F. C., & Hegg, R. V. (1984). The relationship of chronological age, body build and sexual maturation to hand-grip strength in school boys, ages ten through seventeen years. Eugene, OR: *Proceeding of the 1984 Olympic Scientific Congress.*

Beunen, G., Beul, G., Ostyn, M., Renson, R., Simons, J., & Gerven, D. (1978). Age of menarche and motor performance in girls aged 11 through 18. *Medicine and Sport, 11,* 118–123.

Beunen, G., & Malina, R. M. (1988). Growth and physical performance relative to the timing of the adolescent spurt. In K. B. Pandolf (Ed.), *Exercise and Sport Sciences Reviews.* New York: Macmillan.

Beunen, G., Malina, R. M., Van't Hof, M. A., Simons, J., Ostyn, M., Renson, R., & Van Gerven, D. (1988). *Adolescent growth and motor performance: A longi-*

tudinal study of Belgian boys. Champaign, IL: Human Kinetics.

Buckler, J. (1990). *A longitudinal study of adolescent growth.* London: Springer-Verlag.

Buskirk, E. R., Andersen, K. L., & Brozek, F. (1956). Unilateral activity and bone and muscle development in the forearm. *Research Quarterly, 27,* 127–131.

Carter, J. E. (1980). *The Heath-Carter somatotype method.* San Diego: San Diego State University Syllabus Service.

Chumlea, W. C., Roche, A. F., & Mukherjee, D. (1984). *Nutritional assessment of the elderly through anthropometry.* Columbus, OH: Ross Laboratories.

Clarke, H. H. (1971). *Physical and motor tests in the Medford boy's growth study.* Englewood Cliffs, NJ: Prentice-Hall.

Demirjian, A. (1979). Dental development: A measure of physical maturity. In F. E. Johnston, A. F. Roche, & C. Susanne (Eds), *Human physical growth and maturation.* New York: Plenum Press.

Dintiman, G., & Ward, R. (1988). *Sport speed.* Champaign, IL: Leisure Press.

Dyson, G. H. (1964). *The mechanics of athletics,* 3rd ed. London: University of London Press.

Greulich, W. W., & Pyle, S. I. (1959). *Radiographic atlas of skeletal development of the hand and wrist,* 2nd ed. Palo Alto, CA: Stanford University Press.

Hale, C. J. (1956). Physiologic maturity of Little League baseball players. *Research Quarterly, 27,* 276–284.

Haubenstricker, J. L., & Sapp, M. M. (1980). A longitudinal look at physical growth and motor performance: Implications for elementary and middle school activity programs. Detroit: Paper presented at the meeting of the American Alliance for Health, Physical Education, Recreation, and Dance.

Heath, B. H. & Carter, J. E. L. (1967). A modified somatotype method. *American Journal of Physical Anthropology, 27,* 57–74.

Isaacs, L. D. (1976). The anatomical changes of the center of gravity during development: Implications to physical education. Unpublished manuscript, University of Maryland.

Jaffe, M., & Kosakov, C. (1982). The motor development of fat babies. *Clinical Pediatrics, 27,* 619–621.

Johnston, F. E. (1974). Control of age at menarche. *Human Biology, 46,* 159–171.

Klafs, C. E., & Lyon, M. J. (1978). *The female athlete: A coach's guide to conditioning and training.* St. Louis: Mosby.

Korgman, W. M. (1959). Maturation age of 55 boys in the Little League world series. *Research Quarterly, 30,* 54–56.

Kugler, P. N., Kelso, J. A., & Turvey, M. T. (1982). On the control and coordination of naturally developing systems. In J. A. Kelso and J. E. Clark (Eds.), *The development of movement control and coordination.* New York: Wiley & Sons.

Loucks, A. B. (1988) Osteoporosis prevention begins in childhood. In E. W. Brown & C. F. Branta (Eds), *Competitive sports for children and youth.* Champaign, IL: Human Kinetics.

Lowrey, G. H. (1986). *Growth & Development of children,* 8th ed. Chicago: Year Book Medical Publishers.

Malina, R. M. (1975). *Growth and development: The first twenty years.* Minneapolis: Burgess.

———. (1984). Maturational considerations in elite young athletes. Eugene, OR: *Proceeding of the 1984 Olympic Scientific Congress.*

Malina, R. M., Bouchard, C., Shoup, R. F., Demirjian, A., & Lariviere, G. (1979). Age at menarche, family size, and birth order in athletes at the Montreal Olympic Games, 1976. *Medicine and Science in Sport, 11,* 354–358.

Malina, R. M., & Bouchard, C. (1991). *Growth, maturation, and physical activity.* Champaign, IL: Human Kinetics.

Martorell, R., Rivera, J., Kaplowitz, H., & Pollitt, E. (1992). Long-term consequences of growth retardation during early childhood. In M. Hernandez & J. Argente (Eds.), *Human growth: Basic and clinical aspects.* Amsterdam: Elsevier Science Publishers.

Meredith, H. V. (1978). *Human body growth in the first ten years of life.* Columbia, SC: State Printing Company.

Moore, W. M. (1978). Physical growth. In T. R. Johnson, W. M. Moore, & J. E. Jeffries (Eds.), *Children are different: Developmental physiology,* 2nd ed. Columbus, OH: Ross Laboratories.

National Center for Health Statistics (1973a). Height and weight of youths 12–17 years, United States. *Vital and Health Statistics,* ser. 11, no. 124.

———. (1973b). Body weight, stature, and sitting height:: White and Negro youths 12–17 years, United States. *Vital and Health Statistics,* ser. 11, no. 126.

———. (1974). Body dimensions and proportions, White and Negro children 6–11 years, United States. *Vital and Health Statistics,* ser. 11, no. 143.

———. (1979). Weight and height of adults 18–74 years of age, United States 1971–74. *Vital and Health Statistics,* ser. 11, no. 211.

Newell, K. M. (1984). Physical constraints to development of motor skills. In J. R. Thomas (Ed.), *Motor development during adulthood and adolescence.* Minneapolis: Burgess.

Norval, M. A. (1947). Relationship of weight and length of infants at birth to the age at which they begin to walk alone. *Journal of Pediatrics, 30,* 676–678.

Olson, W. (1959). *Child development.* Boston: Heath.

Ostyn, M., Simons, J., Beunen, G., Renson, R., & Van Gerven, D. (Eds.) (1980). *Motor development of Belgian secondary schoolboys.* Leuven: Leuven University Press.

Oxendine, J. B. (1984). *Psychology of motor learning.* Englewood Cliffs, NJ: Prentice-Hall.

Palmer, C. E. (1929). The center of gravity in the developmental period of man. *Anatomical Records, 42,* 31.

Parizkova, J. (1968). Longitudinal study of the development of body composition and body build in boys of various physical activity. *Human Biology, 40,* 212–225.

Rauh, J. L., & Brookman, R. R. (1978). Adolescent developmental stages. In T. R. Johnston, W. M. Moore, & J. E. Jeffries (Eds.), *Children are different: Developmental physiology,* 2nd ed. Columbus, OH: Ross Laboratories.

Roche, A. F. (1979). The measurement of skeletal maturation. In F. E. Johnston, A. F. Roche, & C. Susanne (Eds.), *Human physical growth and maturation.* New York: Plenum Press.

Roche, A. F., & Himes, J. H. (1980). Incremental growth charts. *American Journal of Clinical Nutrition, 33,* 2041–2052.

Roche, A. F., & Malina, R. M. (Eds.) (1983). *Manual of physical status and performance in childhood,* vol. 1. New York: Plenum Press.

Roche, A. F. (1992). *Growth, maturation and body composition: The fels longitudinal study 1929–1991.* Cambridge, GB: Cambridge University Press.

Sheldon, W. H. (1940). *The varieties of human physique.* New York: Harper & Row.

Shirley, M. M. (1931). *The first two years: A study of twenty-five babies.* Minneapolis: University of Minnesota Press.

Sinclair, D. (1985). *Human growth after birth,* 4th ed. New York: Oxford University Press.

Sveger, T. (1978). Does overnutrition or obesity during the first year affect weight at age four? *Acta, Paediatr, Scand., 67,* 465–467.

Tanner, J. M. (1990). *Fetus into man.* Cambridge, MA: Harvard University Press.

Tanner, J. M., Whitehouse, R. H., Marshall, W. A., Healy, M. J., & Goldstein, H. (1975). *Assessment of skeletal maturity and prediction of adult height (TW 2 method).* New York: Academic Press.

Todd, T. W. (1937). *Atlas of skeletal maturation.* St. Louis: Mosby.

Vose, G. P. (1974). Review of roentgenographic bone demineralization studies of the Gemini space flights. *American Journal of Roentgenology, 121,* 1–4.

Wales, J., & Taitz, L. (1992). Patterns of growth in abused children. In M. Hernandez & J. Argente (Eds.), *Human growth: Basic and clinical aspects.* Amsterdam: Elsevier Science Publishers.

Wells, C. L., & Plowman, S. A. (1988). Relationship between training, menarche, and amenorrhea. In E. W. Brown & C. F. Branta (Eds.), *Competitive sports for children and youth.* Champaign, IL: Human Kinetics.

CHAPTER 8

Adrian, M. J. (1981). Flexibility in the aging adult. In E. Smith & R. Serfass (Eds.), *Exercise and aging.* Hillside, NJ: Enslow Publishers.

Alexander, M. J., Ready, A. E., & Fougere-Mailey, G. (1985). The fitness levels of females in various age groups. *Canadian Journal of Health, Physical Education, and Recreation, 51,* 8–12.

American Academy of Pediatrics (1990). Strength training, weight and power lifting, and body building by children and adolescents. *Pediatrics, 86,* 801–802.

American College of Sports Medicine (1990). The recommended quantity and quality of exercise for developing and maintaining cardiorespiratory and muscular fitness in health adults. *Medicine & Science in Sports & Exercise, 22,* 265–274.

American Orthopaedic Society for Sports Medicine (1985). *Strength training for young athletes.* Washington, DC: Press Release.

Armstrong, N. (1992). Are American children and youth fit? Some international perspectives. *Research Quarterly for Exercise and Sport, 63,* 449–450.

Asmussen, E. (1973). Growth in muscular strength and power. In G. L. Rarick (Ed.), *Physical activity: Human growth and development.* New York: Academic Press.

Astrand, P. O., & Rodahl, K. (1986). *Textbook of work physiology,* 3rd ed. New York, NY: McGraw Hill.

Bar-Or, O. (1983). *Pediatric sports medicine for the practitioner.* New York: Springer-Verlag.

———. (1989). Trainability of the prepubescent child. *Physician and Sportsmedicine, 17,* 65–82.

Barry, H. C. Rich, B. S. E., & Carlson, R. T. (1993). How exercise can benefit older patients: A practical approach. *The Physician and Sportsmedicine, 21,* 124–140.

Blair, S. N., Clark, D. G., Cureton, K. J., & Powell, K. E. (1989). Exercise and fitness in childhood: Implications for a lifetime of health. In C. V. Gisolfi & D. R. Lamb (Eds.), *Perspectives in exercise science and sports medicine: Youth, exercise, and sport.* Indianapolis: Benchmark.

Bonnet, F. P., & Rocour-Brumioul, D. (1981). Normal growth of human adipose tissue. In F. P. Bonnet (Ed.). *Adipose tissue in childhood.* Boca Raton, FL: CRC Press.

Bouchard, C., Malina, R. M., Hollmann, W., & Leblanc, C. (1977). Submaximal working capacity, heart size and body size in 8 to 18 years. *European Journal of Applied Physiology, 36,* 115–126.

Chumlea, W. C., Roche, A. F., & Mukherjee, D. (1984). *Nutritional assessment of the elderly through anthropometry.* Columbus, OH: Ross Laboratories.

Clarke, D. H., Hunt, M. Q., & Dotson, C. O. (1992). Muscular strength and endurance as a function of age and activity level. *Research Quarterly for Exercise and Sport, 63,* 302–310.

Clarke, D. H., & Vaccaro, P. (1979). The effect of swimming training on muscular performance and body composition in children. *Research Quarterly, 50,* 9–17.

Cunningham, D. A., Paterson, D. H., & Blimkie, C. J. (1984). The development of the cardiorespiratory system with growth and physical activity. In R. A. Boileau (Ed.), *Advances in pediatric sport sciences.* Champaign, IL: Human Kinetics.

Dennison, B. A., Straus, J. H., Mellits, E. D., & Charney, E. (1988). Childhood physical fitness tests: Predictor of adult physical activity levels? *Pediatrics, 82,* 324–330.

deVries, H. A. (1983). Exercise and the physiology of aging. In H. Eckert and H. Montoye (Eds.), *The academy papers.* Champaign, IL: Human Kinetics.

deVries, H. A., & Adams, G. M. (1972). Comparison of exercise responses in old and young men, II: Ventilatory mechanics. *Journal of Gerontology, 27,* 349–352.

Docherty, D., & Bell, R. D. (1985). The relationship between flexibility and linearity measures in boys and girls 6–15 years of age. *Journal of Human Movement Studies, 11,* 279–288.

Dotson, C. O, & Ross, J. G. (1985). Relationships between activity patterns and fitness. *Journal of Physical Education, Recreation, and Dance, 56,* 86–89.

Dummer, G. M., Clarke, D. H., Vaccaro, P., Vander Velden, L., Goldfarb, A. H., & Sockler, J. M. (1985). Age-related differences in muscular strength and muscular endurance among female masters swimmers. *Research Quarterly for Exercise and Sport, 56,* 97–110.

Ekblom, B. (1969). Effects of physical training in adolescent boys. *Journal of Applied Physiology, 27,* 350–355.

Faigenbaum, A. D., Zaichkowsky, L. D., Westcott, W. L., Micheli, L. J., & Fehlandt, A. F. (1993). The effects of a twice-a-week strength training program on children. *Pediatric Exercise Science, 5,* 339–346.

Fiatarone, M. A., Marks, E. C., Ryan, N. D., Meredith, C. N., Lipsitz, L. A., & Evans, W. J. (1990). High intensity strength training in nonagenarians: Effect on skeletal muscle. *Journal of the American Medical Association, 263,* 3029–3034.

Fitzgerald, P. L. (1985). Exercise for the elderly. In L. Goldberg and D. Elliott (Eds.), *The medical clinics of North America.* Philadelphia: Saunders.

Fohlin, L., Davies, C., Freyschuss, U., Bjarke, B., & Thoren, C. (1978). Body dimensions and exercise performance in anorexia nervosa patients. In J. Borms & M. Hebbelinck (Eds.), *Pediatric work physiology.* New York: Karger.

Fox, E. L. (1994). *Sports physiology.* Philadelphia: Saunders.

Fox, E. L., Kirby, T. E., & Fox, A. R. (1987). *Bases of fitness.* New York: Macmillan.

Germain, N. W., & Blair, S. N. (1983). Variability of shoulder flexion with age, activity and sex. *American Corrective Therapy Journal, 37.* 156–160.

Isaacs, L. D., Pohlman, R., & Craig, B. (1994). Effects of resistance training on strength development in prepubescent females. *Medicine & Science in Sports & Exercise, 26* (5 Supplement).

Isaacs, L. D. (1989). The role of an active lifestyle in maintaining movement proficiency. *Journal Times, California Association for Health, Physical Education, Recreation, and Dance, 51,* 7–8.

Jaffe, M., & Kosakov, C. (1982). The motor development of fat babies. *Clinical Pediatrics, 21,* 619–621.

Kannel, W. B., & Gordon, T. (1977). Physiological and medical concomitants of obesity: The Framingham study. In G. Bray (Ed.), *Obesity in America.* Washington, DC: U.S. Department of Health, Education and Welfare.

Kenney, R. A. (1982). *Physiology of aging*. Chicago: Year Book Medical Publishers.

Keogh, J., & Sugden, D. (1985). *Movement skill development*. New York: Macmillan.

Lohman, T. G. (1982). Body composition methodology in sports medicine. *Physician and Sportsmedicine, 10,* 47–58.

Malina, R. M., & Bouchard, C. (1991). *Growth, maturation, and physical activity*. Champaign, IL: Human Kinetics.

Metcalf, J. A., & Roberts, S. O. (1993). Strength training and the immature athlete: An overview. *Pediatric Nursing, 19,* 325–332.

Metheny, E. (1941). The present status of strength testing for children of elementary school and preschool age. *Research Quarterly, 12,* 115–130.

Micheli, L. J. (1988). Strength training in the young athlete. In E. W. Brown & C. F. Branta (Eds.), *Competitive sports for children and youth*. Champaign, IL: Human Kinetics.

Montoye, H. J., Willis, P. W., & Cunningham, D. A. (1974). Heart rate response to submaximal exercise: Relation to age and sex. In J. L. Willems et al. (Eds.), *Cardiac function and aging*. New York: MSS Information Corporation.

Mortimer, J. A., Pirozzolo, F. J., & Maletta, G. J. (1982). Overview of the aging motor system. In J. Mortimer, F. Pirozollo, & G. Maletta (Eds.), *The aging motor system*. New York: Praeger.

Mrzena, B., & Macek, M. (1978). Use of treadmill and working capacity assessment of preschool children. In J. Borms & M. Hebbelinck (Eds.), *Pediatric work physiology*. New York: Karger.

Munnings, F. (1993). Strength training: Not only for the young. *The Physician and Sportsmedicine, 21,* 133–140.

Munns, K. (1981). Effects of exercise on the range of joint motion in elderly subjects. In E. Smith & R. Serfass (Eds.), *Exercise and aging*. Hillside, NJ: Enslow Publishers.

National Strength and Conditioning Association (1985). Position statement on prepubescent strength training. *National Strength Conditioning Association Journal, 7,* 27–31.

Newman, S. L. (1985). Clinical assessment of adipose tissue in youth. In A. Roche (Ed.), *Body-composition assessments in youth and adults*. Columbus, OH: Ross Laboratories.

Nielsen, B., Nielsen, K., Behrendt-Hansen, M., & Asmussen, A. (1980). Training of functional muscular strength in girls 7–19 years old. In K. Berg and B. O. Eriksson (Eds.). *Children and exercise IX*. Champaign, IL: Human Kinetics.

Ozmun, J. C., Mikesky, A. E., & Surburg, P. R. (1994). Neuromuscular adaptions following prepubescent strength training. *Medicine and Science in Sports and Exercise, 26,* 510–514.

Parsons, D., Foster, V., Harman, F., Dickinson, A., Oliva, P., & Westerlind, K. (1992). Balance and strength changes in elderly subjects after heavy-resistance strength training. *Medicine & Science in Sports & Exercise, 24,* (5 supplement): S21.

Pate, R. R., Burgess, M. L., Woods, J. A., Ross, J. G., & Baumgartner, T. (1993). Validity of field tests of upper body muscular strength. *Research Quarterly for Exercise and Sport, 64,* 17–24.

Pate, R. R. & Ross, J. G. (1987). Factors associated with health-related fitness. *Journal of Physical Education, Recreation, and Dance, 58,* 93–95.

Pate, R. R., Ross, J. G., Baumgartner, T. A., & Sparks, R. E. (1987). The modified pull-up test. *Journal of Physical Education, Recreation, and Dance, 58,* 71–73.

Pate, R. R., & Shephard, R. J. (1989). Characteristics of physical fitness in youth. In C. V. Gisolfi & D. R. Lamb (Eds.), *Perspectives in exercise science and sport medicine: Youth, exercise and sport*. Indianapolis: Benchmark.

Payne, V. G., & Morrow, J. R. (1993). Exercise and VO_2 max in children: A meta-analysis. *Research Quarterly for Exercise and Sport, 64,* 305–313.

Pissanos, B. W., Moore, J. B., & Reeve, T. G. (1983). Age, sex, and body composition as predictors of children's performance on basic motor abilities and health-related fitness items. *Perceptual and Motor Skills, 56,* 71–77.

Pollock, M. L. (1974). Physiological characteristics of older champion track athletes. *Research Quarterly, 45,* 363–373.

Pollock, M. L., Dawson, G. A., Miller, H. S., Ward, A., Cooper, D., Headley, W., Linnerud, A. C., & Nomier, M. (1976). Physiologic responses of men 49 to 65 years of age to endurance training. *Journal of the American Geriatrics Society, 24,* 97–104.

Raithel, K. S. (1988). Are American children really unfit? (Part 1 of 2). *Physician and Sportsmedicine, 16,* 146–148, 150–152, 154.

Robinson, S., Dill, D. B., Ross, J. C., Robinson, R. D., Wagner, J. A., & Tzankoff, S. P. (1973). Training and physiological aging in man. *Federation Proceedings, 32,* 1628–1634.

Robinson, S., Dill, D. B., Tzankoff, S. P., Wagner, J. A., & Robinson, R. D. (1975). Longitudinal studies of aging in 37 men. *Journal of Applied Physiology, 38*, 263–267.

Rogers, M. C., & Evans, W. J. (1993). Changes in skeletal muscle with aging: Effects of exercise training. In J. O. Holloszy (Ed.), *Exercise and Sport Sciences Reviews:* Vol. 21, Baltimore: Williams & Wilkins.

Ross, J. G., Dotson, C. O., Gilbert, G. G., & Katz, S. J. (1985). New standards for fitness measurement. *Journal of Physical Education, Recreation, and Dance, 56*, 62–69.

Ross, J. G., & Gilbert, G. G. (1985). The national children and youth fitness study: A summary of findings. *Journal of Physical Education, Recreation, and Dance, 56*, 45–50.

Ross, J. G., & Pate, R. R. (1987). The national children and youth fitness study II: A summary of findings. *Journal of Physical Education, Recreation, and Dance, 58*, 51–56.

Ross, J. G., Pate, R. R., Delphy, L. A., Gold, R. S., & Svilar, M. (1987). New health-related fitness norms. *Journal of Physical Education, Recreation, and Dance, 58*, 66–70.

Ross, J. G., Pate, R. R., Lohman, T. G., & Christenson, G. M. (1987). Changes in the body composition of children. *Journal of Physical Education, Recreation, and Dance, 58*, 74–77.

Rowland, T. W. (1985). Aerobic response to endurance training in prepubescent children: A critical analysis. *Medicine and Sciences in Sports and Exercise, 17*, 493–497.

Rowland, T. W. (1993). Aerobic exercise testing protocols. In T. W. Rowland (Ed.). *Pediatric laboratory exercise testing: Clinical guidelines.* Champaign, IL: Human Kinetics.

Rutenfranz, J., Anderson, K. L., Seliger, V., Klimmer, F., Berndt, I., & Ruppel, M. (1981). Maximum aerobic power and body composition during the puberty growth period: Similarities and differences between children of two European countries. *European Journal of Pediatrics, 136*, 123–133.

Sale, D. G. (1989). Strength training in children. In C. V. Gisolfi & D. R. Lamb (Eds.), *Perspectives in exercise science and sport medicine: Youth, exercise, and sport.* Indianapolis: Benchmark.

Servidio, F. J., Bartels, R. L., & Hamlin, R. L. (1985). The effects of weight training using Olympic style lifts on various physiological variables in pre-pubescent boys. *Medicine and Science in Sports and Exercise, 17*, 288.

Sewall, L., & Micheli, L. J. (1986). Strength training for children. *Journal of Pediatric Orthopedics, 6*, 143–146.

Shephard, R. J. (1994). *Aerobic fitness & health.* Champaign, IL: Human Kinetics.

Shephard, R. J. (1977). *Endurance fitness*, 2nd ed. Toronto: University of Toronto Press.

———. (1978). *Human physiological work capacity.* London: Cambridge University Press.

———. (1981). Cardiovascular limitations in the aged. In E. L. Smith and R. C. Serfass (Eds.), *Exercise and aging.* Hillside, NJ: Enslow Publishers.

Shirley, M. (1931). *The first two years: A study of twenty-five babies.* Minneapolis: University of Minnesota Press.

Sims, E. A. H. (1977). Definitions, criteria, and prevalence of obesity. In G. Bray (Ed.), *Obesity in America.* Washington, DC: U.S. Department of Health, Education and Welfare.

Sinclair, D. (1985). *Human growth after birth*, 4th ed. Oxford: Oxford University Press.

Slaughter, M. H., Lohman, T. G., & Misner, J. E. (1977). Relationship of somatotype and body composition to physical performance in 7- to 12-year-old boys. *Research Quarterly, 48*, 159–167.

Smith, E. L., & Gilligan, C. (1983). Physical activity prescription for the older adult. *Physician and Sportsmedicine, 11*, 91–101.

Stewart, K. J., & Gutin, B. (1976). Effects of physical training on cardiorespiratory fitness in children. *Research Quarterly, 47*, 110–120.

Stones, M. J., & Kozma, A. (1985). Physical performance. In N. Charness (Ed.), *Aging and human performance.* New York: John Wiley & Sons.

Tanner, S. M. (1993). Weighing the risks: Strength training for children and adolescents. *The Physician and Sportsmedicine, 21*, 105–116.

Thomas, J. R., Nelson, J. K., & Church, G. (1991). A developmental analysis of gender differences in health related physical fitness, *Pediatric Exercise Science, 3*, 28–42.

Thoren, C. (1978). Working capacity in anorexia nervosa. In J. Borms & M. Hebbelinck (Eds.), *Pediatric work physiology.* New York: Karger.

Timiras, P. S. (1972). *Developmental physiology and aging.* New York: Macmillan.

Tomonaga, M. (1977). Histochemical and ultrastructural changes in senile human skeletal muscle. *Journal of the American Geriatrics Society, 25*, 125–131.

U. S. National Senior Sports Organization, (1993). *U.S. national senior sports classic IV: The senior olympics—results book.* Chesterfield, MO.

Vaughan, V. C. (1975). The cardiovascular system. In V. Vaughan and R. McKay (Eds.), *Nelson textbook of pediatrics,* 10th ed. Philadelphia: Saunders.

Vrijens, J. (1978). Muscle strength development in pre- and postpubescent age. In J. Borms & M. Hebbelinck (Eds.), *Pediatric work physiology.* New York: Karger.

Weber, D. G., Kohl, H. W., Meredith, M. D., & Blair, S. N. (1986). An automated system for assessing physical fitness in school children. In *Health statistics make a difference.* Department of Health and Human Services Publication No. (PHS) 86–1214. Hyattsville, MO: National Center for Health Statistics, 145–148.

Weltman, A., Janney, C., Rians, C. B., Strand, K., Berg, B., Tippett, S., Wise, J., Cahill, B. R., & Katch, F. I. (1986). The effects of hydraulic resistance strength training in pre-pubescent males. *Medicine and Science in Sports and Exercise, 18,* 629–638.

Whitbourne, S. K. (1985). *The aging body: Physiological changes and psychological consequences.* New York: Springer-Verlag.

CHAPTER 9

Adams, G. L. (1965). Effect of eye dominance on baseball batting. *Research Quarterly, 36,* 3–9.

Adelson, E., & Fraiberg, S. (1976). Sensory deficit and motor development in infants blind from birth. In Z. S. Jastrzembska (Ed.), *The effects of blindness and other impairments on early development.* New York: The American Foundation for the Blind.

Andrew, J. M. (1978). Development of vision. In T. R. Johnson, W. M. Moore, & J. E. Jeffries (Eds.), *Children are different.* Columbus, OH: Ross Laboratories.

Atkinson, J., & Braddick, O. (1974). The development of visual function. In J. A. Davis & J. Dobbing (Eds.), *Scientific foundations of paediatrics.* Baltimore, MD: University Park Press.

Beals, R. P., Mayyasi, A. M., Templeton, A. E., & Johnson, W. L. (1971). The relationship between basketball shooting performance and certain visual attributes. *American Journal of Optometry and Archives of American Academy of Optometry, 48,* 585–590.

Bower, T. G. (1982). *Development in infancy,* 2nd ed. San Francisco: Freeman.

Burg, A. (1968). Lateral visual field as related to age and sex. *Journal of Applied Psychology, 52,* 10–15.

Christina, R. W., Feltz, D. L., Hatfield, B. D., & Daniels, F. S. (1981). Demographic and physical characteristics of shooters. In G. C. Roberts & D. M. Landers (Eds.), *Psychology of motor behavior and sport.* Champaign, IL: Human Kinetics.

Corbin, C. B. (1980). *A textbook of motor development,* 2nd ed. Dubuque, IA: Brown.

Davids, K. (1987). The development of peripheral vision in ball games: An analysis of single- and dual-task paradigms. *Journal of Human Movement Studies, 13,* 175–284.

Dorfman, P. W. (1977). Timing and anticipation: A developmental perspective. *Journal of Motor Behavior, 9,* 67–79.

Gibson, E. J., & Walk, R. D. (1960). The visual cliff. *Scientific American, 4,* 67–71.

Graybiel, A., Jokl, E., & Trapp, C. (1955). Russian studies of vision in relation to physical activity and sport. *Research Quarterly, 26,* 480–485.

Haywood, K. M., & Trick, L. R. (1983). Age-related visual changes and their implications for the motor skill performance of older adults. Minneapolis: Paper presented at the meeting of the American Alliance for Health, Physical Education, Recreation, and Dance.

Hobson, R., & Henderson, N. T. (1941). A preliminary study of the visual field in athletics. *Iowa Academy of Science, 48,* 331–337.

Humphrey, T. (1964). Some correlations between the appearance of human fetal reflexes and the development of the nervous system. *Progress in Brain Research, 4,* 93–133.

Humphrey, T. (1970). The development of human fetal activity and its relation to postnatal behavior. In H. Reese & L. Lipsitt (Eds.), *Advances in child development and behavior* (Vol. 5). New York: Academic Press.

Ikeda, M., & Takevchi, T. (1975). Influence of foveal load on the functional visual field. *Perception and Psychophysics, 18,* 255–260.

Isaacs, L. D. (1983). Coincidence-anticipation in simple catching. *Journal of Human Movement Studies, 9,* 195–201.

———. (1984). Players' success in T-baseball. *Perceptual and Motor Skills, 59,* 852–854.

———. (1987). Modifying the Bassin anticipation timer. *Journal of Human Movement Studies, 13,* 461–465.

———. (1990). Effects of angle of approach on coincidence-anticipation timing within a two-target display. Manuscript submitted for publication.

Jan. R. E., Freeman, R. D., & Scott, E. P. (1977). *Visual impairment in children and adolescents.* New York: Grune & Stratton.

Johansson, R. S., & Westling, G. (1988). Programmed and triggered actions to rapid load changes during precision grip. *Experimental Brain Research, 271,* 1–15.

Leader, L., Baillie, P. Bahia, M., & Elsebeth, V. (1982). The assessment and significance of habituation to repeated stimulus by the human fetus. *Early Human Development, 7,* 211–219.

Lipsitt, L. P. (1978). Sensory and learning processes of newborns: Implications for behavioral disabilities. *Allied Health Behavior Science, 1,* 493–522.

Lowenfeld, B. (1981). *Berthold Lowenfeld on blindness and blind people.* New York: The American Foundation for the Blind.

Lowrey, G. H. (1978). *Growth and development of children,* 7th ed. Chicago: Year Book Medical Publishers.

Macfarlane, A., Harris, P., & Barnes, I. (1976). Central and peripheral vision in early infancy. *Journal of Experimental Child Psychology, 21,* 532–538.

Magill, R. A. (1985). *Motor learning: Concepts and applications,* 2nd ed. Dubuque, IA: Brown.

Miller, J., & Ludvigh, E. (1953). *Dynamic visual acuity when the required pursuit movement of the eye is in a vertical plane. Jt. Prof. Rep.* No. NM001.075.01.02, United States Naval School of Aviation Medicine, Pensacola, FL.

Morris, G. S. (1977). Dynamic visual acuity: Implications for the physical educator and coach. *Motor Skills: Theory into Practice, 2,* 15–20.

———. (1980). *Elementary physical education: Toward inclusion.* Salt Lake City, UT: Brighton Publishing Company.

Morris, G. S., & Kreighbaum, E. (1977). Dynamic visual acuity of varsity women volleyball and basketball players. *Research Quarterly, 48,* 480–483.

Oxendine, J. B. (1984). *Psychology of motor learning.* 2nd ed. Englewood Cliffs, NJ: Prentice-Hall.

Payne, V. G. (1988). Effects of direction of stimulus approach, eye dominance, and gender on coincidence-anticipation timing performance. *Journal of Human Movement Studies, 15,* 17–25.

Reisman, J. E. (1987). Touch, motion, and proprioception. In P. Salapatek and L. Cohen (Eds.), *Handbook of infant perception: From sensation to perception* (Vol. 1), New York: Academic Press.

Sage, G. H. (1984). *Motor learning and control: A neuropsychological approach.* Dubuque, IA: Brown.

Sanderson, F. H. (1972). Perceptual studies: Visual acuity and sporting performance. In H. T. A. Whiting (Ed.), *Readings in sport psychology.* Lafayette, IN: Balt Publishers.

Sanderson, F. H., & Whiting, H. T. A. (1974). Dynamic visual acuity and performance in a catching task. *Journal of Motor Behavior, 6,* 87–94.

———. (1978). Dynamic visual acuity: A possible factor in catching performance. *Journal of Motor Behavior, 10,* 7–14.

Schmidt, R. A. (1988). *Motor control and learning: A behavioral emphasis* (2nd ed.), Champaign, IL: Human Kinetics.

Seiderman, A., & Schneider, S. (1983). *The athletic eye.* New York: Hearst Books.

Shephard, R. J. (1978). *Physical activity and aging.* Chicago: Year Book Medical Publishers.

Shick, J. (1971). Relationship between depth perception and hand-eye dominance and free-throw shooting in college women. *Perceptual and Motor Skills, 33,* 539–542.

Siegel, J. S. (1980). Recent and prospective trends for elderly population and some implications for health care. In S. G. Haynes & M. Feinleib (Eds.), Second conference on the epidemiology of aging. Washington, DC: U.S. Dept. of Health Services (NIH Publication no. 80969).

Smith, C. G., Gallie, B. L., & Morin, J. D. (1983). Normal and abnormal development of the eye. In J. S. Crawford & J. D. Morin (Eds.), *The eye in childhood.* New York: Grune & Stratton.

Troster, H., & Brambring, M. (1993). Early motor development in blind infants. *Journal of Applied Developmental Psychology, 14,* 83–106.

Vlahov, E. (1977a). The effects of different workload varying in intensity and duration on resolution acuity. Unpublished doctoral dissertation, University of Maryland.

———. (1977b). Effect of the Harvard step test on visual acuity. *Perceptual and Motor Skills, 45,* 369–370.

Wade, M. G. (1980). Coincidence-anticipation of young normal and handicapped children. *Journal of Motor Behavior, 12,* 103–112.

Weale, R. A. (1963). *The aging eye.* London: Lewis.

Whipple, D. V. (1966). *Dynamics of development: Euthenic pediatrics.* New York: McGraw-Hill.

Whiting, H. T. A. (1971). *Acquiring ball skill: A psychological interpretation.* Philadelphia: Lea & Febiger.

Whiting, H. T. A., & Sanderson, F. H. (1972). The effect of exercise on the visual and auditory acuity of table-tennis players. *Journal of Motor Behavior, 4,* 163–169.

Williams, H. G. (1983). *Perceptual and motor development.* Englewood Cliffs, NJ: Prentice-Hall.

Wolf, E., & Nadroski, A. S. (1971). Extent of the visual field—Changes with age and oxygen tension. *Arch. Ophth., 86,* 637–642.

Yarbas, A. L. (1967). *Eye movements and vision.* New York: Plenum Press.

CHAPTER 10

Barnes, M. R., Crutchfield, C. A., & Heriza, C. B. (1984). *The neurophysiological basis of patient treatment: Volume II, Reflexes in motor development.* Atlanta: Stokesville.

Bower, T. G. R. (1976). Repetitive processes in child development. *Scientific American,* Nov., 38–47.

Capute, A. J., Palmer, F. B., Shapiro, B. F., Wachtel, R. C., Ross, A., & Accardo, P. J. (1984). Primitive Reflex Profile: A Quantitation of primitive reflexes in infancy. *Developmental Medicine and Child Neurology, 26,* 375–383.

Coley, I. L. (1978). *Pediatric assessment of self-care activities.* St. Louis: Mosby.

Fiorentino, M. R. (1963). *Reflex testing methods for evaluating c. n. s. development.* Springfield, IL: Thomas.

———. (1981). *A basis for sensorimotor development: The influence of the primitive, postural reflexes on the development and distribution of tone.* Springfield, IL: Thomas.

Frankenburg, W. K., Thornton, S. M., & Cohrs, M. E. (1981). *Pediatric developmental diagnosis.* New York: Thieme-Stratton.

Lord, L. (1977). Normal motor development in infants. In M. J. Krajicek & A. I. Tearney (Eds.), *Detection of developmental problems in children.* Baltimore, MD: University Park Press.

Lorton, J. W., & Lorton, E. L. (1984). *Human development through the lifespan.* Monterey, CA: Brooks/Cole.

Payne, V. G. (1985). *Infant reflexes in human motor development* (videotape). Evanston, IL: Journal Films, Inc.

Thelen, E. (1979). Rhythmical stereotypies in normal human infants. *Animal Behavior, 27,* 699–715.

Twitchell, T. E. (1970). Reflex mechanisms in the development of prehension. In K. J. Connolly (Ed.), *Mechanisms of motor skill development.* New York: Academic Press.

Wyke, B. (1975). The neurological basis of movement: A developmental review. In K. Holt (Ed.), *Movement and child development.* Philadelphia: Lippincott.

Zelazo, P. (1976). From reflexive to instrumental behavior. In L. P. Lipsitt (Ed.), *Developmental psychobiology: The significance of injury.* Hillsdale, NJ: Erlbaum.

CHAPTER 11

Bower, T. G. R. (1977). *A primer of infant development.* San Francisco: Freeman.

———. (1982). *Development in infancy,* 2nd ed. San Francisco: Freeman.

Bruner, J. S. (1970). The growth and structure of skill. In K. J. Conolly (Ed.), *Mechanisms of motor skill development.* New York: Academic Press.

Clifton, R. K., Muir, D. W., Ashmead, D. H., & Clarkson, M. G. (1993). Is visually guided reaching in early infancy a myth? *Child Development, 64.* 1099–1110.

Cratty, B. J. (1986). *Perceptual and motor development in infants and children,* 2nd ed. Englewood Cliffs, NJ: Prentice-Hall.

Eckert, H. M. (1973). Age changes in motor skills. In G. L. Rarick (Ed.), *Physical activity: Human growth and development.* New York: Academic Press.

Gallahue, D. L., (1989). *Understanding motor development: Infants, children, adolescents.* Indianapolis: Benchmark.

Gallahue, D. L., Werner, P. H., & Luedke, G. C. (1975). *A conceptual approach to moving and learning.* New York: Wiley.

Garn, S. M. (1966). *De genetica medica, pars II.* L. Gedda (Ed.), Rome: Gregor Mendel Institute, 415–434.

Gesell, A., Ames, L. B. (1940). The ontogenetic organization of prone behavior in human infancy. *Journal of Genetic Psychology, 56,* 247–263.

Hottinger, W. L. (1980). Motor development: Conception to age 5. In C. B. Corbin (Ed.), *A textbook of motor development,* 2nd ed. Dubuque, IA: Brown.

Humphrey, T. (1969). Postnatal repetition of human prenatal activity responses with some suggestions for their neuroanatomical basis. In R. J. Robinson (Ed.), *Brain and early behavior.* New York: Academic Press.

Keogh, J., & Sugden, D. (1985). *Movement skill development.* New York: Macmillan.

Mounoud, P., & Bower, T. G. R. (1974). Conservation of weight in infants. *Cognition, 3,* 229–240.

Norval, M. A. (1947). Relationship of weight and length of infants at birth to the age at which they begin to walk. *Journal of Pediatrics, 30,* 676–678.

Perris, E., & Clifton, R. (1988). Reaching in the dark toward sound as a measure of auditory localization in infants. *Infant Behavior and Development, 11,* 473–491.

Rochat, P. (1992). Self-sitting and reaching in 5- and 8-month-old infants: The impact of posture and its development on early eye-hand coordination. *Journal of Motor Behavior, 24*(2), 210–220.

Shirley, M. M. (1931). *The first two years: A study of twenty-five babies. Volume 1: Postural and locomotor development.* Minneapolis: University Minnesota Press.

Stack, K., Muir, D., Sherriff, F., & Roman, J. (1989). Development of infant reaching in the dark to luminous object and "invisible sounds." *Perception, 18,* 69–82.

Wyke, B. (1975). The neurological basis of movement: A developmental review. In K. Holt (Ed.), *Movement and child development.* Philadelphia: Lippincott.

Zaichowsky, L. D., Zaichowsky, L. B., & Martinek, T. J. (1980). *Growth and development: The child and physical activity.* St. Louis: Mosby.

CHAPTER 12

Abercrombie, M. L. J. (1970). Learning to draw. In K. J. Connolly (Ed.), *Mechanisms of motor skill development.* London: Academic Press.

Ayres, A. J. (1978). *Southern California sensory-motor integration test manual.* Los Angeles: Western Psychological Services.

Bernbaum, M., & Goodnow, J. (1974). Relationships among perpetual-motor tasks: Tracing and copying. *Journal of Educational Psychology, 66,* 731–735.

Birch, H. G., & Lefford, A. (1967. Visual differentiation, intersensory integration, and voluntary motor control. *Monographs of the Society for Research in Child Development, 32.*

Blote, A. W. (1988). The development of writing behavior. Personal monograph.

Blote, A. W., & van Der Heijden, P. G. M. (1988). A follow-up study of writing posture and writing movement of young children. *Journal of Human Movement Studies, 14,* 57–74.

Blote, A. W., Zielstra, E. M., & Zoetewey, M. W. (1987). Writing posture and writing movement of children in kindergarten. *Journal of Human Movement Studies, 13,* 323–341.

Bondareff, W. (1985). The neural basis of aging. In J. E. Birren and K. W. Schaie (Eds.), *Handbook of the psychology of aging.* New York: Van Nostrand.

Bushnell, E. W., & Boudreau, J. P. (1993). Motor development and the mind: The potential role of motor abilities as determinants of aspects of perceptual development. *Child Development, 64,* 1005–1021.

Clarkson, P. M., & Kroll, W. (1978). Practice effects on fractionated response time related to age and activity level, *Journal of Motor Behavior, 10,* 275–286.

Cratty, B. J. (1986). *Perceptual and motor development in infants and children.* 3rd ed. Englewood Cliffs, NJ: Prentice-Hall.

De Ajuriaguerra, J., Auzias, M., Coumes, F., Denner, A., Lavondes-Monod, V., Perron, R., & Stambak, M. (1979). *Children's handwriting: The development of handwriting and problems in handwriting.* Paris: Delachauz et Niestle.

Denckla, M. B. (1973). Development of speed in repetitive and successive finger movements in normal children. *Developmental Medicine and Child Neurology, 15,* 635–645.

————. (1974). Development of motor coordination in normal children. *Developmental Medicine and Child Neurology, 16,* 729–741.

Elliott, J. M., & Connolly, K. J. (1984). A classification of manipulative hand movements. *Developmental Medicine and Child Neurology, 26,* 283–296.

Halverson, H. M. (1931). An experimental study of prehension in infants by means of systematic cinema records. *Genetic Psychology Manuscripts, 10,* 107–286.

Hohlstein, R. R. (1974). The development of prehension in normal infants. Unpublished master's thesis, University of Wisconsin, Madison.

Kellogg, R. (1969). *Analyzing children's art.* Palo Alto, CA.: Mayfield.

Lederman, S. J., & Klatzky, R. L. (1987). Hand movement: A window into haptic object recognition. *Cognitive Psychology, 22,* 421–459.

Newell, K. M., Scully, D. M., & McDonald, P. V. (1989). Task constraints and infant grip configurations. *Developmental Psychobiology, 22*(8), 817–832.

Newell, K. M., Scully, D. M., Tenenbaum, F., & Hardiman, S. (1989). Body scale and the development of prehension. *Developmental Psychobiology, 22*(1), 1–13.

Noller, K., & Ingrisano, D. (1984). Cross-sectional study of gross and fine motor development. *Physical Therapy, 64*(3), 308–316.

Normand, R., Kerr, R., & Metiviei, G. (1987). Exercise, aging, and fine motor performance: An assessment. *Journal of Sports Medicine, 27,* 488–496.

Reimer, D. C., Eaves, L. C., Richards, R., & Chrichton, J. (1975). Name printing as a test of developmental maturity. *Developmental Medicine and Child Neurology, 17,* 486–492.

Rosenbloom, L., & Horton, M. E. (1971). The maturation of fine prehension in young children. *Developmental Medicine and Child Neurology, 13,* 38.

Saida, Y., & Miyashita, M. (1979). Development of fine motor skill in children: Manipulation of a pencil in young children aged 2 to 6 years. *Journal of Human Movement Studies, 5,* 104–113.

Salthouse, T. (1985). Speed of behavior and its implication for cognition. In J. E. Birren and K. W. Schaie (Eds.), *Handbook of psychology of aging.* New York: Van Nostrand.

Spirduso, W. W. (1977). Reaction and movement time as a function of age and physical activity level. *Journal of Gerontology, 30,* 435–440.

Stennet, R. G., Smythe, P. C., & Hardy, M. (1972). Developmental trends in letter printing skills. *Perceptual and Motor Skills, 34,* 182–186.

Williams, H. G. (1983). *Perceptual and motor development.* Englewood Cliffs, NJ: Prentice-Hall.

Ziviani, J. (1983). Qualitative changes in dynamic tripod grip between seven and fourteen years of age. *Developmental Medicine and Child Neurology, 25,* 778–782.

CHAPTER 13

American Alliance for Health, Physical Education, and Recreation (1976). *Youth fitness test manual.* Washington, DC: AAHPER.

Atwater, A. E. (1973). Cinematographic analysis of human movement. In J. H. Wilmore (Ed.), *Exercise and sport sciences reviews, 1,* 217–257. New York: Academic Press.

Bernstein, N. (1967). *The coordination and regulation of movements.* New York: Pergamon Press.

Branta, C., Haubenstricker, J., & Seefeldt, V. (1984). Age changes in motor skills during childhood and adolescence. In R. L. Terjung (Ed.). *Exercise and sport sciences review.* New York: Macmillan.

Burnett, C. N., & Johnson, E. W. (1971). Development of gait in childhood: Part II. *Developmental Medicine and Child Neurology, 13,* 207–215.

DiNucci, J. M. (1976). Gross motor performance: A comprehensive analysis of age and sex differences among children ages six to nine years. In J. Broekhoff (Ed.),

Physical education, sports and the sciences. Eugene, Ore.: Microform Publications.

Engel, G. M., & Staheli, L. T. (1974). The natural history of torsion and other factors influencing gait in childhood. *Clinical Orthopaedics and Related Research,* Mar.–Apr., 12–17.

Felton, E. A. (1960). A kinesiological comparison of good and poor performers in the standing broad jump. Unpublished master's thesis, University of Illinois, Urbana.

Fortney, V. L. (1983). The kinematics and kinetics of the running pattern of two-, four-, and six-year-old children. *Research Quarterly for Exercise and Sport, 54,* 126–135.

Fountain, C., Ulrich, B., Haubenstricker, J., & Seefeldt, V. (1981). Relationship of developmental stage and running velocity in children 2 1/2 to 5 years of age. Chicago: Paper presented at the Midwest District convention of the American Alliance for Health, Physical Education, Recreation, and Dance.

Frederick, S. D. (1977). Performance of selected motor tasks by three, four and five year old children. Unpublished doctoral dissertation, Indiana University, Bloomington.

Halverson, L., & Williams, K. (1985). Developmental sequences for hopping over distance: A prelongitudinal screening. *Research Quarterly for Exercise and Sport, 56,* 37–44.

Haubenstricker, J., Branta, C., Seefeldt, V., Brakora, L., & Kiger, J. (1989). Prelongitudinal screening of a developmental sequence for hopping. Boston: Paper presented at the annual convention of the American Alliance for Health, Physical Education, Recreation, and Dance.

Haubenstricker, J., Henn, J., & Seefeldt, V. (1975). Developmental sequence of hopping (rev. ed.). Unpublished materials, Michigan State University, East Lansing, MI.

Haubenstricker, J., Seefeldt, V., & Branta, C. (1983). Preliminary validation of a developmental sequence for the standing long jump. Minneapolis: Paper presented at the annual convention of the American Alliance for Health, Physical Education, Recreation, and Dance.

Hellebrandt, F. A., Rarick, G. L., Glassow, R., & Carns, M. L. (1961). Physiological analysis of basic motor skills: Growth and development of jumping. *American Journal of Physical Medicine, 40,* 14–25.

James, S. L., & Brubaker, C. E. (1973). Biomechanical and neuromuscular aspects of running. In J. H.

Wilmore (Ed.), *Exercise and Sport Sciences Reviews, 1,* 189–216. New York: Academic Press.

Keogh, J., & Sugden, D. (1985). *Movement skill development.* New York: Macmillan.

Milne, C., Seefeldt, V., & Reuschlein, P. (1976). Relationship between grade, sex, race, and motor performance in young children. *Research Quarterly, 47,* 726–730.

Morris, A. M., Williams, J. M., Atwater, A. E., & Wilmore, J. H. (1982). Age and sex differences in motor performance of 3 through 6 year old children. *Research Quarterly for Exercise and Sport, 53,* 214–221.

Murray, M. P., Drought, A. B., & Kory, R. C. (1964). Walking patterns of normal men. *Journal of Bone and Joint Surgery, 46-A,* 335–360.

Payne, V. G. (1985). Teaching elementary physical Education: Recognizing stages of the fundamental movement patterns (videotape). Northbrook, IL: Hubbard Scientific Publications.

Roberton, M. A. (1983). Changing motor patterns during childhood. In J. Thomas (Ed.), *Motor development during childhood and adolescence.* Minneapolis: Burgess.

Roberton, M. A., & Halverson, L. E. (1984). *Developing children—their changing movement.* Philadelphia: Lea & Febiger.

Roberton, M. A., & Langendorfer, S. (1980). Testing motor development sequences across 9–14 years. In C. Nadeau, W. Halliwell, K. Newell, & G. Roberts (Eds.), *Psychology of motor behavior and sport—1979.* Champaign, IL: Human Kinetics.

Roberton, M. A., Williams, K., & Langendorfer, S. (1980).Prelongitudinal screening of motor development sequences. *Research Quarterly for Exercise and Sport, 51,* 724–731.

Sapp, M. (1980). *The development of galloping in young children: A preliminary study.* Unpublished master's project, Michigan State University, East Lansing.

Scrutton, D. S. (1969). Footprint sequences of normal children under five years old. *Developmental Medicine and Child Neurology, 11,* 44–53.

Seefeldt, V., & Haubenstricker, J. (1974). Developmental sequence of hopping. Unpublished materials, Michigan State University, East Lansing, MI.

Seefeldt, V., & Haubenstricker, J. (1982). Patterns, phases, or stages: An analytical model for the study of developmental movement. In J. A. S. Kelso & J. E. Clark (Eds.), *The development of movement control and coordination.* New York: John Wiley & Sons.

Seefeldt, V., Reuschlein, P., & Vogel, P. (1972). Sequencing motor skills within the physical education curriculum. Houston: Paper presented at the American Association for Health, Physical Education, and Recreation.

Statham, L., & Murray, M. P. (1971). Early walking patterns of normal children. *Clinical Orthopaedics and Related Research,* Sept. 8–24.

Sutherland, D. H. (1984). *Gait disorders in childhood and adolescence.* Baltimore: Williams & Wilkins.

Van Sant, A. (in progress). *Development of the standing long jump.* Motor Development and Child Study Laboratory, Department of Physical Education and Dance, University of Wisconsin, Madison.

Van Slooten, P. H. (1973). Performance of selected motor-coordination tasks by young boys and girls in six socioeconomic groups. Unpublished doctoral dissertation, Indiana University, Bloomington.

Wickstrom, R. L. (1983). *Fundamental motor patterns,* 3rd ed. Philadelphia: Lea & Febiger.

Zimmerman, H. M. (1956). Characteristic likenesses and differences between skilled and nonskilled performance of standing broad jump. *Research Quarterly, 27,* 352–362.

CHAPTER 14

Bruce, R. D. (1966). The effects of variation in ball trajectory upon the catching performance of elementary school children. Unpublished doctoral dissertation. University of Wisconsin, Madison.

Burton, A. W., Greer, N. L., & Wiese, D. M. (1992). Changes in overhand throwing patterns as a function of ball size. *Pediatric Exercise Science, 4,* 50–67.

Burton, A. W., Greer, N. L., & Wiese-Bjornstal, D. M. (1993). Variations in grasping and throwing patterns as a function of ball size. *Pediatric Exercise Science, 5,* 25–41.

Butterfield, S. A., & Loovis, E. M. (1993). Influence of age, sex, balance, and sport participation on development of throwing by children in grades K–8. *Perceptual and Motor Skills, 76,* 459–464.

Deach, D. (1950). Genetic development of motor skills in children two through six years of age. Unpublished doctoral dissertation, University of Michigan, Ann Arbor.

East, W. B., & Hensley, L. D. (1985). The effects of selected sociocultural factors upon the overhand-throwing performance of prepubescent children. In J. E. Clark and J. H. Humphrey (Eds.), *Motor development: Current selected research.* Volume 1. Princeton Book Company.

Espenschade, A. S., & Eckert, H. M. (1980). *Motor development,* 2nd ed. Columbus, OH: Merrill.

Fischman, M. G., Moore, J. B., & Steel, K. H. (1992). Children's one-hand catching as a function of age, gender, and ball location. *Research Quarterly for Exercise and Sport, 63,* 349–355.

Frederick, S. D. (1977). Performance of selected motor tasks by three, four and five year old children. Unpublished doctoral dissertation, Indiana University, Bloomington.

Gavnishy, B. (1970). Vision and sporting results. *Journal of Sports Medicine and Physical Fitness, 10,* 260–264.

Ghosh, A. (1973). Ocular problems in athletics: Role of opthalmology in sports medicine. *Journal of Sports Medicine and Physical Fitness, 13,* 111–118.

Gutteridge, M. (1939). A study of motor achievements of young children. *Archives of Psychology, 244,* 1–178.

Halverson, L. E., & Roberton, M. A. (1979). The effects of instruction on overhand throwing development in children. In G. Roberts & K. Newell (Eds.), *Psychology of motor behavior and sport—1978.* Champaign, IL: Human Kinetics.

Halverson, L. E., Roberton, M. A., & Langendorfer, S. (1982). Development of the overarm throw: Movement and ball velocity changes by seventh grade. *Research Quarterly for Exercise and Sport, 53,* 198–205.

Halverson, L. E., Roberton, M. A., Safrit, M. J., & Roberts, T. W. (1977). Effect of guided practice on overhand-throw ball velocities of kindergarten children. *Research Quarterly, 48,* 311–318.

Harper, C. J. (1979). Learning to observe children's motor development. Part III: Observing children's motor development in the gymnasium. New Orleans: Paper presented at the national convention of the American Alliance for Health, Physical Education, and Recreation.

Harper, C. J., & Struna, N. L. (1973). Case studies in the development of one-handed striking. Minneapolis: Paper presented at the American Alliance for Health, Physical Education, and Recreation.

Haubenstricker, J., Branta, C., & Seefeldt, V. (1983). Preliminary validation of developmental sequences for throwing and catching. East Lansing, Mich.: Paper presented at the annual conference of the North American Society for the Psychology of Sport and Physical Activity.

Haubenstricker, J., Branta, C., Seefeldt, V., Brakora, L., & Kiger, J. (1989). Prelongitudinal screening of a developmental sequence for hopping. Boston: Paper presented at the annual convention of the American Alliance for Health, Physical Education, Recreation, and Dance.

Haubenstricker, J., Henn, J., & Seefeldt, V. (1975). Developmental sequence of hopping (rev. ed.). Unpublished materials, Michigan State University, East Lansing.

Haubenstricker, J., Seefeldt, V., & Branta, C. (1983). Preliminary validation of a developmental sequence for the standing long jump. Minneapolis: Paper presented at the annual convention of the American Alliance for Health, Physical Education, Recreation, and Dance.

Haubenstricker, J., Seefeldt, V., Fountain, C., & Sapp, M. (1981). Preliminary validation of a developmental sequence for kicking. Chicago: Paper presented at the Midwest District convention of the American Alliance for Health, Physical Education, Recreation, and Dance.

Hellweg, D. A. (1972). An analysis of perceptual and performance characteristics of the catching skill in 6–7 year old children. Unpublished doctoral dissertation, University of Wisconsin, Madison.

Isaacs, L. D. (1980). Effects of ball size, ball color, and preferred color on catching by young children. *Perceptual and Motor Skills, 51,* 583–586.

Kay, H. (1970). Analyzing motor skill performance. In K. Connolly (Ed.), *Mechanisms of motor skill development.* New York: Academic Press.

Langendorfer, S. (1980). Longitudinal evidence for developmental changes in the preparatory phase of the overarm throw for force. Detroit: Paper presented at the Research Section of the American Alliance for Health, Physical Education, Recreation, and Dance.

———. (1982). Developmental relationships between throwing and striking: A prelongitudinal test of motor stage theory. Unpublished doctoral dissertation, University of Wisconsin, Madison.

Leme, S., & Shambes, G. (1978). Immature throwing patterns in normal adult women. *Journal of Human Movement Studies, 4,* 85–93.

Luedke, G. C. (1980). Range of motion as the focus of teaching the overhand throwing pattern to children. Unpublished doctoral dissertation, Indiana University, Bloomington.

McCaskill, C. L., & Wellman, B. L. (1938). A study of common motor achievements at the preschool ages. *Child Development, 9,* 141–150.

McClenaghan, B. A., & Gallahue, D. L. (1978). *Fundamental movement: A developmental and remedial approach.* Philadelphia: Saunders.

Morris, G. S. D. (1976). Effects ball and background color have upon the catching performance of elementary school children. *Research Quarterly, 47,* 409–416.

Nelson, J. D., Thomas, J. R., Nelson, K. R., & Abraharm, P. C. (1986). Gender differences in children's throwing performance: Biology and environment. *Research Quarterly for Exercise and Sport, 57,* 280–287.

Nelson, K. R., Thomas, J. R., & Nelson, J. K. (1991). Longitudinal change in throwing performance: Gender differences. *Research Quarterly for Exercise and Sport, 62,* 105–108.

Nessler, J. (1973). Length of time necessary to view a ball while catching it. *Journal of Motor Behavior, 5,* 179–185.

Payne, V. G. (1982). Current status of research on object reception as a function of ball size. *Perceptual and Motor Skills, 55,* 953–954.

———. (1985a). Effects of object size and experimental design on object reception by children in the first grade. *Journal of Human Movement Studies, 11,* 1–9.

———. (1985b). Teaching elementary physical education: Recognizing stages of the fundamental movement patterns (videotape). Northbrook, IL: Hubbard Scientific Publications.

Payne, V. G., & Koslow, R. (1981). Effects of varying ball diameters on catching ability of young children. *Perceptual and Motor Skills, 53,* 739–744.

Ridenour, M. V. (1974). Influence of object size, speed, and direction on the perception of a moving object. *Research Quarterly, 45,* 293–301.

Roberton, M. A. (1977). Stability of stage categorizations across trials: Implications for the "stage theory" of overarm throw development. *Journal of Human Movement Studies, 3,* 49–59.

———. (1978). Longitudinal evidence for developmental stages in the forceful overarm throw. *Journal of Human Movement Studies, 4,* 167–175.

Roberton, M. A., & Langendorfer, S. (1980). Testing motor development sequences across 9–14 years. In C. Nadeau, W. Halliwell, K. Newell, & G. Roberts (Eds.), *Psychology of motor behavior and sport—1979.* Champaign, IL: Human Kinetics.

———. (1983). Changing motor patterns during childhood. In J. Thomas (Ed.), *Motor development during childhood and adolescence.* Minneapolis: Burgess.

Roberton, M. A., & DiRocco, P. (1981). Validating a motor skill sequence for mentally retarded children. *American Corrective Therapy Journal, 35,* 148–154.

Roberton, M. A., & Halverson, L. E. (1984). *Developing children—their changing movement.* Philadelphia: Lea & Febiger.

Roberton, M. A., Halverson, L. E., Langendorfer, S., & Williams, K. (1979). Longitudinal changes in children's overarm throw ball velocities. *Research Quarterly for Exercise and Sport, 50,* 256–264.

Seefeldt, V. (1972a). Developmental sequence of catching skill. Houston: Paper presented at the annual convention of the American Association for Health, Physical Education, and Recreation.

———. (1972b). Developmental sequence of kicking. Unpublished materials, Michigan State University, East Lansing.

———. (1974b). Developmental sequence of striking with a bat. Unpublished materials, Michigan State University, East Lansing.

———. & Haubenstricker, J. (1975a). Developmental sequence of kicking (rev. ed.). Unpublished materials, Michigan State University, East Lansing.

———. & Haubenstricker, J. (1975b). Developmental sequence of punting. Unpublished materials, Michigan State University, East Lansing.

———. & Haubenstricker, J. (1976). Developmental sequence of throwing (rev. ed.) Unpublished manuscript, Michigan State University, East Lansing.

———. & Haubenstricker, J. (1982). Patterns, phases, or stages: An analytical model for the study of developmental movement. In J. A. S. Kelso & J. E. Clark (Eds.), *The development of movement control and coordination.* New York: John Wiley & Sons.

Seefeldt, V., Reuschlein, P., & Vogel, P. (1972). Sequencing motor skills within the physical education curriculum. Houston: Paper presented at the American Association for Health, Physical Education, and Recreation.

Smith, H. (1970). Implications for movement education experiences drawn from perceptual-motor research. *Journal of Health, Physical Education, and Recreation, 41,* 30–33.

Strohmeyer, H. S., Williams, K., & Schaub-George, D. (1991). Developmental sequences for catching a small ball: A prelongitudinal screening. *Research Quarterly for Exercise and Sport, 62,* 257–266.

Thomas, J. R., & French, K. E. (1985). Gender differences across age in motor performance: A meta-analysis. *Psychological Bulletin, 98,* 260–282.

Thomas, J. R., & Marzke, M. W. (1992). The development of gender differences in throwing: Is human evolution a factor? In R. W. Cristina and H. M. Eckert (Eds.), *Enhancing human performance in sport: New concepts and developments.* (Academy Papers No. 25), Champaign, IL: Human Kinetics.

Van Slooten, P. H. (1973). Performance of selected motor-coordination tasks by young boys and girls in six socioeconomic groups. Unpublished doctoral dissertation, Indiana University, Bloomington.

Victors, E. E. (1961). A cinematographical analysis of catching behavior of a selected group of seven and nine year old boys. Unpublished doctoral dissertation, University of Wisconsin, Madison.

Warner, A. P. (1952). The motor ability of third, fourth, and fifth grade boys in the elementary school. Unpublished doctoral dissertation. University of Michigan, Ann Arbor.

Wellman, B. L. (1937). Motor achievements of preschool children. *Childhood Education, 13,* 311–316.

Whiting, H. T. A., Gill, E. B., & Stephenson, J. M. (1970). Critical time intervals for taking in flight information in a ball-catching task. *Ergonomics, 13,* 265–272.

Wickstrom, R. L. (1968). Developmental motor patterns in young children. Unpublished film study.

———. (1980). Acquisition of a ball-handling skill. Detroit: Paper presented at the Research Section of the American Alliance for Health, Physical Education, Recreation, and Dance.

———. (1983). *Fundamental motor patterns,* 3rd ed. Philadelphia: Lea & Febiger.

Wild, M. (1938). The behavior pattern of throwing and some observations concerning its course of development in children. *Research Quarterly, 9,* 20–24.

Williams, H. G. (1968). The effects of systematic variation of speed and direction of object flight and of skill and age classification upon visuoperceptual judgments of moving objects in three dimensional space. Unpublished doctoral dissertation, University of Wisconsin, Madison.

Williams, J. G. (1992a). Effects of instruction and practice on ball catching skill: Single-subject study of an 8-year-old. *Perceptual and Motor Skills, 75,* 392–394.

Williams, J. G. (1992b). Catching action: Visuomotor adaptations in children. *Perceptual and Motor Skills, 75,* 211–219.

CHAPTER 15

American Academy of Pediatrics (1988). *Recommendations for participation in competitive sports: Committee on sports medicine.* Elk Grove Village, IL.

Athletic Footwear Association (1990). *American youth and sports participation.* North Palm Beach, FL: Athletic Footwear Association.

Barnes, L. (1979). Preadolescent training: How young is too young? *Physician and Sportsmedicine, 10,* 114–119.

Blitzer, C. M., Johnson, R. J., Ettlinger, C. F., & Aggebor, K. (1984). Downhill skiing injuries in children. *American Journal of Sports Medicine, 12,* 142–147.

Brown, E. W. (1982). Teaching novice coaches a developmental approach to skill acquisition. In R. H. Cox (Ed.), *Educating youth sport coaches: Solutions to a national dilemma.* Reston, VA: AAHPERD Publications.

Clain, M. R., & Hershman, E. B. (1989). Overuse injuries in children and adolescents. *Physician and Sportsmedicine, 17,* 111–123.

Conn, J., & Razor, J. (1989). Certification of coaches—a legal and moral responsibility. *Physical Educator, 46,* 161–165.

Dishman, R. K. (1989). Exercise and sport psychology in youth 6 to 18 years of age. In C. V. Gisolfi & D. R. Lamb (Eds.), *Perspectives in exercise science and sports medicine: Youth, exercise, and sport.* Indianapolis: Benchmark.

Dyment, P. G. (Ed.), (1991). *Sports medicine: Health care for young athletes,* (2nd ed.). Elk Grove Village, IL: American Academy of Pediatrics.

Feltz, D. (1984). Competence motivation in youth sports. Eugene, Ore.: Paper presented at the meeting of the Olympic Scientific Congress.

Feltz, D. L., & Petlichkoff, L. (1983). Perceived competence among interscholastic sport participants and dropouts. *Canadian Journal of Applied Sport Sciences, 8,* 231–235.

Galton, L. (1980). *Your child in sports.* New York: Franklin Watts.

Garrick, J. G., & Requa, R. K. (1979). Injury patterns of children and adolescent skiers. *American Journal of Sports Medicine, 1,* 245–248.

Gill, D. L., Gross, J. B., & Huddleston, S. (1983). Participation motivation in youth sports. *International Journal of Sport Psychology, 14,* 1–14.

Godshall, R. W. (1975). Junior league football: Risk vs. benefits. *Journal of Sports Medicine, 3,* 139–144.

Goldberg, B., Rosenthal, P. P., Robertson, L. S., & Nicholas, J. A. (1988). Injuries in youth football. *Pediatrics, 81,* 255–261.

Goldberg, B., Whitman, P., Gleim, G., & Nicholas, J. (1979). Children's sports injuries: Are they avoidable? *Physician and Sportsmedicine, 7,* 93–97.

Gould, D. (1987). Understanding attrition in children's sport. In D. Gould & M. Weiss (Eds.), *Advances in pediatric sport sciences: Behavioral issues.* Champaign, IL: Human Kinetics.

Gould, D., Feltz, D., Horn, T., & Weiss, M. R. (1982). Reasons for discontinuing involvement in competitive youth swimming. *Journal of Sport Behavior, 5,* 155–165.

Gould, D., & Petlichkoff, L. (1988). Participation motivation and attrition in youth athletes. In F. L. Smoll, R. A. Magill, & M. J. Ash (Eds.), *Children in sport,* 3rd ed. Champaign, IL: Human Kinetics.

Gugenheim, J. J., Stanley, R. F., Woods, G. W., & Tullos, H. S. (1976). Little League survey: The Houston study. *American Journal of Sports Medicine, 4,* 189–200.

Hansen, H., & Gauthier, R. (1988). Reasons for involvement of Canadian hockey coaches in minor hockey. *Physical Educator, 45,* 147–153.

Harter, S. (1978). Effectance motivation reconsidered: Toward a developmental model. *Human Development, 21,* 34–64.

———. (1982). The perceived competence scale for children. *Child Development, 53,* 87–97.

Isaacs, L. D. (1981). Factors affecting children's basketball shooting performance: A log-linear analysis. *Carnegie Research Papers,* Dec., 29–32.

———. (1984). Players' success in T-baseball. *Perceptual and Motor Skills, 59,* 852–854.

Jeffers, P. (1980) A marathon runner: Thoughts on children's running. *The Main Artery,* Feb.–Mar., 2.

Johnson, R. J., Ettlinger, C. F., Campbell, K. J., et al. (1980). Trends in skiing injuries: Analysis of a 6-year study (1972 to 1978). *American Journal of Sports Medicine, 8,* 106–113.

Kibler, W. B. (1993). Injuries in adolescent and preadolescent soccer players. *Medicine & Science in Sports & Exercise, 25,* 1330–1332.

Kimiecik, J. C. (1988). Who needs coaches' education? Us coaches do. *Physician and Sportsmedicine, 16,* 124–136.

Klint, K., & Weiss, M. R. (1986). Dropping in and dropping out: Participation motives of current and former youth gymnasts. *Canadian Journal of Applied Sport Sciences, 11,* 106–114.

Kozar, B., & Lord, R. H. (1988). Overuse injuries in young athletes: A "growing" problem. In F. L. Smoll, R. A. Magill, & M. J. Ash (Eds.), *Children in sport,* 3rd ed. Champaign, IL: Human Kinetics.

Larson, R. L., Singer, K. M., Bergstrom, R., & Thomas, S. (1976). Little League survey: The Eugene study. *American Journal of Sports Medicine, 4,* 201–209.

Lopiano, D. (1986). The certified coach: A central figure. *Journal of Physical Education, Recreation, and Dance, 57*(3), 34–38.

Martens, R. (1978). *Joy and sadness in children's sports.* Champaign, IL: Human Kinetics.

———. (1988). Youth sports in the USA. In F. L. Smoll, R. A. Magill, & M. J. Ash (Eds.), *Children in sport,* 3rd ed. Champaign, IL: Human Kinetics.

Martens, R., Christina, R. W., Harvey, J. S., & Sharkey, B. J. (1981). *Coaching young athletes.* Champaign, IL: Human Kinetics.

Mueller, F. O., & Blyth, C. S. (1986). An update on football deaths and catastrophic injuries. *Physician and Sportsmedicine, 14,* 139–142.

National Federation of State High Schools, (1993). *Large increase in girls' programs hikes sports participation to 5.4 million.* National Federation News.

Nilsson, S., & Roaas, A. (1978). Soccer injuries in adolescents. *American Journal of Sports Medicine, 6,* 258–361.

Oppliger, R. A., Landry, G. L., Foster, S. W., & Lambrecht, A. C. (1993). Bulimic behaviors among interscholastic wrestlers: A statewide survey. *Pediatrics, 91,* 826–831.

Passer, M. W. (1982). Psychological stress in youth sports. In R. A. Magill, M. J. Ash, & F. L. Smoll (Eds.), *Children in sport.* Champaign, IL: Human Kinetics.

Pate, R. R. (1993). Physical activity in children and youth: Relationship to obesity. *Contemporary Nutrition, 18,* 1–2.

Paulson, W. (1980). *Coaching cooperative youth sports: A values education approach.* La Grange, IL: Youth Sports Press.

Richmond Times Dispatch (1979). Infant Olympians sought, Dec. 2, 22.

Roberts, G. C., Kleiber, D. A., & Duda, J. L. (1981). An analysis of motivation in children's sport: The role of perceived competence in participation. *Journal of Sport Psychology, 3,* 206–216.

Sabock, R. J., & Chandler-Garvin, P. B. (1986). Coaching certification: United States requirements. *Journal of Physical Education, Recreation, and Dance, 57,* 57–59.

Sapp, M., & Haubenstricker, J. (1978). Motivation for joining and reasons for not continuing in youth sports programs in Michigan. Kansas City, MO: Paper presented to the national convention of the American Alliance for Health, Physical Education, and Recreation.

Seefeldt, V. (1987). *Handbook for youth sport coaches.* Reston, VA: American Alliance for Health, Physical Education, Recreation, and Dance.

Shaffer, T. E. (1982). The young athlete. In R. A. Magill, M. J. Ash, and F. L. Smoll (Eds.), *Children in sport.* Champaign, IL: Human Kinetics.

Shively, R. A., Grana, W. A., & Ellis, D. (1981). High school sports injuries. *Physician and Sportsmedicine, 9,* 46–50.

Silverstein, B. M. (1979). Injuries in youth league football. *Physician and Sportsmedicine, 7,* 105–111.

Simon, J., & Martens, R. (1979). Children's anxiety in sport and nonsport evaluative activities. *Journal of Sport Psychology, 1,* 160–169.

Sisley, B. L., & Wiese, D. M. (1987). Current status: Requirements for interscholastic coaches. *Journal of Physical Education, Recreation, and Dance, 58,* 73–85.

Smith, R. E., Smoll, F. L., & Hunt, E. (1977). A system for the behavioral assessment of athletic coaches. *Research Quarterly, 48,* 401–407.

Smoll, F. L., & Smith, R. E. (1984). Improving the quality of coach-player interaction. In J. R. Thomas (Ed.), *Motor development during childhood and adolescence.* Minneapolis: Burgess.

Thomas, J. R. (Ed.) (1977). *Youth sports guide for coaches and parents.* Washington, D.C.: Manufacturers Life Insurance Company and National Association for Sport and Physical Education, AAHPERD Publications.

Ulrich, B. D. (1987). Perceptions of physical competence, motor competence, and participation in organized sport: Their interrelationships in young children. *Research Quarterly for Exercise and Sport, 58,* 57–67.

Wankel, L. M., & Kreisel, P. S. J. (1985). Factors underlying enjoyment of youth sports: Sport and age group comparisons. *Journal of Sport Psychology, 7,* 51–64.

Wild, S. (1992). Choosing a junior tennis program. *CrossCourt News, July/August,* 3.

Williams, R. (1980). Why children get hurt. *Sport Scene, 7,* 1.

CHAPTER 16

Aniansson. A. (1980). *Muscle function in old age with special reference to muscle morphology, effect of training and capacity in activities of daily living.* Goteborg, Sweden: Goteborg University.

Anshel, M. H. (1989). An information processing approach for teaching motor skills to the elderly. In A. C. Ostrow (Ed.), *Aging and motor behavior.* Indianapolis: Benchmark.

Backman, L., & Molander, B. (1989). The relationship between level of arousal and cognitive operations during motor behavior in young and older adults. In A. C. Ostrow (Ed.), *Aging and motor behavior.* Indianapolis: Benchmark.

Barry, H. C., Rich, B. S., & Carlson, R. T. (1993). How exercise can benefit older patients: A practical approach. *The Physician and Sportsmedicine, 21,* 124–140.

Birren, J. E., Woods, A. M., & Williams, M. V. (1980). Behavioral slowing with age: Causes, organization and consequences. In L. W. Poon (Ed.), *Aging in the '80s.* Washington, DC: American Psychological Association, 293–308.

Corbin, C. B. (1980). *A textbook of motor development.* Dubuque, Iowa: Brown.

Cratty, B. J. (1986). Perceptual and motor development in infants and children, 3rd ed. Englewood Cliffs, NJ: Prentice-Hall.

Cunningham, D. A., Montoye, H. J., Metzer, H. L., & Keller, J. B. (1968). Active leisure time activities as related to age among males in a total population. *Journal of Gerontology, 23,* 551–556

Degnan, F., & Payne, V. G. (1994). Age and peak performance in adulthood: 1953-93. Unpublished manuscript.

Eckert, H. M. (1987). *Motor development.* Indianapolis: Benchmark.

Faulkner, J. A., Maxwell, L. C., & Lieberman, D. A. (1972). Histochemical characteristics of muscle fibers from trained and detrained guinea pigs. *American Journal of Physiology, 222,* 836–840.

Gallahue, D. L. (1989). *Understanding motor development: Infants, children, adolescents.* Indianapolis: Benchmark.

Hagberg, J. M. (1994). Physical activity, fitness, health, and aging. In C. Bouchard, R. J. Shephard, and T. Stephens (Eds.), *Physical activity, fitness, and health: International proceedings and consensus statement.* Champaign, IL: Human Kinetics.

Hasselkus, B. R., & Shambes, G. M. (1975). Aging and postural sway in women. *Journal of Gerontology, 30,* 661–667.

Haywood, K. (1993). *Lifespan motor development.* Champaign, IL: Human Kinetics.

Heitmann, H. M. (1982). Older adult physical education: Research implications for instruction. *Quest, 34(1),* 34–42.

Hertzog, C. (1991). Age, information processing speed, and intelligence. In K. W. Schaie and M. P. Lawton (Eds.), *Annual review of gerontology and geriatrics,* New York: Springer.

Hodgkins, J. (1962). Influence of age and the speed of reaction and movement in females. Journal of Gerontology, 17, 385–389.

Hutman, L. P., & Sekuler, R. (1980). Spatial vision and aging. II. Criterion effects. *Journal of Gerontology, 35,* 700–706.

Jarvik, L. F., & Cohen, D. (1973). A biobehavioral approach to internal changes with aging. In C. Eisdorfer and M. P. Lawton (Eds.), *The psychology of adult development and aging.* Washington, DC: American Psychological Association.

Keogh, J., & Sugden, D. (1985). *Movement skill development.* New York: Macmillan.

Khattab, E. (1980). The effect of aging on selected kinematic and kinetic parameters of gait. In J. M. Cooper and B. Haven (Eds.) *Proceedings of the biomechanics symposium.* Indianapolis: Indiana University. Indiana State Board of Health. 348–349.

Klinger, A. (1980). Temporal and spatial characteristics of movement patterns of women over 60. Detroit: Paper presented at the National Conference of the American Alliance of Health, Physical Education, Recreation, and Dance.

Lehman, H. C. (1953). *Age and achievement.* Princeton, NJ: Princeton University Press.

Murray, M., Drought, A. B., & Kory, R. C. (1964). Walking patterns of normal men. *Journal of Bone and Joint Surgery, 46-A,* 335–360.

Overstall, P. W., Exton-Smith, A. N., Imms, F. J., & Johnson, A. L. (1977). Falls in the elderly related to postural imbalance. *British Medical Journal, I,* 261–264.

Potash, M., & Jones, B. (1977). Aging and decision criteria for the detection of tones in noise. *Journal of Gerontology, 35,* 436–440.

Rabitt, P., & Rogers, M. (1965). Age and choice between responses in a self-paced repetitive task. *Ergonomics, 8,* 435–444.

Reigel, P. S. (1981). Athletic records and human endurance. *American Scientist, 69,* 285–290.

Salthouse, T. A. (1979). Adult age and the speed-accuracy tradeoff. *Ergonomics, 22,* 811–821.

Salthouse, T. A., & Somberg, B. L. (1982). Skilled performance: Effects of adult age and experience on elementary processes. *Journal of Experimental Psychology: General, III,* 176-207.

Schmidt, R. A. (1991). *Motor learning and performance: From principles to practice.* Champaign, IL: Human Kinetics.

———. (1988). *Motor control and learning: A behavioral emphasis.* 2nd ed. Champaign, IL: Human Kinetics.

Shephard, R. J. (1978). *Physical activity and aging.* Chicago: Year Book Medical Publishers.

Sidney, K. H., & Shephard, R. J. (1977). Activity patterns of elderly men and women. *Journal of Gerontology, 32,* 25–32.

Spirduso, W. W. (1982). Physical fitness in relation to motor aging. In F. J. Pirozzolo and G. J. Maletta (Eds.), *The aging motor system.* New York: Praeger.

———. (1985). Age as a limiting factor in human neuromuscular performance. In D. H. Clarke and H. M. Eckert (Eds). *The academy papers: Limits of human performance.* Champaign, IL: Human Kinetics.

Stephens, T., & Caspersen, C. J. (1994). The demography of physical activity. In C. Bouchard, R. J. Shepherd, and T. Stephens (Eds.), *Physical activity, fitness, and health: International proceedings and consensus statement.* Champaign, IL: Human Kinetics

Stones, M. J., & Kozma, A. (1981). Adult age trends in athletic performances. *Experimental Aging Research, 7,* 269–279

Surburg, P. (1976). Aging and effect of physical and mental practice upon acquisition and retention of motor skill. *Journal of Gerontology, 31,* 64–67.

Thomas, J. R. (1984). *Motor development during childhood and adolescence.* Minneapolis: Burgess.

Ubell, E. (1984). How to prepare for old age. *Parade Magazine.* Nov. 25.

Welford, A. T. (1982). Motor skills and aging. In F. J. Pirozzolo and G. J. Maletta (Eds.). *The aging motor system.* New York: Praeger.

Williams, H. G. (1983). *Perceptual and motor development.* Englewood Cliffs, NJ: Prentice-Hall.

Woollacott, M. H. (1989). Aging, posture control, and movement preparation. In M. H. Woollacott and A. Shumway-Cook (Eds.), *Development of posture and gait across the lifespan.* Columbia, SC: University of South Carolina Press.

Woollacott, M. H., Shumway-Cook, A., & Nasher, L. (1982). Postural reflexes and aging. In F. J. Pirozzolo and G. J. Maletta (Eds.). *The aging motor system.* New York: Praeger.

Zaichowsky, L. D., Zaichowsky, L. B., & Martinek, T. J. (1980). *Growth and development: The child and physical activity.* St. Louis: Mosby.

CHAPTER 17

American Alliance for Health, Physical Education, Recreation, and Dance (1976). *Youth fitness test manual.* Washington, DC.

———. (1980). *Health-related physical fitness test manual.* Reston, VA.

———. (1988). *Physical Best: The American alliance physical fitness education & assessment program.* Reston, VA.

Arnheim, D. D., & Sinclair, W. A. (1979). *The clumsy child: A program of motor therapy,* 2nd ed. St. Louis: Mosby.

Bagnato, S. J., & Neisworth, J. T. (1981). *Linking developmental assessment and curricula: Prescriptions for early intervention.* Rockville, MD: Aspen Publication.

Bayley, N. (1969). *Manual for the Bayley Scales of Infant Development.* New York: The Psychological Corporation.

Brigance, A. H. (1978). *Brigance Diagnostic Inventory of Early Development.* Worcester, MA: Curriculum Associates.

Bruininks, R. H. (1978). *Bruininks-Oseretsky Test of Motor Proficiency.* Circle Pines, MN: American Guidance Service.

Conoley, J. C., & Kramer, J. J. (Eds.). (1989). *The tenth mental measurements yearbook.* Lincoln, NE: University of Nebraska Press.

DiRocco, P. (1979). Physical education and the handicapped: Developmental approach. *Physical Education, 36,* 127–131.

Frankenburg, W. K., & Dodds, J. B. (1967). The Denver Developmental Screening Test. *Journal of Pediatrics, 71,* 181–191.

Frankenburg, W. K., & Dodds, J., & Archer, P. (1990). *Denver II technical manual.* Denver, CO: Denver Developmental Materials, Inc.

Frankenburg, W. K., Dodds, J., Archer, P., Shapiro, H., & Bresnick, B. (1992). The Denver II: A major revision and restandardization of the Denver Developmental Screening Test. *Pediatrics, 89,* 91–97.

Gesell, A., & Ames, L. B. (1940). The ontogenetic organization of prone behavior in human infancy. *Journal of Genetic Psychology, 56,* 247–263.

Hastad, D. N., & Lacy, A. G. (1994). *Measurement and evaluation in contemporary physical education.* 2nd ed. Scottsdale, AZ: Gorsuch, Scarisbrick, Publishers.

Haubenstricker, J. (1984). The assessment of motor skills in grades 4 to 6. Anaheim, CA: Paper presented at the ARAPCS Measurement and Evaluation Council at the AAHPERD Convention.

———. (1990). Summary of fundamental motor skill stage characteristics: Motor performance study—MSU. Unpublished materials, Michigan State University, East Lansing, MI.

Haubenstricker, J., Seefeldt, V., Fountain, C., & Sapp, M. (1981). The efficiency of the Bruininks-Oseretsky test of motor proficiency in discriminating between normal children and those with gross motor dysfunction. Boston: Paper presented at the Motor Development Academy at the AAHPERD Convention.

Hoffman, H. (1975). *The Bayley Scales of Infant Development: Modification for youngsters with handicapping conditions.* Connack, NY: Suffolk Rehabilitation Center.

Jansma, P. (Ed.) (1981). *The psychomotor domain and the seriously handicapped.* Washington, DC: University Press of America.

Jenkot, V. K. (1986). *Feasibility of large-scale implementation of the component approach for assessment of fundamental motor skills in grades K–3.* Unpublished doctoral dissertation, University of North Carolina at Greensboro, Greensboro, NC.

Kraus, H., & Hirschland, R. P. (1954). Minimum muscular fitness test in school children. *Research Quarterly, 25,* 177–188.

Langendorfer, S. (1986). Books and media review: Test of gross motor development. *Adapted Physical Activity Quarterly, 3,* 186–190.

Linder, T. W. (1993a). *Transdisciplinary play-based assessment: A functional approach to working with young children* (rev. ed.). Baltimore, MD: Paul H. Brookes Publishing Co.

———. (1993b). *Transdisciplinary play-based intervention.* Baltimore, MD: Paul H. Brookes Publishing Co.

Loovis, E. M., & Ersing, W. F. (1979). *Assessing and programming gross motor development for children,* 2nd ed. Loudonville, OH: Mohican Textbook Publishing.

McClenaghan, B., & Gallahue, D. (1978). Fundamental movement: A developmental and remedial approach. Philadelphia: Saunders.

Miles, B. H., Nierengarten, M. E., & Nearing, R. J. (1988). A review of the eleven most often-cited instruments used in adapted physical education. *Clinical Kinesiology.* April–May–June, 33–41

Osness, W. H. (1989). The AAHPERD fitness task force: History and philosophy. *Journal of Physical Education, Recreation, and Dance, 60,* 64–65.

Pate, R. R. (1985). *Norms for college students: Health-related physical fitness test.* Reston, VA.

Pate, R. R., Ross, J. G., Baumgartner, T. A., & Sparks, R. E. (1987). The modified pull-up test. *Journal of Physical Education, Recreation, and Dance, 58,* 71–73

Roach, E. G., & Hephart, N. C. (1966). *The Purdue Perceptual-Motor Survey.* Columbus, OH: Merrill.

Roberton, M. A., & Halverson, L. E. (1984). *Developing children–Their changing movement.* Philadelphia: Lea & Febiger.

Ross, J. G., Dotson, C. O., Gilbert, G. G., & Katz, S. J. (1985). New standards for fitness measurement. *Journal of Physical Education, Recreation, and Dance, 56,* 62–66.

Ross, J. G., Pate, R. R., Delpy, L. A., Gold, R. S., & Svilar, M. (1987). New health-related fitness norms. *Journal of Physical Education, Recreation, and Dance, 58,* 66–70.

Safrit, M. J. (1990). *Introduction to measurement in physical education and exercise science,* 2nd ed. St. Louis: Times Mirror/Mosby.

Seefeldt, V., & Haubenstricker, J. (1974). *Developmental sequence of skipping.* Unpublished materials, Michigan State University, East Lansing, MI.

Sherrill, C. (1986). *Adapted physical education and recreation: A multidisciplinary approach,* 3rd ed. Dubuque, IA: Brown.

Sherrill, C. (1993). *Adapted physical activity, recreation and sport: Crossdisciplinary and lifespan.* Madison, WI: W. C. Brown & Benchmark Publishers.

Strand, B. N., & Wilson, R. (1993). *Assessing sport skills.* Champaign, IL: Human Kinetics.

Texas Governor's Commission on Physical Fitness (1973). *Physical fitness–motor ability test.* Austin, TX.

Ulrich, D. A. (1985a). *Test of gross motor development.* Austin, TX.: Pro-Ed.

———. (1985b). *Current assessment practices in adapted physical education.* Washington, DC: Paper presented at the annual meeting of the National Consortium on Physical Education and Recreation for the Handicapped.

Werder, J. K., & Kalakian, L. H. (1985). *Assessment in adapted physical education.* Minneapolis: Burgess.

Wessel, J. A. (1976). *I CAN: Implementation guide.* Northbrook, IL: Hubbard.

CHAPTER 18

American Academy of Orthopedic Surgeons (1991). *Play it safe: A guide to playground safety.* Rosemont, IL.

Bowers, L., & Bruya, L. D. (1988). Twenty one results: Seventeen safety problems. In L. Bruya and S. Langendorfer (Eds.), *Where our children play: Elementary school playground equipment.* Reston, VA: American Alliance for Health, Physical Education, Recreation, and Dance.

Bruya, L. & Langendorfer, S. (Eds.), (1988). *Where our children play: Elementary school playground equipment.* Reston, VA: AAHPERD

Burton, A. W., Greer, N. L., & Wiese, D. M. (1992). Changes in overhand throwing patterns as a function of ball size. *Pediatric Exercise Science, 4,* 50–67

Burton, A. W., Greer, N. L. & Wiese-Bjornstal, D. M. (1993). Variations in grasping and throwing patterns as a function of ball size. *Pediatric Exercise Science, 5,* 24–41.

Dunn, J. M., Morehouse, J. W., & Fredericks, H. D. (1985). *Physical education for the severely handicapped: A systematic approach to a data based gymnasium.* Austin, TX: Pro-ed.

Duston, D. (May 25, 1992). *Breaking the fall at playgrounds not just kids' stuff.* Dayton, OH: Dayton Daily News.

Frost, J. (1990). Young children and playground safety. In S. Wortham and J. Frost (Eds.), *Playgrounds for young children: National survey and perspectives.* Reston, VA: American Alliance for Health, Physical Education, Recreation, and Dance.

Haywood, K. M. (1978). *Children's basketball performance with regulation and junior-sized basketballs.* St. Louis: University of Missouri.

Herkowitz, J. (1978). The design and evaluation of playspaces for children. In M. V. Ridenour (Ed.), *Motor development: Issues and applications.* Princeton, NJ: Princeton Book Company.

————. (1984) Developmentally engineered equipment and playgrounds. In J. Thomas (Ed.), *Motor development during childhood and adolescence.* Minneapolis: Burgess.

Isaacs, L. D., & Karpman, M. B. (1981). Factors affecting children's basketball shooting performance: A log-linear analysis. *Carnegie Research Papers,* 29–32.

Magill, R. A. (1993). *Motor learning: Concepts and applications.* 4th ed. Dubuque, IA: Brown.

Rasor, D. (1994). *Blood management, Sport Pulse,* 13(1), Dayton, OH: St. Elizabeth Sports Medicine Center.

Siedentop, D., Herkowitz, J., & Rink, J. (1984). *Elementary physical education methods.* Englewood Cliffs, NJ: Prentice-Hall.

Wright, E. J. (1967). Effects of light and heavy equipment on acquisition of sport-type skills by young children. *Research Quarterly, 38,* 705–714.

Author Index

Subject Index

role of, 189–191
search, 194
startle, 196
stepping, 200
stepping reflex, 199
sucking, 194
swimming, 200–201
symmetric tonic neck, 196
Infant walkers, 101, 108, 120
Information processing
levels of, 371–372
theory of, 6
Injuries
birth, 94
from youth sports participation, 302–309
infant walkers and, 108
maternal exercise and, 94–95
overuse, 307–308
playground, 161–162
Integration, defined, 16
Intellectual decline, theories of, 35–37
Interception, visual, 179–181
Intrinsic movements of the hands, 223
Intuitive substage, in Piaget's theory, 31
Isometric force, 154
Isotonic force, 154

Johnny and Jimmy, 108–111, 120
Joint receptors, 184
Jumping, 254–255, 258–259
and hopping, 255–257, 259–262
developmental sequences of
component approach, 256–257
total body approach, 258–259
flight phase in, 254
landing phase in, 254–255
preparatory phase in, 254
take-off phase in, 254

Kicking
assessment of, total body approach, 292–293
Kinesiology, 1
Knee height, 122–123
nomogram for, 124
Knee jerk, reflex, 184

Knowledge
and sport performance, 37–38
declarative, 37
of results, 372
procedural, 37

Labyrinthine reflex, 203
Language development, 30–31
Large for gestational age (LGA), 93–94, 97
Laterality, 70
Leap, 254
Length caliper, 135
Lettering, development of, 239
Level of fixity, 110
Lifespan reflexes, 189
Little League elbow, 307–308
Locomotion
prone, 211–213
upright, 213–214
Locomotion skills, fundamental, 243–267
galloping, 259, 263–264
hopping, 255, 257, 259–262
jumping, 254–259
leaping, 254
running, 247–254
skipping, 259, 264–266
sliding, 259, 264
walking, 243, 246
Long-term memory, 371–372
Longitudinal design, 10

Macula, defined, 172
Males
gender role identity and, 50–52
genitalia development in, 144–145
Manipulation, 189
categories of, 223, 225
defined, 223, 225, 241
Manual control, 208
Maternal exercise, 94–97
fetal responses to, 95–97
injuries from, 94–95
Maternal nutrition, 90–92
Maturation
defined, 15
dental, 142–143
genitalia, 144